HOMER

WORLD CLASSICS LIBRARY

HOMER

The Iliad and The Odyssey

SIRIUS

SIRIUS

This edition published in 2021 by Sirius Publishing, a division of
Arcturus Publishing Limited,
26/27 Bickels Yard, 151–153 Bermondsey Street,
London SE1 3HA

ISBN: 978-1-83940-696-6
AD007838UK

Printed in China

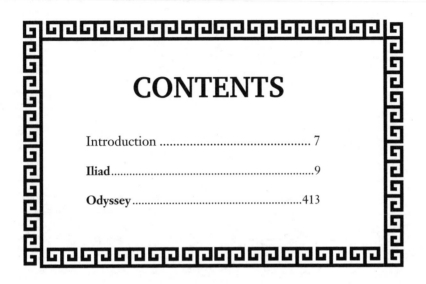

CONTENTS

INTRODUCTION

Homer's first biographers placed his birth around the Sack of Troy, which is traditionally dated sometime in the 12th or 11th centuries BC. For the ancient Greeks he was the legendary poet of *The Iliad* and *The Odyssey* – epic poems which laid the foundations for Greek culture. By the 3rd or 2nd centuries BC Homer's existence was called into question. In order to determine the truth, attempts have been made to locate his date and place of birth. Many cities vied to be the home of such a legendary poet including Smyrna, Rhodes, Athens and Argos. Was the difficulty in locating his birthplace because he was not a real person or because his fame spawned myths of its own? Was he the son of a river and a nymph? And did he use many of his own experiences as a wandering balladeer as inspiration for the epic journey in *The Odyssey?*

With little evidence of such a man having ever lived, it is now believed that the texts attributed to him were likely be the works of many poets working within the oral tradition, though perhaps first written down by one man we now know as Homer. Regardless of authorship, these two works composed sometime around the 8th century BC are cornerstones of the Western canon. Originally written as epic poems, the translations presented here are in prose, allowing the texts to be more accessible.

The earlier work, *The Iliad* – though it takes place over a period of only a few weeks during the later years of the Trojan War – reveals much about the causes and events of the long siege and conflict, and sees the Gods failing in their bid to stay out of the affairs of men. The Trojan War, much like Homer, has been a topic of debate, believed by the ancient Greeks to be a real historic event exaggerated for poetic effect. By 1870 the war and existence of Troy itself were thought to be pure fiction though the remains of Troy were excavated later that decade by Heinrich Schliemann and his wife Sophia. Recent studies believe that the war is likely based in reality but that we will never know the true details.

This version of *The Iliad* was translated in 1898 by the celebrated late-Victorian author Samuel Butler, who influenced the writings of H. G. Wells, Aldous Huxley, and E. M. Forster to name but a few. He is most famed for his satirical Utopian novel *Erewhon* written in 1872.

The more popular of the two works, *The Odyssey*, tells the story of the gallant Odysseus, King of Ithaca, as he journeys home following the fall of Troy. Odysseus' journey is beset by many obstacles, both divine and natural, and its tales of heroics and adventure filled with the gods and monsters of myth have proven endlessly fascinating to readers.

This version was translated by T.E. Lawrence – the famed Lawrence of Arabia – in 1932. His major work *Seven Pillars of Wisdom* (1926) told the story of his experiences as a liaison officer with rebel forces during the Arab revolt (1916–1918) and it was this work that gave rise to his famous nickname.

Considered vitally important by the ancient Greeks, the Homeric texts fell out of favour in the middle ages. However, many translations, adaptions and derivatives remained popular, and it continued to inspire works such as William Shakespeare's *Troilus and Cressida*. A resurgence during the renaissance saw them recognised as the first and foremost works in the Western canon. They have since been adapted in forms as various as James Joyce's modernist novel *Ulysses*, the Coen Brothers crime-comedy film *O Brother, Where art Thou?* through 2018's feminist reworkings *The Silence of the Girls* by Pat Barker and Madeleine Miller's *Circe*. These influential texts continue to be read, enjoyed, and translated across the globe as timeless classics.

THE
ILIAD

Contents

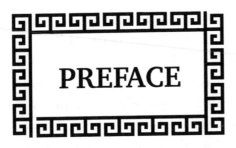

PREFACE

The Head Master of one of our foremost public schools told me not long since, that he had been asked what canons he thought it most essential to observe in translating from English into Latin. His answer was, that in the first place the Latin must be idiomatic, in the second it must flow, and in the third it must keep as near as it could to the English from which it was being translated.

I said, 'Then you hold that if either the Latin or the English must perforce give place, it is the English that should yield rather than the Latin?'

This, he replied, was his opinion; and surely the very sound canons above given apply to all translation. The genius of the language into which a translation is being made is the first thing to be considered; if the original was readable, the translation must be so also, or however good it may be as a construe, it is not a translation.

It follows that a translation should depart hardly at all from the modes of speech current in the translator's own times, inasmuch as nothing is readable, for long, which affects any other diction than that of the age in which it is written. We know the charm of the Elizabethan translations, but he who would attempt one that shall vie with these must eschew all Elizabethanisms that are not good Victorianisms also.

For the charm of the Elizabethans does not lie in their Elizabethanisms; these are but as the mosses and lichens which Time will grow upon our Victorian literature as surely as he has grown them upon the Elizabethan – upon such of it, at least, as has not been jerry-built. Shakespeare tells us that it is Time's glory to stamp the seal of time on aged things. No doubt; but he will have no hands stamp it save his own; he will rot an artificial ruin, but he will not glorify it; if he is to hallow any work it must be frankly secular when he deigns to take it in hand – by this I mean honestly after the manner of its own age and country. The Elizabethans probably knew this too well to know that they knew it, but whether they knew it or no they did not lard a crib with Chaucerisms and think that they were translating. They aimed fearlessly and without taint of affectation at making a dead author living to a generation other than his own. To do this they transfused their blood into his cold veins, and quickened him with their own livingness.

Then the life is theirs not his? In part no doubt it is so; but if they have loved him well enough, his life will have entered into them and possessed them. They will have given him of their life, and he will have paid them in their own coin. If, however, the mouth of the ox who treads out the corn may not be muzzled, and if there is to be a certain give and take between a dead author and his translator, it follows that a translator should be allowed greater liberty when the work he is translating belongs to an age and country widely remote from his own. For a poem's prosperity is like a jest's – it is in the ear of him that hears it. It takes two people to say a thing – a sayee as well as a sayer – and by parity of reasoning a poem's original audience and environment are integral parts of the poem itself. Poem and audience are as ego and non-ego; they blend into one another. Change either, and some corresponding change, spiritual rather than literal, will be necessary in the other, if the original harmony between them is to be preserved.

Happily in the cases both of the Iliad and the Odyssey we can see clearly enough that the audiences did not differ so widely from ourselves as we might expect after an interval of some three thousand years. But they differ, especially in the case of the Iliad, and the difference necessitates a greater amount of freedom on the part of a translator than would be tolerable if it did not exist.

Freedom of another kind is further involved in the initial liberty of rendering in prose a work that was composed in verse. Prose differs from verse much as singing from speaking or dancing from walking, and what is right in the one is often wrong in the other. Prose, for example, does not permit that iteration of epithet and title, sometimes due merely to the requirements of metre, and sometimes otiose, which abounds in the Iliad without in any way disfiguring it. We look, indeed, for the iteration and enjoy it. We are never weary of being told that Juno is white-armed, Minerva grey-eyed, and Agamemnon king of men; but had Homer written in prose he would not have told us these things so often. Therefore, though frequently allowing common form epithets and titles to recur, I have not less frequently suppressed them.

Lest, however, the reader should imagine that I have departed from the letter of the Iliad more than I have, I will give the first fifty lines or so of the best prose translation that has yet been made – I mean that of Messrs. Leaf, Lang, and Myers, to which throughout my work I have been greatly indebted. Often have they saved me from error, and rarely have I found occasion to differ from them as to the meaning of a passage. I do not believe that I have translated a single paragraph without reference to them, but this said, a comparison of their opening paragraphs with my own will show the kind of way in which I differ from them as to the manner in which Homer should be translated.

Their translation (here, by Dr Leaf) opens thus:—

Sing, goddess, the wrath of Achilles Peleus' son, the ruinous wrath that brought on the Achaians woes innumerable, and hurled down into Hades many strong souls of heroes, and gave their bodies to be a prey to dogs and all winged fowls; and so the counsel of Zeus wrought out its accomplishment from the day when strife first parted Atreides king of men and noble Achilles.

Who then among the gods set the twain at strife and variance? Even the son of Leto and of Zeus; for he in anger at the king sent a sore plague upon the host, that the folk began to perish, because Atreides had done dishonour to Chryses the priest. For he had come to the Achaians' fleet ships to win his daughter's freedom, and brought a ransom beyond telling; and bare in his hands the fillet of Apollo the Far-darter upon a golden staff; and made his prayer unto all the Achaians, and most of all to the two sons of Atreus, orderers of the host: 'Ye sons of Atreus and all ye well-greaved Achaians, now may the gods that dwell in the mansions of Olympus grant you to lay waste the city of Priam, and to fare happily homeward; only set ye my dear child free, and accept the ransom in reverence to the son of Zeus, far-darting Apollo.'

Then all the other Achaians cried assent, to reverence the priest and accept his goodly ransom; yet the thing pleased not the heart of Agamemnon son of Atreus, but he roughly sent him away, and laid stern charge upon him, saying, 'Let me not find thee, old man, amid the hollow ships, whether tarrying now or returning again hereafter, lest the staff and fillet of the god avail thee naught. And her will I not set free; nay, ere that shall old age come on her in our house, in Argos, far from her native land, where she shall ply the loom and serve my couch. But depart, provoke me not, that thou mayest the rather go in peace.'

So said he, and the old man was afraid and obeyed his word, and fared silently along the shore of the loud-sounding sea. Then went that aged man apart and prayed aloud to King Apollo, whom Leto of the fair locks bare, 'Hear me, god of the silver bow, that standest over Chryse and holy Killa, and rulest Tenedos with might, O Smintheus! If ever I built a temple gracious in thine eyes, or if ever I burnt to thee fat flesh of thighs of bulls or goats, fulfil thou this my desire; let the Danaans pay by thine arrows for my tears.'

So spake he in prayer, and Phœbus Apollo heard him, and came down from the peaks of Olympus wroth at heart, bearing on his shoulders his bow and covered quiver. And the arrows clanged upon his shoulders in his wrath, as the god moved; and he descended like to night. Then he sate him aloof from the ships, and let an arrow fly; and there was heard a dread clanging of the silver bow. First did he assail the mules and fleet dogs, but afterward, aiming at the men his piercing dart, he smote; and the pyres of the dead burnt continually in multitude.

I have given the foregoing extract with less compunction, by reason of the reflection, ever present with me, that not a few readers – nor these the least cultured – will prefer Dr Leaf's translation to my own. Throughout my work I have taken the same kind of liberties as those that the reader will readily detect if he compares Dr Leaf's rendering with mine. But I do not believe that I have anywhere taken greater ones. The difference between us in the prayer of Chryses, where Dr Leaf translates 'If ever I built a temple,' &c., while I render 'If ever I decked your temple with garlands,' &c., is not a case in point, for it is due to my preferring Liddell and Scott's translation. I very readily admit that Dr Leaf has in the main kept more closely to the words of Homer, but I believe him to have lost more of the spirit of the original through his abandonment (no doubt deliberate) of all attempt at stately, and at the same time easy, musical, flow of language, than he has gained in adherence to the letter – to which, after all, neither he nor any man can adhere.

These last words may suggest that I claim graces which Dr Leaf has not attained. I can make no such claim. All I claim is to have done my best towards making the less sanguinary parts of the Iliad interesting to English readers. The more sanguinary parts cannot be made interesting; indeed I doubt whether they can ever have been so, or even been intended to be so, to a highly cultivated audience. They had to be written, and they were written; but it is clear that Homer often wrote them with impatience, and that actual warfare was as distasteful to him as it was foreign to his experience. Happily there is much less fighting in the Iliad than people generally think.

One word more and I have done. I have burdened my translation with as few notes as possible, intending to reserve what I have to say about the Iliad generally for another work to be undertaken when my complete translation of the Odyssey has been printed. Lastly, the reception of my recent book, 'The Authoress of the Odyssey,' has convinced me that the general reader much prefers the Latinised names of gods and heroes to those which it has of late years been attempted to popularise: I have no hesitation, therefore, in adhering to the nomenclature to which Pope, Mr Gladstone, and Lord Derby have long since familiarised the public.

August 8, 1898.

THE ILIAD OF HOMER

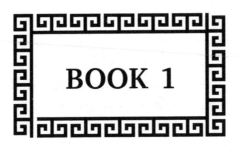

BOOK 1

The quarrel between Agamemnon and Achilles – Achilles withdraws from the war, and sends his mother Thetis to ask Jove to help the Trojans – Scene between Jove and Juno on Olympus.

Sing, O goddess, the anger of Achilles son of Peleus, that brought countless ills upon the Achæans. Many a brave soul did it send hurrying down to Hades, and many a hero did it yield a prey to dogs and vultures, for so were the counsels of Jove fulfilled from the day on which the son of Atreus, king of men, and great Achilles, first fell out with one another.

And which of the gods was it that set them on to quarrel? It was the son of Jove and Leto; for he was angry with the king and sent a pestilence upon the host to plague the people, because the son of Atreus had dishonoured Chryses his priest. Now Chryses had come to the ships of the Achæans to free his daughter, and had brought with him a great ransom: moreover he bore in his hand the sceptre of Apollo wreathed with a suppliant's wreath, and he besought the Achæans, but most of all the two sons of Atreus, who were their chiefs.

'Sons of Atreus,' he cried, 'and all other Achæans, may the gods who dwell in Olympus grant you to sack the city of Priam, and to reach your homes in safety; but free my daughter, and accept a ransom for her, in reverence to Apollo, son of Jove.'

On this the rest of the Achæans with one voice were for respecting the priest and taking the ransom that he offered; but not so Agamemnon, who spoke fiercely to him and sent him roughly away. 'Old man,' said he, 'let me not find you tarrying about our ships, nor yet coming hereafter. Your sceptre of the god and your wreath shall profit you nothing. I will not free her. She shall grow old in my house at Argos far from her own home, busying herself with her loom and visiting my couch; so go, and do not provoke me or it shall be the worse for you.'

The old man feared him and obeyed. Not a word he spoke, but went by the shore of the sounding sea and prayed apart to King Apollo whom lovely Leto had borne. 'Hear me,' he cried, 'O god of the silver bow, that protectest Chryse and holy Cilla and rulest Tenedos with thy might, hear me oh thou of Sminthe. If I have ever decked your temple with garlands, or burned your thigh-bones in fat of bulls or goats, grant my prayer, and let your arrows avenge these my tears upon the Danaans.'

Thus did he pray, and Apollo heard his prayer. He came down furious from the summits of Olympus, with his bow and his quiver upon his shoulder, and the arrows rattled on his back with the rage that trembled within him. He sat himself down away from the ships with a face as dark as night, and his silver bow rang death as he shot his arrow in the midst of them. First he smote their mules and their hounds, but presently he aimed his shafts at the people themselves, and all day long the pyres of the dead were burning.

For nine whole days he shot his arrows among the people, but upon the tenth day Achilles called them in assembly – moved thereto by Juno, who saw the Achæans in their death-throes and had compassion upon them. Then, when they were got together, he rose and spoke among them.

'Son of Atreus,' said he, 'I deem that we should now turn roving home if we would escape destruction, for we are being cut down by war and pestilence at once. Let us ask some priest or prophet, or some reader of dreams (for dreams, too, are of Jove) who can tell us why Phœbus Apollo is so angry, and say whether it is for some vow that we have broken, or hecatomb that we have not offered, and whether he will accept the savour of lambs and goats without blemish, so as to take away the plague from us.'

With these words he sat down, and Calchas son of Thestor, wisest of augurs, who knew things past, present, and to come, rose to speak. He it was who had guided the Achæans with their fleet to Ilius, through the prophesyings with which Phœbus Apollo had inspired him. With all sincerity and goodwill he addressed them thus:—

'Achilles, loved of heaven, you bid me tell you about the anger of King Apollo, I will therefore do so; but consider first and swear that you will stand by me heartily in word and deed, for I know that I shall offend one who rules the Argives with might, and to whom all the Achæans are in subjection. A plain man cannot stand against the anger of a king, who if he swallow his displeasure now, will yet nurse revenge till he has wreaked it. Consider, therefore, whether or no you will protect me.'

And Achilles answered, 'Fear not, but speak as it is borne in upon you from heaven, for by Apollo, Calchas, to whom you pray, and whose oracles you reveal to us, not a Danaan at our ships shall lay his hand upon you, while I yet live to look upon the face of the earth – no, not though you name Agamemnon himself, who is by far the foremost of the Achæans.'

Thereon the seer spoke boldly. 'The god,' he said, 'is angry neither about vow nor hecatomb, but for his priest's sake, whom Agamemnon has dishonoured, in that he would not free his daughter nor take a ransom for her; therefore has he sent these evils upon us, and will yet send others. He will not deliver the Danaans from this pestilence till Agamemnon has restored the girl without fee or ransom to her father, and has sent a holy hecatomb to Chryse. Thus we may perhaps appease him.'

With these words he sat down, and Agamemnon rose in anger. His heart was black with rage, and his eyes flashed fire as he scowled on Calchas and said, 'Seer of evil, you never yet prophesied smooth things concerning me, but have ever loved to foretell that which was evil.

You have brought me neither comfort nor performance; and now you come seeing among the Danaans, and saying that Apollo has plagued us because I would not take a ransom for this girl, the daughter of Chryses. I have set my heart on keeping her in my own house, for I love her better even than my own wife Clytemnestra, whose peer she is alike in form and feature, in understanding and accomplishments. Still I will give her up if I must, for I would have the people live, not die; but you must find me a prize instead, or I alone among the Argives shall be without one. This is not well; for you behold, all of you, that my prize is to go elsewhither.'

And Achilles answered, 'Most noble son of Atreus, covetous beyond all mankind, how shall the Achæans find you another prize? We have no common store from which to take one. Those we took from the cities have been awarded; we cannot disallow the awards that have been made already. Give this girl, therefore, to the god, and if ever Jove grants us to sack the city of Troy we will requite you three and four-fold.'

Then Agamemnon said, 'Achilles, valiant though you be, you shall not thus outwit me. You shall not overreach and you shall not persuade me. Are you to keep your own prize, while I sit tamely under my loss and give up the girl at your bidding? Let the Achæans find me a prize in fair exchange to my liking, or I will come and take your own, or that of Ajax or of Ulysses; and he to whomsoever I may come shall rue my coming. But of this we will take thought hereafter; for the present, let us draw a ship into the sea, and find a crew for her expressly; let us put a hecatomb on board, and let us send Chryseis also; further, let some chief man among us be in command, either Ajax, or Idomeneus, or yourself, son of Peleus, mighty warrior that you are, that we may offer sacrifice and appease the anger of the god.'

Achilles scowled at him and answered, 'You are steeped in insolence and lust of gain. With what heart can any of the Achæans do your bidding, either on foray or in open fighting? I came not warring here for any ill the Trojans had done me. I have no quarrel with them. They have not raided my cattle nor my horses, nor cut down my harvests on the rich plains of Phthia; for between me and them there is a great space, both mountain and sounding sea. We have followed you, Sir Insolence! for your pleasure, not ours – to gain satisfaction from the Trojans for your shameless self and for Menelaus. You forget this, and threaten to rob me of the prize for which I have toiled, and which the sons of the Achæans have given me. Never when the Achæans sack any rich city of the Trojans do I receive so good a prize as you do, though it is my hands that do the better part of the fighting. When the sharing comes, your share is far the largest, and I, forsooth, must go back to my ships, take what I can get and be thankful, when my labour of fighting is done. Now, therefore, I shall go back to Phthia; it will be much better for me to return home with my ships, for I will not stay here dishonoured to gather gold and substance for you.'

And Agamemnon answered, 'Fly if you will, I shall make you no prayers to stay you. I have others here who will do me honour, and above all Jove, the lord of counsel. There is no king here so hateful to me as you are, for you are ever quarrelsome and ill affected. What though you be brave? Was it not heaven that made you so? Go home, then, with your ships and comrades to lord it over the Myrmidons. I care neither for you nor for your anger; and thus will I do: since Phœbus Apollo is taking Chryseis from me, I shall send her with my ship and my followers, but I shall come to your tent and take your own prize Briseis, that you may learn how much stronger I am than you are, and that another may fear to set himself up as equal or comparable with me.'

The son of Peleus was furious, and his heart within his shaggy breast was divided whether to draw his sword, push the others aside, and kill the son of Atreus, or to restrain himself and check his anger. While he was thus in two minds, and was drawing his mighty sword from its scabbard, Minerva came down from heaven (for Juno had sent her in the love she bore to them both), and seized the son of Peleus by his yellow hair, visible to him alone, for of the others no man could see her. Achilles turned in amaze, and by the fire that flashed from her eyes at once knew that she was Minerva. 'Why are you here,' said he, 'daughter of ægis-bearing[1] Jove? To see the pride of Agamemnon, son of Atreus? Let me tell you – and it shall surely be – he shall pay for this insolence with his life.'

And Minerva said, 'I come from heaven, if you will hear me, to bid you stay your anger. Juno has sent me, who cares for both of you alike. Cease, then, this brawling, and do not draw your sword; rail at him if you will, and your railing will not be vain, for I tell you – and it shall surely be – that you shall hereafter receive gifts three times as splendid by reason of this present insult. Hold, therefore, and obey.'

'Goddess,' answered Achilles, 'however angry a man may be, he must do as you two command him. This will be best, for the gods ever hear the prayers of him who has obeyed them.'

He stayed his hand on the silver hilt of his sword, and thrust it back into the scabbard as Minerva bade him. Then she went back to Olympus among the other gods, and to the house of ægis-bearing Jove.

But the son of Peleus again began railing at the son of Atreus, for he was still in a rage. 'Wine-bibber,' he cried, 'with the face of a dog and the heart of a hind, you never dare to go out with the host in fight, nor yet with our chosen men in ambuscade. You shun this as you do death itself. You had rather go round and rob his prizes from any man who contradicts you. You devour your people, for you are king over a feeble folk; otherwise, son of Atreus, hence-forward you would insult no man. Therefore I say, and swear it with a great oath – nay, by this my sceptre which shall sprout neither leaf nor shoot, nor bud anew from the day on which it left its parent stem upon the mountains – for the axe stripped it of leaf and bark, and now the sons of the Achæans bear it as judges and guardians of the decrees of heaven – so surely and solemnly do I swear that hereafter they shall look fondly for Achilles and shall not find him. In the day of your distress, when your men fall dying by the murderous hand of Hector, you shall not know how to help them, and shall rend your heart with rage for the hour when you offered insult to the bravest of the Achæans.'

With this the son of Peleus dashed his gold-bestudded sceptre on the ground and took his seat, while the son of Atreus was beginning fiercely from his place upon the other side. Then uprose smooth-tongued Nestor, the facile speaker of the Pylians, and the words fell from his lips sweeter than honey. Two generations of men born and bred in Pylos had passed away under his rule, and he was now reigning over the third. With all sincerity and goodwill, therefore, he addressed them thus:—

'Of a truth,' he said, 'a great sorrow has befallen the Achæan land. Surely Priam with his sons would rejoice, and the Trojans be glad at heart if they could hear this quarrel between you two, who are so excellent in fight and counsel. I am older than either of you; therefore be guided by me. Moreover I have been the familiar friend of men even greater than you are, and they did not disregard my counsels. Never again can I behold such men as Pirithoüs and Dryas shepherd of his people, or as Cæneus, Exadius, godlike Polyphemus, and Theseus son of Ægeus, peer of the immortals. These were the mightiest men ever born upon this earth: mightiest were they, and when they fought the fiercest tribes of mountain savages they utterly overthrew them. I came from distant Pylos, and went about among them, for they would have me come, and I fought as it was in me to do. Not a man now living could withstand them, but they heard my words, and were persuaded by them. So be it also with yourselves, for this is the more excellent way. Therefore, Agamemnon, though you be strong, take not this girl away, for the sons of the Achæans have already given her to Achilles; and you, Achilles, strive not further with the king, for no man who by the grace of Jove wields a sceptre has like honour with Agamemnon. You are strong, and have a goddess for your mother; but Agamemnon is stronger than you, for he has more people under him. Son of Atreus, check your anger, I implore you; end this quarrel with Achilles, who in the day of battle is a tower of strength to the Achæans.'

And Agamemnon answered, 'Sir, all that you have said is true, but this fellow must needs become our lord and master: he must be lord of all, king of all, and captain of all, and this shall hardly be. Granted that the gods have made him a great warrior, have they also given him the right to speak with railing?'

Achilles interrupted him. 'I should be a mean coward,' he cried, 'were I to give in to you in all things. Order other people about, not me, for I shall obey no longer. Furthermore I say – and lay my saying to your heart – I shall fight neither you nor any man about this girl, for those that take were those also that gave. But of all else that is at my ship you shall carry away nothing by force. Try, that others may see; if you do, my spear shall be reddened with your blood.'

When they had quarrelled thus angrily, they rose, and broke up the assembly at the ships of the Achæans. The son of Peleus went back to his tents and ships with the son of Menœtius and his company, while Agamemnon drew a vessel into the water and chose a crew of twenty oarsmen. He escorted Chryseis on board and sent moreover a hecatomb for the god. And Ulysses went as captain.

These, then, went on board and sailed their ways over the sea. But the son of Atreus bade the people purify themselves; so they purified themselves and cast their filth into the sea. Then they offered hecatombs of bulls and goats without blemish on the sea-shore, and the smoke with the savour of their sacrifice rose curling up towards heaven.

Thus did they busy themselves throughout the host. But Agamemnon did not forget the threat that he had made Achilles, and called his trusty messengers and squires Talthybius and Eurybates. 'Go,' said he, 'to the tent of Achilles, son of Peleus; take Briseis by the hand and bring her hither; if he will not give her I shall come with others and take her – which will press him harder.'

He charged them straightly further and dismissed them, whereon they went their way sorrowfully by the seaside, till they came to the tents and ships of the Myrmidons. They found Achilles sitting by his tent and his ships, and ill-pleased he was when he beheld them. They stood fearfully and reverently before him, and never a word did they speak, but he knew them and said, 'Welcome, heralds, messengers of gods and men; draw near; my quarrel is not with you but with Agamemnon who has sent you for the girl Briseis. Therefore, Patroclus, bring her and give her to them, but let them be witnesses by the blessed gods, by mortal men, and by the fierceness of Agamemnon's anger, that if ever again there be need of me to save the people from ruin, they shall seek and they shall not find. Agamemnon is mad with rage and knows not how to look before and after that the Achæans may fight by their ships in safety.'

Patroclus did as his dear comrade had bidden him. He brought Briseis from the tent and gave her over to the heralds, who took her with them to the ships of the Achæans – and the woman was loth to go. Then Achilles went all alone by the side of the hoar sea, weeping and looking out upon the boundless waste of waters. He raised his hands in prayer to his immortal mother, 'Mother,' he cried, 'you bore me doomed to live but for a little season; surely Jove, who thunders from Olympus, might have made that little glorious. It is not so. Agamemnon, son of Atreus, has done me dishonour, and has robbed me of my prize by force.'

As he spoke he wept aloud, and his mother heard him where she was sitting in the depths of the sea hard by the old man her father. Forthwith she rose as it were a grey mist out of the waves, sat down before him as he stood weeping, caressed him with her hand, and said, 'My son, why are you weeping? What is it that grieves you? Keep it not from me, but tell me, that we may know it together.'

Achilles drew a deep sigh and said, 'You know it; why tell you what you know well already? We went to Thebe the strong city of Eëtion, sacked it, and brought hither the spoil. The sons of the Achæans shared it duly among themselves, and chose lovely Chryseis as the meed of Agamemnon; but Chryses, priest of Apollo, came to the ships of the Achæans to free his daughter, and brought with him a great ransom: moreover he bore in his hand the sceptre of Apollo, wreathed with a suppliant's wreath, and he besought the Achæans, but most of all the two sons of Atreus who were their chiefs.

'On this the rest of the Achæans with one voice were for respecting the priest and taking the ransom that he offered; but not so Agamemnon, who spoke fiercely to him and sent him roughly away. So he went back in anger, and Apollo, who loved him dearly, heard his prayer. Then the god sent a deadly dart upon the Argives, and the people died thick on one another, for the arrows went everywhither among the wide host of the Achæans. At last a seer in the fulness of his knowledge declared to us the oracles of Apollo, and I was myself first to say that we should appease him. Whereon the son of Atreus rose in anger, and threatened that which he has since done. The Achæans are now taking the girl in a ship to Chryse, and sending gifts of sacrifice to the god; but the heralds have just taken from my tent the daughter of Briseus, whom the Achæans had awarded to myself.

'Help your brave son, therefore, if you are able. Go to Olympus, and if you have ever done him service in word or deed, implore the aid of Jove. Ofttimes in my father's house have I heard you glory in that you alone of the immortals saved the son of Saturn from ruin, when the others, with Juno, Neptune, and Pallas Minerva would have put him in bonds. It was you, goddess, who delivered him by calling to Olympus the hundred-handed monster whom gods call Briareus, but men Ægæon, for he is stronger even than his father; when therefore he took his seat all-glorious beside the son of Saturn, the other gods were afraid, and did not bind him. Go, then, to him, remind him of all this, clasp his knees, and bid him give succour to the Trojans. Let the Achæans be hemmed in at the sterns of their ships, and perish on the sea-shore, that they may reap what joy they may of their king, and that Agamemnon may rue his blindness in offering insult to the foremost of the Achæans.'

Thetis wept and answered, 'My son, woe is me that I should have borne or suckled you. Would indeed that you had lived your span free from all sorrow at your ships, for it is all too brief; alas, that you should be at once short of life and long of sorrow above your peers: woe, therefore, was the hour in which I bore you; nevertheless I will go to the snowy heights of Olympus, and tell this tale to Jove, if he will hear our prayer: meanwhile stay where you are with your ships, nurse your anger against the Achæans, and hold aloof from fight. For Jove went yesterday to Oceanus, to a feast among the Ethiopians, and the other gods went with him. He will return to Olympus twelve days hence; I will then go to his mansion paved with bronze and will beseech him; nor do I doubt that I shall be able to persuade him.'

On this she left him, still furious at the loss of her that had been taken from him. Meanwhile Ulysses reached Chryse with the hecatomb. When they had come inside the harbour they furled the sails and laid them in the ship's hold; they slackened the forestays, lowered the mast into its place, and rowed the ship to the place where they would have her lie; there they cast out their mooring-stones and made fast the hawsers. They then got out upon the sea-shore and landed the hecatomb for Apollo; Chryseis also left the ship, and Ulysses led her to the altar to deliver her into the hands of her father. 'Chryses,' said he, 'King Agamemnon has sent me to bring you back your child, and to offer sacrifice to Apollo on behalf of the Danaans, that we may propitiate the god, who has now brought much sorrow upon the Argives.'

So saying he gave the girl over to her father, who received her gladly, and they ranged the holy hecatomb all orderly round the altar of the god. They washed their hands and took up the barley-meal to sprinkle over the victims, while Chryses lifted up his hands and prayed aloud on their behalf. 'Hear me,' he cried, 'O god of the silver bow, that protectest Chryse and holy Cilla, and rulest Tenedos with thy might. Even as thou didst hear me aforetime when I prayed, and didst press hardly upon the Achæans, so hear me yet again, and stay this fearful pestilence from the Danaans.'

Thus did he pray, and Apollo heard his prayer. When they had done praying and sprinkling the barley-meal, they drew back the heads of the victims and killed and flayed them. They cut out the thigh-bones, wrapped them round in two layers of fat, set some pieces of raw meat on the top of them, and then Chryses laid them on the wood fire and poured wine over them, while the young men stood near him with five-pronged spits in their hands. When the thigh-bones were burned and they had tasted the inward meats, they cut the rest up small, put the pieces upon the spits, roasted them till they were done, and drew them off: then, when they had finished their work and the feast was ready, they ate it, and every man had his full share, so that all were satisfied. As soon as they had had enough to eat and drink, pages filled the mixing-bowl with wine and water and handed it round, after giving every man his drink-offering.

Thus all day long the young men worshipped the god with song, hymning him and chaunting the joyous pæan, and the god took pleasure in their voices; but when the sun went down, and it came on dark, they laid themselves down to sleep by the stern cables of the ship, and when the child of morning, rosy-fingered Dawn, appeared they again set sail for the host of the Achæans. Apollo sent them a fair wind, so they raised their mast and hoisted their white sails aloft. As the sail bellied with the wind the ship flew through the deep blue water, and the foam hissed against her bows as she sped onward. When they reached the wide-stretching host of the Achæans, they drew the vessel ashore, high and dry upon the sands, set her strong props beneath her, and went their ways to their own tents and ships.

But Achilles abode at his ships and nursed his anger. He went not to the honourable assembly, and sallied not forth to fight, but gnawed at his own heart, pining for battle and the war-cry.

Now after twelve days the immortal gods came back in a body to Olympus, and Jove led the way. Thetis was not unmindful of the charge her son had laid upon her, so she rose from under the sea and went through great heaven with early morning to Olympus, where she found the mighty son of Saturn sitting all alone upon its topmost ridges. She sat herself down before him, and with her left hand seized his knees, while with her right she caught him under the chin, and besought him, saying:—

'Father Jove, if I ever did you service in word or deed among the immortals, hear my prayer, and do honour to my son, whose life is to be cut short so early. King Agamemnon has dishonoured him by taking his prize and keeping her. Honour him then yourself, Olympian lord of counsel, and grant victory to the Trojans, till the Achæans give my son his due and load him with riches in requital.'

Jove sat for a while silent, and without a word, but Thetis still kept firm hold of his knees, and besought him a second time. 'Incline your head,' said she, 'and promise me surely, or else deny me – for you have nothing to fear – that I may learn how greatly you disdain me.'

At this Jove was much troubled and answered, 'I shall have trouble if you set me quarrelling with Juno, for she will provoke me with her taunting speeches; even now she is always railing at me before the other gods and accusing me of giving aid to the Trojans. Go back now, lest she should find out. I will consider the matter, and will bring it about as you wish. See, I incline my head that you may believe me. This is the most solemn token that I can give to any god. I never recall my word, or deceive, or fail to do what I say, when I have nodded my head.'

As he spoke the son of Saturn bowed his dark brows, and the ambrosial locks swayed on his immortal head, till vast Olympus reeled.

When the pair had thus laid their plans, they parted – Jove to his own house, while the goddess quitted the splendour of Olympus, and plunged into the depths of the sea. The gods rose from their seats, before the coming of their sire. Not one of them dared to remain sitting, but all stood up as he came among them. There, then, he took his seat. But Juno, when she saw him, knew that he and the old merman's daughter, silver-footed Thetis, had been hatching mischief, so she at once began to upbraid him. 'Trickster,' she cried, 'which of the gods have you been taking into your counsels now? You are always settling matters in secret behind my back, and have never yet told me, if you could help it, one word of your intentions.'

'Juno,' replied the sire of gods and men, 'you must not expect to be informed of all my counsels. You are my wife, but you would find it hard to understand them. When it is proper for you to hear, there is no one, god or man, who will be told sooner, but when I mean to keep a matter to myself, you must not pry nor ask questions.'

'Dread son of Saturn,' answered Juno, 'what are you talking about? I? Pry and ask questions? Never. I let you have your own way in everything. Still, I have a strong misgiving that the old merman's daughter Thetis has been talking you over, for she was with you and had hold of your knees this self-same morning. I believe, therefore, that you have been promising her to give glory to Achilles, and to kill much people at the ships of the Achæans.'

'Wife,' said Jove, 'I can do nothing but you suspect me and find it out. You will take nothing by it, for I shall only dislike you the more, and it will go harder with you. Granted that it is as you say; I mean to have it so; sit down and hold your tongue as I bid you, for if I once begin to lay my hands about you, though all heaven were on your side it would profit you nothing.'

On this Juno was frightened, so she curbed her stubborn will and sat down in silence. But the heavenly beings were disquieted throughout the house of Jove, till the cunning workman Vulcan began to try and pacify his mother Juno. 'It will be intolerable,' said he, 'if you two fall to wrangling and setting heaven in an uproar about a pack of mortals. If such ill counsels are to prevail, we shall have no pleasure at our banquet. Let me then advise my mother – and she must herself know that it will be better – to make friends with my dear father Jove, lest he again scold her and disturb our feast. If the Olympian Thunderer wants to hurl us all from our seats, he can do so, for he is far the strongest, so give him fair words, and he will then soon be in a good humour with us.'

As he spoke, he took a double cup of nectar, and placed it in his mother's hand. 'Cheer up, my dear mother,' said he, 'and make the best of it. I love you dearly, and should be very sorry to see you get a thrashing; however grieved I might be, I could not help you, for there is no standing against Jove. Once before when I was trying to help you, he caught me by the foot and flung me from the heavenly threshold. All day long from morn till eve, was I falling, till at sunset I came to ground in the island of Lemnos, and there I lay, with very little life left in me, till the Sintians came and tended me.'

Juno smiled at this, and as she smiled she took the cup from her son's hands. Then Vulcan drew sweet nectar from the mixing-bowl, and served it round among the gods, going from left to right; and the blessed gods laughed out a loud applause as they saw him bustling about the heavenly mansion.

Thus through the livelong day to the going down of the sun they feasted, and every one had his full share, so that all were satisfied. Apollo struck his lyre, and the Muses lifted up their sweet voices, calling and answering one another. But when the sun's glorious light had faded, they went home to bed, each in his own abode, which lame Vulcan with his consummate skill had fashioned for them. So Jove, the Olympian Lord of Thunder, hied him to the bed in which he always slept; and when he had got on to it he went to sleep, with Juno of the golden throne by his side.

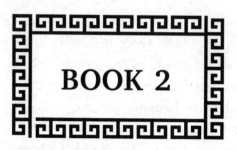

BOOK 2

Jove sends a lying dream to Agamemnon, who thereon calls the chiefs in assembly, and proposes to sound the mind of his army – In the end they march to fight – Catalogue of the Achæan and Trojan forces.

Now the other gods and the armed warriors on the plain slept soundly, but Jove was wakeful, for he was thinking how to do honour to Achilles, and destroy much people at the ships of the Achæans. In the end he deemed it would be best to send a lying dream to King Agamemnon; so he called one to him and said to it, 'Lying Dream, go to the ships of the Achæans, into the tent of Agamemnon, and say to him word for word as I now bid you. Tell him to get the Achæans instantly under arms, for he shall take Troy. There are no longer divided counsels among the gods; Juno has brought them to her own mind, and woe betides the Trojans.'

The dream went when it had heard its message, and soon reached the ships of the Achæans. It sought Agamemnon son of Atreus and found him in his tent, wrapped in a profound slumber. It hovered over his head in the likeness of Nestor, son of Neleus, whom Agamemnon honoured above all his councillors, and said:—

'You are sleeping, son of Atreus; one who has the welfare of his host and so much other care upon his shoulders should dock his sleep. Hear me at once, for I come as a messenger from Jove, who, though he be not near, yet takes thought for you and pities you. He bids you get the Achæans instantly under arms, for you shall take Troy. There are no longer divided counsels among the gods; Juno has brought them over to her own mind, and woe betides the Trojans at the hands of Jove. Remember this, and when you wake see that it does not escape you.'

The dream then left him, and he thought of things that were surely not to be accomplished. He thought that on that same day he was to take the city of Priam, but he little knew what was in the mind of Jove, who had many another hard-fought fight in store alike for Danaans and Trojans. Then presently he woke, with the divine message still ringing in his ears; so he sat upright, and put on his soft shirt so fair and new, and over this his heavy cloak. He bound his sandals on to his comely feet, and slung his silver-studded sword about his shoulders; then he took the imperishable staff of his father, and sallied forth to the ships of the Achæans.

The goddess Dawn now wended her way to vast Olympus that she might herald day to Jove and to the other immortals, and Agamemnon sent the criers round to call the people in assembly; so they called them and the people gathered thereon. But first he summoned a meeting of the elders at the ship of Nestor king of Pylos, and when they were assembled he laid a cunning counsel before them.

'My friends,' said he, 'I have had a dream from heaven in the dead of night, and its face and figure resembled none but Nestor's. It hovered over my head and said, 'You are sleeping, son of Atreus; one who has the welfare of his host and so much other care upon his shoulders should dock his sleep. Hear me at once, for I am a messenger from Jove, who, though he be not near, yet takes thought for you and pities you. He bids you get the Achæans instantly under arms, for you shall take Troy. There are no longer divided counsels among the gods; Juno has brought them over to her own mind, and woe betides the Trojans at the hands of Jove. Remember this.' The dream then vanished and I awoke. Let us now, therefore, arm the sons of the Achæans. But it will be well that I should first sound them, and to this end I will tell them to fly with their ships; but do you others go about among the host and prevent their doing so.'

He then sat down, and Nestor the prince of Pylos with all sincerity and goodwill addressed them thus: 'My friends,' said he, 'princes and councillors of the Argives, if any other man of the Achæans had told us of this dream we should have declared it false, and would have had nothing to do with it. But he who has seen it is the foremost man among us; we must therefore set about getting the people under arms.'

With this he led the way from the assembly, and the other sceptred kings rose with him in obedience to the word of Agamemnon; but the people pressed forward to hear. They swarmed like bees that sally from some hollow cave and flit in countless throng among the spring flowers, bunched in knots and clusters; even so did the mighty multitude pour from ships and tents to the assembly, and range themselves upon the wide-watered shore, while among them ran Wildfire Rumour, messenger of Jove, urging them ever to the fore. Thus they gathered in a pell-mell of mad confusion, and the earth groaned under the tramp of men as the people sought their places. Nine heralds went crying about among them to stay their tumult and bid them listen to the kings, till at last they were got into their several places and ceased their clamour. Then King Agamemnon rose, holding his sceptre. This was the work of Vulcan, who gave it to Jove the son of Saturn. Jove gave it to Mercury, slayer of Argus, guide and guardian. King Mercury gave it to Pelops, the mighty charioteer, and Pelops to Atreus, shepherd of his people. Atreus, when he died, left it to Thyestes, rich in flocks, and Thyestes in his turn left it to be borne by Agamemnon, that he might be lord of all Argos and of the isles. Leaning, then, on his sceptre, he addressed the Argives.

'My friends,' he said, 'heroes, servants of Mars, the hand of heaven has been laid heavily upon me. Cruel Jove gave me his solemn promise that I should sack the city of Priam before returning, but he has played me false, and is now bidding me go ingloriously back to Argos with the loss of much people. Such is the will of Jove, who has laid many a proud city in the dust, as he will yet lay others, for his power is above all. It will be a sorry tale hereafter that an Achæan host, at once so great and valiant, battled in vain against men fewer in number than themselves; but as yet the end is not in sight. Think that the Achæans and Trojans have sworn to a solemn covenant, and that they have each been numbered – the Trojans by the roll of their householders, and we by companies of ten; think further that each of our companies desired to have a Trojan householder to pour out their wine; we are so greatly more in number that full many a company would have to go without its cup-bearer. But they have in the town many allies from other places, and it is these that hinder me from being able to sack the rich city of Ilius. Nine of Jove's years are gone; the timbers of our ships have rotted; their tackling is sound no longer. Our wives and little ones at home look anxiously for our coming, but the work that we came hither to do has not been done. Now, therefore, let us all do as I say: let us sail back to our own land, for we shall not take Troy.'

With these words he moved the hearts of the multitude, so many of them as knew not the cunning counsel of Agamemnon. They surged to and fro like the waves of the Icarian Sea, when the east and south winds break from heaven's clouds to lash them; or as when the west wind sweeps over a field of corn and the ears bow beneath the blast, even so were they swayed as they flew with loud cries towards the ships, and the dust from under their feet rose heavenward. They cheered each other on to draw the ships into the sea; they cleared the channels in front of them; they began taking away the stays from underneath them, and the welkin rang with their glad cries, so eager were they to return.

Then surely the Argives would have returned after a fashion that was not fated. But Juno said to Minerva, 'Alas, daughter of ægis-bearing Jove, unweariable, shall the Argives fly home to their own land over the broad sea, and leave Priam and the Trojans the glory of still keeping Helen, for whose sake so many of the Achæans have died at Troy, far from their homes? Go about at once among the host, and speak fairly to them, man by man, that they draw not their ships into the sea.'

Minerva was not slack to do her bidding. Down she darted from the topmost summits of Olympus, and in a moment she was at the ships of the Achæans. There she found Ulysses, peer of Jove in counsel, standing alone. He had not as yet laid a hand upon his ship, for he was grieved and sorry; so she went close up to him and said, 'Ulysses, noble son of Laertes, are you going to fling yourselves into your ships, and be off home to your own land in this way? Will you leave Priam and the Trojans the glory of still keeping Helen, for whose sake so many of the Achæans have died at Troy, far from their homes? Go about at once among the host, and speak fairly to them, man by man, that they draw not their ships into the sea.'

Ulysses knew the voice as that of the goddess; he flung his cloak from him and set off to run. His servant Eurybates, a man of Ithaca, who waited on him, took charge of the cloak, whereon Ulysses went straight up to Agamemnon and received from him his ancestral, imperishable staff. With this he went about among the ships of the Achæans.

Whenever he met a king or chieftain, he stood by him and spoke him fairly. 'Sir,' said he, 'this flight is cowardly and unworthy. Stand to your post, and bid your people also keep their places. You do not yet know the full mind of Agamemnon; he was sounding us, and ere long will visit the Achæans with his displeasure. We were not all of us at the council to hear what he then said; see to it lest he be angry and do us a mischief; for the pride of kings is great, and the hand of Jove is with them.'

But when he came across any common man who was making a noise, he struck him with his staff and rebuked him, saying, 'Sirrah, hold your peace, and listen to better men than yourself. You are a coward and no soldier; you are nobody either in fight or council; we cannot all be kings; it is not well that there should be many masters; one man must be supreme – one king to whom the son of scheming Saturn has given the sceptre of sovereignty over you all.'

Thus masterfully did he go about among the host, and the people hurried back to the council from their tents and ships with a sound as the thunder of surf when it comes crashing down upon the shore, and all the sea is in an uproar.

The rest now took their seats and kept to their own several places, but Thersites still went on wagging his unbridled tongue – a man of many words, and those unseemly; a monger of sedition, a railer against all who were in authority, who cared not what he said, so that he might set the Achæans in a laugh. He was the ugliest man of all those that came before Troy – bandy-legged, lame of one foot, with his two shoulders rounded and hunched over his chest. His head ran up to a point, but there was little hair on the top of it. Achilles and Ulysses hated him worst of all, for it was with them that he was most wont to wrangle; now, however, with a shrill squeaky voice he began heaping his abuse on Agamemnon. The Achæans were angry and disgusted, yet none the less he kept on brawling and bawling at the son of Atreus.

'Agamemnon,' he cried, 'what ails you now, and what more do you want? Your tents are filled with bronze and with fair women, for whenever we take a town we give you the pick of them. Would you have yet more gold, which some Trojan is to give you as a ransom for his son, when I or another Achæan has taken him prisoner? or is it some young girl to hide away and lie with? It is not well that you, the ruler of the Achæans, should bring them into such misery. Weakling cowards, women rather than men, let us sail home, and leave this fellow here at Troy to stew in his own meeds of honour, and discover whether we were of any service to him or no. Achilles is a much better man than he is, and see how he has treated him – robbing him of his prize and keeping it himself. Achilles takes it meekly and shows no fight; if he did, son of Atreus, you would never again insult him.'

Thus railed Thersites, but Ulysses at once went up to him and rebuked him sternly. 'Check your glib tongue, Thersites,' said he, 'and babble not a word further. Chide not with princes when you have none to back you. There is no viler creature come before Troy with the sons of Atreus. Drop this chatter about kings, and neither revile them nor keep harping about going home. We do not yet know how things are going to be, nor whether the Achæans are to return with good success or evil. How dare you gibe at Agamemnon because the Danaans have awarded him so many prizes? I tell you, therefore – and it shall surely be – that if I again catch you talking such nonsense, I will either forfeit my own head and be no more called father of Telemachus, or I will take you, strip you stark naked, and whip you out of the assembly till you go blubbering back to the ships.'

On this he beat him with his staff about the back and shoulders till he dropped and fell a-weeping. The golden sceptre raised a bloody weal on his back, so he sat down frightened and in pain, looking foolish as he wiped the tears from his eyes. The people were sorry for him, yet they laughed heartily, and one would turn to his neighbour saying, 'Ulysses has done many a good thing ere now in fight and council, but he never did the Argives a better turn than when he stopped this fellow's mouth from prating further. He will give the kings no more of his insolence.'

Thus said the people. Then Ulysses rose, sceptre in hand, and Minerva in the likeness of a herald bade the people be still, that those who were far off might hear him and consider his council. He therefore with all sincerity and goodwill addressed them thus:—

'King Agamemnon, the Achæans are for making you a by-word among all mankind. They forget the promise they made you when they set out from Argos, that you should not return till you had sacked the town of Troy, and, like children or widowed women, they murmur and would set off homeward. True it is that they have had toil enough to be disheartened. A man chafes at having to stay away from his wife even for a single month, when he is on shipboard, at the mercy of wind and sea, but it is now nine long years that we have been kept here; I cannot, therefore, blame the Achæans if they turn restive; still we shall be shamed if we go home empty after so long a stay – therefore, my friends, be patient yet a little longer that we may learn whether the prophesyings of Calchas were false or true.

'All who have not since perished must remember as though it were yesterday or the day before, how the ships of the Achæans were detained in Aulis when we were on our way hither to make war on Priam and the Trojans. We were ranged round about a fountain offering hecatombs to the gods upon their holy altars, and there was a fine plane-tree from beneath which there welled a stream of pure water. Then we saw a prodigy; for Jove sent a fearful serpent out of the ground, with blood-red stains upon its back, and it darted from under the altar on to the plane-tree. Now there was a brood of young sparrows, quite small, upon the topmost bough, peeping out from under the leaves, eight in all, and their mother that hatched them made nine. The serpent ate the poor cheeping things, while the old bird flew about lamenting her little ones; but the serpent threw his coils about her and caught her by the wing as she was screaming. Then, when he had eaten both the sparrow and her young, the god who had sent him made him become a sign; for the son of scheming Saturn turned him into stone, and we stood there wondering at that which had come to pass. Seeing, then, that such a fearful portent had broken in upon our hecatombs, Calchas forthwith declared to us the oracles of heaven. "Why, Achæans," said he, "are you thus speechless? Jove has sent us this sign, long in coming, and long ere it be fulfilled, though its fame shall last for ever. As the serpent ate the eight fledglings and the sparrow that hatched them, which makes nine, so shall we fight nine years at Troy, but in the tenth shall take the town." This was what he said, and now it is all coming true. Stay here, therefore, all of you, till we take the city of Priam.'

On this the Argives raised a shout, till the ships rang again with the uproar. Nestor, knight of Gerene, then addressed them. 'Shame on you,' he cried, 'to stay talking here like children, when you should fight like men. Where are our covenants now, and where the oaths that we have taken? Shall our counsels be flung into the fire, with our drink-offerings and the right hands of fellowship wherein we have put our trust? We waste our time in words, and for all our talking here shall be no further forward. Stand, therefore, son of Atreus, by your own steadfast purpose; lead the Argives on to battle, and leave this handful of men to rot, who scheme, and scheme in vain, to get back to Argos ere they have learned whether Jove be true or a liar. For the mighty son of Saturn surely promised that we should succeed, when we Argives set sail to bring death and destruction upon the Trojans. He showed us favourable signs by flashing his lightning on our right hands; therefore let none make haste to go till he has first lain with the wife of some Trojan, and avenged the toil and sorrow that he has suffered for the sake of Helen. Nevertheless, if any man is in such haste to be at home again, let him lay his hand to his ship that he may meet his doom in the sight of all. But, O king, consider and give ear to my counsel, for the word that I say may not be neglected lightly. Divide your men, Agamemnon, into their several tribes and clans, that clans and tribes may stand by and help one another. If you do this, and if the Achæans obey you, you will find out who, both chiefs and peoples, are brave, and who are cowards; for they will vie one against the other. Thus you shall also learn whether it is through the counsel of heaven or the cowardice of man that you shall fail to take the town.'

And Agamemnon answered, 'Nestor, you have again outdone the sons of the Achæans in counsel. Would, by Father Jove, Minerva, and Apollo, that I had among them ten more such councillors, for the city of King Priam would then soon fall beneath our hands, and we should sack it. But the son of Saturn afflicts me with bootless wranglings and strife. Achilles and I are quarrelling about this girl, in which matter I was the first to offend; if we can be of one mind again, the Trojans will not stave off destruction for a day. Now, therefore, get your morning meal, that our hosts may join in fight. Whet well your spears; see well to the ordering of your shields; give good feeds to your horses, and look your chariots carefully over, that we may do battle the livelong day; for we shall have no rest, not for a moment, till night falls to part us. The bands that bear your shields shall be wet with the sweat upon your shoulders, your hands shall weary upon your spears, your horses shall steam in front of your chariots, and if I see any man shirking the fight, or trying to keep out of it at the ships, there shall be no help for him, but he shall be a prey to dogs and vultures.'

Thus he spoke, and the Achæans roared applause. As when the waves run high before the blast of the south wind and break on some lofty headland, dashing against it and buffeting it without ceasing, as the storms from every quarter drive them, even so did the Achæans rise and hurry in all directions to their ships. There they lighted their fires at their tents and got dinner, offering sacrifice every man to one or other of the gods, and praying each one of them that he might live to come out of the fight. Agamemnon, king of men, sacrificed a fat five-year-old bull to the mighty son of Saturn, and invited the princes and elders of his host. First he asked Nestor and King Idomeneus, then the two Ajaxes and the son of Tydeus, and sixthly Ulysses, peer of gods in counsel; but Menelaus came of his own accord, for he knew how busy his brother then was. They stood round the bull with the barley-meal in their hands, and Agamemnon prayed, saying, 'Jove, most glorious, supreme, that dwellest in heaven, and ridest upon the storm-cloud, grant that the sun may not go down, nor the night fall, till the palace of Priam is laid low, and its gates are consumed with fire. Grant that my sword may pierce the shirt of Hector about his heart, and that full many of his comrades may bite the dust as they fall dying round him.'

Thus he prayed, but the son of Saturn would not fulfil his prayer. He accepted the sacrifice, yet none the less increased their toil continually. When they had done praying and sprinkling the barley-meal upon the victim, they drew back its head, killed it, and then flayed it. They cut out the thigh-bones, wrapped them round in two layers of fat, and set pieces of raw meat on the top of them. These they burned upon the split logs of firewood, but they spitted the inward meats, and held them in the flames to cook. When the thigh-bones were burned, and they had tasted the inward meats, they cut the rest up small, put the pieces upon spits, roasted them till they were done, and drew them off; then, when they had finished their work and the feast was ready, they ate it, and every man had his full share, so that all were satisfied. As soon as they had had enough to eat and drink, Nestor, knight of Gerene, began to speak. 'King Agamemnon,' said he, 'let us not stay talking here, nor be slack in the work that heaven has put into our hands. Let the heralds summon the people to gather at their several ships; we will then go about among the host, that we may begin fighting at once.'

Thus did he speak and Agamemnon heeded his words. He at once sent the criers round to call the people in assembly. So they called them, and the people gathered thereon. The chiefs about the son of Atreus chose their men and marshalled them, while Minerva went among them holding her priceless ægis that knows neither age nor death. From it there waved a hundred tassels of pure gold, all deftly woven, and each one of them worth a hundred oxen. With this she darted furiously everywhere among the hosts of the Achæans, urging them forward, and putting courage into the heart of each, so that he might fight and do battle without ceasing. Thus war became sweeter in their eyes even than returning home in their ships. As when some great forest fire is raging upon a mountain top and its light is seen afar, even so as they marched the gleam of their armour flashed up into the firmament of heaven.

They were like great flocks of geese, or cranes, or swans on the plain about the waters of Cayster, that wing their way hither and thither, glorying in the pride of flight, and crying as they settle till the fen is alive with their screaming. Even thus did their tribes pour from ships and tents on to the plain of the Scamander; and the ground rang as brass under the feet of men and horses. They stood as thick upon the flower-bespangled field as leaves that bloom in summer.

As countless swarms of flies buzz around a herdsman's homestead in the time of spring when the pails are drenched with milk, even so did the Achæans swarm on to the plain to charge the Trojans and destroy them.

The chiefs disposed their men this way and that before the fight began, drafting them out as easily as goatherds draft their flocks when they have got mixed while feeding; and among them went King Agamemnon, with a head and face like Jove the lord of thunder, a waist like Mars, and a chest like that of Neptune. As some great bull that lords it over the herds upon the plain, even so did Jove make the son of Atreus stand peerless among the multitude of heroes.

And now, O Muses, dwellers in the mansions of Olympus, tell me – for you are goddesses and are in all places so that you see all things, while we know nothing but by report – who were the chiefs and princes of the Danaans? As for the common soldiers, they were so many that I could not name every single one of them though I had ten tongues, and though my voice failed not and my heart were of bronze within me, unless you, O Olympian Muses, daughters of ægis-bearing Jove, were to recount them to me. Nevertheless, I will tell the captains of the ships and all the fleet together.

Peneleōs, Leïtus, Arcesilaus, Prothoënor, and Clonius were captains of the Bœotians. These were they that dwelt in Hyria and rocky Aulis, and who held Schœnus, Scolus, and the highlands of Eteonus, with Thespeia, Graia, and the fair city of Mycalessus. They also held Harma, Eilesium, and Erythræ; and they had Eleon, Hyle, and Peteon; Ocalea and the strong fortress of Medeon; Copæ, Eutrēsis, and Thisbe the haunt of doves; Coronea, and the pastures of Haliartus; Platæa and Glisas; the fortress of Thebes the less; holy Onchestus with its famous grove of Neptune; Arne rich in vineyards; Midea, sacred Nisa, and Anthedon upon the sea. From these there came fifty ships, and in each there were a hundred and twenty young men of the Bœotians.

Ascalaphus and Ialmenus, sons of Mars, led the people that dwelt in Aspledon and Orchomenus the realm of Minyas. Astyoche a noble maiden bore them in the house of Actor son of Azeus; for she had gone with Mars secretly into an upper chamber, and he had lain with her. With these there came thirty ships.

The Phocēans were led by Schedius and Epistrophus, sons of mighty Iphitus the son of Naubolus. These were they that held Cyparissus, rocky Pytho, holy Crisa, Daulis, and Panopeus; they also that dwelt in Anemorea and Hyampolis, and about the waters of the river Cephissus, and Lilæa by the springs of the Cephissus; with their chieftains came forty ships, and they marshalled the forces of the Phocēans, which were stationed next to the Bœotians, on their left.

Ajax, the fleet son of Oïleus, commanded the Locrians. He was not so great, nor nearly so great, as Ajax the son of Telamon. He was a little man, and his breastplate was made of linen, but in use of the spear he excelled all the Hellenes and the Achæans. These dwelt in Cynus, Opoüs, Calliarus, Bessa, Scarphe, fair Augeæ, Tarphe, and Thronium about the river Boagrius. With him there came forty ships of the Locrians who dwell beyond Eubœa.

The fierce Abantes held Eubœa with its cities, Chalcis, Eretria, Histiæa rich in vines, Cerinthus upon the sea, and the rock-perched town of Dium; with them were also the men of Carystus and Styra; Elephenor of the race of Mars was in command of these; he was son of Chalcōdon, and chief over all the Abantes. With him they came, fleet of foot and wearing their hair long behind, brave warriors, who would ever strive to tear open the corslets of their foes with their long ashen spears. Of these there came fifty ships.

And they that held the strong city of Athens, the people of great Erechtheus, who was born of the soil itself, but Jove's daughter, Minerva, fostered him, and established him at Athens in her own rich sanctuary. There, year by year, the Athenian youths worship him with sacrifices of bulls and rams. These were commanded by Menestheus, son of Peteōs. No man living could equal him in the marshalling of chariots and foot soldiers. Nestor could alone rival him, for he was older. With him there came fifty ships.

Ajax brought twelve ships from Salamis, and stationed them alongside those of the Athenians.

The men of Argos, again, and those who held the walls of Tiryns, with Hermione, and Asine upon the gulf; Trœzene, Eïonæ, and the vineyard lands of Epidaurus; the Achæan youths, moreover, who came from Ægina and Mases; these were led by Diomed of the loud battle-cry, and Sthenelus son of famed Capaneus. With them in command was Euryalus, son of king Mecisteus, son of Talaus; but Diomed was chief over them all. With these there came eighty ships.

Those who held the strong city of Mycenæ, rich Corinth and Cleonæ; Orneæ, Aræthyrea, and Licyon, where Adrastus reigned of old; Hyperesia, high Gonoëssa, and Pellene; Ægium and all the coast-land round about Helice; these sent a hundred ships under the command of King Agamemnon, son of Atreus. His force was far both finest and most numerous, and in their midst was the king himself, all glorious in his armour of gleaming bronze – foremost among the heroes, for he was the greatest king, and had most men under him.

And those that dwelt in Lacedæmon, lying low among the hills, Pharis, Sparta,[2] with Messe the haunt of doves; Bryseæ, Augeæ, Amyclæ, and Helos upon the sea; Laas, moreover, and Œtylus; these were led by Menelaus of the loud battle-cry, brother to Agamemnon, and of them there were sixty ships, drawn up apart from the others. Among them went Menelaus himself, strong in zeal, urging his men to fight; for he longed to avenge the toil and sorrow that he had suffered for the sake of Helen.

The men of Pylos and Arēne, and Thryum where is the ford of the river Alpheus; strong Aipy, Cyparisseis, and Amphigenea; Pteleum, Helos, and Dorium, where the Muses met Thamyris, and stilled his minstrelsy for ever. He was returning from Œchalia, where Eurytus lived and reigned, and boasted that he would surpass even the Muses, daughters of ægis-bearing Jove, if they should sing against him; whereon they were angry, and maimed him. They robbed him of his divine power of song, and thenceforth he could strike the lyre no more. These were commanded by Nestor, knight of Gerene, and with him there came ninety ships.

And those that held Arcadia, under the high mountain of Cyllene, near the tomb of Æpytus, where the people fight hand to hand; the men of Pheneus also, and Orchomenus rich in flocks; of Rhipæ, Stratie, and bleak Enispe; of Tegea and fair Mantinea; of Stymphelus and

Parrhasia; of these King Agapenor son of Ancæus was commander, and they had sixty ships. Many Arcadians, good soldiers, came in each one of them, but Agamemnon found them the ships in which to cross the sea, for they were not a people that occupied their business upon the waters.

The men, moreover, of Buprasium and of Elis, so much of it as is enclosed between Hyrmine, Myrsinus upon the sea-shore, the rock Olene and Alesium. These had four leaders, and each of them had ten ships, with many Epeans on board. Their captains were Amphimachus and Thalpius – the one, son of Cteatus, and the other, of Eurytus – both of the race of Actor. The two others were Diōres, son of Amarynces, and Polyxenus, son of King Agasthenes, son of Augeas.

And those of Dulichium with the sacred Echinean islands, who dwelt beyond the sea off Elis; these were led by Meges, peer of Mars, and the son of valiant Phyleus, dear to Jove, who quarrelled with his father, and went to settle in Dulichium. With him there came forty ships.

Ulysses led the brave Cephallenians, who held Ithaca, Neritum with its forests, Crocylea, rugged Ægilips, Samos and Zacynthus, with the mainland also that was over against the islands. These were led by Ulysses, peer of Jove in counsel, and with him there came twelve ships.

Thoas, son of Andræmon, commanded the Ætolians, who dwelt in Pleuron, Olenus, Pylene, Chalcis by the sea, and rocky Calydon, for the great king Œneus had now no sons living, and was himself dead, as was also golden-haired Meleager, who had been set over the Ætolians to be their king. And with Thoas there came forty ships.

The famous spearsman Idomeneus led the Cretans, who held Cnossus, and the well-walled city of Gortys; Lyctus also, Miletus and Lycastus that lies upon the chalk; the populous towns of Phæstus and Rhytium, with the other peoples that dwelt in the hundred cities of Crete. All these were led by Idomeneus, and by Meriones, peer of murderous Mars. And with these there came eighty ships.

Tlepolemus, son of Hercules, a man both brave and large of stature, brought nine ships of lordly warriors from Rhodes. These dwelt in

Rhodes which is divided among the three cities of Lindus, Ielysus, and Cameirus, that lies upon the chalk. These were commanded by Tlepolemus, son of Hercules by Astyochea, whom he had carried off from Ephyra, on the river Selleïs, after sacking many cities of valiant warriors. When Tlepolemus grew up, he killed his father's uncle Licymnius, who had been a famous warrior in his time, but was then grown old. On this he built himself a fleet, gathered a great following, and fled beyond the sea, for he was menaced by the other sons and grandsons of Hercules. After a voyage, during which he suffered great hardship, he came to Rhodes, where the people divided into three communities, according to their tribes, and were dearly loved by Jove, the lord of gods and men; wherefore the son of Saturn showered down great riches upon them.

And Nireus brought three ships from Syme – Nireus, who was the handsomest man that came up under Ilius of all the Danaans after the son of Peleus – but he was a man of no substance, and had but a small following.

And those that held Nisyrus, Crapathus, and Casus, with Cos, the city of Eurypylus, and the Calydnian islands, these were commanded by Pheidippus and Antiphus, two sons of King Thessalus the son of Hercules. And with them there came thirty ships.

Those again who held Pelasgic Argos, Alos, Alope, and Trachis; and those of Phthia and Hellas the land of fair women, who were called Myrmidons, Hellenes, and Achæans; these had fifty ships, over which Achilles was in command. But they now took no part in the war, inasmuch as there was no one to marshal them; for Achilles stayed by his ships, furious about the loss of the girl Briseis, whom he had taken from Lyrnessus at his own great peril, when he had sacked Lyrnessus and Thebe, and had overthrown Mynes and Epistrophus, sons of king Evenor, son of Selepus. For her sake Achilles was still grieving, but ere long he was again to join them.

And those that held Phylace and the flowery meadows of Pyrasus, sanctuary of Ceres; Iton, the mother of sheep; Antrum upon the sea, and Pteleum that lies upon the grass lands. Of these brave Protesilaus had been captain while he was yet alive, but he was now lying under the earth. He had left a wife behind him in Phylace to tear her cheeks in sorrow, and his house was only half finished, for he was slain by a Dardanian warrior while leaping foremost of the Achæans upon the soil of Troy. Still, though his people mourned their chieftain, they were not without a leader, for Podarces, of the race of Mars, marshalled them; he was son of Iphiclus, rich in sheep, who was the son of Phylacus, and he was own brother to Protesilaus, only younger, Protesilaus being at once the elder and the more valiant. So the people were not without a leader, though they mourned him whom they had lost. With him there came forty ships.

And those that held Pheræ by the Bœbean lake, with Bœbe, Glaphyræ, and the populous city of Iolcus, these with their eleven ships were led by Eumelus, son of Admetus, whom Alcestis bore to him, loveliest of the daughters of Pelias.

And those that held Methone and Thaumacia, with Melibœa and rugged Olizon, these were led by the skilful archer Philoctetes, and they had seven ships, each with fifty oarsmen all of them good archers; but Philoctetes was lying in great pain in the Island of Lemnos, where the sons of the Achæans left him, for he had been bitten by a poisonous water snake. There he lay sick and sorry, and full soon did the Argives come to miss him. But his people, though they felt his loss, were not leaderless, for Medon, the bastard son of Oïleus by Rhene, set them in array.

Those, again, of Tricca and the stony region of Ithome, and they that held Œchalia, the city of Œchalian Eurytus, these were commanded by the two sons of Æsculapius, skilled in the art of healing, Podalirius and Machaon. And with them there came thirty ships.

The men, moreover, of Ormenius, and by the fountain of Hypereia, with those that held Asterius, and the white crests of Titanus, these were led by Eurypylus, the son of Euæmon, and with them there came forty ships.

Those that held Argissa and Gyrtone, Orthe, Elone, and the white city of Oloösson, of these brave Polypœtes was leader. He was son of Pirithoüs, who was son of Jove himself, for Hippodameia bore him to Pirithoüs on the day when he took his revenge on the shaggy mountain savages, and drove them from Mt Pelion to the Aithices. But Polypœtes was not sole in command, for with him was Leonteus, of the race of Mars, who was son of Coronus, the son of Cæneus. And with these there came forty ships.

Guneus brought two and twenty ships from Cyphus, and he was followed by the Enienes and the valiant Peræbi, who dwelt about wintry Dodona, and held the lands round the lovely river Titaresius, which sends its waters into the Peneus. They do not mingle with the silver eddies of the Peneus, but flow on the top of them like oil; for the Titaresius is a branch of dread Orcus and of the river Styx.

Of the Magnetes, Prothoüs son of Tenthredon was commander. They were they that dwelt about the river Peneus and Mt Pelion. Prothoüs, fleet of foot, was their leader, and with him there came forty ships.

Such were the chiefs and princes of the Danaans. Who, then, O Muse, was the foremost, whether man or horse, among those that followed after the sons of Atreus?

Of the horses, those of the son of Pheres were by far the finest. They were driven by Eumelus, and were as fleet as birds. They were of the same age and colour, and perfectly matched in height. Apollo, of the silver bow, had bred them in Perea – both of them mares, and terrible as Mars in battle. Of the men, Ajax, son of Telamon, was much the foremost so long as Achilles' anger lasted, for Achilles excelled him greatly and he had also better horses; but Achilles was now holding aloof at his ships by reason of his quarrel with Agamemnon, and his people passed their time upon the sea shore, throwing discs or aiming with spears at a mark, and in archery. Their horses stood each by his own chariot, champing lotus and wild celery. The chariots were housed under cover, but their owners, for lack of leadership, wandered hither and thither about the host and went not forth to fight.

Thus marched the host like a consuming fire, and the earth groaned beneath them as when the lord of thunder is angry and lashes the land about Typhœus among the Arimi, where they say Typhœus lies. Even so did the earth groan beneath them as they sped over the plain.

And now Iris, fleet as the wind, was sent by Jove to tell the bad news among the Trojans. They were gathered in assembly, old and young, at Priam's gates, and Iris came close up to Priam, speaking with the voice of Priam's son Polites, who, being fleet of foot, was stationed as watchman for the Trojans on the tomb of old Æsyetes, to look out for any sally of the Achæans. In his likeness Iris spoke, saying, 'Old man, you talk idly, as in time of peace, while war is at hand. I have been in many a battle, but never yet saw such a host as is now advancing. They are crossing the plain to attack the city as thick as leaves or as the sands of the sea. Hector, I charge you above all others, do as I say. There are many allies dispersed about the city of Priam from distant places and speaking divers tongues. Therefore, let each chief give orders to his own people, setting them severally in array and leading them forth to battle.'

Thus she spoke, but Hector knew that it was the goddess, and at once broke up the assembly. The men flew to arms; all the gates were opened, and the people thronged through them, horse and foot, with the tramp as of a great multitude.

Now there is a high mound before the city, rising by itself upon the plain. Men call it Batieia, but the gods know that it is the tomb of lithe Myrine. Here the Trojans and their allies divided their forces.

Priam's son, great Hector of the gleaming helmet, commanded the Trojans, and with him were arrayed by far the greater number and most valiant of those who were longing for the fray.

The Dardanians were led by brave Æneas, whom Venus bore to Anchises, when she, goddess though she was, had lain with him upon the mountain slopes of Ida. He was not alone, for with him were the two sons of Antenor, Archilochus and Acamas, both skilled in all the arts of war.

They that dwelt in Telea under the lowest spurs of Mt Ida, men of substance, who drink the limpid waters of the Æsepus, and are of Trojan blood – these were led by Pandarus son of Lycaon, whom Apollo had taught to use the bow.

They that held Adresteia and the land of Apæsus, with Pityeia, and the high mountain of Tereia – these were led by Adrestus and Amphius, whose breastplate was of linen. These were the sons of Merops of Percote, who excelled in all kinds of divination. He told them not to take part in the war, but they gave him no heed, for fate lured them to destruction.

They that dwelt about Percote and Practius, with Sestos, Abydos, and Arisbe – these were led by Asius, son of Hyrtacus, a brave commander – Asius, the son of Hyrtacus, whom his powerful dark bay steeds, of the breed that comes from the river Selleïs, had brought from Arisbe.

Hippothoüs led the tribes of Pelasgian spearsmen, who dwelt in fertile Larisa – Hippothoüs, and Pylæus of the race of Mars, two sons of the Pelasgian Lethus, son of Teutamus.

Acamas and the warrior Peiroüs commanded the Thracians and those that came from beyond the mighty stream of the Hellespont.

Euphemus, son of Trœzenus, the son of Ceos, was captain of the Ciconian spearsmen.

Pyræchmes led the Pæonian archers from distant Amydon, by the broad waters of the river Axius, the fairest that flow upon the earth.

The Paphlagonians were commanded by stout-hearted Pylæmenes from Enetæ, where the mules run wild in herds. These were they that held Cytorus and the country round Sesamus, with the cities by the river Parthenius, Cromna, Ægialus, and lofty Erithini.

Odius and Epistrophus were captains over the Halizoni from distant Alybe, where there are mines of silver.

Chromis, and Ennomus the augur, led the Mysians, but his skill in augury availed not to save him from destruction, for he fell by the hand of the fleet descendant of Æacus in the river, where he slew others also of the Trojans.

Phorcys, again, and noble Ascanius led the Phrygians from the far country of Ascania, and both were eager for the fray.

Mesthles and Antiphus commanded the Meonians, sons of Talæmenes, born to him of the Gygæan lake. These led the Meonians, who dwelt under Mt Tmolus.

Nastes led the Carians, men of a strange speech. These held Miletus and the wooded mountain of Phthires, with the water of the river Mæander and the lofty crests of Mt Mycale. These were commanded by Nastes and Amphimachus, the brave sons of Nomion. He came into the fight with gold about him, like a girl; fool that he was, his gold was of no avail to save him, for he fell in the river by the hand of the fleet descendant of Æacus, and Achilles bore away his gold.

Sarpedon and Glaucus led the Lycians from their distant land, by the eddying waters of the Xanthus.

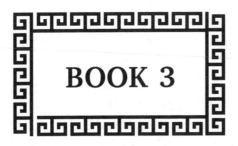

BOOK 3

Alexandrus, also called Paris, challenges Menelaus – Helen and
Priam view the Achæans from the wall – The covenant – Paris
and Menelaus fight, and Paris is worsted – Venus carries him off
to save him – Scene between him and Helen.

When the companies were thus arrayed, each under its own captain,
the Trojans advanced as a flight of wild fowl or cranes that scream
overhead when rain and winter drive them over the flowing waters of
Oceanus to bring death and destruction on the Pygmies, and they
wrangle in the air as they fly; but the Achæans marched silently, in
high heart, and minded to stand by one another.

As when the south wind spreads a curtain of mist upon the moun-
tain tops, bad for shepherds but better than night for thieves, and a
man can see no further than he can throw a stone, even so rose the
dust from under their feet as they made all speed over the plain.

When they were close up with one another, Alexandrus came forward
as champion on the Trojan side. On his shoulders he bore the skin of
a panther, his bow, and his sword, and he brandished two spears shod
with bronze as a challenge to the bravest of the Achæans to meet him
in single fight. Menelaus saw him thus stride out before the ranks, and
was glad as a hungry lion that lights on the carcase of some goat or
horned stag, and devours it there and then, though dogs and youths
set upon him. Even thus was Menelaus glad when his eyes caught sight
of Alexandrus, for he deemed that now he should be revenged. He
sprang, therefore, from his chariot, clad in his suit of armour.

Alexandrus quailed as he saw Menelaus come forward, and shrank in fear of his life under cover of his men. As one who starts back affrighted, trembling and pale, when he comes suddenly upon a serpent in some mountain glade, even so did Alexandrus plunge into the throng of Trojan warriors, terror-stricken at the sight of the son of Atreus.

Then Hector upbraided him. 'Paris,' said he, 'evil-hearted Paris, fair to see, but woman-mad, and false of tongue, would that you had never been born, or that you had died unwed. Better so, than live to be disgraced and looked askance at. Will not the Achæans mock at us and say that we have sent one to champion us who is fair to see but who has neither wit nor courage? Did you not, such as you are, get your following together and sail beyond the seas? Did you not from a far country carry off a lovely woman wedded among a people of warriors – to bring sorrow upon your father, your city, and your whole country, but joy to your enemies, and hang-dog shame-facedness to yourself? And now can you not dare face Menelaus and learn what manner of man he is whose wife you have stolen? Where indeed would be your lyre and your love-tricks, your comely locks and your fair favour, when you were lying in the dust before him? The Trojans are a weak-kneed people, or ere this you would have had a shirt of stones for the wrongs you have done them.'

And Alexandrus answered, 'Hector, your rebuke is just. You are hard as the axe which a shipwright wields at his work, and cleaves the timber to his liking. As the axe in his hand, so keen is the edge of your scorn. Still, taunt me not with the gifts that golden Venus has given me; they are precious; let not a man disdain them, for the gods give them where they are minded, and none can have them for the asking. If you would have me do battle with Menelaus, bid the Trojans and Achæans take their seats, while he and I fight in their midst for Helen and all her wealth. Let him who shall be victorious and prove to be the better man take the woman and all she has, to bear them to his home, but let the rest swear to a solemn covenant of peace whereby you Trojans shall stay here in Troy, while the others go home to Argos and the land of the Achæans.'

When Hector heard this he was glad, and went about among the Trojan ranks holding his spear by the middle to keep them back, and they all sat down at his bidding: but the Achæans still aimed at him with stones and arrows, till Agamemnon shouted to them saying, 'Hold, Argives, shoot not, sons of the Achæans; Hector desires to speak.'

They ceased taking aim and were still, whereon Hector spoke. 'Hear from my mouth,' said he, 'Trojans and Achæans, the saying of Alexandrus, through whom this quarrel has come about. He bids the Trojans and Achæans lay their armour upon the ground, while he and Menelaus fight in the midst of you for Helen and all her wealth. Let him who shall be victorious and prove to be the better man take the woman and all she has, to bear them to his own home, but let the rest swear to a solemn covenant of peace.'

Thus he spoke, and they all held their peace, till Menelaus of the loud battle-cry addressed them. 'And now,' he said, 'hear me too, for it is I who am the most aggrieved. I deem that the parting of Achæans and Trojans is at hand, as well it may be, seeing how much you have suffered for my quarrel with Alexandrus and the wrong he did me. Let him who shall die, die, and let the others fight no more. Bring, then, two lambs, a white ram and a black ewe, for Earth and Sun, and we will bring a third for Jove. Moreover, you shall bid Priam come, that he may swear to the covenant himself; for his sons are high-handed and ill to trust, and the oaths of Jove must not be transgressed or taken in vain. Young men's minds are light as air, but when an old man comes he looks before and after, deeming that which shall be fairest upon both sides.'

The Trojans and Achæans were glad when they heard this, for they thought that they should now have rest. They backed their chariots toward the ranks, got out of them, and put off their armour, laying it down upon the ground; and the hosts were near to one another with a little space between them. Hector sent two messengers to the city to bring the lambs and to bid Priam come, while Agamemnon told Talthybius to fetch the other lamb from the ships, and he did as Agamemnon had said.

Meanwhile Iris went to Helen in the form of her sister-in-law, wife of the son of Antenor, for Helicaon, son of Antenor, had married Laodice, the fairest of Priam's daughters. She found her in her own room, working at a great web of purple linen, on which she was embroidering the battles between Trojans and Achæans, that Mars had made them fight for her sake. Iris then came close up to her and said, 'Come hither, child, and see the strange doings of the Trojans and Achæans; till now they have been warring upon the plain, mad with lust of battle, but now they have left off fighting, and are leaning upon their shields, sitting still with their spears planted beside them. Alexandrus and Menelaus are going to fight about yourself, and you are to be the wife of him who is the victor.'

Thus spoke the goddess, and Helen's heart yearned after her former husband, her city, and her parents. She threw a white mantle over her head, and hurried from her room, weeping as she went, not alone, but attended by two of her handmaids, Æthræ, daughter of Pittheus, and Clymene. And straightway they were at the Scæan gates.

The two sages, Ucalegon and Antenor, elders of the people, were seated by the Scæan gates, with Priam, Panthoüs, Thymœtes, Lampus, Clytius, and Hiketaon of the race of Mars. These were too old to fight, but they were fluent orators, and sat on the tower like cicales that chirrup delicately from the boughs of some high tree in a wood. When they saw Helen coming towards the tower, they said softly to one another, 'Small wonder that Trojans and Achæans should endure so much and so long, for the sake of a woman so marvellously and divinely lovely. Still, fair though she be, let them take her and go, or she will breed sorrow for us and for our children after us.'

But Priam bade her draw nigh. 'My child,' said he, 'take your seat in front of me that you may see your former husband, your kinsmen and your friends. I lay no blame upon you, it is the gods, not you who are to blame. It is they that have brought about this terrible war with the Achæans. Tell me, then, who is yonder huge hero so great and goodly? I have seen men taller by a head, but none so comely and so royal. Surely he must be a king.'

'Sir,' answered Helen, 'father of my husband, dear and reverend in my eyes, would that I had chosen death rather than to have come here with your son, far from my bridal chamber, my friends, my darling daughter, and all the companions of my girlhood. But it was not to be, and my lot is one of tears and sorrow. As for your question, the hero of whom you ask is Agamemnon, son of Atreus, a good king and a brave soldier, brother-in-law as surely as that he lives, to my abhorred and miserable self.'

The old man marvelled at him and said, 'Happy son of Atreus, child of good fortune. I see that the Achæans are subject to you in great multitudes. When I was in Phrygia I saw much horsemen, the people of Otreus and of Mygdon, who were camping upon the banks of the river Sangarius; I was their ally, and with them when the Amazons, peers of men, came up against them, but even they were not so many as the Achæans.'

The old man next looked upon Ulysses; 'Tell me,' he said, 'who is that other, shorter by a head than Agamemnon, but broader across the chest and shoulders? His armour is laid upon the ground, and he stalks in front of the ranks as it were some great woolly ram ordering his ewes.'

And Helen answered, 'He is Ulysses, a man of great craft, son of Laertes. He was born in rugged Ithaca, and excels in all manner of stratagems and subtle cunning.'

On this Antenor said, 'Madam, you have spoken truly. Ulysses once came here as envoy about yourself, and Menelaus with him. I received them in my own house, and therefore know both of them by sight and conversation. When they stood up in presence of the assembled Trojans, Menelaus was the broader shouldered, but when both were seated Ulysses had the more royal presence. After a time they delivered their message, and the speech of Menelaus ran trippingly on the tongue; he did not say much, for he was a man of few words, but he spoke very clearly and to the point, though he was the younger man of the two; Ulysses, on the other hand, when he rose to speak, was at first silent and kept his eyes fixed upon the ground. There was no play nor graceful movement of his sceptre; he kept it straight and stiff like a man unpractised in oratory – one might have taken him for a mere churl or simpleton; but when he raised his voice, and the words came driving from his deep chest like winter snow before the wind, then there was none to touch him, and no man thought further of what he looked like.'

Priam then caught sight of Ajax and asked, 'Who is that great and goodly warrior whose head and broad shoulders tower above the rest of the Argives?'

'That,' answered Helen, 'is huge Ajax, bulwark of the Achæans, and on the other side of him, among the Cretans, stands Idomeneus looking like a god, and with the captains of the Cretans round him. Often did Menelaus receive him as a guest in our house when he came visiting us from Crete. I see, moreover, many other Achæans whose names I could tell you, but there are two whom I can nowhere find, Castor, breaker of horses, and Pollux the mighty boxer; they are children of my mother, and own brothers to myself. Either they have not left Lacedæmon, or else, though they have brought their ships, they will not show themselves in battle for the shame and disgrace that I have brought upon them.'

She knew not that both these heroes were already lying under the earth in their own land of Lacedæmon.

Meanwhile the heralds were bringing the holy oath-offerings through the city – two lambs and a goatskin of wine, the gift of earth; and Idæus brought the mixing bowl and the cups of gold. He went up to Priam and said, 'Son of Laomedon, the princes of the Trojans and Achæans bid you come down on to the plain and swear to a solemn covenant. Alexandrus and Menelaus are to fight for Helen in single combat, that she and all her wealth may go with him who is the victor. We are to swear to a solemn covenant of peace whereby we others shall dwell here in Troy, while the Achæans return to Argos and the land of the Achæans.'

The old man trembled as he heard, but bade his followers yoke the horses, and they made all haste to do so. He mounted the chariot, gathered the reins in his hand, and Antenor took his seat beside him; they then drove through the Scæan gates on to the plain. When they reached the ranks of the Trojans and Achæans they left the chariot, and with measured pace advanced into the space between the hosts.

Agamemnon and Ulysses both rose to meet them. The attendants brought on the oath-offerings and mixed the wine in the mixing-bowls; they poured water over the hands of the chieftains, and the son of Atreus drew the dagger that hung by his sword, and cut wool from the lambs' heads; this the men-servants gave about among the Trojan and Achæan princes, and the son of Atreus lifted up his hands in prayer. 'Father Jove,' he cried, 'that rulest in Ida, most glorious in power, and thou, O Sun, that seest and givest ear to all things, Earth and Rivers, and ye who in the realms below chastise the soul of him that has broken his oath, witness these rites and guard them, that they be not vain. If Alexandrus kills Menelaus, let him keep Helen and all her wealth, while we sail home with our ships; but if Menelaus kills Alexandrus, let the Trojans give back Helen and all that she has; let them moreover pay such fine to the Achæans as shall be agreed upon, in testimony among those that shall be born hereafter. And if Priam and his sons refuse such fine when Alexandrus has fallen, then will I stay here and fight on till I have got satisfaction.'

As he spoke he drew his knife across the throats of the victims, and laid them down gasping and dying upon the ground, for the knife had reft them of their strength. Then they poured wine from the mixing-bowl into the cups, and prayed to the everlasting gods, saying, Trojans and Achæans among one another, 'Jove, most great and glorious, and ye other everlasting gods, grant that the brains of them who shall first sin against their oaths – of them and their children – may be shed upon the ground even as this wine, and let their wives become the slaves of strangers.'

Thus they prayed, but not as yet would Jove grant them their prayer. Then Priam, descendant of Dardanus, spoke, saying, 'Hear me, Trojans and Achæans, I will now go back to the wind-beaten city of Ilius: I dare not with my own eyes witness this fight between my son and Menelaus, for Jove and the other immortals alone know which shall fall.'

On this he laid the two lambs on his chariot and took his seat. He gathered the reins in his hand, and Antenor sat beside him; the two then went back to Ilius. Hector and Ulysses measured the ground, and cast lots from a helmet of bronze to see which should take aim first. Meanwhile the two hosts lifted up their hands and prayed, saying, 'Father Jove, that rulest from Ida, most glorious in power, grant that he who first brought about this war between us may die, and enter the house of Hades, while we others remain at peace and abide by our oaths.'

Great Hector now turned his head aside while he shook the helmet, and the lot of Paris flew out first. The others took their several stations, each by his horses and the place where his arms were lying, while Alexandrus, husband of lovely Helen, put on his goodly armour. First he greaved his legs with greaves of good make and fitted with ancle-clasps of silver; after this he donned the cuirass of his brother Lycaon, and fitted it to his own body; he hung his silver-studded sword of bronze about his shoulders, and then his mighty shield. On his comely head he set his helmet, well-wrought, with a crest of horse-hair that nodded menacingly above it, and he grasped a redoubtable spear that suited his hands. In like fashion Menelaus also put on his armour.

When they had thus armed, each amid his own people, they strode fierce of aspect into the open space, and both Trojans and Achæans were struck with awe as they beheld them. They stood near one another on the measured ground, brandishing their spears, and each furious against the other. Alexandrus aimed first, and struck the round shield of the son of Atreus, but the spear did not pierce it, for the shield turned its point. Menelaus next took aim, praying to Father Jove as he did so. 'King Jove,' he said, 'grant me revenge on Alexandrus who has wronged me; subdue him under my hand that in ages yet to come a man may shrink from doing ill deeds in the house of his host.'

He poised his spear as he spoke, and hurled it at the shield of Alexandrus. Through shield and cuirass it went, and tore the shirt by his flank, but Alexandrus swerved aside, and thus saved his life. Then the son of Atreus drew his sword, and drove at the projecting part of his helmet, but the sword fell shivered in three or four pieces from his hand, and he cried, looking towards Heaven, 'Father Jove, of all gods thou are the most despiteful; I made sure of my revenge, but the sword has broken in my hand, my spear has been hurled in vain, and I have not killed him.'

With this he flew at Alexandrus, caught him by the horsehair plume of his helmet, and began dragging him towards the Achæans. The strap of the helmet that went under his chin was choking him, and Menelaus would have dragged him off to his own great glory had not Jove's daughter Venus been quick to mark and to break the strap of oxhide, so that the empty helmet came away in his hand. This he flung to his comrades among the Achæans, and was again springing upon Alexandrus to run him through with a spear, but Venus snatched him up in a moment (as a god can do), hid him under a cloud of darkness, and conveyed him to his own bedchamber.

Then she went to call Helen, and found her on a high tower with the Trojan women crowding round her. She took the form of an old woman who used to dress wool for her when she was still in Lacedæmon, and of whom she was very fond. Thus disguised she plucked her by her perfumed robe and said, 'Come hither; Alexandrus says you are to go to the house; he is on his bed in his own room, radiant with beauty and dressed in gorgeous apparel. No one would think he had just come from fighting, but rather that he was going to a dance, or had done dancing and was sitting down.'

With these words she moved the heart of Helen to anger. When she marked the beautiful neck of the goddess, her lovely bosom, and sparkling eyes, she marvelled at her and said, 'Goddess, why do you thus beguile me? Are you going to send me afield still further to some man whom you have taken up in Phrygia or fair Meonia? Menelaus has just vanquished Alexandrus, and is to take my hateful self back with him. You are come here to betray me. Go sit with Alexandrus yourself; henceforth be goddess no longer; never let your feet carry you back to Olympus; worry about him and look after him till he make you his wife, or, for the matter of that, his slave – but me? I shall not go; I can garnish his bed no longer; I should be a by-word among all the women of Troy. Besides, I have trouble on my mind.'

Venus was very angry, and said, 'Bold hussy, do not provoke me; if you do, I shall leave you to your fate and hate you as much as I have loved you. I will stir up fierce hatred between Trojans and Achæans, and you shall come to a bad end.'

At this Helen was frightened. She wrapped her mantle about her and went in silence, following the goddess and unnoticed by the Trojan women.

When they came to the house of Alexandrus the maid-servants set about their work, but Helen went into her own room, and the laughter-loving goddess took a seat and set it for her facing Alexandrus. On this Helen, daughter of ægis-bearing Jove, sat down, and with eyes askance began to upbraid her husband.

'So you are come from the fight,' said she; 'would that you had fallen rather by the hand of that brave man who was my husband. You used to brag that you were a better man with your hands and spear than Menelaus; go, then, and challenge him again – but I should advise you not to do so, for if you are foolish enough to meet him in single combat, you will soon fall by his spear.'

And Paris answered, 'Wife, do not vex me with your reproaches. This time, with the help of Minerva, Menelaus has vanquished me; another time I may myself be victor, for I too have gods that will stand by me. Come, let us lie down together and make friends. Never yet was I so passionately enamoured of you as at this moment – not even when I first carried you off from Lacedæmon and sailed away with you – not even when I had converse with you upon the couch of love in the island of Cranaë was I so enthralled by my desire of you as now.' On this he led her towards the bed, and his wife went with him.

Thus they laid themselves on the bed together; but the son of Atreus strode among the throng, looking everywhere for Alexandrus, and no man, neither of the Trojans nor of the allies, could find him. If they had seen him they were in no mind to hide him, for they all of them hated him as they did death itself. Then Agamemnon, king of men, spoke, saying, 'Hear me, Trojans, Dardanians, and allies. The victory has been with Menelaus; therefore give back Helen with all her wealth, and pay such fine as shall be agreed upon, in testimony among them that shall be born hereafter.'

Thus spoke the son of Atreus, and the Achæans shouted in applause.

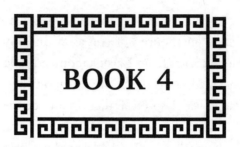

BOOK 4

A quarrel in Olympus – Minerva goes down and persuades Pandarus to violate the oaths by wounding Menelaus with an arrow – Agamemnon makes a speech and sends for Machaon – He then goes about among his captains and upbraids Ulysses and Sthenelus, who each of them retort fiercely – Diomed checks Sthenelus, and the two hosts then engage, with great slaughter on either side.

Now the gods were sitting with Jove in council upon the golden floor while Hebe went round pouring out nectar for them to drink, and as they pledged one another in their cups of gold they looked down upon the town of Troy. The son of Saturn then began to tease Juno, talking at her so as to provoke her. 'Menelaus,' said he, 'has two good friends among the goddesses, Juno of Argos, and Minerva of Alalcomene, but they only sit still and look on, while Venus keeps ever by Alexandrus' side to defend him in any danger; indeed she has just rescued him when he made sure that it was all over with him – for the victory really did lie with Menelaus. We must consider what we shall do about all this; shall we set them fighting anew or make peace between them? If you will agree to this last Menelaus can take back Helen and the city of Priam may remain still inhabited.'

Minerva and Juno muttered their discontent as they sat side by side hatching mischief for the Trojans. Minerva scowled at her father, for she was in a furious passion with him, and said nothing, but Juno could not contain herself. 'Dread son of Saturn,' said she, 'what, pray, is the meaning of all this? Is my trouble, then, to go for nothing, and the sweat that I have sweated, to say nothing of my horses, while getting the people together against Priam and his children? Do as you will, but we other gods shall not all of us approve your counsel.'

Jove was angry and answered, 'My dear, what harm have Priam and his sons done you that you are so hotly bent on sacking the city of Ilius? Will nothing do for you but you must go within their walls and eat Priam raw, with his sons and all the other Trojans to boot? Have it your own way then; for I would not have this matter become a bone of contention between us. I say further, and lay my saying to your heart, if ever I want to sack a city belonging to friends of yours, you must not try to stop me; you will have to let me do it, for I am giving in to you sorely against my will. Of all inhabited cities under the sun and stars of heaven, there was none that I so much respected as Ilius with Priam and his whole people. Equitable feasts were never wanting about my altar, nor the savour of burning fat, which is the honour due to ourselves.'

'My own three favourite cities,' answered Juno, 'are Argos, Sparta, and Mycenæ. Sack them whenever you may be displeased with them. I shall not defend them and I shall not care. Even if I did, and tried to stay you, I should take nothing by it, for you are much stronger than I am, but I will not have my own work wasted. I too am a god and of the same race with yourself. I am Saturn's eldest daughter, and am honourable not on this ground only, but also because I am your wife, and you are king over the gods. Let it be a case, then, of give-and-take between us, and the rest of the gods will follow our lead. Tell Minerva to go and take part in the fight at once, and let her contrive that the Trojans shall be the first to break their oaths and set upon the Achæans.'

The sire of gods and men heeded her words, and said to Minerva, 'Go at once into the Trojan and Achæan hosts, and contrive that the Trojans shall be the first to break their oaths and set upon the Achæans.'

This was what Minerva was already eager to do, so down she darted from the topmost summits of Olympus. She shot through the sky as some brilliant meteor which the son of scheming Saturn has sent as a sign to mariners or to some great army, and a fiery train of light follows in its wake. The Trojans and Achæans were struck with awe as they beheld, and one would turn to his neighbour, saying, 'Either we shall again have war and din of combat, or Jove the lord of battle will now make peace between us.'

Thus did they converse. Then Minerva took the form of Laodocus, son of Antenor, and went through the ranks of the Trojans to find Pandarus, the redoubtable son of Lycaon. She found him standing among the stalwart heroes who had followed him from the banks of the Æsopus, so she went close up to him and said, 'Brave son of Lycaon, will you do as I tell you? If you dare send an arrow at Menelaus you will win honour and thanks from all the Trojans, and especially from prince Alexandrus – he would be the first to requite you very handsomely if he could see Menelaus mount his funeral pyre, slain by an arrow from your hand. Take your aim then, and pray to Lycian Apollo, the famous archer; vow that when you get home to your strong city of Zelea you will offer a hecatomb of firstling lambs in his honour.'

His fool's heart was persuaded, and he took his bow from its case. This bow was made from the horns of a wild ibex which he had killed as it was bounding from a rock; he had stalked it, and it had fallen as the arrow struck it to the heart. Its horns were sixteen palms long, and a worker in horn had made them into a bow, smoothing them well down, and giving them tips of gold. When Pandarus had strung his bow he laid it carefully on the ground, and his brave followers held their shields before him lest the Achæans should set upon him before he had shot Menelaus. Then he opened the lid of his quiver and took out a winged arrow that had never yet been shot, fraught with the pangs of death. He laid the arrow on the string and prayed to Lycian Apollo, the famous archer, vowing that when he got home to his strong city of Zelea he would offer a hecatomb of firstling lambs in his honour. He laid the notch of the arrow on the oxhide bowstring, and drew both notch and string to his breast till the arrow-head was near the bow; then when the bow was arched into a half-circle he let fly, and the bow twanged, and the string sang as the arrow flew gladly on over the heads of the throng.

But the blessed gods did not forget thee, O Menelaus, and Jove's daughter, driver of the spoil, was the first to stand before thee and ward off the piercing arrow. She turned it from his skin as a mother whisks a fly from off her child when it is sleeping sweetly; she guided it to the part where the golden buckles of the belt that passed over his double cuirass were fastened, so the arrow struck the belt that went tightly round him. It went right through this and through the cuirass of cunning workmanship; it also pierced the belt beneath it, which he wore next his skin to keep out darts or arrows; it was this that served him in the best stead, nevertheless the arrow went through it and grazed the top of the skin, so that blood began flowing from the wound.

As when some woman of Meonia or Caria strains purple dye on to a piece of ivory that is to be the cheek-piece of a horse, and is to be laid up in a treasure-house – many a knight is fain to bear it, but the king keeps it as an ornament of which both horse and driver may be proud – even so, O Menelaus, were your shapely thighs and your legs down to your fair ancles stained with blood.

When King Agamemnon saw the blood flowing from the wound he was afraid, and so was brave Menelaus himself till he saw that the barbs of the arrow and the thread that bound the arrow-head to the shaft were still outside the wound. Then he took heart, but Agamemnon heaved a deep sigh as he held Menelaus's hand in his own, and his comrades made moan in concert. 'Dear brother,' he cried, 'I have been the death of you in pledging this covenant and letting you come forward as our champion. The Trojans have trampled on their oaths and have wounded you; nevertheless the oath, the blood of lambs, the drink offerings, and the right hands of fellowship in which we have put our trust shall not be vain. If he that rules Olympus fulfil it not here and now, he will yet fulfil it hereafter, and they shall pay dearly with their lives and with their wives and children. The day will surely come when mighty Ilius shall be laid low, with Priam and Priam's people, when the son of Saturn from his high throne shall overshadow them with his awful ægis in punishment of their present treachery. This shall surely be; but how, Menelaus, shall I mourn you, if it be your lot now to die? I should return to Argos as a by-word, for the Achæans will at once go home. We shall leave Priam and the Trojans the glory of still keeping Helen, and the earth will rot your bones as you lie here at Troy with your purpose not fulfilled. Then shall some braggart Trojan leap upon your tomb and say, "Ever thus may Agamemnon wreak his vengeance; he brought his army in vain; he is gone home to his own land with empty ships, and has left Menelaus behind him." Thus will one of them say, and may the earth then swallow me.'

But Menelaus reassured him and said, 'Take heart, and do not alarm the people; the arrow has not struck me in a mortal part, for my outer belt of burnished metal first stayed it, and under this my cuirass and the belt of mail which the bronze-smiths made me.'

And Agamemnon answered, 'I trust, dear Menelaus, that it may be even so, but the surgeon shall examine your wound and lay herbs upon it to relieve your pain.'

He then said to Talthybius, 'Talthybius, tell Machaon, son to the great physician Æsculapius, to come and see Menelaus immediately. Some Trojan or Lycian archer has wounded him with an arrow to our dismay, and to his own great glory.'

Talthybius did as he was told, and went about the host trying to find Machaon. Presently he found him standing amid the brave warriors who had followed him from Tricca; thereon he went up to him and said, 'Son of Æsculapius, King Agamemnon says you are to come and see Menelaus immediately. Some Trojan or Lycian archer has wounded him with an arrow to our dismay and to his own great glory.'

Thus did he speak, and Machaon was moved to go. They passed through the spreading host of the Achæans and went on till they came to the place where Menelaus had been wounded and was lying with the chieftains gathered in a circle round him. Machaon passed into the middle of the ring and at once drew the arrow from the belt, bending its barbs back through the force with which he pulled it out. He undid the burnished belt, and beneath this the cuirass and the belt of mail which the bronze-smiths had made; then, when he had seen the wound, he wiped away the blood and applied some soothing drugs which Chiron had given to Æsculapius out of the good will he bore him.

While they were thus busy about Menelaus, the Trojans came forward against them, for they had put on their armour, and now renewed the fight.

You would not have then found Agamemnon asleep nor cowardly and unwilling to fight, but eager rather for the fray. He left his chariot rich with bronze and his panting steeds in charge of Eurymedon, son of Ptolemæus the son of Peiræus, and bade him hold them in readiness against the time his limbs should weary of going about and giving orders to so many, for he went among the ranks on foot. When he saw men hasting to the front he stood by them and cheered them on. 'Argives,' said he, 'slacken not one whit in your onset; father Jove will be no helper of liars; the Trojans have been the first to break their oaths and to attack us; therefore they shall be devoured of vultures; we shall take their city and carry off their wives and children in our ships.'

But he angrily rebuked those whom he saw shirking and disinclined to fight. 'Argives,' he cried, 'cowardly miserable creatures, have you no shame to stand here like frightened fawns who, when they can no longer scud over the plain, huddle together, but show no fight? You are as dazed and spiritless as deer. Would you wait till the Trojans reach the sterns of our ships as they lie on the shore, to see whether the son of Saturn will hold his hand over you to protect you?'

Thus did he go about giving his orders among the ranks. Passing through the crowd, he came presently on the Cretans, arming round Idomeneus, who was at their head, fierce as a wild boar, while Meriones was bringing up the battalions that were in the rear. Agamemnon was glad when he saw him, and spoke him fairly. 'Idomeneus,' said he,

'I treat you with greater distinction than I do any other of the Achæans, whether in war or in other things, or at table. When their princes are mixing my choicest wine in the mixing-bowls, they have each of them a fixed allowance, but your cup is kept always full like my own, that you may drink whenever you are minded. Go, therefore, into battle, and show yourself the man you have been always proud to be.'

Idomeneus answered, 'I will be a trusty comrade, as I promised you from the first I would be. Urge on the other Achæans, that we may join battle at once, for the Trojans have trampled upon their covenants. Death and destruction shall be theirs, seeing they have been the first to break their oaths and to attack us.'

The son of Atreus went on, glad at heart, till he came upon the two Ajaxes arming themselves amid a host of foot-soldiers. As when a goatherd from some high post watches a storm drive over the deep before the west wind – black as pitch is the offing and a mighty whirlwind draws towards him, so that he is afraid and drives his flock into a cave, – even thus did the ranks of stalwart youths move in a dark mass to battle under the Ajaxes, horrid with shield and spear. Glad was King Agamemnon when he saw them. 'No need,' he cried, 'to give orders to such leaders of the Argives as you are, for of your own selves you spur your men on to fight with might and main. Would, by father Jove, Minerva, and Apollo that all were so minded as you are, for the city of Priam would then soon fall beneath our hands, and we should sack it.'

With this he left them and went onward to Nestor, the facile speaker of the Pylians, who was marshalling his men and urging them on, in company with Pelagon, Alastor, Chromius, Hæmon, and Bias shepherd of his people. He placed his knights with their chariots and horses in the front rank, while the foot-soldiers, brave men and many, whom he could trust, were in the rear. The cowards he drove into the middle, that they might fight whether they would or no. He gave his orders to the knights first, bidding them hold their horses well in hand, so as to avoid confusion. 'Let no man,' he said, 'relying on his strength or horsemanship, get before the others and engage singly with the Trojans, nor yet let him lag behind, or you will weaken your attack; but let each when he meets an enemy's chariot throw his spear from his own; this will be much the best; this is how the men of old took towns and strongholds; in this wise were they minded.'

Thus did the old man charge them, for he had been in many a fight, and King Agamemnon was glad. 'I wish,' he said to him, 'that your limbs were as supple and your strength as sure as your judgment is; but age, the common enemy of mankind, has laid his hand upon you; would that it had fallen upon some other, and that you were still young.'

And Nestor, knight of Gerene, answered, 'Son of Atreus, I too would gladly be the man I was when I slew mighty Ereuthalion; but the gods will not give us everything at one and the same time. I was then young, and now I am old; still I can go with my knights and give them that counsel which old men have a right to give. The wielding of the spear I leave to those who are younger and stronger than myself.'

Agamemnon went his way rejoicing, and presently found Menestheus, son of Peteos, tarrying in his place, and with him were the Athenians loud of tongue in battle. Near him also tarried cunning Ulysses, with his sturdy Cephallenians round him; they had not yet heard the battle-cry, for the ranks of Trojans and Achæans had only just begun to move, so they were standing still, waiting for some other columns of the Achæans to attack the Trojans and begin the fighting. When he saw this Agamemnon rebuked them and said, 'Son of Peteos, and you other, steeped in cunning, heart of guile, why stand you here cowering and waiting on others? You two should be of all men foremost when there is hard fighting to be done, for you are ever foremost to accept my invitation when we councillors of the Achæans are holding feast. You are glad enough then to take your fill of roast meats and to drink wine as long as you please, whereas now you would not care though you saw ten columns of Achæans engage the enemy in front of you.'

Ulysses glared at him and answered, 'Son of Atreus, what are you talking about? How can you say that we are slack? When the Achæans are in full fight with the Trojans, you shall see, if you care to do so, that the father of Telemachus will join battle with the foremost of them. You are talking idly.'

When Agamemnon saw that Ulysses was angry, he smiled pleasantly at him and withdrew his words. 'Ulysses,' said he, 'noble son of Laertes, excellent in all good counsel, I have neither fault to find nor orders to give you, for I know your heart is right, and that you and I are of a mind. Enough; I will make you amends for what I have said, and if any ill has now been spoken may the gods bring it to nothing.'

He then left them and went on to others. Presently he saw the son of Tydeus, noble Diomed, standing by his chariot and horses, with Sthenelus the son of Capaneus beside him; whereon he began to upbraid him. 'Son of Tydeus,' he said, 'why stand you cowering here upon the brink of battle? Tydeus did not shrink thus, but was ever ahead of his men when leading them on against the foe – so, at least, say they that saw him in battle, for I never set eyes upon him myself. They say that there was no man like him. He came once to Mycenæ, not as an enemy but as a guest, in company with Polynices to recruit his forces, for they were levying war against the strong city of Thebes, and prayed our people for a body of picked men to help them. The men of Mycenæ were willing to let them have one, but Jove dissuaded them by showing them unfavourable omens. Tydeus, therefore, and Polynices went their way. When they had got as far as the deep-meadowed and rush-grown banks of the Æsopus, the Achæans sent Tydeus as their envoy, and he found the Cadmeans gathered in great numbers to a banquet in the house of Eteocles. Stranger though he was, he knew no fear on finding himself single-handed among so many, but challenged them to contests of all kinds, and in each one of them was at once victorious, so mightily did Minerva help him. The Cadmeans were incensed at his success, and set a force of fifty youths with two captains – the godlike hero Mæon, son of Hæmon, and Polyphontes, son of Autophonus – at their head, to lie in wait for him on his return journey; but Tydeus slew every man of them, save only Mæon, whom he let go in obedience to heaven's omens. Such was Tydeus of Ætolia. His son can talk more glibly, but he cannot fight as his father did.'

Diomed made no answer, for he was shamed by the rebuke of Agamemnon; but the son of Capaneus took up his words and said, 'Son of Atreus, tell no lies, for you can speak truth if you will. We boast ourselves as even better men than our fathers; we took seven-gated Thebes, though the wall was stronger and our men were fewer in number, for we trusted in the omens of the gods and in the help of Jove, whereas they perished through their own sheer folly; hold not, then, our fathers in like honour with us.'

Diomed looked sternly at him and said, 'Hold your peace, my friend, as I bid you. It is not amiss that Agamemnon should urge the Achæans forward, for the glory will be his if we take the city, and his the shame if we are vanquished. Therefore let us acquit ourselves with valour.'

As he spoke he sprang from his chariot, and his armour rang so fiercely about his body that even a brave man might well have been scared to hear it.

As when some mighty wave that thunders on the beach when the west wind has lashed it into fury – it has reared its head afar and now comes crashing down on the shore; it bows its arching crest high over the jagged rocks and spews its salt foam in all directions – even so did the serried phalanxes of the Danaans march steadfastly to battle. The chiefs gave orders each to his own people, but the men said never a word; no man would think it, for huge as the host was, it seemed as though there was not a tongue among them, so silent were they in their obedience; and as they marched the armour about their bodies glistened in the sun. But the clamour of the Trojan ranks was as that of many thousand ewes that stand waiting to be milked in the yards of some rich flockmaster, and bleat incessantly in answer to the bleating of their lambs; for they had not one speech nor language, but their tongues were diverse, and they came from many different places. These were inspired of Mars, but the others by Minerva – and with them came Panic, Rout, and Strife whose fury never tires, sister and friend of murderous Mars, who, from being at first but low in stature, grows till she uprears her head to heaven, though her feet are still on earth. She it was that went about among them and flung down discord to the waxing of sorrow with even hand between them.

When they were got together in one place shield clashed with shield and spear with spear in the rage of battle. The bossed shields beat one upon another, and there was a tramp as of a great multitude – death-cry and shout of triumph of slain and slayers, and the earth ran red with blood. As torrents swollen with rain course madly down their deep channels till the angry floods meet in some gorge, and the shepherd on the hillside hears their roaring from afar – even such was the toil and uproar of the hosts as they joined in battle.

First Antilochus slew an armed warrior of the Trojans, Echepolus, son of Thalysius, fighting in the foremost ranks. He struck at the projecting part of his helmet and drove the spear into his brow; the point of bronze pierced the bone, and darkness veiled his eyes; headlong as a tower he fell amid the press of the fight, and as he dropped King Elephenor, son of Chalcodon and captain of the proud Abantes, began dragging him out of reach of the darts that were falling around him, in haste to strip him of his armour. But his purpose was not for long; Agenor saw him haling the body away, and smote him in the side with his bronze-shod spear – for as he stooped his side was left unprotected by his shield – and thus he perished. Then the fight between Trojans and Achæans grew furious over his body, and they flew upon each other like wolves, man and man crushing one upon the other.

Forthwith Ajax, son of Telamon, slew the fair youth Simöeisius, son of Anthemion, whom his mother bore by the banks of the Simois, as she was coming down from Mt Ida, where she had been with her parents to see their flocks. Therefore he was named Simöeisius, but he did not live to pay his parents for his rearing, for he was cut off untimely by the spear of mighty Ajax, who struck him in the breast by the right nipple as he was coming on among the foremost fighters;

the spear went right through his shoulder, and he fell as a poplar that has grown straight and tall in a meadow by some mere, and its top is thick with branches. Then the wheelwright lays his axe to its roots that he may fashion a felloe for the wheel of some goodly chariot, and it lies seasoning by the waterside. In such wise did Ajax fell to earth Simöeisius, son of Anthemion. Thereon Antiphus of the gleaming corslet, son of Priam, hurled a spear at Ajax from amid the crowd and missed him, but he hit Leucus, the brave comrade of Ulysses, in the groin, as he was dragging the body of Simöeisius over to the other side; so he fell upon the body and loosed his hold upon it. Ulysses was furious when he saw Leucus slain, and strode in full armour through the front ranks till he was quite close; then he glared round about him and took aim, and the Trojans fell back as he did so. His dart was not sped in vain, for it struck Democoön, the bastard son of Priam, who had come to him from Abydos, where he had charge of his father's mares. Ulysses, infuriated by the death of his comrade, hit him with his spear on one temple, and the bronze point came through on the other side of his forehead, Thereon darkness veiled his eyes, and his armour rang rattling round him as he fell heavily to the ground. Hector, and they that were in front, then gave ground while the Argives raised a shout and drew off the dead, pressing further forward as they did so. But Apollo looked down from Pergamus and called aloud to the Trojans, for he was displeased. 'Trojans,' he cried, 'rush on the foe, and do not let yourselves be thus beaten by the Argives. Their skins are not stone nor iron that when you hit them you do them no harm. Moreover, Achilles, the son of lovely Thetis, is not fighting, but is nursing his anger at the ships.'

Thus spoke the mighty god, crying to them from the city, while Jove's redoubtable daughter, the Trito-born, went about among the host of the Achæans, and urged them forward whenever she beheld them slackening.

Then fate fell upon Diores, son of Amarynceus, for he was struck by a jagged stone near the ancle of his right leg. He that hurled it was

Peiroüs, son of Imbrasus, captain of the Thracians, who had come from Ænus; the bones and both the tendons were crushed by the pitiless stone. He fell to the ground on his back, and in his death throes stretched out his hands towards his comrades. But Peiroüs, who had wounded him, sprang on him and thrust a spear into his belly, so that his bowels came gushing out upon the ground, and darkness veiled his eyes. As he was leaving the body, Thoas of Ætolia struck him in the chest near the nipple, and the point fixed itself in his lungs. Thoas came close up to him, pulled the spear out of his chest, and then drawing his sword, smote him in the middle of the belly so that he died; but he did not strip him of his armour, for his Thracian comrades, men who wear their hair in a tuft at the top of their heads, stood round the body and kept him off with their long spears for all his great stature and valour; so he was driven back. Thus the two corpses lay stretched on earth near to one another, the one captain of the Thracians and the other of the Epeans; and many another fell round them.

And now no man would have made light of the fighting if he could have gone about among it scatheless and unwounded, with Minerva leading him by the hand, and protecting him from the storm of spears and arrows. For many Trojans and Achæans on that day lay stretched side by side face downwards upon the earth.

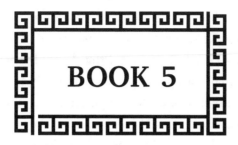

BOOK 5

The exploits of Diomed, who, though wounded by Pandarus, continues fighting – He kills Pandarus and wounds Æneas – Venus rescues Æneas, but being wounded by Diomed, commits him to the care of Apollo and goes to Olympus, where she is tended by her mother Dione – Mars encourages the Trojans, and Æneas returns to the fight cured of his wound – Minerva and Juno help the Achæans, and by the advice of the former Diomed wounds Mars, who returns to Olympus to get cured.

Then Pallas Minerva put valour into the heart of Diomed, son of Tydeus, that he might excel all the other Argives, and cover himself with glory. She made a stream of fire flare from his shield and helmet like the star that shines most brilliantly in summer after its bath in the waters of Oceanus – even such a fire did she kindle upon his head and shoulders as she bade him speed into the thickest hurly-burly of the fight.

Now there was a certain rich and honourable man among the Trojans, priest of Vulcan, and his name was Dares. He had two sons, Phegeus and Idæus, both of them skilled in all the arts of war. These two came forward from the main body of Trojans, and set upon Diomed, he being on foot, while they fought from their chariot. When they were close up to one another, Phegeus took aim first, but his spear went over Diomed's left shoulder without hitting him. Diomed then threw, and his spear sped not in vain, for it hit Phegeus on the breast near the nipple, and he fell from his chariot. Idæus did not dare to bestride his brother's body, but sprang from the chariot and took to flight, or he would have shared his brother's fate; whereon Vulcan saved him by wrapping him in a cloud of darkness, that his old father might not be utterly overwhelmed with grief; but the son of Tydeus drove off with the horses, and bade his followers take them to the ships. The Trojans were scared when they saw the two sons of Dares, one of them in flight and the other lying dead by his chariot. Minerva, therefore, took Mars by the hand and said, 'Mars, Mars, bane of men, bloodstained stormer of cities, may we not now leave the Trojans and Achæans to fight it out, and see to which of the two Jove will vouchsafe the victory? Let us go away, and thus avoid his anger.'

So saying, she drew Mars out of the battle, and set him down upon the steep banks of the Scamander. Upon this the Danaans drove the Trojans back, and each one of their chieftains killed his man. First King Agamemnon flung mighty Odius, captain of the Halizoni, from his chariot. The spear of Agamemnon caught him on the broad of his back, just as he was turning in flight; it struck him between the shoulders and went right through his chest, and his armour rang rattling round him as he fell heavily to the ground.

Then Idomeneus killed Phæsus, son of Borus the Meonian, who had come from Varne. Mighty Idomeneus speared him on the right shoulder as he was mounting his chariot, and the darkness of death enshrouded him as he fell heavily from the car.

The squires of Idomeneus spoiled him of his armour, while Menelaus, son of Atreus, killed Scamandrius the son of Strophius, a mighty huntsman and keen lover of the chase. Diana herself had taught him how to kill every kind of wild creature that is bred in mountain forests, but neither she nor his famed skill in archery could now save him, for the spear of Menelaus struck him in the back as he was flying; it struck him between the shoulders and went right through his chest, so that he fell headlong and his armour rang rattling round him.

Meriones then killed Phereclus the son of Tecton, who was the son of Hermon, a man whose hand was skilled in all manner of cunning workmanship, for Pallas Minerva had dearly loved him. He it was that made the ships for Alexandrus, which were the beginning of all mischief, and brought evil alike both on the Trojans and on Alexandrus himself; for he heeded not the decrees of heaven. Meriones overtook him as he was flying, and struck him on the right buttock. The point of the spear went through the bone into the bladder, and death came upon him as he cried aloud and fell forward on his knees.

Meges, moreover, slew Pedæus, son of Antenor, who, though he was a bastard, had been brought up by Theano as one of her own children, for the love she bore her husband. The son of Phyleus got close up to him and drove a spear into the nape of his neck: it went under his tongue all among his teeth, so he bit the cold bronze, and fell dead in the dust.

And Eurypylus, son of Euæmon, killed Hypsenor, the son of noble Dolopion, who had been made priest of the river Scamander, and was honoured among the people as though he were a god. Eurypylus gave him chase as he was flying before him, smote him with his sword upon the arm, and lopped his strong hand from off it. The bloody hand fell to the ground, and the shades of death, with fate that no man can withstand, came over his eyes.

Thus furiously did the battle rage between them. As for the son of Tydeus, you could not say whether he was more among the Achæans or the Trojans. He rushed across the plain like a winter torrent that has burst its barrier in full flood; no dykes, no walls of fruitful vineyards can embank it when it is swollen with rain from heaven, but in a moment it comes tearing onward, and lays many a field waste that many a strong man's hand has reclaimed – even so were the dense phalanxes of the Trojans driven in rout by the son of Tydeus, and many though they were, they dared not abide his onslaught.

Now when the son of Lycaon saw him scouring the plain and driving the Trojans pell-mell before him, he aimed an arrow and hit the front part of his cuirass near the shoulder: the arrow went right through the metal and pierced the flesh, so that the cuirass was covered with blood. On this the son of Lycaon shouted in triumph, 'Knights Trojans, come on; the bravest of the Achæans is wounded, and he will not hold out much longer if King Apollo was indeed with me when I sped from Lycia huther.'

Thus did he vaunt; but his arrow had not killed Diomed, who withdrew and made for the chariot and horses of Sthenelus, the son of Capaneus. 'Dear son of Capaneus,' said he, 'come down from your chariot, and draw the arrow out of my shoulder.'

Sthenelus sprang from his chariot, and drew the arrow from the wound, whereon the blood came spouting out through the hole that had been made in his shirt. Then Diomed prayed, saying, 'Hear me, daughter of ægis-bearing Jove, unweariable, if ever you loved my father well and stood by him in the thick of a fight, do the like now by me; grant me to come within a spear's throw of that man and kill him. He has been too quick for me and has wounded me; and now he is boasting that I shall not see the light of the sun much longer.'

Thus he prayed, and Pallas Minerva heard him; she made his limbs supple and quickened his hands and his feet. Then she went close up to him and said, 'Fear not, Diomed, to do battle with the Trojans, for I have set in your heart the spirit of your knightly father Tydeus. Moreover, I have withdrawn the veil from your eyes, that you may know gods and men apart. If, then, any other god comes here and offers you battle, do not fight him; but should Jove's daughter Venus come, strike her with your spear and wound her.'

When she had said this Minerva went away, and the son of Tydeus again took his place among the foremost fighters, three times more fierce even than he had been before. He was like a lion that some mountain shepherd has wounded, but not killed, as he is springing over the wall of a sheep-yard to attack the sheep. The shepherd has roused the brute to fury but cannot defend his flock, so he takes shelter under cover of the buildings, while the sheep, panic-stricken on being deserted, are smothered in heaps one on top of the other, and the angry lion leaps out over the sheep-yard wall. Even thus did Diomed go furiously about among the Trojans.

He killed Astynoüs, and Hypeiron shepherd of his people, the one with a thrust of his spear, which struck him above the nipple, the other with a sword-cut on the collar-bone, that severed his shoulder from his neck and back. He let both of them lie, and went in pursuit of Abas and Polyidus, sons of the old reader of dreams Eurydamas: they never came back for him to read them any more dreams, for mighty Diomed made an end of them. He then gave chase to Xanthus and Thoön, the two sons of Phænops, both of them very dear to him, for he was now worn out with age, and begat no more sons to inherit his possessions. But Diomed took both their lives and left their father sorrowing bitterly, for he nevermore saw them come home from battle alive, and his kinsmen divided his wealth among themselves.

Then he came upon two sons of Priam, Echemmon and Chromius, as they were both in one chariot. He sprang upon them as a lion fastens on the neck of some cow or heifer when the herd is feeding in a coppice. For all their vain struggles he flung them both from their chariot and stripped the armour from their bodies. Then he gave their horses to his comrades to take them back to the ships.

When Æneas saw him thus making havoc among the ranks, he went through the fight amid the rain of spears to see if he could find Pandarus. When he had found the brave son of Lycaon he said, 'Pandarus, where is now your bow, your winged arrows, and your renown as an archer, in respect of which no man here can rival you nor is there any in Lycia that can beat you? Lift then your hands to Jove and send an arrow at this fellow who is going so masterfully about, and has done such deadly work among the Trojans. He has killed many a brave man – unless indeed he is some god who is angry with the Trojans about their sacrifices, and has set his hand against them in his displeasure.'

And the son of Lycaon answered, 'Æneas, I take him for none other than the son of Tydeus. I know him by his shield, the visor of his helmet, and by his horses. It is possible that he may be a god, but if he is the man I say he is, he is not making all this havoc without heaven's help, but has some god by his side who is shrouded in a cloud of darkness, and who turned my arrow aside when it had hit him. I have taken aim at him already and hit him on the right shoulder; my arrow went through the breastpiece of his cuirass; and I made sure I should send him hurrying to the world below, but it seems that I have not killed him. There must be a god who is angry with me. Moreover I have neither horse nor chariot. In my father's stables there are eleven excellent chariots, fresh from the builder, quite new, with cloths spread over them; and by each of them there stand a pair of horses, champing barley and rye; my old father Lycaon urged me again and again when I was at home and on the point of starting, to take chariots and horses with me that I might lead the Trojans in battle, but I would not listen to him; it would have been much better if I had done so, but I was thinking about the horses, which had been used to eat their fill, and I was afraid that in such a great gathering of men they might be ill-fed, so I left them at home and came on foot to Ilius armed only with my bow and arrows. These, it seems, are of no use, for I have already hit two chieftains, the sons of Atreus and of Tydeus, and though I drew blood surely enough, I have only made them still more furious. I did ill to take my bow down from its peg on the day I led my band of Trojans to Ilius in Hector's service, and if ever I get home again to set eyes on my native place, my wife, and the greatness of my house, may some one cut my head off then and there if I do not break the bow and set it on a hot fire – such pranks as it plays me.'

Æneas answered, 'Say no more. Things will not mend till we two go against this man with chariot and horses and bring him to a trial of arms. Mount my chariot, and note how cleverly the horses of Tros can speed hither and thither over the plain in pursuit or flight. If Jove again vouchsafes glory to the son of Tydeus they will carry us safely back to the city. Take hold, then, of the whip and reins while I stand upon the car to fight, or else do you wait this man's onset while I look after the horses.'

'Æneas,' replied the son of Lycaon, 'take the reins and drive; if we have to fly before the son of Tydeus the horses will go better for their own driver. If they miss the sound of your voice when they expect it they may be frightened, and refuse to take us out of the fight. The son of Tydeus will then kill both of us and take the horses. Therefore drive them yourself and I will be ready for him with my spear.'

They then mounted the chariot and drove full-speed towards the son of Tydeus. Sthenelus, son of Capaneus, saw them coming and said to Diomed, 'Diomed, son of Tydeus, man after my own heart, I see two heroes speeding towards you, both of them men of might – the one a skilful archer, Pandarus, son of Lycaon, the other, Æneas, whose sire is Anchises, while his mother is Venus. Mount the chariot and let us retreat. Do not, I pray you, press so furiously forward, or you may get killed.'

Diomed looked angrily at him and answered: 'Talk not of flight, for I shall not listen to you: I am of a race that knows neither flight nor fear, and my limbs are as yet unwearied. I am in no mind to mount, but will go against them even as I am; Pallas Minerva bids me be afraid of no man, and even though one of them escape, their steeds shall not take both back again. I say further, and lay my saying to your heart – if Minerva sees fit to vouchsafe me the glory of killing both, stay your horses here and make the reins fast to the rim of the chariot; then be sure you spring upon Æneas' horses and drive them from the Trojan to the Achæan ranks. They are of the stock that great Jove gave to Tros in payment for his son Ganymede, and are the finest that live and move under the sun. King Anchises stole the blood by putting his mares to them without Laomedon's knowledge, and they bore him six foals. Four are still in his stables, but he gave the other two to Æneas. We shall win great glory if we can take them.'

Thus did they converse, but the other two had now driven close up to them, and the son of Lycaon spoke first. 'Great and mighty son,' said he, 'of noble Tydeus, my arrow failed to lay you low, so I will now try with my spear.'

He poised his spear as he spoke and hurled it from him. It struck the shield of the son of Tydeus; the bronze point pierced it and passed on till it reached the breastplate. Thereon the son of Lycaon shouted out and said, 'You are hit clean through the belly; you will not stand out for long, and the glory of the fight is mine.'

But Diomed all undismayed made answer, 'You have missed, not hit, and before you two see the end of this matter one or other of you shall glut tough-shielded Mars with his blood.'

With this he hurled his spear, and Minerva guided it on to Pandarus's nose near the eye. It went crashing in among his white teeth; the bronze point cut through the root of his tongue, coming out under his chin, and his glistening armour rang rattling round him as he fell heavily to the ground. The horses started aside for fear, and he was reft of life and strength.

Æneas sprang from his chariot armed with shield and spear, fearing lest the Achæans should carry off the body. He bestrode it as a lion in the pride of strength, with shield and spear before him and a cry of battle on his lips – resolute to kill the first that should dare face him. But the son of Tydeus caught up a mighty stone, so huge and great that as men now are it would take two to lift it; nevertheless he bore it aloft with ease unaided, and with this he struck Æneas on the groin where the hip turns in the joint that is called the 'cup-bone.' The stone crushed this joint, and broke both the sinews, while its jagged edges tore away all the flesh. The hero fell on his knees, and propped himself with his hand resting on the ground till the darkness of night fell upon his eyes. And now Æneas, king of men, would have perished then and there, had not his mother, Jove's daughter Venus, who had conceived him by Anchises when he was herding cattle, been quick to mark, and thrown her two white arms about the body of her dear son. She protected him by covering him with a fold of her own fair garment, lest some Danaan should drive a spear into his breast and kill him.

Thus, then, did she bear her dear son out of the fight. But the son of Capaneus was not unmindful of the orders that Diomed had given him. He made his own horses fast, away from the hurly-burly, by binding the reins to the rim of the chariot. Then he sprang upon

Æneas's horses and drove them from the Trojan to the Achæan ranks. When he had so done he gave them over to his chosen comrade Deipylus, whom he valued above all others as the one who was most like-minded with himself, to take them on to the ships. He then remounted his own chariot, seized the reins, and drove with all speed in search of the son of Tydeus.

Now the son of Tydeus was in pursuit of the Cyprian goddess, spear in hand, for he knew her to be feeble and not one of those goddesses that can lord it among men in battle like Minerva or Enyo the waster of cities, and when at last after a long chase he caught her up, he flew at her and thrust his spear into the flesh of her delicate hand. The point tore through the ambrosial robe which the Graces had woven for her, and pierced the skin between her wrist and the palm of her hand, so that the immortal blood, or ichor, that flows in the veins of the blessed gods, came pouring from the wound; for the gods do not eat bread nor drink wine, hence they have no blood such as ours, and are immortal. Venus screamed aloud, and let her son fall, but Phœbus Apollo caught him in his arms, and hid him in a cloud of darkness, lest some Danaan should drive a spear into his breast and kill him; and Diomed shouted out as he left her, 'Daughter of Jove, leave war and battle alone, can you not be contented with beguiling silly women? If you meddle with fighting you will get what will make you shudder at the very name of war.'

The goddess went dazed and discomfited away, and Iris, fleet as the wind, drew her from the throng, in pain and with her fair skin all besmirched. She found fierce Mars waiting on the left of the battle, with his spear and his two fleet steeds resting on a cloud; whereon she fell on her knees before her brother and implored him to let her have his horses. 'Dear brother,' she cried, 'save me, and give me your horses to take me to Olympus where the gods dwell. I am badly wounded by a mortal, the son of Tydeus, who would now fight even with father Jove.'

Thus she spoke, and Mars gave her his gold-bedizened steeds. She mounted the chariot sick and sorry at heart, while Iris sat beside her and took the reins in her hand. She lashed her horses on and they flew forward nothing loth, till in a trice they were at high Olympus, where the gods have their dwelling. There she stayed them, unloosed them from the chariot, and gave them their ambrosial forage; but Venus flung herself on to the lap of her mother Dione, who threw her arms about her and caressed her, saying, 'Which of the heavenly beings has been treating you in this way, as though you had been doing something wrong in the face of day?'

And laughter-loving Venus answered, 'Proud Diomed, the son of Tydeus, wounded me because I was bearing my dear son Æneas, whom I love best of all mankind, out of the fight. The war is no longer one between Trojans and Achæans, for the Danaans have now taken to fighting with the immortals.'

'Bear it, my child,' replied Dione, 'and make the best of it. We dwellers in Olympus have to put up with much at the hands of men, and we lay much suffering on one another. Mars had to suffer when Otus and Ephialtes, children of Aloeus, bound him in cruel bonds, so that he lay thirteen months imprisoned in a vessel of bronze. Mars would have then perished had not fair Eëribœa, stepmother to the sons of Aloeus, told Mercury, who stole him away when he was already well-nigh worn out by the severity of his bondage. Juno, again, suffered when the mighty son of Amphitryon wounded her on the right breast with a three-barbed arrow, and nothing could assuage her pain. So, also, did huge Hades, when this same man, the son of ægis-bearing Jove, hit him with an arrow even at the gates of hell, and hurt him badly. Thereon Hades went to the house of Jove on great Olympus, angry and full of pain; and the arrow in his brawny shoulder caused him great anguish till Pæëon healed him by spreading soothing herbs on the wound, for Hades was not of mortal mould. Daring, head-strong, evil-doer who recked not of his sin in shooting the gods that dwell in Olympus. And now Minerva has egged this son of Tydeus on against yourself, fool that he is for not reflecting that no man who fights with gods will live long or hear his children prattling about his knees when he returns from battle. Let, then, the son of Tydeus see that he does not have to fight with one who is stronger than you are. Then shall his brave wife Ægialeia, daughter of Adrestus, rouse her whole house from sleep, wailing for the loss of her wedded lord, Diomed the bravest of the Achæans.'

So saying, she wiped the ichor from the wrist of her daughter with both hands, whereon the pain left her, and her hand was healed. But Minerva and Juno, who were looking on, began to taunt Jove with their mocking talk, and Minerva was first to speak. 'Father Jove,' said she, 'do not be angry with me, but I think the Cyprian must have been persuading some one of the Achæan women to go with the Trojans of whom she is so very fond, and while caressing one or other of them she must have torn her delicate hand with the gold pin of the woman's brooch.'

The sire of gods and men smiled, and called golden Venus to his side. 'My child,' said he, 'it has not been given you to be a warrior. Attend, henceforth, to your own delightful matrimonial duties, and leave all this fighting to Mars and to Minerva.'

Thus did they converse. But Diomed sprang upon Æneas, though he knew him to be in the very arms of Apollo. Not one whit did he fear the mighty god, so set was he on killing Æneas and stripping him of his armour. Thrice did he spring forward with might and main to slay him, and thrice did Apollo beat back his gleaming shield. When he was coming on for the fourth time, as though he were a god, Apollo shouted to him with an awful voice and said, 'Take heed, son of Tydeus, and draw off; think not to match yourself against gods, for men that walk the earth cannot hold their own with the immortals.'

The son of Tydeus then gave way for a little space, to avoid the anger of the god, while Apollo took Æneas out of the crowd and set him in sacred Pergamus, where his temple stood. There, within the mighty sanctuary, Latona and Diana healed him and made him glorious to behold, while Apollo of the silver bow fashioned a wraith in the likeness of Æneas, and armed as he was. Round this the Trojans and

Achæans hacked at the bucklers about one another's breasts, hewing each other's round shields and light hide-covered targets. Then Phœbus Apollo said to Mars, 'Mars, Mars, bane of men, blood-stained stormer of cities, can you not go to this man, the son of Tydeus, who would now fight even with father Jove, and draw him out of the battle? He first went up to the Cyprian and wounded her in the hand near her wrist, and afterwards sprang upon me too, as though he were a god.'

He then took his seat on the top of Pergamus, while murderous Mars went about among the ranks of the Trojans, cheering them on, in the likeness of fleet Acamas chief of the Thracians. 'Sons of Priam,' said he, 'how long will you let your people be thus slaughtered by the Achæans? Would you wait till they are at the walls of Troy? Æneas the son of Anchises has fallen, he whom we held in as high honour as Hector himself. Help me, then, to rescue our brave comrade from the stress of the fight.'

With these words he put heart and soul into them all. Then Sarpedon rebuked Hector very sternly. 'Hector,' said he, 'where is your prowess now? You used to say that though you had neither people nor allies you could hold the town alone with your brothers and brothers-in-law. I see not one of them here; they cower as hounds before a lion; it is we, your allies, who bear the brunt of the battle. I have come from afar, even from Lycia and the banks of the river Xanthus, where I have left my wife, my infant son, and much wealth to tempt whoever is needy; nevertheless, I head my Lycian soldiers and stand my ground against any who would fight me though I have nothing here for the Achæans to plunder, while you look on, without even bidding your men stand firm in defence of their wives. See that you fall not into the hands of your foes as men caught in the meshes of a net, and they sack your fair city forthwith. Keep this before your mind night and day, and beseech the captains of your allies to hold on without flinching, and thus put away their reproaches from you.'

So spoke Sarpedon, and Hector smarted under his words. He sprang from his chariot clad in his suit of armour, and went about among the host brandishing his two spears, exhorting the men to fight and raising the terrible cry of battle. Then they rallied and again faced the Achæans, but the Argives stood compact and firm, and were not driven back. As the breezes sport with the chaff upon some goodly threshing-floor, when men are winnowing – while yellow Ceres blows with the wind to sift the chaff from the grain, and the chaff-heaps grow whiter and whiter – even so did the Achæans whiten in the dust which the horses' hoofs raised to the firmament of heaven, as their drivers turned them back to battle, and they bore down with might upon the foe. Fierce Mars, to help the Trojans, covered them in a veil of darkness, and went about everywhere among them, inasmuch as Phœbus Apollo had told him that when he saw Pallas Minerva leave the fray he was to put courage into the hearts of the Trojans – for it was she who was helping the Danaans. Then Apollo sent Æneas forth from his rich sanctuary, and filled his heart with valour, whereon he took his place among his comrades, who were overjoyed at seeing him alive, sound, and of a good courage; but they could not ask him how it had all happened, for they were too busy with the turmoil raised by Mars and by Strife, who raged insatiably in their midst.

The two Ajaxes, Ulysses, and Diomed cheered the Danaans on, fearless of the fury and onset of the Trojans. They stood as still as clouds which the son of Saturn has spread upon the mountain tops when there is no air and fierce Boreas sleeps with the other boisterous winds whose shrill blasts scatter the clouds in all directions – even so did the Danaans stand firm and unflinching against the Trojans. The son of Atreus went about among them and exhorted them. 'My friends,' said he, 'quit yourselves like brave men, and shun dishonour in one another's eyes amid the stress of battle. They that shun dishonour more often live than get killed, but they that fly save neither life nor name.'

As he spoke he hurled his spear and hit one of those who were in the front rank, the comrade of Æneas, Deicoön son of Pergasus, whom the Trojans held in no less honour than the sons of Priam, for he was ever quick to place himself among the foremost. The spear of King

Agamemnon struck his shield and went right through it, for the shield stayed it not. It drove through his belt into the lower part of his belly, and his armour rang rattling round him as he fell heavily to the ground.

Then Æneas killed two champions of the Danaans, Crethon and Orsilochus. Their father was a rich man who lived in the strong city of Phere and was descended from the river Alpheus, whose broad stream flows through the land of the Pylians. The river begat Orsilochus, who ruled over much people and was father to Diocles, who in his turn begat twin sons, Crethon and Orsilochus, well skilled in all the arts of war. These, when they grew up, went to Ilius with the Argive fleet in the cause of Menelaus and Agamemnon sons of Atreus, and there they both of them fell. As two lions whom their dam has reared in the depths of some mountain forest to plunder homesteads and carry off sheep and cattle till they get killed by the hand of man, so were these two vanquished by Æneas, and fell like high pine-trees to the ground.

Brave Menelaus pitied them in their fall, and made his way to the front, clad in gleaming bronze and brandishing his spear, for Mars egged him on to do so with intent that he should be killed by Æneas; but Antilochus the son of Nestor saw him and sprang forward, fearing that the king might come to harm and thus bring all their labour to nothing; when, therefore, Æneas and Menelaus were setting their hands and spears against one another eager to do battle, Antilochus placed himself by the side of Menelaus. Æneas, bold though he was, drew back on seeing the two heroes side by side in front of him, so they drew the bodies of Crethon and Orsilochus to the ranks of the Achæans and committed the two poor fellows into the hands of their comrades. They then turned back and fought in the front ranks.

They killed Pylæmenes peer of Mars, leader of the Paphlagonian warriors. Menelaus struck him on the collar-bone, as he was standing on his chariot, while Antilochus hit his charioteer and squire Mydon, the son of Atymnius, who was turning his horses in flight. He hit him with a stone upon the elbow, and the reins, enriched with white ivory, fell from his hands into the dust. Antilochus rushed towards him and struck him on the temples with his sword, whereon he fell head first from the chariot to the ground. There he stood for a while with his head and shoulders buried deep in the dust – for he had fallen on sandy soil – till his horses kicked him and laid him flat on the ground, as Antilochus lashed them and drove them off to the host of the Achæans.

But Hector marked them from across the ranks, and with a loud cry rushed towards them, followed by the strong battalions of the Trojans. Mars and dread Enyo led them on, she fraught with ruthless turmoil of battle, while Mars wielded a monstrous spear, and went about, now in front of Hector and now behind him.

Diomed shook with passion as he saw them. As a man crossing a wide plain is dismayed to find himself on the brink of some great river rolling swiftly to the sea – he sees its boiling waters and starts back in fear – even so did the son of Tydeus give ground. Then he said to his men, 'My friends, how can we wonder that Hector wields the spear so well? Some god is ever by his side to protect him, and now Mars is with him in the likeness of mortal man. Keep your faces therefore towards the Trojans, but give ground backwards, for we dare not fight with gods.'

As he spoke the Trojans drew close up, and Hector killed two men, both in one chariot, Menesthes and Anchialus, heroes well versed in war. Ajax son of Telamon pitied them in their fall; he came close up and hurled his spear, hitting Amphius the son of Selagus, a man of great wealth who lived in Pæsus and owned much corn-growing land, but his lot had led him to come to the aid of Priam and his sons. Ajax struck him in the belt; the spear pierced the lower part of his belly, and he fell heavily to the ground. Then Ajax ran towards him to strip him of his armour, but the Trojans rained spears upon him, many of which fell upon his shield. He planted his heel upon the body and drew out his spear, but the darts pressed so heavily upon him that he could not strip the goodly armour from his shoulders. The Trojan

HOMER

chieftains, moreover, many and valiant, came about him with their spears, so that he dared not stay; great, brave and valiant though he was, they drove him from them and he was beaten back.

Thus, then, did the battle rage between them. Presently the strong hand of fate impelled Tlepolemus, the son of Hercules, a man both brave and of great stature, to fight Sarpedon; so the two, son and grandson of great Jove, drew near to one another, and Tlepolemus spoke first. 'Sarpedon,' said he, 'councillor of the Lycians, why should you come skulking here – you who are a man of peace? They lie who call you son of ægis-bearing Jove, for you are little like those who were of old his children. Far other was Hercules, my own brave and lion-hearted father, who came here for the horses of Laomedon, and though he had six ships only, and few men to follow him, sacked the city of Ilius and made a wilderness of her highways. You are a coward, and your people are falling from you. For all your strength, and all your coming from Lycia, you will be no help to the Trojans but will pass the gates of Hades vanquished by my hand.'

And Sarpedon, captain of the Lycians, answered, 'Tlepolemus, your father overthrew Ilius by reason of Laomedon's folly in refusing payment to one who had served him well. He would not give your father the horses which he had come so far to fetch. As for yourself, you shall meet death by my spear. You shall yield glory to myself, and your soul to Hades of the noble steeds.'

Thus spoke Sarpedon, and Tlepolemus upraised his spear. They threw at the same moment, and Sarpedon struck his foe in the middle of his throat; the spear went right through, and the darkness of death fell upon his eyes. Tlepolemus's spear struck Sarpedon on the left thigh with such force that it tore through the flesh and grazed the bone, but his father as yet warded off destruction from him.

His comrades bore Sarpedon out of the fight, in great pain by the weight of the spear that was dragging from his wound. They were in such haste and stress as they bore him that no one thought of drawing the spear from his thigh so as to let him walk uprightly. Meanwhile the Achæans carried off the body of Tlepolemus, whereon Ulysses was moved to pity, and panted for the fray as he beheld them. He doubted whether to pursue the son of Jove, or to make slaughter of the Lycian rank and file; it was not decreed, however, that he should slay the son of Jove; Minerva, therefore, turned him against the main body of the Lycians. He killed Cœranus, Alastor, Chromius, Alcandrus, Halius, Noëmon, and Prytanis, and would have slain yet more, had not great Hector marked him, and sped to the front of the fight clad in his suit of mail, filling the Danaans with terror. Sarpedon was glad when he saw him coming, and besought him, saying, 'Son of Priam, let me not lie here to fall into the hands of the Danaans. Help me, and since I may not return home to gladden the hearts of my wife and of my infant son, let me die within the walls of your city.'

Hector made him no answer, but rushed onward to fall at once upon the Achæans and kill many among them. His comrades then bore Sarpedon away and laid him beneath Jove's spreading oak tree. Pelagon his friend and comrade drew the spear out of his thigh, but Sarpedon fainted and a mist came over his eyes. Presently he came to himself again, for the breath of the north wind as it played upon him gave him new life, and brought him out of the deep swoon into which he had fallen.

Meanwhile the Argives were neither driven towards their ships by Mars and Hector, nor yet did they attack them; when they knew that Mars was with the Trojans they retreated, but kept their faces still turned towards the foe. Who, then, was first and who last to be slain by Mars and Hector? They were valiant Teuthras, and Orestes the renowned charioteer, Trechus the Ætolian warrior, Œnomaus, Helenus the son of Œnops, and Oresbius of the gleaming girdle, who was possessed of great wealth, and dwelt by the Cephisian lake with the other Bœotians who lived near him, owners of a fertile country.

Now when the goddess Juno saw the Argives thus falling, she said to Minerva, 'Alas, daughter of ægis-bearing Jove, unweariable, the promise we made Menelaus that he should not return till he had sacked the city of Ilius will be of none effect if we let Mars rage thus furiously. Let us go into the fray at once.'

Minerva did not gainsay her. Thereon the august goddess, daughter of great Saturn, began to harness her gold-bedizened steeds. Hebe with all speed fitted on the eight-spoked wheels of bronze that were on either side of the iron axle-tree. The felloes of the wheels were of gold, imperishable, and over these there was a tire of bronze, wondrous to behold. The naves of the wheels were silver, turning round the axle upon either side. The car itself was made with plaited bands of gold and silver, and it had a double top-rail running all round it. From the body of the car there went a pole of silver, on to the end of which she bound the golden yoke, with the bands of gold that were to go under the necks of the horses. Then Juno put her steeds under the yoke, eager for battle and the war-cry.

Meanwhile Minerva flung her richly embroidered vesture, made with her own hands, on to her father's threshold, and donned the shirt of Jove, arming herself for battle. She threw her tasselled ægis about her shoulders, wreathed round with Rout as with a fringe, and on it were Strife, and Strength, and Panic whose blood runs cold; moreover there was the head of the dread monster Gorgon, grim and awful to behold, portent of ægis-bearing Jove. On her head she set her helmet of gold, with four plumes, and coming to a peak both in front and behind – decked with the emblems of a hundred cities; then she stepped into her flaming chariot and grasped the spear, so stout and sturdy and strong, with which she quells the ranks of heroes who have displeased her. Juno lashed the horses on, and the gates of heaven bellowed as they flew open of their own accord – gates over which the Hours preside, in whose hands are Heaven and Olympus, either to open the dense cloud that hides them, or to close it. Through these the goddesses drove their obedient steeds, and found the son of Saturn sitting all alone on the topmost ridges of Olympus. There Juno stayed her horses, and spoke to Jove the son of Saturn, lord of all. 'Father Jove,' said she, 'are you not angry with Mars for these high doings? See how great and goodly a host of the Achæans he has destroyed to my great grief, and without either right or reason, while the Cyprian and Apollo are enjoying it all at their ease and setting this unrighteous madman on to do further mischief. I hope, Father Jove, that you will not be angry if I hit Mars hard, and chase him out of the battle.'

And Jove answered, 'Set Minerva on to him, for she punishes him more often than any one else does.'

Juno did as he had said. She lashed her horses, and they flew forward nothing loth midway betwixt earth and sky. As far as a man can see when he looks out upon the sea from some high beacon, so far can the loud-neighing horses of the gods spring at a single bound. When they reached Troy and the place where its two flowing streams Simois and Scamander meet, there Juno stayed them and took them from the chariot. She hid them in a thick cloud, and Simois made ambrosia spring up for them to eat; the two goddesses then went on, flying like turtledoves in their eagerness to help the Argives. When they came to the part where the bravest and most in number were gathered about mighty Diomed, fighting like lions or wild boars of great strength and endurance, there Juno stood still and raised a shout like that of brazen-voiced Stentor, whose cry was as loud as that of fifty men together. 'Argives,' she cried; 'shame on you, cowardly creatures, brave in semblance only; as long as Achilles was fighting, his spear was so deadly that the Trojans dared not show themselves outside the Dardanian gates, but now they sally far from the city and fight even at your ships.'

With these words she put heart and soul into them all, while Minerva sprang to the side of the son of Tydeus, whom she found near his chariot and horses, cooling the wound that Pandarus had given him. For the sweat caused by the band that bore the weight of his shield irritated the hurt: his arm was weary with pain, and he was lifting up the strap to wipe away the blood. The goddess laid her hand on the yoke of his horses and said, 'The son of Tydeus is not such another as his father. Tydeus was a little man, but he could fight, and rushed madly into the fray even when I told him not to do so. When he went all unattended as envoy to the city of Thebes among the Cadmeans, I bade him feast in their houses and be at peace; but with that high spirit which was ever present with him, he challenged the youth of the Cadmeans, and at once beat them in all that he attempted, so mightily did I help him. I stand by you too to protect you, and I bid you be instant in fighting the Trojans; but either you are tired out, or you are afraid and out of heart, and in that case I say that you are no true son of Tydeus the son of Œneus.'

Diomed answered, 'I know you, goddess, daughter of ægis-bearing Jove, and will hide nothing from you. I am not afraid nor out of heart, nor is there any slackness in me. I am only following your own instructions; you told me not to fight any of the blessed gods; but if Jove's daughter Venus came into battle I was to wound her with my spear. Therefore I am retreating, and bidding the other Argives gather in this place, for I know that Mars is now lording it in the field.'

'Diomed, son of Tydeus,' replied Minerva, 'man after my own heart, fear neither Mars nor any other of the immortals, for I will befriend you. Nay, drive straight at Mars, and smite him in close combat; fear not this raging madman, villain incarnate, first on one side and then on the other. But now he was holding talk with Juno and myself, saying he would help the Argives and attack the Trojans; nevertheless he is with the Trojans, and has forgotten the Argives.'

With this she caught hold of Sthenelus and lifted him off the chariot on to the ground. In a second he was on the ground, whereupon the goddess mounted the car and placed herself by the side of Diomed. The oaken axle groaned aloud under the burden of the awful goddess and the hero; Pallas Minerva took the whip and reins, and drove straight at Mars. He was in the act of stripping huge Periphas, son of Ochesius and bravest of the Ætolians. Bloody Mars was stripping him of his armour, and Minerva donned the helmet of Hades, that he might not see her; when, therefore, he saw Diomed, he made straight for him and let Periphas lie where he had fallen. As soon as they were at close quarters he let fly with his bronze spear over the reins and yoke, thinking to take Diomed's life, but Minerva caught the spear in her hand and made it fly harmlessly over the chariot. Diomed then threw, and Pallas Minerva drove the spear into the pit of Mars's stomach where his under-girdle went round him. There Diomed wounded him, tearing his fair flesh and then drawing his spear out again. Mars roared as loudly as nine or ten thousand men in the thick of a fight, and the Achæans and Trojans were struck with panic, so terrible was the cry he raised.

As a dark cloud in the sky when it comes on to blow after heat, even so did Diomed son of Tydeus see Mars ascend into the broad heavens. With all speed he reached high Olympus, home of the gods, and in great pain sat down beside Jove the son of Saturn. He showed Jove the immortal blood that was flowing from his wound, and spoke piteously, saying, 'Father Jove, are you not angered by such doings? We gods are continually suffering in the most cruel manner at one another's hands while helping mortals; and we all owe you a grudge for having begotten that mad termagant of a daughter, who is always committing outrage of some kind. We other gods must all do as you bid us, but her you neither scold nor punish; you encourage her because the pestilent creature is your daughter. See how she has been inciting proud Diomed to vent his rage on the immortal gods. First he went up to the Cyprian and wounded her in the hand near her wrist, and then he sprang upon me too as though he were a god. Had I not run for it I must either have lain there for long enough in torments among the ghastly corpses, or have been beaten alive with spears till I had no more strength left in me.'

Jove looked angrily at him and said, 'Do not come whining here, Sir Facing-both-ways. I hate you worst of all the gods in Olympus, for you are ever fighting and making mischief. You have the intolerable and stubborn spirit of your mother Juno: it is all I can do to manage her, and it is her doing that you are now in this plight: still, I cannot let you remain longer in such great pain; you are my own offspring, and it was by me that your mother conceived you; if, however, you had been the son of any other god, you are so destructive that by this time you should have been lying lower than the Titans.'

He then bade Pæëon heal him, whereon Pæëon spread pain-killing herbs upon his wound and cured him, for he was not of mortal mould. As the juice of the fig-tree curdles milk, and thickens it in a moment though it is liquid, even so instantly did Pæëon cure fierce Mars. Then Hebe washed him, and clothed him in goodly raiment, and he took his seat by his father Jove all glorious to behold.

But Juno of Argos and Minerva of Alalcomene, now that they had put a stop to the murderous doings of Mars, went back again to the house of Jove.

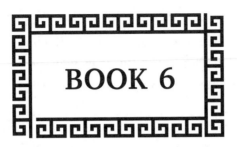

BOOK 6

Glaucus and Diomed – The story of Bellerophon –
Hector and Andromache.

The fight between Trojans and Achæans was now left to rage as it
would, and the tide of war surged hither and thither over the plain as
they aimed their bronze-shod spears at one another between the streams
of Simois and Xanthus.

First, Ajax son of Telamon, tower of strength to the Achæans, broke
a phalanx of the Trojans, and came to the assistance of his comrades
by killing Acamas son of Eussorus, the best man among the Thracians,
being both brave and of great stature. The spear struck the projecting
peak of his helmet: its bronze point then went through his forehead
into the brain, and darkness veiled his eyes.

Then Diomed killed Axylus son of Teuthranus, a rich man who lived
in the strong city of Arisbe, and was beloved by all men; for he had a
house by the roadside, and entertained every one who passed; howbeit
not one of his guests stood before him to save his life, and Diomed
killed both him and his squire Calesius, who was then his charioteer
– so the pair passed beneath the earth.

Euryalus killed Dresus and Opheltius, and then went in pursuit of
Æsepus and Pedasus, whom the naiad nymph Abarbarea had borne
to noble Bucolion. Bucolion was eldest son to Laomedon, but he was
a bastard. While tending his sheep he had converse with the nymph,
and she conceived twin sons; these the son of Mecisteus now slew,
and he stripped the armour from their shoulders. Polypœtes then

killed Astyalus, Ulysses Pidytes of Percote, and Teucer Aretaon. Ablerus fell by the spear of Nestor's son Antilochus, and Agamemnon, king of men, killed Elatus who dwelt in Pedasus by the banks of the river Satnioeis. Leïtus killed Phylacus as he was flying, and Eurypylus slew Melanthus.

Then Menelaus of the loud war-cry took Adrestus alive, for his horses ran into a tamarisk bush, as they were flying wildly over the plain, and broke the pole from the car; they went on towards the city along with the others in full flight, but Adrestus rolled out, and fell in the dust flat on his face by the wheel of his chariot. Menelaus came up to him spear in hand, but Adrestus caught him by the knees begging for his life. 'Take me alive,' he cried, 'son of Atreus, and you shall have a full ransom for me: my father is rich and has much treasure of gold, bronze, and wrought iron laid by in his house. From this store he will give you a large ransom should he hear of my being alive and at the ships of the Achæans.'

Thus did he plead, and Menelaus was for yielding and giving him to a squire to take to the ships of the Achæans, but Agamemnon came running up to him and rebuked him. 'My good Menelaus,' said he, 'this is no time for giving quarter. Has, then, your house fared so well at the hands of the Trojans? Let us not spare a single one of them – not even the child unborn and in its mother's womb; let not a man of them be left alive, but let all in Ilius perish, unheeded and forgotten.'

Thus did he speak, and his brother was persuaded by him, for his words were just. Menelaus, therefore, thrust Adrestus from him, whereon King Agamemnon struck him in the flank, and he fell: then the son of Atreus planted his foot upon his breast to draw his spear from the body.

Meanwhile Nestor shouted to the Argives, saying, 'My friends, Danaan warriors, servants of Mars, let no man lag that he may spoil the dead, and bring back much booty to the ships. Let us kill as many as we can; the bodies will lie upon the plain, and you can despoil them later at your leisure.'

With these words he put heart and soul into them all. And now the Trojans would have been routed and driven back into Ilius, had not Priam's son Helenus, wisest of augurs, said to Hector and Æneas, 'Hector and Æneas, you two are the mainstays of the Trojans and Lycians, for you are foremost at all times, alike in fight and counsel; hold your ground here, and go about among the host to rally them in front of the gates, or they will fling themselves into the arms of their wives, to the great joy of our foes. Then, when you have put heart into all our companies, we will stand firm here and fight the Danaans however hard they press us, for there is nothing else to be done. Meanwhile do you, Hector, go to the city and tell our mother what is happening. Tell her to bid the matrons gather at the temple of Minerva in the acropolis; let her then take her key and open the doors of the sacred building; there, upon the knees of Minerva, let her lay the largest, fairest robe she has in her house – the one she sets most store by; let her, moreover, promise to sacrifice twelve yearling heifers that have never yet felt the goad, in the temple of the goddess, if she will take pity on the town, with the wives and little ones of the Trojans, and keep the son of Tydeus from falling on the goodly city of Ilius; for he fights with fury and fills men's souls with panic. I hold him mightiest of them all; we did not fear even their great champion Achilles, son of a goddess though he be, as we do this man: his rage is beyond all bounds, and there is none can vie with him in prowess.'

Hector did as his brother bade him. He sprang from his chariot, and went about everywhere among the host, brandishing his spears, urging the men on to fight, and raising the dread cry of battle. Thereon they rallied and again faced the Achæans, who gave ground and ceased their murderous onset, for they deemed that some one of the immortals had come down from starry heaven to help the Trojans, so strangely had they rallied. And Hector shouted to the Trojans, 'Trojans and allies, be men, my friends, and fight with might and main, while I go to Ilius and tell the old men of our council and our wives to pray to the gods and vow hecatombs in their honour.'

With this he went his way, and the black rim of hide that went round his shield beat against his neck and his ancles.

Then Glaucus son of Hippolochus, and the son of Tydeus went into the open space between the hosts to fight in single combat. When they were close up to one another Diomed of the loud war-cry was the first to speak. 'Who, my good sir,' said he, 'who are you among men? I have never seen you in battle until now, but you are daring beyond all others if you abide my onset. Woe to those fathers whose sons face my might. If, however, you are one of the immortals and have come down from heaven, I will not fight you; for even valiant Lycurgus, son of Dryas, did not live long when he took to fighting with the gods. He it was that drove the nursing women who were in charge of frenzied Bacchus through the land of Nysa, and they flung their thyrsi on the ground as murderous Lycurgus beat them with his ox-goad. Bacchus himself plunged terror-stricken into the sea, and Thetis took him to her bosom to comfort him, for he was scared by the fury with which the man reviled him. Thereon the gods who live at ease were angry with Lycurgus and the son of Saturn struck him blind, nor did he live much longer after he had become hateful to the immortals. Therefore I will not fight with the blessed gods; but if you are of them that eat the fruit of the ground, draw near and meet your doom.'

And the son of Hippolochus answered, 'Mighty son of Tydeus, why ask me of my lineage? Men come and go as leaves year by year upon the trees. Those of autumn the wind sheds upon the ground, but when spring returns the forest buds forth with fresh ones. Even so is it with the generations of mankind, the new spring up as the old are passing away. If, then, you would learn my descent, it is one that is well known to many. There is a city in the heart of Argos, pasture land of horses, called Ephyra, where Sisyphus lived, who was the craftiest of all mankind. He was the son of Æolus, and had a son named Glaucus, who was father to Bellerophon, whom heaven endowed with the most surpassing comeliness and beauty. But Prœtus devised his ruin, and being stronger than he, drove him from the land of the Argives, over which Jove had made him ruler. For Antea, wife of Prœtus, lusted after him, and would have had him lie with her in secret; but Bellerophon was an honourable man and would not, so she told lies about him to Prœtus. 'Prœtus,' said she, 'kill Bellerophon or die, for he would have had converse with me against my will.' The king was angered, but shrank from killing Bellerophon, so he sent him to Lycia with lying letters of introduction, written on a folded tablet, and containing much ill against the bearer. He bade Bellerophon show these letters to his father-in-law, to the end that he might thus perish; Bellerophon therefore went to Lycia, and the gods convoyed him safely.

'When he reached the river Xanthus, which is in Lycia, the king received him with all goodwill, feasted him nine days, and killed nine heifers in his honour, but when rosy-fingered morning appeared upon the tenth day, he questioned him and desired to see the letter from his son-in-law Prœtus. When he had received the wicked letter he first commanded Bellerophon to kill that savage monster, the Chimæra, who was not a human being, but a goddess, for she had the head of a lion and the tail of a serpent, while her body was that of a goat, and she breathed forth flames of fire; but Bellerophon slew her, for he was guided by signs from heaven. He next fought the far-famed Solymi, and this, he said, was the hardest of all his battles. Thirdly, he killed the Amazons, women who were the peers of men, and as he was returning thence the king devised yet another plan for his destruction; he picked the bravest warriors in all Lycia, and placed them in ambuscade, but not a man ever came back, for Bellerophon killed every one of them. Then the king knew that he must be the valiant offspring of a god, so he kept him in Lycia, gave him his daughter in marriage, and made him of equal honour in the kingdom with himself; and the Lycians gave him a piece of land, the best in all the country, fair with vineyards and tilled fields, to have and to hold.

'The king's daughter bore Bellerophon three children, Isander, Hippolochus, and Laodameia. Jove, the lord of counsel, lay with Laodameia, and she bore him noble Sarpedon; but when Bellerophon came to be hated by all the gods, he wandered all desolate and dismayed upon the Alean plain, gnawing at his own heart, and shunning the path of man. Mars, insatiate of battle, killed his son Isander while he was fighting the Solymi; his daughter was killed by Diana of the golden reins, for she was angered with her; but Hippolochus was father to myself, and when he sent me to Troy he urged me again and again to fight ever among the foremost and outvie my peers, so as not to shame the blood of my fathers who were the noblest in Ephyra and in all Lycia. This, then, is the descent I claim.'

Thus did he speak, and the heart of Diomed was glad. He planted his spear in the ground, and spoke to him with friendly words. 'Then,' he said, 'you are an old friend of my father's house. Great Œneus once entertained Bellerophon for twenty days, and the two exchanged presents. Œneus gave a belt rich with purple, and Bellerophon a double cup, which I left at home when I set out for Troy. I do not remember Tydeus, for he was taken from us while I was yet a child, when the army of the Achæans was cut to pieces before Thebes. Henceforth, however, I must be your host in middle Argos, and you mine in Lycia, if I should ever go there; let us avoid one another's spears even during a general engagement; there are many noble Trojans and allies whom I can kill, if I overtake them and heaven delivers them into my hand; so again with yourself, there are many Achæans whose lives you may take if you can; we two, then, will exchange armour, that all present may know of the old ties that subsist between us.'

With these words they sprang from their chariots, grasped one another's hands, and plighted friendship. But the son of Saturn made Glaucus take leave of his wits, for he exchanged golden armour for bronze, the worth of a hundred head of cattle for the worth of nine.

Now when Hector reached the Scæan gates and the oak tree, the wives and daughters of the Trojans came running towards him to ask after their sons, brothers, kinsmen, and husbands: he told them to set about praying to the gods, and many were made sorrowful as they heard him.

Presently he reached the splendid palace of King Priam, adorned with colonnades of hewn stone. In it there were fifty bedchambers – all of hewn stone – built near one another, where the sons of Priam slept, each with his wedded wife. Opposite these, on the other side the courtyard, there were twelve upper rooms also of hewn stone for Priam's daughters, built near one another, where his sons-in-law slept with their wives. When Hector got there, his fond mother came up to him with Laodice the fairest of her daughters. She took his hand within her own and said, 'My son, why have you left the battle to come hither? Are the Achæans, woe betide them, pressing you hard about the city that you have thought fit to come and uplift your hands to Jove from the citadel? Wait till I can bring you wine that you may make offering to Jove and to the other immortals, and may then drink and be refreshed. Wine gives a man fresh strength when he is wearied, as you now are with fighting on behalf of your kinsmen.'

And Hector answered, 'Honoured mother, bring no wine, lest you unman me and I forget my strength. I dare not make a drink-offering to Jove with unwashed hands; one who is bespattered with blood and filth may not pray to the son of Saturn. Get the matrons together, and go with offerings to the temple of Minerva driver of the spoil; there, upon the knees of Minerva, lay the largest and fairest robe you have in your house – the one you set most store by; promise, moreover, to sacrifice twelve yearling heifers that have never yet felt the goad, in the temple of the goddess, if she will take pity on the town, with the wives and little ones of the Trojans, and keep the son of Tydeus from off the goodly city of Ilius, for he fights with fury, and fills men's souls with panic. Go, then, to the temple of Minerva, while I seek Paris and exhort him, if he will hear my words. Would that the earth might open her jaws and swallow him, for Jove bred him to be the bane of the Trojans, and of Priam and Priam's sons. Could I but see him go down into the house of Hades, my heart would forget its heaviness.'

His mother went into the house and called her waiting-women who gathered the matrons throughout the city. She then went down into her fragrant store-room, where her embroidered robes were kept, the work of Sidonian women, whom Alexandrus had brought over from Sidon when he sailed the seas upon that voyage during which he carried off noble Helen. Hecuba took out the largest robe, and the one that was most beautifully enriched with embroidery, as an offering to Minerva: it glittered like a star, and lay at the very bottom of the chest. With this she went on her way and many matrons with her.

When they reached the temple of Minerva, lovely Theano, daughter of Cisseus and wife of Antenor, opened the doors, for the Trojans had made her priestess of Minerva. The women lifted up their hands to the goddess with a loud cry, and Theano took the robe to lay it upon the knees of Minerva, praying the while to the daughter of great Jove. 'Holy Minerva,' she cried, 'protectress of our city, mighty goddess, break the spear of Diomed and lay him low before the Scæan gates. Do this, and we will sacrifice twelve heifers that have never yet known the goad, in your temple, if you will have pity upon the town, with the wives and little ones of the Trojans.' Thus she prayed, but Pallas Minerva granted not her prayer.

While they were thus praying to the daughter of great Jove, Hector went to the fair house of Alexandrus, which he had had built for him by the foremost builders in the land. They had built him his house, storehouse, and courtyard near those of Priam and Hector on the acropolis. Here Hector entered, with a spear eleven cubits long in his hand; the bronze point gleamed in front of him, and was fastened to the shaft of the spear by a ring of gold. He found Alexandrus within the house, busied about his armour, his shield and cuirass, and handling his curved bow; there, too, sat Argive Helen with her women, setting them their several tasks; and as Hector saw him he rebuked him with words of scorn. 'Sir,' said he, 'you do ill to nurse this rancour; the people perish fighting round this our town; you would yourself chide one whom you saw shirking his part in the combat. Up then, or ere long the city will be in a blaze.'

And Alexandrus answered, 'Hector, your rebuke is just; listen therefore, and believe me when I tell you that I am not here so much through rancour or ill-will towards the Trojans, as from a desire to indulge my grief. My wife was even now gently urging me to battle, and I hold it better that I should go, for victory is ever fickle. Wait, then, while I put on my armour, or go first and I will follow. I shall be sure to overtake you.'

Hector made no answer, but Helen tried to soothe him. 'Brother,' said she, 'to my abhorred and sinful self, would that a whirlwind had caught me up on the day my mother brought me forth, and had borne me to some mountain or to the waves of the roaring sea that should have swept me away ere this mischief had come about. But, since the gods have devised these evils, would, at any rate, that I had been wife to a better man – to one who could smart under dishonour and men's evil speeches. This fellow was never yet to be depended upon, nor never will be, and he will surely reap what he has sown. Still, brother, come in and rest upon this seat, for it is you who bear the brunt of that toil that has been caused by my hateful self and by the sin of Alexandrus – both of whom Jove has doomed to be a theme of song among those that shall be born hereafter.'

And Hector answered, 'Bid me not be seated, Helen, for all the goodwill you bear me. I cannot stay. I am in haste to help the Trojans, who miss me greatly when I am not among them; but urge your husband, and of his own self also let him make haste to overtake me before I am out of the city. I must go home to see my household, my wife and my little son, for I know not whether I shall ever again return to them, or whether the gods will cause me to fall by the hands of the Achæans.'

Then Hector left her, and forthwith was at his own house. He did not find Andromache, for she was on the wall with her child and one of her maids, weeping bitterly. Seeing, then, that she was not within, he stood on the threshold of the women's rooms and said, 'Women, tell me, and tell me true, where did Andromache go when she left the house? Was it to my sisters, or to my brothers' wives? or is she at the temple of Minerva where the other women are propitiating the awful goddess?'

His good housekeeper answered, 'Hector, since you bid me tell you truly, she did not go to your sisters nor to your brothers' wives, nor yet to the temple of Minerva, where the other women are propitiating the awful goddess, but she is on the high wall of Ilius, for she had heard the Trojans were being hard pressed, and that the Achæans were in great force: therefore she went to the wall in frenzied haste, and the nurse went with her carrying the child.'

Hector hurried from the house when she had done speaking, and went down the streets by the same way that he had come. When he had gone through the city and had reached the Scæan gates through which he would go out on to the plain, his wife came running towards him, Andromache, daughter of great Eëtion who ruled in Thebe under the wooded slopes of Mt Placus, and was king of the Cilicians. His daughter had married Hector, and now came to meet him with a nurse who carried his little child in her bosom – a mere babe, Hector's darling son, and lovely as a star. Hector had named him Scamandrius, but the people called him Astyanax,³ for his father stood alone as chief guardian of Ilius. Hector smiled as he looked upon the boy, but he did not speak, and Andromache stood by him weeping and taking his hand in her own. 'Dear husband,' said she, 'your valour will bring you to destruction; think on your infant son, and on my hapless self who ere long shall be your widow – for the Achæans will set upon you in a body and kill you. It would be better for me, should I lose you, to lie dead and buried, for I shall have nothing left to comfort me when you are gone, save only sorrow. I have neither father nor mother now. Achilles slew my father when he sacked Thebe the goodly city of the Cilicians. He slew him, but did not for very shame despoil him; when he had burned him in his wondrous armour, he raised a barrow over his ashes and the mountain nymphs, daughters of ægis-bearing Jove, planted a grove of elms about his tomb. I had seven brothers in my father's house, but on the same day they all went within the house of Hades. Achilles killed them as they were with their sheep and cattle. My mother – her who had been queen of all the land under Mt Placus – he brought hither with the spoil, and freed her for a great sum, but the archer-queen Diana took her in the house of your father. Nay – Hector – you who to me are father, mother, brother, and dear husband – have mercy upon me; stay here upon this wall; make not your child fatherless, and your wife a widow; as for the host, place them near the fig-tree, where the city can be best scaled, and the wall is weakest. Thrice have the bravest of them come thither and assailed it, under the two Ajaxes, Idomeneus, the sons of Atreus, and the brave son of Tydeus, either of their own bidding, or because some soothsayer had told them.'

And Hector answered, 'Wife, I too have thought upon all this, but with what face should I look upon the Trojans, men or women, if I shirked battle like a coward? I cannot do so: I know nothing save to fight bravely in the forefront of the Trojan host and win renown alike for my father and myself. Well do I know that the day will surely come when mighty Ilius shall be destroyed with Priam and Priam's people, but I grieve for none of these – not even for Hecuba, nor King Priam, nor for my brothers many and brave who may fall in the dust before their foes – for none of these do I grieve as for yourself when the day shall come on which some one of the Achæans shall rob you for ever of your freedom, and bear you weeping away. It may be that you will have to ply the loom in Argos at the bidding of a mistress, or to fetch water from the springs Messeïs or Hypereia, treated brutally by some cruel task-master; then will one say who sees you weeping, "She was wife to Hector, the bravest warrior among the Trojans during the war before Ilius." On this your tears will break forth anew for him who would have put away the day of captivity from you. May I lie dead under the barrow that is heaped over my body ere I hear your cry as they carry you into bondage.'

He stretched his arms towards his child, but the boy cried and nestled in his nurse's bosom, scared at the sight of his father's armour, and at the horse-hair plume that nodded fiercely from his helmet. His father and mother laughed to see him, but Hector took the helmet from his head and laid it all gleaming upon the ground. Then he took his darling child, kissed him, and dandled him in his arms, praying over him the while to Jove and to all the gods. 'Jove,' he cried, 'grant that this my child may be even as myself, chief among the Trojans; let him be not less excellent in strength, and let him rule Ilius with his might. Then may one say of him as he comes from battle, "The son is far better than the father." May he bring back the blood-stained spoils of him whom he has laid low, and let his mother's heart be glad.'

With this he laid the child again in the arms of his wife, who took him to her own soft bosom, smiling through her tears. As her husband watched her his heart yearned towards her and he caressed her fondly, saying, 'My own wife, do not take these things too bitterly to heart. No one can hurry me down to Hades before my time, but if a man's hour is come, be he brave or be he coward, there is no escape for him when he has once been born. Go, then, within the house, and busy yourself with your daily duties, your loom, your distaff, and the ordering of your servants; for war is man's matter, and mine above all others of them that have been born in Ilius.'

He took his plumed helmet from the ground, and his wife went back again to her house, weeping bitterly and often looking back towards him. When she reached her home she found her maidens within, and bade them all join in her lament; so they mourned Hector in his own house though he was yet alive, for they deemed that they should never see him return safe from battle, and from the furious hands of the Achæans.

Paris did not remain long in his house. He donned his goodly armour overlaid with bronze, and hasted through the city as fast as his feet could take him. As a horse, stabled and full fed, breaks loose and gallops gloriously over the plain to the place where he is wont to bathe in the fair-flowing river – he holds his head high, and his mane streams upon his shoulders as he exults in his strength and flies like the wind to the haunts and feeding ground of the mares – even so went forth Paris from high Pergamus, gleaming like sunlight in his armour, and he laughed aloud as he sped swiftly on his way. Forthwith he came upon his brother Hector, who was then turning away from the place where he had held converse with his wife, and he was himself the first to speak. 'Sir,' said he, 'I fear that I have kept you waiting when you are in haste, and have not come as quickly as you bade me.'

'My good brother,' answered Hector, 'you fight bravely, and no man with any justice can make light of your doings in battle. But you are careless and wilfully remiss. It grieves me to the heart to hear the ill that the Trojans speak about you, for they have suffered much on your account. Let us be going, and we will make things right hereafter, should Jove vouchsafe us to set the cup of our deliverance before the ever-living gods of heaven in our own homes, when we have chased the Achæans from Troy.'

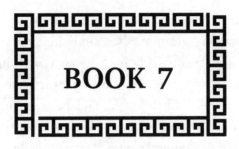

BOOK 7

Hector and Ajax fight – Hector is getting worsted when night comes on and parts them – They exchange presents – The burial of the dead, and the building of a wall round their ships by the Achæans – The Achæans buy their wine of Agamemnon and Menelaus.

With these words Hector passed through the gates, and his brother Alexandrus with him, both eager for the fray. As when heaven sends a breeze to sailors who have long looked for one in vain, and have laboured at their oars till they are faint with toil, even so welcome was the sight of these two heroes to the Trojans.

Thereon Alexandrus killed Menesthius the son of Areïthoüs; he lived in Arne, and was son of Areïthoüs the Mace-man, and of Phylomedusa. Hector threw a spear at Eioneus and struck him dead with a wound in the neck under the bronze rim of his helmet. Glaucus, moreover, son of Hippolochus, captain of the Lycians, in hard hand-to-hand fight smote Iphinoüs son of Dexius on the shoulder, as he was springing on to his chariot behind his fleet mares; so he fell to earth from the car, and there was no life left in him.

When, therefore, Minerva saw these men making havoc of the Argives, she darted down to Ilius from the summits of Olympus, and Apollo, who was looking on from Pergamus, went out to meet her; for he wanted the Trojans to be victorious. The pair met by the oak tree, and King Apollo son of Jove was first to speak. 'What would you have,' said he, 'daughter of great Jove, that your proud spirit has sent you hither from Olympus? Have you no pity upon the Trojans, and would you incline the scales of victory in favour of the Danaans? Let me persuade you – for it will be better thus – stay the combat for to-day, but let them renew the fight hereafter till they compass the doom of Ilius, since you goddesses have made up your minds to destroy the city.'

And Minerva answered, 'So be it, Far-Darter; it was in this mind that I came down from Olympus to the Trojans and Achæans. Tell me, then, how do you propose to end this present fighting?'

Apollo, son of Jove, replied, 'Let us incite great Hector to challenge some one of the Danaans in single combat; on this the Achæans will be shamed into finding a man who will fight him.'

Minerva assented, and Helenus son of Priam divined the counsel of the gods; he therefore went up to Hector and said, 'Hector son of Priam, peer of gods in counsel, I am your brother, let me then persuade you. Bid the other Trojans and Achæans all of them take their seats, and challenge the best man among the Achæans to meet you in single combat. I have heard the voice of the ever-living gods, and the hour of your doom is not yet come.'

Hector was glad when he heard this saying, and went in among the Trojans, grasping his spear by the middle to hold them back, and they all sat down. Agamemnon also bade the Achæans be seated. But Minerva and Apollo, in the likeness of vultures, perched on father Jove's high oak tree, proud of their men; and the ranks sat close ranged together, bristling with shield and helmet and spear. As when the rising west wind furs the face of the sea and the waters grow dark beneath it, so sat the companies of Trojans and Achæans upon the plain. And Hector spoke thus:—

'Hear me, Trojans and Achæans, that I may speak even as I am minded; Jove on his high throne has brought our oaths and covenants to nothing, and foreshadows ill for both of us, till you either take the towers of Troy, or are yourselves vanquished at your ships. The princes of the Achæans are here present in the midst of you; let him, then, that will fight me stand forward as your champion against Hector. Thus I say, and may Jove be witness between us. If your champion slay me, let him strip me of my armour and take it to your ships, but let him send my body home that the Trojans and their wives may give me my dues of fire when I am dead. In like manner if Apollo vouchsafe me glory and I slay your champion, I will strip him of his armour and take it to the city of Ilius, where I will hang it in the temple of Apollo, but I will give up his body, that the Achæans may bury him at their ships, and build him a mound by the wide waters of the Hellespont. Then will one say hereafter as he sails his ship over the sea, "This is the monument of one who died long since – a champion who was slain by mighty Hector." Thus will one say, and my fame shall not be lost.'

Thus did he speak, but they all held their peace, ashamed to decline the challenge, yet fearing to accept it, till at last Menelaus rose and rebuked them, for he was angry. 'Alas,' he cried, 'vain braggarts, women forsooth not men, double-dyed indeed will be the stain upon us if no man of the Danaans will now face Hector. May you be turned every man of you into earth and water as you sit spiritless and inglorious in your places. I will myself go out against this man, but the upshot of the fight will be from on high in the hands of the immortal gods.'

With these words he put on his armour; and then, O Menelaus, your life would have come to an end at the hands of Hector, for he was far the better man, had not the princes of the Achæans sprung upon you and checked you. King Agamemnon caught him by the right hand and said, 'Menelaus, you are mad; a truce to this folly. Be patient in spite of passion, do not think of fighting a man so much stronger than yourself as Hector son of Priam, who is feared by many another as well as you. Even Achilles, who is far more doughty than you are, shrank from meeting him in battle. Sit down among your own people, and the Achæans will send some other champion to fight Hector; fearless and fond of battle though he be, I ween his knees will bend gladly under him if he comes out alive from the hurly-burly of this fight.'

With these words of reasonable counsel he persuaded his brother, whereon his squires gladly stripped the armour from off his shoulders. Then Nestor rose and spoke, 'Of a truth,' said he, 'the Achæan land is fallen upon evil times. The old knight Peleus, counsellor and orator among the Myrmidons, loved when I was in his house to question me concerning the race and lineage of all the Argives. How would it not grieve him could he hear of them as now quailing before Hector? Many a time would he lift his hands in prayer that his soul might leave his body and go down within the house of Hades. Would, by father Jove, Minerva, and Apollo, that I were still young and strong as when the Pylians and Arcadians were gathered in fight by the rapid river Celadon under the walls of Pheia, and round about the waters of the river Iardanus. The godlike hero Ereuthalion stood forward as their champion, with the armour of King Areïthoüs upon his shoulders – Areïthoüs whom men and women had surnamed 'the Mace-man,' because he fought neither with bow nor spear, but broke the battalions of the foe with his iron mace. Lycurgus killed him, not in fair fight, but by entrapping him in a narrow way where his mace served him in no stead; for Lycurgus was too quick for him and speared him through the middle, so he fell to earth on his back. Lycurgus then spoiled him of the armour which Mars had given him, and bore it in battle thenceforward; but when he grew old and stayed at home, he gave it to his faithful squire Ereuthalion, who in this same armour challenged the foremost men among us. The others quaked and quailed, but my high spirit bade me fight him though none other would venture; I was the youngest man of them all; but when I fought him Minerva vouchsafed me victory. He was the biggest and strongest man that ever I killed, and covered much ground as he lay sprawling upon the earth. Would that I were still young and strong as I then was, for the son of Priam would then soon find one who would face him. But you, foremost among the whole host though you be, have none of you any stomach for fighting Hector.'

Thus did the old man rebuke them, and forthwith nine men started to their feet. Foremost of all uprose King Agamemnon, and after him brave Diomed the son of Tydeus. Next were the two Ajaxes, men clothed in valour as with a garment, and then Idomeneus, and Meriones his brother in arms. Thoas the son of Andræmon, and Ulysses also rose. Then Nestor knight of Gerene again spoke, saying: 'Cast lots among you to see who shall be chosen. If he come alive out of this fight he will have done good service alike to his own soul and to the Achæans.'

Thus he spoke, and when each of them had marked his lot, and had thrown it into the helmet of Agamemnon son of Atreus, the people lifted their hands in prayer, and thus would one of them say as he looked into the vault of heaven, 'Father Jove, grant that the lot fall on Ajax, or on the son of Tydeus, or upon the king of rich Mycene himself.'

As they were speaking, Nestor knight of Gerene shook the helmet, and from it there fell the very lot which they wanted – the lot of Ajax. The herald bore it about and showed it to all the chieftains of the Achæans, going from left to right; but they none of them owned it. When, however, in due course he reached the man who had written upon it and had put it into the helmet, brave Ajax held out his hand, and the herald gave him the lot. When Ajax saw his mark he knew it and was glad; he threw it to the ground and said, 'My friends, the lot is mine, and I rejoice, for I shall vanquish Hector. I will put on my armour; meanwhile, pray to King Jove in silence among yourselves that the Trojans may not hear you – or aloud if you will, for we fear no man. None shall overcome me, neither by force nor cunning, for I was born and bred in Salamis, and can hold my own in all things.'

With this they fell praying to King Jove the son of Saturn, and thus would one of them say as he looked into the vault of heaven, 'Father Jove that rulest from Ida, most glorious in power, vouchsafe victory to Ajax, and let him win great glory: but if you wish well to Hector also and would protect him, grant to each of them equal fame and prowess.'

Thus they prayed, and Ajax armed himself in his suit of gleaming bronze. When he was in full array he sprang forward as monstrous Mars when he takes part among men whom Jove has set fighting with one another – even so did huge Ajax, bulwark of the Achæans, spring forward with a grim smile on his face as he brandished his long spear and strode onward. The Argives were elated as they beheld him, but the Trojans trembled in every limb, and the heart even of Hector beat quickly, but he could not now retreat and withdraw into the ranks behind him, for he had been the challenger. Ajax came up bearing his shield in front of him like a wall – a shield of bronze with seven folds of oxhide – the work of Tychius, who lived in Hyle and was by far the best worker in leather. He had made it with the hides of seven full-fed bulls, and over these he had set an eighth layer of bronze. Holding this shield before him, Ajax son of Telamon came close up to Hector, and menaced him saying, 'Hector, you shall now learn, man to man, what kind of champions the Danaans have among them even besides lion-hearted Achilles cleaver of the ranks of men. He now abides at the ships in anger with Agamemnon shepherd of his people, but there are many of us who are well able to face you; therefore begin the fight.'

And Hector answered, 'Noble Ajax, son of Telamon, captain of the host, treat me not as though I were some puny boy or woman that cannot fight. I have been long used to the blood and butcheries of battle. I am quick to turn my leathern shield either to right or left, for this I deem the main thing in battle. I can charge among the chariots and horsemen, and in hand-to-hand fighting can delight the heart of Mars; howbeit I would not take such a man as you are off his guard – but I will smite you openly if I can.'

He poised his spear as he spoke, and hurled it from him. It struck the sevenfold shield in its outermost layer – the eighth, which was of bronze – and went through six of the layers but in the seventh hide it stayed. Then Ajax threw in his turn, and struck the round shield of the son of Priam. The terrible spear went through his gleaming shield, and pressed onward through his cuirass of cunning workmanship; it pierced the shirt against his side, but he swerved and thus saved his life. They then each of them drew out the spear from his shield, and fell on one another like savage lions or wild boars of great strength and endurance: the son of Priam struck the middle of Ajax's shield, but the bronze did not break, and the point of his dart was turned. Ajax then sprang forward and pierced the shield of Hector; the spear went through it and staggered him as he was springing forward to attack; it gashed his neck and the blood came pouring from the wound, but even so Hector did not cease fighting; he gave ground, and with his brawny hand seized a stone, rugged and huge, that was lying upon the plain; with this he struck the shield of Ajax on the boss that was in its middle, so that the bronze rang again. But Ajax in turn caught up a far larger stone, swung it aloft, and hurled it with prodigious force. This millstone of a rock broke Hector's shield inwards and threw him down on his back with the shield crushing him under it, but Apollo raised him at once. Thereon they would have hacked at one another in close combat with their swords, had not heralds, messengers of gods and men, come forward, one from the Trojans and the other from the Achæans – Talthybius and Idæus both of them honourable men; these parted them with their staves, and the good herald Idæus said, 'My sons, fight no longer, you are both of you valiant, and both are dear to Jove; we know this; but night is now falling, and the behests of night may not be well gainsaid.'

Ajax son of Telamon answered, 'Idæus, bid Hector say so, for it was he that challenged our princes. Let him speak first and I will accept his saying.'

Then Hector said, 'Ajax, heaven has vouchsafed you stature and strength, and judgement; and in wielding the spear you excel all others of the Achæans. Let us for this day cease fighting; hereafter we will fight anew till heaven decide between us, and give victory to one or to the other; night is now falling, and the behests of night may not be well gainsaid. Gladden, then, the hearts of the Achæans at your ships, and more especially those of your own followers and clansmen, while

I, in the great city of King Priam, bring comfort to the Trojans and their women, who vie with one another in their prayers on my behalf. Let us, moreover, exchange presents, that it may be said among Achæans and Trojans, "They fought with might and main, but were reconciled and parted in friendship."'

On this he gave Ajax a silver-studded sword with its sheath and leathern baldric, and in return Ajax gave him a girdle dyed with purple. Thus they parted, the one going to the host of the Achæans, and the other to that of the Trojans, who rejoiced when they saw their hero come to them safe and unharmed from the strong hands of mighty Ajax. They led him, therefore, to the city as one that had been saved beyond their hopes. On the other side the Achæans brought Ajax elated with victory to Agamemnon.

When they reached the quarters of the son of Atreus, Agamemnon sacrificed for them a five-year-old bull in honour of Jove the son of Saturn. They flayed the carcase, made it ready, and divided it into joints; these they cut carefully up into smaller pieces, putting them on the spits, roasting them sufficiently, and then drawing them off. When they had done all this and had prepared the feast, they ate it, and every man had his full and equal share, so that all were satisfied, and King Agamemnon gave Ajax some slices cut lengthways down the loin, as a mark of special honour. As soon as they had had enough to eat and drink, old Nestor whose counsel was ever truest began to speak; with all sincerity and goodwill, therefore, he addressed them thus:—

'Son of Atreus, and other chieftains, inasmuch as many of the Achæans are now dead, whose blood Mars has shed by the banks of the Scamander, and their souls have gone down to the house of Hades, it will be well when morning comes that we should cease fighting; we will then wheel our dead together with oxen and mules and burn them not far from the ships, that when we sail hence we may take the bones of our comrades home to their children. Hard by the funeral pyre we will build a barrow that shall be raised from the plain for all in common; near this let us set about building a high wall, to shelter ourselves and our ships, and let it have well-made gates that there may be a way through them for our chariots. Close outside we will dig a deep trench all round it to keep off both horse and foot, that the Trojan chieftains may not bear hard upon us.'

Thus he spoke, and the princes shouted in applause. Meanwhile the Trojans held a council, angry and full of discord, on the acropolis by the gates of King Priam's palace; and wise Antenor spoke. 'Hear me,' he said, 'Trojans, Dardanians, and allies, that I may speak even as I am minded. Let us give up Argive Helen and her wealth to the sons of Atreus, for we are now fighting in violation of our solemn covenants, and shall not prosper till we have done as I say.'

He then sat down and Alexandrus husband of lovely Helen rose to speak. 'Antenor,' said he, 'your words are not to my liking; you can find a better saying than this if you will; if, however, you have spoken in good earnest, then indeed has heaven robbed you of your reason. I will speak plainly, and hereby notify to the Trojans that I will not give up the woman; but the wealth that I brought home with her from Argos I will restore, and will add yet further of my own.'

On this, when Paris had spoken and taken his seat, Priam of the race of Dardanus, peer of gods in council, rose and with all sincerity and goodwill addressed them thus: 'Hear me, Trojans, Dardanians, and allies, that I may speak even as I am minded. Get your suppers now as hitherto throughout the city, but keep your watches and be wakeful. At daybreak let Idæus go to the ships, and tell Agamemnon and Menelaus sons of Atreus the saying of Alexandrus through whom this quarrel has come about; and let him also be instant with them that they now cease fighting till we burn our dead; hereafter we will fight anew, till heaven decide between us and give victory to one or to the other.'

Thus did he speak, and they did even as he had said. They took supper in their companies and at daybreak Idæus went his way to the ships. He found the Danaans, servants of Mars, in council at the stern of Agamemnon's ship, and took his place in the midst of them. 'Son of Atreus,' he said, 'and princes of the Achæan host, Priam and the other noble Trojans have sent me to tell you the saying of Alexandrus through whom this quarrel has come about, if so be that you may find it acceptable. All the treasure he took with him in his ships to Troy – would that he had sooner perished – he will restore, and will add yet further of his own, but he will not give up the wedded wife of Menelaus, though the Trojans would have him do so. Priam bade me inquire further if you will cease fighting till we burn our dead; hereafter we will fight anew, till heaven decide between us and give victory to one or to the other.'

They all held their peace, but presently Diomed of the loud war-cry spoke, saying, 'Let there be no taking, neither treasure, nor yet Helen, for even a child may see that the doom of the Trojans is at hand.'

The sons of the Achæans shouted applause at the words that Diomed had spoken, and thereon King Agamemnon said to Idæus, 'Idæus, you have heard the answer the Achæans make you – and I with them. But as concerning the dead, I give you leave to burn them, for when men are once dead there should be no grudging them the rites of fire. Let Jove the mighty husband of Juno be witness to this covenant.'

As he spoke he upheld his sceptre in the sight of all the gods, and Idæus went back to the strong city of Ilius. The Trojans and Dardanians were gathered in council waiting his return; when he came, he stood in their midst and delivered his message. As soon as they heard it they set about their twofold labour, some to gather the corpses, and others to bring in wood. The Argives on their part also hastened from their ships, some to gather the corpses, and others to bring in wood.

The sun was beginning to beat upon the fields, fresh risen into the vault of heaven from the slow still currents of deep Oceanus, when the two armies met. They could hardly recognise their dead, but they washed the clotted gore from off them, shed tears over them, and lifted them upon their waggons. Priam had forbidden the Trojans to wail aloud, so they heaped their dead sadly and silently upon the pyre, and having burned them went back to the city of Ilius. The Achæans in like manner heaped their dead sadly and silently on the pyre, and having burned them went back to their ships.

Now in the twilight when it was not yet dawn, chosen bands of the Achæans were gathered round the pyre and built one barrow that was raised in common for all, and hard by this they built a high wall to shelter themselves and their ships; they gave it strong gates that there might be a way through them for their chariots, and close outside it they dug a trench deep and wide, and they planted it within with stakes.

Thus did the Achæans toil, and the gods, seated by the side of Jove the lord of lightning, marvelled at their great work; but Neptune, lord of the earthquake, spoke, saying, 'Father Jove, what mortal in the whole world will again take the gods into his counsel? See you not how the Achæans have built a wall about their ships and driven a trench all round it, without offering hecatombs to the gods? The fame of this wall will reach as far as dawn itself, and men will no longer think anything of the one which Phœbus Apollo and myself built with so much labour for Laomedon.'

Jove was displeased and answered, 'What, O shaker of the earth, are you talking about? A god less powerful than yourself might be alarmed at what they are doing, but your fame reaches as far as dawn itself. Surely when the Achæans have gone home with their ships, you can shatter their wall and fling it into the sea; you can cover the beach with sand again, and the great wall of the Achæans will then be utterly effaced.'

Thus did they converse, and by sunset the work of the Achæans was completed; they then slaughtered oxen at their tents and got their supper. Many ships had come with wine from Lemnos, sent by Euneüs the son of Jason, born to him by Hypsipyle. The son of Jason freighted them with ten thousand measures of wine, which he sent specially to the sons of Atreus, Agamemnon and Menelaus. From this supply the Achæans bought their wine, some with bronze, some with iron, some with hides, some with whole heifers, and some again with captives. They spread a goodly banquet and feasted the whole night through, as also did the Trojans and their allies in the city. But all the time Jove boded them ill and roared with his portentous thunder. Pale fear got hold upon them, and they spilled the wine from their cups on to the ground, nor did any dare drink till he had made offerings to the most mighty son of Saturn. Then they laid themselves down to rest and enjoyed the boon of sleep.

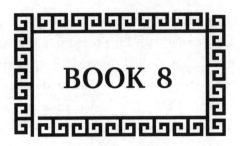

BOOK 8

Jove forbids the gods to interfere further – There is an even fight till midday, but then Jove inclines the scales of victory in favour of the Trojans, who eventually chase the Achæans within their wall – Juno and Minerva set out to help the Trojans: Jove sends Iris to turn them back, but later on he promises Juno that she shall have her way in the end – Hector's triumph is stayed by nightfall – The Trojans bivouac on the plain.

Now when Morning, clad in her robe of saffron, had begun to suffuse light over the earth, Jove called the gods in council on the topmost crest of serrated Olympus. Then he spoke and all the other gods gave ear. 'Hear me,' said he, 'gods and goddesses, that I may speak even as I am minded. Let none of you neither goddess nor god try to cross me, but obey me every one of you that I may bring this matter to an end. If I see any one acting apart and helping either Trojans or Danaans, he shall be beaten inordinately ere he come back again to Olympus; or I will hurl him down into dark Tartarus far into the deepest pit under the earth, where the gates are iron and the floor bronze, as far beneath Hades as heaven is high above the earth, that you may learn how much the mightiest I am among you. Try me and find out for yourselves. Hang me a golden chain from heaven, and lay hold of it all of you, gods and goddesses together – tug as you will, you will not drag Jove the supreme counsellor from heaven to earth; but were I to pull at it myself I should draw you up with earth and sea into the bargain, then would I bind the chain about some pinnacle of Olympus and leave you all dangling in the mid firmament. So far am I above all others either of gods or men.'

They were frightened and all of them held their peace, for he had spoken masterfully; but at last Minerva answered, 'Father, son of Saturn, king of kings, we all know that your might is not to be gainsaid, but we are also sorry for the Danaan warriors, who are perishing and coming to a bad end. We will, however, since you so bid us, refrain from actual fighting, but we will make serviceable suggestions to the Argives that they may not all of them perish in your displeasure.'

Jove smiled at her and answered, ' Take heart, my child, Trito-born; I am not really in earnest, and I wish to be kind to you.'

With this he yoked his fleet horses, with hoofs of bronze and manes of glittering gold. He girded himself also with gold about the body, seized his gold whip and took his seat in his chariot. Thereon he lashed his horses and they flew forward nothing loth midway twixt earth and starry heaven. After a while he reached many-fountained Ida, mother of wild beasts, and Gargarus, where are his grove and fragrant altar. There the father of gods and men stayed his horses, took them from the chariot, and hid them in a thick cloud; then he took his seat all glorious upon the topmost crests, looking down upon the city of Troy and the ships of the Achæans.

The Achæans took their morning meal hastily at the ships, and afterwards put on their armour. The Trojans on the other hand likewise armed themselves throughout the city, fewer in numbers but nevertheless eager perforce to do battle for their wives and children. All the gates were flung wide open, and horse and foot sallied forth with the tramp as of a great multitude.

When they were got together in one place, shield clashed with shield, and spear with spear, in the conflict of mail-clad men. Mighty was the din as the bossed shields pressed hard on one another – death-cry and shout of triumph of slain and slayers, and the earth ran red with blood.

Now so long as the day waxed and it was still morning their weapons beat against one another, and the people fell, but when the sun had reached mid-heaven, the sire of all balanced his golden scales, and put two fates of death within them, one for the Trojans and the other for the Achæans. He took the balance by the middle, and when he lifted it up the day of the Achæans sank; the death-fraught scale of the Achæans settled down upon the ground, while that of the Trojans rose heavenwards. Then he thundered aloud from Ida, and sent the glare of his lightning upon the Achæans; when they saw this, pale fear fell upon them and they were sore afraid.

Idomeneus dared not stay nor yet Agamemnon, nor did the two Ajaxes, servants of Mars, hold their ground. Nestor knight of Gerene alone stood firm, bulwark of the Achæans, not of his own will, but one of his horses was disabled. Alexandrus husband of lovely Helen had hit it with an arrow just on the top of its head where the mane begins to grow away from the skull, a very deadly place. The horse bounded in his anguish as the arrow pierced his brain, and his struggles threw the others into confusion. The old man instantly began cutting the traces with his sword, but Hector's fleet horses bore down upon him through the rout with their bold charioteer, even Hector himself, and the old man would have perished there and then had not Diomed been quick to mark, and with a loud cry called Ulysses to help him.

'Ulysses,' he cried, 'noble son of Laertes, where are you flying to, with your back turned like a coward? See that you are not struck with a spear between the shoulders. Stay here and help me to defend Nestor from this man's furious onset.'

Ulysses would not give ear, but sped onward to the ships of the Achæans, and the son of Tydeus flinging himself alone into the thick of the fight took his stand before the horses of the son of Neleus. 'Sir,' said he, 'these young warriors are pressing you hard, your force is spent, and age is heavy upon you, your squire is naught, and your horses are slow to move. Mount my chariot and see what the horses of Tros can do – how cleverly they can scud hither and thither over the plain either in flight or in pursuit. I took them from the hero Æneas. Let our squires attend to your own steeds, but let us drive mine straight at the Trojans, that Hector may learn how furiously I too can wield my spear.'

Nestor knight of Gerene hearkened to his words. Thereon the doughty squires, Sthenelus and kind-hearted Eurymedon, saw to Nestor's horses, while the two both mounted Diomed's chariot. Nestor took the reins in his hands and lashed the horses on; they were soon close up with Hector, and the son of Tydeus aimed a spear at him as he was charging full speed towards them. He missed him, but struck his charioteer and squire Eniopeus son of noble Thebæus in the breast by the nipple while the reins were in his hands, so that he died there and then, and the horses swerved as he fell headlong from the chariot. Hector was greatly grieved at the loss of his charioteer, but let him lie for all his sorrow, while he went in quest of another driver; nor did his steeds have to go long without one, for he presently found brave Archeptolemus the son of Iphitus, and made him get up behind the horses, giving the reins into his hand.

All had then been lost and no help for it, for they would have been penned up in Ilius like sheep, had not the sire of gods and men been quick to mark, and hurled a fiery flaming thunderbolt which fell just in front of Diomed's horses with a flare of burning brimstone. The horses were frightened and tried to back beneath the car, while the reins dropped from Nestor's hands. Then he was afraid and said to Diomed, 'Son of Tydeus, turn your horses in flight; see you not that the hand of Jove is against you? To-day he vouchsafes victory to Hector; to-morrow, if it so please him, he will again grant it to ourselves; no man, however brave, may thwart the purpose of Jove, for he is far stronger than any.'

Diomed answered, 'All that you have said is true; there is a grief however which pierces me to the very heart, for Hector will talk among the Trojans and say, "The son of Tydeus fled before me to the ships." This is the vaunt he will make, and may earth then swallow me.'

'Son of Tydeus,' replied Nestor, 'what mean you? Though Hector say that you are a coward the Trojans and Dardanians will not believe him, nor yet the wives of the mighty warriors whom you have laid low.'

So saying he turned the horses back through the thick of the battle, and with a cry that rent the air the Trojans and Hector rained their darts after them. Hector shouted to him and said, 'Son of Tydeus, the Danaans have done you honour hitherto as regards your place at table, the meals they give you, and the filling of your cup with wine. Henceforth they will despise you, for you are become no better than a woman. Be off, girl and coward that you are, you shall not scale our walls through any flinching upon my part; neither shall you carry off our wives in your ships, for I shall kill you with my own hand.'

The son of Tydeus was in two minds whether or no to turn his horses round again and fight him. Thrice did he doubt, and thrice did Jove thunder from the heights of Ida in token to the Trojans that he would turn the battle in their favour. Hector then shouted to them and said, 'Trojans, Lycians, and Dardanians, lovers of close fighting, be men, my friends, and fight with might and with main; I see that Jove is minded to vouchsafe victory and great glory to myself, while he will deal destruction upon the Danaans. Fools, for having thought of building this weak and worthless wall. It shall not stay my fury; my horses will spring lightly over their trench, and when I am at their ships forget not to bring me fire that I may burn them, while I slaughter the Argives who will be all dazed and bewildered by the smoke.'

Then he cried to his horses, 'Xanthus and Podargus, and you Æthon and goodly Lampus, pay me for your keep now and for all the honey-sweet corn with which Andromache daughter of great Eëtion has fed you, and for the way in which she has mixed wine and water for you to drink whenever you would, before doing so even for me who am her own husband. Haste in pursuit, that we may take the shield of Nestor, the fame of which ascends to heaven, for it is of solid gold, arm-rods and all, and that we may strip from the shoulders of Diomed the cuirass which Vulcan made him. Could we take these two things, the Achæans would set sail in their ships this self-same night.'

Thus did he vaunt, but Queen Juno made high Olympus quake as she shook with rage upon her throne. Then said she to the mighty god Neptune, 'What now, wide ruling lord of the earthquake? Can you find no compassion in your heart for the dying Danaans, who bring you many a welcome offering to Helice and to Ægæ? Wish them well then. If all of us who are with the Danaans were to drive the Trojans back and keep Jove from helping them, he would have to sit there sulking alone on Ida.'

King Neptune was greatly troubled and answered, 'Juno, rash of tongue, what are you talking about? We other gods must not set ourselves against Jove, for he is far stronger than we are.'

Thus did they converse; but the whole space enclosed by the ditch, from the ships even to the wall, was filled with horses and warriors, who were pent up there by Hector son of Priam, now that the hand of Jove was with him. He would even have set fire to the ships and burned them, had not Queen Juno put it into the mind of Agamemnon, to bestir himself and to encourage the Achæans. To this end he went round the ships and tents carrying a great purple cloak, and took his stand by the huge black hull of Ulysses' ship, which was middlemost of all; it was from this place that his voice would carry farthest, on the one hand towards the tents of Ajax son of Telamon, and on the other towards those of Achilles – for these two heroes, well assured of their own strength, had valorously drawn up their ships at the two ends of the line. From this spot then, with a voice that could be heard afar, he shouted to the Danaans, saying, 'Argives, shame on you cowardly creatures, brave in semblance only; where are now our vaunts that we should prove victorious – the vaunts we made so vaingloriously in Lemnos, when we ate the flesh of horned cattle and filled our mixing-bowls to the brim? You vowed that you would each of you stand against a hundred or two hundred men, and now you prove no match even for one – for Hector, who will be ere long setting our ships in a blaze. Father Jove, did you ever so ruin a great king and rob him so utterly of his greatness? yet, when to my sorrow I was coming hither, I never let my ship pass your altars without offering the fat and thigh-bones of heifers upon every one of them, so eager was I to sack the city of Troy. Vouchsafe me then this prayer – suffer us to escape at any rate with our lives, and let not the Achæans be so utterly vanquished by the Trojans.'

Thus did he pray, and father Jove pitying his tears vouchsafed him that his people should live, not die; forthwith he sent them an eagle, most unfailingly portentous of all birds, with a young fawn in its talons; the eagle dropped the fawn by the altar on which the Achæans sacrificed to Jove the lord of omens; when, therefore, the people saw that the bird had come from Jove, they sprang more fiercely upon the Trojans and fought more boldly.

There was no man of all the many Danaans who could then boast that he had driven his horses over the trench and gone forth to fight sooner than the son of Tydeus; long before any one else could do so he slew an armed warrior of the Trojans, Agelaus the son of Phradmon. He had turned his horses in flight, but the spear struck him in the back midway between his shoulders and went right through his chest, and his armour rang rattling round him as he fell forward from his chariot.

After him came Agamemnon and Menelaus, sons of Atreus, the two Ajaxes clothed in valour as with a garment, Idomeneus and his companion in arms Meriones, peer of murderous Mars, and Eurypylus the brave son of Euæmon. Ninth came Teucer with his how, and took his place under cover of the shield of Ajax son of Telamon. When Ajax lifted his shield Teucer would peer round, and when he had hit any one in the throng, the man would fall dead; then Teucer would hie back to Ajax as a child to its mother, and again duck down under his shield.

Which of the Trojans did brave Teucer first kill? Orsilochus, and then Ormenus and Ophelestes, Dætor, Chromius, and godlike Lycophontes, Amopaon son of Polyæmon, and Melanippus. All these in turn did he lay low upon the earth, and King Agamemnon was glad when he saw him making havoc of the Trojans with his mighty bow. He went up to him and said, 'Teucer, man after my own heart, son of Telamon, captain among the host, shoot on, and be at once the saving of the Danaans and the glory of your father Telamon, who brought you up and took care of you in his own house when you were a child, bastard though you were. Cover him with glory though he is far off; I will promise and I will assuredly perform; if ægis-bearing Jove and Minerva grant me to sack the city of Ilius, you shall have the next best meed of honour after my own – a tripod, or two horses with their chariot, or a woman who shall go up into your bed.'

And Teucer answered, 'Most noble son of Atreus, you need not urge me; from the moment we began to drive them back to Ilius, I have never ceased so far as in me lies to look out for men whom I can shoot and kill; I have shot eight barbed shafts, and all of them have been buried in the flesh of warlike youths, but this mad dog I cannot hit.'

As he spoke he aimed another arrow straight at Hector, for he was bent on hitting him; nevertheless he missed him, and the arrow hit Priam's brave son Gorgythion in the breast. His mother, fair Castianeira, lovely as a goddess, had been married from Æsyme, and now he bowed his head as a garden poppy in full bloom when it is weighed down by showers in spring – even thus heavily bowed his head beneath the weight of his helmet.

Again he aimed at Hector, for he was longing to hit him, and again his arrow missed, for Apollo turned it aside; but he hit Hector's brave charioteer Archeptolemus in the breast, by the nipple, as he was driving furiously into the fight. The horses swerved aside as he fell headlong from the chariot, and there was no life left in him. Hector was greatly grieved at the loss of his charioteer, but for all his sorrow he let him lie where he fell, and bade his brother Cebriones, who was hard by, take the reins. Cebriones did as he had said. Hector thereon with a loud cry sprang from his chariot to the ground, and seizing a great stone made straight for Teucer with intent to kill him. Teucer had just taken an arrow from his quiver and had laid it upon the bow-string, but Hector struck him with the jagged stone as he was taking aim and drawing the string to his shoulder; he hit him just where the collar-bone divides the neck from the chest, a very deadly place, and broke the sinew of his arm so that his wrist was powerless, and the bow dropped from his hand as he fell forward on his knees. Ajax saw that his brother had fallen, and running towards him bestrode him and sheltered him with his shield. Meanwhile his two trusty squires, Mecisteus son of Echius, and Alastor, came up and bore him to the ships groaning in his great pain.

Jove now again put heart into the Trojans, and they drove the Achæans to their deep trench with Hector in all his glory at their head. As a hound grips a wild boar or lion in flank or buttock when he gives him chase, and watches warily for his wheeling, even so did Hector follow close upon the Achæans, ever killing the hindmost as they rushed panic-stricken onwards. When they had fled through the set stakes and trench and many Achæans had been laid low at the hands of the Trojans, they halted at their ships, calling upon one another and praying every man instantly as they lifted up their hands to the gods; but Hector wheeled his horses this way and that, his eyes glaring like those of Gorgo or murderous Mars.

Juno when she saw them had pity upon them, and at once said to Minerva, 'Alas, child of ægis-bearing Jove, shall you and I take no more thought for the dying Danaans, though it be the last time we ever do so? See how they perish and come to a bad end before the onset of but a single man. Hector the son of Priam rages with intolerable fury, and has already done great mischief.'

Minerva answered, 'Would, indeed, this fellow might die in his own land, and fall by the hands of the Achæans; but my father Jove is mad with spleen, ever foiling me, ever headstrong and unjust. He forgets how often I saved his son[4] when he was worn out by the labours Eurystheus had laid on him. He would weep till his cry came up to heaven, and then Jove would send me down to help him; if I had had the sense to foresee all this, when Eurystheus sent him to the house of Hades, to fetch the hell-hound from Erebus, he would never have come back alive out of the deep waters of the river Styx. And now Jove hates me, while he lets Thetis have her way because she kissed his knees and took hold of his beard, when she was begging him to do honour to Achilles. I shall know what to do next time he begins calling me his grey-eyed darling. Get our horses ready, while I go within the house of ægis-bearing Jove and put on my armour; we shall then find out whether Priam's son Hector will be glad to meet us in the highways of battle, or whether the Trojans will glut hounds and vultures with the fat of their flesh as they lie dead by the ships of the Achæans.'

Thus did she speak and white-armed Juno, daughter of great Saturn, obeyed her words; she set about harnessing her gold-bedizened steeds, while Minerva daughter of ægis-bearing Jove flung her richly embroidered vesture, made with her own hands, on to the threshold of her father, and donned the shirt of Jove, arming herself for battle. Then she stepped into her flaming chariot, and grasped the spear so stout and sturdy and strong with which she quells the ranks of heroes who have displeased her. Juno lashed her horses, and the gates of heaven bellowed as they flew open of their own accord – gates over which the Hours preside, in whose hands are heaven and Olympus, either to open the dense cloud that hides them or to close it. Through these the goddesses drove their obedient steeds.

But father Jove when he saw them from Ida was very angry, and sent winged Iris with a message to them. 'Go,' said he, 'fleet Iris, turn them back, and see that they do not come near me, for if we come to fighting there will be mischief. This is what I say, and this is what I mean to do. I will lame their horses for them; I will hurl them from their chariot, and will break it in pieces. It will take them all ten years to heal the wounds my lightning shall inflict upon them; my grey-eyed daughter will then learn what quarrelling with her father means. I am less surprised and angry with Juno, for whatever I say she always contradicts me.'

With this Iris went her way, fleet as the wind, from the heights of Ida to the lofty summits of Olympus. She met the goddesses at the outer gates of its many valleys and gave them her message. 'What,' said she, 'are you about? Are you mad? The son of Saturn forbids your going. This is what he says, and this is what he means to do, he will lame your horses for you, he will hurl you from your chariot, and will break it in pieces. It will take you all ten years to heal the wounds his lightning will inflict upon you, that you may learn, grey-eyed goddess, what quarrelling with your father means. He is less hurt and angry with Juno, for whatever he says she always contradicts him – but you, bold hussy, will you really dare to raise your huge spear in defiance of Jove?'

With this she left them, and Juno said to Minerva, 'Of a truth, child of ægis-bearing Jove, I am not for fighting men's battles further in defiance of Jove. Let them live or die as luck will have it, and let Jove mete out his judgements upon the Trojans and Danaans according to his own pleasure.'

She turned her steeds; the Hours presently unyoked them, made them fast to their ambrosial mangers, and leaned the chariot against the end wall of the courtyard. The two goddesses then sat down upon their golden thrones, amid the company of the other gods; but they were very angry.

Presently father Jove drove his chariot to Olympus, and entered the assembly of gods. The mighty lord of the earthquake unyoked his horses for him, set the car upon its stand, and threw a cloth over it. Jove then sat down upon his golden throne and Olympus reeled beneath him. Minerva and Juno sat alone, apart from Jove, and neither spoke nor asked him questions, but Jove knew what they meant, and said, 'Minerva and Juno, why are you so angry? Are you fatigued with killing so many of your dear friends the Trojans? Be this as it may, such is the might of my hands that all the gods in Olympus cannot turn me; you were both of you trembling all over ere ever you saw the fight and its terrible doings. I tell you therefore – and it would have surely been – I should have struck you with lightning, and your chariots would never have brought you back again to Olympus.'

Minerva and Juno groaned in spirit as they sat side by side and brooded mischief for the Trojans. Minerva sat silent without a word, for she was in a furious passion and bitterly incensed against her father; but Juno could not contain herself and said, 'What, dread son of Saturn, are you talking about? We know how great your power is, nevertheless we have compassion upon the Danaan warriors who are perishing and coming to a bad end. We will, however, since you so bid us, refrain from actual fighting, but we will make serviceable suggestions to the Argives, that they may not all of them perish in your displeasure.'

And Jove answered, 'To-morrow morning, Juno, if you choose to do so, you will see the son of Saturn destroying large numbers of the Argives, for fierce Hector shall not cease fighting till he has roused the son of Peleus when they are fighting in dire straits at their ships' sterns about the body of Patroclus. Like it or no, this is how it is decreed; for aught I care, you may go to the lowest depths beneath earth and sea, where Iapetus and Saturn dwell in lone Tartarus with neither ray of light nor breath of wind to cheer them. You may go on and on till you get there, and I shall not care one whit for your displeasure; you are the greatest vixen living.'

Juno made him no answer. The sun's glorious orb now sank into Oceanus and drew down night over the land. Sorry indeed were the Trojans when light failed them, but welcome and thrice prayed for did darkness fall upon the Achæans.

Then Hector led the Trojans back from the ships, and held a council on the open space near the river, where there was a spot clear of corpses. They left their chariots and sat down on the ground to hear the speech he made them. He grasped a spear eleven cubits long, the bronze point of which gleamed in front of it, while the ring round the spear-head was of gold. Spear in hand he spoke. 'Hear me,' said he, 'Trojans, Dardanians, and allies. I deemed but now that I should destroy the ships and all the Achæans with them ere I went back to Ilius, but darkness came on too soon. It was this alone that saved them and their ships upon the sea-shore. Now, therefore, let us obey the behests of night, and prepare our suppers. Take your horses out of their chariots and give them their feeds of corn; then make speed to bring sheep and cattle from the city; bring wine also and corn for your horses and gather much wood, that from dark till dawn we may burn watchfires whose flare may reach to heaven. For the Achæans may try to fly beyond the sea by night, and they must not embark scatheless and unmolested; many a man among them must take a dart with him to nurse at home, hit with spear or arrow as he is leaping on board his ship, that others may fear to bring war and weeping upon the Trojans. Moreover let the heralds tell it about the city that the growing youths and grey-bearded men are to camp upon its heaven-built walls. Let the women each of them light a great fire in her house, and let watch be safely kept lest the town be entered by surprise while the host is outside. See to it, brave Trojans, as I have said, and let this suffice for the moment; at daybreak I will instruct you further. I pray in hope to Jove and to the gods that we may then drive those fate-sped hounds from our land, for 'tis the fates that have borne them and their ships hither. This night, therefore, let us keep watch, but with early morning let us put on our armour and rouse fierce war at the ships of the Achæans; I shall then know whether brave Diomed the son of Tydeus will drive me back from the ships to the wall, or whether I shall myself slay him and carry off his blood-stained spoils. To-morrow let him show his mettle, and abide my spear if he dare. I ween that at break of day, he shall be among the first to fall and many another of his comrades round him. Would that I were as sure of being immortal and never growing old, and of being worshipped like Minerva and Apollo, as I am that this day will bring evil to the Argives.'

Thus spoke Hector and the Trojans shouted applause. They took their sweating steeds from under the yoke, and made them fast each by his own chariot. They made haste to bring sheep and cattle from the city, they brought wine also and corn from their houses and gathered much wood. They then offered unblemished hecatombs to the immortals, and the wind carried the sweet savour of sacrifice to heaven – but the blessed gods partook not thereof, for they bitterly hated Ilius with Priam and Priam's people. Thus high in hope they sat through the livelong night by the highways of war, and many a watchfire did they kindle. As when the stars shine clear, and the moon is bright – there is not a breath of air, not a peak nor glade nor jutting headland but it stands out in the ineffable radiance that breaks from the serene of heaven; the stars can all of them be told and the heart of the shepherd is glad – even thus shone the watchfires of the Trojans before Ilius midway between the ships and the river Xanthus. A thousand camp-fires gleamed upon the plain, and in the glow of each there sat fifty men, while the horses, champing oats and corn beside their chariots, waited till dawn should come.

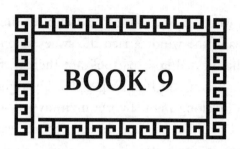

BOOK 9

The Embassy to Achilles.

Thus did the Trojans watch. But Panic, comrade of blood-stained Rout, had taken fast hold of the Achæans, and their princes were all of them in despair. As when the two winds that blow from Thrace – the north and the northwest – spring up of a sudden and rouse the fury of the main – in a moment the dark waves uprear their heads and scatter their sea-wrack in all directions – even thus troubled were the hearts of the Achæans.

The son of Atreus in dismay bade the heralds call the people to a council man by man, but not to cry the matter aloud; he made haste also himself to call them, and they sat sorry at heart in their assembly. Agamemnon shed tears as it were a running stream or cataract on the side of some sheer cliff; and thus, with many a heavy sigh he spoke to the Achæans. 'My friends,' said he, 'princes and councillors of the Argives, the hand of heaven has been laid heavily upon me. Cruel Jove gave me his solemn promise that I should sack the city of Troy before returning, but he has played me false, and is now bidding me go ingloriously back to Argos with the loss of much people. Such is the will of Jove, who has laid many a proud city in the dust as he will yet lay others, for his power is above all. Now, therefore, let us all do as I say and sail back to our own country, for we shall not take Troy.'

Thus he spoke, and the sons of the Achæans for a long while sat sorrowful there, but they all held their peace, till at last Diomed of the loud battle-cry made answer saying, 'Son of Atreus, I will chide your folly, as is my right in council. Be not then aggrieved that I should do so. In the first place you attacked me before all the Danaans and said that I was a coward and no soldier. The Argives young and old know that you did so. But the son of scheming Saturn endowed you by halves only. He gave you honour as the chief ruler over us, but valour, which is the highest both right and might, he did not give you. Sir, think you that the sons of the Achæans are indeed as unwarlike and cowardly as you say they are? If your own mind is set upon going home – go – the way is open to you; the many ships that followed you from Mycene stand ranged upon the sea-shore; but the rest of us will stay here till we have sacked Troy. Nay though these too should turn homeward with their ships, Sthenelus and myself will still fight on till we reach the goal of Ilius, for heaven was with us when we came.'

The sons of the Achæans shouted applause at the words of Diomed, and presently Nestor rose to speak. 'Son of Tydeus,' said he, 'in war your prowess is beyond question, and in council you excel all who are of your own years; no one of the Achæans can make light of what you say nor gainsay it, but you have not yet come to the end of the whole matter. You are still young – you might be the youngest of my own children – still you have spoken wisely and have counselled the chief of the Achæans not without discretion; nevertheless I am older than you and I will tell you everything; therefore let no man, not even King Agamemnon, disregard my saying, for he that foments civil discord is a clanless, heartless outlaw.

'Now, however, let us obey the behests of night and get our suppers, but let the sentinels every man of them camp by the trench that is without the wall. I am giving these instructions to the young men; when they have been attended to, do you, son of Atreus, give your orders, for you are the most royal among us all. Prepare a feast for your councillors; it is right and reasonable that you should do so; there is abundance of wine in your tents, which the ships of the Achæans bring from Thrace daily. You have everything at your disposal where-with to entertain guests, and you have many subjects. When many are got together, you can be guided by him whose counsel is wisest – and sorely do we need shrewd and prudent counsel, for the foe has lit his watchfires hard by our ships. Who can be other than dismayed? This night will either be the ruin of our host, or save it.'

Thus did he speak, and they did even as he had said. The sentinels went out in their armour under command of Nestor's son Thrasymedes, a captain of the host, and of the bold warriors Ascalaphus and Ialmenus: there were also Meriones, Aphareus and Deïpyrus, and the son of Creion, noble Lycomedes. There were seven captains of the sentinels, and with each there went a hundred youths armed with long spears: they took their places midway between the trench and the wall, and when they had done so they lit their fires and got every man his supper.

The son of Atreus then bade many councillors of the Achæans to his quarters and prepared a great feast in their honour. They laid their hands on the good things that were before them, and as soon as they had had enough to eat and drink, old Nestor, whose counsel was ever truest, was the first to lay his mind before them. He, therefore, with all sincerity and goodwill addressed them thus.

'With yourself, most noble son of Atreus, king of men, Agamemnon, will I both begin my speech and end it, for you are king over much people. Jove, moreover, has vouchsafed you to wield the sceptre and to uphold righteousness, that you may take thought for your people under you; therefore it behoves you above all others both to speak and to give ear, and to carry out the counsel of another who shall have been minded to speak wisely. All turns on you and on your commands, therefore I will say what I think will be best. No man will be of a truer mind than that which has been mine from the hour when you, sir, angered Achilles by taking the girl Briseis from his tent against my judgement. I urged you not to do so, but you yielded to your own pride, and dishonoured a hero whom heaven itself had honoured – for you still hold the prize that had been awarded to him. Now, however, let us think how we may appease him, both with presents and fair speeches that may conciliate him.'

And King Agamemnon answered, 'Sir, you have reproved my folly justly. I was wrong. I own it. One whom heaven befriends is in himself a host, and Jove has shown that he befriends this man by destroying much people of the Achæans. I was blinded with passion and yielded to my worser mind; therefore I will make amends, and will give him great gifts by way of atonement. I will tell them in the presence of you all. I will give him seven tripods that have never yet been on the fire, and ten talents of gold. I will give him twenty iron cauldrons and twelve strong horses that have won races and carried off prizes. Rich, indeed, both in land and gold is he that has as many prizes as my horses have won me. I will give him seven excellent workwomen, Lesbians, whom I chose for myself when he took Lesbos – all of surpassing beauty. I will give him these, and with them her whom I erewhile took from him, the daughter of Briseus; and I swear a great oath that I never went up into her couch, nor have been with her after the manner of men and women.

'All these things will I give him now down, and if hereafter the gods vouchsafe me to sack the city of Priam, let him come when we Achæans are dividing the spoil, and load his ship with gold and bronze to his liking; furthermore let him take twenty Trojan women, the loveliest after Helen herself. Then, when we reach Achæan Argos, wealthiest of all lands, he shall be my son-in-law and I will show him like honour with my own dear son Orestes, who is being nurtured in all abundance. I have three daughters, Chrysothemis, Laodice, and Iphianassa, let him take the one of his choice, freely and without gifts of wooing, to the house of Peleus; I will add such dower to boot as no man ever yet gave his daughter, and will give him seven well-established cities, Cardamyle, Enope, and Hire, where there is grass; holy Pheræ and the rich meadows of Anthea; Æpea also, and the vine-clad slopes of Pedasus, all near the sea, and on the borders of sandy Pylos. The men that dwell there are rich in cattle and sheep; they will honour him with gifts as though he were a god, and be obedient to his comfortable ordinances. All this will I do if he will now forgo his anger. Let him then yield – it is only

Hades who is utterly ruthless and unyielding, and hence he is of all gods the one most hateful to mankind. Moreover I am older and more royal than himself. Therefore, let him now obey me.'

Then Nestor answered, 'Most noble son of Atreus, king of men, Agamemnon. The gifts you offer are no small ones, let us then send chosen messengers, who may go to the tent of Achilles son of Peleus without delay. Let those go whom I shall name. Let Phœnix, dear to Jove, lead the way; let Ajax and Ulysses follow, and let the heralds Odius and Eurybates go with them. Now bring water for our hands, and bid all keep silence while we pray to Jove the son of Saturn, if so be that he may have mercy upon us.'

Thus did he speak, and his saying pleased them well. Men-servants poured water over the hands of the guests, while pages filled the mixing-bowls with wine and water, and handed it round after giving every man his drink-offering; then, when they had made their offerings, and had drunk each as much as he was minded, the envoys set out from the tent of Agamemnon son of Atreus; and Nestor, looking first to one and then to another, but most especially at Ulysses, was instant with them that they should prevail with the noble son of Peleus.

They went their way by the shore of the sounding sea, and prayed earnestly to earth-encircling Neptune that the high spirit of the son of Æacus might incline favourably towards them. When they reached the ships and tents of the Myrmidons, they found Achilles playing on a lyre, fair, of cunning workmanship, and its cross-bar was of silver. It was part of the spoils which he had taken when he sacked the city of Eëtion, and he was now diverting himself with it and singing the feats of heroes. He was alone with Patroclus, who sat opposite to him and said nothing, waiting till he should cease singing. Ulysses and Ajax now came in – Ulysses leading the way – and stood before him. Achilles sprang from his seat with the lyre still in his hand, and Patroclus, when he saw the strangers, rose also. Achilles then greeted them saying, 'All hail and welcome – you must come upon some great matter, you, who for all my anger are still dearest to me of the Achæans.'

With this he led them forward, and bade them sit on seats covered with purple rugs; then he said to Patroclus who was close by him, 'Son of Menœtius, set a larger bowl upon the table, mix less water with the wine, and give every man his cup, for these are very dear friends, who are now under my roof.'

Patroclus did as his comrade bade him; he set the chopping-block in front of the fire, and on it he laid the loin of a sheep, the loin also of a goat, and the chine of a fat hog. Automedon held the meat while Achilles chopped it; he then sliced the pieces and put them on spits while the son of Menœtius made the fire burn high. When the flame had died down, he spread the embers, laid the spits on top of them, lifting them up and setting them upon the spit-racks; and he sprinkled them with salt. When the meat was roasted, he set it on platters, and handed bread round the table in fair baskets, while Achilles dealt them their portions. Then Achilles took his seat facing Ulysses against the opposite wall, and bade his comrade Patroclus offer sacrifice to the gods; so he cast the offerings into the fire, and they laid their hands upon the good things that were before them. As soon as they had had enough to eat and drink, Ajax made a sign to Phœnix, and when he saw this, Ulysses filled his cup with wine and pledged Achilles.

'Hail,' said he, 'Achilles, we have had no scant of good cheer, neither in the tent of Agamemnon, nor yet here; there has been plenty to eat and drink, but our thought turns upon no such matter. Sir, we are in the face of great disaster, and without your help know not whether we shall save our fleet or lose it. The Trojans and their allies have camped hard by our ships and by the wall; they have lit watchfires throughout their host and deem that nothing can now prevent them from falling on our fleet. Jove, moreover, has sent his lightnings on their right; Hector, in all his glory, rages like a maniac; confident that Jove is with him he fears neither god nor man, but is gone raving mad, and prays for the approach of day. He vows that he will hew the high sterns of our ships in pieces, set fire to their hulls, and make havoc of the Achæans while they are dazed and smothered in smoke; I much fear that heaven will make good his boasting, and it will prove our lot to perish at Troy far from our home in Argos. Up, then, and late though it be, save the sons of the Achæans who faint before the fury of the Trojans. You will repent bitterly hereafter if you do not, for when the harm is done there will be no curing it; consider ere it be too late, and save the Danaans from destruction.

'My good friend, when your father Peleus sent you from Phthia to Agamemnon, did he not charge you saying, "Son, Minerva and Juno will make you strong if they choose, but check your high temper, for the better part is in goodwill. Eschew vain quarrelling, and the Achæans old and young will respect you more for doing so." These were his words, but you have forgotten them. Even now, however, be appeased, and put away your anger from you. Agamemnon will make you great amends if you will forgive him; listen, and I will tell you what he has said in his tent that he will give you. He will give you seven tripods that have never yet been on the fire, and ten talents of gold; twenty iron cauldrons, and twelve strong horses that have won races and carried off prizes. Rich indeed both in land and gold is he who has as many prizes as these horses have won for Agamemnon. Moreover he will give you seven excellent workwomen, Lesbians, whom he chose for himself, when you took Lesbos – all of surpassing beauty. He will give you these, and with them her whom he erewhile took from you, the daughter of Briseus, and he will swear a great oath, he has never gone up into her couch nor been with her after the manner of men and women. All these things will he give you now down, and if here-after the gods vouchsafe him to sack the city of Priam, you can come when we Achæans are dividing the spoil, and load your ship with gold and bronze to your liking. You can take twenty Trojan women, the loveliest after Helen herself. Then, when we reach Achæan Argos, wealthiest of all lands, you shall be his son-in-law, and he will show you like honour with his own dear son Orestes, who is being nurtured in all abundance. Agamemnon has three daughters, Chrysothemis, Laodice, and Iphianassa; you may take the one of your choice, freely and without gifts of wooing, to the house of Peleus; he will add such dower to boot as no man ever yet gave his daughter, and will give you seven well-established cities, Cardamyle, Enope, and Hire where there is grass; holy Pheræ and the rich meadows of Anthea; Æpea also, and the vine-clad slopes of Pedasus, all near the sea, and on the borders of sandy Pylos. The men that dwell there are rich in cattle and sheep; they will honour you with gifts as though you were a god, and be obedient to your comfortable ordinances. All this will he do if you will now forgo your anger. Moreover, though you hate both him and his gifts with all your heart, yet pity the rest of the Achæans who are being harassed in all their host; they will honour you as a god, and you will earn great glory at their hands. You might even kill Hector; he will come within your reach, for he is infatuated, and declares that not a Danaan whom the ships have brought can hold his own against him.'

Achilles answered, 'Ulysses, noble son of Laertes, I should give you formal notice plainly and in all fixity of purpose that there be no more of this cajoling, from whatsoever quarter it may come. Him do I hate even as the gates of hell who says one thing while he hides another in his heart; therefore I will say what I mean. I will be appeased neither by Agamemnon son of Atreus nor by any other of the Danaans, for I see that I have no thanks for all my fighting. He that fights fares no better than he that does not; coward and hero are held in equal honour, and death deals like measure to him who works and him who is idle. I have taken nothing by all my hardships – with my life ever in my hand; as a bird when she has found a morsel takes it to her nestlings, and herself fares hardly, even so many a long night have I been wakeful, and many a bloody battle have I waged by day against those who were fighting for their women. With my ships I have taken twelve cities, and eleven round about Troy have I stormed with my men by land; I took great store of wealth from every one of them, but I gave all up to Agamemnon son of Atreus. He stayed where he was by his ships, yet of what came to him he gave little, and kept much himself.

'Nevertheless he did distribute some meeds of honour among the chieftains and kings, and these have them still; from me alone of the Achæans did he take the woman in whom I delighted – let him keep her and sleep with her. Why, pray, must the Argives needs fight the Trojans? What made the son of Atreus gather the host and bring them? Was it not for the sake of Helen? Are the sons of Atreus the only men in the world who love their wives? Any man of common right feeling will love and cherish her who is his own, as I this woman, with my whole heart, though she was but a fruitling of my spear. Agamemnon has taken her from me; he has played me false; I know him; let him tempt me no further, for he shall not move me. Let him look to you, Ulysses, and to the other princes to save his ships from burning. He has done much without me already. He has built a wall; he has dug a trench deep and wide all round it, and he has planted it within with stakes; but even so he stays not the murderous might of Hector. So long as I fought among the Achæans Hector suffered not the battle to range far from the city walls; he would come to the Scæan gates and to the oak tree, but no further. Once he stayed to meet me – and hardly did he escape my onset: now, however, since I am in no mood to fight him, I will to-morrow offer sacrifice to Jove and to all the gods; I will draw my ships into the water and then victual them duly; to-morrow morning, if you care to look, you will see my ships on the Hellespont, and my men rowing out to sea with might and main. If great Neptune vouchsafes me a fair passage, in three days I shall be in Phthia. I have much there that I left behind me when I came here to my sorrow, and I shall bring back still further store of gold, of red copper, of fair women, and of iron, my share of the spoils that we have taken; but one prize, he who gave has insolently taken away. Tell him all as I now bid you, and tell him in public that the Achæans may hate him and beware of him should he think that he can yet dupe others – for his effrontery never fails him.

'As for me, hound that he is, he dares not look me in the face. I will take no counsel with him, and will undertake nothing in common with him. He has wronged me and deceived me enough, he shall not cozen me further; let him go his own way, for Jove has robbed him of his reason. I loathe his presents, and for himself care not one straw. He may offer me ten or even twenty times what he has now done, nay – not though it be all that he has in the world, both now or ever shall have; he may promise me the wealth of Orchomenus or of Egyptian Thebes, which is the richest city in the whole world, for it has a hundred gates through each of which two hundred men may drive at once with their chariots and horses; he may offer me gifts as the sands of the sea or the dust of the plain in multitude, but even so he shall not move me till I have been revenged in full for the bitter wrong he has done me. I will not marry his daughter; she may be fair as Venus, and skilful as Minerva, but I will have none of her: let another take her, who may be a good match for her and who rules a larger kingdom. If the gods spare me to return home, Peleus will find me a wife; there are Achæan women in Hellas and Phthia, daughters of kings that have cities under them; of these I can take whom I will and marry her. Many a time was I minded when at home in Phthia to woo and wed a woman who would make me a suitable wife, and to enjoy the riches of my old father Peleus. My life is more to me than all the wealth of Ilius while it was yet at peace before the Achæans went there, or than all the treasure that lies on the stone floor of Apollo's temple beneath the cliffs of Pytho. Cattle and sheep are to be had for harrying, and a man may buy both tripods and horses if he wants them, but when his life has once left him it can neither be bought nor harried back again.

'My mother Thetis tells me that there are two ways in which I may meet my end. If I stay here and fight, I shall not return alive but my name will live for ever: whereas if I go home my name will die, but it will be long ere death shall take me. To the rest of you, then, I say, "Go home, for you will not take Ilius." Jove has held his hand over her to protect her, and her people have taken heart. Go, therefore, as in duty bound, and tell the princes of the Achæans the message that I have sent them; tell them to find some other plan for the saving of their ships and people, for so long as my displeasure lasts the one that they have now hit upon may not be. As for Phœnix, let him sleep here that he may sail with me in the morning if he so will. But I will not take him by force.'

They all held their peace, dismayed at the sternness with which he had denied them, till presently the old knight Phœnix in his great fear for the ships of the Achæans, burst into tears and said, 'Noble Achilles, if you are now minded to return, and in the fierceness of your anger will do nothing to save the ships from burning, how, my son, can I remain here without you? Your father Peleus bade me go with you when he sent you as a mere lad from Phthia to Agamemnon. You knew nothing neither of war nor of the arts whereby men make their mark in council, and he sent me with you to train you in all excellence of speech and action. Therefore, my son, I will not stay here without you – no, not though heaven itself vouchsafe to strip my years from off me, and make me young as I was when I first left Hellas the land of fair women. I was then flying the anger of my father Amyntor, son of Ormenus, who was furious with me in the matter of his concubine, of whom he was enamoured to the wronging of his wife my mother. My mother, therefore, prayed me without ceasing to lie with the woman myself, that so she might hate my father, and in the course of time I yielded. But my father soon came to know, and cursed me bitterly, calling the dread Erinyes to witness. He prayed that no son of mine might ever sit upon my knees – and the gods, Jove of the world below and awful Proserpine, fulfilled his curse. I took counsel to kill him, but some god stayed my rashness and bade me think on men's evil tongues and how I should be branded as the murderer of my father: nevertheless I could not bear to stay in my father's house with him so bitter against me. My cousins and clansmen came about me, and pressed me sorely to remain; many a sheep and many an ox did they slaughter, and many a fat hog did they set down to roast before the fire; many a jar, too, did they broach of my father's wine. Nine whole nights did they set a guard over me taking it in turns to watch, and they kept a fire always burning, both in the cloister of the outer court and in the inner court at the doors of the room wherein I lay; but when the darkness of the tenth night came, I broke through the closed doors of my room, and climbed the wall of the outer court after passing quickly and unperceived through the men on guard and the women servants. I then fled through Hellas till I came to fertile Phthia, mother of sheep, and to King Peleus, who made me welcome and treated me as a father treats an only son who will be heir to all his wealth. He made me rich and set me over much people, establishing me on the borders of Phthia where I was chief ruler over the Dolopians.

'It was I, Achilles, who had the making of you; I loved you with all my heart: for you would eat neither at home nor when you had gone out elsewhere, till I had first set you upon my knees, cut up the dainty morsel that you were to eat, and held the wine-cup to your lips. Many a time have you slobbered your wine in baby helplessness over my shirt; I had infinite trouble with you, but I knew that heaven had vouchsafed me no offspring of my own, and I made a son of you, Achilles, that in my hour of need you might protect me. Now, therefore, I say battle with your pride and beat it; cherish not your anger for ever; the might and majesty of heaven are more than ours, but even heaven may be appeased; and if a man has sinned he prays the gods, and reconciles them to himself by his piteous cries and by frankincense, with drink-offerings and the savour of burnt sacrifice. For prayers are as daughters to great Jove; halt, wrinkled, with eyes askance, they follow in the footsteps of sin, who, being fierce and fleet of foot, leaves them far behind him, and ever baneful to mankind outstrips them even to the ends of the world; but nevertheless the prayers come hobbling and healing after. If a man has pity upon these daughters of Jove when they draw near him, they will bless him and hear him too when he is praying; but if he deny them and will not listen to them, they go to Jove the son of Saturn and pray that he may presently fall into sin – to his ruing bitterly hereafter. Therefore, Achilles, give these daughters of Jove due reverence, and bow before them as all good men will bow. Were not the son of Atreus offering you gifts and promising others later – if he were still furious and implacable – I am not he that would bid you throw off your anger and help the Achæans, no matter how great their need; but he is giving much now, and more hereafter; he has sent his captains to urge his suit, and has chosen those who of all the Argives are most acceptable to you; make not then their words and their coming to be of none effect. Your anger has been righteous so far. We have heard in song how heroes of old time quarrelled when they were roused to fury, but still they could be won by gifts, and fair words could soothe them.

'I have an old story in my mind – a very old one – but you are all friends and I will tell it. The Curetes and the Ætolians were fighting and killing one another round Calydon – the Ætolians defending the city and the Curetes trying to destroy it. For Diana of the golden throne was angry and did them hurt because Œneus had not offered her his harvest first-fruits. The other gods had all been feasted with hecatombs, but to the daughter of great Jove alone he had made no sacrifice. He had forgotten her, or somehow or other it had escaped him, and this was a grievous sin. Thereon the archer goddess in her displeasure sent a prodigious creature against him – a savage wild boar with great white tusks that did much harm to his orchard lands, uprooting apple-trees in full bloom and throwing them to the ground. But Meleager son of Œneus got huntsmen and hounds from many cities and killed it – for it was so monstrous that not a few were needed, and many a man did it stretch upon his funeral pyre. On this the goddess set the Curetes and the Ætolians fighting furiously about the head and skin of the boar.

'So long as Meleager was in the field things went badly with the Curetes, and for all their numbers they could not hold their ground under the city walls; but in the course of time Meleager was angered as even a wise man will sometimes be. He was incensed with his mother Althæa, and therefore stayed at home with his wedded wife fair Cleopatra, who was daughter of Marpessa daughter of Euenus, and of

Ides the strongest man then living. He it was who took his bow and faced King Apollo himself for fair Marpessa's sake; her father and mother then named her Alcyone, because her mother had mourned with the plaintive strains of the halcyon-bird when Phœbus Apollo had carried her off. Meleager, then, stayed at home with Cleopatra, nursing the anger which he felt by reason of his mother's curses. His mother, grieving for the death of her brother, prayed the gods, and beat the earth with her hands, calling upon Hades and on awful Proserpine; she went down upon her knees and her bosom was wet with tears as she prayed that they would kill her son – and Erinys that walks in darkness and knows no ruth heard her from Erebus.

'Then was heard the din of battle about the gates of Calydon, and the dull thump of the battering against their walls. Thereon the elders of the Ætolians besought Meleager; they sent the chiefest of their priests, and begged him to come out and help them, promising him a great reward. They bade him choose fifty plough-gates, the most fertile in the plain of Calydon, the one-half vineyard and the other open plough-land. The old warrior Œneus implored him, standing at the threshold of his room and beating the doors in supplication. His sisters and his mother herself besought him sore, but he the more refused them; those of his comrades who were nearest and dearest to him also prayed him, but they could not move him till the foe was battering at the very doors of his chamber, and the Curetes had scaled the walls and were setting fire to the city. Then at last his sorrowing wife detailed the horrors that befall those whose city is taken; she reminded him how the men are slain, and the city is given over to the flames, while the women and children are carried into captivity; when he heard all this, his heart was touched, and he donned his armour to go forth. Thus of his own inward motion he saved the city of the Ætolians; but they now gave him nothing of those rich rewards that they had offered earlier, and though he saved the city he took nothing by it. Be not then, my son, thus minded; let not heaven lure you into any such course. When the ships are burning it will be a harder matter to save them. Take the gifts, and go, for the Achæans will then honour you as a god; whereas if you fight without taking them, you may beat the battle back, but you will not be held in like honour.'

And Achilles answered, 'Phœnix, old friend and father, I have no need of such honour. I have honour from Jove himself, which will abide with me at my ships while I have breath in my body, and my limbs are strong. I say further – and lay my saying to your heart – vex me no more with this weeping and lamentation, all in the cause of the son of Atreus. Love him so well, and you may lose the love I bear you. You ought to help me rather in troubling those that trouble me; be king as much as I am, and share like honour with myself; the others shall take my answer; stay here yourself and sleep comfortably in your bed; at daybreak we will consider whether to remain or go.'

On this he nodded quietly to Patroclus as a sign that he was to prepare a bed for Phœnix, and that the others should take their leave. Ajax son of Telamon then said, 'Ulysses, noble son of Laertes, let us be gone, for I see that our journey is vain. We must now take our answer, unwelcome though it be, to the Danaans who are waiting to receive it. Achilles is savage and remorseless; he is cruel, and cares nothing for the love his comrades lavished upon him more than on all the others. He is implacable – and yet if a man's brother or son has been slain he will accept a fine by way of amends from him that killed him, and the wrong-doer having paid in full remains in peace among his own people; but as for you, Achilles, the gods have put a wicked unforgiving spirit in your heart, and this all about one single girl, whereas we now offer you the seven best we have, and much else into the bargain. Be then of a more gracious mind, respect the hospitality of your own roof. We are with you as messengers from the host of the Danaans, and would fain be held nearest and dearest to yourself of all the Achæans.'

'Ajax,' replied Achilles, 'noble son of Telamon, you have spoken much to my liking, but my blood boils when I think it all over, and remember how the son of Atreus treated me with contumely as though

I were some vile tramp, and that too in the presence of the Argives. Go, then, and deliver your message; say that I will have no concern with fighting, till Hector, son of noble Priam, reaches the tents of the Myrmidons in his murderous course, and flings fire upon their ships. For all his lust of battle, I take it he will be held in check when he is at my own tent and ship.'

On this they took every man his double cup, made their drink-offerings, and went back to the ships, Ulysses leading the way. But Patroclus told his men and the maid-servants to make ready a comfortable bed for Phænix; they therefore did so with sheepskins, a rug, and a sheet of fine linen. The old man then laid himself down and waited till morning came. But Achilles slept in an inner room, and beside him the daughter of Phorbas lovely Diomedè, whom he had carried off from Lesbos. Patroclus lay on the other side of the room, and with him fair Iphis whom Achilles had given him when he took Scyros the city of Enyeüs.

When the envoys reached the tents of the son of Atreus, the Achæans rose, pledged them in cups of gold, and began to question, them. King Agamemnon was the first to do so. 'Tell me, Ulysses,' said he, 'will he save the ships from burning, or did he refuse, and is he still furious?'

Ulysses answered, 'Most noble son of Atreus, king of men, Agamemnon, Achilles will not be calmed, but is more fiercely angry than ever, and spurns both you and your gifts. He bids you take counsel with the Achæans to save the ships and host as you best may; as for himself, he said that at daybreak he should draw his ships into the water. He said further that he should advise every one to sail home likewise, for that you will not reach the goal of Ilius. "Jove," he said, "has laid his hand over the city to protect it, and the people have taken heart." This is what he said, and the others who were with me can tell you the same story – Ajax and the two heralds, men, both of them, who may be trusted. The old man Phœnix stayed where he was to sleep, for so Achilles would have it, that he might go home with him in the morning if he so would; but he will not take him by force.'

They all held their peace, sitting for a long time silent and dejected, by reason of the sternness with which Achilles had refused them, till presently Diomed said, 'Most noble son of Atreus, king of men, Agamemnon, you ought not to have sued the son of Peleus nor offered him gifts. He is proud enough as it is, and you have encouraged him in his pride still further. Let him stay or go as he will. He will fight later when he is in the humour, and heaven puts it in his mind to do so. Now, therefore, let us all do as I say; we have eaten and drunk our fill, let us then take our rest, for in rest there is both strength and stay. But when fair rosy-fingered morn appears, forthwith bring out your host and your horsemen in front of the ships, urging them on, and yourself fighting among the foremost.'

Thus he spoke, and the other chieftains approved his words. They then made their drink-offerings and went every man to his own tent, where they lay down to rest and enjoyed the boon of sleep.

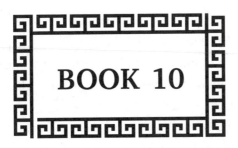

BOOK 10

Ulysses and Diomed go out as spies, and meet Dolon, who gives them information: they then kill him, and profiting by what he had told them, kill Rhesus king of the Thracians and take his horses.

Now the other princes of the Achæans slept soundly the whole night through, but Agamemnon son of Atreus was troubled, so that he could get no rest. As when fair Juno's lord flashes his lightning in token of great rain or hail or snow when the snow-flakes whiten the ground, or again as a sign that he will open the wide jaws of hungry war, even so did Agamemnon heave many a heavy sigh, for his soul trembled within him. When he looked upon the plain of Troy he marvelled at the many watchfires burning in front of Ilius, and at the sound of pipes and flutes and of the hum of men, but when presently he turned towards the ships and hosts of the Achæans, he tore his hair by handfuls before Jove on high, and groaned aloud for the very disquietness of his soul. In the end he deemed it best to go at once to Nestor son of Neleus, and see if between them they could find any way of saving the Achæans from destruction. He therefore rose, put on his shirt, bound his sandals about his comely feet, flung the skin of a huge tawny lion over his shoulders – a skin that reached his feet – and took his spear in his hand.

Neither could Menelaus sleep, for he, too, boded ill for the Argives who for his sake had sailed from far over the seas to fight the Trojans. He covered his broad back with the skin of a spotted panther, put a casque of bronze upon his head, and took his spear in his brawny hand. Then he went to rouse his brother, who was by far the most powerful of the Achæans, and was honoured by the people as though he were a god. He found him by the stern of his ship already putting his goodly array about his shoulders, and right glad was he that his brother had come.

Menelaus spoke first. 'Why,' said he, 'my dear brother, are you thus arming? Are you going to send any of our comrades to exploit the Trojans? I greatly fear that no one will do you this service, and spy upon the enemy alone in the dead of night. It will be a deed of great daring.'

And King Agamemnon answered, 'Menelaus, we both of us need shrewd counsel to save the Argives and our ships, for Jove has changed his mind, and inclines towards Hector's sacrifices rather than ours. I never saw nor heard tell of any man as having wrought such ruin in one day as Hector has now wrought against the sons of the Achæans – and that too of his own unaided self, for he is son neither to god nor goddess. The Argives will rue it long and deeply. Run, therefore, with all speed by the line of the ships, and call Ajax and Idomeneus. Meanwhile I will go to Nestor, and bid him rise and go about among the companies of our sentinels to give them their instructions; they will listen to him sooner than to any man, for his own son, and Meriones brother in arms to Idomeneus, are captains over them. It was to them more particularly that we gave this charge.'

Menelaus replied, 'How do I take your meaning? Am I to stay with them and wait your coming, or shall I return here as soon as I have given your orders?' 'Wait,' answered King Agamemnon, 'for there are so many paths about the camp that we might miss one another. Call every man on your way, and bid him be stirring; name him by his lineage and by his father's name, give each all titular observance, and stand not too much upon your own dignity; we must take our full share of toil, for at our birth Jove laid this heavy burden upon us.'

With these instructions he sent his brother on his way, and went on to Nestor shepherd of his people. He found him sleeping in his tent hard by his own ship; his goodly armour lay beside him – his shield, his two spears and his helmet; beside him also lay the gleaming girdle with which the old man girded himself when he armed to lead his people into battle – for his age stayed him not. He raised himself on his elbow and looked up at Agamemnon. 'Who is it,' said he, 'that goes thus about the host and the ships alone and in the dead of night, when men are sleeping? Are you looking for one of your mules or for some comrade? Do not stand there and say nothing, but speak. What is your business?'

And Agamemnon answered, 'Nestor, son of Neleus, honour to the Achæan name, it is I, Agamemnon son of Atreus, on whom Jove has laid labour and sorrow so long as there is breath in my body and my limbs carry me. I am thus abroad because sleep sits not upon my eyelids, but my heart is big with war and with the jeopardy of the Achæans. I am in great fear for the Danaans. I am at sea, and without sure counsel; my heart beats as though it would leap out of my body, and my limbs fail me. If then you can do anything – for you too cannot sleep – let us go the round of the watch, and see whether they are drowsy with toil and sleeping to the neglect of their duty. The enemy is encamped hard by, and we know not but he may attack us by night.'

Nestor replied, 'Most noble son of Atreus, king of men, Agamemnon, Jove will not do all for Hector that Hector thinks he will; he will have troubles yet in plenty if Achilles will lay aside his anger. I will go with you, and we will rouse others, either the son of Tydeus, or Ulysses, or fleet Ajax and the valiant son of Phyleus. Some one had also better go and call Ajax and King Idomeneus, for their ships are not near at hand but the farthest of all. I cannot however refrain from blaming Menelaus, much as I love him and respect him – and I will say so plainly, even at the risk of offending you – for sleeping and leaving all this trouble to yourself. He ought to be going about imploring aid from all the princes of the Achæans, for we are in extreme danger.'

And Agamemnon answered, 'Sir, you may sometimes blame him justly, for he is often remiss and unwilling to exert himself – not indeed from sloth, nor yet heedlessness, but because he looks to me and expects me to take the lead. On this occasion, however, he was awake before I was, and came to me of his own accord. I have already sent him to call the very men whom you have named. And now let us be going. We shall find them with the watch outside the gates, for it was there I said that we would meet them.'

'In that case,' answered Nestor, 'the Argives will not blame him nor disobey his orders when he urges them to fight or gives them instructions.'

With this he put on his shirt, and bound his sandals about his comely feet. He buckled on his purple coat, of two thicknesses, large, and of a rough shaggy texture, grasped his redoubtable bronze-shod spear, and wended his way along the line of the Achæan ships. First he called loudly to Ulysses peer of gods in counsel and woke him, for he was soon roused by the sound of the battle-cry. He came outside his tent and said, 'Why do you go thus alone about the host, and along the line of the ships in the stillness of the night? What is it that you find so urgent?' And Nestor knight of Gerene answered, 'Ulysses, noble son of Laertes, take it not amiss, for the Achæans are in great straits. Come with me and let us wake some other, who may advise well with us whether we shall fight or fly.'

On this Ulysses went at once into his tent, put his shield about his shoulders and came out with them. First they went to Diomed son of Tydeus, and found him outside his tent clad in his armour with his comrades sleeping round him and using their shields as pillows; as for their spears, they stood upright on the spikes of their butts that were driven into the ground, and the burnished bronze flashed afar like the lightning of father Jove. The hero was sleeping upon the skin of an ox, with a piece of fine carpet under his head; Nestor went up to him and stirred him with his heel to rouse him, upbraiding him and urging him to bestir himself. 'Wake up,' he exclaimed, 'son of Tydeus. How can you sleep on in this way? Can you not see that the Trojans are encamped on the brow of the plain hard by our ships, with but a little space between us and them?'

On these words Diomed leaped up instantly and said, 'Old man, your heart is of iron; you rest not one moment from your labours. Are there no younger men among the Achæans who could go about to rouse the princes? There is no tiring you.'

And Nestor knight of Gerene made answer, 'My son, all that you have said is true. I have good sons, and also much people who might call the chieftains, but the Achæans are in the gravest danger; life and death are balanced as it were on the edge of a razor. Go then, for you are younger than I, and of your courtesy rouse Ajax and the fleet son of Phyleus.'

Diomed threw the skin of a great tawny lion about his shoulders – a skin that reached his feet – and grasped his spear. When he had roused the heroes, he brought them back with him; they then went the round of those who were on guard, and found the captains not sleeping at their posts but wakeful and sitting with their arms about them. As sheep dogs that watch their flocks when they are yarded, and hear a wild beast coming through the mountain forest towards them – forthwith there is a hue and cry of dogs and men, and slumber is broken – even so was sleep chased from the eyes of the Achæans as they kept the watches of the wicked night, for they turned constantly towards the plain whenever they heard any stir among the Trojans. The old man was glad and bade them be of good cheer, 'Watch on, my children,' said he, 'and let not sleep get hold upon you, lest our enemies triumph over us.'

With this he passed the trench, and with him the other chiefs of the Achæans who had been called to the council. Meriones and the brave son of Nestor went also, for the princes bade them. When they were beyond the trench that was dug round the wall they held their meeting on the open ground where there was a space clear of corpses, for it was here that when night fell Hector had turned back from his onslaught on the Argives. They sat down, therefore, and held debate with one another.

Nestor spoke first. 'My friends,' said he, 'is there any man bold enough to venture among the Trojans, and cut off some straggler, or bring us news of what the enemy mean to do – whether they will stay here by the ships away from the city, or whether, now that they have worsted the Achæans, they will retire within their walls. If he could learn all this and come back safely here, his fame would be high as heaven in the mouths of all men, and he would be rewarded richly; for the chiefs from all our ships would each of them give him a black ewe with her lamb – which is a present of surpassing value – and he would be asked as a guest to all feasts and clan-gatherings.'

They all held their peace, but Diomed of the loud war-cry spoke saying, 'Nestor, gladly will I visit the host of the Trojans over against us, but if another will go with me I shall do so in greater confidence and comfort. When two men are together, one of them may see some opportunity which the other has not caught sight of; if a man is alone he is less full of resource, and his wit is weaker.'

On this several offered to go with Diomed. The two Ajaxes, servants of Mars, Meriones, and the son of Nestor all wanted to go, so did Menelaus son of Atreus; Ulysses also wished to go among the host of the Trojans, for he was ever full of daring, and thereon Agamemnon king of men spoke thus: 'Diomed,' said he, 'son of Tydeus, man after my own heart, choose your comrade for yourself – take the best man of those that have offered, for many would now go with you. Do not through delicacy reject the better man, and take the worst out of respect for his lineage, because he is of more royal blood.'

He said this because he feared for Menelaus. Diomed answered, 'If you bid me take the man of my own choice, how in that case can I fail to think of Ulysses, than whom there is no man more eager to face all kinds of danger – and Pallas Minerva loves him well? If he were to go with me we should pass safely through fire itself, for he is quick to see and understand.'

'Son of Tydeus,' replied Ulysses, 'say neither good nor ill about me, for you are among Argives who know me well. Let us be going, for the night wanes and dawn is at hand. The stars have gone forward, two-thirds of the night are already spent, and the third is alone left us.'

They then put on their armour. Brave Thrasymedes provided the son of Tydeus with a sword and a shield (for he had left his own at his ship) and on his head he set a helmet of bull's hide without either peak or crest; it is called a skull-cap and is a common headgear. Meriones found a bow and quiver for Ulysses, and on his head he set a leathern helmet that was lined with a strong plaiting of leathern thongs, while on the outside it was thickly studded with boar's teeth, well and skilfully set into it; next the head there was an inner lining of felt. This helmet had been stolen by Autolycus out of Eleon when he broke into the house of Amyntor son of Ormenus. He gave it to Amphidamas of Cythera to take to Scandea, and Amphidamas gave it as a guest-gift to Molus, who gave it to his son Meriones; and now it was set upon the head of Ulysses.

When the pair had armed, they set out, and left the other chieftains behind them. Pallas Minerva sent them a heron by the wayside upon their right hands; they could not see it for the darkness, but they heard its cry. Ulysses was glad when he heard it and prayed to Minerva: 'Hear me,' he cried, 'daughter of ægis-bearing Jove, you who spy out all my ways and who are with me in all my hardships; befriend me in this mine hour, and grant that we may return to the ships covered with glory after having achieved some mighty exploit that shall bring sorrow to the Trojans.'

Then Diomed of the loud war-cry also prayed: 'Hear me too,' said he, 'daughter of Jove, unwearie; be with me even as you were with my noble father Tydeus when he went to Thebes as envoy sent by the Achæans. He left the Achæans by the banks of the river Æsopus, and went to the city bearing a message of peace to the Cadmeians; on his return thence, with your help, goddess, he did great deeds of daring, for you were his ready helper. Even so guide me and guard me now, and in return I will offer you in sacrifice a broad-browed heifer of a year old, unbroken, and never yet brought by man under the yoke. I will gild her horns and will offer her up to you in sacrifice.'

Thus they prayed, and Pallas Minerva heard their prayer. When they had done praying to the daughter of great Jove, they went their way like two lions prowling by night amid the armour and blood-stained bodies of them that had fallen.

Neither again did Hector let the Trojans sleep; for he too called the princes and councillors of the Trojans that he might set his counsel before them. 'Is there one,' said he, 'who for a great reward will do me the service of which I will tell you? He shall be well paid if he will. I will give him a chariot and a couple of horses, the fleetest that can be found at the ships of the Achæans, if he will dare this thing; and he will win infinite honour to boot; he must go to the ships and find out whether they are still guarded as heretofore, or whether now that we have beaten them the Achæans design to fly, and through sheer exhaustion are neglecting to keep their watches.'

They all held their peace; but there was among the Trojans a certain man named Dolon, son of Eumedes, the famous herald – a man rich in gold and bronze. He was ill-favoured, but a good runner, and was an only son among five sisters. He it was that now addressed the Trojans. 'I, Hector,' said he, 'will go to the ships and will exploit them. But first hold up your sceptre and swear that you will give me the chariot, bedight with bronze, and the horses that now carry the noble son of Peleus. I will make you a good scout, and will not fail you. I will go through the host from one end to the other till I come to the ship of Agamemnon, where I take it the princes of the Achæans are now consulting whether they shall fight or fly.'

When he had done speaking Hector held up his sceptre, and swore him his oath saying, 'May Jove the thundering husband of Juno bear witness that no other Trojan but yourself shall mount those steeds, and that you shall have your will with them for ever.'

The oath he swore was bootless, but it made Dolon more keen on going. He hung his bow over his shoulder, and as an overall he wore the skin of a grey wolf, while on his head he set a cap of ferret skin. Then he took a pointed javelin, and left the camp for the ships, but he was not to return with any news for Hector. When he had left the horses and the troops behind him, he made all speed on his way, but

Ulysses perceived his coming and said to Diomed, 'Diomed, here is some one from the camp; I am not sure whether he is a spy, or whether it is some thief who would plunder the bodies of the dead; let him get a little past us, we can then spring upon him and take him. If, however, he is too quick for us, go after him with your spear and hem him in towards the ships away from the Trojan camp, to prevent his getting back to the town.'

With this they turned out of their way and lay down among the corpses. Dolon suspected nothing and soon passed them, but when he had got about as far as the distance by which a mule-ploughed furrow exceeds one that has been ploughed by oxen (for mules can plough fallow land quicker than oxen) they ran after him, and when he heard their footsteps he stood still, for he made sure they were friends from the Trojan camp come by Hector's orders to bid him return; when, however, they were only a spear's cast, or less, away from him, he saw that they were enemies and ran away as fast as his legs could take him. The others gave chase at once, and as a couple of well-trained hounds press forward after a doe or hare that runs screaming in front of them, even so did the son of Tydeus and Ulysses pursue Dolon and cut him off from his own people. But when he had fled so far towards the ships that he would soon have fallen in with the outposts, Minerva infused fresh strength into the son of Tydeus for fear some other of the Achæans might have the glory of being first to hit him, and he might himself be only second; he therefore sprang forward with his spear and said, 'Stand, or I shall throw my spear, and in that case I shall soon make an end of you.'

He threw as he spoke, but missed his aim on purpose. The dart flew over the man's right shoulder, and then stuck in the ground. He stood stock still, trembling and in great fear; his teeth chattered, and he turned pale with fear. The two came breathless up to him and seized his hands, whereon he began to weep and said, 'Take me alive; I will ransom myself; we have great store of gold, bronze, and wrought iron, and from this my father will satisfy you with a very large ransom, should he hear of my being alive at the ships of the Achæans.'

'Fear not,' replied Ulysses, 'let no thought of death be in your mind; but tell me, and tell me true, why are you thus going about alone in the dead of night away from your camp and towards the ships, while other men are sleeping? Is it to plunder the bodies of the slain, or did Hector send you to spy out what was going on at the ships? Or did you come here of your own mere notion?'

Dolon answered, his limbs trembling beneath him: 'Hector, with his vain flattering promises, lured me from my better judgement. He said he would give me the horses of the noble son of Peleus and his bronze-bedizened chariot; he bade me go through the darkness of the flying night, get close to the enemy, and find out whether the ships are still guarded as heretofore, or whether, now that we have beaten them, the Achæans design to fly, and through sheer exhaustion are neglecting to keep their watches.'

Ulysses smiled at him and answered, 'You had indeed set your heart upon a great reward, but the horses of the descendant of Æacus are hardly to be kept in hand or driven by any other mortal man than Achilles himself, whose mother was an immortal. But tell me, and tell me true, where did you leave Hector when you started? Where lies his armour and his horses? How, too, are the watches and sleeping-ground of the Trojans ordered? What are their plans? Will they stay here by the ships and away from the city, or now that they have worsted the Achæans, will they retire within their walls?'

And Dolon answered, 'I will tell you truly all. Hector and the other councillors are now holding conference by the monument of great Ilus, away from the general tumult; as for the guards about which you ask me, there is no chosen watch to keep guard over the host. The Trojans have their watchfires, for they are bound to have them; they, therefore, are awake and keep each other to their duty as sentinels; but the allies who have come from other places are asleep and leave it to the Trojans to keep guard, for their wives and children are not here.'

Ulysses then said, 'Now tell me; are they sleeping among the Trojan troops, or do they lie apart? Explain this that I may understand it.'

'I will tell you truly all,' replied Dolon. 'To the sea-ward lie the Carians, the Pæonian bowmen, the Leleges, the Cauconians, and the noble Pelasgi. The Lysians and proud Mysians, with the Phrygians and Meonians, have their place on the side towards Thymbra; but why ask about all this? If you want to find your way into the host of the Trojans, there are the Thracians, who have lately come here and lie apart from the others at the far end of the camp; and they have Rhesus son of Eïoneus for their king. His horses are the finest and strongest that I have ever seen, they are whiter than snow and fleeter than any wind that blows. His chariot is bedight with silver and gold, and he has brought his marvellous golden armour, of the rarest workmanship – too splendid for any mortal man to carry, and meet only for the gods. Now, therefore, take me to the ships or bind me securely here, until you come back and have proved my words whether they be false or true.'

Diomed looked sternly at him and answered, 'Think not, Dolon, for all the good information you have given us, that you shall escape now you are in our hands, for if we ransom you or let you go, you will come some second time to the ships of the Achæans either as a spy or as an open enemy, but if I kill you and make an end of you, you will give no more trouble.'

On this Dolon would have caught him by the beard to beseech him further, but Diomed struck him in the middle of his neck with his sword and cut through both sinews so that his head fell rolling in the dust while he was yet speaking. They took the ferret-skin cap from his head, and also the wolf-skin, the bow, and his long spear. Ulysses hung them up aloft in honour of Minerva the goddess of plunder, and prayed saying, 'Accept these, goddess, for we give them to you in preference to all the gods in Olympus: therefore speed us still further towards the horses and sleeping-ground of the Thracians.'

With these words he took up the spoils and set them upon a tamarisk tree, and they marked the place by pulling up reeds and gathering boughs of tamarisk that they might not miss it as they came back through the flying hours of darkness. The two then went onwards amid the fallen armour and the blood, and came presently to the company of Thracian soldiers, who were sleeping, tired out with their day's toil; their goodly armour was lying on the ground beside them all orderly in three rows; and each man had his yoke of horses beside him. Rhesus was sleeping in the middle, and hard by him his horses were made fast to the topmost rim of his chariot. Ulysses from some way off saw him and said, 'This, Diomed, is the man, and these are the horses about which Dolon whom we killed told us. Do your very utmost; dally not about your armour, but loose the horses at once – or else kill the men yourself, while I see to the horses.'

Thereon Minerva put courage into the heart of Diomed, and he smote them right and left. They made a hideous groaning as they were being hacked about, and the earth was red with their blood. As a lion springs furiously upon a flock of sheep or goats when he finds them without their shepherd, so did the son of Tydeus set upon the Thracian soldiers till he had killed twelve. As he killed them Ulysses came and drew them aside by their feet one by one, that the horses might go forward freely without being frightened as they passed over the dead bodies, for they were not yet used to them. When the son of Tydeus came to the king, he killed him too (which made thirteen), as he was breathing hard, for by the counsel of Minerva an evil dream, the seed of Œneus, hovered that night over his head. Meanwhile Ulysses untied the horses, made them fast one to another and drove them off, striking them with his bow, for he had forgotten to take the whip from the chariot. Then he whistled as a sign to Diomed.

But Diomed stayed where he was, thinking what other daring deed he might accomplish. He was doubting whether to take the chariot in which the king's armour was lying, and draw it out by the pole, or to lift the armour out and carry it off; or whether again, he should not kill some more Thracians. While he was thus hesitating Minerva came up to him and said, 'Get back, Diomed, to the ships, or you may be driven thither, should some other god rouse the Trojans.'

Diomed knew that it was the goddess, and at once sprang upon the horses. Ulysses beat them with his bow and they flew onward to the ships of the Achæans.

But Apollo kept no blind look-out when he saw Minerva with the son of Tydeus. He was angry with her, and coming to the host of the Trojans he roused Hippocoön, a counsellor of the Thracians and a noble kinsman of Rhesus. He started up out of his sleep and saw that the horses were no longer in their place, and that the men were gasping in their death-agony; on this he groaned aloud, and called upon his friend by name. Then the whole Trojan camp was in an uproar as the people kept hurrying together, and they marvelled at the deeds of the heroes who had now got away towards the ships.

When they reached the place where they had killed Hector's scout, Ulysses stayed his horses, and the son of Tydeus, leaping to the ground, placed the blood-stained spoils in the hands of Ulysses and remounted: then he lashed the horses onwards, and they flew forward nothing loth towards the ships as though of their own free will. Nestor was first to hear the tramp of their feet. 'My friends,' said he, 'princes and coun-sellors of the Argives, shall I guess right or wrong? – but I must say what I think: there is a sound in my ears as of the tramp of horses. I hope it may be Diomed and Ulysses driving in horses from the Trojans, but I much fear that the bravest of the Argives may have come to some harm at their hands.'

He had hardly done speaking when the two men came in and dismounted, whereon the others shook hands right gladly with them and congratulated them. Nestor knight of Gerene was first to question them. 'Tell me,' said he, 'renowned Ulysses, how did you two come by these horses? Did you steal in among the Trojan forces, or did some god meet you and give them to you? They are like sunbeams. I am well conversant with the Trojans, for old warrior though I am I never hold back by the ships, but I never yet saw or heard of such horses as these are. Surely some god must have met you and given them to you, for you are both of you dear to Jove, and to Jove's daughter Minerva.'

And Ulysses answered, 'Nestor son of Neleus, honour to the Achæan name, heaven, if it so will, can give us even better horses than these, for the gods are far mightier than we are. These horses, however, about which you ask me, are freshly come from Thrace. Diomed killed their king with the twelve bravest of his companions. Hard by the ships we took a thirteenth man – a scout whom Hector and the other Trojans had sent as a spy upon our ships.'

He laughed as he spoke and drove the horses over the ditch, while the other Achæans followed him gladly. When they reached the strongly built quarters of the son of Tydeus, they tied the horses with thongs of leather to the manger, where the steeds of Diomed stood eating their sweet corn, but Ulysses hung the blood-stained spoils of Dolon at the stern of his ship, that they might prepare a sacred offering to Minerva. As for themselves, they went into the sea and washed the sweat from their bodies, and from their necks and thighs. When the sea-water had taken all the sweat from off them, and had refreshed them, they went into the baths and washed themselves. After they had so done and had anointed themselves with oil, they sat down to table, and drawing from a full mixing-bowl, made a drink-offering of wine to Minerva.

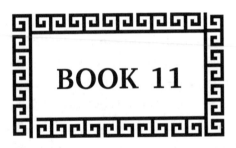

BOOK 11

In the forenoon the fight is equal, but Agamemnon turns the fortune of the day towards the Achæans until he gets wounded and leaves the field – Hector then drives everything before him till he is wounded by Diomed – Paris wounds Diomed – Ulysses, Nestor, and Idomeneus perform prodigies of valour – Machaon is wounded – Nestor drives him off in his chariot – Achilles sees the pair driving towards the camp and sends Patroclus to ask who it is that is wounded – This is the beginning of evil for Patroclus – Nestor makes a long speech.

And now as Dawn rose from her couch beside Tithonus, harbinger of light alike to mortals and immortals, Jove sent fierce Discord with the ensign of war in her hands to the ships of the Achæans. She took her stand by the huge black hull of Ulysses' ship which was middlemost of all, so that her voice might carry farthest on either side, on the one hand towards the tents of Ajax son of Telamon, and on the other towards those of Achilles – for these two heroes, well-assured of their own strength, had valorously drawn up their ships at the two ends of the line. There she took her stand, and raised a cry both loud and shrill that filled the Achæans with courage, giving them heart to fight resolutely and with all their might, so that they had rather stay there and do battle than go home in their ships.

The son of Atreus shouted aloud and bade the Argives gird themselves for battle while he put on his armour. First he girded his goodly greaves about his legs, making them fast with ancle-clasps of silver;

and about his chest he set the breastplate which Cinyras had once given him as a guest-gift. It had been noised abroad as far as Cyprus that the Achæans were about to sail for Troy, and therefore he gave it to the king. It had ten courses of dark cyanus,[5] twelve of gold, and ten of tin. There were serpents of cyanus that reared themselves up towards the neck, three upon either side, like the rainbows which the son of Saturn has set in heaven as a sign to mortal men. About his shoulders he threw his sword, studded with bosses of gold; and the scabbard was of silver with a chain of gold wherewith to hang it. He took moreover the richly-dight shield that covered his body when he was in battle – fair to see, with ten circles of bronze running all round it. On the body of the shield there were twenty bosses of white tin, with another of dark cyanus in the middle: this last was made to show a Gorgon's head, fierce and grim, with Rout and Panic on either side. The band for the arm to go through was of silver, on which there was a writhing snake of cyanus with three heads that sprang from a single neck, and went in and out among one another. On his head Agamemnon set a helmet, with a peak before and behind, and four plumes of horse-hair that nodded menacingly above it; then he grasped two redoubtable bronze-shod spears, and the gleam of his armour shot from him as a flame into the firmament, while Juno and Minerva thundered in honour of the king of rich Mycene.

Every man now left his horses in charge of his charioteer to hold them in readiness by the trench, while he went into battle on foot clad in full armour, and a mighty uproar rose on high into the dawning. The chiefs were armed and at the trench before the horses got there, but these came up presently. The son of Saturn sent a portent of evil sound about their host, and the dew fell red with blood, for he was about to send many a brave man hurrying down to Hades.

The Trojans, on the other side upon the rising slope of the plain, were gathered round great Hector, noble Polydamas, Æneas who was honoured by the Trojans like an immortal, and the three sons of Antenor, Polybus, Agenor, and young Acamas beauteous as a god.

Hector's round shield showed in the front rank, and as some baneful star that shines for a moment through a rent in the clouds and is again hidden beneath them; even so was Hector now seen in the front ranks and now again in the hindermost, and his bronze armour gleamed like the lightning of ægis-bearing Jove.

And now as a band of reapers mow swathes of wheat or barley upon a rich man's land, and the sheaves fall thick before them, even so did the Trojans and Achæans fall upon one another; they were in no mood for yielding but fought like wolves, and neither side got the better of the other. Discord was glad as she beheld them, for she was the only god that went among them; the others were not there, but stayed quietly each in his own home among the dells and valleys of Olympus. All of them blamed the son of Saturn for wanting to give victory to the Trojans, but father Jove heeded them not: he held aloof from all, and sat apart in his all-glorious majesty, looking down upon the city of the Trojans, the ships of the Achæans, the gleam of bronze, and alike upon the slayers and on the slain.

Now so long as the day waxed and it was still morning, their darts rained thick on one another and the people perished, but as the hour drew nigh when a woodman working in some mountain forest will get his midday meal – for he has felled till his hands are weary; he is tired out, and must now have food – then the Danaans with a cry that rang through all their ranks, broke the battalions of the enemy. Agamemnon led them on, and slew first Bienor, a leader of his people, and afterwards his comrade and charioteer Oïleus, who sprang from his chariot and was coming full towards him; but Agamemnon struck him on the forehead with his spear; his bronze visor was of no avail against the weapon, which pierced both bronze and bone, so that his brains were battered in and he was killed in full fight.

Agamemnon stripped their shirts from off them and left them with their breasts all bare to lie where they had fallen. He then went on to kill Isus and Antiphus two sons of Priam, the one a bastard, the other born in wedlock; they were in the same chariot – the bastard driving, while noble Antiphus fought beside him. Achilles had once taken both of them prisoners in the glades of Ida, and had bound them with fresh withes as they were shepherding, but he had taken a ransom for them; now, however, Agamemnon son of Atreus smote Isus in the chest above the nipple with his spear, while he struck Antiphus hard by the ear and threw him from his chariot. Forthwith he stripped their goodly armour from off them and recognised them, for he had already seen them at the ships when Achilles brought them in from Ida. As a lion fastens on the fawns of a hind and crushes them in his great jaws, robbing them of their tender life while he is on his way back to his lair – the hind can do nothing for them even though she be close by, for she is in an agony of fear, and flies through the thick forest, sweating, and at her utmost speed before the mighty monster – so, no man of the Trojans could help Isus and Antiphus, for they were themselves flying in panic before the Argives.

Then King Agamemnon took the two sons of Antimachus, Pisander and brave Hippolochus. It was Antimachus who had been foremost in preventing Helen's being restored to Menelaus, for he was largely bribed by Alexandrus; and now Agamemnon took his two sons, both in the same chariot, trying to bring their horses to a stand – for they had lost hold of the reins and the horses were mad with fear. The son of Atreus sprang upon them like a lion, and the pair besought him from their chariot. 'Take us alive,' they cried, 'son of Atreus, and you shall receive a great ransom for us. Our father Antimachus has great store of gold, bronze, and wrought iron, and from this he will satisfy you with a very large ransom should he hear of our being alive at the ships of the Achæans.'

With such piteous words and tears did they beseech the king, but they heard no pitiful answer in return. 'If,' said Agamemnon, 'you are sons of Antimachus, who once at a council of Trojans proposed that Menelaus and Ulysses, who had come to you as envoys, should be killed and not suffered to return, you shall now pay for the foul iniquity of your father.'

As he spoke he felled Pisander from his chariot to the earth, smiting him on the chest with his spear, so that he lay face uppermost upon the ground. Hippolochus fled, but him too did Agamemnon smite; he cut off his hands and his head – which he sent rolling in among the crowd as though it were a ball. There he let them both lie, and wherever the ranks were thickest thither he flew, while the other Achæans followed. Foot soldiers drove the foot soldiers of the foe in rout before them, and slew them; horsemen did the like by horsemen, and the thundering tramp of the horses raised a cloud of dust from off the plain. King Agamemnon followed after, ever slaying them and cheering on the Achæans. As when some mighty forest is all ablaze – the eddying gusts whirl fire in all directions till the thickets shrivel and are consumed before the blast of the flame – even so fell the heads of the flying Trojans before Agamemnon son of Atreus, and many a noble pair of steeds drew an empty chariot along the highways of war, for lack of drivers who were lying on the plain, more useful now to vultures than to their wives.

Jove drew Hector away from the darts and dust, with the carnage and din of battle; but the son of Atreus sped onwards, calling out lustily to the Danaans. They flew on by the tomb of old Ilus, son of Dardanus, in the middle of the plain, and past the place of the wild fig-tree making always for the city – the son of Atreus still shouting, and with hands all bedrabbled in gore; but when they had reached the Scæan gates and the oak tree, there they halted and waited for the others to come up. Meanwhile the Trojans kept on flying over the middle of the plain like a herd of cows maddened with fright when a lion has attacked them in the dead of night – he springs on one of them, seizes her neck in the grip of his strong teeth and then laps up her blood and gorges himself upon her entrails – even so did King Agamemnon son of Atreus pursue the foe, ever slaughtering the hindmost as they fled pell-mell before him. Many a man was flung headlong from his chariot by the hand of the son of Atreus, for he wielded his spear with fury.

But when he was just about to reach the high wall and the city, the father of gods and men came down from heaven and took his seat, thunderbolt in hand, upon the crest of many-fountained Ida. He then told Iris of the golden wings to carry a message for him. 'Go,' said he, 'fleet Iris, and speak thus to Hector – say that so long as he sees Agamemnon heading his men and making havoc of the Trojan ranks, he is to keep aloof and bid the others bear the brunt of the battle, but when Agamemnon is wounded either by spear or arrow, and takes to his chariot, then will I vouchsafe him strength to slay till he reach the ships and night falls at the going down of the sun.'

Iris hearkened and obeyed. Down she went to strong Ilius from the crests of Ida, and found Hector son of Priam standing by his chariot and horses. Then she said, 'Hector son of Priam, peer of gods in counsel, father Jove has sent me to bear you this message – so long as you see Agamemnon heading his men and making havoc of the Trojan ranks, you are to keep aloof and bid the others bear the brunt of the battle, but when Agamemnon is wounded either by spear or arrow, and takes to his chariot, then will Jove vouchsafe you strength to slay, till you reach the ships, and till night falls at the going down of the sun.'

When she had thus spoken Iris left him, and Hector sprang full armed from his chariot to the ground, brandishing his spear as he went about everywhere among the host, cheering his men on to fight, and stirring the dread strife of battle. The Trojans then wheeled round, and again met the Achæans, while the Argives on their part strengthened their battalions. The battle was now in array and they stood face to face with one another, Agamemnon ever pressing forward in his eagerness to be ahead of all others.

Tell me now ye Muses that dwell in the mansions of Olympus, who, whether of the Trojans or of their allies, was first to face Agamemnon? It was Iphidamas son of Antenor, a man both brave and of great stature, who was brought up in fertile Thrace the mother of sheep. Cisses, his mother's father, brought him up in his own house when he was a child – Cisses, father to fair Theano. When he reached manhood, Cisses would have kept him there, and was for giving him his daughter in marriage, but as soon as he had married he set out to fight the Achæans with twelve ships that followed him: these he had left at Percote and had come on by land to Ilius. He it was that now met Agamemnon son of Atreus. When they were close up with one another, the son of Atreus missed his aim, and Iphidamas hit him on the girdle below the cuirass and then flung himself upon him, trusting to his strength of arm; the girdle, however, was not pierced, nor nearly so, for the point of the spear struck against the silver and was turned aside as though it had been lead: King Agamemnon caught it from his hand, and drew it towards him with the fury of a lion; he then drew his sword, and killed Iphidamas by striking him on the neck. So there the poor fellow lay, sleeping a sleep as it were of bronze, killed in the defence of his fellow-citizens, far from his wedded wife, of whom he had had no joy though he had given much for her: he had given a hundred head of cattle down, and had promised later on to give a thousand sheep and goats mixed, from the countless flocks of which he was possessed. Agamemnon son of Atreus then despoiled him, and carried off his armour into the host of the Achæans.

When noble Cöon, Antenor's eldest son, saw this, sore indeed were his eyes at the sight of his fallen brother. Unseen by Agamemnon he got beside him, spear in hand, and wounded him in the middle of his arm below the elbow, the point of the spear going right through the arm. Agamemnon was convulsed with pain, but still not even for this did he leave off struggling and fighting, but grasped his spear that flew as fleet as the wind, and sprang upon Cöon who was trying to drag off the body of his brother – his father's son – by the foot, and was crying for help to all the bravest of his comrades; but Agamemnon struck him with a bronze-shod spear and killed him as he was dragging the dead body through the press of men under cover of his shield: he then cut off his head, standing over the body of Iphidamas. Thus did the sons of Antenor meet their fate at the hands of the son of Atreus, and go down into the house of Hades.

As long as the blood still welled warm from his wound Agamemnon went about attacking the ranks of the enemy with spear and sword and with great handfuls of stone, but when the blood had ceased to flow and the wound grew dry, the pain became great. As the sharp pangs which the Eilithuiæ, goddesses of childbirth, daughters of Juno and dispensers of cruel pain, send upon a woman when she is in labour – even so sharp were the pangs of the son of Atreus. He sprang on to his chariot, and bade his charioteer drive to the ships, for he was in great agony. With a loud clear voice he shouted to the Danaans, 'My friends, princes and counsellors of the Argives, defend the ships yourselves, for Jove has not suffered me to fight the whole day through against the Trojans.'

With this the charioteer turned his horses towards the ships, and they flew forward nothing loth. Their chests were white with foam and their bellies with dust, as they drew the wounded king out of the battle.

When Hector saw Agamemnon quit the field, he shouted to the Trojans and Lycians saying, 'Trojans, Lycians, and Dardanian warriors, be men, my friends, and acquit yourselves in battle bravely; their best man has left them, and Jove has vouchsafed me a great triumph; charge the foe with your chariots that you may win still greater glory.'

With these words he put heart and soul into them all, and as a huntsman hounds his dogs on against a lion or wild boar, even so did Hector, peer of Mars, hound the proud Trojans on against the Achæans. Full of hope he plunged in among the foremost, and fell on the fight like some fierce tempest that swoops down upon the sea, and lashes its deep blue waters into fury.

What, then, is the full tale of those whom Hector son of Priam killed in the hour of triumph which Jove then vouchsafed him? First Asæus, Autonoüs, and Opites; Dolops son of Clytius, Opheltius and Agelaus; Æsymnus, Orus and Hipponoüs steadfast in battle; these chieftains of the Achæans did Hector slay, and then he fell upon the rank and file. As when the west wind hustles the clouds of the white south and beats them down with the fierceness of its fury – the waves of the sea roll high, and the spray is flung aloft in the rage of the wandering wind – even so thick were the heads of them that fell by the hand of Hector.

All had then been lost and no help for it, and the Achæans would have fled pell-mell to their ships, had not Ulysses cried out to Diomed, 'Son of Tydeus, what has happened to us that we thus forget our prowess? Come, my good fellow, stand by my side and help me, we shall be shamed for ever if Hector takes the ships.'

And Diomed answered, 'Come what may, I will stand firm; but we shall have scant joy of it, for Jove is minded to give victory to the Trojans rather than to us.'

With these words he struck Thymbræus from his chariot to the ground, smiting him in the left breast with his spear, while Ulysses killed Molion who was his squire. These they let lie, now that they had stopped their fighting; the two heroes then went on playing havoc with the foe, like two wild boars that turn in fury and rend the hounds that hunt them. Thus did they turn upon the Trojans and slay them, and the Achæans were thankful to have breathing time in their flight from Hector.

They then took two princes with their chariot, the two sons of Merops of Percote, who excelled all others in the arts of divination. He had forbidden his sons to go to the war, but they would not obey him, for fate lured them to their fall. Diomed son of Tydeus slew them both and stripped them of their armour, while Ulysses killed Hippodamus and Hypeirochus.

And now the son of Saturn as he looked down from Ida ordained that neither side should have the advantage, and they kept on killing one another. The son of Tydeus speared Agastrophus son of Pæon in the hip-joint with his spear. His chariot was not at hand for him to fly with, so blindly confident had he been. His squire was in charge of it at some distance and he was fighting on foot among the foremost until he lost his life. Hector soon marked the havoc Diomed and

Ulysses were making, and bore down upon them with a loud cry, followed by the Trojan ranks; brave Diomed was dismayed when he saw them, and said to Ulysses who was beside him, 'Great Hector is bearing down upon us and we shall be undone; let us stand firm and wait his onset.'

He poised his spear as he spoke and hurled it, nor did he miss his mark. He had aimed at Hector's head near the top of his helmet, but bronze was turned by bronze, and Hector was untouched, for the spear was stayed by the visored helm made with three plates of metal, which Phœbus Apollo had given him. Hector sprang back with a great bound under cover of the ranks; he fell on his knees and propped himself with his brawny hand leaning on the ground, for darkness had fallen on his eyes. The son of Tydeus having thrown his spear dashed in among the foremost fighters, to the place where he had seen it strike the ground; meanwhile Hector recovered himself and springing back into his chariot mingled with the crowd, by which means he saved his life. But Diomed made at him with his spear and said, 'Dog, you have again got away though death was close on your heels. Phœbus Apollo, to whom I ween you pray ere you go into battle, has again saved you, nevertheless I will meet you and make an end of you hereafter, if there is any god who will stand by me too and be my helper. For the present I must pursue those whom I can lay hands on.'

As he spoke he began stripping the spoils from the son of Pæon, but Alexandrus husband of lovely Helen aimed an arrow at him, leaning against a pillar of the monument which men had raised to Ilus son of Dardanus, a ruler in days of old. Diomed had taken the cuirass from off the breast of Agastrophus, his heavy helmet also, and the shield from off his shoulders, when Paris drew his bow and let fly an arrow that sped not from his hand in vain, but pierced the flat of Diomed's right foot, going right through it and fixing itself in the ground. Thereon Paris with a hearty laugh sprang forward from his hiding-place, and taunted him saying, 'You are wounded – my arrow has not been shot in vain; would that it had hit you in the belly and killed you, for thus the Trojans, who fear you as goats fear a lion, would have had a truce from evil.'

Diomed all undaunted answered, 'Archer, you who without your bow are nothing, slanderer and seducer, if you were to be tried in single combat fighting in full armour, your bow and your arrows would serve you in little stead. Vain is your boast in that you have scratched the sole of my foot. I care no more than if a girl or some silly boy had hit me. A worthless coward can inflict but a light wound; when I wound a man though I but graze his skin it is another matter, for my weapon will lay him low. His wife will tear her cheeks for grief and his children will be fatherless: there will he rot, reddening the earth with his blood, and vultures, not women, will gather round him.'

Thus he spoke, but Ulysses came up and stood over him. Under this cover he sat down to draw the arrow from his foot, and sharp was the pain he suffered as he did so. Then he sprang on to his chariot and bade the charioteer drive him to the ships, for he was sick at heart.

Ulysses was now alone; not one of the Argives stood by him, for they were all panic-stricken. 'Alas,' said he to himself in his dismay, 'what will become of me? It is ill if I turn and fly before these odds, but it will be worse if I am left alone and taken prisoner, for the son of Saturn has struck the rest of the Danaans with panic. But why talk to myself in this way? Well do I know that though cowards quit the field, a hero, whether he wound or be wounded, must stand firm and hold his own.'

While he was thus in two minds, the ranks of the Trojans advanced and hemmed him in, and bitterly did they come to rue it. As hounds and lusty youths set upon a wild boar that sallies from his lair whetting his white tusks – they attack him from every side and can hear the gnashing of his jaws, but for all his fierceness they still hold their ground – even so furiously did the Trojans attack Ulysses. First he sprang spear in hand upon Deïopites and wounded him on the shoulder with a downward blow; then he killed Thoön and Ennomus. After these he struck Chersidamas in the loins under his shield as he had just sprung down from his chariot; so he fell in the dust and clutched the earth in the hollow of his hand. These he let lie, and went on to wound Charops son of Hippasus own brother to noble Socus. Socus, hero that he was, made all speed to help him, and when he was close to Ulysses he said, 'Far-famed Ulysses, insatiable of craft and toil, this day you shall either boast of having killed both the sons of Hippasus and stripped them of their armour, or you shall fall before my spear.'

With these words he struck the shield of Ulysses. The spear went through the shield and passed on through his richly wrought cuirass, tearing the flesh from his side, but Pallas Minerva did not suffer it to pierce the entrails of the hero. Ulysses knew that his hour was not yet come, but he gave ground and said to Socus, 'Wretch, you shall now surely die. You have stayed me from fighting further with the Trojans, but you shall now fall by my spear, yielding glory to myself, and your soul to Hades of the noble steeds.'

Socus had turned in flight, but as he did so, the spear struck him in the back midway between the shoulders, and went right through his chest. He fell heavily to the ground and Ulysses vaunted over him saying, 'O Socus, son of Hippasus tamer of horses, death has been too quick for you and you have not escaped him: poor wretch, not even in death shall your father and mother close your eyes, but the ravening vultures shall enshroud you with the flapping of their dark wings and devour you. Whereas even though I fall the Achæans will give me my due rites of burial.'

So saying he drew Socus's heavy spear out of his flesh and from his shield, and the blood welled forth when the spear was withdrawn so that he was much dismayed. When the Trojans saw that Ulysses was bleeding they raised a great shout and came on in a body towards him; he therefore gave ground, and called his comrades to come and help him. Thrice did he cry as loudly as man can cry, and thrice did brave Menelaus hear him; he turned, therefore, to Ajax who was close beside him and said, 'Ajax, noble son of Telamon, captain of your people, the cry of Ulysses rings in my ears, as though the Trojans had cut him off and were worsting him while he is single-handed. Let us make our way through the throng; it will be well that we defend him; I fear he may come to harm for all his valour if he be left without support, and the Danaans would miss him sorely.'

He led the way and mighty Ajax went with him. The Trojans had gathered round Ulysses like ravenous mountain jackals round the carcase of some horned stag that has been hit with an arrow – the stag has fled at full speed so long as his blood was warm and his strength has lasted, but when the arrow has overcome him, the savage jackals devour him in the shady glades of the forest. Then heaven sends a fierce lion thither, whereon the jackals fly in terror and the lion robs them of their prey – even so did Trojans many and brave gather round crafty Ulysses, but the hero stood at bay and kept them off with his spear. Ajax then came up with his shield before him like a wall, and stood hard by, whereon the Trojans fled in all directions. Menelaus took Ulysses by the hand, and led him out of the press while his squire brought up his chariot, but Ajax rushed furiously on the Trojans and killed Doryclus, a bastard son of Priam; then he wounded Pandocus, Lysandrus, Pyrasus, and Pylartes; as some swollen torrent comes rushing in full flood from the mountains on to the plain, big with the rain of heaven – many a dry oak and many a pine does it engulf, and much mud does it bring down and cast into the sea – even so did brave Ajax chase the foe furiously over the plain, slaying both men and horses.

Hector did not yet know what Ajax was doing, for he was fighting on the extreme left of the battle by the banks of the river Scamander, where the carnage was thickest and the war-cry loudest round Nestor and brave Idomeneus. Among these Hector was making great slaughter with his spear and furious driving, and was destroying the ranks that were opposed to him; still the Achæans would have given no ground, had not Alexandrus husband of lovely Helen stayed the prowess of Machaon shepherd of his people, by wounding him in the right shoulder with a triple-barbed arrow. The Achæans were in great fear that as the fight had turned against them the Trojans might take him prisoner, and Idomeneus said to Nestor, 'Nestor son of Neleus, honour to the Achæan name, mount your chariot at once; take Machaon with you and drive your horses to the ships as fast as you can. A physician is worth more than several other men put together, for he can cut out arrows and spread healing herbs.'

Nestor knight of Gerene did as Idomeneus had counselled; he at once mounted his chariot, and Machaon son of the famed physician Æsculapius went with him. He lashed his horses and they flew onward nothing loth towards the ships, as though of their own free will.

Then Cebriones seeing the Trojans in confusion said to Hector from his place beside him, 'Hector, here are we two fighting on the extreme wing of the battle, while the other Trojans are in pell-mell rout, they and their horses. Ajax son of Telamon is driving them before him; I know him by the breadth of his shield: let us turn our chariot and horses thither, where horse and foot are fighting most desperately, and where the cry of battle is loudest.'

With this he lashed his goodly steeds, and when they felt the whip they drew the chariot full speed among the Achæans and Trojans, over the bodies and shields of those that had fallen: the axle was bespattered with blood, and the rail round the car was covered with splashes both from the horses' hoofs and from the tyres of the wheels. Hector tore his way through and flung himself into the thick of the fight, and his presence threw the Danaans into confusion, for his spear was not long idle; nevertheless though he went among the ranks with sword and spear, and throwing great stones, he avoided Ajax son of Telamon, for Jove would have been angry with him if he had fought a better man than himself.

Then father Jove from his high throne struck fear into the heart of Ajax, so that he stood there dazed and threw his shield behind him – looking fearfully at the throng of his foes as though he were some wild beast, and turning hither and thither but crouching slowly backwards. As peasants with their hounds chase a lion from their stockyard, and watch by night to prevent his carrying off the pick of their herd – he makes his greedy spring, but in vain, for the darts from many a strong hand fall thick around him, with burning brands that scare him for all his fury, and when morning comes he slinks foiled and angry away – even so did Ajax, sorely against his will, retreat angrily before the Trojans, fearing for the ships of the Achæans. Or as some lazy ass that has had many a cudgel broken about his back, when he gets into a field begins eating the corn – boys beat him but he is too many for them, and though they lay about with their sticks they cannot hurt him; still when he has had his fill they at last drive him from the field – even so did the Trojans and their allies pursue great Ajax, ever smiting the middle of his shield with their darts. Now and again he would turn and show fight, keeping back the battalions of the Trojans, and then he would again retreat; but he prevented any of them from making his way to the ships. Single-handed he stood midway between the Trojans and Achæans: the spears that sped from their hands stuck some of them in his mighty shield, while many, though thirsting for his blood, fell to the ground ere they could reach him to the wounding of his fair flesh.

Now when Eurypylus the brave son of Euæmon saw that Ajax was being overpowered by the rain of arrows, he went up to him and hurled his spear. He struck Apisaon son of Phausius in the liver below the midriff, and laid him low. Eurypylus sprang upon him, and stripped the armour from his shoulders; but when Alexandrus saw him, he aimed an arrow at him which struck him in the right thigh; the arrow broke, but the point that was left in the wound dragged on the thigh; he drew back, therefore, under cover of his comrades to save his life, shouting as he did so to the Danaans, 'My friends, princes and counsellors of the Argives, rally to the defence of Ajax who is being overpowered, and I doubt whether he will come out of the fight alive. Hither, then, to the rescue of great Ajax son of Telamon.'

Even so did he cry when he was wounded; thereon the others came near, and gathered round him, holding their shields upwards from their shoulders so as to give him cover. Ajax then made towards them, and turned round to stand at bay as soon as he had reached his men.

Thus then did they fight as it were a flaming fire. Meanwhile the mares of Neleus, all in a lather with sweat, were bearing Nestor out of the fight, and with him Machaon shepherd of his people. Achilles saw and took note, for he was standing on the stern of his ship watching the hard stress and struggle of the fight. He called from the ship to his comrade Patroclus, who heard him in the tent and came out looking like Mars himself – here indeed was the beginning of the ill that presently befell him. 'Why,' said he, 'Achilles, do you call me? what do you want with me?' And Achilles answered, 'Noble son of Menœtius, man after my own heart, I take it that I shall now have the Achæans praying at my knees, for they are in great straits; go, Patroclus, and ask Nestor who it is that he is bearing away wounded from the field; from his back I should say it was Machaon son of Æsculapius, but I could not see his face for the horses went by me at full speed.'

Patroclus did as his dear comrade had bidden him, and set off running by the ships and tents of the Achæans.

When Nestor and Machaon had reached the tents of the son of Neleus, they dismounted, and an esquire, Eurymedon, took the horses from the chariot. The pair then stood in the breeze by the seaside to dry the sweat from their shirts, and when they had so done they came inside and took their seats. Fair Hecamedè, whom Nestor had had awarded to him from Tenedos when Achilles took it, mixed them a mess; she was daughter of wise Arsinöus, and the Achæans had given her to Nestor because he excelled all of them in counsel. First she set for them a fair and well-made table that had feet of cyanus; on it there was a vessel of bronze and an onion to give relish to the drink, with honey and cakes of barley-meal. There was also a cup of rare workmanship which the old man had brought with him from home, studded with bosses of gold; it had four handles, on each of which there were two golden doves feeding, and it had two feet to stand on. Any one else would hardly have been able to lift it from the table when it was full, but Nestor could do so quite easily. In this the woman, as fair as a goddess, mixed them a mess with Pramnian wine; she grated goat's-milk cheese into it with a bronze grater, threw in a handful of white barley-meal, and having thus prepared the mess she bade them drink it. When they had done so and had thus quenched their thirst, they fell talking with one another, and at this moment Patroclus appeared at the door.

When the old man saw him he sprang from his seat, seized his hand, led him into the tent, and bade him take his place among them; but Patroclus stood where he was and said, 'Noble sir, I may not stay, you cannot persuade me to come in; he that sent me is not one to be trifled with, and he bade me ask who the wounded man was whom you were bearing away from the field. I can now see for myself that he is Machaon shepherd of his people. I must go back and tell Achilles. You, sir, know what a terrible man he is, and how ready to blame even where no blame should lie.'

And Nestor answered, 'Why should Achilles care to know how many of the Achæans may be wounded? He recks not of the dismay that reigns in our host; our most valiant chieftains lie disabled, brave Diomed son of Tydeus is wounded; so are Ulysses and Agamemnon; Eurypylus has been hit with an arrow in the thigh, and I have just been bringing this man from the field – he too wounded with an arrow; nevertheless Achilles, so valiant though he be, cares not and knows no ruth. Will he wait till the ships, do what we may, are in a blaze, and we perish one upon the other? As for me, I have no strength nor stay in me any longer; would that I were still young and strong as in the days when there was a fight between us and the men of Elis about some cattle-raiding. I then killed Itymoneus the valiant son of Hypeirochus a dweller in Elis, as I was driving in the spoil; he was hit by a dart thrown by my hand while fighting in the front rank in defence of his cows, so he fell and the country people around him were in great fear. We drove off a vast quantity of booty from the plain, fifty herds of cattle and as many flocks of sheep; fifty droves also of pigs, and as many wide-spreading flocks of goats. Of horses moreover we seized a hundred and fifty, all of them mares, and many had foals running with them.

All these did we drive by night to Pylus the city of Neleus, taking them within the city; and the heart of Neleus was glad in that I had taken so much, though it was the first time I had ever been in the field. At daybreak the heralds went round crying that all in Elis to whom there was a debt owing should come; and the leading Pylians assembled to divide the spoils. There were many to whom the Epeans owed chattels, for we men of Pylus were few and had been oppressed with wrong; in former years Hercules had come, and had laid his hand heavy upon us, so that all our best men had perished. Neleus had had twelve sons, but I alone was left; the others had all been killed. The Epeans presuming upon all this had looked down upon us and had done us much evil. My father chose a herd of cattle and a great flock of sheep – three hundred in all – and he took their shepherds with him, for there was a great debt due to him in Elis, to wit four horses, winners of prizes. They and their chariots with them had gone to the games and were to run for a tripod, but King Augeas took them, and sent back their driver grieving for the loss of his horses. Neleus was angered by what he had both said and done, and took great value in return, but he divided the rest, that no man might have less than his full share.

'Thus did we order all things, and offer sacrifices to the gods throughout the city; but three days afterwards the Epeans came in a body, many in number, they and their chariots, in full array, and with them the two Moliones in their armour, though they were still lads and unused to fighting. Now there is a certain town, Thryoëssa, perched upon a rock on the river Alpheus, the border city of Pylus; this they would destroy, and pitched their camp about it, but when they had crossed their whole plain, Minerva darted down by night from Olympus and bade us set ourselves in array; and she found willing soldiers in Pylos, for the men meant fighting. Neleus would not let me arm, and hid my horses, for he said that as yet I could know nothing about war; nevertheless Minerva so ordered the fight that, all on foot as I was, I fought among our mounted forces and vied with the foremost of them.

There is a river Minyeius that falls into the sea near Arene, and there they that were mounted (and I with them) waited till morning, when the companies of foot soldiers came up with us in force. Thence in full panoply and equipment we came towards noon to the sacred waters of the Alpheus, and there we offered victims to almighty Jove, with a bull to Alpheus, another to Neptune, and a herd-heifer to Minerva. After this we took supper in our companies, and laid us down to rest each in his armour by the river.

'The Epeans were beleaguering the city and were determined to take it, but ere this might be there was a desperate fight in store for them. When the sun's rays began to fall upon the earth we joined battle, praying to Jove and to Minerva, and when the fight had begun, I was the first to kill my man and take his horses – to wit the warrior Mulius. He was son-in-law to Augeas, having married his eldest daughter, golden-haired Agamedé, who knew the virtues of every herb which grows upon the face of the earth. I speared him as he was coming towards me, and when he fell headlong in the dust, I sprang upon his chariot and took my place in the front ranks. The Epeans fled in all directions when they saw the captain of their horsemen (the best man they had) laid low, and I swept down on them like a whirlwind, taking fifty chariots – and in each of them two men bit the dust, slain by my spear. I should have even killed the two Moliones sons of Actor, unless their real father, Neptune lord of the earthquake, had hidden them in a thick mist and borne them out of the fight. Thereon Jove vouchsafed the Pylians a great victory, for we chased them far over the plain, killing the men and bringing in their armour, till we had brought our horses to Buprasium rich in wheat and to the Olenian rock, with the hill that is called Alision, at which point Minerva turned the people back. There I slew the last man and left him; then the Achæans drove their horses back from Buprasium to Pylos and gave thanks to Jove among the gods, and among mortal men to Nestor.

'Such was I among my peers, as surely as ever was, but Achilles is for keeping all his valour for himself; bitterly will he rue it hereafter when the host is being cut to pieces. My good friend, did not Menœtius charge you thus, on the day when he sent you from Phthia to Agamemnon? Ulysses and I were in the house, inside, and heard all that he said to you; for we came to the fair house of Peleus while beating up recruits throughout all Achæa, and when we got there we found Menœtius and yourself, and Achilles with you. The old knight Peleus was in the outer court, roasting the fat thigh-bones of a heifer to Jove the lord of thunder; and he held a gold chalice in his hand from which he poured drink-offerings of wine over the burning sacrifice. You two were busy cutting up the heifer, and at that moment we stood at the gates, whereon Achilles sprang to his feet, led us by the hand into the house, placed us at table, and set before us such hospitable entertainment as guests expect. When we had satisfied ourselves with meat and drink, I said my say and urged both of you to join us. You were ready enough to do so, and the two old men charged you much and straitly. Old Peleus bade his son Achilles fight ever among the foremost and outvie his peers, while Menœtius the son of Actor spoke thus to you: "My son," said he, "Achilles is of nobler birth than you are, but you are older than he, though he is far the better man of the two. Counsel him wisely, guide him in the right way, and he will follow you to his own profit." Thus did your father charge you, but you have forgotten; nevertheless, even now, say all this to Achilles if he will listen to you. Who knows but with heaven's help you may talk him over, for it is good to take a friend's advice. If, however, he is fearful about some oracle, or if his mother has told him something from Jove, then let him send you, and let the rest of the Myrmidons follow with you, if perchance you may bring light and saving to the Danaans. And let him send you into battle clad in his own armour, that the Trojans may mistake you for him and leave off fighting; the sons of the Achæans may thus have time to get their breath, for they are hard pressed and there is little breathing time in battle. You, who are fresh, might easily drive a tired enemy back to his walls and away from the tents and ships.'

With these words he moved the heart of Patroclus, who set off running by the line of the ships to Achilles, descendant of Æacus. When he had got as far as the ships of Ulysses, where was their place of assembly and court of justice, with their altars dedicated to the gods, Eurypylus son of Euæmon met him, wounded in the thigh with an arrow, and limping out of the fight. Sweat rained from his head and shoulders, and black blood welled from his cruel wound, but his mind did not wander. The son of Menœtius when he saw him had compassion upon him and spoke piteously saying, 'O unhappy princes and counsellors of the Danaans, are you then doomed to feed the hounds of Troy with your fat, far from your friends and your native land? say, noble Eurypylus, will the Achæans be able to hold great Hector in check, or will they fall now before his spear?'

Wounded Eurypylus made answer, 'Noble Patroclus, there is no hope left for the Achæans but they will perish at their ships. All they that were princes among us are lying struck down and wounded at the hands of the Trojans, who are waxing stronger and stronger. But save me and take me to your ship; cut out the arrow from my thigh; wash the black blood from off it with warm water, and lay upon it those gracious herbs which, so they say, have been shown you by Achilles, who was himself shown them by Chiron, most righteous of all the centaurs. For of the physicians Podalirius and Machaon, I hear that the one is lying wounded in his tent and is himself in need of healing, while the other is fighting the Trojans upon the plain.'

'Hero Eurypylus,' replied the brave son of Menœtius, 'how may these things be? What can I do? I am on my way to bear a message to noble Achilles from Nestor of Gerene, bulwark of the Achæans, but even so I will not be unmindful of your distress.'

With this he clasped him round the middle and led him into the tent, and a servant, when he saw him, spread bullock-skins on the ground for him to lie on. He laid him at full length and cut out the sharp arrow from his thigh; he washed the black blood from the wound with warm water; he then crushed a bitter herb, rubbing it between his hands, and spread it upon the wound; this was a virtuous herb which killed all pain; so the wound presently dried and the blood left off flowing.

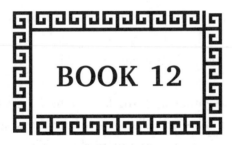

BOOK 12

The Trojans and their allies break the wall, led on by Hector.

So the son of Menœtius was attending to the hurt of Eurypylus within the tent, but the Argives and Trojans still fought desperately, nor were the trench and the high wall above it, to keep the Trojans in check longer. They had built it to protect their ships, and had dug the trench all round it that it might safeguard both the ships and the rich spoils which they had taken, but they had not offered hecatombs to the gods. It had been built without the consent of the immortals, and therefore it did not last. So long as Hector lived and Achilles nursed his anger, and so long as the city of Priam remained untaken, the great wall of the Achæans stood firm; but when the bravest of the Trojans were no more, and many also of the Argives, though some were yet left alive – when, moreover, the city was sacked in the tenth year, and the Argives had gone back with their ships to their own country – then Neptune and Apollo took counsel to destroy the wall, and they turned on to it the streams of all the rivers from Mount Ida into the sea, Rhesus, Heptaporus, Caresus, Rhodius, Grenicus, Æsopus, and goodly Scamander, with Simois, where many a shield and helm had fallen, and many a hero of the race of demigods had bitten the dust. Phœbus Apollo turned the mouths of all these rivers together and made them flow for nine days against the wall, while Jove rained the whole time that he might wash it sooner into the sea. Neptune himself, trident in hand, surveyed the work and threw into the sea all the foundations of beams and stones which the Achæans had laid with so much toil; he made all level by the mighty stream of the Hellespout, and then when he had swept the wall away he spread a great beach of sand over the place where it had been. This done he turned the rivers back into their old courses.

This was what Neptune and Apollo were to do in after time; but as yet battle and turmoil were still raging round the wall till its timbers rang under the blows that rained upon them. The Argives, cowed by the scourge of Jove, were hemmed in at their ships in fear of Hector the mighty minister of Rout, who as heretofore fought with the force and fury of a whirlwind. As a lion or wild boar turns fiercely on the dogs and men that attack him, while these form a solid wall and shower their javelins as they face him – his courage is all undaunted, but his high spirit will be the death of him; many a time does he charge at his pursuers to scatter them, and they fall back as often as he does so – even so did Hector go about among the host exhorting his men, and cheering them on to cross the trench.

But the horses dared not do so, and stood neighing upon its brink, for the width frightened them. They could neither jump it nor cross it, for it had overhanging banks all round upon either side, above which there were the sharp stakes that the sons of the Achæans had planted so close and strong as a defence against all who would assail it; a horse, therefore, could not get into it and draw his chariot after him, but those who were on foot kept trying their very utmost. Then Polydamas went up to Hector and said, 'Hector, and you other captains of the Trojans and allies, it is madness for us to try and drive our horses across the trench; it will be very hard to cross, for it is full of sharp stakes, and beyond these there is the wall. Our horses therefore cannot get down into it, and would be of no use if they did; moreover it is a narrow place and we should come to harm. If, indeed, great Jove is minded to help the Trojans, and in his anger will utterly destroy the Achæans, I would myself gladly see them perish now and here far from Argos; but if they should rally and we are driven back from the ships pell-mell into the trench there will be not so much as a man get back to the city to tell the tale. Now, therefore, let us all do as I say; let our squires hold our horses by the trench, but let us follow Hector in a body on foot, clad in full armour, and if the day of their doom is at hand the Achæans will not be able to withstand us.'

Thus spoke Polydamas and his saying pleased Hector, who sprang in full armour to the ground, and all the other Trojans, when they saw him do so, also left their chariots. Each man then gave his horses over to his charioteer in charge to hold them ready for him at the trench. Then they formed themselves into companies, made themselves ready, and in five bodies followed their leaders. Those that went with Hector and Polydamas were the bravest and most in number, and the most determined to break through the wall and fight at the ships. Cebriones was also joined with them as third in command, for Hector had left his chariot in charge of a less valiant soldier. The next company was led by Paris, Alcathoüs, and Agenor; the third by Helenus and Deïphobus, two sons of Priam, and with them was the hero Asius – Asius the son of Hyrtacus, whose great black horses of the breed that comes from the river Selleis had brought him from Arisbe. Æneas the valiant son of Anchises led the fourth; he and the two sons of Antenor, Archelochus and Acamas, men well versed in all the arts of war. Sarpedon was captain over the allies, and took with him Glaucus and Asteropæus whom he deemed most valiant after himself – for he was far the best man of them all. These helped to array one another in their ox-hide shields, and then charged straight at the Danaans, for they felt sure that they would not hold out longer and that they should themselves now fall upon the ships.

The rest of the Trojans and their allies now followed the counsel of Polydamas, but Asius son of Hyrtacus would not leave his horses and his esquire behind him; in his foolhardiness he took them on with him towards the ships, nor did he fail to come by his end in consequence. Nevermore was he to return to wind-beaten Ilius, exulting in his chariot and his horses; ere he could do so, death of ill-omened name had overshadowed him and he had fallen by the spear of

Idomeneus the noble son of Deucalion. He had driven towards the left wing of the ships, by which way the Achæans used to return with their chariots and horses from the plain. Hither he drove and found the gates with their doors opened wide, and the great bar down – for the gatemen kept them open so as to let those of their comrades enter who might be flying towards the ships. Hither of set purpose did he direct his horses, and his men followed him with a loud cry, for they felt sure that the Achæans would not hold out longer, and that they should now fall upon the ships. Little did they know that at the gates they should find two of the bravest chieftains, proud sons of the fighting Lapithæ – the one, Polypœtes, mighty son of Pirithoüs, and the other Leonteus, peer of murderous Mars. These stood before the gates like two high oak trees upon the mountains, that tower from their wide-spreading roots, and year after year battle with wind and rain – even so did these two men await the onset of great Asius confidently and without flinching. The Trojans led by him and by Iamenus, Orestes, Adamas the son of Asius, Thöon and Œnomaus, raised a loud cry of battle and made straight for the wall, holding their shields of dry ox-hide above their heads; for a while the two defenders remained inside and cheered the Achæans on to stand firm in the defence of their ships; when, however, they saw that the Trojans were attacking the wall, while the Danaans were crying out for help and being routed, they rushed outside and fought in front of the gates like two wild boars upon the mountains that abide the attack of men and dogs, and charging on either side break down the wood all round them tearing it up by the roots, and one can hear the clattering of their tusks, till some one hits them and makes an end of them – even so did the gleaming bronze rattle about their breasts, as the weapons fell upon them; for they fought with great fury, trusting to their own prowess and to those who were on the wall above them. These threw great stones at their assailants in defence of themselves, their tents, and their ships. The stones fell thick as the flakes of snow which some fierce blast drives from the dark clouds and showers down in sheets upon the earth – even so fell the weapons from the hands alike of Trojans and Achæans. Helmet and shield rang out as the great stones rained upon them, and Asius the son of Hyrtacus in his dismay cried aloud and smote his two thighs. 'Father Jove,' he cried, 'of a truth you too are altogether given to lying. I made sure the Argive heroes could not withstand us, whereas like slim-waisted wasps, or bees that have their nests in the rocks by the wayside – they leave not the holes wherein they have built undefended, but fight for their little ones against all who would take them – even so these men, though they be but two, will not be driven from the gates, but stand firm either to slay or be slain.'

He spoke, but moved not the mind of Jove, whose counsel it then was to give glory to Hector. Meanwhile the rest of the Trojans were fighting about the other gates; I, however, am no god to be able to tell about all these things, for the battle raged everywhere about the stone wall as it were a fiery furnace. The Argives, discomfited though they were, were forced to defend their ships, and all the gods who were defending the Achæans were vexed in spirit; but the Lapithæ kept on fighting with might and main.

Thereon Polypœtes, mighty son of Pirithoüs, hit Damasus with a spear upon his cheek-pierced helmet. The helmet did not protect him, for the point of the spear went through it, and broke the bone, so that the brain inside was scattered about, and he died fighting. He then slew Pylon and Ormenus. Leonteus, of the race of Mars, killed Hippomachus the son of Antimachus by striking him with his spear upon the girdle. He then drew his sword and sprang first upon Antiphates whom he killed in close combat, and who fell face upwards on the earth. After him he killed Menon, Iamenus, and Orestes, and laid them low one after the other.

While they were busy stripping the armour from these heroes, the youths who were led on by Polydamas and Hector (and these were the greater part and the most valiant of those that were trying to break through the wall and fire the ships) were still standing by the trench, uncertain what they should do; for they had seen a sign from heaven when they had essayed to cross it – a soaring eagle that flew skirting the left wing of their host, with a monstrous blood-red snake in its talons still alive and struggling to escape. The snake was still bent on revenge, wriggling and twisting itself backwards till it struck the bird that held it, on the neck and breast; whereon the bird being in pain, let it fall, dropping it into the middle of the host, and then flew down the wind with a sharp cry. The Trojans were struck with terror when they saw the snake, portent of ægis-bearing Jove, writhing in the midst of them, and Polydamas went up to Hector and said, 'Hector, at our councils of war you are ever given to rebuke me, even when I speak wisely, as though it were not well, forsooth, that one of the people should cross your will either in the field or at the council board; you would have them support you always: nevertheless I will say what I think will be best; let us not now go on to fight the Danaans at their ships, for I know what will happen if this soaring eagle which skirted the left wing of our host with a monstrous blood-red snake in its talons (the snake being still alive) was really sent as an omen to the Trojans on their essaying to cross the trench. The eagle let go her hold; she did not succeed in taking it home to her little ones, and so will it be with ourselves; even though by a mighty effort we break through the gates and wall of the Achæans, and they give way before us, still we shall not return in good order by the way we came, but shall leave many a man behind us whom the Achæans will do to death in defence of their ships. Thus would any seer who was expert in these matters, and was trusted by the people, read the portent.'

Hector looked fiercely at him and said, 'Polydamas, I like not of your reading. You can find a better saying than this if you will. If, however, you have spoken in good earnest, then indeed has heaven robbed you of your reason. You would have me pay no heed to the counsels of Jove, nor to the promises he made me – and he bowed his head in confirmation; you bid me be ruled rather by the flight of wild-fowl. What care I whether they fly towards dawn or dark, and whether they be on my right hand or on my left? Let us put our trust rather in the counsel of great Jove, king of mortals and immortals. There is one omen, and one only – that a man should fight for his country. Why are you so fearful? Though we be all of us slain at the ships of the Argives you are not likely to be killed yourself, for you are not steadfast nor courageous. If you will not fight, or would talk others over from doing so, you shall fall forthwith before my spear.'

With these words he led the way, and the others followed after with a cry that rent the air. Then Jove the lord of thunder sent the blast of a mighty wind from the mountains of Ida, that bore the dust down towards the ships; he thus lulled the Achæans into security, and gave victory to Hector and to the Trojans, who, trusting to their own might and to the signs he had shown them, essayed to break through the great wall of the Achæans. They tore down the breastworks from the walls, and overthrew the battlements; they upheaved the buttresses, which the Achæans had set in front of the wall in order to support it; when they had pulled these down they made sure of breaking through the wall, but the Danaans still showed no sign of giving ground; they still fenced the battlements with their shields of ox-hide, and hurled their missiles down upon the foe as soon as any came below the wall.

The two Ajaxes went about everywhere on the walls cheering on the Achæans, giving fair words to some while they spoke sharply to any one whom they saw to be remiss. 'My friends,' they cried, 'Argives one and all – good, bad, and indifferent, for there was never fight yet, in which all were of equal prowess – there is now work enough, as you very well know, for all of you. See that you none of you turn in flight towards the ships, daunted by the shouting of the foe, but press forward and keep one another in heart, if it may so be that Olympian Jove the lord of lightning will vouchsafe us to repel our foes, and drive them back towards the city.'

Thus did the two go about shouting and cheering the Achæans on. As the flakes that fall thick upon a winter's day, when Jove is minded to snow and to display these his arrows to mankind – he lulls the wind to rest, and snows hour after hour till he has buried the tops of the high mountains, the headlands that jut into the sea, the grassy plains, and the tilled fields of men; the snow lies deep upon the forelands and havens of the grey sea, but the waves as they come rolling in stay it that it can come no further, though all else is wrapped as with a mantle so heavy are the heavens with snow – even thus thickly did the stones fall on one side and on the other, some thrown at the Trojans, and some by the Trojans at the Achæans; and the whole wall was in an uproar.

Still the Trojans and brave Hector would not yet have broken down the gates and the great bar, had not Jove turned his son Sarpedon against the Argives as a lion against a herd of horned cattle. Before him he held his shield of hammered bronze, that the smith had beaten so fair and round, and had lined with ox hides which he had made fast with rivets of gold all round the shield; this he held in front of him, and brandishing his two spears came on like some lion of the wilderness, who has been long famished for want of meat and will dare break even into a well-fenced homestead to try and get at the sheep. He may find the shepherds keeping watch over their flocks with dogs and spears, but he is in no mind to be driven from the fold till he has had a try for it; he will either spring on a sheep and carry it off, or be hit by a spear from some strong hand – even so was Sarpedon fain to attack the wall and break down its battlements. Then he said to Glaucus son of Hippolochus, 'Glaucus, why in Lycia do we receive especial honour as regards our place at table? Why are the choicest portions served us and our cups kept brimming, and why do men look up to us as though we were gods? Moreover we hold a large estate by the banks of the river Xanthus, fair with orchard lawns and wheat-growing land; it becomes us, therefore, to take our stand at the head of all the Lycians and bear the brunt of the fight, that one may say to another, "Our princes in Lycia eat the fat of the land and drink the best of wine, but they are fine fellows; they fight well and are ever at the front in battle." My good friend, if, when we were once out of this fight, we could escape old age and death thenceforward and for ever, I should neither press forward myself nor bid you do so, but death in ten thousand shapes hangs ever over our heads, and no man can elude him; therefore let us go forward and either win glory for ourselves, or yield it to another.'

Glaucus heeded his saying, and the pair forthwith led on the host of Lycians. Menestheus son of Peteos was dismayed when he saw them, for it was against his part of the wall that they came – bringing destruction with them; he looked along the wall for some chieftain to support his comrades and saw the two Ajaxes, men ever eager for the fray, and Teucer, who had just come from his tent, standing near them; but he could not make his voice heard by shouting to them, so great an uproar was there from clashing shields and helmets and the battering of gates with a din which reached the skies. For all the gates had been closed, and the Trojans were hammering at them to try and break their way through them. Menestheus, therefore, sent Thoötes with a message to Ajax. 'Run, good Thoötes,' said he, 'and call Ajax, or better still bid both come, for it will be all over with us here directly; the leaders of the Lycians are upon us, men who have ever fought desperately here-tofore. But if the pair have too much on their hands to let them both come, at any rate let Ajax son of Telamon do so, and let Teucer the famous bowman come with him.'

The messenger did as he was told, and set off running along the wall of the Achæans. When he reached the Ajaxes he said to them, 'Sirs, princes of the Argives, the son of noble Peteos bids you come to him for a while and help him. You had better both come if you can, or it will be all over with him directly; the leaders of the Lycians are upon him, men who have ever fought desperately here-tofore; if you have too much on your hands to let both come, at any rate let Ajax son of Telamon do so, and let Teucer the famous bowman come with him.'

Great Ajax, son of Telamon, heeded the message, and at once spoke to the son of Oïleus. 'Ajax,' said he, 'do you two, yourself and brave Lycomedes, stay here and keep the Danaans in heart to fight their hardest. I will go over yonder, and bear my part in the fray, but I will come back here at once as soon as I have given them the help they need.'

With this, Ajax son of Telamon set off, and Teucer his brother by the same father went also, with Pandion to carry Teucer's bow. They went along inside the wall, and when they came to the tower where Menestheus was (and hard pressed indeed did they find him) the brave captains and leaders of the Lycians were storming the battlements as it were a thick dark cloud, fighting in close quarters, and raising the battle-cry aloud.

First, Ajax son of Telamon killed brave Epicles, a comrade of Sarpedon, hitting him with a jagged stone that lay by the battlements at the very top of the wall. As men now are, even one who is in the bloom of youth could hardly lift it with his two hands, but Ajax raised it high aloft and flung it down, smashing Epicles' four-crested helmet so that the bones of his head were crushed to pieces, and he fell from the high wall as though he were diving, with no more life left in him. Then Teucer wounded Glaucus the brave son of Hippolochus as he was coming on to attack the wall. He saw his shoulder bare and aimed an arrow at it, which made Glaucus leave off fighting. Thereon he sprang covertly down for fear some of the Achæans might see that he was wounded and taunt him. Sarpedon was stung with grief when he saw Glaucus leave him, still he did not leave off fighting, but aimed his spear at Alcmaon the son of Thestor and hit him. He drew his spear back again and Alcmaon came down headlong after it with his bronzed armour rattling round him. Then Sarpedon seized the battlement in his strong hands, and tugged at it till it all gave way together, and a breach was made through which many might pass.

Ajax and Teucer then both of them attacked him. Teucer hit him with an arrow on the band that bore the shield which covered his body, but Jove saved his son from destruction that he might not fall by the ships' sterns. Meanwhile Ajax sprang on him and pierced his shield, but the spear did not go clean through, though it hustled him back that he could come on no further. He therefore retired a little space from the battlement, yet without losing all his ground, for he still thought to cover himself with glory. Then he turned round and shouted to the brave Lycians saying, 'Lycians, why do you thus fail me? For all my prowess I cannot break through the wall and open a way to the ships single-handed. Come close on behind me, for the more there are of us the better.'

The Lycians, shamed by his rebuke, pressed closer round him who was their counsellor and their king. The Argives on their part got their men in fighting order within the wall, and there was a deadly struggle between them. The Lycians could not break through the wall and force their way to the ships, nor could the Danaans drive the Lycians from the wall now that they had once reached it. As two men, measuring-rods in hand, quarrel about their boundaries in a field that they own in common, and stickle for their rights though they be but in a mere strip, even so did the battlements now serve as a bone of contention, and they beat one another's round shields for their possession. Many a man's body was wounded with the pitiless bronze, as he turned round and bared his back to the foe, and many were struck clean through their shields; the wall and battlements were everywhere deluged with the blood alike of Trojans and of Achæans. But even so the Trojans could not rout the Achæans, who still held on; and as some honest hard-working woman weighs wool in her balance and sees that the scales be true, for she would gain some pitiful earnings for her little ones, even so was the fight balanced evenly between them till the time came when Jove gave the greater glory to Hector son of Priam, who was first to spring towards the wall of the Achæans. As he did so, he cried aloud to the Trojans, 'Up, Trojans, break the wall of the Argives, and fling fire upon their ships.'

Thus did he hound them on, and in one body they rushed straight at the wall as he had bidden them, and scaled the battlements with sharp spears in their hands. Hector laid hold of a stone that lay just outside the gates and was thick at one end but pointed at the other;

two of the best men in a town, as men now are, could hardly raise it from the ground and put it on to a waggon, but Hector lifted it quite easily by himself, for the son of scheming Saturn made it light for him. As a shepherd picks up a ram's fleece with one hand and finds it no burden, so easily did Hector lift the great stone and drive it right at the doors that closed the gates so strong and so firmly set. These doors were double and high, and were kept closed by two cross-bars to which there was but one key. When he had got close up to them, Hector strode towards them that his blow might gain in force and struck them in the middle, leaning his whole weight against them. He broke both hinges, and the stone fell inside by reason of its great weight. The portals re-echoed with the sound, the bars held no longer, and the doors flew open, one one way, and the other the other, through the force of the blow. Then brave Hector leaped inside with a face as dark as that of flying night. The gleaming bronze flashed fiercely about his body and he had two spears in his hand. None but a god could have withstood him as he flung himself into the gateway, and his eyes glared like fire. Then he turned round towards the Trojans and called on them to scale the wall, and they did as he bade them – some of them at once climbing over the wall, while others passed through the gates. The Danaans then fled panic-stricken towards their ships, and all was uproar and confusion.

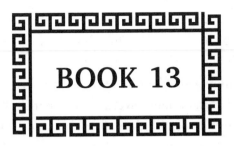

BOOK 13

Neptune helps the Achæans – The feats of Idomeneus –
Hector at the ships.

Now when Jove had thus brought Hector and the Trojans to the ships, he left them to their never-ending toil, and turned his keen eyes away, looking elsewhither towards the horse-breeders of Thrace, the Mysians, fighters at close quarters, the noble Hippemolgi, who live on milk, and the Abians, justest of mankind. He no longer turned so much as a glance towards Troy, for he did not think that any of the immortals would go and help either Trojans or Danaans.

But King Neptune had kept no blind look-out; he had been looking admiringly on the battle from his seat on the topmost crests of wooded Samothrace, whence he could see all Ida, with the city of Priam and the ships of the Achæans. He had come from under the sea and taken his place here, for he pitied the Achæans who were being overcome by the Trojans; and he was furiously angry with Jove.

Presently he came down from his post on the mountain top, and as he strode swiftly onwards the high hills and the forest quaked beneath the tread of his immortal feet. Three strides he took, and with the fourth he reached his goal – Ægæ, where is his glittering golden palace, imperishable, in the depths of the sea. When he got there, he yoked his fleet brazen-footed steeds with their manes of gold all flying in the wind; he clothed himself in raiment of gold, grasped his gold whip, and took his stand upon his chariot. As he went his way over the waves the sea-monsters left their lairs, for they knew their lord, and came gambolling round him from every quarter of the deep, while the sea in her gladness opened a path before his chariot. So lightly did the horses fly that the bronze axle of the car was not even wet beneath it; and thus his bounding steeds took him to the ships of the Achæans.

Now there is a certain huge cavern in the depths of the sea midway between Tenedos and rocky Imbrus; here Neptune lord of the earthquake stayed his horses, unyoked them, and set before them their ambrosial forage. He hobbled their feet with hobbles of gold which none could either unloose or break, so that they might stay there in that place until their lord should return. This done he went his way to the host of the Achæans.

Now the Trojans followed Hector son of Priam in close array like a storm-cloud or flame of fire, fighting with might and main and raising the cry of battle; for they deemed that they should take the ships of the Achæans and kill all their chiefest heroes then and there. Meanwhile earth-encircling Neptune lord of the earthquake cheered on the Argives, for he had come up out of the sea and had assumed the form and voice of Calchas.

First he spoke to the two Ajaxes, who were doing their best already, and said, 'Ajaxes, you two can be the saving of the Achæans if you will put out all your strength and not let yourselves be daunted. I am not afraid that the Trojans, who have got over the wall in force, will be victorious in any other part, for the Achæans can hold all of them in check, but I much fear that some evil will befall us here where furious Hector, who boasts himself the son of great Jove himself, is leading them on like a pillar of flame. May some god, then, put it into your hearts to make a firm stand here, and to incite others to do the like. In this case you will drive him from the ships even though he be inspired by Jove himself.'

As he spoke the earth-encircling lord of the earthquake struck both of them with his sceptre and filled their hearts with daring. He made their legs light and active, as also their hands and their feet. Then, as the soaring falcon poises on the wing high above some sheer rock, and presently swoops down to chase some bird over the plain, even so did Neptune lord of the earthquake wing his flight into the air and leave them. Of the two, swift Ajax son of Oïleus was the first to know who it was that had been speaking with them, and said to Ajax son of Telamon, 'Ajax, this is one of the gods that dwell on Olympus, who in the likeness of the prophet is bidding us fight hard by our ships. It was not Calchas the seer and diviner of omens; I knew him at once by his feet and knees as he turned away, for the gods are soon recognised. Moreover I feel the lust of battle burn more fiercely within me, while my hands and my feet under me are more eager for the fray.'

And Ajax son of Telamon answered, 'I too feel my hands grasp my spear more firmly; my strength is greater, and my feet more nimble; I long, moreover, to meet furious Hector son of Priam, even in single combat.'

Thus did they converse, exulting in the hunger after battle with which the god had filled them. Meanwhile the earth-encircler roused the Achæans, who were resting in the rear by the ships overcome at once by hard fighting and by grief at seeing that the Trojans had got over the wall in force. Tears began falling from their eyes as they beheld them, for they made sure that they should not escape destruction; but the lord of the earthquake passed lightly about among them and urged their battalions to the front.

First he went up to Teucer and Leïtus, the hero Peneleos, and Thoas and Deïpyrus; Meriones also and Antilochus, valiant warriors; all these did he exhort. 'Shame on you young Argives,' he cried, 'it was on your prowess I relied for the saving of our ships; if you fight not with might and main, this very day will see us overcome by the Trojans. Of a truth my eyes behold a great and terrible portent which I had never thought to see – the Trojans at our ships – they, who heretofore were like panic-stricken hinds, the prey of jackals and wolves in a forest, with no strength but in flight for they cannot defend themselves. Hitherto the Trojans dared not for one moment face the attack of the Achæans, but now they have sallied far from their city and are fighting at our very ships through the cowardice of our leader and the disaffection of the people themselves, who in their discontent care not to fight in defence of the ships but are being slaughtered near them. True, King Agamemnon son of Atreus is the cause of our disaster by having insulted the son of Peleus, still this is no reason why we should leave off fighting. Let us be quick to heal, for the hearts of the brave heal quickly. You do ill to be thus remiss, you, who are the finest soldiers in our whole army. I blame no man for keeping out of battle if he is a weakling, but I am indignant with such men as you are. My good friends, matters will soon become even worse through this slackness; think, each one of you, of his own honour and credit, for the hazard of the fight is extreme. Great Hector is now fighting at our ships; he has broken through the gates and the strong bolt that held them.'

Thus did the earth-encircler address the Achæans and urge them on. Thereon round the two Ajaxes there gathered strong bands of men, of whom not even Mars nor Minerva marshaller of hosts could make light if they went among them, for they were the picked men of all those who were now awaiting the onset of Hector and the Trojans. They made a living fence, spear to spear, shield to shield, buckler to buckler, helmet to helmet, and man to man. The horse-hair crests on their gleaming helmets touched one another as they nodded forward, so closely serried were they; the spears they brandished in their strong hands were interlaced, and their hearts were set on battle.

The Trojans advanced in a dense body, with Hector at their head pressing right on as a rock that comes thundering down the side of some mountain from whose brow the winter torrents have torn it; the foundations of the dull thing have been loosened by floods of rain, and as it bounds headlong on its way it sets the whole forest in an uproar; it swerves neither to right nor left till it reaches level ground, but then for all its fury it can go no further – even so easily did Hector for a while seem as though he would career through the tents and ships of the Achæans till he had reached the sea in his murderous course; but the closely serried battalions stayed him when he reached them, for the sons of the Achæans thrust at him with swords and spears pointed at both ends, and drove him from them so that he staggered and gave ground; thereon he shouted to the Trojans, 'Trojans, Lycians, and Dardanians, fighters in close combat, stand firm: the Achæans have set themselves as a wall against me, but they will not check me for long; they will give ground before me if the mightiest of the gods, the thundering spouse of Juno, has indeed inspired my onset.'

With these words he put heart and soul into them all. Deïphobus son of Priam went about among them intent on deeds of daring with his round shield before him, under cover of which he strode quickly forward. Meriones took aim at him with a spear, nor did he fail to hit the broad orb of ox-hide; but he was far from piercing it for the spear broke in two pieces long ere he could do so; moreover Deïphobus had seen it coming and had held his shield well away from him. Meriones drew back under cover of his comrades, angry alike at having failed to vanquish Deïphobus, and having broken his spear. He turned therefore towards the ships and tents to fetch a spear which he had left behind in his tent.

The others continued fighting, and the cry of battle rose up into the heavens. Teucer son of Telamon was the first to kill his man, to wit, the warrior Imbrius son of Mentor rich in horses. Until the Achæans came he had lived in Pedæum, and had married Medesicaste a bastard daughter of Priam; but on the arrival of the Danaan fleet he had gone back to Ilius, and was a great man among the Trojans, dwelling near Priam himself, who gave him like honour with his own sons. The son of Telamon now struck him under the ear with a spear which he then drew back again, and Imbrius fell headlong as an ashtree when it is felled on the crest of some high mountain beacon, and its delicate green foliage comes toppling down to the ground. Thus did he fall with his bronze-dight armour ringing harshly round him, and Teucer sprang forward with intent to strip him of his armour; but as he was doing so, Hector took aim at him with a spear. Teucer saw the spear coming and swerved aside, whereon it hit Amphimachus, son of Cteatus son of Actor, in the chest as he was coming into battle, and his armour rang rattling round him as he fell heavily to the ground. Hector sprang forward to take Amphimachus's helmet from off his temples, and in a moment Ajax threw a spear at him, but did not wound him, for he was encased all over in his terrible armour; nevertheless the spear struck the boss of his shield with such force as to drive him back from the two corpses, which the Achæans then drew off. Stichius and Menestheus, captains of the Athenians, bore away Amphimachus to the host of the Achæans, while the two brave and impetuous Ajaxes did the like by Imbrius. As two lions snatch a goat from the hounds that have it in their fangs, and bear it through thick brushwood high above the ground in their jaws, thus did the Ajaxes bear aloft the body of Imbrius, and strip it of its armour. Then the son of Oïleus severed the head from the neck in revenge for the death of Amphimachus, and sent it whirling over the crowd as though it had been a ball, till it fell in the dust at Hector's feet.

Neptune was exceedingly angry that his grandson Amphimachus should have fallen; he therefore went to the tents and ships of the Achæans to urge the Danaans still further, and to devise evil for the Trojans. Idomeneus met him, as he was taking leave of a comrade, who had just come to him from the fight, wounded in the knee. His fellow-soldiers bore him off the field, and Idomeneus having given orders to the physicians went on to his tent, for he was still thirsting for battle. Neptune spoke in the likeness and with the voice of Thoas son of Andræmon who ruled the Ætolians of all Pleuron and high Calydon, and was honoured among his people as though he were a god. 'Idomeneus,' said he, 'lawgiver to the Cretans, what has now become of the threats with which the sons of the Achæans used to threaten the Trojans?'

And Idomeneus chief among the Cretans answered, 'Thoas, no one, so far as I know, is in fault, for we can all fight. None are held back neither by fear nor slackness, but it seems to be the will of almighty Jove that the Achæans should perish ingloriously here far from Argos: you, Thoas, have been always staunch, and you keep others in heart if you see any fail in duty; be not then remiss now, but exhort all to do their utmost.'

To this Neptune lord of the earthquake made answer, 'Idomeneus, may he never return from Troy, but remain here for dogs to batten upon, who is this day wilfully slack in fighting. Get your armour and go, we must make all haste together if we may be of any use, though we are only two. Even cowards gain courage from companionship, and we two can hold our own with the bravest.'

Therewith the god went back into the thick of the fight, and Idomeneus when he had reached his tent donned his armour, grasped his two spears, and sallied forth. As the lightning which the son of Saturn brandishes from bright Olympus when he would show a sign to mortals, and its gleam flashes far and wide – even so did his armour gleam about him as he ran. Meriones his sturdy squire met him while he was still near his tent (for he was going to fetch his spear) and Idomeneus said:—

'Meriones, fleet son of Molus, best of comrades, why have you left the field? Are you wounded, and is the point of the weapon hurting you? or have you been sent to fetch me? I want no fetching; I had far rather fight than stay in my tent.'

'Idomeneus,' answered Meriones, 'I come for a spear, if I can find one in my tent; I have broken the one I had, in throwing it at the shield of Deïphobus.'

And Idomeneus captain of the Cretans answered, 'You will find one spear, or twenty if you so please, standing up against the end wall of my tent. I have taken them from Trojans whom I have killed, for I am not one to keep my enemy at arm's length; therefore I have spears, bossed shields, helmets, and burnished corslets.'

Then Meriones said, 'I too in my tent and at my ship have spoils taken from the Trojans, but they are not at hand. I have been at all times valorous, and wherever there has been hard fighting have held my own among the foremost. There may be those among the Achæans who do not know how I fight, but you know it well enough yourself.'

Idomeneus answered, 'I know you for a brave man: you need not tell me. If the best men at the ships were being chosen to go on an ambush – and there is nothing like this for showing what a man is made of; it comes out then who is cowardly and who brave; the coward will change colour at every touch and turn; he is full of fears, and keeps shifting his weight first on one knee and then on the other; his heart beats fast as he thinks of death, and one can hear the chattering of his teeth; whereas the brave man will not change colour nor be frightened on finding himself in ambush, but is all the time longing to go into action – if the best men were being chosen for such a service, no one could make light of your courage nor feats of arms. If you were struck by a dart or smitten in close combat, it would not be from behind, in your neck nor back, but the weapon would hit you in the chest or belly as you were pressing forward to a place in the front ranks. But let us no longer stay here talking like children, lest we be ill spoken of; go, fetch your spear from the tent at once.'

On this Meriones, peer of Mars, went to the tent and got himself a spear of bronze. He then followed after Idomeneus, big with great deeds of valour. As when baneful Mars sallies forth to battle, and his son Panic so strong and dauntless goes with him, to strike terror even into the heart of a hero – the pair have gone from Thrace to arm themselves among the Ephyri or the brave Phlegyans, but they will not listen to both the contending hosts, and will give victory to one side or to the other – even so did Meriones and Idomeneus, captains of men, go out to battle clad in their bronze armour. Meriones was first to speak. 'Son of Deucalion,' said he, 'where would you have us begin fighting? On the right wing of the host, in the centre, or on the left wing, where I take it the Achæans will be weakest?'

Idomeneus answered, 'There are others to defend the centre – the two Ajaxes and Teucer, who is the finest archer of all the Achæans, and is good also in a hand-to-hand fight. These will give Hector son of Priam enough to do; fight as he may, he will find it hard to vanquish their indomitable fury, and fire the ships, unless the son of Saturn fling a firebrand upon them with his own hand. Great Ajax son of Telamon will yield to no man who is in mortal mould and eats the grain of Ceres, if bronze and great stones can overthrow him. He would not yield even to Achilles in hand-to-hand fight, and in fleetness of foot there is none to beat him; let us turn therefore towards the left wing, that we may know forthwith whether we are to give glory to some other, or he to us.'

Meriones, peer of fleet Mars, then led the way till they came to the part of the host which Idomeneus had named.

Now when the Trojans saw Idomeneus coming on like a flame of fire, him and his squire clad in their richly wrought armour, they shouted and made towards him all in a body, and a furious hand-to-hand fight raged under the ships' sterns. Fierce as the shrill winds that whistle upon a day when dust lies deep on the roads, and the gusts raise it into a thick cloud – even such was the fury of the combat, and might and main did they hack at each other with spear and sword throughout the host. The field bristled with the long and deadly spears which they bore. Dazzling was the sheen of their gleaming helmets, their fresh-burnished breastplates, and glittering shields as they joined battle with one another. Iron indeed must be his courage who could take pleasure in the sight of such a turmoil, and look on it without being dismayed.

Thus did the two mighty sons of Saturn devise evil for mortal heroes. Jove was minded to give victory to the Trojans and to Hector, so as to do honour to fleet Achilles, nevertheless he did not mean to utterly overthrow the Achæan host before Ilius, and only wanted to glorify Thetis and her valiant son. Neptune on the other hand went about among the Argives to incite them, having come up from the grey sea in secret, for he was grieved at seeing them vanquished by the Trojans, and was furiously angry with Jove. Both were of the same race and country, but Jove was elder born and knew more, therefore Neptune feared to defend the Argives openly, but in the likeness of man, he kept on encouraging them throughout their host. Thus, then, did these two devise a knot of war and battle, that none could unloose or break, and set both sides tugging at it, to the failing of men's knees beneath them.

And now Idomeneus, though his hair was already flecked with grey, called loud on the Danaans and spread panic among the Trojans as he leaped in among them. He slew Othryoneus from Cabesus, a sojourner, who had but lately come to take part in the war. He sought Cassandra the fairest of Priam's daughters in marriage, but offered no gifts of wooing, for he promised a great thing, to wit, that he would drive the sons of the Achæans willy nilly from Troy; old King Priam had given his consent and promised her to him, whereon he fought on the strength of the promises thus made to him. Idomeneus aimed a spear, and hit him as he came striding on. His cuirass of bronze did not protect him, and the spear stuck in his belly, so that he fell heavily to the ground. Then Idomeneus vaunted over him saying, 'Othryoneus, there is no one in the world whom I shall admire more than I do you, if you indeed perform what you have promised Priam son of Dardanus in return for his daughter. We too will make you an offer; we will give you the loveliest daughter of the son of Atreus, and will bring her from Argos for you to marry, if you will sack the goodly city of Ilius in company with ourselves; so come along with me, that we may make a covenant at the ships about the marriage, and we will not be hard upon you about gifts of wooing.'

With this Idomeneus began dragging him by the foot through the thick of the fight, but Asius came up to protect the body, on foot, in front of his horses, which his esquire drove so close behind him that he could feel their breath upon his shoulder. He was longing to strike down Idomeneus, but ere he could do so Idomeneus smote him with his spear in the throat under the chin, and the bronze point went clean through it. He fell as an oak, or poplar, or pine which shipwrights have felled for ship's timber upon the mountains with whetted axes – even thus did he lie full length in front of his chariot and horses, grinding his teeth and clutching at the bloodstained dust. His charioteer was struck with panic and did not dare turn his horses round and escape: thereupon Antilochus hit him in the middle of his body with a spear; his cuirass of bronze did not protect him, and the spear stuck in his belly. He fell gasping from his chariot and Antilochus, great Nestor's son, drove his horses from the Trojans to the Achæans.

Deïphobus then came close up to Idomeneus to avenge Asius, and took aim at him with a spear, but Idomeneus was on the look-out and avoided it, for he was covered by the round shield he always bore – a shield of ox-hide and bronze with two arm-rods on the inside. He crouched under cover of this, and the spear flew over him, but the shield rang out as the spear grazed it, and the weapon sped not in vain from the strong hand of Deïphobus, for it struck Hypsenor son of Hippasus, shepherd of his people, in the liver under the midriff, and his limbs failed beneath him. Deïphobus vaunted over him and cried with a loud voice saying, 'Of a truth Asius has not fallen unavenged; he will be glad even while passing into the house of Hades, strong warden of the gate, that I have sent some one to escort him.'

Thus did he vaunt, and the Argives were stung by his saying. Noble Antilochus was more angry than any one, but grief did not make him forget his friend and comrade. He ran up to him, bestrode him, and covered him with his shield; then two of his staunch comrades, Mecisteus son of Echius, and Alastor stooped down, and bore him away groaning heavily to the ships. But Idomeneus ceased not his fury. He kept on striving continually either to enshroud some Trojan in the darkness of death, or himself to fall while warding off the evil day from the Achæans. Then fell Alcathoüs son of noble Æsyetes: he was son-in-law to Anchises, having married his eldest daughter Hippodameia who was the darling of her father and mother, and excelled all her generation in beauty, accomplishments, and understanding, wherefore the bravest man in all Troy had taken her to wife – him did Neptune lay low by the hand of Idomeneus, blinding his bright eyes and binding his strong limbs in fetters so that he could neither go back nor to one side, but stood stock still like a pillar or lofty tree when Idomeneus struck him with a spear in the middle of his chest. The coat of mail that had hitherto protected his body was now broken, and rang harshly as the spear tore through it. He fell heavily to the ground, and the spear stuck in his heart, which still beat, and made the butt-end of the spear quiver till dread Mars put an end to his life. Idomeneus vaunted over him and cried with a loud voice saying, 'Deïphobus, since you are in a mood to vaunt, shall we cry quits now that we have killed three men to your one? Nay, sir, stand in fight with me yourself, that you may learn what manner of Jove-begotten man am I that have come hither. Jove first begot Minos chief ruler in Crete, and Minos in his turn begot a son, noble Deucalion; Deucalion begot me to be a ruler over many men in Crete, and my ships have now brought me hither, to be the bane of yourself, your father, and the Trojans.'

Thus did he speak, and Deïphobus was in two minds, whether to go back and fetch some other Trojan to help him, or to take up the challenge single-handed. In the end, he deemed it best to go and fetch Æneas, whom he found standing in the rear, for he had long been aggrieved with Priam because in spite of his brave deeds he did not give him his due share of honour. Deïphobus went up to him and said, 'Æneas, prince among the Trojans, if you know any ties of kinship, help me now to defend the body of your sister's husband; come with me to the rescue of Alcathoüs, who being husband to your sister brought you up when you were a child in his house, and now Idomeneus has slain him.'

With these words he moved the heart of Æneas, and he went in pursuit of Idomeneus, big with great deeds of valour; but Idomeneus was not to be thus daunted as though he were a mere child; he held his ground as a wild boar at bay upon the mountains, who abides the coming of a great crowd of men in some lonely place – the bristles stand upright on his back, his eyes flash fire, and he whets his tusks in his eagerness to defend himself against hounds and men – even so did famed Idomeneus hold his ground and budge not at the coming of Æneas. He cried aloud to his comrades looking towards Ascalaphus,

Aphareus, Deïpyrus, Meriones, and Antilochus, all of them brave soldiers – 'Hither my friends,' he cried, 'and leave me not single-handed – I go in great fear by fleet Æneas, who is coming against me, and is a redoubtable dispenser of death in battle. Moreover he is in the flower of youth when a man's strength is greatest; if I was of the same age as he is and in my present mind, either he or I should soon bear away the prize of victory.'

On this, all of them as one man stood near him, shield on shoulder. Æneas on the other side called to his comrades, looking towards Deïphobus, Paris, and Agenor, who were leaders of the Trojans along with himself, and the people followed them as sheep follow the ram when they go down to drink after they have been feeding, and the heart of the shepherd is glad – even so was the heart of Æneas gladdened when he saw his people follow him.

Then they fought furiously in close combat about the body of Alcathoüs, wielding their long spears; and the bronze armour about their bodies rang fearfully as they took aim at one another in the press of the fight, while the two heroes Æneas and Idomeneus, peers of Mars, outvied every one in their desire to hack at each other with sword and spear. Æneas took aim first, but Idomeneus was on the look-out and avoided the spear, so that it sped from Æneas' strong hand in vain, and fell quivering in the ground. Idomeneus meanwhile smote Œnomaus in the middle of his belly, and broke the plate of his corslet, whereon his bowels came gushing out and he clutched the earth in the palms of his hands as he fell sprawling in the dust. Idomeneus drew his spear out of the body, but could not strip him of the rest of his armour for the rain of darts that were showered upon him: moreover his strength was now beginning to fail him so that he could no longer charge, and could neither spring forward to recover his own weapon nor swerve aside to avoid one that was aimed at him; therefore, though he still defended himself in hand-to-hand fight, his heavy feet could not bear him swiftly out of the battle. Deïphobus aimed a spear at him as he was retreating slowly from the field, for his bitterness against him was as fierce as ever, but again he missed him, and hit Ascalaphus, the son of Mars; the spear went through his shoulder, and he clutched the earth in the palms of his hands as he fell sprawling in the dust.

Grim Mars of awful voice did not yet know that his son had fallen, for he was sitting on the summits of Olympus under the golden clouds, by command of Jove, where the other gods were also sitting, forbidden to take part in the battle. Meanwhile men fought furiously about the body. Deïphobus tore the helmet from off his head, but Meriones sprang upon him, and struck him on the arm with a spear so that the visored helmet fell from his hand and came ringing down upon the ground. Thereon Meriones sprang upon him like a vulture, drew the spear from his shoulder, and fell back under cover of his men. Then Polites, own brother of Deïphobus, passed his arms around his waist, and bore him away from the battle till he got to his horses that were standing in the rear of the fight with the chariot and their driver. These took him towards the city groaning and in great pain, with the blood flowing from his arm.

The others still fought on, and the battle-cry rose to heaven without ceasing. Æneas sprang on Aphareus son of Caletor, and struck him with a spear in his throat which was turned towards him; his head fell on one side, his helmet and shield came down along with him, and death, life's foe, was shed around him. Antilochus spied his chance, flew forward towards Thoön, and wounded him as he was turning round. He laid open the vein that runs all the way up the back to the neck; he cut this vein clean away throughout its whole course, and Thoön fell in the dust face upwards, stretching out his hands imploringly towards his comrades. Antilochus sprang upon him and stripped the armour from his shoulders, glaring round him fearfully as he did so. The Trojans came about him on every side and struck his broad and gleaming shield, but could not wound his body, for Neptune stood guard over the son of Nestor, though the darts fell thickly round him. He was never clear of the foe, but was always in the thick of the fight;

his spear was never idle; he poised and aimed it in every direction, so eager was he to hit some one from a distance or to fight him hand to hand.

As he was thus aiming among the crowd, he was seen by Adamas son of Asius, who rushed towards him and struck him with a spear in the middle of his shield, but Neptune made its point without effect, for he grudged him the life of Antilochus. One half, therefore, of the spear stuck fast like a charred stake in Antilochus's shield, while the other lay on the ground. Adamas then sought shelter under cover of his men, but Meriones followed after and hit him with a spear midway between the private parts and the navel, where a wound is particularly painful to wretched mortals. There did Meriones transfix him, and he writhed convulsively about the spear as some bull whom mountain herdsmen have bound with ropes of withes and are taking away perforce. Even so did he move convulsively for a while, but not for very long, till Meriones came up and drew the spear out of his body, and his eyes were veiled in darkness.

Helenus then struck Deïpyrus with a great Thracian sword, hitting him on the temple in close combat and tearing the helmet from his head; the helmet fell to the ground, and one of those who were fighting on the Achæan side took charge of it as it rolled at his feet, but the eyes of Deïpyrus were closed in the darkness of death.

On this Menelaus was grieved, and made menacingly towards Helenus, brandishing his spear; but Helenus drew his bow, and the two attacked one another at one and the same moment, the one with his spear, and the other with his bow and arrow. The son of Priam hit the breastplate of Menelaus's corslet, but the arrow glanced from off it. As black beans or pulse come pattering down on to a threshing-floor from the broad winnowing-shovel, blown by shrill winds and shaken by the shovel – even so did the arrow glance off and recoil from the shield of Menelaus, who in his turn wounded the hand with which Helenus carried his bow; the spear went right through his hand and stuck in the bow itself, so that to save his life he retreated under cover of his men, with his hand dragging by his side – for the spear weighed it down till Agenor drew it out and bound the hand carefully up in a woollen sling which his esquire had with him.

Pisander then made straight at Menelaus – his evil destiny luring him on to his doom, for he was to fall in fight with you, O Menelaus. When the two were hard by one another the spear of the son of Atreus turned aside and he missed his aim; Pisander then struck the shield of brave Menelaus but could not pierce it, for the shield stayed the spear and broke the shaft; nevertheless he was glad and made sure of victory; forthwith, however, the son of Atreus drew his sword and sprang upon him. Pisander then seized the bronze battle-axe, with its long and polished handle of olive wood that hung by his side under his shield, and the two made at one another. Pisander struck the peak of Menelaus's crested helmet just under the crest itself, and Menelaus hit Pisander as he was coming towards him, on the forehead, just at the rise of his nose; the bones cracked and his two gore-bedrabbled eyes fell by his feet in the dust. He fell backwards to the ground, and Menelaus set his heel upon him, stripped him of his armour, and vaunted over him saying, 'Even thus shall you Trojans leave the ships of the Achæans, proud and insatiate of battle though you be: nor shall you lack any of the disgrace and shame which you have heaped upon myself. Cowardly she-wolves that you are, you feared not the anger of dread Jove, avenger of violated hospitality, who will one day destroy your city; you stole my wedded wife and wickedly carried off much treasure when you were her guest, and now you would fling fire upon our ships, and kill our heroes. A day will come when, rage as you may, you shall be stayed. O father Jove, you, who they say are above all both gods and men in wisdom, and from whom all things that befall us do proceed, how can you thus favour the Trojans – men so proud and overweening, that they are never tired of fighting? All things pall after a while – sleep, love, sweet song, and stately dance – still these are things of which a man would surely have his fill rather than of battle, whereas it is of battle that the Trojans are insatiate.'

So saying Menelaus stripped the blood-stained armour from the body of Pisander, and handed it over to his men; then he again ranged himself among those who were in the front of the fight.

Harpalion son of King Pylæmenes then sprang upon him; he had come to fight at Troy along with his father, but he did not go home again. He struck the middle of Menelaus's shield with his spear but could not pierce it, and to save his life drew back under cover of his men, looking round him on every side lest he should be wounded. But Meriones aimed a bronze-tipped arrow at him as he was leaving the field, and hit him on the right buttock; the arrow pierced the bone through and through, and penetrated the bladder, so he sat down where he was and breathed his last in the arms of his comrades, stretched like a worm upon the ground and watering the earth with the blood that flowed from his wound. The brave Paphlagonians tended him with all due care; they raised him into his chariot, and bore him sadly off to the city of Troy; his father went also with him weeping bitterly, but there was no ransom that could bring his dead son to life again.

Paris was deeply grieved by the death of Harpalion, who was his host when he went among the Paphlagonians; he aimed an arrow, therefore, in order to avenge him. Now there was a certain man named Euchenor, son of Polyidus the prophet, a brave man and wealthy, whose home was in Corinth. This Euchenor had set sail for Troy well knowing that it would be the death of him, for his good old father Polyidus had often told him that he must either stay at home and die of a terrible disease, or go with the Achæans and perish at the hands of the Trojans; he chose, therefore, to avoid incurring the heavy fine the Achæans would have laid upon him, and at the same time to escape the pain and suffering of disease. Paris now smote him on the jaw under his ear, whereon the life went out of him and he was enshrouded in the darkness of death.

Thus then did they fight as it were a flaming fire. But Hector had not yet heard, and did not know that the Argives were making havoc of his men on the left wing of the battle, where the Achæans ere long would have triumphed over them, so vigorously did Neptune cheer them on and help them. He therefore held on at the point where he had first forced his way through the gates and the wall, after breaking through the serried ranks of Danaan warriors. It was here that the ships of Ajax and Protesilaus were drawn up by the sea-shore; here the wall was at its lowest, and the fight both of man and horse raged most fiercely. The Bœotians and the Ionians with their long tunics, the Locrians, the men of Phthia, and the famous force of the Epeans could hardly stay Hector as he rushed on towards the ships, nor could they drive him from them, for he was as a wall of fire. The chosen men of the Athenians were in the van, led by Menestheus son of Peteos, with whom were also Pheidas, Stichius, and stalwart Bias: Meges son of Phyleus, Amphion, and Dracius commanded the Epeans, while Medon and staunch Podarces led the men of Phthia. Of these, Medon was bastard son to Oïleus and brother of Ajax, but he lived in Phylace away from his own country, for he had killed the brother of his stepmother Eriopis, the wife of Oïleus; the other, Podarces, was the son of Iphiclus son of Phylacus. These two stood in the van of the Phthians, and defended the ships along with the Bœotians.

Ajax son of Oïleus never for a moment left the side of Ajax son of Telamon, but as two swart oxen both strain their utmost at the plough which they are drawing in a fallow field, and the sweat steams upwards from about the roots of their horns – nothing but the yoke divides them as they break up the ground till they reach the end of the field – even so did the two Ajaxes stand shoulder to shoulder by one another. Many and brave comrades followed the son of Telamon, to relieve him of his shield when he was overcome with sweat and toil, but the Locrians did not follow so close after the son of Oïleus, for they could not hold their own in a hand-to-hand fight. They had no bronze helmets with plumes of horse-hair, neither had they shields nor ashen spears, but they had come to Troy armed with bows, and with slings of twisted wool from which they showered their missiles to break the ranks of the Trojans. The others, therefore, with their heavy armour bore the brunt of the fight with the Trojans and with Hector, while the Locrians shot from behind, under their cover; and thus the Trojans began to lose heart, for the arrows threw them into confusion.

The Trojans would now have been driven in sorry plight from the ships and tents back to windy Ilius, had not Polydamas presently said to Hector, 'Hector, there is no persuading you to take advice. Because heaven has so richly endowed you with the arts of war, you think that you must therefore excel others in counsel; but you cannot thus claim pre-eminence in all things. Heaven has made one man an excellent soldier; of another it has made a dancer or a singer and player on the lyre; while yet in another Jove has implanted a wise understanding of which men reap fruit to the saving of many, and he himself knows more about it than any one; therefore I will say what I think will be best. The fight has hemmed you in as with a circle of fire, and even now that the Trojans are within the wall some of them stand aloof in full armour, while others are fighting scattered and outnumbered near the ships. Draw back, therefore, and call your chieftains round you, that we may advise together whether to fall now upon the ships in the hope that heaven may vouchsafe us victory, or to beat a retreat while we can yet safely do so. I greatly fear that the Achæans will pay us their debt of yesterday in full, for there is one abiding at their ships who is never weary of battle, and who will not hold aloof much longer.'

Thus spoke Polydamas, and his words pleased Hector well. He sprang in full armour from his chariot and said, 'Polydamas, gather the chieftains here; I will go yonder into the fight, but will return at once when I have given them their orders.'

He then sped onward, towering like a snowy mountain, and with a loud cry flew through the ranks of the Trojans and their allies. When they heard his voice they all hastened to gather round Polydamas the excellent son of Panthoüs, but Hector kept on among the foremost, looking everywhere to find Deïphobus and prince Helenus, Adamas son of Asius, and Asius son of Hyrtacus; living, indeed, and scatheless he could no longer find them, for the two last were lying by the sterns of the Achæan ships, slain by the Argives, while the others had been also stricken and wounded by them; but upon the left wing of the dread battle he found Alexandrus, husband of lovely Helen, cheering his men and urging them on to fight. He went up to him and upbraided him. 'Paris,' said he, 'evil-hearted Paris, fair to see but woman-mad and false of tongue, where are Deïphobus and King Helenus? Where are Adamas son of Asius, and Asius son of Hyrtacus? Where too is Othryoneus? Ilius is undone and will now surely fall!'

Alexandrus answered, 'Hector, why find fault when there is no one to find fault with? I should hold aloof from battle on any day rather than this, for my mother bore me with nothing of the coward about me. From the moment when you set our men fighting about the ships we have been staying here and doing battle with the Danaans. Our comrades about whom you ask me are dead; Deïphobus and King Helenus alone have left the field, wounded both of them in the hand, but the son of Saturn saved them alive. Now, therefore, lead on where you would have us go, and we will follow with right goodwill; you shall not find us fail you in so far as our strength holds out, but no man can do more than in him lies, no matter how willing he may be.'

With these words he satisfied his brother, and the two went towards the part of the battle where the fight was thickest, about Cebriones, brave Polydamas, Phalces, Orthæus, godlike Polyphetes, Palmys, Ascanius, and Morys son of Hippotion, who had come from fertile Ascania on the preceding day to relieve other troops. Then Jove urged them on to fight. They flew forth like the blasts of some fierce wind that strike earth in the van of a thunderstorm – they buffet the salt sea into an uproar; many and mighty are the great waves that come crashing in one after the other upon the shore with their arching heads all crested with foam – even so did rank behind rank of Trojans arrayed in gleaming armour follow their leaders onward. The way was led by Hector son of Priam, peer of murderous Mars, with his round shield before him – his shield of ox-hides covered with plates of bronze – and his gleaming helmet upon his temples. He kept stepping forward under cover of his shield in every direction, making trial of the ranks to see if they would give way before him, but he could not daunt the courage of the Achæans. Ajax was the first to stride out and challenge him. 'Sir,' he cried, 'draw near; why do you think thus vainly to dismay the Argives? We Achæans are excellent soldiers, but the scourge of Jove has fallen heavily upon us. Your heart, forsooth, is set on destroying our ships, but we too have hands that can keep you at bay, and your own fair town shall be sooner taken and sacked by ourselves. The time is near when you shall pray Jove and all the gods in your flight, that your steeds may be swifter than hawks as they raise the dust on the plain and bear you back to your city.'

As he was thus speaking a bird flew by upon his right hand, and the host of the Achæans shouted, for they took heart at the omen. But Hector answered, 'Ajax, braggart and false of tongue, would that I were as sure of being son for evermore to ægis-bearing Jove, with Queen Juno for my mother, and of being held in like honour with Minerva and Apollo, as I am that this day is big with the destruction of the Achæans; and you shall fall among them if you dare abide my spear; it shall rend your fair body and bid you glut our hounds and birds of prey with your fat and your flesh, as you fall by the ships of the Achæans.'

With these words he led the way and the others followed after with a cry that rent the air, while the host shouted behind them. The Argives on their part raised a shout likewise, nor did they forget their prowess, but stood firm against the onslaught of the Trojan chieftains, and the cry from both the hosts rose up to heaven and to the brightness of Jove's presence.

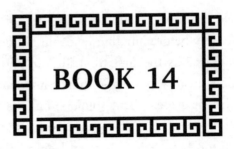

BOOK 14

Agamemnon proposes that the Achæans should sail home, and is
rebuked by Ulysses – Juno beguiles Jupiter – Hector is wounded.

Nestor was sitting over his wine, but the cry of battle did not escape
him, and he said to the son of Æsculapius, 'What, noble Machaon, is
the meaning of all this? The shouts of men fighting by our ships grow
stronger and stronger; stay here, therefore, and sit over your wine,
while fair Hecamedé heats you a bath and washes the clotted blood
from off you. I will go at once to the look-out station and see what it
is all about.'

As he spoke he took up the shield of his son Thrasymedes that was
lying in his tent, all gleaming with bronze, for Thrasymedes had taken
his father's shield; he grasped his redoubtable bronze-shod spear, and
as soon as he was outside saw the disastrous rout of the Achæans who,
now that their wall was overthrown, were flying pell-mell before the
Trojans. As when there is a heavy swell upon the sea, but the waves
are dumb – they keep their eyes on the watch for the quarter whence
the fierce winds may spring upon them, but they stay where they are
and set neither this way nor that, till some particular wind sweeps
down from heaven to determine them – even so did the old man ponder
whether to make for the crowd of Danaans, or go in search of
Agamemnon. In the end he deemed it best to go to the son of Atreus;
but meanwhile the hosts were fighting and killing one another, and
the hard bronze rattled on their bodies, as they thrust at one another
with their swords and spears.

The wounded kings, the son of Tydeus, Ulysses, and Agamemnon son of Atreus, fell in with Nestor as they were coming up from their ships – for theirs were drawn up some way from where the fighting was going on, being on the shore itself inasmuch as they had been beached first, while the wall had been built behind the hindermost. The stretch of the shore, wide though it was, did not afford room for all the ships, and the host was cramped for space, therefore they had placed the ships in rows one behind the other, and had filled the whole opening of the bay between the two points that formed it. The kings, leaning on their spears, were coming out to survey the fight, being in great anxiety, and when old Nestor met them they were filled with dismay. Then King Agamemnon said to him, 'Nestor son of Neleus, honour to the Achæan name, why have you left the battle to come hither? I fear that what dread Hector said will come true, when he vaunted among the Trojans saying that he would not return to Ilius till he had fired our ships and killed us; this is what he said, and now it is all coming true. Alas! others of the Achæans, like Achilles, are in anger with me that they refuse to fight by the sterns of our ships.'

Then Nestor knight of Gerene answered, 'It is indeed as you say; it is all coming true at this moment, and even Jove who thunders from on high cannot prevent it. Fallen is the wall on which we relied as an impregnable bulwark both for us and our fleet. The Trojans are fighting stubbornly and without ceasing at the ships; look where you may you cannot see from what quarter the rout of the Achæans is coming; they are being killed in a confused mass and the battle-cry ascends to heaven; let us think, if counsel can be of any use, what we had better do; but I do not advise our going into battle ourselves, for a man cannot fight when he is wounded.'

And King Agamemnon answered, 'Nestor, if the Trojans are indeed fighting at the rear of our ships, and neither the wall nor the trench has served us – over which the Danaans toiled so hard, and which they deemed would be an impregnable bulwark both for us and our fleet – I see it must be the will of Jove that the Achæans should perish ingloriously here, far from Argos. I knew when Jove was willing to defend us, and I know now that he is raising the Trojans to like honour with the gods, while us, on the other hand, he has bound hand and foot. Now, therefore, let us all do as I say; let us bring down the ships that are on the beach and draw them into the water; let us make them fast to their mooring-stones a little way out, against the fall of night – if even by night the Trojans will desist from fighting; we may then draw down the rest of the fleet. There is nothing wrong in flying ruin even by night. It is better for a man that he should fly and be saved than be caught and killed.'

Ulysses looked fiercely at him and said, 'Son of Atreus, what are you talking about? Wretch, you should have commanded some other and baser army, and not been ruler over us to whom Jove has allotted a life of hard fighting from youth to old age, till we every one of us perish. Is it thus that you would quit the city of Troy, to win which we have suffered so much hardship? Hold your peace, lest some other of the Achæans hear you say what no man who knows how to give good counsel, no king over so great a host as that of the Argives should ever have let fall from his lips. I despise your judgement utterly for what you have been saying. Would you, then, have us draw down our ships into the water while the battle is raging, and thus play further into the hands of the conquering Trojans? It would be ruin; the Achæans will not go on fighting when they see the ships being drawn into the water, but will cease attacking and keep turning their eyes towards them; your counsel, therefore, Sir captain, would be our destruction.'

Agamemnon answered, 'Ulysses, your rebuke has stung me to the heart. I am not, however, ordering the Achæans to draw their ships into the sea whether they will or no. Some one, it may be, old or young, can offer us better counsel which I shall rejoice to hear.'

Then said Diomed, 'Such an one is at hand; he is not far to seek, if you will listen to me and not resent my speaking though I am younger than any of you. I am by lineage son to a noble sire, Tydeus, who lies buried at Thebes. For Portheus had three noble sons, two of whom,

Agrius and Melas, abode in Pleuron and rocky Calydon. The third was the knight Œneus, my father's father, and he was the most valiant of them all. Œneus remained in his own country, but my father (as Jove and the other gods ordained it) migrated to Argos. He married into the family of Adrastus, and his house was one of great abundance, for he had large estates of rich corn-growing land, with much orchard ground as well, and he had many sheep; moreover he excelled all the Argives in the use of the spear. You must yourselves have heard whether these things are true or no; therefore when I say well despise not my words as though I were a coward or of ignoble birth. I say, then, let us go to the fight as we needs must, wounded though we be. When there, we may keep out of the battle and beyond the range of the spears lest we get fresh wounds in addition to what we have already, but we can spur on others, who have been indulging their spleen and holding aloof from battle hitherto.'

Thus did he speak; whereon they did even as he had said and set out, King Agamemnon leading the way.

Meanwhile Neptune had kept no blind look-out, and came up to them in the semblance of an old man. He took Agamemnon's right hand in his own and said, 'Son of Atreus, I take it Achilles is glad now that he sees the Achæans routed and slain, for he is utterly without remorse – may he come to a bad end and heaven confound him. As for yourself, the blessed gods are not yet so bitterly angry with you but that the princes and counsellors of the Trojans shall again raise the dust upon the plain, and you shall see them flying from the ships and tents towards their city.'

With this he raised a mighty cry of battle, and sped forward to the plain. The voice that came from his deep chest was as that of nine or ten thousand men when they are shouting in the thick of a fight, and it put fresh courage into the hearts of the Achæans to wage war and do battle without ceasing.

Juno of the golden throne looked down as she stood upon a peak of Olympus and her heart was gladdened at the sight of him who was at once her brother and her brother-in-law, hurrying hither and thither amid the fighting. Then she turned her eyes to Jove as he sat on the topmost crests of many-fountained Ida, and loathed him. She set herself to think how she might hoodwink him, and in the end she deemed that it would be best for her to go to Ida and array herself in rich attire, in the hope that Jove might become enamoured of her, and wish to embrace her. While he was thus engaged a sweet and careless sleep might be made to steal over his eyes and senses.

She went, therefore, to the room which her son Vulcan had made her, and the doors of which he had cunningly fastened by means of a secret key so that no other god could open them. Here she entered and closed the doors behind her. She cleansed all the dirt from her fair body with ambrosia, then she anointed herself with olive oil, ambrosial, very soft, and scented specially for herself – if it were so much as shaken in the bronze-floored house of Jove, the scent pervaded the universe of heaven and earth. With this she anointed her delicate skin, and then she plaited the fair ambrosial locks that flowed in a stream of golden tresses from her immortal head. She put on the wondrous robe which Minerva had worked for her with consummate art, and had embroidered with manifold devices; she fastened it about her bosom with golden clasps, and she girded herself with a girdle that had a hundred tassels: then she fastened her earrings, three brilliant pendants that glistened most beautifully, through the pierced lobes of her ears, and threw a lovely new veil over her head. She bound her sandals on to her feet, and when she had arrayed herself perfectly to her satisfaction, she left her room and called Venus to come aside and speak to her. 'My dear child,' said she, 'will you do what I am going to ask of you, or will you refuse me because you are angry at my being on the Danaan side, while you are on the Trojan?'

Jove's daughter Venus answered, 'Juno, august queen of goddesses, daughter of mighty Saturn, say what you want, and I will do it for you at once, if I can, and if it can be done at all.'

Then Juno told her a lying tale and said, 'I want you to endow me with some of those fascinating charms, the spells of which bring all things mortal and immortal to your feet. I am going to the world's end to visit Oceanus (from whom all we gods proceed) and mother Tethys: they received me in their house, took care of me, and brought me up, having taken me over from Rhæa when Jove imprisoned great Saturn in the depths that are under earth and sea. I must go and see them that I may make peace between them; they have been quarrelling, and are so angry that they have not slept with one another this long while; if I can bring them round and restore them to one another's embraces, they will be grateful to me and love me for ever afterwards.'

Thereon laughter-loving Venus said, 'I cannot and must not refuse you, for you sleep in the arms of Jove who is our king.'

As she spoke she loosed from her bosom the curiously embroidered girdle into which all her charms had been wrought – love, desire, and that sweet flattery which steals the judgement even of the most prudent. She gave the girdle to Juno and said, 'Take this girdle wherein all my charms reside and lay it in your bosom. If you will wear it I promise you that your errand, be it what it may, will not be bootless.'

When she heard this Juno smiled, and still smiling she laid the girdle in her bosom.

Venus now went back into the house of Jove, while Juno darted down from the summits of Olympus. She passed over Pieria and fair Emathia, and went on and on till she came to the snowy ranges of the Thracian horsemen, over whose topmost crests she sped without ever setting foot to ground. When she came to Athos she went on over the waves of the sea till she reached Lemnos, the city of noble Thoas. There she met Sleep, own brother to Death, and caught him by the hand, saying, 'Sleep, you who lord it alike over mortals and immortals, if you ever did me a service in times past, do one for me now, and I shall be grateful to you ever after. Close Jove's keen eyes for me in slumber while I hold him clasped in my embrace, and I will give you a beautiful golden seat, that can never fall to pieces; my club-footed son Vulcan shall make it for you, and he shall give it a footstool for you to rest your fair feet upon when you are at table.'

Then Sleep answered, 'Juno, great queen of goddesses, daughter of mighty Saturn, I would lull any other of the gods to sleep without compunction, not even excepting the waters of Oceanus from whom all of them proceed, but I dare not go near Jove, nor send him to sleep unless he bids me. I have had one lesson already through doing what you asked me, on the day when Jove's mighty son Hercules set sail from Ilius after having sacked the city of the Trojans. At your bidding I suffused my sweet self over the mind of ægis-bearing Jove, and laid him to rest; meanwhile you hatched a plot against Hercules, and set the blasts of the angry winds beating upon the sea, till you took him to the goodly city of Cos away from all his friends. Jove was furious when he awoke, and began hurling the gods about all over the house; he was looking more particularly for myself, and would have flung me down through space into the sea where I should never have been heard of any more, had not Night who cows both men and gods protected me. I fled to her and Jove left off looking for me in spite of his being so angry, for he did not dare do anything to displease Night. And now you are again asking me to do something on which I cannot venture.'

And Juno said, 'Sleep, why do you take such notions as those into your head? Do you think Jove will be as anxious to help the Trojans, as he was about his own son? Come, I will marry you to one of the youngest of the Graces, and she shall be your own – Pasithea, whom you have always wanted to marry.'

Sleep was pleased when he heard this, and answered, 'Then swear it to me by the dread waters of the river Styx; lay one hand on the bounteous earth, and the other on the sheen of the sea, so that all the gods who dwell down below with Saturn may be our witnesses, and see that you really do give me one of the youngest of the Graces – Pasithea, whom I have always wanted to marry.'

Juno did as he had said. She swore, and invoked all the gods of the nether world, who are called Titans, to witness. When she had completed her oath, the two enshrouded themselves in a thick mist and sped lightly forward, leaving Lemnos and Imbrus behind them. Presently they reached many-fountained Ida, mother of wild beasts, and Lectum where they left the sea to go on by land, and the tops of the trees of the forest soughed under the going of their feet. Here Sleep halted, and ere Jove caught sight of him he climbed a lofty pine-tree – the tallest that reared its head towards heaven on all Ida. He hid himself behind the branches and sat there in the semblance of the sweet-singing bird that haunts the mountains and is called Chalcis by the gods, but men call it Cymindis. Juno then went to Gargarus, the topmost peak of Ida, and Jove, driver of the clouds, set eyes upon her. As soon as he did so he became inflamed with the same passionate desire for her that he had felt when they had first enjoyed each other's embraces, and slept with one another without their dear parents knowing anything about it. He went up to her and said, 'What do you want that you have come hither from Olympus – and that too with neither chariot nor horses to convey you?'

Then Juno told him a lying tale and said, 'I am going to the world's end, to visit Oceanus, from whom all we gods proceed, and mother Tethys; they received me into their house, took care of me, and brought me up. I must go and see them that I may make peace between them: they have been quarrelling, and are so angry that they have not slept with one another this long time. The horses that will take me over land and sea are stationed on the lowermost spurs of many-fountained Ida, and I have come here from Olympus, on purpose to consult you. I was afraid you might be angry with me later on, if I went to the house of Oceanus without letting you know.'

And Jove said, 'Juno, you can choose some other time for paying your visit to Oceanus – for the present let us devote ourselves to love and to the enjoyment of one another. Never yet have I been so over-powered by passion neither for goddess nor mortal woman as I am at this moment for yourself – not even when I was in love with the wife of Ixion who bore me Pirithoüs, peer of gods in counsel, nor yet with Danaë the daintily-ancled daughter of Acrisius, who bore me the famed hero Perseus. Then there was the daughter of Phœnix, who bore me Minos and Rhadamanthus: there was Semele, and Alcmena in Thebes by whom I begot my lion-hearted son Hercules, while Semele became mother to Bacchus the comforter of mankind. There was queen Ceres again, and lovely Leto, and yourself – but with none of these was I ever so much enamoured as I now am with you.'

Juno again answered him with a lying tale. 'Most dread son of Saturn,' she exclaimed, 'what are you talking about? Would you have us enjoy one another here on the top of Mount Ida, where everything can be seen? What if one of the ever-living gods should see us sleeping together, and tell the others? It would be such a scandal that when I had risen from your embraces I could never show myself inside your house again; but if you are so minded, there is a room which your son Vulcan has made me, and he has given it good strong doors; if you would so have it, let us go thither and lie down.'

And Jove answered, 'Juno, you need not be afraid that either god or man will see you, for I will enshroud both of us in such a dense golden cloud, that the very sun for all his bright piercing beams shall not see through it.'

With this the son of Saturn caught his wife in his embrace; whereon the earth sprouted them a cushion of young grass, with dew-bespangled lotus, crocus, and hyacinth, so soft and thick that it raised them well above the ground. Here they laid themselves down and overhead they were covered by a fair cloud of gold, from which there fell glittering dew-drops.

Thus, then, did the sire of all things repose peacefully on the crest of Ida, overcome at once by sleep and love, and he held his spouse in his arms. Meanwhile Sleep made off to the ships of the Achæans, to tell earth-encircling Neptune, lord of the earthquake. When he had found him he said, 'Now, Neptune, you can help the Danaans with a will, and give them victory though it be only for a short time while

Jove is still sleeping. I have sent him into a sweet slumber, and Juno has beguiled him into going to bed with her.'

Sleep now departed and went his ways to and fro among mankind, leaving Neptune more eager than ever to help the Danaans. He darted forward among the first ranks and shouted saying, 'Argives, shall we let Hector son of Priam have the triumph of taking our ships and covering himself with glory? This is what he says that he shall now do, seeing that Achilles is still in dudgeon at his ships. We shall get on very well without him if we keep each other in heart and stand by one another. Now, therefore, let us all do as I say. Let us each take the best and largest shield we can lay hold of, put on our helmets, and sally forth with our longest spears in our hands; I will lead you on, and Hector son of Priam, rage as he may, will not dare to hold out against us. If any good staunch soldier has only a small shield, let him hand it over to a worse man, and take a larger one for himself.'

Thus did he speak, and they did even as he had said. The son of Tydeus, Ulysses, and Agamemnon, wounded though they were, set the others in array, and went about everywhere effecting the exchanges of armour; the most valiant took the best armour, and gave the worse to the worse man. When they had donned their bronze armour they marched on with Neptune at their head. In his strong hand he grasped his terrible sword, keen of edge and flashing like lightning; woe to him who comes across it in the day of battle; all men quake for fear and keep away from it.

Hector on the other side set the Trojans in array. Thereon Neptune and Hector waged fierce war on one another – Hector on the Trojan and Neptune on the Argive side. Mighty was the uproar as the two forces met; the sea came rolling in towards the ships and tents of the Achæans, but waves do not thunder on the shore more loudly when driven before the blast of Boreas, nor do the flames of a forest fire roar more fiercely when it is well alight upon the mountains, nor does the wind bellow with ruder music as it tears on through the tops of the oaks when it is blowing its hardest, than the terrible shout which the Trojans and Achæans raised as they sprang upon one another.

Hector first aimed his spear at Ajax, who was turned full towards him, nor did he miss his aim. The spear struck him where two bands passed over his chest – the band of his shield and that of his silver-studded sword – and these protected his body. Hector was angry that his spear should have been hurled in vain, and withdrew under cover of his men. As he was thus retreating, Ajax son of Telamon struck him with a stone, of which there were many lying about under the men's feet as they fought – brought there to give support to the ships' sides as they lay on the shore. Ajax caught up one of them and struck Hector above the rim of his shield close to his neck; the blow made him spin round like a top and reel in all directions. As an oak falls headlong when uprooted by the lightning flash of father Jove, and there is a terrible smell of brimstone – no man can help being dismayed if he is standing near it, for a thunderbolt is a very awful thing – even so did Hector fall to earth and bite the dust. His spear fell from his hand, but his shield and helmet were made fast about his body, and his bronze armour rang about him.

The sons of the Achæans came running with a loud cry towards him, hoping to drag him away, and they showered their darts on the Trojans, but none of them could wound him before he was surrounded and covered by the princes Polydamas, Æneas, Agenor, Sarpedon captain of the Lycians, and noble Glaucus: of the others, too, there was not one who was unmindful of him, and they held their round shields over him to cover him. His comrades then lifted him off the ground and bore him away from the battle to the place where his horses stood waiting for him at the rear of the fight with their driver and the chariot; these then took him towards the city groaning and in great pain. When they reached the ford of the fair stream of Xanthus, begotten of Immortal Jove, they took him from off his chariot and laid him down on the ground; they poured water over him, and as they did so he breathed again and opened his eyes. Then kneeling on his knees he vomited blood, but soon fell back on to the ground, and his eyes were again closed in darkness for he was still stunned by the blow.

When the Argives saw Hector leaving the field, they took heart and set upon the Trojans yet more furiously. Ajax fleet son of Oïleus began by springing on Satnius son of Enops and wounding him with his spear: a fair naiad nymph had borne him to Enops as he was herding cattle by the banks of the river Satnïoeis. The son of Oïleus came up to him and struck him in the flank so that he fell, and a fierce fight between Trojans and Danaans raged round his body. Polydamas son of Panthoüs drew near to avenge him, and wounded Prothoënor son of Areïlycus on the right shoulder; the terrible spear went right through his shoulder, and he clutched the earth as he fell in the dust. Polydamas vaunted loudly over him saying, 'Again I take it that the spear has not sped in vain from the strong hand of the son of Panthoüs; an Argive has caught it in his body, and it will serve him for a staff as he goes down into the house of Hades.'

The Argives were maddened by this boasting. Ajax son of Telamon was more angry than any, for the man had fallen close beside him; so he aimed at Polydamas as he was retreating, but Polydamas saved himself by swerving aside and the spear struck Archelochus son of Antenor, for heaven counselled his destruction; it struck him where the head springs from the neck at the top joint of the spine, and severed both the tendons at the back of the head. His head, mouth, and nostrils reached the ground long before his legs and knees could do so, and Ajax shouted to Polydamas saying, 'Think, Polydamas, and tell me truly whether this man is not as well worth killing as Prothoënor was: he seems rich, and of rich family, a brother, it may be, or son of the knight Antenor, for he is very like him.'

But he knew well who it was, and the Trojans were greatly angered. Acamas then bestrode his brother's body and wounded Promachus the Bœotian with his spear, for he was trying to drag his brother's body away. Acamas vaunted loudly over him saying, 'Argive archers, braggarts that you are, toil and suffering shall not be for us only, but some of you too shall fall here as well as ourselves. See how Promachus now sleeps, vanquished by my spear; payment for my brother's blood has not been long delayed; a man, therefore, may well be thankful if he leaves a kinsman in his house behind him to avenge his fall.'

His taunts infuriated the Argives, and Peneleos was more enraged than any of them. He sprang towards Acamas, but Acamas did not stand his ground, and he killed Ilioneus son of the rich flock-master Phorbas, whom Mercury had favoured and endowed with greater wealth than any other of the Trojans. Ilioneus was his only son, and Peneleos now wounded him in the eye under his eye-brows, tearing the eye-ball from its socket: the spear went right through the eye into the nape of the neck, and he fell, stretching out both hands before him. Peneleos then drew his sword and smote him on the neck, so that both head and helmet came tumbling down to the ground with the spear still sticking in the eye; he then held up the head, as though it had been a poppy-head, and showed it to the Trojans, vaunting over them as he did so. 'Trojans,' he cried, 'bid the father and mother of noble Ilioneus make moan for him in their house, for the wife also of Promachus son of Alegenor will never be gladdened by the coming of her dear husband when we Argives return with our ships from Troy.'

As he spoke fear fell upon them, and every man looked round about to see whither he might fly for safety.

Tell me now, O Muses that dwell on Olympus, who was the first of the Argives to bear away blood-stained spoils after Neptune lord of the earthquake had turned the fortune of war. Ajax son of Telamon was first to wound Hyrtius son of Gyrtius, captain of the staunch Mysians. Antilochus killed Phalces and Mermerus, while Meriones slew Morys and Hippotion, Teucer also killed Prothoön and Periphetes. The son of Atreus then wounded Hyperenor shepherd of his people, in the flank, and the bronze point made his entrails gush out as it tore in among them; on this his life came hurrying out of him at the place where he had been wounded, and his eyes were closed in darkness. Ajax son of Oïleus killed more than any other, for there was no man so fleet as he to pursue flying foes when Jove had spread panic among them.

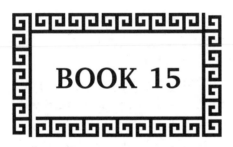

BOOK 15

Jove awakes, tells Apollo to heal Hector, and the Trojans again become victorious.

But when their flight had taken them past the trench and the set stakes, and many had fallen by the hands of the Danaans, the Trojans made a halt on reaching their chariots, routed and pale with fear. Jove now woke on the crests of Ida, where he was lying with golden-throned Juno by his side, and starting to his feet he saw the Trojans and Achæans, the one thrown into confusion, and the others driving them pell-mell before them with King Neptune in their midst. He saw Hector lying on the ground with his comrades gathered round him, gasping for breath, wandering in mind and vomiting blood, for it was not the feeblest of the Achæans who struck him.

The sire of gods and men had pity on him, and looked fiercely on Juno. 'I see, Juno,' said he, 'you mischief-making trickster, that your cunning has stayed Hector from fighting and has caused the rout of his host. I am in half a mind to thrash you, in which case you will be the first to reap the fruits of your scurvy knavery. Do you not remember how once upon a time I had you hanged? I fastened two anvils on to your feet, and bound your hands in a chain of gold which none might break, and you hung in mid-air among the clouds. All the gods in Olympus were in a fury, but they could not reach you to set you free; when I caught any one of them I gripped him and hurled him from the heavenly threshold till he came fainting down to earth; yet even this did not relieve my mind from the incessant anxiety which I felt about noble Hercules whom you and Boreas had spitefully conveyed beyond the seas to Cos, after suborning the tempests; but I rescued him, and notwithstanding all his mighty labours I brought him back again to Argos. I would remind you of this that you may learn to leave off being so deceitful, and discover how much you are likely to gain by the embraces out of which you have come here to trick me.'

Juno trembled as he spoke, and said, 'May heaven above and earth below be my witnesses, with the waters of the river Styx – and this is the most solemn oath that a blessed god can take – nay, I swear also by your own almighty head and by our bridal bed – things over which I could never possibly perjure myself – that Neptune is not punishing Hector and the Trojans and helping the Achæans through any doing of mine; it is all of his own mere motion because he was sorry to see the Achæans hard pressed at their ships: if I were advising him, I should tell him to do as you bid him.'

The sire of gods and men smiled and answered, 'If you, Juno, were always to support me when we sit in council of the gods, Neptune, like it or no, would soon come round to your and my way of thinking. If, then, you are speaking the truth and mean what you say, go among the rank and file of the gods, and tell Iris and Apollo lord of the bow, that I want them – Iris, that she may go to the Achæan host and tell Neptune to leave off fighting and go home, and Apollo, that he may send Hector again into battle and give him fresh strength; he will thus forget his present sufferings, and drive the Achæans back in confusion till they fall among the ships of Achilles son of Peleus. Achilles will then send his comrade Patroclus into battle, and Hector will kill him in front of Ilius after he has slain many warriors, and among them my own noble son Sarpedon. Achilles will kill Hector to avenge Patroclus, and from that time I will bring it about that the Achæans shall persistently drive the Trojans back till they fulfil the counsels of Minerva and take Ilius. But I will not stay my anger, nor permit any god to help the Danaans till I have accomplished the desire of the son of Peleus, according to the promise I made by bowing my head on the day when Thetis touched my knees and besought me to give him honour.'

Juno heeded his words and went from the heights of Ida to great Olympus. Swift as the thought of one whose fancy carries him over vast continents, and he says to himself, 'Now I will be here, or there,' and he would have all manner of things – even so swiftly did Juno wing her way till she came to high Olympus and went in among the gods who were gathered in the house of Jove. When they saw her they all of them came up to her, and held out their cups to her by way of greeting. She let the others be, but took the cup offered her by lovely Themis, who was first to come running up to her. 'Juno,' said she, 'why are you here? And you seem troubled – has your husband the son of Saturn been frightening you?'

And Juno answered, 'Themis, do not ask me about it. You know what a proud and cruel disposition my husband has. Lead the gods to table, where you and all the immortals can hear the wicked designs which he has avowed. Many a one, mortal and immortal, will be angered by them, however peaceably he may be feasting now.'

On this Juno sat down, and the gods were troubled throughout the house of Jove. Laughter sat on her lips but her brow was furrowed with care, and she spoke up in a rage. 'Fools that we are,' she cried, 'to be thus madly angry with Jove; we keep on wanting to go up to him and stay him by force or by persuasion, but he sits aloof and cares for nobody, for he knows that he is much stronger than any other of the immortals. Make the best, therefore, of whatever ills he may choose to send each one of you; Mars, I take it, has had a taste of them already, for his son Ascalaphus has fallen in battle – the man whom of all others he loved most dearly and whose father he owns himself to be.'

When he heard this Mars smote his two sturdy thighs with the flat of his hands, and said in anger, 'Do not blame me, you gods that dwell in heaven, if I go to the ships of the Achæans and avenge the death of my son, even though it end in my being struck by Jove's lightning and lying in blood and dust among the corpses.'

As he spoke he gave orders to yoke his horses Panic and Rout, while he put on his armour. On this, Jove would have been roused to still more fierce and implacable enmity against the other immortals, had not Minerva, alarmed for the safety of the gods, sprung from her seat and hurried outside. She tore the helmet from his head and the shield from his shoulders, and she took the bronze spear from his strong hand and set it on one side; then she said to Mars, 'Madman, you are undone; you have ears that hear not, or you have lost all judgement and understanding; have you not heard what Juno has said on coming straight from the presence of Olympian Jove? Do you wish to go through all kinds of suffering before you are brought back sick and sorry to Olympus, after having caused infinite mischief to all us others? Jove would instantly leave the Trojans and Achæans to themselves; he would come to Olympus to punish us, and would grip us up one after another, guilty or not guilty. Therefore lay aside your anger for the death of your son; better men than he have either been killed already or will fall hereafter, and one cannot protect every one's whole family.'

With these words she took Mars back to his seat. Meanwhile Juno called Apollo outside, with Iris the messenger of the gods. 'Jove,' she said to them, 'desires you to go to him at once on Mt Ida; when you have seen him you are to do as he may then bid you.'

Thereon Juno left them and resumed her seat inside, while Iris and Apollo made all haste on their way. When they reached many-fountained Ida, mother of wild beasts, they found Jove seated on topmost Gargarus with a fragrant cloud encircling his head as with a diadem.

They stood before his presence, and he was pleased with them for having been so quick in obeying the orders his wife had given them.

He spoke to Iris first. 'Go,' said he, 'fleet Iris, tell King Neptune what I now bid you – and tell him true. Bid him leave off fighting, and either join the company of the gods, or go down into the sea. If he takes no heed and disobeys me, let him consider well whether he is strong enough to hold his own against me if I attack him. I am older and much stronger than he is; yet he is not afraid to set himself up as on a level with myself, of whom all the other gods stand in awe.'

Iris, fleet as the wind, obeyed him, and as the cold hail or snowflakes that fly from out the clouds before the blast of Boreas, even so did she wing her way till she came close up to the great shaker of the earth. Then she said, 'I have come, O dark-haired king that holds the world in his embrace, to bring you a message from Jove. He bids you leave off fighting, and either join the company of the gods or go down into the sea; if, however, you take no heed and disobey him, he says he will come down here and fight you. He would have you keep out of his reach, for he is older and much stronger than you are, and yet you are not afraid to set yourself up as on a level with himself, of whom all the other gods stand in awe.'

Neptune was very angry and said, 'Great heavens! strong as Jove may be, he has said more than he can do if he has threatened violence against me, who am of like honour with himself. We were three brothers whom Rhea bore to Saturn – Jove, myself, and Hades who rules the world below. Heaven and earth were divided into three parts, and each of us was to have an equal share. When we cast lots, it fell to me to have my dwelling in the sea for evermore; Hades took the darkness of the realms under the earth, while air and sky and clouds were the portion that fell to Jove; but earth and great Olympus are the common property of all. Therefore I will not walk as Jove would have me. For all his strength, let him keep to his own third share and be contented without threatening to lay hands upon me as though I were nobody. Let him keep his bragging talk for his own sons and daughters, who must perforce obey him.'

Iris fleet as the wind then answered, 'Am I really, Neptune, to take this daring and unyielding message to Jove, or will you reconsider your answer? Sensible people are open to argument, and you know that the Erinyes always range themselves on the side of the older person.'

Neptune answered, 'Goddess Iris, your words have been spoken in season. It is well when a messenger shows so much discretion.

Nevertheless it cuts me to the very heart that any one should rebuke so angrily another who is his own peer, and of like empire with himself. Now, however, I will give way in spite of my displeasure; furthermore let me tell you, and I mean what I say – if contrary to the desire of myself, Minerva driver of the spoil, Juno, Mercury, and King Vulcan, Jove spares steep Ilius, and will not let the Achæans have the great triumph of sacking it, let him understand that he will incur our implacable resentment.'

Neptune now left the field to go down under the sea, and sorely did the Achæans miss him. Then Jove said to Apollo, 'Go, dear Phœbus, to Hector, for Neptune who holds the earth in his embrace has now gone down under the sea to avoid the severity of my displeasure. Had he not done so those gods who are below with Saturn would have come to hear of the fight between us. It is better for both of us that he should have curbed his anger and kept out of my reach, for I should have had much trouble with him. Take, then, your tasselled ægis, and shake it furiously, so as to set the Achæan heroes in a panic; take, moreover, brave Hector, O Far-Darter, into your own care, and rouse him to deeds of daring, till the Achæans are sent flying back to their ships and to the Hellespont. From that point I will think it well over, how the Achæans may have a respite from their troubles.'

Apollo obeyed his father's saying, and left the crests of Ida, flying like a falcon, bane of doves and swiftest of all birds. He found Hector no longer lying upon the ground, but sitting up, for he had just come to himself again. He knew those who were about him, and the sweat and hard breathing had left him from the moment when the will of ægis-bearing Jove had revived him. Apollo stood beside him and said, 'Hector, son of Priam, why are you so faint, and why are you here away from the others? Has any mishap befallen you?'

Hector in a weak voice answered, 'And which, kind sir, of the gods are you, who now ask me thus? Do you not know that Ajax struck me on the chest with a stone as I was killing his comrades at the ships of the Achæans, and compelled me to leave off fighting? I made sure that this very day I should breathe my last and go down into the house of Hades.'

Then King Apollo said to him, 'Take heart; the son of Saturn has sent you a mighty helper from Ida to stand by you and defend you, even me, Phœbus Apollo of the golden sword, who have been guardian hitherto not only of yourself but of your city. Now, therefore, order your horsemen to drive their chariots to the ships in great multitudes. I will go before your horses to smooth the way for them, and will turn the Achæans in flight.'

As he spoke he infused great strength into the shepherd of his people. And as a horse, stabled and full-fed, breaks loose and gallops gloriously over the plain to the place where he is wont to take his bath in the river – he tosses his head, and his mane streams over his shoulders as in all the pride of his strength he flies full speed to the pastures where the mares are feeding – even so Hector, when he heard what the god said, urged his horsemen on, and sped forward as fast as his limbs could take him. As country peasants set their hounds on to a horned stag or wild goat – he has taken shelter under rock or thicket, and they cannot find him, but, lo, a bearded lion whom their shouts have roused stands in their path, and they are in no further humour for the chase – even so the Achæans were still charging on in a body, using their swords and spears pointed at both ends, but when they saw Hector going about among his men they were afraid, and their hearts fell down into their feet.

Then spoke Thoas son of Andræmon, leader of the Ætolians, a man who could throw a good throw, and who was staunch also in close fight, while few could surpass him in debate when opinions were divided. He then with all sincerity and goodwill addressed them thus: 'What, in heaven's name, do I now see? Is it not Hector come to life again? Every one made sure he had been killed by Ajax son of Telamon, but it seems that one of the gods has again rescued him. He has killed many of us Danaans already, and I take it will yet do so, for the hand of Jove must be with him or he would never dare show himself so masterful in the forefront of the battle. Now, therefore, let us all do as I say; let us order the main body of our forces to fall back upon the ships, but let those of us who profess to be the flower of the army stand firm, and see whether we cannot hold Hector back at the point of our spears as soon as he comes near us; I conceive that he will then think better of it before he tries to charge into the press of the Danaans.'

Thus did he speak, and they did even as he had said. Those who were about Ajax and King Idomeneus, the followers moreover of Teucer, Meriones, and Meges peer of Mars called all their best men about them and sustained the fight against Hector and the Trojans, but the main body fell back upon the ships of the Achæans.

The Trojans pressed forward in a dense body, with Hector striding on at their head. Before him went Phœbus Apollo shrouded in cloud about his shoulders. He bore aloft the terrible ægis with its shaggy fringe, which Vulcan the smith had given Jove to strike terror into the hearts of men. With this in his hand he led on the Trojans.

The Argives held together and stood their ground. The cry of battle rose high from either side, and the arrows flew from the bowstrings. Many a spear sped from strong hands and fastened in the bodies of many a valiant warrior, while others fell to earth midway, before they could taste of man's fair flesh and glut themselves with blood. So long as Phœbus Apollo held his ægis quietly and without shaking it, the weapons on either side took effect and the people fell, but when he shook it straight in the face of the Danaans and raised his mighty battle-cry their hearts fainted within them and they forgot their former prowess. As when two wild beasts spring in the dead of night on a herd of cattle or a large flock of sheep when the herdsman is not there – even so were the Danaans struck helpless, for Apollo filled them with panic and gave victory to Hector and the Trojans.

The fight then became more scattered and they killed one another where they best could. Hector killed Stichius and Arcesilaus, the one, leader of the Bœotians, and the other, friend and comrade of Menestheus. Æneas killed Medon and Iasus. The first was bastard son to Oïleus, and brother to Ajax, but he lived in Phylace away from his own country, for he had killed a man, a kinsman of his stepmother Eriopis whom Oïleus had married. Iasus had become a leader of the Athenians, and was son of Sphelus the son of Boucolos. Polydamas killed Mecisteus, and Polites Echius, in the front of the battle, while Agenor slew Clonius. Paris struck Deïochus from behind in the lower part of the shoulder, as he was flying among the foremost, and the point of the spear went clean through him.

While they were spoiling these heroes of their armour, the Achæans were flying pell-mell to the trench and the set stakes, and were forced back within their wall. Hector then cried out to the Trojans, 'Forward to the ships, and let the spoils be. If I see any man keeping back on the other side the wall away from the ships I will have him killed: his kinsmen and kinswomen shall not give him his dues of fire, but dogs shall tear him in pieces in front of our city.'

As he spoke he laid his whip about his horses' shoulders and called to the Trojans throughout their ranks; the Trojans shouted with a cry that rent the air, and kept their horses neck and neck with his own. Phœbus Apollo went before, and kicked down the banks of the deep trench into its middle so as to make a great broad bridge, as broad as the throw of a spear when a man is trying his strength. The Trojan battalions poured over the bridge, and Apollo with his redoubtable ægis led the way. He kicked down the wall of the Achæans as easily as a child who playing on the sea-shore has built a house of sand and then kicks it down again and destroys it – even so did you, O Apollo, shed toil and trouble upon the Argives, filling them with panic and confusion.

Thus then were the Achæans hemmed in at their ships, calling out to one another and raising their hands with loud cries every man to heaven. Nestor of Gerene, tower of strength to the Achæans, lifted up his hands to the starry firmament of heaven, and prayed more fervently than any of them. 'Father Jove,' said he, 'if ever any one in wheat-growing Argos burned you fat thigh-bones of sheep or heifer and prayed that he might return safely home, whereon you bowed your head to him in assent, bear it in mind now, and suffer not the Trojans to triumph thus over the Achæans.'

All-counselling Jove thundered loudly in answer to the prayer of the aged son of Neleus. When the Trojans heard Jove thunder they flung themselves yet more fiercely on the Achæans. As a wave breaking over the bulwarks of a ship when the sea runs high before a gale – for it is the force of the wind that makes the waves so great – even so did the Trojans spring over the wall with a shout, and drive their chariots onwards. The two sides fought with their double-pointed spears in hand-to-hand encounter – the Trojans from their chariots, and the Achæans climbing up into their ships and wielding the long pikes that were lying on the decks ready for use in a sea-fight, jointed and shod with bronze.

Now Patroclus, so long as the Achæans and Trojans were fighting about the wall, but were not yet within it and at the ships, remained sitting in the tent of good Eurypylus, entertaining him with his conversation and spreading herbs over his wound to ease his pain. When, however, he saw the Trojans swarming through the breach in the wall, while the Achæans were clamouring and struck with panic, he cried aloud, and smote his two thighs with the flat of his hands. 'Eurypylus,' said he in his dismay, 'I know you want me badly, but I cannot stay with you any longer, for there is hard fighting going on; a servant shall take care of you now, for I must make all speed to Achilles, and induce him to fight if I can; who knows but with heaven's help I may persuade him. A man does well to listen to the advice of a friend.'

When he had thus spoken he went his way. The Achæans stood firm and resisted the attack of the Trojans, yet though these were fewer in number, they could not drive them back from the ships, neither could the Trojans break the Achæan ranks and make their way in among the tents and ships. As a carpenter's line gives a true edge to a piece of ship's timber, in the hand of some skilled workman whom Minerva has instructed in all kinds of useful arts – even so level was the issue of the fight between the two sides, as they fought some round one ship and some round another.

Hector made straight for Ajax, and the two fought fiercely about the same ship. Hector could not force Ajax back and fire the ship, nor yet could Ajax drive Hector from the spot to which heaven had brought him.

Then Ajax struck Caletor son of Clytius in the chest with a spear as he was bringing fire towards the ship. He fell heavily to the ground and the torch dropped from his hand. When Hector saw his cousin fallen in front of the ship he shouted to the Trojans and Lycians saying, 'Trojans, Lycians, and Dardanians good in close fight, bate not a jot, but rescue the son of Clytius lest the Achæans strip him of his armour now that he has fallen.'

He then aimed a spear at Ajax, and missed him, but he hit Lycophron a follower of Ajax, who came from Cythera, but was living with Ajax inasmuch as he had killed a man among the Cythereans. Hector's spear struck him on the head below the ear, and he fell headlong from the ship's prow on to the ground with no life left in him. Ajax shook with rage and said to his brother, 'Teucer, my good fellow, our trusty comrade the son of Mastor has fallen, he who came to live with us from Cythera and whom we honoured as much as our own parents. Hector has just killed him; fetch your deadly arrows at once and the bow which Phœbus Apollo gave you.'

Teucer heard him and hastened towards him with his bow and quiver in his hands. Forthwith he showered his arrows on the Trojans, and hit Cleitus the son of Pisenor, comrade of Polydamas the noble son of Panthoüs, with the reins in his hands as he was attending to his horses; he was in the middle of the very thickest part of the fight, doing good service to Hector and the Trojans, but evil had now come upon him, and not one of those who were fain to do so could avert it, for the arrow struck him on the back of the neck. He fell from his chariot and his horses shook the empty car as they swerved aside. King Polydamas saw what had happened, and was the first to come up to the horses; he gave them in charge to Astynoüs son of Protiaon, and ordered him to look on, and to keep the horses near at hand. He then went back and took his place in the front ranks.

Teucer then aimed another arrow at Hector, and there would have been no more fighting at the ships if he had hit him and killed him then and there: Jove, however, who kept watch over Hector, had his eyes on Teucer, and deprived him of his triumph, by breaking his bowstring for him just as he was drawing it and about to take his aim; on this the arrow went astray and the bow fell from his hands. Teucer shook with anger and said to his brother, 'Alas, see how heaven thwarts us in all we do; it has broken my bowstring and snatched the bow from my hand, though I strung it this self-same morning that it might serve me for many an arrow.'

Ajax son of Telamon answered, 'My good fellow, let your bow and your arrows be, for Jove has made them useless in order to spite the Danaans. Take your spear, lay your shield upon your shoulder, and both fight the Trojans yourself and urge others to do so. They may be successful for the moment but if we fight as we ought they will find it a hard matter to take the ships.'

Teucer then took his bow and put it by in his tent. He hung a shield four hides thick about his shoulders, and on his comely head he set his helmet well wrought with a crest of horse-hair that nodded menacingly above it; he grasped his redoubtable bronze-shod spear, and forthwith he was by the side of Ajax.

When Hector saw that Teucer's bow was of no more use to him, he shouted out to the Trojans and Lycians, 'Trojans, Lycians, and Dardanians good in close fight, be men, my friends, and show your mettle here at the ships, for I see the weapon of one of their chieftains made useless by the hand of Jove. It is easy to see when Jove is helping people and means to help them still further, or again when he is bringing them down and will do nothing for them; he is now on our side, and is going against the Argives. Therefore swarm round the ships and fight. If any of you is struck by spear or sword and loses his life, let him die; he dies with honour who dies fighting for his country and he will leave his wife and children safe behind him, with his house and allotment unplundered if only the Achæans can be driven back to their own land, they and their ships.'

With these words he put heart and soul into them all. Ajax on the other side exhorted his comrades saying, 'Shame on you Argives, we are now utterly undone, unless we can save ourselves by driving the enemy from our ships. Do you think, if Hector takes them, that you will be able to get home by land? Can you not hear him cheering on his whole host to fire our fleet, and bidding them remember that they are not at a dance but in battle? Our only course is to fight them with might and main; we had better chance it, life or death, once for all, than fight long and without issue hemmed in at our ships by worse men than ourselves.'

With these words he put life and soul into them all. Hector then killed Schedius son of Perimedes, leader of the Phocēans, and Ajax killed Laodamas captain of foot soldiers and son to Antenor. Polydamas killed Otus of Cyllene a comrade of the son of Phyleus and chief of the proud Epeans. When Meges saw this he sprang upon him, but Polydamas crouched down, and he missed him, for Apollo would not suffer the son of Panthoüs to fall in battle; but the spear hit Croesmus in the middle of his chest, whereon he fell heavily to the ground, and Meges stripped him of his armour. At that moment the valiant soldier Dolops son of Lampus sprang upon him; Lampus was son of Laomedon and noted for his valour, while his son Dolops was versed in all the ways of war. He then struck the middle of the son of Phyleus' shield with his spear, setting on him at close quarters, but his good corslet made with plates of metal saved him; Phyleus had brought it from Ephyra and the river Selleïs, where his host, King Euphetes, had given it him to wear in battle and protect him. It now served to save the life of his son. Then Meges struck the topmost crest of Dolops's bronze helmet with his spear and tore away its plume of horse-hair, so that all newly dyed with scarlet as it was it tumbled down into the dust. While he was still fighting and confident of victory, Menelaus came up to help Meges, and got by the side of Dolops unperceived; he then speared him in the shoulder, from behind, and the point, driven so furiously, went through into his chest, whereon he fell headlong. The two then made towards him to strip him of his armour, but Hector called on all his brothers for help, and he especially upbraided brave Melanippus son of Hiketaon, who erewhile used to pasture his herds of cattle in Percote before the war broke out; but when the ships of the Danaans came, he went back to Ilius, where he was eminent among the Trojans, and lived near Priam who treated him as one of his own sons. Hector now rebuked him and said, 'Why, Melanippus, are we thus remiss? do you take no note of the death of your kinsman, and do you not see how they are trying to take Dolops's armour? Follow me; there must be no fighting the Argives from a distance now, but we must do so in close combat till either we kill them or they take the high wall of Ilius and slay her people.'

He led on as he spoke, and the hero Melanippus followed after. Meanwhile Ajax son of Telamon was cheering on the Argives. 'My friends,' he cried, 'be men, and fear dishonour; quit yourselves in battle so as to win respect from one another. Men who respect each other's good opinion are less likely to be killed than those who do not, but in flight there is neither gain nor glory.'

Thus did he exhort men who were already bent upon driving back the Trojans. They laid his words to heart and hedged the ships as with a wall of bronze, while Jove urged on the Trojans. Menelaus of the loud battle-cry urged Antilochus on. 'Antilochus,' said he, 'you are young and there is none of the Achæans more fleet of foot or more valiant than you are. See if you cannot spring upon some Trojan and kill him.'

He hurried away when he had thus spurred Antilochus, who at once darted out from the front ranks and aimed a spear, after looking carefully round him. The Trojans fell back as he threw, and the dart did not speed from his hand without effect, for it struck Melanippus the proud son of Hiketaon in the breast by the nipple as he was coming forward, and his armour rang rattling round him as he fell heavily to the ground. Antilochus sprang upon him as a dog springs on a fawn which a hunter has hit as it was breaking away from its covert, and killed it. Even so, O Melanippus, did stalwart Antilochus spring upon you to strip you of your armour; but noble Hector marked him, and came running up to him through the thick of the battle. Antilochus, brave soldier though he was, would not stay to face him, but fled like some savage creature which knows it has done wrong, and flies, when it has killed a dog or a man who is herding his cattle, before a body of men can be gathered to attack it. Even so did the son of Nestor fly, and the Trojans and Hector with a cry that rent the air showered their weapons after him; nor did he turn round and stay his flight till he had reached his comrades.

The Trojans, fierce as lions, were still rushing on towards the ships in fulfilment of the behests of Jove who kept spurring them on to new deeds of daring, while he deadened the courage of the Argives and defeated them by encouraging the Trojans. For he meant giving glory to Hector son of Priam, and letting him throw fire upon the ships, till he had fulfilled the unrighteous prayer that Thetis had made him; Jove, therefore, bided his time till he should see the glare of a blazing ship. From that hour he was about so to order it that the Trojans should be driven back from the ships and to vouchsafe glory to the Achæans. With this purpose he inspired Hector son of Priam, who was eager enough already, to assail the ships. His fury was as that of Mars, or as when a fire is raging in the glades of some dense forest upon the mountains; he foamed at the mouth, his eyes glared under his terrible eye-brows, and his helmet quivered on his temples by reason of the fury with which he fought. Jove from heaven was with him, and though he was but one against many, vouchsafed him victory and glory; for he was doomed to an early death, and already Pallas Minerva was hurrying on the hour of his destruction at the hands of the son of Peleus. Now, however, he kept trying to break the ranks of the enemy wherever he could see them thickest, and in the goodliest armour; but do what he might he could not break through them, for they stood as a tower foursquare, or as some high cliff rising from the grey sea that braves the anger of the gale, and of the waves that thunder up against it. He fell upon them like flames of fire from every quarter. As when a wave, raised mountain high by wind and storm, breaks over a ship and covers it deep in foam, the fierce winds roar against the mast, the hearts of the sailors fail them for fear, and they are saved but by a very little from destruction – even so were the hearts of the Achæans fainting within them. Or as a savage lion attacking a herd of cows while they are feeding by thousands in the low-lying meadows by some wide-watered shore – the herdsman is at his wits' end how to protect his herd and keeps going about now in the van and now in the rear of his cattle, while the lion springs into the thick of them and fastens on a cow so that they all tremble for fear – even so were the Achæans utterly panic-stricken by Hector and father Jove. Nevertheless Hector only killed Periphetes of Mycenæ; he was son of Copreus who was wont to take the orders of King Eurystheus to mighty Hercules, but the son was a far better man than the father in every way; he was fleet of foot, a valiant warrior, and in understanding ranked among the foremost men of Mycenæ. He it was who then afforded Hector a triumph, for as he was turning back he stumbled against the rim of his shield which reached his feet, and served to keep the javelins off him. He tripped against this and fell face upward, his helmet ringing loudly about his head as he did so. Hector saw him fall and ran up to him; he then thrust a spear into his chest, and killed him close to his own comrades. These, for all their sorrow, could not help him for they were themselves terribly afraid of Hector.

They had now reached the ships and the prows of those that had been drawn up first were on every side of them, but the Trojans came pouring after them. The Argives were driven back from the first row of ships, but they made a stand by their tents without being broken up and scattered; shame and fear restrained them. They kept shouting incessantly to one another, and Nestor of Gerene, tower of strength to the Achæans, was loudest in imploring every man by his parents, and beseeching him to stand firm.

'Be men, my friends,' he cried, 'and respect one another's good opinion. Think, all of you, on your children, your wives, your property, and your parents whether these be alive or dead. On their behalf though they are not here, I implore you to stand firm, and not to turn in flight.'

With these words he put heart and soul into them all. Minerva lifted the thick veil of darkness from their eyes, and much light fell upon them, alike on the side of the ships and on that where the fight was raging. They could see Hector and all his men, both those in the rear who were taking no part in the battle, and those who were fighting by the ships.

Ajax could not bring himself to retreat along with the rest, but strode from deck to deck with a great sea-pike in his hands twelve cubits long and jointed with rings. As a man skilled in feats of horsemanship couples four horses together and comes tearing full speed along the public way from the country into some large town – many both men and women marvel as they see him for he keeps all the time changing his horse, springing from one to another without ever missing his feet while the horses are at a gallop – even so did Ajax go striding from one ship's deck to another, and his voice went up into the heavens. He kept on shouting his orders to the Danaans and exhorting them to defend their ships and tents; neither did Hector remain within the main body of the Trojan warriors, but as a dun eagle swoops down upon a flock of wild-fowl feeding near a river – geese, it may be, or cranes, or long-necked swans – even so did Hector make straight for a dark-prowed ship, rushing right towards it; for Jove with his mighty hand impelled him forward, and roused his people to follow him.

And now the battle again raged furiously at the ships. You would have thought the men were coming on fresh and unwearied, so fiercely did they fight; and this was the mind in which they were – the Achæans did not believe they should escape destruction but thought themselves doomed, while there was not a Trojan but his heart beat high with the hope of firing the ships and putting the Achæan heroes to the sword.

Thus were the two sides minded. Then Hector seized the stern of the good ship that had brought Protesilaus to Troy, but never bore him back to his native land. Round this ship there raged a close hand-to-hand fight between Danaans and Trojans. They did not fight at a distance with bows and javelins, but with one mind hacked at one another in close combat with their mighty swords and spears pointed at both ends; they fought moreover with keen battle-axes and with hatchets. Many a good stout blade hilted and scabbarded with iron, fell from hand or shoulder as they fought, and the earth ran red with blood. Hector, when he had seized the ship, would not loose his hold but held on to its curved stern and shouted to the Trojans, 'Bring fire, and raise the battle-cry all of you with a single voice. Now has Jove vouchsafed us a day that will pay us for all the rest; this day we shall take the ships which came hither against heaven's will, and which have caused us such infinite suffering through the cowardice of our councillors, who when I would have done battle at the ships held me back and forbade the host to follow me; if Jove did then indeed warp our judgements, himself now commands me and cheers me on.'

As he spoke thus the Trojans sprang yet more fiercely on the Achæans, and Ajax no longer held his ground, for he was overcome by the darts that were flung at him, and made sure that he was doomed. Therefore he left the raised deck at the stern, and stepped back on to the seven-foot bench of the oarsmen. Here he stood on the look-out, and with his spear held back any Trojan whom he saw bringing fire to the ships. All the time he kept on shouting at the top of his voice and exhorting the Danaans. 'My friends,' he cried, 'Danaan heroes, servants of Mars, be men my friends, and fight with might and with main. Can we hope to find helpers hereafter, or a wall to shield us more surely than the one we have? There is no strong city within reach, whence we may draw fresh forces to turn the scales in our favour. We are on the plain of the armed Trojans with the sea behind us, and far from our own country. Our salvation, therefore, is in the might of our hands and in hard fighting.'

As he spoke he wielded his spear with still greater fury, and when any Trojan made towards the ships with fire at Hector's bidding, he would be on the look-out for him, and drive at him with his long spear. Twelve men did he thus kill in hand-to-hand fight before the ships.

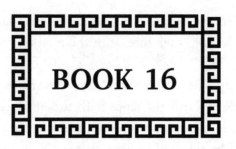

BOOK 16

Fire being now thrown on the ship of Protesilaus, Patroclus fights in the armour of Achilles – He drives the Trojans back, but is in the end killed by Euphorbus and Hector.

Thus did they fight about the ship of Protesilaus. Then Patroclus drew near to Achilles with tears welling from his eyes, as from some spring whose crystal stream falls over the ledges of a high precipice. When Achilles saw him thus weeping he was sorry for him and said, 'Why, Patroclus, do you stand there weeping like some silly child that comes running to her mother, and begs to be taken up and carried – she catches hold of her mother's dress to stay her though she is in a hurry, and looks tearfully up until her mother carries her – even such tears, Patroclus, are you now shedding. Have you anything to say to the Myrmidons or to myself? or have you had news from Phthia which you alone know? They tell me Menœtius son of Actor is still alive, as also Peleus son of Æacus, among the Myrmidons – men whose loss we two should bitterly deplore; or are you grieving about the Argives and the way in which they are being killed at the ships, through their own high-handed doings? Do not hide anything from me but tell me that both of us may know about it.'

Then, O knight Patroclus, with a deep sigh you answered, 'Achilles, son of Peleus, foremost champion of the Achæans, do not be angry, but I weep for the disaster that has now befallen the Argives. All those who have been their champions so far are lying at the ships, wounded by sword or spear. Brave Diomed son of Tydeus has been hit with a spear, while famed Ulysses and Agamemnon have received sword-wounds; Eurypylus again has been struck with an arrow in the thigh; skilled apothecaries are attending to these heroes, and healing them of their wounds; are you still, O Achilles, so inexorable? May it never be my lot to nurse such a passion as you have done, to the baning of your own good name. Who in future story will speak well of you unless you now save the Argives from ruin? You know no pity; knight Peleus was not your father nor Thetis your mother, but the grey sea bore you and the sheer cliffs begot you, so cruel and remorseless are you. If however you are kept back through knowledge of some oracle, or if your mother Thetis has told you something from the mouth of Jove, at least send me and the Myrmidons with me, if I may bring deliverance to the Danaans. Let me moreover wear your armour; the Trojans may thus mistake me for you and quit the field, so that the hard-pressed sons of the Achæans may have breathing time – which while they are fighting may hardly be. We who are fresh might soon drive tired men back from our ships and tents to their own city.'

He knew not what he was asking, nor that he was suing for his own destruction. Achilles was deeply moved and answered, 'What, noble Patroclus, are you saying? I know no prophesyings which I am heeding, nor has my mother told me anything from the mouth of Jove, but I am cut to the very heart that one of my own rank should dare to rob me because he is more powerful than I am. This, after all that I have gone through, is more than I can endure. The girl whom the sons of the Achæans chose for me, whom I won as the fruit of my spear on having sacked a city – her has King Agamemnon taken from me as though I were some common vagrant. Still, let bygones be bygones: no man may keep his anger for ever; I said I would not relent till battle and the cry of war had reached my own ships; nevertheless, now gird my armour about your shoulders, and lead the Myrmidons to battle, for the dark cloud of Trojans has burst furiously over our fleet; the Argives are driven back on to the beach, cooped within a narrow space, and the whole people of Troy has taken heart to sally out against them, because they see not the visor of my helmet gleaming near them. Had they seen this, there would not have been a creek nor grip[6] that had not been filled with their dead as they fled back again. And so it would have been, if only King Agamemnon had dealt fairly by me. As it is the Trojans have beset our host. Diomed son of Tydeus no longer wields his spear to defend the Danaans, neither have I heard the voice of the son of Atreus coming from his hated head, whereas that of murderous Hector rings in my ears as he gives orders to the Trojans, who triumph over the Achæans and fill the whole plain with their cry of battle. But even so, Patroclus, fall upon them and save the fleet, lest the Trojans fire it and prevent us from being able to return. Do, however, as I now bid you, that you may win me great honour from all the Danaans, and that they may restore the girl to me again and give me rich gifts into the bargain. When you have driven the Trojans from the ships, come back again. Though Juno's thundering husband should put triumph within your reach, do not fight the Trojans further in my absence, or you will rob me of glory that should be mine. And do not for lust of battle go on killing the Trojans nor lead the Achæans on to Ilius, lest one of the ever-living gods from Olympus attack you – for Phœbus Apollo loves them well; return when you have freed the ships from peril, and let others wage war upon the plain. Would, by father Jove, Minerva, and Apollo, that not a single man of all the Trojans might be left alive, nor yet of the Argives, but that we two might be alone left to tear aside the mantle that veils the brow of Troy.'

Thus did they converse. But Ajax could no longer hold his ground for the shower of darts that rained upon him; the will of Jove and the javelins of the Trojans were too much for him; the helmet that gleamed about his temples rang with the continuous clatter of the missiles that kept pouring on to it and on to the cheek-pieces that protected his face. Moreover his left shoulder was tired with having held his shield so long, yet for all this, let fly at him as they would, they could not make him give ground. He could hardly draw his breath, the sweat rained from every pore of his body, he had not a moment's respite, and on all sides he was beset by danger upon danger.

And now, tell me, O Muses that hold your mansions on Olympus, how fire was thrown upon the ships of the Achæans. Hector came close up and let drive with his great sword at the ashen spear of Ajax. He cut it clean in two just behind where the point was fastened on to the shaft of the spear. Ajax, therefore, had now nothing but a headless spear, while the bronze point flew some way off and came ringing down on to the ground. Ajax knew the hand of heaven in this, and was dismayed at seeing that Jove had now left him utterly defenceless and was willing victory for the Trojans. Therefore he drew back, and the Trojans flung fire upon the ship which was at once wrapped in flame.

The fire was now flaring about the ship's stern, whereon Achilles smote his two thighs and said to Patroclus, 'Up, noble knight, for I see the glare of hostile fire at our fleet; up, lest they destroy our ships, and there be no way by which we may retreat. Gird on your armour at once while I call our people together.'

As he spoke Patroclus put on his armour. First he greaved his legs with greaves of good make, and fitted with ancle-clasps of silver; after this he donned the cuirass of the son of Æacus, richly inlaid and studded. He hung his silver-studded sword of bronze about his shoulders, and then his mighty shield. On his comely head he set his helmet, well wrought, with a crest of horse-hair that nodded menacingly above it. He grasped two redoubtable spears that suited his hands, but he did not take the spear of noble Achilles, so stout and strong, for none other of the Achæans could wield it, though Achilles could do so easily. This was the ashen spear from Mount Pelion, which Chiron had cut upon a mountain top and had given to Peleus, wherewith to deal out death among heroes. He bade Automedon yoke his horses with all speed, for he was the man whom he held in honour next after Achilles, and on whose support in battle he could rely most firmly. Automedon therefore yoked the fleet horses Xanthus and Balius, steeds that could fly like the wind: these were they whom the harpy Podarge bore to the west wind, as she was grazing in a meadow by the waters of the river Oceanus. In the side traces he set the noble horse Pedasus, whom Achilles had brought away with him when he sacked the city of Eëtion, and who, mortal steed though he was, could take his place along with those that were immortal.

Meanwhile Achilles went about everywhere among the tents, and bade his Myrmidons put on their armour. Even as fierce ravening wolves that are feasting upon a horned stag which they have killed upon the mountains, and their jaws are red with blood – they go in a pack to lap water from the clear spring with their long thin tongues, and they reek of blood and slaughter; they know not what fear is, for it is hunger drives them – even so did the leaders and counsellors of the Myrmidons gather round the good squire of the fleet descendant of Æacus, and among them stood Achilles himself cheering on both men and horses.

Fifty ships had noble Achilles brought to Troy, and in each there was a crew of fifty oarsmen. Over these he set five captains whom he could trust, while he was himself commander over them all. Menesthius of the gleaming corslet, son to the river Spercheius that streams from heaven, was captain of the first company. Fair Polydora daughter of Peleus bore him to ever-flowing Spercheius – a woman mated with a god – but he was called son of Borus son of Perieres, with whom his mother was living as his wedded wife, and who gave great wealth to gain her. The second company was led by noble Eudorus, son to an unwedded woman. Polymele, daughter of Phylas the graceful dancer, bore him; the mighty slayer of Argos was enamoured of her as he saw her among the singing women at a dance held in honour of Diana the rushing huntress of the golden arrows; he therefore – Mercury, giver of all good – went with her into an upper chamber, and lay with her in secret, whereon she bore him a noble son Eudorus, singularly fleet of foot and in fight valiant. When Ilithuia goddess of the pains of child-birth brought him to the light of day, and he saw the face of the sun, mighty Echecles son of Actor took the mother to wife, and gave great wealth to gain her, but her father Phylas brought the child up, and took care of him, doting as fondly upon him as though he were his own son. The third company was led by Pisander son of Mæmalus, the finest spearman among all the Myrmidons next to Achilles' own comrade Patroclus. The old knight Phœnix was captain of the fourth company, and Alcimedon, noble son of Laërceus, of the fifth.

When Achilles had chosen his men and had stationed them all with their captains, he charged them straitly saying, 'Myrmidons, remember your threats against the Trojans while you were at the ships in the time of my anger, and you were all complaining of me. "Cruel son of Peleus," you would say, "your mother must have suckled you on gall, so ruthless are you. You keep us here at the ships against our will; if you are so relentless it were better we went home over the sea." Often have you gathered and thus chided with me. The hour is now come for those high feats of arms that you have so long been pining for, therefore keep high hearts each one of you to do battle with the Trojans.'

With these words he put heart and soul into them all, and they serried their companies yet more closely when they heard the words of their king. As the stones which a builder sets in the wall of some high house which is to give shelter from the winds – even so closely were the helmets and bossed shields set against one another. Shield pressed on shield, helm on helm, and man on man; so close were they that the horse-hair plumes on the gleaming ridges of their helmets touched each other as they bent their heads.

In front of them all two men put on their armour – Patroclus and Automedon – two men, with but one mind to lead the Myrmidons. Then Achilles went inside his tent and opened the lid of the strong chest which silver-footed Thetis had given him to take on board ship, and which she had filled with shirts, cloaks to keep out the cold, and good thick rugs. In this chest he had a cup of rare workmanship, from which no man but himself might drink, nor would he make offering from it to any other god save only to father Jove. He took the cup from the chest and cleansed it with sulphur; this done he rinsed it in clean water, and after he had washed his hands he drew wine. Then he stood in the middle of the court and prayed, looking towards heaven, and making his drink-offering of wine; nor was he unseen of Jove whose joy is in thunder. 'King Jove,' he cried, 'lord of Dodona, god of the Pelasgi, who dwellest afar, you who hold wintry Dodona in your sway, where your prophets the Selli dwell around you with their feet unwashed and their couches made upon the ground – if you heard me when I prayed to you aforetime, and did me honour while you sent disaster on the Achæans, vouchsafe me now the fulfilment of yet this further prayer. I shall stay here where my ships are lying, but I shall send my comrade into battle at the head of many Myrmidons. Grant, O all-seeing Jove, that victory may go with him; put your courage into his heart that Hector may learn whether my squire is man enough to fight alone, or whether his might is only then so indomitable when I myself enter the turmoil of war. Afterwards when he has chased the fight and the cry of battle from the ships, grant that he may return unharmed, with his armour and his comrades, fighters in close combat.'

Thus did he pray, and all-counselling Jove heard his prayer. Part of it he did indeed vouchsafe him – but not the whole. He granted that Patroclus should thrust back war and battle from the ships, but refused to let him come safely out of the fight.

When he had made his drink-offering and had thus prayed, Achilles went inside his tent and put back the cup into his chest.

Then he again came out, for he still loved to look upon the fierce fight that raged between the Trojans and Achæans.

Meanwhile the armed band that was about Patroclus marched on till they sprang high in hope upon the Trojans. They came swarming out like wasps whose nests are by the roadside, and whom silly children love to tease, whereon any one who happens to be passing may get stung – or again, if a wayfarer going along the road vexes them by accident, every wasp will come flying out in a fury to defend his little ones – even with such rage and courage did the Myrmidons swarm from their ships, and their cry of battle rose heavenwards. Patroclus called out to his men at the top of his voice, 'Myrmidons, followers of Achilles son of Peleus, be men my friends, fight with might and with main, that we may win glory for the son of Peleus, who is far the foremost man at the ships of the Argives – he, and his close fighting followers. The son of Atreus King Agamemnon will thus learn his folly in showing no respect to the bravest of the Achæans.'

With these words he put heart and soul into them all, and they fell in a body upon the Trojans. The ships rang again with the cry which the Achæans raised, and when the Trojans saw the brave son of Menœtius and his squire all gleaming in their armour, they were daunted and their battalions were thrown into confusion, for they thought the fleet son of Peleus must now have put aside his anger, and have been reconciled to Agamemnon; every one, therefore, looked round about to see whither he might fly for safety.

Patroclus first aimed a spear into the middle of the press where men were packed most closely, by the stern of the ship of Protesilaus. He hit Pyræchmes who had led his Pæonian horsemen from the Amydon and the broad waters of the river Axius; the spear struck him on the right shoulder, and with a groan he fell backwards in the dust; on this his men were thrown into confusion, for by killing their leader, who was the finest soldier among them, Patroclus struck panic into them all. He thus drove them from the ship and quenched the fire that was then blazing – leaving the half-burnt ship to lie where it was. The Trojans were now driven back with a shout that rent the skies, while the Danaans poured after them from their ships, shouting also without ceasing. As when Jove, gatherer of the thunder-cloud, spreads a dense canopy on the top of some lofty mountain, and all the peaks, the jutting headlands, and forest glades show out in the great light that flashes from the bursting heavens, even so when the Danaans had now driven back the fire from their ships, they took breath for a little while; but the fury of the fight was not yet over, for the Trojans were not driven back in utter rout, but still gave battle, and were ousted from their ground only by sheer fighting.

The fight then became more scattered, and the chieftains killed one another when and how they could. The valiant son of Menœtius first drove his spear into the thigh of Areïlycus just as he was turning round; the point went clean through, and broke the bone so that he fell forward. Meanwhile Menelaus struck Thoas in the chest, where it was exposed near the rim of his shield, and he fell dead. The son of Phyleus saw Amphiclus about to attack him, and ere he could do so took aim at the upper part of his thigh, where the muscles are thicker than in any other part; the spear tore through all the sinews of the leg, and his eyes were closed in darkness. Of the sons of Nestor one, Antilochus, speared Atymnius, driving the point of the spear through his throat, and down he fell. Maris then sprang on Antilochus in hand-to-hand fight to avenge his brother, and bestrode the body spear in hand; but valiant Thrasymedes was too quick for him, and in a moment had struck him in the shoulder ere he could deal his blow; his aim was true, and the spear severed all the muscles at the root of his arm, and tore them right down to the bone, so he fell heavily to the ground and his eyes were closed in darkness. Thus did these two noble comrades of Sarpedon go down to Erebus slain by the two sons of Nestor; they were the warrior sons of Amisodorus, who had reared the invincible Chimæra, to the bane of many. Ajax son of Oïleus sprang on Cleobulus and took him alive as he was entangled in the crush; but he killed him then and there by a sword-blow on the neck. The sword reeked with his blood, while dark death and the strong hand of fate gripped him and closed his eyes.

Peneleos and Lycon now met in close fight, for they had missed each other with their spears. They had both thrown without effect, so now they drew their swords. Lycon struck the plumed crest of Peneleos' helmet but his sword broke at the hilt, while Peneleos smote Lycon on the neck under the ear. The blade sank so deep that the head was held on by nothing but the skin, and there was no more life left in him. Meriones gave chase to Acamas on foot and caught him up just as he was about to mount his chariot; he drove a spear through his right shoulder so that he fell headlong from the car, and his eyes were closed in darkness. Idomeneus speared Erymas in the mouth; the bronze point of the spear went clean through it beneath the brain, crashing in among the white bones and smashing them up. His teeth were all of them knocked out and the blood came gushing in a stream from both his eyes; it also came gurgling up from his mouth and nostrils, and the darkness of death enfolded him round about.

Thus did these chieftains of the Danaans each of them kill his man. As ravening wolves seize on kids or lambs, fastening on them when they are alone on the hillsides and have strayed from the main flock through the carelessness of the shepherd – and when the wolves see this they pounce upon them at once because they cannot defend themselves – even so did the Danaans now fall on the Trojans, who fled with ill-omened cries in their panic and had no more fight left in them.

Meanwhile great Ajax kept on trying to drive a spear into Hector, but Hector was so skilful that he held his broad shoulders well under cover of his ox-hide shield, ever on the look-out for the whizzing of the arrows and the heavy thud of the spears. He well knew that the fortunes of the day had changed, but still stood his ground and tried to protect his comrades.

As when a cloud goes up into heaven from Olympus, rising out of a clear sky when Jove is brewing a gale – even with such panic-stricken rout did the Trojans now fly, and there was no order in their going. Hector's fleet horses bore him and his armour out of the fight, and he left the Trojan host penned in by the deep trench against their will. Many a yoke of horses snapped the pole of their chariots in the trench and left their master's car behind them. Patroclus gave chase, calling impetuously on the Danaans and full of fury against the Trojans, who, being now no longer in a body, filled all the ways with their cries of panic and rout; the air was darkened with the clouds of dust they raised, and the horses strained every nerve in their flight from the tents and ships towards the city.

Patroclus kept on heading his horses wherever he saw most men flying in confusion, cheering on his men the while. Chariots were being smashed in all directions, and many a man came tumbling down from his own car to fall beneath the wheels of that of Patroclus, whose immortal steeds, given by the gods to Peleus, sprang over the trench at a bound as they sped onward. He was intent on trying to get near Hector, for he had set his heart on spearing him, but Hector's horses were now hurrying him away. As the whole dark earth bows before some tempest on an autumn day when Jove rains his hardest to punish men for giving crooked judgement in their courts, and driving justice therefrom without heed to the decrees of heaven – all the rivers run full and the torrents tear many a new channel as they roar headlong from the mountains to the dark sea, and it fares ill with the works of men – even such was the stress and strain of the Trojan horses in their flight.

Patroclus now cut off the battalions that were nearest to him and drove them back to the ships. They were doing their best to reach the city, but he would not let them, and bore down on them between the river and the ships and wall. Many a fallen comrade did he then avenge. First he hit Pronoüs with a spear on the chest where it was exposed near the rim of his shield, and he fell heavily to the ground. Next he sprang on Thestor son of Enops, who was sitting all huddled up in his chariot, for he had lost his head and the reins had been torn out of his hands. Patroclus went up to him and drove a spear into his right jaw; he thus hooked him by the teeth and the spear pulled him over the rim of his car, as one who sits at the end of some jutting rock and draws a strong fish out of the sea with a hook and a line – even so with his spear did he pull Thestor all gaping from his chariot; he then threw him down on his face and he died while falling. On this, as Erylaus was coming on to attack him, he struck him full on the head with a stone, and his brains were all battered inside his helmet, whereon he fell headlong to the ground and the pangs of death took hold upon him. Then he laid low, one after the other, Erymas, Amphoterus, Epaltes, Tlepolemus, Echius son of Damastor, Pyris, Ipheus, Euippus and Polymelus son of Argeas.

Now when Sarpedon saw his comrades, men who wore ungirdled tunics, being overcome by Patroclus son of Menœtius, he rebuked the Lycians saying, 'Shame on you, where are you flying to? Show your mettle; I will myself meet this man in fight and learn who it is that is so masterful; he has done us much hurt, and has stretched many a brave man upon the ground.'

He sprang from his chariot as he spoke, and Patroclus, when he saw this, leaped on to the ground also. The two then rushed at one another with loud cries like eagle-beaked crook-taloned vultures that scream and tear at one another in some high mountain fastness.

The son of scheming Saturn looked down upon them in pity and said to Juno who was his wife and sister, 'Alas, that it should be the lot of Sarpedon whom I love so dearly to perish by the hand of Patroclus. I am in two minds whether to catch him up out of the fight and set him down safe and sound in the fertile land of Lycia, or to let him now fall by the hand of the son of Menœtius.'

And Juno answered, 'Most dread son of Saturn, what is this that you are saying? Would you snatch a mortal man, whose doom has long been fated, out of the jaws of death? Do as you will, but we shall not all of us be of your mind. I say further, and lay my saying to your heart, that if you send Sarpedon safely to his own home, some other of the gods will be also wanting to escort his son out of battle, for there are many sons of gods fighting round the city of Troy, and you will make every one jealous. If, however, you are fond of him and pity him, let him indeed fall by the hand of Patroclus, but as soon as the life is gone out of him, send Death and sweet Sleep to bear him off the field and take him to the broad lands of Lycia, where his brothers and his kinsmen will bury him with mound and pillar, in due honour to the dead.'

The sire of gods and men assented, but he shed a rain of blood upon the earth in honour of his son whom Patroclus was about to kill on the rich plain of Troy far from his home.

When they were now come close to one another Patroclus struck Thrasydemus, the brave squire of Sarpedon, in the lower part of the belly, and killed him. Sarpedon then aimed a spear at Patroclus and missed him, but he struck the horse Pedasus in the right shoulder, and it screamed aloud as it lay, groaning in the dust until the life went out of it. The other two horses began to plunge; the pole of the chariot cracked, and they got entangled in the reins through the fall of the horse that was yoked along with them; but Automedon knew what to do; without the loss of a moment he drew the keen blade that hung by his sturdy thigh and cut the third horse adrift; whereon the other two righted themselves, and pulling hard at the reins again went together into battle.

Sarpedon now took a second aim at Patroclus, and again missed him, the point of the spear passed over his left shoulder without hitting him. Patroclus then aimed in his turn, and the spear sped not from his hand in vain, for he hit Sarpedon just where the midriff surrounds the everbeating heart. He fell like some oak or silver poplar or tall pine to which woodmen have laid their axes upon the mountains to make timber for ship-building – even so did he lie stretched at full length in front of his chariot and horses, moaning and clutching at the blood-stained dust. As when a lion springs with a bound upon a herd of cattle and fastens on a great black bull which dies bellowing in its clutches – even so did the leader of the Lycian warriors struggle in death as he fell by the hand of Patroclus. He called on his trusty comrade and said, 'Glaucus, my brother, hero among heroes, put forth all your strength, fight with might and main, now if ever quit yourself like a valiant soldier. First go about among the Lycian captains and bid them fight for Sarpedon; then yourself also do battle to save my armour from being taken. My name will haunt you henceforth and for ever if the Achæans rob me of my armour now that I have fallen at their ships. Do your very utmost and call all my people together.'

Death closed his eyes as he spoke. Patroclus planted his heel on his breast and drew the spear from his body, whereon his senses came out along with it, and he drew out both spear-point and Sarpedon's soul at the same time. Hard by the Myrmidons held his snorting steeds, who were wild with panic at finding themselves deserted by their lords.

Glaucus was overcome with grief when he heard what Sarpedon said, for he could not help him. He had to support his arm with his other hand, being in great pain through the wound which Teucer's arrow had given him when Teucer was defending the wall as he, Glaucus, was assailing it. Therefore he prayed to far-darting Apollo saying, 'Hear me O king from your seat, may be in the rich land of Lycia, or may be in Troy, for in all places you can hear the prayer of one who is in distress, as I now am. I have a grievous wound; my hand is aching with pain; there is no staunching the blood, and my whole arm drags by reason of my hurt, so that I cannot grasp my sword nor go among my foes and fight them, though our prince, Jove's son Sarpedon, is slain. Jove defended not his son, do you, therefore, O king, heal me of my wound, ease my pain and grant me strength both to cheer on the Lycians and to fight along with them round the body of him who has fallen.'

Thus did he pray, and Apollo heard his prayer. He eased his pain, staunched the black blood from the wound, and gave him new strength. Glaucus perceived this, and was thankful that the mighty god had answered his prayer; forthwith, therefore, he went among the Lycian captains, and bade them come to fight about the body of Sarpedon. From these he strode on among the Trojans to Polydamas son of Panthoüs and Agenor; he then went in search of Æneas and Hector, and when he had found them he said, 'Hector, you have utterly forgotten your allies, who languish here for your sake far from friends and home while you do nothing to support them. Sarpedon leader of the Lycian warriors has fallen – he who was at once the right and might of Lycia; Mars has laid him low by the spear of Patroclus. Stand by him, my friends, and suffer not the Myrmidons to strip him of his armour, nor to treat his body with contumely in revenge for all the Danaans whom we have speared at the ships.'

As he spoke the Trojans were plunged in extreme and ungovernable grief; for Sarpedon, alien though he was, had been one of the main

stays of their city, both as having much people with him, and as himself
the foremost among them all. Led by Hector, who was infuriated by
the fall of Sarpedon, they made instantly for the Danaans with all their
might, while the undaunted spirit of Patroclus son of Menœtius cheered
on the Achæans. First he spoke to the two Ajaxes, men who needed
no bidding. 'Ajaxes,' said he, 'may it now please you to show yourselves
the men you always have been, or even better – Sarpedon is fallen – he
who was first to overleap the wall of the Achæans; let us take the body
and outrage it; let us strip the armour from his shoulders, and kill his
comrades if they try to rescue his body.'

He spoke to men who of themselves were full eager; both sides,
therefore, the Trojans and Lycians on the one hand, and the Myrmidons
and Achæans on the other, strengthened their battalions, and fought
desperately about the body of Sarpedon, shouting fiercely the while.
Mighty was the din of their armour as they came together, and Jove
shed a thick darkness over the fight, to increase the fury of the battle
over the body of his son.

At first the Trojans made some headway against the Achæans, for
one of the best men among the Myrmidons was killed, Epeigeus, son
of noble Agacles who had erewhile been king in the good city of Budeum;
but presently, having killed a valiant kinsman of his own, he took refuge
with Peleus and Thetis, who sent him to Ilius the land of noble steeds
to fight the Trojans under Achilles. Hector now struck him on the head
with a stone just as he had caught hold of the body, and his brains
inside his helmet were all battered in, so that he fell face foremost upon
the body of Sarpedon, and there died. Patroclus was enraged by the
death of his comrade, and sped through the front ranks as swiftly as a
hawk that swoops down on a flock of daws or starlings. Even so swiftly,
O noble knight Patroclus, did you make straight for the Lycians and
Trojans to avenge your comrade. Forthwith he struck Sthenelaus the
son of Ithæmenes on the neck with a stone, and broke the tendons that
join it to the head and spine. On this Hector and the front rank of his
men gave ground. As far as a man can throw a javelin when competing

for some prize, or even in battle – so far did the Trojans now retreat before the Achæans. Glaucus, captain of the Lycians, was the first to rally them, by killing Bathycles son of Chalcon who lived in Hellas and was the richest man among the Myrmidons. Glaucus turned round suddenly, just as Bathycles who was pursuing him was about to lay hold of him, and drove his spear right into the middle of his chest, whereon he fell heavily to the ground, and the fall of so good a man filled the Achæans with dismay, while the Trojans were exultant, and came up in a body round the corpse. Nevertheless the Achæans, mindful of their prowess, bore straight down upon them.

Meriones then killed a helmed warrior of the Trojans, Laogonus son of Onetor, who was priest of Jove of Mt Ida, and was honoured by the people as though he were a god. Meriones struck him under the jaw and ear, so that life went out of him and the darkness of death laid hold upon him. Æneas then aimed a spear at Meriones, hoping to hit him under the shield as he was advancing, but Meriones saw it coming and stooped forward to avoid it, whereon the spear flew past him and the point stuck in the ground, while the butt-end went on quivering till Mars robbed it of its force. The spear, therefore, sped from Æneas's hand in vain and fell quivering to the ground. Æneas was angry and said, 'Meriones, you are a good dancer, but if I had hit you my spear would soon have made an end of you.'

And Meriones answered, 'Æneas, for all your bravery, you will not be able to make an end of every one who comes against you. You are only a mortal like myself, and if I were to hit you in the middle of your shield with my spear, however strong and self-confident you may be, I should soon vanquish you, and you would yield your life to Hades of the noble steeds.'

On this the son of Menœtius rebuked him and said, 'Meriones, hero though you be, you should not speak thus; taunting speeches, my good friend, will not make the Trojans draw away from the dead body; some of them must go under ground first; blows for battle, and words for council; fight, therefore, and say nothing.'

He led the way as he spoke and the hero went forward with him. As the sound of woodcutters in some forest glade upon the mountains – and the thud of their axes is heard afar – even such a din now rose from earth – clash of bronze armour and of good ox-hide shields, as men smote each other with their swords and spears pointed at both ends. A man had need of good eyesight now to know Sarpedon, so covered was he from head to foot with spears and blood and dust. Men swarmed about the body, as flies that buzz round the full milk-pails in spring when they are brimming with milk – even so did they gather round Sarpedon; nor did Jove turn his keen eyes away for one moment from the fight, but kept looking at it all the time, for he was settling how best to kill Patroclus, and considering whether Hector should be allowed to end him now in the fight round the body of Sarpedon, and strip him of his armour, or whether he should let him give yet further trouble to the Trojans. In the end, he deemed it best that the brave squire of Achilles son of Peleus should drive Hector and the Trojans back towards the city and take the lives of many. First, therefore, he made Hector turn faint-hearted, whereon he mounted his chariot and fled, bidding the other Trojans fly also, for he saw that the scales of Jove had turned against him. Neither would the brave Lycians stand firm; they were dismayed when they saw their king lying struck to the heart amid a heap of corpses – for when the son of Saturn made the fight wax hot many had fallen above him. The Achæans, therefore, stripped the gleaming armour from his shoulders and the brave son of Menœtius gave it to his men to take to the ships. Then Jove lord of the storm-cloud said to Apollo, 'Dear Phœbus, go, I pray you, and take Sarpedon out of range of the weapons; cleanse the black blood from off him, and then bear him a long way off where you may wash him in the river, anoint him with ambrosia, and clothe him in immortal raiment; this done, commit him to the arms of the two fleet messengers, Death, and Sleep, who will carry him straightway to the rich land of Lycia, where his brothers and kinsmen will inter him, and will raise both mound and pillar to his memory, in due honour to the dead.'

Thus he spoke. Apollo obeyed his father's saying, and came down from the heights of Ida into the thick of the fight; forthwith he took Sarpedon out of range of the weapons, and then bore him a long way off, where he washed him in the river, anointed him with ambrosia and clothed him in immortal raiment; this done, he committed him to the arms of the two fleet messengers, Death, and Sleep, who presently set him down in the rich land of Lycia.

Meanwhile Patroclus, with many a shout to his horses and to Automedon, pursued the Trojans and Lycians in the pride and foolishness of his heart. Had he but obeyed the bidding of the son of Peleus, he would have escaped death and have been scatheless; but the counsels of Jove pass man's understanding; he will put even a brave man to flight and snatch victory from his grasp, or again he will set him on to fight, as he now did when he put a high spirit into the heart of Patroclus.

Who then first, and who last, was slain by you, O Patroclus, when the gods had now called you to meet your doom? First Adrestus, Autonoüs, Echeclus, Perimus the son of Megas, Epistor and Melanippus; after these he killed Elasus, Mulius, and Pylartes. These he slew, but the rest saved themselves by flight.

The sons of the Achæans would now have taken Troy by the hands of Patroclus, for his spear flew in all directions, had not Phœbus Apollo taken his stand upon the wall to defeat his purpose and to aid the Trojans. Thrice did Patroclus charge at an angle of the high wall, and thrice did Apollo beat him back, striking his shield with his own immortal hands. When Patroclus was coming on like a god for yet a fourth time, Apollo shouted to him with an awful voice and said, 'Draw back, noble Patroclus, it is not your lot to sack the city of the Trojan chieftains, nor yet will it be that of Achilles who is a far better man than you are.' On hearing this, Patroclus withdrew to some distance and avoided the anger of Apollo.

Meanwhile Hector was waiting with his horses inside the Scæan gates, in doubt whether to drive out again and go on fighting, or to

call the army inside the gates. As he was thus doubting Phœbus Apollo
drew near him in the likeness of a young and lusty warrior Asius, who
was Hector's uncle, being own brother to Hecuba, and son of Dymas
who lived in Phrygia by the waters of the river Sangarius; in his like-
ness Jove's son Apollo now spoke to Hector saying. 'Hector, why have
you left off fighting? It is ill done of you. If I were as much better a
man than you, as I am worse, you should soon rue your slackness.
Drive straight towards Patroclus, if so be that Apollo may grant you
a triumph over him, and you may kill him.'

With this the god went back into the hurly-burly, and Hector bade
Cebriones drive again into the fight. Apollo passed in among them,
and struck panic into the Argives, while he gave triumph to Hector
and the Trojans. Hector let the other Danaans alone and killed no
man, but drove straight at Patroclus. Patroclus then sprang from his
chariot to the ground, with a spear in his left hand, and in his right a
jagged stone as large as his hand could hold. He stood still and threw
it, nor did it go far without hitting some one; the cast was not in vain,
for the stone struck Cebriones, Hector's charioteer, a bastard son of
Priam, as he held the reins in his hands. The stone hit him on the
forehead and drove his brows into his head, for the bone was smashed,
and his eyes fell to the ground at his feet. He dropped dead from his
chariot as though he were diving, and there was no more life left in
him. Over him did you then vaunt, O knight Patroclus, saying, 'Bless
my heart, how active he is, and how well he dives. If we had been at
sea this fellow would have dived from the ship's side and brought up
as many oysters as the whole crew could stomach, even in rough water,
for he has dived beautifully off his chariot on to the ground. It seems,
then, that there are divers also among the Trojans.'

As he spoke he flung himself on Cebriones with the spring, as it
were, of a lion that while attacking a stockyard is himself struck in the
chest, and his courage is his own bane – even so furiously, O Patroclus,
did you then spring upon Cebriones. Hector sprang also from his
chariot to the ground. The pair then fought over the body of Cebriones.

As two famished lions fight fiercely on some high mountain over the body of a stag that they have killed, even so did these two mighty warriors, Patroclus son of Menœtius and brave Hector, hack and hew at one another over the corpse of Cebriones. Hector would not let him go when he had once got him by the head, while Patroclus kept fast hold of his feet, and a fierce fight raged between the other Danaans and Trojans. As the east and south wind buffet one another when they beat upon some dense forest on the mountains – there is beech and ash and spreading cornel; the tops of the trees roar as they beat on one another, and one can hear the boughs cracking and breaking – even so did the Trojans and Achæans spring upon one another and lay about each other, and neither side would give way. Many a pointed spear fell to ground and many a winged arrow sped from its bow-string about the body of Cebriones; many a great stone, moreover, beat on many a shield as they fought around his body, but there he lay in the whirling clouds of dust, all huge and hugely, heedless of his driving now.

So long as the sun was still high in mid-heaven the weapons of either side were alike deadly, and the people fell; but when he went down towards the time when men loose their oxen, the Achæans proved to be beyond all forecast stronger, so that they drew Cebriones out of range of the darts and tumult of the Trojans, and stripped the armour from his shoulders. Then Patroclus sprang like Mars with fierce intent and a terrific shout upon the Trojans, and thrice did he kill nine men; but as he was coming on like a god for a fourth time, then, O Patroclus, was the hour of your end approaching, for Phœbus fought you in fell earnest. Patroclus did not see him as he moved about in the crush, for he was enshrouded in thick darkness, and the god struck him from behind on his back and his broad shoulders with the flat of his hand, so that his eyes turned dizzy. Phœbus Apollo beat the helmet from off his head, and it rolled rattling off under the horses' feet, where its horse-hair plumes were all begrimed with dust and blood. Never indeed had that helmet fared so before, for it had served to protect the head and comely forehead of the godlike hero Achilles. Now, however, Zeus delivered it over to be worn by Hector. Nevertheless the end of Hector also was near. The bronze-shod spear, so great and so strong, was broken in the hand of Patroclus, while his shield that covered him from head to foot fell to the ground as did also the band that held it, and Apollo undid the fastenings of his corslet.

On this his mind became clouded; his limbs failed him, and he stood as one dazed; whereon Euphorbus son of Panthoüs a Dardanian, the best spearman of his time, as also the finest horseman and fleetest runner, came behind him and struck him in the back with a spear, midway between the shoulders. This man as soon as ever he had come up with his chariot had dismounted twenty men, so proficient was he in all the arts of war – he it was, O knight Patroclus, that first drove a weapon into you, but he did not quite overpower you. Euphorbus then ran back into the crowd, after drawing his ashen spear out of the wound; he would not stand firm and wait for Patroclus, unarmed though he now was, to attack him; but Patroclus unnerved, alike by the blow the god had given him and by the spear-wound, drew back under cover of his men in fear for his life. Hector on this, seeing him to be wounded and giving ground, forced his way through the ranks, and when close up with him struck him in the lower part of the belly with a spear, driving the bronze point right through it, so that he fell heavily to the ground to the great grief of the Achæans. As when a lion has fought some fierce wild-boar and worsted him – the two fight furiously upon the mountains over some little fountain at which they would both drink, and the lion has beaten the boar till he can hardly breathe – even so did Hector son of Priam take the life of the brave son of Menœtius who had killed so many, striking him from close at hand, and vaunting over him the while. 'Patroclus,' said he, 'you deemed that you should sack our city, rob our Trojan women of their freedom, and carry them off in your ships to your own country. Fool; Hector and his fleet horses were ever straining their utmost to defend them. I am foremost of all the Trojan warriors to stave the day of bondage from off them; as for you, vultures shall devour you here. Poor wretch,

Achilles with all his bravery availed you nothing; and yet I ween when you left him he charged you straitly saying, "Come not back to the ships, knight Patroclus, till you have rent the blood-stained shirt of murderous Hector about his body." Thus I ween did he charge you, and your fool's heart answered him "yea" within you.'

Then, as the life ebbed out of you, you answered, O knight Patroclus: 'Hector, vaunt as you will, for Jove the son of Saturn and Apollo have vouchsafed you victory; it is they who have vanquished me so easily, and they who have stripped the armour from my shoulders; had twenty such men as you attacked me, all of them would have fallen before my spear. Fate and the son of Leto have overpowered me, and among mortal men Euphorbus; you are yourself third only in the killing of me. I say further, and lay my saying to your heart, you too shall live but for a little season; death and the day of your doom are close upon you, and they will lay you low by the hand of Achilles son of Æacus.'

When he had thus spoken his eyes were closed in death, his soul left his body and flitted down to the house of Hades, mourning its sad fate and bidding farewell to the youth and vigour of its manhood. Dead though he was, Hector still spoke to him saying, 'Patroclus, why should you thus foretell my doom? Who knows but Achilles, son of lovely Thetis, may be smitten by my spear and die before me?'

As he spoke he drew the bronze spear from the wound, planting his foot upon the body, which he thrust off and let lie on its back. He then went spear in hand after Automedon, squire of the fleet descendant of Æacus, for he longed to lay him low, but the immortal steeds which the gods had given as a rich gift to Peleus bore him swiftly from the field.

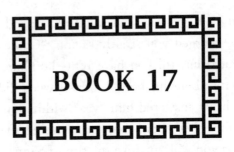

BOOK 17

The fight around the body of Patroclus.

Brave Menelaus son of Atreus now came to know that Patroclus had fallen, and made his way through the front ranks clad in full armour to bestride him. As a cow stands lowing over her first calf, even so did yellow-haired Menelaus bestride Patroclus. He held his round shield and his spear in front of him, resolute to kill any who should dare face him. But the son of Panthoüs had also noted the body, and came up to Menelaus saying, 'Menelaus, son of Atreus, draw back, leave the body, and let the blood-stained spoils be. I was first of the Trojans and their brave allies to drive my spear into Patroclus, let me, therefore, have my full glory among the Trojans, or I will take aim and kill you.'

To this Menelaus answered in great anger, 'By father Jove, boasting is an ill thing. The pard is not more bold, nor the lion nor savage wild-boar, which is fiercest and most dauntless of all creatures, than are the proud sons of Panthoüs. Yet Hyperenor did not see out the days of his youth when he made light of me and withstood me, deeming me the meanest soldier among the Danaans. His own feet never bore him back to gladden his wife and parents. Even so shall I make an end of you too, if you withstand me; get you back into the crowd and do not face me, or it shall be worse for you. Even a fool may be wise after the event.'

Euphorbus would not listen, and said, 'Now indeed, Menelaus, shall you pay for the death of my brother over whom you vaunted, and whose wife you widowed in her bridal chamber, while you brought grief unspeakable on his parents. I shall comfort these poor people if I bring your head and armour and place them in the hands of Panthoüs and noble Phrontis. The time is come when this matter shall be fought out and settled, for me or against me.'

As he spoke he struck Menelaus full on the shield, but the spear did not go through, for the shield turned its point. Menelaus then took aim, praying to father Jove as he did so; Euphorbus was drawing back, and Menelaus struck him about the roots of his throat, leaning his whole weight on the spear, so as to drive it home. The point went clean through his neck, and his armour rang rattling round him as he fell heavily to the ground. His hair which was like that of the Graces, and his locks so deftly bound in bands of silver and gold, were all bedrabbled with blood. As one who has grown a fine young olive tree in a clear space where there is abundance of water – the plant is full of promise, and though the winds beat upon it from every quarter it puts forth its white blossoms till the blasts of some fierce hurricane sweep down upon it and level it with the ground – even so did Menelaus strip the fair youth Euphorbus of his armour after he had slain him. Or as some fierce lion upon the mountains in the pride of his strength fastens on the finest heifer in a herd as it is feeding – first he breaks her neck with his strong jaws, and then gorges on her blood and entrails; dogs and shepherds raise a hue and cry against him, but they stand aloof and will not come close to him, for they are pale with fear – even so no one had the courage to face valiant Menelaus. The son of Atreus would have then carried off the armour of the son of Panthoüs with ease, had not Phœbus Apollo been angry, and in the guise of Mentes chief of the Cicons incited Hector to attack him. 'Hector,' said he, 'you are now going after the horses of the noble son of Æacus, but you will not take them; they cannot be kept in hand and driven by mortal man, save only by Achilles, who is son to an immortal mother. Meanwhile Menelaus son of Atreus has bestridden the body of Patroclus and killed the noblest of the Trojans, Euphorbus son of Panthoüs, so that he can fight no more.'

⌐⌐

The god then went back into the toil and turmoil, but the soul of Hector was darkened with a cloud of grief; he looked along the ranks and saw Euphorbus lying on the ground with the blood still flowing from his wound, and Menelaus stripping him of his armour. On this he made his way to the front like a flame of fire, clad in his gleaming armour, and crying with a loud voice. When the son of Atreus heard him, he said to himself in his dismay, 'Alas! what shall I do? I may not let the Trojans take the armour of Patroclus who has fallen fighting on my behalf, lest some Danaan who sees me should cry shame upon me. Still if for my honour's sake I fight Hector and the Trojans single-handed, they will prove too many for me, for Hector is bringing them up in force. Why, however, should I thus hesitate? When a man fights in despite of heaven with one whom a god befriends, he will soon rue it. Let no Danaan think ill of me if I give place to Hector, for the hand of heaven is with him. Yet, if I could find Ajax, the two of us would fight Hector and heaven too, if we might only save the body of Patroclus for Achilles son of Peleus. This, of many evils would be the least.'

While he was thus in two minds, the Trojans came up to him with Hector at their head; he therefore drew back and left the body, turning about like some bearded lion who is being chased by dogs and men from a stockyard with spears and hue and cry, whereon he is daunted and slinks sulkily off – even so did Menelaus son of Atreus turn and leave the body of Patroclus. When among the body of his men, he looked around for mighty Ajax son of Telamon, and presently saw him on the extreme left of the fight, cheering on his men and exhorting them to keep on fighting, for Phœbus Apollo had spread a great panic among them. He ran up to him and said, 'Ajax, my good friend, come with me at once to dead Patroclus, if so be that we may take the body to Achilles – as for his armour, Hector already has it.'

These words stirred the heart of Ajax, and he made his way among the front ranks, Menelaus going with him. Hector had stripped Patroclus of his armour, and was dragging him away to cut off his head and take the body to fling before the dogs of Troy. But Ajax came up with his shield like a wall before him, on which Hector withdrew under shelter of his men, and sprang on to his chariot, giving the armour over to the Trojans to take to the city, as a great trophy for himself; Ajax, therefore, covered the body of Patroclus with his broad shield and bestrode him; as a lion stands over his whelps if hunters have come upon him in a forest when he is with his little ones – in the pride and fierceness of his strength he draws his knit brows down till they cover his eyes – even so did Ajax bestride the body of Patroclus, and by his side stood Menelaus son of Atreus, nursing great sorrow in his heart.

Then Glaucus son of Hippolochus looked fiercely at Hector and rebuked him sternly. 'Hector,' said he, 'you make a brave show, but in fight you are sadly wanting. A runaway like yourself has no claim to so great a reputation. Think how you may now save your town and citadel by the hands of your own people born in Ilius; for you will get no Lycians to fight for you, seeing what thanks they have had for their incessant hardships. Are you likely, sir, to do anything to help a man of less note, after leaving Sarpedon, who was at once your guest and comrade in arms, to be the spoil and prey of the Danaans? So long as he lived he did good service both to your city and yourself; yet you had no stomach to save his body from the dogs. If the Lycians will listen to me, they will go home and leave Troy to its fate. If the Trojans had any of that daring fearless spirit which lays hold of men who are fighting for their country and harassing those who would attack it, we should soon bear off Patroclus into Ilius. Could we get this dead man away and bring him into the city of Priam, the Argives would readily give up the armour of Sarpedon, and we should get his body to boot. For he whose squire has been now killed is the foremost man at the ships of the Achæans – he and his close-fighting followers. Nevertheless you dared not make a stand against Ajax, nor face him, eye to eye, with battle all round you, for he is a braver man than you are.'

Hector scowled at him and answered, 'Glaucus, you should know better. I have held you so far as a man of more understanding than any in all Lycia, but now I despise you for saying that I am afraid of Ajax. I fear neither battle nor the din of chariots, but Jove's will is stronger than ours; Jove at one time makes even a strong man draw back and snatches victory from his grasp, while at another he will set him on to fight. Come hither then, my friend, stand by me and see indeed whether I shall play the coward the whole day through as you say, or whether I shall not stay some even of the boldest Danaans from fighting round the body of Patroclus.'

As he spoke he called loudly on the Trojans saying, 'Trojans, Lycians, and Dardanians, fighters in close combat, be men, my friends, and fight might and main, while I put on the goodly armour of Achilles, which I took when I killed Patroclus.'

With this Hector left the fight, and ran full speed after his men who were taking the armour of Achilles to Troy, but had not yet got far. Standing for a while apart from the woeful fight, he changed his armour. His own he sent to the strong city of Ilius and to the Trojans, while he put on the immortal armour of the son of Peleus, which the gods had given to Peleus, who in his age gave it to his son; but the son did not grow old in his father's armour.

When Jove, lord of the storm-cloud, saw Hector standing aloof and arming himself in the armour of the son of Peleus, he wagged his head and muttered to himself saying, 'Alas! poor wretch, you arm in the armour of a hero, before whom many another trembles, and you reck nothing of the doom that is already close upon you. You have killed his comrade so brave and strong, but it was not well that you should strip the armour from his head and shoulders. I do indeed endow you with great might now, but as against this you shall not return from battle to lay the armour of the son of Peleus before Andromache.'

The son of Saturn bowed his portentous brows, and Hector fitted the armour to his body, while terrible Mars entered into him, and filled his whole body with might and valour. With a shout he strode in among the allies, and his armour flashed about him so that he seemed to all of them like the great son of Peleus himself. He went about among them and cheered them on – Mesthles, Glaucus, Medon, Thersilochus, Asteropæus, Deisenor and Hippothoüs, Phorcys, Chromius and Ennomus the augur. All these did he exhort saying, 'Hear me, allies from other cities who are here in your thousands, it was not in order to have a crowd about me that I called you hither each from his several city, but that with heart and soul you might defend the wives and little ones of the Trojans from the fierce Achæans. For this do I oppress my people with your food and the presents that make you rich. Therefore turn, and charge at the foe, to stand or fall as is the game of war; whoever shall bring Patroclus, dead though he be, into the hands of the Trojans, and shall make Ajax give way before him, I will give him one half of the spoils while I keep the other. He will thus share like honour with myself.'

When he had thus spoken they charged full weight upon the Danaans with their spears held out before them, and the hopes of each ran high that he should force Ajax son of Telamon to yield up the body – fools that they were, for he was about to take the lives of many. Then Ajax said to Menelaus, 'My good friend Menelaus, you and I shall hardly come out of this fight alive. I am less concerned for the body of Patroclus, who will shortly become meat for the dogs and vultures of Troy, than for the safety of my own head and yours. Hector has wrapped us round in a storm of battle from every quarter, and our destruction seems now certain. Call then upon the princes of the Danaans if there is any who can hear us.'

Menelaus did as he said, and shouted to the Danaans for help at the top of his voice. 'My friends,' he cried, 'princes and counsellors of the Argives, all you who with Agamemnon and Menelaus drink at the public cost, and give orders each to his own people as Jove vouchsafes him power and glory, the fight is so thick about me that I cannot distinguish you severally; come on, therefore, every man unbidden, and think it shame that Patroclus should become meat and morsel for Trojan hounds.'

Fleet Ajax son of Oïleus heard him and was first to force his way through the fight and run to help him. Next came Idomeneus and Meriones his esquire, peer of murderous Mars. As for the others that came into the fight after these, who of his own self could name them?

The Trojans with Hector at their head charged in a body. As a great wave that comes thundering in at the mouth of some heaven-born river, and the rocks that jut into the sea ring with the roar of the breakers that beat and buffet them – even with such a roar did the Trojans come on; but the Achæans in singleness of heart stood firm about the son of Menœtius, and fenced him with their bronze shields. Jove, moreover, hid the brightness of their helmets in a thick cloud, for he had borne no grudge against the son of Menœtius while he was still alive and squire to the descendant of Æacus; therefore he was loth to let him fall a prey to the dogs of his foes the Trojans, and urged his comrades on to defend him.

At first the Trojans drove the Achæans back, and they withdrew from the dead man daunted. The Trojans did not succeed in killing any one, nevertheless they drew the body away. But the Achæans did not lose it long, for Ajax, foremost of all the Danaans after the son of Peleus alike in stature and prowess, quickly rallied them and made towards the front like a wild boar upon the mountains when he stands at bay in the forest glades and routs the hounds and lusty youths that have attacked him – even so did Ajax son of Telamon passing easily in among the phalanxes of the Trojans, disperse those who had bestridden Patroclus and were most bent on winning glory by dragging him off to their city. At this moment Hippothoüs brave son of the Pelasgian Lethus, in his zeal for Hector and the Trojans, was dragging the body off by the foot through the press of the fight, having bound a strap round the sinews near the ancle; but a mischief soon befell him from which none of those could save him who would have gladly done so, for the son of Telamon sprang forward and smote him on his bronze-cheeked helmet. The plumed headpiece broke about the point of the weapon, struck at once by the spear and by the strong hand of Ajax, so that the bloody brain came oozing out through the crest-socket. His strength then failed him and he let Patroclus' foot drop from his hand, as he fell full length dead upon the body; thus he died far from the fertile land of Larissa, and never repaid his parents the cost of bringing him up, for his life was cut short early by the spear of mighty Ajax. Hector then took aim at Ajax with a spear, but he saw it coming and just managed to avoid it; the spear passed on and struck Schedius son of noble Iphitus, captain of the Phocēans, who dwelt in famed Panopeus and reigned over much people; it struck him under the middle of the collar-bone; the bronze point went right through him, coming out at the bottom of his shoulder-blade, and his armour rang rattling round him as he fell heavily to the ground. Ajax in his turn struck noble Phorcys son of Phænops in the middle of the belly as he was bestriding Hippothoüs, and broke the plate of his cuirass; whereon the spear tore out his entrails and he clutched the ground in his palm as he fell to earth. Hector and those who were in the front rank then gave ground, while the Argives raised a loud cry of triumph, and drew off the bodies of Phorcys and Hippothoüs which they stripped presently of their armour.

The Trojans would now have been worsted by the brave Achæans and driven back to Ilius through their own cowardice, while the Argives, so great was their courage and endurance, would have achieved a triumph even against the will of Jove, if Apollo had not roused Æneas, in the likeness of Periphas son of Epytus, an attendant who had grown old in the service of Æneas' aged father, and was at all times devoted to him. In his likeness, then, Apollo said, 'Æneas, can you not manage, even though heaven be against us, to save high Ilius? I have known men, whose numbers, courage, and self-reliance have saved their people in spite of Jove, whereas in this case he would much rather give victory to us than to the Danaans, if you would only fight instead of being so terribly afraid.'

Æneas knew Apollo when he looked straight at him, and shouted to Hector saying, 'Hector and all other Trojans and allies, shame on us if we are beaten by the Achæans and driven back to Ilius through our own cowardice. A god has just come up to me and told me that Jove the supreme disposer will be with us. Therefore let us make for the Danaans, that it may go hard with them ere they bear away dead Patroclus to the ships.'

As he spoke he sprang out far in front of the others, who then rallied and again faced the Achæans. Æneas speared Leiocritus son of Arisbas, a valiant follower of Lycomedes, and Lycomedes was moved with pity as he saw him fall; he therefore went close up, and speared Apisaon son of Hippasus shepherd of his people in the liver under the midriff, so that he died; he had come from fertile Pæonia and was the best man of them all after Asteropæus. Asteropæus flew forward to avenge him and attack the Danaans, but this might no longer be, inasmuch as those about Patroclus were well covered by their shields, and held their spears in front of them, for Ajax had given them strict orders that no man was either to give ground, or to stand out before the others, but all were to hold well together about the body and fight hand to hand. Thus did huge Ajax bid them, and the earth ran red with blood as the corpses fell thick on one another alike on the side of the Trojans and allies, and on that of the Danaans; for these last, too, fought no bloodless fight though many fewer of them perished, through the care they took to defend and stand by one another.

Thus did they fight as it were a flaming fire; it seemed as though it had gone hard even with the sun and moon, for they were hidden over all that part where the bravest heroes were fighting about the dead son of Menœtius, whereas the other Danaans and Achæans fought at their ease in full daylight with brilliant sunshine all round them, and there was not a cloud to be seen neither on plain nor mountain. These last moreover would rest for a while and leave off fighting, for they were some distance apart and beyond the range of one another's weapons, whereas those who were in the thick of the fray suffered both from battle and darkness. All the best of them were being worn out by the great weight of their armour, but the two valiant heroes,

Thrasymedes and Antilochus, had not yet heard of the death of Patroclus, and believed him to be still alive and leading the van against the Trojans; they were keeping themselves in reserve against the death or rout of their own comrades, for so Nestor had ordered when he sent them from the ships into battle.

Thus through the livelong day did they wage fierce war, and the sweat of their toil rained ever on their legs under them, and on their hands and eyes, as they fought over the squire of the fleet son of Peleus. It was as when a man gives a great ox-hide all drenched in fat to his men, and bids them stretch it; whereon they stand round it in a ring and tug till the moisture leaves it, and the fat soaks in for the many that pull at it, and it is well stretched – even so did the two sides tug the dead body hither and thither within the compass of but a little space – the Trojans steadfastly set on dragging it into Ilius, while the Achæans were no less so on taking it to their ships; and fierce was the fight between them. Not Mars himself the lord of hosts, nor yet Minerva, even in their fullest fury could make light of such a battle.

Such fearful turmoil of men and horses did Jove on that day ordain round the body of Patroclus. Meanwhile Achilles did not know that he had fallen, for the fight was under the wall of Troy a long way off the ships. He had no idea, therefore, that Patroclus was dead, and deemed that he would return alive as soon as he had gone close up to the gates. He knew that he was not to sack the city neither with nor without himself, for his mother had often told him this when he had sat alone with her, and she had informed him of the counsels of great Jove. Now, however, she had not told him how great a disaster had befallen him in the death of the one who was far dearest to him of all his comrades.

The others still kept on charging one another round the body with their pointed spears and killing each other. Then would one say, 'My friends, we can never again show our faces at the ships – better, and greatly better, that earth should open and swallow us here in this place, than that we should let the Trojans have the triumph of bearing off Patroclus to their city.'

The Trojans also on their part spoke to one another saying, 'Friends, though we fall to a man beside this body, let none shrink from fighting.' With such words did they exhort each other. They fought and fought, and an iron clank rose through the void air to the brazen vault of heaven. The horses of the descendant of Æacus stood out of the fight and wept when they heard that their driver had been laid low by the hand of murderous Hector. Automedon, valiant son of Diores, lashed them again and again; many a time did he speak kindly to them, and many a time did he upbraid them, but they would neither go back to the ships by the waters of the broad Hellespont, nor yet into battle among the Achæans; they stood with their chariot stock still, as a pillar set over the tomb of some dead man or woman, and bowed their heads to the ground. Hot tears fell from their eyes as they mourned the loss of their charioteer, and their noble manes drooped all wet from under the yoke-straps on either side the yoke.

The son of Saturn saw them and took pity upon their sorrow. He wagged his head, and muttered to himself, saying, 'Poor things, why did we give you to King Peleus who is a mortal, while you are yourselves ageless and immortal? Was it that you might share the sorrows that befall mankind? for of all creatures that live and move upon the earth there is none so pitiable as he is – still, Hector son of Priam shall drive neither you nor your chariot. I will not have it. It is enough that he should have the armour over which he vaunts so vainly. Furthermore I will give you strength of heart and limb to bear Automedon safely to the ships from battle, for I shall let the Trojans triumph still further, and go on killing till they reach the ships; whereon night shall fall and darkness overshadow the land.'

As he spoke he breathed heart and strength into the horses so that they shook the dust from out of their manes, and bore their chariot swiftly into the fight that raged between Trojans and Achæans. Behind them fought Automedon full of sorrow for his comrade, as a vulture amid a flock of geese. In and out, and here and there, full speed he dashed amid the throng of the Trojans, but for all the fury of his pursuit he killed no man, for he could not wield his spear and keep his horses in hand when alone in the chariot; at last, however, a comrade, Alcimedon, son of Laerces son of Hæmon caught sight of him and came up behind his chariot. 'Automedon,' said he, 'what god has put this folly into your heart and robbed you of your right mind, that you fight the Trojans in the front rank single-handed? He who was your comrade is slain, and Hector plumes himself on being armed in the armour of the descendant of Æacus.'

Automedon son of Diores answered, 'Alcimedon, there is no one else who can control and guide the immortal steeds so well as you can, save only Patroclus – while he was alive – peer of gods in counsel. Take then the whip and reins, while I go down from the car and fight.'

Alcimedon sprang on to the chariot, and caught up the whip and reins, while Automedon leaped from off the car. When Hector saw him he said to Æneas who was near him, 'Æneas, counsellor of the mail-clad Trojans, I see the steeds of the fleet son of Æacus come into battle with weak hands to drive them. I am sure, if you think well, that we might take them; they will not dare face us if we both attack them.'

The valiant son of Anchises was of the same mind, and the pair went right on, with their shoulders covered under shields of tough dry ox-hide, overlaid with much bronze. Chromius and Aretus went also with them, and their hearts beat high with hope that they might kill the men and capture the horses – fools that they were, for they were not to return scatheless from their meeting with Automedon, who prayed to father Jove and was forthwith filled with courage and strength abounding. He turned to his trusty comrade Alcimedon and said, 'Alcimedon, keep your horses so close up that I may feel their breath upon my back; I doubt that we shall not stay Hector son of Priam till he has killed us and mounted behind the horses; he will then either spread panic among the ranks of the Achæans, or himself be killed among the foremost.'

On this he cried out to the two Ajaxes and Menelaus, 'Ajaxes captains of the Argives, and Menelaus, give the dead body over to them that are best able to defend it, and come to the rescue of us living; for Hector and Æneas who are the two best men among the Trojans, are pressing us hard in the full tide of war. Nevertheless the issue lies on the lap of heaven, I will therefore hurl my spear and leave the rest to Jove.'

He poised and hurled as he spoke, whereon the spear struck the round shield of Aretus, and went right through it for the shield stayed it not, so that it was driven through his belt into the lower part of his belly. As when some sturdy youth, axe in hand, deals his blow behind the horns of an ox and severs the tendons at the back of its neck so that it springs forward and then drops, even so did Aretus give one bound and then fall on his back – the spear quivering in his body till it made an end of him. Hector then aimed a spear at Automedon but he saw it coming and stooped forward to avoid it, so that it flew past him and the point stuck in the ground, while the butt-end went on quivering till Mars robbed it of its force. They would then have fought hand to hand with swords had not the two Ajaxes forced their way through the crowd when they heard their comrade calling, and parted them for all their fury – for Hector, Æneas, and Chromius were afraid and drew back, leaving Aretus to lie there struck to the heart. Automedon, peer of fleet Mars, then stripped him of his armour and vaunted over him saying, 'I have done little to assuage my sorrow for the son of Menœtius, for the man I have killed is not so good as he was.'

As he spoke he took the blood-stained spoils and laid them upon his chariot; then he mounted the car with his hands and feet all steeped in gore as a lion that has been gorging upon a bull.

And now the fierce groanful fight again raged about Patroclus, for Minerva came down from heaven and roused its fury by the command of far-seeing Jove, who had changed his mind and sent her to encourage the Danaans. As when Jove bends his bright bow in heaven in token to mankind either of war or of the chill storms that stay men from their labour and plague the flocks – even so, wrapped in such radiant raiment, did Minerva go in among the host and speak man by man to each. First she took the form and voice of Phœnix and spoke to Menelaus son of Atreus, who was standing near her. 'Menelaus,' said she, 'it will be shame and dishonour to you, if dogs tear the noble comrade of Achilles under the walls of Troy. Therefore be staunch, and urge your men to be so also.'

Menelaus answered, 'Phœnix, my good old friend, may Minerva vouchsafe me strength and keep the darts from off me, for so shall I stand by Patroclus and defend him; his death has gone to my heart, but Hector is as a raging fire and deals his blows without ceasing, for Jove is now granting him a time of triumph.'

Minerva was pleased at his having named herself before any of the other gods. Therefore she put strength into his knees and shoulders, and made him as bold as a fly, which, though driven off will yet come again and bite if it can, so dearly does it love man's blood – even so bold as this did she make him as he stood over Patroclus and threw his spear. Now there was among the Trojans a man named Podes, son of Eëtion, who was both rich and valiant. Hector held him in the highest honour for he was his comrade and boon companion; the spear of Menelaus struck this man in the girdle just as he had turned in flight, and went right through him. Whereon he fell heavily forward, and Menelaus son of Atreus drew off his body from the Trojans into the ranks of his own people.

Apollo then went up to Hector and spurred him on to fight, in the likeness of Phænops son of Asius who lived in Abydos and was the most favoured of all Hector's guests. In his likeness Apollo said, 'Hector, who of the Achæans will fear you henceforward now that you have quailed before Menelaus who has ever been rated poorly as a soldier? Yet he has now got a corpse away from the Trojans single-handed, and has slain your own true comrade, a man brave among the foremost, Podes son of Eëtion.

A dark cloud of grief fell upon Hector as he heard, and he made his way to the front clad in full armour. Thereon the son of Saturn seized his bright tasselled ægis, and veiled Ida in cloud: he sent forth his lightnings and his thunders, and as he shook his ægis he gave victory to the Trojans and routed the Achæans.

The panic was begun by Peneleos the Bœotian, for while keeping his face turned ever towards the foe he had been hit with a spear on the upper part of the shoulder; a spear thrown by Polydamas had grazed the top of the bone, for Polydamas had come up to him and struck him from close at hand. Then Hector in close combat struck Leïtus son of noble Alectryon in the hand by the wrist, and disabled him from fighting further. He looked about him in dismay, knowing that never again should he wield spear in battle with the Trojans. While Hector was in pursuit of Leïtus, Idomeneus struck him on the breast-plate over his chest near the nipple; but the spear broke in the shaft, and the Trojans cheered aloud. Hector then aimed at Idomeneus son of Deucalion as he was standing on his chariot, and very narrowly missed him, but the spear hit Coiranus, a follower and charioteer of Meriones who had come with him from Lyctus. Idomeneus had left the ships on foot and would have afforded a great triumph to the Trojans if Coiranus had not driven quickly up to him, he therefore brought life and rescue to Idomeneus, but himself fell by the hand of murderous Hector. For Hector hit him on the jaw under the ear; the end of the spear drove out his teeth and cut his tongue in two pieces, so that he fell from his chariot and let the reins fall to the ground. Meriones gathered them up from the ground and took them into his own hands, then he said to Idomeneus, 'Lay on, till you get back to the ships, for you must see that the day is no longer ours.'

On this Idomeneus lashed the horses to the ships, for fear had taken hold upon him.

Ajax and Menelaus noted how Jove had turned the scale in favour of the Trojans, and Ajax was first to speak. 'Alas,' said he, 'even a fool may see that father Jove is helping the Trojans. All their weapons strike home; no matter whether it be a brave man or a coward that hurls them, Jove speeds all alike, whereas ours fall each one of them without effect. What, then, will be best both as regards rescuing the body, and our return to the joy of our friends who will be grieving as they look hitherwards; for they will make sure that nothing can now check the terrible hands of Hector, and that he will fling himself upon our ships. I wish that some one would go and tell the son of Peleus at once, for I do not think he can have yet heard the sad news that the dearest of his friends has fallen. But I can see not a man among the Achæans to send, for they and their chariots are alike hidden in darkness. O father Jove, lift this cloud from over the sons of the Achæans; make heaven serene, and let us see; if you will that we perish, let us fall at any rate by daylight.'

Father Jove heard him and had compassion upon his tears. Forthwith he chased away the cloud of darkness, so that the sun shone out and all the fighting was revealed. Ajax then said to Menelaus, 'Look, Menelaus, and if Antilochus son of Nestor be still living, send him at once to tell Achilles that by far the dearest to him of all his comrades has fallen.'

Menelaus heeded his words and went his way as a lion from a stock-yard – the lion is tired of attacking the men and hounds, who keep watch the whole night through and will not let him feast on the fat of their herd. In his lust of meat he makes straight at them but in vain, for darts from strong hands assail him, and burning brands which daunt him for all his hunger, so in the morning he slinks sulkily away – even so did Menelaus sorely against his will leave Patroclus, in great fear lest the Achæans should be driven back in rout and let him fall into the hands of the foe. He charged Meriones and the two Ajaxes straitly saying, 'Ajaxes and Meriones, leaders of the Argives, now indeed remember how good Patroclus was; he was ever courteous while alive, bear it in mind now that he is dead.'

With this Menelaus left them, looking round him as keenly as an eagle, whose sight they say is keener than that of any other bird – however high he may be in the heavens, not a hare that runs can escape him by crouching under bush or thicket, for he will swoop down upon it and make an end of it – even so, O Menelaus, did your keen eyes range round the mighty host of your followers to see if you could find the son of Nestor still alive. Presently Menelaus saw him on the extreme left of the battle cheering on his men and exhorting them to fight boldly. Menelaus went up to him and said, 'Antilochus, come here and listen to sad news, which I would indeed were untrue. You must see with your own eyes that heaven is heaping calamity upon the Danaans, and giving victory to the Trojans. Patroclus has fallen, who was the bravest of the Achæans, and sorely will the Danaans miss him. Run instantly to the ships and tell Achilles, that he may come to rescue the body and bear it to the ships. As for the armour, Hector already has it.'

Antilochus was struck with horror. For a long time he was speechless; his eyes filled with tears and he could find no utterance, but he did as Menelaus had said, and set off running as soon as he had given his armour to a comrade, Laodocus, who was wheeling his horses round, close beside him.

Thus, then, did he run weeping from the field, to carry the bad news to Achilles son of Peleus. Nor were you, O Menelaus, minded to succour his harassed comrades, when Antilochus had left the Pylians – and greatly did they miss him – but he sent them noble Thrasymedes, and himself went back to Patroclus. He came running up to the two Ajaxes and said, 'I have sent Antilochus to the ships to tell Achilles, but rage against Hector as he may, he cannot come, for he cannot fight without armour. What then will be our best plan both as regards rescuing the dead, and our own escape from death amid the battle-cries of the Trojans?'

Ajax answered, 'Menelaus, you have said well: do you, then, and Meriones stoop down, raise the body, and bear it out of the fray, while we two behind you keep off Hector and the Trojans, one in heart as in name, and long used to fighting side by side with one another.'

On this Menelaus and Meriones took the dead man in their arms and lifted him high aloft with a great effort. The Trojan host raised a hue and cry behind them when they saw the Achæans bearing the body away, and flew after them like hounds attacking a wounded boar at the loo of a band of young huntsmen. For a while the hounds fly at him as though they would tear him in pieces, but now and again he turns on them in a fury, scaring and scattering them in all directions – even so did the Trojans for a while charge in a body, striking with sword and with spears pointed at both the ends, but when the two Ajaxes faced them and stood at bay, they would turn pale and no man dared press on to fight further about the dead.

In this wise did the two heroes strain every nerve to bear the body to the ships out of the fight. The battle raged round them like fierce flames that when once kindled spread like wildfire over a city, and the houses fall in the glare of its burning – even such was the roar and tramp of men and horses that pursued them as they bore Patroclus from the field. Or as mules that put forth all their strength to draw some beam or great piece of ship's timber down a rough mountain-track, and they pant and sweat as they go – even so did Menelaus and Meriones pant and sweat as they bore the body of Patroclus. Behind them the two Ajaxes held stoutly out. As some wooded mountain-spur that stretches across a plain will turn water and check the flow even of a great river, nor is there any stream strong enough to break through it – even so did the two Ajaxes face the Trojans and stem the tide of their fighting though they kept pouring on towards them – and foremost among them all was Æneas son of Anchises with valiant Hector. As a flock of daws or starlings fall to screaming and chattering when they see a falcon, foe to all small birds, come soaring near them, even so did the Achæan youth raise a babel of cries as they fled before Æneas and Hector, unmindful of their former prowess. In the rout of the Danaans much goodly armour fell round about the trench, and of fighting there was no end.

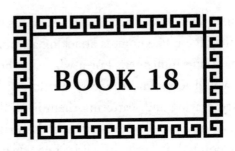

BOOK 18

The grief of Achilles over Patroclus – The visit of Thetis to Vulcan and the armour that he made for Achilles.

Thus then did they fight as it were a flaming fire. Meanwhile the fleet runner Antilochus, who had been sent as messenger, reached Achilles, and found him sitting by his tall ships and boding that which was indeed too surely true. 'Alas,' said he to himself in the heaviness of his heart, 'why are the Achæans again scouring the plain and flocking towards the ships? Heaven grant the gods be not now bringing that sorrow upon me of which my mother Thetis spoke, saying that while I was yet alive the bravest of the Myrmidons should fall before the Trojans, and see the light of the sun no longer. I fear the brave son of Menœtius has fallen through his own daring – and yet I bade him return to the ships as soon as he had driven back those that were bringing fire against them, and not join battle with Hector.'

As he was thus pondering, the son of Nestor came up to him and told his sad tale, weeping bitterly the while. 'Alas,' he cried, 'son of noble Peleus, I bring you bad tidings, would indeed that they were untrue. Patroclus has fallen, and a fight is raging about his naked body – for Hector holds his armour.'

A dark cloud of grief fell upon Achilles as he listened. He filled both hands with dust from off the ground, and poured it over his head, disfiguring his comely face, and letting the refuse settle over his shirt so fair and new. He flung himself down all huge and hugely at full length, and tore his hair with his hands. The bondswomen whom

Achilles and Patroclus had taken captive screamed aloud for grief, beating their breasts, and with their limbs failing them for sorrow. Antilochus bent over him the while, weeping and holding both his hands as he lay groaning for he feared that he might plunge a knife into his own throat. Then Achilles gave a loud cry and his mother heard him as she was sitting in the depths of the sea by the old man her father, whereon she screamed, and all the goddesses daughters of Nereus that dwelt at the bottom of the sea, came gathering round her. There were Glauce, Thalia and Cymodoce, Nesaia, Speo, Thoë and dark-eyed Halië, Cymothoë, Actæa and Limnorea, Melite, Iæra, Amphithoë and Agave, Doto and Proto, Pherusa and Dynamene, Dexamene, Amphinome and Callianeira, Doris, Panope, and the famous sea-nymph Galatea, Nemertes, Apseudes and Callianassa. There were also Clymene, Ianeira and Ianassa, Mæra, Oreithuia and Amatheia of the lovely locks, with other Nereids who dwell in the depths of the sea. The crystal cave was filled with their multitude and they all beat their breasts while Thetis led them in their lament.

'Listen,' she cried, 'sisters, daughters of Nereus, that you may hear the burden of my sorrows. Alas, woe is me, woe in that I have borne the most glorious of offspring. I bore him fair and strong, hero among heroes, and he shot up as a sapling; I tended him as a plant in a goodly garden, and sent him with his ships to Ilius to fight the Trojans, but never shall I welcome him back to the house of Peleus. So long as he lives to look upon the light of the sun he is in heaviness, and though I go to him I cannot help him. Nevertheless I will go, that I may see my dear son and learn what sorrow has befallen him though he is still holding aloof from battle.'

She left the cave as she spoke, while the others followed weeping after, and the waves opened a path before them. When they reached the rich plain of Troy, they came up out of the sea in a long line on to the sands, at the place where the ships of the Myrmidons were drawn up in close order round the tents of Achilles. His mother went up to him as he lay groaning; she laid her hand upon his head and spoke piteously, saying, 'My son, why are you thus weeping? What sorrow has now befallen you? Tell me; hide it not from me. Surely Jove has granted you the prayer you made him, when you lifted up your hands and besought him that the Achæans might all of them be pent up at their ships, and rue it bitterly in that you were no longer with them.'

Achilles groaned and answered, 'Mother, Olympian Jove has indeed vouchsafed me the fulfilment of my prayer, but what boots it to me, seeing that my dear comrade Patroclus has fallen – he whom I valued more than all others, and loved as dearly as my own life? I have lost him; aye, and Hector when he had killed him stripped him of the wondrous armour, so glorious to behold, which the gods gave to Peleus when they laid you in the couch of a mortal man. Would that you were still dwelling among the immortal sea-nymphs, and that Peleus had taken to himself some mortal bride. For now you shall have grief infinite by reason of the death of that son whom you can never welcome home – nay, I will not live nor go about among mankind unless Hector fall by my spear, and thus pay me for having slain Patroclus son of Menœtius.'

Thetis wept and answered, 'Then, my son, is your end near at hand – for your own death awaits you full soon after that of Hector.'

Then said Achilles in his great grief, 'I would die here and now, in that I could not save my comrade. He has fallen far from home, and in his hour of need my hand was not there to help him. What is there for me? Return to my own land I shall not, and I have brought no saving neither to Patroclus nor to my other comrades of whom so many have been slain by mighty Hector; I stay here by my ships a bootless burden upon the earth, I, who in fight have no peer among the Achæans, though in council there are better than I. Therefore, perish strife both from among gods and men, and anger, wherein even a righteous man will harden his heart – which rises up in the soul of a man like smoke, and the taste thereof is sweeter than drops of honey. Even so has Agamemnon angered me. And yet – so be it, for it is over;

I will force my soul into subjection as I needs must; I will go; I will pursue Hector who has slain him whom I loved so dearly, and will then abide my doom when it may please Jove and the other gods to send it. Even Hercules, the best beloved of Jove – even he could not escape the hand of death, but fate and Juno's fierce anger laid him low, as I too shall lie when I am dead if a like doom awaits me. Till then I will win fame, and will bid Trojan and Dardanian women wring tears from their tender cheeks with both their hands in the grievousness of their great sorrow; thus shall they know that he who has held aloof so long will hold aloof no longer. Hold me not back, therefore, in the love you bear me, for you shall not move me.'

Then silver-footed Thetis answered, 'My son, what you have said is true. It is well to save your comrades from destruction, but your armour is in the hands of the Trojans; Hector bears it in triumph upon his own shoulders. Full well I know that his vaunt shall not be lasting, for his end is close at hand; go not, however, into the press of battle till you see me return hither; to-morrow at break of day I shall be here, and will bring you goodly armour from King Vulcan.'

On this she left her brave son, and as she turned away she said to the sea-nymphs her sisters, 'Dive into the bosom of the sea and go to the house of the old sea-god my father. Tell him everything; as for me, I will go to the cunning workman Vulcan on high Olympus, and ask him to provide my son with a suit of splendid armour.'

When she had so said, they dived forthwith beneath the waves, while silver-footed Thetis went her way that she might bring the armour for her son.

Thus, then, did her feet bear the goddess to Olympus, and meanwhile the Achæans were flying with loud cries before murderous Hector till they reached the ships and the Hellespont, and they could not draw the body of Mars's servant Patroclus out of reach of the weapons that were showered upon him, for Hector son of Priam with his host and horsemen had again caught up to him like the flame of a fiery furnace; thrice did brave Hector seize him by the feet, striving with might and main to draw him away and calling loudly on the Trojans, and thrice did the two Ajaxes, clothed in valour as with a garment, beat him from off the body; but all undaunted he would now charge into the thick of the fight, and now again he would stand still and cry aloud, but he would give no ground. As upland shepherds that cannot chase some famished lion from a carcase, even so could not the two Ajaxes scare Hector son of Priam from the body of Patroclus.

And now he would even have dragged it off and have won imperishable glory, had not Iris fleet as the wind, winged her way as messenger from Olympus to the son of Peleus and bidden him arm. She came secretly without the knowledge of Jove and of the other gods, for Juno sent her, and when she had got close to him she said, 'Up, son of Peleus, mightiest of all mankind; rescue Patroclus about whom this fearful fight is now raging by the ships. Men are killing one another, the Danaans in defence of the dead body, while the Trojans are trying to hale it away, and take it to windy Ilius: Hector is the most furious of them all; he is for cutting the head from the body and fixing it on the stakes of the wall. Up, then, and bide here no longer; shrink from the thought that Patroclus may become meat for the dogs of Troy. Shame on you, should his body suffer any kind of outrage.'

And Achilles said, 'Iris, which of the gods was it that sent you to me?'

Iris answered, 'It was Juno the royal spouse of Jove, but the son of Saturn does not know of my coming, nor yet does any other of the immortals who dwell on the snowy summits of Olympus.'

Then fleet Achilles answered her saying, 'How can I go up into the battle? They have my armour. My mother forbade me to arm till I should see her come, for she promised to bring me goodly armour from Vulcan; I know no man whose arms I can put on, save only the shield of Ajax son of Telamon, and he surely must be fighting in the front rank and wielding his spear about the body of dead Patroclus.'

Iris said, 'We know that your armour has been taken, but go as you are; go to the deep trench and show yourself before the Trojans, that they may fear you and cease fighting. Thus will the fainting sons of the

Achæans gain some brief breathing-time, which in battle may hardly be.'

Iris left him when she had so spoken. But Achilles dear to Jove arose, and Minerva flung her tasselled ægis round his strong shoulders; she crowned his head with a halo of golden cloud from which she kindled a glow of gleaming fire. As the smoke that goes up into heaven from some city that is being beleaguered on an island far out at sea – all day long do men sally from the city and fight their hardest, and at the going down of the sun the line of beacon-fires blazes forth, flaring high for those that dwell near them to behold, if so be that they may come with their ships and succour them – even so did the light flare from the head of Achilles, as he stood by the trench, going beyond the wall – but he did not join the Achæans for he heeded the charge which his mother laid upon him.

There did he stand and shout aloud. Minerva also raised her voice from afar, and spread terror unspeakable among the Trojans. Ringing as the note of a trumpet that sounds alarm when the foe is at the gates of a city, even so brazen was the voice of the son of Æacus, and when the Trojans heard its clarion tones they were dismayed; the horses turned back with their chariots for they boded mischief, and their drivers were awe-struck by the steady flame which the grey-eyed goddess had kindled above the head of the great son of Peleus.

Thrice did Achilles raise his loud cry as he stood by the trench, and thrice were the Trojans and their brave allies thrown into confusion; whereon twelve of their noblest champions fell beneath the wheels of their chariots and perished by their own spears. The Achæans to their great joy then drew Patroclus out of reach of the weapons, and laid him on a litter: his comrades stood mourning round him, and among them fleet Achilles who wept bitterly as he saw his true comrade lying dead upon his bier. He had sent him out with horses and chariots into battle, but his return he was not to welcome.

Then Juno sent the busy sun, loth though he was, into the waters of Oceanus; so he set, and the Achæans had rest from the tug and turmoil of war.

Now the Trojans when they had come out of the fight, unyoked their horses and gathered in assembly before preparing their supper. They kept their feet, nor would any dare to sit down, for fear had fallen upon them all because Achilles had shown himself after having held aloof so long from battle. Polydamas son of Panthoüs was first to speak, a man of judgement, who alone among them could look both before and after. He was comrade to Hector, and they had been born upon the same night; with all sincerity and goodwill, therefore, he addressed them thus:—

'Look to it well, my friends; I would urge you to go back now to your city and not wait here by the ships till morning, for we are far from our walls. So long as this man was at enmity with Agamemnon the Achæans were easier to deal with, and I would have gladly camped by the ships in the hope of taking them; but now I go in great fear of the fleet son of Peleus; he is so daring that he will never bide here on the plain whereon the Trojans and Achæans fight with equal valour, but he will try to storm our city and carry off our women. Do then as I say, and let us retreat. For this is what will happen. The darkness of night will for a time stay the son of Peleus, but if he find us here in the morning when he sallies forth in full armour, we shall have knowledge of him in good earnest. Glad indeed will he be who can escape and get back to Ilius, and many a Trojan will become meat for dogs and vultures – may I never live to hear it. If we do as I say, little though we may like it, we shall have strength in counsel during the night, and the great gates with the doors that close them will protect the city. At dawn we can arm and take our stand on the walls; he will then rue it if he sallies from the ships to fight us. He will go back when he has given his horses their fill of being driven all whithers under our walls, and will be in no mind to try and force his way into the city. Neither will he ever sack it, dogs shall devour him ere he do so.'

Hector looked fiercely at him and answered, 'Polydamas, your words are not to my liking in that you bid us go back and be pent within the city. Have you not had enough of being cooped up behind walls? In the old days the city of Priam was famous the whole world over for its wealth of gold and bronze, but our treasures are wasted out of our houses, and much goods have been sold away to Phrygia and fair Meonia, for the hand of Jove has been laid heavily upon us. Now, therefore, that the son of scheming Saturn has vouchsafed me to win glory here and to hem the Achæans in at their ships, prate no more in this fool's wise among the people. You will have no man with you; it shall not be; do all of you as I now say; – take your suppers in your companies throughout the host, and keep your watches and be wakeful every man of you. If any Trojan is uneasy about his possessions, let him gather them and give them out among the people. Better let these, rather than the Achæans, have them. At daybreak we will arm and fight about the ships; granted that Achilles has again come forward to defend them, let it be as he will, but it shall go hard with him. I shall not shun him, but will fight him, to fall or conquer. The god of war deals out like measure to all, and the slayer may yet be slain.'

Thus spoke Hector; and the Trojans, fools that they were, shouted in applause, for Pallas Minerva had robbed them of their understanding. They gave ear to Hector with his evil counsel, but the wise words of Polydamas no man would heed. They took their supper throughout the host, and meanwhile through the whole night the Achæans mourned Patroclus, and the son of Peleus led them in their lament. He laid his murderous hands upon the breast of his comrade, groaning again and again as a bearded lion when a man who was chasing deer has robbed him of his young in some dense forest; when the lion comes back he is furious, and searches dingle and dell to track the hunter if he can find him, for he is mad with rage – even so with many a sigh did Achilles speak among the Myrmidons saying, 'Alas! vain were the words with which I cheered the hero Menœtius in his own house; I said that I would bring his brave son back again to Opöeis after he had sacked Ilius and taken his share of the spoils – but Jove does not give all men their heart's desire. The same soil shall be reddened here at Troy by the blood of us both, for I too shall never be welcomed home by the old knight Peleus, nor by my mother Thetis, but even in this place shall the earth cover me. Nevertheless, O Patroclus, now that I am left behind you, I will not bury you, till I have brought hither the head and armour of mighty Hector who has slain you. Twelve noble sons of Trojans will I behead before your bier to avenge you; till I have done so you shall lie as you are by the ships, and fair women of Troy and Dardanus, whom we have taken with spear and strength of arm when we sacked men's goodly cities, shall weep over you both night and day.'

Then Achilles told his men to set a large tripod[7] upon the fire that they might wash the clotted gore from off Patroclus. Thereon they set a tripod full of bath water on to a clear fire: they threw sticks on to it to make it blaze, and the water became hot as the flame played about the belly of the tripod. When the water in the cauldron was boiling they washed the body, anointed it with oil, and closed its wounds with ointment that had been kept nine years. Then they laid it on a bier and covered it with a linen cloth from head to foot, and over this they laid a fair white robe. Thus all night long did the Myrmidons gather round Achilles to mourn Patroclus.

Then Jove said to Juno his sister-wife, 'So, Queen Juno, you have gained your end, and have roused fleet Achilles. One would think that the Achæans were of your own flesh and blood.'

And Juno answered, 'Dread son of Saturn, why should you say this thing? May not a man though he be only mortal and knows less than we do, do what he can for another person? And shall not I – foremost of all goddesses both by descent and as wife to you who reign in heaven – devise evil for the Trojans if I am angry with them?'

Thus did they converse. Meanwhile Thetis came to the house of Vulcan, imperishable, star-bespangled, fairest of the abodes in heaven, a house of bronze wrought by the lame god's own hands. She found him busy with his bellows, sweating and hard at work, for he was making twenty tripods that were to stand by the wall of his house, and he set wheels of gold under them all that they might go of their own selves to the assemblies of the gods, and come back again – marvels indeed to see. They were finished all but the ears of cunning workmanship which yet remained to be fixed to them: these he was now fixing, and he was hammering at the rivets. While he was thus at work silver-footed Thetis came to the house. Charis, of graceful head-dress, wife to the far-famed lame god, came towards her as soon as she saw her, and took her hand in her own, saying, 'Why have you come to our house, Thetis, honoured and ever welcome – for you do not visit us often? Come inside and let me set refreshment before you.'

The goddess led the way as she spoke, and bade Thetis sit on a richly decorated seat inlaid with silver; there was a footstool also under her feet. Then she called Vulcan and said, 'Vulcan, come here, Thetis wants you'; and the far-famed lame god answered, 'Then it is indeed an august and honoured goddess who has come here; she it was that took care of me when I was suffering from the heavy fall which I had through my cruel mother's anger – for she would have got rid of me because I was lame. It would have gone hardly with me had not Eurynome, daughter of the ever-encircling waters of Oceanus, and Thetis, taken me to their bosom. Nine years did I stay with them, and many beautiful works in bronze, brooches, spiral armlets, cups, and chains, did I make for them in their cave, with the roaring waters of Oceanus foaming as they rushed ever past it; and no one knew, neither of gods nor men, save only Thetis and Eurynome who took care of me. If, then, Thetis has come to my house I must make her due requital for having saved me; entertain her, therefore, with all hospitality, while I put by my bellows and all my tools.'

On this the mighty monster hobbled off from his anvil, his thin legs plying lustily under him. He set the bellows away from the fire, and gathered his tools into a silver chest. Then he took a sponge and washed his face and hands, his shaggy chest and brawny neck; he donned his shirt, grasped his strong staff, and limped towards the door. There were golden handmaids also who worked for him, and were like real young women, with sense and reason, voice also and strength, and all the learning of the immortals; these busied themselves as the king bade them, while he drew near to Thetis, seated her upon a goodly seat, and took her hand in his own, saying, 'Why have you come to our house, Thetis honoured and ever welcome – for you do not visit us often? Say what you want, and I will do it for you at once if I can, and if it can be done at all.'

Thetis wept and answered, 'Vulcan, is there another goddess in Olympus whom the son of Saturn has been pleased to try with so much affliction as he has me? Me alone of the marine goddesses did he make subject to a mortal husband, Peleus son of Æacus, and solely against my will did I submit to the embraces of one who was but mortal, and who now stays at home worn out with age. Neither is this all. Heaven vouchsafed me a son, hero among heroes, and he shot up as a sapling. I tended him as a plant in a goodly garden and sent him with his ships to Ilius to fight the Trojans, but never shall I welcome him back to the house of Peleus. So long as he lives to look upon the light of the sun, he is in heaviness, and though I go to him I cannot help him; King Agamemnon has made him give up the maiden whom the sons of the Achæans had awarded him, and he wastes with sorrow for her sake. Then the Trojans hemmed the Achæans in at their ships' sterns and would not let them come forth; the elders, therefore, of the Argives besought Achilles and offered him great treasure, whereon he refused to bring deliverance to them himself, but put his own armour on Patroclus and sent him into the fight with much people after him. All day long they fought by the Scæan gates and would have taken the city there and then, had not Apollo vouchsafed glory to Hector and slain the valiant son of Menœtius after he had done the Trojans much evil. Therefore I am suppliant at your knees if haply you may be pleased to provide my son, whose end is near at hand, with helmet and shield, with goodly greaves fitted with ancle-clasps, and with a breastplate, for he lost his own when his true comrade fell at the hands of the Trojans, and he now lies stretched on earth in the bitterness of his soul.'

And Vulcan answered, 'Take heart, and be no more disquieted about this matter; would that I could hide him from death's sight when his hour is come, so surely as I can find him armour that shall amaze the eyes of all who behold it.'

When he had so said he left her and went to his bellows, turning them towards the fire and bidding them do their office. Twenty bellows blew upon the melting-pots, and they blew blasts of every kind, some fierce to help him when he had need of them, and others less strong as Vulcan willed it in the course of his work. He threw tough copper into the fire, and tin, with silver and gold; he set his great anvil on its block, and with one hand grasped his mighty hammer while he took the tongs in the other.

First he shaped the shield so great and strong, adorning it all over and binding it round with a gleaming circuit in three layers; and the baldric was made of silver. He made the shield in five thicknesses, and with many a wonder did his cunning hand enrich it.

He wrought the earth, the heavens, and the sea; the moon also at her full and the untiring sun, with all the signs that glorify the face of heaven – the Pleiads, the Hyads, huge Orion, and the Bear, which men also call the Wain and which turns round ever in one place, facing Orion, and alone never dips into the stream of Oceanus.

He wrought also two cities, fair to see and busy with the hum of men. In the one were weddings and wedding-feasts, and they were going about the city with brides whom they were escorting by torch-light from their chambers. Loud rose the cry of Hymen, and the youths danced to the music of flute and lyre, while the women stood each at her house door to see them.

Meanwhile the people were gathered in assembly, for there was a quarrel, and two men were wrangling about the blood-money for a man who had been killed, the one saying before the people that he had paid damages in full, and the other that he had not been paid. Each was trying to make his own case good, and the people took sides, each man backing the side that he had taken; but the heralds kept them back, and the elders sate on their seats of stone in a solemn circle, holding the staves which the heralds had put into their hands. Then they rose and each in his turn gave judgement, and there were two talents laid down, to be given to him whose judgement should be deemed the fairest.

About the other city there lay encamped two hosts in gleaming armour, and they were divided whether to sack it, or to spare it and accept the half of what it contained. But the men of the city would not yet consent, and armed themselves for a surprise; their wives and little children kept guard upon the walls, and with them were the men who were past fighting through age; but the others sallied forth with Mars and Pallas Minerva at their head – both of them wrought in gold and clad in golden raiment, great and fair with their armour as befitting gods, while they that followed were smaller. When they reached the place where they would lay their ambush, it was on a riverbed to which live stock of all kinds would come from far and near to water; here, then, they lay concealed, clad in full armour. Some way off them there were two scouts who were on the look-out for the coming of sheep or cattle, which presently came, followed by two shepherds who were playing on their pipes, and had not so much as a thought of danger. When those who were in ambush saw this, they cut off the flocks and herds and killed the shepherds. Meanwhile the besiegers, when they heard much noise among the cattle as they sat in council, sprang to their horses, and made with all speed towards them; when they reached them they set battle in array by the banks of the river, and the hosts aimed their bronze-shod spears at one another. With them were Strife and Riot, and fell Fate who was dragging three men after her, one with a fresh wound, and the other unwounded, while the third was dead, and she was dragging him along by his heel: and her robe was bedrabbled in men's blood. They went in and out with one another and fought as though they were living people haling away one another's dead.

He wrought also a fair fallow field, large and thrice ploughed already. Many men were working at the plough within it, turning their oxen to and fro, furrow after furrow. Each time that they turned on reaching the headland a man would come up to them and give them a cup of wine, and they would go back to their furrows looking forward to the time when they should again reach the headland. The part that they had ploughed was dark behind them, so that the field, though it was of gold, still looked as if it were being ploughed – very curious to behold.

He wrought also a field of harvest corn, and the reapers were reaping with sharp sickles in their hands. Swathe after swathe fell to the ground in a straight line behind them, and the binders bound them in bands of twisted straw. There were three binders, and behind them there were boys who gathered the cut corn in armfuls and kept on bringing them to be bound: among them all the owner of the land stood by in silence and was glad. The servants were getting a meal ready under an oak, for they had sacrificed a great ox, and were busy cutting him up, while the women were making a porridge of much white barley for the labourers' dinner.

He wrought also a vineyard, golden and fair to see, and the vines were loaded with grapes. The bunches overhead were black, but the vines were trained on poles of silver. He ran a ditch of dark metal all round it, and fenced it with a fence of tin; there was only one path to it, and by this the vintagers went when they would gather the vintage. Youths and maidens all blithe and full of glee, carried the luscious fruit in plaited baskets; and with them there went a boy who made sweet music with his lyre, and sang the Linus-song[8] with his clear boyish voice.

He wrought also a herd of horned cattle. He made the cows of gold and tin, and they lowed as they came full speed out of the yards to go and feed among the waving reeds that grow by the banks of the river. Along with the cattle there went four shepherds, all of them in gold, and their nine fleet dogs went with them. Two terrible lions had fastened on a bellowing bull that was with the foremost cows, and bellow as he might they haled him, while the dogs and men gave chase: the lions tore through the bull's thick hide and were gorging on his blood and bowels, but the herdsmen were afraid to do anything, and only hounded on their dogs; the dogs dared not fasten on the lions but stood by barking and keeping out of harm's way.

The god wrought also a pasture in a fair mountain dell, and a large flock of sheep, with a homestead and huts, and sheltered sheepfolds.

Furthermore he wrought a green, like that which Dædalus once made in Cnossus for lovely Ariadne. Hereon there danced youths and maidens whom all would woo, with their hands on one another's wrists. The maidens wore robes of light linen, and the youths well-woven shirts that were slightly oiled. The girls were crowned with garlands, while the young men had daggers of gold that hung by silver baldrics; sometimes they would dance deftly in a ring with merry twinkling feet, as it were a potter sitting at his work and making trial of his wheel to see whether it will run, and sometimes they would go all in line with one another, and much people was gathered joyously about the green. There was a bard also to sing to them and play his lyre, while two tumblers went about performing in the midst of them when the man struck up with his tune.

All round the outermost rim of the shield he set the mighty stream of the river Oceanus.

Then when he had fashioned the shield so great and strong, he made a breastplate also that shone brighter than fire. He made a helmet, close fitting to the brow, and richly worked, with a golden plume overhanging it; and he made greaves also of beaten tin.

Lastly, when the famed lame god had made all the armour, he took it and set it before the mother of Achilles; whereon she darted like a falcon from the snowy summits of Olympus and bore away the gleaming armour from the house of Vulcan.

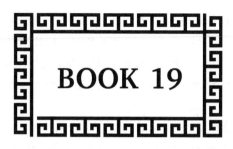

BOOK 19

Achilles is reconciled with Agamemnon, puts on the armour which Vulcan had made him, and goes out to fight.

Now when Dawn in robe of saffron was hasting from the streams of Oceanus, to bring light to mortals and immortals, Thetis reached the ships with the armour that the god had given her. She found her son fallen about the body of Patroclus and weeping bitterly. Many also of his followers were weeping round him, but when the goddess came among them she clasped his hand in her own, saying, 'My son, grieve as we may we must let this man lie, for it is by heaven's will that he has fallen; now, therefore, accept from Vulcan this rich and goodly armour, which no man has ever yet borne upon his shoulders.'

As she spoke she set the armour before Achilles, and it rang out bravely as she did so. The Myrmidons were struck with awe, and none dared look full at it, for they were afraid; but Achilles was roused to still greater fury, and his eyes gleamed with a fierce light, for he was glad when he handled the splendid present which the god had made him. Then, as soon as he had satisfied himself with looking at it, he said to his mother, 'Mother, the god has given me armour, meet handiwork for an immortal and such as no man living could have fashioned; I will now arm, but I much fear that flies will settle upon the son of Menœtius and breed worms about his wounds, so that his body, now he is dead, will be disfigured and the flesh will rot.'

Silver-footed Thetis answered, 'My son, be not disquieted about this matter. I will find means to protect him from the swarms of noisome flies that prey on the bodies of men who have been killed in battle. He may lie for a whole year, and his flesh shall still be as sound as ever, or even sounder. Call, therefore, the Achæan heroes in assembly; unsay your anger against Agamemnon; arm at once, and fight with might and main.'

As she spoke she put strength and courage into his heart, and she then dropped ambrosia and red nectar into the wounds of Patroclus, that his body might suffer no change.

Then Achilles went out upon the sea-shore, and with a loud cry called on the Achæan heroes. On this even those who as yet had stayed always at the ships, the pilots and helmsmen, and even the stewards who were about the ships and served out rations, all came to the place of assembly because Achilles had shown himself after having held aloof so long from fighting. Two sons of Mars, Ulysses and the son of Tydeus, came limping, for their wounds still pained them; nevertheless they came, and took their seats in the front row of the assembly. Last of all came Agamemnon, king of men, he too wounded, for Coön son of Antenor had struck him with a spear in battle.

When the Achæans were got together Achilles rose and said, 'Son of Atreus, surely it would have been better alike for both you and me, when we two were in such high anger about Briseis, surely it would have been better, had Diana's arrow slain her at the ships on the day when I took her after having sacked Lyrnessus. For so, many an Achæan the less would have bitten dust before the foe in the days of my anger. It has been well for Hector and the Trojans, but the Achæans will long indeed remember our quarrel. Now, however, let it be, for it is over. If we have been angry, necessity has schooled our anger. I put it from me: I dare not nurse it for ever; therefore, bid the Achæans arm forthwith that I may go out against the Trojans, and learn whether they will be in a mind to sleep by the ships or no. Glad, I ween, will he be to rest his knees who may fly my spear when I wield it.'

Thus did he speak, and the Achæans rejoiced in that he had put away his anger.

Then Agamemnon spoke, rising in his place, and not going into the middle of the assembly. 'Danaan heroes,' said he, 'servants of Mars, it is well to listen when a man stands up to speak, and it is not seemly to interrupt him, or it will go hard even with a practised speaker. Who can either hear or speak in an uproar? Even the finest orator will be disconcerted by it. I will expound to the son of Peleus, and do you other Achæans heed me and mark me well. Often have the Achæans spoken to me of this matter and upbraided me, but it was not I that did it: Jove, and Fate, and Erinys that walks in darkness struck me mad when we were assembled on the day that I took from Achilles the meed that had been awarded to him. What could I do? All things are in the hand of heaven, and Folly, eldest of Jove's daughters, shuts men's eyes to their destruction. She walks delicately, not on the solid earth, but hovers over the heads of men to make them stumble or to ensnare them.

'Time was when she fooled Jove himself, who they say is greatest whether of gods or men; for Juno, woman though she was, beguiled him on the day when Alcmena was to bring forth mighty Hercules in the fair city of Thebes. He told it out among the gods saying, "Hear me all gods and goddesses, that I may speak even as I am minded; this day shall an Ilithuia, helper of women who are in labour, bring a man child into the world who shall be lord over all that dwell about him who are of my blood and lineage." Then said Juno all crafty and full of guile, "You will play false, and will not hold to your word. Swear me, O Olympian, swear me a great oath, that he who shall this day fall between the feet of a woman, shall be lord over all that dwell about him who are of your blood and lineage."

'Thus she spoke, and Jove suspected her not, but swore the great oath, to his much ruing thereafter. For Juno darted down from the high summit of Olympus, and went in haste to Achæan Argos where she knew that the noble wife of Sthenelus son of Perseus then was. She being with child and in her seventh month, Juno brought the child to birth though there was a month still wanting, but she stayed the offspring of Alcmena, and kept back the Ilithuiæ. Then she went to tell Jove the son of Saturn, and said, "Father Jove, lord of the lightning – I have a word for your ear. There is a fine child born this day, Eurystheus, son to Sthenelus the son of Perseus; he is of your lineage; it is well, therefore, that he should reign over the Argives."

'On this Jove was stung to the very quick, and in his rage he caught Folly by the hair, and swore a great oath that never should she again invade starry heaven and Olympus, for she was the bane of all. Then he whirled her round with a twist of his hand, and flung her down from heaven so that she fell on to the fields of mortal men; and he was ever angry with her when he saw his son groaning under the cruel labours that Eurystheus laid upon him. Even so did I grieve when mighty Hector was killing the Argives at their ships, and all the time I kept thinking of Folly who had so baned me. I was blind, and Jove robbed me of my reason; I will now make atonement, and will add much treasure by way of amends. Go, therefore, into battle, you and your people with you. I will give you all that Ulysses offered you yesterday in your tents: or if it so please you, wait, though you would fain fight at once, and my squires shall bring the gifts from my ship, that you may see whether what I give you is enough.'

And Achilles answered, 'Son of Atreus, king of men Agamemnon, you can give such gifts as you think proper, or you can withhold them: it is in your own hands. Let us now set battle in array; it is not well to tarry talking about trifles, for there is a deed which is as yet to do. Achilles shall again be seen fighting among the foremost, and laying low the ranks of the Trojans: bear this in mind each one of you when he is fighting.'

Then Ulysses said, 'Achilles, godlike and brave, send not the Achæans thus against Ilius to fight the Trojans fasting, for the battle will be no brief one, when it is once begun, and heaven has filled both sides with fury; bid them first take food both bread and wine by the ships, for in this there is strength and stay. No man can do battle the livelong day to the going down of the sun if he is without food; however much he

may want to fight his strength will fail him before he knows it; hunger
and thirst will find him out, and his limbs will grow weary under him.
But a man can fight all day if he is full fed with meat and wine; his
heart beats high, and his strength will stay till he has routed all his
foes; therefore, send the people away and bid them prepare their meal;
King Agamemnon will bring out the gifts in presence of the assembly,
that all may see them and you may be satisfied. Moreover let him swear
an oath before the Argives that he has never gone up into the couch
of Briseis, nor been with her after the manner of men and women;
and do you, too, show yourself of a gracious mind; let Agamemnon
entertain you in his tents with a feast of reconciliation, that so you
may have had your dues in full. As for you, son of Atreus, treat people
more righteously in future; it is no disgrace even to a king that he
should make amends if he was wrong in the first instance.'

And King Agamemnon answered, 'Son of Laertes, your words please
me well, for throughout you have spoken wisely. I will swear as you
would have me do; I do so of my own free will, neither shall I take
the name of heaven in vain. Let, then, Achilles wait, though he would
fain fight at once, and do you others wait also, till the gifts come from
my tent and we ratify the oath with sacrifice. Thus, then, do I charge
you: take some noble young Achæans with you, and bring from my
tents the gifts that I promised yesterday to Achilles, and bring the
women also; furthermore let Talthybius find me a boar from those that
are with the host, and make it ready for sacrifice to Jove and to the
sun.'

Then said Achilles, 'Son of Atreus, king of men Agamemnon, see
to these matters at some other season, when there is breathing time
and when I am calmer. Would you have men eat while the bodies of
those whom Hector son of Priam slew are still lying mangled upon
the plain? Let the sons of the Achæans, say I, fight fasting and without
food, till we have avenged them; afterwards at the going down of the
sun let them eat their fill. As for me, Patroclus is lying dead in my
tent, all hacked and hewn, with his feet to the door, and his comrades

are mourning round him. Therefore I can take thought of nothing save only slaughter and blood and the rattle in the throat of the dying.'

Ulysses answered, 'Achilles, son of Peleus, mightiest of all the Achæans, in battle you are better than I, and that more than a little, but in counsel I am much before you, for I am older and of greater knowledge. Therefore be patient under my words. Fighting is a thing of which men soon surfeit, and when Jove, who is war's steward, weighs the upshot, it may well prove that the straw which our sickles have reaped is far heavier than the grain. It may not be that the Achæans should mourn the dead with their bellies; day by day men fall thick and threefold continually; when should we have respite from our sorrow? Let us mourn our dead for a day and bury them out of sight and mind, but let those of us who are left eat and drink that we may arm and fight our foes more fiercely. In that hour let no man hold back, waiting for a second summons; such summons shall bode ill for him who is found lagging behind at our ships; let us rather sally as one man and loose the fury of war upon the Trojans.'

When he had thus spoken he took with him the sons of Nestor, with Meges son of Phyleus, Thoas, Meriones, Lycomedes son of Creontes, and Melanippus, and went to the tent of Agamemnon son of Atreus. The word was not sooner said than the deed was done: they brought out the seven tripods which Agamemnon had promised, with the twenty metal cauldrons and the twelve horses; they also brought the women skilled in useful arts, seven in number, with Briseis, which made eight. Ulysses weighed out the ten talents of gold and then led the way back, while the young Achæans brought the rest of the gifts, and laid them in the middle of the assembly.

Agamemnon then rose, and Talthybius whose voice was like that of a god came up to him with the boar. The son of Atreus drew the knife which he wore by the scabbard of his mighty sword, and began by cutting off some bristles from the boar, lifting up his hands in prayer as he did so. The other Achæans sat where they were all silent and orderly to hear the king, and Agamemnon looked into the vault of heaven and prayed saying, 'I call Jove the first and mightiest of all gods to witness, I call also Earth and Sun and the Erinyes who dwell below and take vengeance on him who shall swear falsely, that I have laid no hand upon the girl Briseis, neither to take her to my bed nor otherwise, but that she has remained in my tents inviolate. If I swear falsely may heaven visit me with all the penalties which it metes out to those who perjure themselves.'

He cut the boar's throat as he spoke, whereon Talthybius whirled it round his head, and flung it into the wide sea to feed the fishes. Then Achilles also rose and said to the Argives, 'Father Jove, of a truth you blind men's eyes and bane them. The son of Atreus had not else stirred me to so fierce an anger, nor so stubbornly taken Briseis from me against my will. Surely Jove must have counselled the destruction of many an Argive. Go, now, and take your food that we may begin fighting.'

On this he broke up the assembly, and every man went back to his own ship. The Myrmidons attended to the presents and took them away to the ship of Achilles. They placed them in his tents, while the stable-men drove the horses in among the others.

Briseis, fair as Venus, when she saw the mangled body of Patroclus, flung herself upon it and cried aloud, tearing her breast, her neck, and her lovely face with both her hands. Beautiful as a goddess she wept and said, 'Patroclus, dearest friend, when I went hence I left you living; I return, O prince, to find you dead; thus do fresh sorrows multiply upon me one after the other. I saw him to whom my father and mother married me, cut down before our city, and my three own dear brothers perished with him on the self-same day; but you, Patroclus, even when Achilles slew my husband and sacked the city of noble Mynes, told me that I was not to weep, for you said you would make Achilles marry me, and take me back with him to Phthia, where we should have a wedding feast among the Myrmidons. You were always kind to me and I shall never cease to grieve for you.'

She wept as she spoke, and the women joined in her lament – making as though their tears were for Patroclus, but in truth each was weeping for her own sorrows. The elders of the Achæans gathered round Achilles and prayed him to take food, but he groaned and would not do so. 'I pray you,' said he, 'if any comrade will hear me, bid me neither eat nor drink, for I am in great heaviness, and will stay fasting even to the going down of the sun.'

On this he sent the other princes away, save only the two sons of Atreus and Ulysses, Nestor, Idomeneus, and the old knight Phœnix, who stayed behind and tried to comfort him in the bitterness of his sorrow: but he would not be comforted till he should have flung himself into the jaws of battle, and he fetched sigh on sigh, thinking ever of Patroclus. Then he said:—

'Hapless and dearest comrade, you it was who would get a good dinner ready for me at once and without delay when the Achæans were hasting to fight the Trojans; now, therefore, though I have meat and drink in my tents, yet will I fast for sorrow. Grief greater than this I could not know, not even though I were to hear of the death of my father, who is now in Phthia weeping for the loss of me his son, who am here fighting the Trojans in a strange land for the accursed sake of Helen, nor yet though I should hear that my son is no more – he who is being brought up in Scyros – if indeed Neoptolemus is still living. Till now I made sure that I alone was to fall here at Troy away from Argos, while you were to return to Phthia, bring back my son with you in your own ship, and show him all my property, my bondsmen, and the greatness of my house – for Peleus must surely be either dead, or what little life remains to him is oppressed alike with the infirmities of age and ever present fear lest he should hear the sad tidings of my death.'

He wept as he spoke, and the elders sighed in concert as each thought on what he had left at home behind him. The son of Saturn looked down with pity upon them, and said presently to Minerva, 'My child, you have quite deserted your hero; is he then gone so clean out of your recollection? There he sits by the ships all desolate for the loss of his dear comrade, and though the others are gone to their dinner he will neither eat nor drink. Go then and drop nectar and ambrosia into his breast, that he may know no hunger.'

With these words he urged Minerva, who was already of the same mind. She darted down from heaven into the air like some falcon sailing on his broad wings and screaming. Meanwhile the Achæans were arming throughout the host, and when Minerva had dropped nectar and ambrosia into Achilles so that no cruel hunger should cause his limbs to fail him, she went back to the house of her mighty father. Thick as the chill snow-flakes shed from the hand of Jove and borne on the keen blasts of the north wind, even so thick did the gleaming helmets, the bossed shields, the strongly plated breastplates, and the ashen spears stream from the ships. The sheen pierced the sky, the whole land was radiant with their flashing armour, and the sound of the tramp of their treading rose from under their feet. In the midst of them all Achilles put on his armour; he gnashed his teeth, his eyes gleamed like fire, for his grief was greater than he could bear. Thus, then, full of fury against the Trojans, did he don the gift of the god, the armour that Vulcan had made him.

First he put on the goodly greaves fitted with ancle-clasps, and next he did on the breastplate about his chest. He slung the silver-studded sword of bronze about his shoulders, and then took up the shield so great and strong that shone afar with a splendour as of the moon. As the light seen by sailors from out at sea, when men have lit a fire in their homestead high up among the mountains, but the sailors are carried out to sea by wind and storm far from the haven where they would be – even so did the gleam of Achilles' wondrous shield strike up into the heavens. He lifted the redoubtable helmet, and set it upon his head, from whence it shone like a star, and the golden plumes which Vulcan had set thick about the ridge of the helmet, waved all around it. Then Achilles made trial of himself in his armour to see whether it fitted him, so that his limbs could play freely under it, and it seemed to buoy him up as though it had been wings.

He also drew his father's spear out of the spear-stand, a spear so great and heavy and strong that none of the Achæans save only Achilles had strength to wield it; this was the spear of Pelian ash from the topmost ridges of Mt Pelion, which Chiron had once given to Peleus, fraught with the death of heroes. Automedon and Alcimus busied themselves with the harnessing of his horses; they made the bands fast about them, and put the bit in their mouths, drawing the reins back towards the chariot. Automedon, whip in hand, sprang up behind the horses, and after him Achilles mounted in full armour, resplendent as the sun-god Hyperion. Then with a loud voice he chided with his father's horses saying, 'Xanthus and Balius, famed offspring of Podarge – this time when we have done fighting be sure and bring your driver safely back to the host of the Achæans, and do not leave him dead on the plain as you did Patroclus.'

Then fleet Xanthus answered from under the yoke – for white-armed Juno had endowed him with human speech – and he bowed his head till his mane touched the ground as it hung down from under the yoke-band. 'Dread Achilles,' said he, 'we will indeed save you now, but the day of your death is near, and the blame will not be ours, for it will be heaven and stern fate that will destroy you. Neither was it through any sloth or slackness on our part that the Trojans stripped Patroclus of his armour; it was the mighty god whom lovely Leto bore that slew him as he fought among the foremost, and vouchsafed a triumph to Hector. We two can fly as swiftly as Zephyrus who they say is fleetest of all winds; nevertheless it is your doom to fall by the hand of a man and of a god.'

When he had thus said the Erinyes stayed his speech, and Achilles answered him in great sadness, saying, 'Why, O Xanthus, do you thus foretell my death? You need not do so, for I well know that I am to fall here, far from my dear father and mother; none the more, however, shall I stay my hand till I have given the Trojans their fill of fighting.'

So saying, with a loud cry he drove his horses to the front.

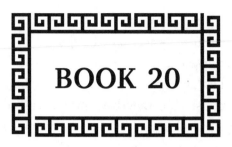

BOOK 20

The gods hold a council and determine to watch the fight from the hill Callicolone, and the barrow of Hercules – A fight between Achilles and Æneas is interrupted by Neptune, who saves Æneas – Achilles kills many Trojans.

Thus, then, did the Achæans arm by their ships round you, O son of Peleus, who were hungering for battle; while the Trojans over against them armed upon the rise of the plain.

Meanwhile Jove from the top of many-delled Olympus, bade Themis gather the gods in council, whereon she went about and called them to the house of Jove. There was not a river absent except Oceanus, nor a single one of the nymphs that haunt fair groves, or springs of rivers and meadows of green grass. When they reached the house of cloud-compelling Jove, they took their seats in the arcades of polished marble which Vulcan with his consummate skill had made for father Jove.

In such wise, therefore, did they gather in the house of Jove. Neptune also, lord of the earthquake, obeyed the call of the goddess, and came up out of the sea to join them. There, sitting in the midst of them, he asked what Jove's purpose might be. 'Why,' said he, 'wielder of the lightning, have you called the gods in council? Are you considering some matter that concerns the Trojans and Achæans – for the blaze of battle is on the point of being kindled between them?'

And Jove answered, 'You know my purpose, shaker of earth, and wherefore I have called you hither. I take thought for them even in their destruction. For my own part I shall stay here seated on Mt Olympus and look on in peace, but do you others go about among Trojans and Achæans, and help either side as you may be severally disposed. If Achilles fights the Trojans without hindrance they will make no stand against him; they have ever trembled at the sight of him, and now that he is roused to such fury about his comrade, he will override fate itself and storm their city.'

Thus spoke Jove and gave the word for war, whereon the gods took their several sides and went into battle. Juno, Pallas Minerva, earth-encircling Neptune, Mercury bringer of good luck and excellent in all cunning – all these joined the host that came from the ships; with them also came Vulcan in all his glory, limping, but yet with his thin legs plying lustily under him. Mars of gleaming helmet joined the Trojans, and with him Apollo of locks unshorn, and the archer goddess Diana, Leto, Xanthus, and laughter-loving Venus.

So long as the gods held themselves aloof from mortal warriors the Achæans were triumphant, for Achilles who had long refused to fight was now with them. There was not a Trojan but his limbs failed him for fear as he beheld the fleet son of Peleus all glorious in his armour, and looking like Mars himself. When, however, the Olympians came to take their part among men, forthwith uprose strong Strife, rouser of hosts, and Minerva raised her loud voice, now standing by the deep trench that ran outside the wall, and now shouting with all her might upon the shore of the sounding sea. Mars also bellowed out upon the other side, dark as some black thunder-cloud, and called on the Trojans at the top of his voice, now from the acropolis, and now speeding up the side of the river Simois till he came to the hill Callicolone.

Thus did the gods spur on both hosts to fight, and rouse fierce contention also among themselves. The sire of gods and men thundered from heaven above, while from beneath Neptune shook the vast earth, and bade the high hills tremble. The spurs and crests of many-fountained Ida quaked, as also the city of the Trojans and the ships of the Achæans. Hades, king of the realms below, was struck with fear; he sprang panic-stricken from his throne and cried aloud in terror lest Neptune, lord of the earthquake, should crack the ground over his head, and lay bare his mouldy mansions to the sight of mortals and immortals – mansions so ghastly grim that even the gods shudder to think of them. Such was the uproar as the gods came together in battle. Apollo with his arrows took his stand to face King Neptune, while Minerva took hers against the god of war; the archer-goddess Diana with her golden arrows, sister of far-darting Apollo, stood to face Juno; Mercury the lusty bringer of good luck faced Leto, while the mighty eddying river whom men call Scamander, but gods Xanthus, matched himself against Vulcan.

The gods, then, were thus ranged against one another. But the heart of Achilles was set on meeting Hector son of Priam, for it was with his blood that he longed above all things else to glut the stubborn lord of battle. Meanwhile Apollo set Æneas on to attack the son of Peleus, and put courage into his heart, speaking with the voice of Lycaon son of Priam. In his likeness, therefore, he said to Æneas, 'Æneas, counsellor of the Trojans, where are now the brave words with which you vaunted over your wine before the Trojan princes, saying that you would fight Achilles son of Peleus in single combat?'

And Æneas answered, 'Why do you thus bid me fight the proud son of Peleus, when I am in no mind to do so? Were I to face him now, it would not be for the first time. His spear has already put me to flight from Ida, when he attacked our cattle and sacked Lyrnessus and Pedasus; Jove indeed saved me in that he vouchsafed me strength to fly, else had I fallen by the hands of Achilles and Minerva, who went before him to protect him and urged him to fall upon the Lelegæ and Trojans. No man may fight Achilles, for one of the gods is always with him as his guardian angel, and even were it not so, his weapon flies ever straight, and fails not to pierce the flesh of him who is against him; if heaven would let me fight him on even terms he should not soon overcome me, though he boasts that he is made of bronze.'

Then said King Apollo, son to Jove, 'Nay, hero, pray to the ever-living gods, for men say that you were born of Jove's daughter Venus, whereas

Achilles is son to a goddess of inferior rank. Venus is child to Jove, while Thetis is but daughter to the old man of the sea. Bring, therefore, your spear to bear upon him, and let him not scare you with his taunts and menaces.'

As he spoke he put courage into the heart of the shepherd of his people, and he strode in full armour among the ranks of the foremost fighters. Nor did the son of Anchises escape the notice of white-armed Juno, as he went forth into the throng to meet Achilles. She called the gods about her, and said, 'Look to it, you two, Neptune and Minerva, and consider how this shall be; Phœbus Apollo has been sending Æneas clad in full armour to fight Achilles. Shall we turn him back at once, or shall one of us stand by Achilles and endow him with strength so that his heart fail not, and he may learn that the chiefs of the immortals are on his side, while the others who have all along been defending the Trojans are but vain helpers? Let us all come down from Olympus and join in the fight, that this day he may take no hurt at the hands of the Trojans. Hereafter let him suffer whatever fate may have spun out for him when he was begotten and his mother bore him. If Achilles be not thus assured by the voice of a god, he may come to fear presently when one of us meets him in battle, for the gods are terrible if they are seen face to face.'

Neptune lord of the earthquake answered her saying, 'Juno, restrain your fury; it is not well; I am not in favour of forcing the other gods to fight us, for the advantage is too greatly on our own side; let us take our places on some hill out of the beaten track, and let mortals fight it out among themselves. If Mars or Phœbus Apollo begin fighting, or keep Achilles in check so that he cannot fight, we, too, will at once raise the cry of battle, and in that case they will soon leave the field and go back vanquished to Olympus among the other gods.'

With these words the dark-haired god led the way to the high earth-barrow of Hercules, built round solid masonry, and made by the Trojans and Pallas Minerva for him to fly to when the sea-monster was chasing him from the shore on to the plain. Here Neptune and those that were with him took their seats, wrapped in a thick cloud of darkness; but the other gods seated themselves on the brow of Callicolone round you, O Phœbus, and Mars the waster of cities.

Thus did the gods sit apart and form their plans, but neither side was willing to begin battle with the other, and Jove from his seat on high was in command over them all. Meanwhile the whole plain was alive with men and horses, and blazing with the gleam of armour. The earth rang again under the tramp of their feet as they rushed towards each other, and two champions, by far the foremost of them all, met between the hosts to fight – to wit, Æneas son of Anchises, and noble Achilles.

Æneas was first to stride forward in attack, his doughty helmet tossing defiance as he came on. He held his strong shield before his breast, and brandished his bronze spear. The son of Peleus from the other side sprang forth to meet him, like some fierce lion that the whole country-side has met to hunt and kill – at first he bodes no ill, but when some daring youth has struck him with a spear, he crouches open-mouthed, his jaws foam, he roars with fury, he lashes his tail from side to side about his ribs and loins, and glares as he springs straight before him, to find out whether he is to slay, or be slain among the foremost of his foes – even with such fury did Achilles burn to spring upon Æneas.

When they were now close up with one another Achilles was first to speak. 'Æneas,' said he, 'why do you stand thus out before the host to fight me? Is it that you hope to reign over the Trojans in the seat of Priam? Nay, though you kill me Priam will not hand his kingdom over to you. He is a man of sound judgement, and he has sons of his own. Or have the Trojans been allotting you a demesne of passing richness, fair with orchard lawns and corn lands, if you should slay me? This you shall hardly do. I have discomfited you once already. Have you forgotten how when you were alone I chased you from your herds helter-skelter down the slopes of Ida? You did not turn round to look behind you; you took refuge in Lyrnessus, but I attacked the city, and with the help of Minerva and father Jove I sacked it and carried its women into captivity, though Jove and the other gods rescued you. You think they will protect you now, but they will not do so; therefore I say go back into the host, and do not face me, or you will rue it. Even a fool may be wise after the event.'

Then Æneas answered, 'Son of Peleus, think not that your words can scare me as though I were a child. I too, if I will, can brag and talk unseemly. We know one another's race and parentage as matters of common fame, though neither have you ever seen my parents nor I yours. Men say that you are son to noble Peleus, and that your mother is Thetis, fair-haired daughter of the sea. I have noble Anchises for my father, and Venus for my mother; the parents of one or other of us shall this day mourn a son, for it will be more than silly talk that shall part us when the fight is over. Learn, then, my lineage if you will – and it is known to many.

'In the beginning Dardanus was the son of Jove, and founded Dardania, for Ilius was not yet stablished on the plain for men to dwell in, and her people still abode on the spurs of many-fountained Ida. Dardanus had a son, King Erichthonius, who was wealthiest of all men living; he had three thousand mares that fed by the water-meadows, they and their foals with them. Boreas was enamoured of them as they were feeding, and covered them in the semblance of a dark-maned stallion. Twelve filly foals did they conceive and bear him, and these, as they sped over the rich plain, would go bounding on over the ripe ears of corn and not break them; or again when they would disport themselves on the broad back of Ocean they could gallop on the crest of a breaker. Erichthonius begat Tros, king of the Trojans, and Tros had three noble sons, Ilus, Assaracus, and Ganymede who was comeliest of mortal men; wherefore the gods carried him off to be Jove's cupbearer, for his beauty's sake, that he might dwell among the immortals. Ilus begat Laomedon, and Laomedon begat Tithonus, Priam, Lampus, Clytius, and Hiketaon of the stock of Mars. But Assaracus was father to Capys, and Capys to Anchises, who was my father, while Hector is son to Priam.

'Such do I declare my blood and lineage, but as for valour, Jove gives it or takes it as he will, for he is lord of all. And now let there be no more of this prating in mid-battle as though we were children. We could fling taunts without end at one another; a hundred-oared galley would not hold them. The tongue can run all whithers and talk all wise; it can go here and there, and as a man says, so shall he be gainsaid. What is the use of our bandying hard words, like women who when they fall foul of one another go out and wrangle in the streets, one half true and the other lies, as rage inspires them? No words of yours shall turn me now that I am fain to fight – therefore let us make trial of one another with our spears.'

As he spoke he drove his spear at the great and terrible shield of Achilles, which rang out as the point struck it. The son of Peleus held the shield before him with his strong hand, and he was afraid, for he deemed that Æneas's spear would go through it quite easily, not reflecting that the god's glorious gifts were little likely to yield before the blows of mortal men; and indeed Æneas's spear did not pierce the shield, for the layer of gold, gift of the god, stayed the point. It went through two layers, but the god had made the shield in five, two of bronze, the two innermost ones of tin, and one of gold; it was in this that the spear was stayed.

Achilles in his turn threw, and struck the round shield of Æneas at the very edge, where the bronze was thinnest; the spear of Pelian ash went clean through, and the shield rang under the blow; Æneas was afraid, and crouched backwards, holding the shield away from him; the spear, however, flew over his back, and stuck quivering in the ground, after having gone through both circles of the sheltering shield. Æneas though he had avoided the spear, stood still, blinded with fear and grief because the weapon had gone so near him; then Achilles sprang furiously upon him, with a cry as of death and with his keen blade drawn, and Æneas seized a great stone, so huge that two men, as men now are, would be unable to lift it, but Æneas wielded it quite easily.

Æneas would then have struck Achilles as he was springing towards him, either on the helmet, or on the shield that covered him, and Achilles would have closed with him and despatched him with his sword, had not Neptune lord of the earthquake been quick to mark, and said forthwith to the immortals, 'Alas, I am sorry for great Æneas, who will now go down to the house of Hades, vanquished by the son of Peleus. Fool that he was to give ear to the counsel of Apollo. Apollo will never save him from destruction. Why should this man suffer when he is guiltless, to no purpose, and in another's quarrel? Has he not at all times offered acceptable sacrifice to the gods that dwell in heaven? Let us then snatch him from death's jaws, lest the son of Saturn be angry should Achilles slay him. It is fated, moreover, that he should escape, and that the race of Dardanus, whom Jove loved above all the sons born to him of mortal women, shall not perish utterly without seed or sign. For now indeed has Jove hated the blood of Priam, while Æneas shall reign over the Trojans, he and his children's children that shall be born hereafter.'

Then answered Juno, 'Earth-shaker, look to this matter yourself, and consider concerning Æneas, whether you will save him, or suffer him, brave though he be, to fall by the hand of Achilles son of Peleus. For of a truth we two, I and Pallas Minerva, have sworn full many a time before all the immortals, that never would we shield Trojans from destruction, not even when all Troy is burning in the flames that the Achæans shall kindle.'

When earth-encircling Neptune heard this he went into the battle amid the clash of spears, and came to the place where Achilles and Æneas were. Forthwith he shed a darkness before the eyes of the son of Peleus, drew the bronze-headed ashen spear from the shield of Æneas, and laid it at the feet of Achilles. Then he lifted Æneas on high from off the earth and hurried him away. Over the heads of many a band of warriors both horse and foot did he soar as the god's hand sped him, till he came to the very fringe of the battle where the Cauconians were arming themselves for fight. Neptune, shaker of the earth, then came near to him and said, 'Æneas, what god has egged you on to this folly in fighting the son of Peleus, who is both a mightier man of valour and more beloved of heaven than you are? Give way before him whensoever you meet him, lest you go down to the house of Hades even though fate would have it otherwise. When Achilles is dead you may then fight among the foremost undaunted, for none other of the Achæans shall slay you.'

The god left him when he had given him these instructions, and at once removed the darkness from before the eyes of Achilles, who opened them wide indeed and said in great anger, 'Alas! what marvel am I now beholding? Here is my spear upon the ground, but I see not him whom I meant to kill when I hurled it. Of a truth Æneas also must be under heaven's protection, although I had thought his boasting was idle. Let him go hang; he will be in no mood to fight me further, seeing how narrowly he has missed being killed. I will now give my orders to the Danaans and attack some other of the Trojans.'

He sprang forward along the line and cheered his men on as he did so. 'Let not the Trojans,' he cried, 'keep you at arm's length, Achæans, but go for them and fight them man for man. However valiant I may be, I cannot give chase to so many and fight all of them. Even Mars, who is an immortal, or Minerva, would shrink from flinging himself into the jaws of such a fight and laying about him; nevertheless, so far as in me lies I will show no slackness of hand or foot nor want of endurance, not even for a moment; I will utterly break their ranks, and woe to the Trojan who shall venture within reach of my spear.'

Thus did he exhort them. Meanwhile Hector called upon the Trojans and declared that he would fight Achilles. 'Be not afraid, proud Trojans,' said he, 'to face the son of Peleus; I could fight gods myself if the battle were one of words only, but they would be more than a match for me, if we had to use our spears. Even so the deed of Achilles will fall somewhat short of his word; he will do in part, and the other part he will clip short. I will go up against him though his hands be as fire – though his hands be fire and his strength iron.'

Thus urged the Trojans lifted up their spears against the Achæans, and raised the cry of battle as they flung themselves into the midst of their ranks. But Phœbus Apollo came up to Hector and said, 'Hector, on no account must you challenge Achilles to single combat; keep a look-out for him while you are under cover of the others and away from the thick of the fight, otherwise he will either hit you with a spear or cut you down at close quarters.'

Thus he spoke, and Hector drew back within the crowd, for he was afraid when he heard what the god had said to him. Achilles then sprang upon the Trojans with a terrible cry, clothed in valour as with a garment. First he killed Iphition son of Otrynteus, a leader of much people whom a naiad nymph had borne to Otrynteus waster of cities, in the land of Hydè under the snowy heights of Mt Tmolus. Achilles struck him full on the head as he was coming on towards him, and split it clean in two; whereon he fell heavily to the ground and Achilles vaunted over him saying, 'You lie low, son of Otrynteus, mighty hero; your death is here, but your lineage is on the Gygæan lake where your father's estate lies, by Hyllus, rich in fish, and the eddying waters of Hermus.'

Thus did he vaunt, but darkness closed the eyes of the other. The chariots of the Achæans cut him up as their wheels passed over him in the front of the battle, and after him Achilles killed Demoleon, a valiant man of war and son to Antenor. He struck him on the temple through his bronze-cheeked helmet. The helmet did not stay the spear, but it went right on, crushing the bone so that the brain inside was shed in all directions, and his lust of fighting was ended. Then he struck Hippodamas in the midriff as he was springing down from his chariot in front of him, and trying to escape. He breathed his last, bellowing like a bull bellows when young men are dragging him to offer him in sacrifice to the King of Helice, and the heart of the earth-shaker is glad: even so did he bellow as he lay dying. Achilles then went in pursuit of Polydorus son of Priam, whom his father had always forbidden to fight because he was the youngest of his sons, the one he loved best, and the fastest runner. He, in his folly and showing off the fleetness of his feet, was rushing about among the front ranks until he lost his life, for Achilles struck him in the middle of the back as he was darting past him: he struck him just at the golden fastenings of his belt and where the two pieces of the double breastplate overlapped. The point of the spear pierced him through and came out by the navel, whereon he fell groaning on to his knees and a cloud of darkness overshadowed him as he sank holding his entrails in his hands.

When Hector saw his brother Polydorus with his entrails in his hands and sinking down upon the ground, a mist came over his eyes, and he could not bear to keep longer at a distance; he therefore poised his spear and darted towards Achilles like a flame of fire. When Achilles saw him he bounded forward and vaunted saying, 'This is he that has wounded my heart most deeply and has slain my beloved comrade. Not for long shall we two quail before one another on the highways of war.'

He looked fiercely on Hector and said, 'Draw near, that you may meet your doom the sooner.' Hector feared him not and answered, 'Son of Peleus, think not that your words can scare me as though I were a child; I too if I will can brag and talk unseemly; I know that you are a mighty warrior, mightier by far than I, nevertheless the issue lies in the lap of heaven whether I, worse man though I be, may not slay you with my spear, for this too has been found keen ere now.'

He hurled his spear as he spoke, but Minerva breathed upon it, and though she breathed but very lightly she turned it back from going towards Achilles, so that it returned to Hector and lay at his feet in front of him. Achilles then sprang furiously on him with a loud cry, bent on killing him, but Apollo caught him up easily as a god can, and hid him in a thick darkness. Thrice did Achilles spring towards him spear in hand, and thrice did he waste his blow upon the air. When he rushed forward for the fourth time as though he were a god, he shouted aloud saying, 'Hound, this time too you have escaped death – but of a truth it came exceedingly near you. Phœbus Apollo, to whom it seems you pray before you go into battle, has again saved you; but if I too have any friend among the gods I will surely make an end of you when I come across you at some other time. Now, however, I will pursue and overtake other Trojans.'

On this he struck Dryops with his spear, about the middle of his neck, and he fell headlong at his feet. There he let him lie and stayed Demouchus son of Philetor, a man both brave and of great stature, by hitting him on the knee with a spear; then he smote him with his sword and killed him. After this he sprang on Laogonus and Dardanus, sons of Bias, and threw them from their chariot, the one with a blow from a thrown spear, while the other he cut down in hand-to-hand fight. There was also Tros the son of Alastor – he came up to Achilles and clasped his knees in the hope that he would spare him and not kill him but let him go, because they were both of the same age. Fool, he might have known that he should not prevail with him, for the man was in no mood for pity or forbearance but was in grim earnest. Therefore when Tros laid hold of his knees and sought a hearing for his prayers, Achilles drove his sword into his liver, and the liver came rolling out, while his bosom was all covered with the black blood that welled from the wound. Thus did death close his eyes as he lay lifeless.

Achilles then went up to Mulius and struck him on the ear with a spear, and the bronze spear-head came right out at the other ear. He also struck Echeclus son of Agenor on the head with his sword, which became warm with the blood, while death and stern fate closed the eyes of Echeclus. Next in order the bronze point of his spear wounded Deucalion in the fore-arm where the sinews of the elbow are united, whereon he waited Achilles' onset with his arm hanging down and death staring him in the face. Achilles cut his head off with a blow from his sword and flung it helmet and all away from him, and the marrow came oozing out of his backbone as he lay. He then went in pursuit of Rhigmus, noble son of Peires, who had come from fertile

Thrace, and struck him through the middle with a spear which fixed itself in his belly, so that he fell headlong from his chariot. He also speared Areïthous squire to Rhigmus in the back as he was turning his horses in flight, and thrust him from his chariot, while the horses were struck with panic.

As a fire raging in some mountain glen after long drought – and the dense forest is in a blaze, while the wind carries great tongues of fire in every direction – even so furiously did Achilles rage, wielding his spear as though he were a god, and giving chase to those whom he would slay, till the dark earth ran with blood. Or as one who yokes broad-browed oxen that they may tread barley in a threshing-floor – and it is soon bruised small under the feet of the lowing cattle – even so did the horses of Achilles trample on the shields and bodies of the slain. The axle underneath and the railing that ran round the car were bespattered with clots of blood thrown up by the horses' hoofs, and from the tyres of the wheels; but the son of Peleus pressed on to win still further glory, and his hands were bedrabbled with gore.

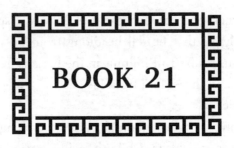

BOOK 21

The fight between Achilles and the river Scamander – The gods fight among themselves – Achilles drives the Trojans within their gates.

Now when they came to the ford of the full-flowing river Xanthus, begotten of immortal Jove, Achilles cut their forces in two: one half he chased over the plain towards the city by the same way that the Achæans had taken when flying panic-stricken on the preceding day with Hector in full triumph; this way did they fly pell-mell, and Juno sent down a thick mist in front of them to stay them. The other half were hemmed in by the deep silver-eddying stream, and fell into it with a great uproar. The waters resounded, and the banks rang again, as they swam hither and thither with loud cries amid the whirling eddies. As locusts flying to a river before the blast of a grass fire – the flame comes on and on till at last it overtakes them and they huddle into the water – even so was the eddying stream of Xanthus filled with the uproar of men and horses, all struggling in confusion before Achilles.

Forthwith the hero left his spear upon the bank, leaning it against a tamarisk bush, and plunged into the river like a god, armed with his sword only. Fell was his purpose as he hewed the Trojans down on every side. Their dying groans rose hideous as the sword smote them, and the river ran red with blood. As when fish fly scared before a huge dolphin, and fill every nook and corner of some fair haven – for he is sure to eat all he can catch – even so did the Trojans cower under the banks of the mighty river, and when Achilles' arms grew weary with killing them, he drew twelve youths alive out of the water, to sacrifice in revenge for Patroclus son of Menœtius. He drew them out like dazed fawns, bound their hands behind them with the girdles of their own shirts, and gave them over to his men to take back to the ships. Then he sprang into the river, thirsting for still further blood.

There he found Lycaon, son of Priam seed of Dardanus, as he was escaping out of the water; he it was whom he had once taken prisoner when he was in his father's vineyard, having set upon him by night, as he was cutting young shoots from a wild fig-tree to make the wicker sides of a chariot. Achilles then caught him to his sorrow unawares, and sent him by sea to Lemnos, where the son of Jason bought him. But a guest-friend, Eëtion of Imbros, freed him with a great sum, and sent him to Arisbe, whence he had escaped and returned to his father's house. He had spent eleven days happily with his friends after he had come from Lemnos, but on the twelfth heaven again delivered him into the hands of Achilles, who was to send him to the house of Hades sorely against his will. He was unarmed when Achilles caught sight of him, and had neither helmet nor shield; nor yet had he any spear, for he had thrown all his armour from him on to the bank, and was sweating with his struggles to get out of the river, so that his strength was now failing him.

Then Achilles said to himself in his surprise, 'What marvel do I see here? If this man can come back alive after having been sold over into Lemnos, I shall have the Trojans also whom I have slain rising from the world below. Could not even the waters of the grey sea imprison him, as they do many another whether he will or no? This time let him taste my spear, that I may know for certain whether mother earth who can keep even a strong man down, will be able to hold him, or whether thence too he will return.'

Thus did he pause and ponder. But Lycaon came up to him dazed and trying hard to embrace his knees, for he would fain live, not die. Achilles thrust at him with his spear, meaning to kill him, but Lycaon ran crouching up to him and caught his knees, whereby the spear passed over his back, and stuck in the ground, hungering though it was for blood. With one hand he caught Achilles' knees as he besought him, and with the other he clutched the spear and would not let it go. Then he said, 'Achilles, have mercy upon me and spare me, for I am your suppliant. It was in your tents that I first broke bread on the day when you took me prisoner in the vineyard; after which you sold me away to Lemnos far from my father and my friends, and I brought you the price of a hundred oxen. I have paid three times as much to gain my freedom; it is but twelve days that I have come to Ilius after much suffering, and now cruel fate has again thrown me into your hands. Surely father Jove must hate me, that he has given me over to you a second time. Short of life indeed did my mother Laothöe bear me, daughter of aged Altes – of Altes who reigns over the warlike Lelegæ and holds steep Pedasus on the river Satniöeis. Priam married his daughter along with many other women and two sons were born of her, both of whom you will have slain. Your spear slew noble Polydorus as he was fighting in the front ranks, and now evil will here befall me, for I fear that I shall not escape you since heaven has delivered me over to you. Furthermore I say, and lay my saying to your heart, spare me, for I am not of the same womb as Hector who slew your brave and noble comrade.'

With such words did the princely son of Priam beseech Achilles; but Achilles answered him sternly. 'Idiot,' said he, 'talk not to me of ransom. Until Patroclus fell I preferred to give the Trojans quarter, and sold beyond the sea many of those whom I had taken alive; but now not a man shall live of those whom heaven delivers into my hands before the city of Ilius – and of all Trojans it shall fare hardest with the sons of Priam. Therefore, my friend, you too shall die. Why should you whine in this way? Patroclus fell, and he was a better man than you are. I too – see you not how I am great and goodly? I am son to a noble father, and have a goddess for my mother, but the hands of doom and death overshadow me all as surely. The day will come, either at dawn or dark, or at the noontide, when one shall take my life also in battle, either with his spear, or with an arrow sped from his bow.'

Thus did he speak, and Lycaon's heart sank within him. He loosed his hold of the spear, and held out both hands before him; but Achilles drew his keen blade, and struck him by the collar-bone on his neck; he plunged his two-edged sword into him to the very hilt, whereon he lay at full length on the ground, with the dark blood welling from him till the earth was soaked. Then Achilles caught him by the foot and flung him into the river to go down stream, vaunting over him the while, and saying, 'Lie there among the fishes, who will lick the blood from your wound and gloat over it; your mother shall not lay you on any bier to mourn you, but the eddies of Scamander shall bear you into the broad bosom of the sea. There shall the fishes feed on the fat of Lycaon as they dart under the dark ripple of the waters – so perish all of you till we reach the citadel of strong Ilius – you in flight, and I following after to destroy you. The river with its broad silver stream shall serve you in no stead, for all the bulls you offered him and all the horses that you flung living into his waters. None the less miserably shall you perish till there is not a man of you but has paid in full for the death of Patroclus and the havoc you wrought among the Achæans whom you have slain while I held aloof from battle.'

So spoke Achilles, but the river grew more and more angry, and pondered within himself how he should stay the hand of Achilles and save the Trojans from disaster. Meanwhile the son of Peleus, spear in hand, sprang upon Asteropæus son of Pelegon to kill him. He was son to the broad river Axius and Peribœa eldest daughter of Acessamenus; for the river had lain with her. Asteropæus stood up out of the water to face him with a spear in either hand, and Xanthus filled him with courage, being angry for the death of the youths whom Achilles was slaying ruthlessly within his waters. When they were close up with one another Achilles was first to speak. 'Who and whence are you,' said he, 'who dare to face me? Woe to the parents whose son stands up against me.' And the son of Pelegon answered, 'Great son of Peleus, why should you ask my lineage. I am from the fertile land of far Pæonia, captain of the Pæonians, and it is now eleven days that I am at Ilius. I am of the blood of the river Axius – of Axius that is the fairest of all rivers that run. He begot the famed warrior Pelegon, whose son men call me. Let us now fight, Achilles.'

Thus did he defy him, and Achilles raised his spear of Pelian ash. Asteropæus failed with both his spears, for he could use both hands alike; with the one spear he struck Achilles' shield, but did not pierce it, for the layer of gold, gift of the god, stayed the point; with the other spear he grazed the elbow of Achilles' right arm drawing dark blood, but the spear itself went by him and fixed itself in the ground, foiled of its bloody banquet. Then Achilles, fain to kill him, hurled his spear at Asteropæus, but failed to hit him and struck the steep bank of the river, driving the spear half its length into the earth. The son of Peleus then drew his sword and sprang furiously upon him. Asteropæus vainly tried to draw Achilles' spear out of the bank by main force; thrice did he tug at it, trying with all his might to draw it out, and thrice he had to leave off trying; the fourth time he tried to bend and break it, but ere he could do so Achilles smote him with his sword and killed him. He struck him in the belly near the navel, so that all his bowels came gushing out on to the ground, and the darkness of death came over him as he lay gasping. Then Achilles set his foot on his chest and spoiled him of his armour, vaunting over him and saying, 'Lie there – begotten of a river though you be, it is hard for you to strive with the offspring of Saturn's son. You declare yourself sprung from the blood of a broad river, but I am of the seed of mighty Jove. My father is Peleus, son of Æacus ruler over the many Myrmidons, and Æacus was the son of Jove. Therefore as Jove is mightier than any river that flows into the sea, so are his children stronger than those of any river whatsoever. Moreover you have a great river hard by if he can be of any use to you, but there is no fighting against Jove the son of Saturn, with whom not even King Achelous can compare, nor the mighty stream of deep-flowing Oceanus, from whom all rivers and seas with all springs and deep wells proceed; even Oceanus fears the lightnings of great Jove, and his thunder that comes crashing out of heaven.'

With this he drew his bronze spear out of the bank, and now that he had killed Asteropæus, he let him lie where he was on the sand, with the dark water flowing over him and the eels and fishes busy nibbling and gnawing the fat that was about his kidneys. Then he went in chase of the Pæonians, who were flying along the bank of the river in panic when they saw their leader slain by the hands of the son of Peleus. Therein he slew Thersilochus, Mydon, Astypylus, Mnesus, Thrasius, Œneus, and Ophelestes, and he would have slain yet others, had not the river in anger taken human form, and spoken to him from out the deep waters saying, 'Achilles, if you excel all in strength, so do you also in wickedness, for the gods are ever with you to protect you: if, then, the son of Saturn has vouchsafed it to you to destroy all the Trojans, at any rate drive them out of my stream, and do your grim work on land. My fair waters are now filled with corpses, nor can I find any channel by which I may pour myself into the sea for I am choked with dead, and yet you go on mercilessly slaying. I am in despair, therefore, O captain of your host, trouble me no further.'

Achilles answered, 'So be it, Scamander, Jove-descended; but I will never cease dealing out death among the Trojans, till I have pent them up in their city, and made trial of Hector face to face, that I may learn whether he is to vanquish me, or I him.'

As he spoke he set upon the Trojans with a fury like that of the gods. But the river said to Apollo, 'Surely, son of Jove, lord of the silver bow, you are not obeying the commands of Jove who charged you straitly that you should stand by the Trojans and defend them, till twilight fades, and darkness is over all the earth.'

Meanwhile Achilles sprang from the bank into mid-stream, whereon the river raised a high wave and attacked him. He swelled his stream into a torrent, and swept away the many dead whom Achilles had slain and left within his waters. These he cast out on to the land, bellowing like a bull the while, but the living he saved alive, hiding them in his mighty eddies. The great and terrible wave gathered about Achilles, falling upon him and beating on his shield, so that he could not keep his feet; he caught hold of a great elm-tree, but it came up by the roots, and tore away the bank, damming the stream with its thick branches and bridging it all across; whereby Achilles struggled out of the stream, and fled full speed over the plain, for he was afraid.

But the mighty god ceased not in his pursuit, and sprang upon him with a dark-crested wave, to stay his hands and save the Trojans from destruction. The son of Peleus darted away a spear's throw from him; swift as the swoop of a black hunter-eagle which is the strongest and fleetest of all birds, even so did he spring forward, and the armour rang loudly about his breast. He fled on in front, but the river with a loud roar came tearing after. As one who would water his garden leads a stream from some fountain over his plants, and all his ground – spade in hand he clears away the dams to free the channels, and the little stones run rolling round and round with the water as it goes merrily down the bank faster than the man can follow – even so did the river keep catching up with Achilles albeit he was a fleet runner, for the gods are stronger than men. As often as he would strive to stand his ground, and see whether or no all the gods in heaven were in league against him, so often would the mighty wave come beating down upon his shoulders, and he would have to keep flying on and on in great dismay; for the angry flood was tiring him out as it flowed past him, and ate the ground from under his feet.

Then the son of Peleus lifted up his voice to heaven saying, 'Father Jove, is there none of the gods who will take pity upon me, and save me from the river? I do not care what may happen to me afterwards. I blame none of the other dwellers on Olympus so severely as I do my dear mother, who has beguiled and tricked me. She told me I was to fall under the walls of Troy by the flying arrows of Apollo; would that Hector, the best man among the Trojans, might there slay me; then should I fall a hero by the hand of a hero; whereas now it seems that

I shall come to a most pitiable end, trapped in this river as though I were some swineherd's boy, who gets carried down a torrent while trying to cross it during a storm.'

As soon as he had spoken thus, Neptune and Minerva came up to him in the likeness of two men, and took him by the hand to reassure him. Neptune spoke first. 'Son of Peleus,' said he, 'be not so exceeding fearful; we are two gods, come with Jove's sanction to assist you, I, and Pallas Minerva. It is not your fate to perish in this river; he will abate presently as you will see; moreover we strongly advise you, if you will be guided by us, not to stay your hand from fighting till you have pent the Trojan host within the famed walls of Ilius – as many of them as may escape. Then kill Hector and go back to the ships, for we will vouchsafe you a triumph over him.'

When they had so said they went back to the other immortals, but Achilles strove onward over the plain, encouraged by the charge the gods had laid upon him. All was now covered with the flood of waters, and much goodly armour of the youths that had been slain was drifting about, as also many corpses, but he forced his way against the stream, speeding right onwards, nor could the broad waters stay him, for Minerva had endowed him with great strength. Nevertheless Scamander did not slacken in his pursuit, but was still more furious with the son of Peleus. He lifted his waters into a high crest and cried aloud to Simois saying, 'Dear brother, let the two of us unite to stay this man, or he will sack the mighty city of King Priam, and the Trojans will not hold out against him. Help me at once; fill your streams with water from their sources, rouse all your torrents to a fury; raise your wave on high, and let snags and stones come thundering down you that we may make an end of this savage creature who is now lording it as though he were a god. Nothing shall serve him longer, not strength nor comeliness, nor his fine armour, which forsooth shall soon be lying low in the deep waters covered over with mud. I will wrap him in sand, and pour tons of shingle round him, so that the Achæans shall not know how to gather his bones for the silt in which

I shall have hidden him, and when they celebrate his funeral they need build no barrow.'

On this he upraised his tumultuous flood high against Achilles, seething as it was with foam and blood and the bodies of the dead. The dark waters of the river stood upright and would have overwhelmed the son of Peleus, but Juno, trembling lest Achilles should be swept away in the mighty torrent, lifted her voice on high and called out to Vulcan her son. 'Crook-foot,' she cried, 'my child, be up and doing, for I deem it is with you that Xanthus is fain to fight; help us at once, kindle a fierce fire; I will then bring up the west and the white south wind in a mighty hurricane from the sea, that shall bear the flames against the heads and armour of the Trojans and consume them, while you go along the banks of Xanthus burning his trees and wrapping him round with fire. Let him not turn you back neither by fair words nor foul, and slacken not till I shout and tell you. Then you may stay your flames.'

On this Vulcan kindled a fierce fire, which broke out first upon the plain and burned the many dead whom Achilles had killed and whose bodies were lying about in great numbers; by this means the plain was dried and the flood stayed. As the north wind, blowing on an orchard that has been sodden with autumn rain, soon dries it, and the heart of the owner is glad – even so the whole plain was dried and the dead bodies were consumed. Then he turned tongues of fire on to the river. He burned the elms, the willows, and the tamarisks, the lotus also, with the rushes and marshy herbage that grew abundantly by the banks of the river. The eels and fishes that go darting about everywhere in the water, these, too, were sorely harassed by the flames that cunning Vulcan had kindled, and the river himself was scalded, so that he spoke saying, 'Vulcan, there is no god can hold his own against you. I cannot fight you when you flare out your flames in this way; strive with me no longer. Let Achilles drive the Trojans out of their city immediately. What have I to do with quarrelling and helping people?'

He was boiling as he spoke, and all his waters were seething. As a cauldron upon a large fire boils when it is melting the lard of some fatted hog, and the lard keeps bubbling up all over when the dry faggots blaze under it – even so were the goodly waters of Xanthus heated with the fire till they were boiling. He could flow no longer but stayed his stream, so afflicted was he by the blasts of fire which cunning Vulcan had raised. Then he prayed to Juno and besought her saying, 'Juno, why should your son vex my stream with such especial fury? I am not so much to blame as all the others are who have been helping the Trojans. I will leave off, since you so desire it, and let your son leave off also. Furthermore I swear that never again will I do anything to save the Trojans from destruction, not even when all Troy is burning in the flames which the Achæans will kindle.'

As soon as Juno heard this she said to her son Vulcan, 'Son Vulcan, hold now your flames; we ought not to use such violence against a god for the sake of mortals.'

When she had thus spoken Vulcan quenched his flames, and the river went back once more into his own fair bed.

Xanthus was now beaten, so these two left off fighting, for Juno stayed them though she was still angry; but a furious quarrel broke out among the other gods, for they were of divided counsels. They fell on one another with a mighty uproar – earth groaned, and the spacious firmament rang out as with a blare of trumpets. Jove heard as he was sitting on Olympus, and laughed for joy when he saw the gods coming to blows among themselves. They were not long about beginning, and Mars piercer of shields opened the battle. Sword in hand he sprang at once upon Minerva and reviled her. 'Why, vixen,' said he, 'have you again set the gods by the ears in the pride and haughtiness of your heart? Have you forgotten how you set Diomed son of Tydeus on to wound me, and yourself took visible spear and drove it into me to the hurt of my fair body? You shall now suffer for what you then did to me.'

As he spoke he struck her on the terrible tasselled ægis – so terrible that not even can Jove's lightning pierce it. Here did murderous Mars strike her with his great spear. She drew back and with her strong hand seized a stone that was lying on the plain – great and rugged and black – which men of old had set for the boundary of a field. With this she struck Mars on the neck, and brought him down. Nine roods did he cover in his fall, and his hair was all soiled in the dust, while his armour rang rattling round him. But Minerva laughed and vaunted over him saying, 'Idiot, have you not learned how far stronger I am than you, but you must still match yourself against me? Thus do your mother's curses now roost upon you, for she is angry and would do you mischief because you have deserted the Achæans and are helping the Trojans.'

She then turned her two piercing eyes elsewhere, whereon Jove's daughter Venus took Mars by the hand and led him away, groaning all the time, for it was only with great difficulty that he had come to himself again. When Queen Juno saw her, she said to Minerva, 'Look, daughter of ægis-bearing Jove, unweariable, that vixen Venus is again taking Mars through the crowd out of the battle; go after her at once.'

Thus she spoke. Minerva sped after Venus with a will, and made at her, striking her on the bosom with her strong hand so that she fell fainting to the ground, and there they both lay stretched at full length. Then Minerva vaunted over her saying, 'May all who help the Trojans against the Argives prove just as redoubtable and stalwart as Venus did when she came across me while she was helping Mars. Had this been so, we should long since have ended the war by sacking the strong city of Ilius.'

Juno smiled as she listened. Meanwhile King Neptune turned to Apollo saying, 'Phœbus, why should we keep each other at arm's length? It is not well, now that the others have begun fighting; it will be disgraceful to us if we return to Jove's bronze-floored mansion on Olympus without having fought each other; therefore come on, you are the younger of the two, and I ought not to attack you, for I am older and have had more experience. Idiot, you have no sense, and forget how we two alone of all the gods fared hardly round about Ilius when we came from Jove's house and worked for Laomedon a whole year at a stated wage and he gave us his orders. I built the Trojans the wall about their city, so wide and fair that it might be impregnable, while you, Phœbus, herded cattle for him in the dales of many-valleyed Ida. When, however, the glad hours brought round the time of payment, mighty Laomedon robbed us of all our hire and sent us off with nothing but abuse. He threatened to bind us hand and foot and sell us over into some distant island. He tried, moreover, to cut off the ears of both of us, so we went away in a rage, furious about the payment he had promised us, and yet withheld; in spite of all this, you are now showing favour to his people, and will not join us in compassing the utter ruin of the proud Trojans with their wives and children.'

And King Apollo answered, 'Lord of the earthquake, you would have no respect for me if I were to fight you about a pack of miserable mortals, who come out like leaves in summer and eat the fruit of the field, and presently fall lifeless to the ground. Let us stay this fighting at once and let them settle it among themselves.'

He turned away as he spoke, for he would lay no hand on the brother of his own father. But his sister the huntress Diana, patroness of wild beasts, was very angry with him and said, 'So you would fly, Far-Darter, and hand victory over to Neptune with a cheap vaunt to boot. Baby, why keep your bow thus idle? Never let me again hear you bragging in my father's house, as you often have done in the presence of the immortals, that you would stand up and fight with Neptune.'

Apollo made her no answer, but Jove's august queen was angry and upbraided her bitterly. 'Bold vixen,' she cried, 'how dare you cross me thus? For all your bow you will find it hard to hold your own against me. Jove made you as a lion among women, and lets you kill them whenever you choose. You will find it better to chase wild beasts and deer upon the mountains than to fight those who are stronger than you are. If you would try war, do so, and find out by pitting yourself against me, how far stronger I am than you are.'

She caught both Diana's wrists with her left hand as she spoke, and with her right she took the bow from her shoulders, and laughed as she beat her with it about the ears while Diana wriggled and writhed under her blows. Her swift arrows were shed upon the ground, and she fled weeping from under Juno's hand as a dove that flies before a falcon to the cleft of some hollow rock, when it is her good fortune to escape. Even so did she fly weeping away, leaving her bow and arrows behind her.

Then the slayer of Argus, guide and guardian, said to Leto, 'Leto, I shall not fight you; it is ill to come to blows with any of Jove's wives. Therefore boast as you will among the immortals that you worsted me in fair fight.'

Leto then gathered up Diana's bow and arrows that had fallen about amid the whirling dust, and when she had got them she made all haste after her daughter. Diana had now reached Jove's bronze-floored mansion on Olympus, and sat herself down with many tears on the knees of her father, while her ambrosial raiment was quivering all about her. The son of Saturn drew her towards him, and laughing pleasantly the while began to question her saying, 'Which of the heavenly beings, my dear child, has been treating you in this cruel manner, as though you had been misconducting yourself in the face of everybody?' and the fair-crowned goddess of the chase answered, 'It was your wife Juno, father, who has been beating me; it is always her doing when there is any quarrelling among the immortals.'

Thus did they converse, and meanwhile Phœbus Apollo entered the strong city of Ilius, for he was uneasy lest the wall should not hold out and the Danaans should take the city then and there, before its hour had come; but the rest of the ever-living gods went back, some angry and some triumphant to Olympus, where they took their seats beside Jove lord of the storm-cloud, while Achilles still kept on dealing out death alike on the Trojans and on their horses. As when the smoke from some burning city ascends to heaven when the anger of the gods has kindled it – there is then toil for all, and sorrow for not a few – even so did Achilles bring toil and sorrow on the Trojans.

Old King Priam stood on a high tower of the wall looking down on huge Achilles as the Trojans fled panic-stricken before him, and there was none to help them. Presently he came down from off the tower and with many a groan went along the wall to give orders to the brave warders of the gate. 'Keep the gates,' said he, 'wide open till the people come flying into the city, for Achilles is hard by and is driving them in rout before him. I see we are in great peril. As soon as our people are inside and in safety, close the strong gates for I fear lest that terrible man should come bounding inside along with the others.'

As he spoke they drew back the bolts and opened the gates, and when these were opened there was a haven of refuge for the Trojans. Apollo then came full speed out of the city to meet them and protect them. Right for the city and the high wall, parched with thirst and grimy with dust, still they fled on, with Achilles wielding his spear furiously behind them. For he was as one possessed, and was thirsting after glory.

Then had the sons of the Achæans taken the lofty gates of Troy if Apollo had not spurred on Agenor, valiant and noble son to Antenor. He put courage into his heart, and stood by his side to guard him, leaning against a beech tree and shrouded in thick darkness. When Agenor saw Achilles he stood still and his heart was clouded with care. 'Alas,' said he to himself in his dismay, 'if I fly before mighty Achilles, and go where all the others are being driven in rout, he will none the less catch me and kill me for a coward. How would it be were I to let Achilles drive the others before him, and then fly from the wall to the plain that is behind Ilius till I reach the spurs of Ida and can hide in the underwood that is thereon? I could then wash the sweat from off me in the river and in the evening return to Ilius. But why commune with myself in this way? Like enough he would see me as I am hurrying from the city over the plain, and would speed after me till he had caught me – I should stand no chance against him, for he is mightiest of all mankind. What, then, if I go out and meet him in front of the city? His flesh too, I take it, can be pierced by pointed bronze. Life is the same in one and all, and men say that he is but mortal despite the triumph that Jove son of Saturn vouchsafes him.'

So saying he stood on his guard and awaited Achilles, for he was now fain to fight him. As a leopardess that bounds from out a thick covert to attack a hunter – she knows no fear and is not dismayed by the baying of the hounds; even though the man be too quick for her and wound her either with thrust or spear, still, though the spear has pierced her she will not give in till she has either caught him in her grip or been killed outright – even so did noble Agenor son of Antenor refuse to fly till he had made trial of Achilles, and took aim at him with his spear, holding his round shield before him and crying with a loud voice. 'Of a truth,' said he, 'noble Achilles, you deem that you shall this day sack the city of the proud Trojans. Fool, there will be trouble enough yet before it, for there is many a brave man of us still inside who will stand in front of our dear parents with our wives and children, to defend Ilius. Here therefore, huge and mighty warrior though you be, here shall you die.'

As he spoke his strong hand hurled his javelin from him, and the spear struck Achilles on the leg beneath the knee; the greave of newly wrought tin rang loudly, but the spear recoiled from the body of him whom it had struck, and did not pierce it, for the god's gift stayed it. Achilles in his turn attacked noble Agenor, but Apollo would not vouchsafe him glory, for he snatched Agenor away and hid him in a thick mist, sending him out of the battle unmolested. Then he craftily drew the son of Peleus away from going after the host, for he put on the semblance of Agenor and stood in front of Achilles, who ran towards him to give him chase and pursued him over the corn lands of the plain, turning him towards the deep waters of the river Scamander. Apollo ran but a little way before him and beguiled Achilles by making him think all the time that he was on the point of overtaking him. Meanwhile the rabble of routed Trojans was thankful to crowd within the city till their numbers thronged it; no longer did they dare wait for one another outside the city walls, to learn who had escaped and who were fallen in fight, but all whose feet and knees could still carry them poured pell-mell into the town.

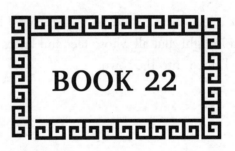

BOOK 22

The death of Hector.

Thus the Trojans in the city, scared like fawns, wiped the sweat from off them and drank to quench their thirst, leaning against the goodly battlements, while the Achæans with their shields laid upon their shoulders drew close up to the walls. But stern fate bade Hector stay where he was before Ilius and the Scæan gates. Then Phœbus Apollo spoke to the son of Peleus saying, 'Why, son of Peleus, do you, who are but man, give chase to me who am immortal? Have you not yet found out that it is a god whom you pursue so furiously? You did not harass the Trojans whom you had routed, and now they are within their walls, while you have been decoyed hither away from them. Me you cannot kill, for death can take no hold upon me.'

Achilles was greatly angered and said, 'You have baulked me, Far-Darter, most malicious of all gods, and have drawn me away from the wall, where many another man would have bitten the dust ere he got within Ilius; you have robbed me of great glory and have saved the Trojans at no risk to yourself, for you have nothing to fear, but I would indeed have my revenge if it were in my power to do so.'

On this, with fell intent he made towards the city, and as the winning horse in a chariot race strains every nerve when he is flying over the plain, even so fast and furiously did the limbs of Achilles bear him onwards. King Priam was first to note him as he scoured the plain, all radiant as the star which men call Orion's Hound,[9] and whose beams blaze forth in time of harvest more brilliantly than those of any other that shines by night; brightest of them all though he be, he yet bodes ill for mortals, for he brings fire and fever in his train – even so did Achilles' armour gleam on his breast as he sped onwards. Priam raised a cry and beat his head with his hands as he lifted them up and shouted out to his dear son, imploring him to return; but Hector still stayed before the gates, for his heart was set upon doing battle with Achilles. The old man reached out his arms towards him and bade him for pity's sake come within the walls. 'Hector,' he cried, 'my son, stay not to face this man alone and unsupported, or you will meet death at the hands of the son of Peleus, for he is mightier than you. Monster that he is; would indeed that the gods loved him no better than I do, for so, dogs and vultures would soon devour him as he lay stretched on earth, and a load of grief would be lifted from my heart, for many a brave son has he reft from me, either by killing them or selling them away in the islands that are beyond the sea: even now I miss two sons from among the Trojans who have thronged within the city, Lycaon and Polydorus, whom Laothoë peerless among women bore me. Should they be still alive and in the hands of the Achæans, we will ransom them with gold and bronze, of which we have store, for the old man Altes endowed his daughter richly; but if they are already dead and in the house of Hades, sorrow will it be to us two who were their parents; albeit the grief of others will be more short-lived unless you too perish at the hands of Achilles. Come, then, my son, within the city, to be the guardian of Trojan men and Trojan women, or you will both lose your own life and afford a mighty triumph to the son of Peleus. Have pity also on your unhappy father while life yet remains to him – on me, whom the son of Saturn will destroy by a terrible doom on the threshold of old age, after I have seen my sons slain and my daughters haled away as captives, my bridal chambers pillaged, little children dashed to earth amid the rage of battle, and my sons' wives dragged away by the cruel hands of the Achæans; in the end fierce hounds will tear me in pieces at my own gates after some one has beaten the life out of my body with sword or spear – hounds that I myself reared and fed at my own table to guard my gates, but who will yet lap my blood and then lie all distraught at my doors. When a young man falls by the sword in battle, he may lie where he is and there is nothing unseemly; let what will be seen, all is honourable in death, but when an old man is slain there is nothing in this world more pitiable than that dogs should defile his grey hair and beard and all that men hide for shame.'

The old man tore his grey hair as he spoke, but he moved not the heart of Hector. His mother hard by wept and moaned aloud as she bared her bosom and pointed to the breast which had suckled him. 'Hector,' she cried, weeping bitterly the while, 'Hector, my son, spurn not this breast, but have pity upon me too: if I have ever given you comfort from my own bosom, think on it now, dear son, and come within the wall to protect us from this man; stand not without to meet him. Should the wretch kill you, neither I nor your richly dowered wife shall ever weep, dear offshoot of myself, over the bed on which you lie, for dogs will devour you at the ships of the Achæans.'

Thus did the two with many tears implore their son, but they moved not the heart of Hector, and he stood his ground awaiting huge Achilles as he drew nearer towards him. As a serpent in its den upon the mountains, full fed with deadly poisons, waits for the approach of man – he is filled with fury and his eyes glare terribly as he goes writhing round his den – even so Hector leaned his shield against a tower that jutted out from the wall and stood where he was, undaunted.

'Alas,' said he to himself in the heaviness of his heart, 'if I go within the gates, Polydamas will be the first to heap reproach upon me, for it was he that urged me to lead the Trojans back to the city on that awful night when Achilles again came forth against us. I would not listen, but it would have been indeed better if I had done so. Now that my folly has destroyed the host, I dare not look Trojan men and Trojan women in the face, lest a worse man should say, "Hector has ruined us by his self-confidence." Surely it would be better for me to return after having fought Achilles and slain him, or to die gloriously here before the city. What, again, if I were to lay down my shield and helmet, lean my spear against the wall and go straight up to noble Achilles? What if I were to promise to give up Helen, who was the fountainhead of all this war, and all the treasure that Alexandrus brought with him in his ships to Troy, aye, and to let the Achæans divide the half of everything that the city contains among themselves? I might make the Trojans, by the mouths of their princes, take a solemn oath that they would hide nothing, but would divide into two shares all that is within the city – but why argue with myself in this way? Were I to go up to him he would show me no kind of mercy; he would kill me then and there as easily as though I were a woman, when I had put off my armour. There is no parleying with him from some rock or oak tree as young men and maidens prattle with one another. Better fight him at once, and learn to which of us Jove will vouchsafe victory.'

Thus did he stand and ponder, but Achilles came up to him as it were Mars himself, plumed lord of battle. From his right shoulder he brandished his terrible spear of Pelian ash, and the bronze gleamed around him like flashing fire or the rays of the rising sun. Fear fell upon Hector as he beheld him, and he dared not stay longer where he was, but fled in dismay from before the gates, while Achilles darted after him at his utmost speed. As a mountain falcon, swiftest of all birds, swoops down upon some cowering dove – the dove flies before him but the falcon with a shrill scream follows close after, resolved to have her – even so did Achilles make straight for Hector with all his might, while Hector fled under the Trojan wall as fast as his limbs could take him.

On they flew along the waggon-road that ran hard by under the wall, past the look-out station, and past the weather-beaten wild fig-tree, till they came to two fair springs which feed the river Scamander. One of these two springs is warm, and steam rises from it as smoke from a burning fire, but the other even in summer is as cold as hail or snow, or the ice that forms on water. Here, hard by the springs, are the goodly washing-troughs of stone, where in the time of peace before the coming of the Achæans the wives and fair daughters of the Trojans used to wash their clothes. Past these did they fly, the one in front and the other giving chase behind him: good was the man that fled, but better far was he that followed after, and swiftly indeed did they run, for the prize was no mere beast for sacrifice or bullock's hide, as it might be for a common foot-race, but they ran for the life of Hector. As horses in a chariot race speed round the turning-posts when they are running for some great prize – a tripod or woman – at the games in honour of some dead hero, so did these two run full speed three times round the city of Priam. All the gods watched them, and the sire of gods and men was the first to speak.

'Alas,' said he, 'my eyes behold a man who is dear to me being pursued round the walls of Troy; my heart is full of pity for Hector, who has burned the thigh-bones of many a heifer in my honour, at one while on the crests of many-valleyed Ida, and again on the citadel of Troy; and now I see noble Achilles in full pursuit of him round the city of Priam. What say you? Consider among yourselves and decide whether we shall now save him or let him fall, valiant though he be, before Achilles, son of Peleus.'

Then Minerva said, 'Father, wielder of the lightning, lord of cloud and storm, what mean you? Would you pluck this mortal whose doom has long been decreed out of the jaws of death? Do as you will, but we others shall not be of a mind with you.'

And Jove answered, 'My child, Trito-born, take heart. I did not speak in full earnest, and I will let you have your way. Do without let or hindrance as you are minded.'

Thus did he urge Minerva who was already eager, and down she darted from the topmost summits of Olympus.

Achilles was still in full pursuit of Hector, as a hound chasing a fawn which he has started from its covert on the mountains, and hunts through glade and thicket. The fawn may try to elude him by crouching under cover of a bush, but he will scent her out and follow her up until he gets her – even so there was no escape for Hector from the fleet son of

Peleus. Whenever he made a set to get near the Dardanian gates and under the walls, that his people might help him by showering down weapons from above, Achilles would gain on him and head him back towards the plain, keeping himself always on the city side. As a man in a dream who fails to lay hands upon another whom he is pursuing – the one cannot escape nor the other overtake – even so neither could Achilles come up with Hector, nor Hector break away from Achilles; nevertheless he might even yet have escaped death had not the time come when Apollo, who thus far had sustained his strength and nerved his running, was now no longer to stay by him. Achilles made signs to the Achæan host, and shook his head to show that no man was to aim a dart at Hector, lest another might win the glory of having hit him and he might himself come in second. Then, at last, as they were nearing the fountains for the fourth time, the father of all balanced his golden scales and placed a doom in each of them, one for Achilles and the other for Hector. As he held the scales by the middle, the doom of Hector fell down deep into the house of Hades – and then Phœbus Apollo left him. Thereon Minerva went close up to the son of Peleus and said, 'Noble Achilles, favoured of heaven, we two shall surely take back to the ships a triumph for the Achæans by slaying Hector, for all his lust of battle. Do what Apollo may as he lies grovelling before his father, ægis-bearing Jove, Hector cannot escape us longer. Stay here and take breath, while I go up to him and persuade him to make a stand and fight you.'

Thus spoke Minerva. Achilles obeyed her gladly, and stood still, leaning on his bronze-pointed ashen spear, while Minerva left him and went after Hector in the form and with the voice of Deïphobus. She came close up to him and said, 'Dear brother, I see you are hard pressed by Achilles who is chasing you at full speed round the city of Priam, let us await his onset and stand on our defence.'

And Hector answered, 'Deïphobus, you have always been dearest to me of all my brothers, children of Hecuba and Priam, but henceforth I shall rate you yet more highly, inasmuch as you have ventured outside the wall for my sake when all the others remain inside.'

Then Minerva said, 'Dear brother, my father and mother went down on their knees and implored me, as did all my comrades, to remain inside, so great a fear has fallen upon them all; but I was in an agony of grief when I beheld you; now, therefore, let us two make a stand and fight, and let there be no keeping our spears in reserve, that we may learn whether Achilles shall kill us and bear off our spoils to the ships, or whether he shall fall before you.'

Thus did Minerva inveigle him by her cunning, and when the two were now close to one another great Hector was first to speak. 'I will no longer fly you, son of Peleus,' said he, 'as I have been doing hitherto. Three times have I fled round the mighty city of Priam, without daring to withstand you, but now, let me either slay or be slain, for I am in the mind to face you. Let us, then, give pledges to one another by our gods, who are the fittest witnesses and guardians of all covenants; let it be agreed between us that if Jove vouchsafes me the longer stay and I take your life, I am not to treat your dead body in any unseemly fashion, but when I have stripped you of your armour, I am to give up your body to the Achæans. And do you likewise.'

Achilles glared at him and answered, 'Fool, prate not to me about covenants. There can be no covenants between men and lions; wolves and lambs can never be of one mind, but hate each other out and out all through. Therefore there can be no understanding between you and me, nor may there be any covenants between us, till one or other shall fall and glut grim Mars with his life's blood. Put forth all your strength; you have need now to prove yourself indeed a bold soldier and man of war. You have no more chance, and Pallas Minerva will forthwith vanquish you by my spear: you shall now pay me in full for the grief you have caused me on account of my comrades whom you have killed in battle.'

He poised his spear as he spoke and hurled it. Hector saw it coming and avoided it; he watched it and crouched down so that it flew over his head and stuck in the ground beyond; Minerva then snatched it up and gave it back to Achilles without Hector's seeing her; Hector thereon said to the son of Peleus, 'You have missed your aim, Achilles, peer of the gods, and Jove has not yet revealed to you the hour of my doom, though you made sure that he had done so. You were a false-tongued liar when you deemed that I should forget my valour and quail before you. You shall not drive your spear into the back of a runaway – drive it, should heaven so grant you power, drive it into me as I make straight towards you; and now for your own part avoid my spear if you can – would that you might receive the whole of it into your body; if you were once dead the Trojans would find the war an easier matter, for it is you who have harmed them most.'

He poised his spear as he spoke and hurled it. His aim was true for he hit the middle of Achilles' shield, but the spear rebounded from it, and did not pierce it. Hector was angry when he saw that the weapon had sped from his hand in vain, and stood there in dismay for he had no second spear. With a loud cry he called Deïphobus and asked him for one, but there was no man; then he saw the truth and said to himself, 'Alas! the gods have lured me on to my destruction. I deemed that the hero Deïphobus was by my side, but he is within the wall, and Minerva has inveigled me; death is now indeed exceedingly near at hand and there is no way out of it – for so Jove and his son Apollo the far-darter have willed it, though heretofore they have been ever ready to protect me. My doom has come upon me; let me not then die ingloriously and without a struggle, but let me first do some great thing that shall be told among men hereafter.'

As he spoke he drew the keen blade that hung so great and strong by his side, and gathering himself together he sprang on Achilles like a soaring eagle which swoops down from the clouds on to some lamb or timid hare – even so did Hector brandish his sword and spring upon Achilles. Achilles mad with rage darted towards him, with his wondrous shield before his breast, and his gleaming helmet, made with four layers of metal, nodding fiercely forward. The thick tresses of gold with which Vulcan had crested the helmet floated round it, and as the evening star that shines brighter than all others through the stillness of night, even such was the gleam of the spear which Achilles poised in his right hand, fraught with the death of noble Hector. He eyed his fair flesh over and over to see where he could best wound it, but all was protected by the goodly armour of which Hector had spoiled Patroclus after he had slain him, save only the throat where the collar-bones divide the neck from the shoulders, and this is a most deadly place: here then did Achilles strike him as he was coming on towards him, and the point of his spear went right through the fleshy part of the neck, but it did not sever his windpipe so that he could still speak. Hector fell headlong, and Achilles vaunted over him saying, 'Hector, you deemed that you should come off scatheless when you were spoiling Patroclus, and recked not of myself who was not with him. Fool that you were: for I, his comrade, mightier far than he, was still left behind him at the ships, and now I have laid you low. The Achæans shall give him all due funeral rites, while dogs and vultures shall work their will upon yourself.'

Then Hector said, as the life ebbed out of him, 'I pray you by your life and knees, and by your parents, let not dogs devour me at the ships of the Achæans, but accept the rich treasure of gold and bronze which my father and mother will offer you, and send my body home, that the Trojans and their wives may give me my dues of fire when I am dead.'

Achilles glared at him and answered, 'Dog, talk not to me neither of knees nor parents; would that I could be as sure of being able to cut your flesh into pieces and eat it raw, for the ill you have done me, as I am that nothing shall save you from the dogs – it shall not be, though they bring ten or twenty-fold ransom and weigh it out for me on the spot, with promise of yet more hereafter. Though Priam son of Dardanus should bid them offer me your weight in gold, even so your mother shall never lay you out and make lament over the son she bore, but dogs and vultures shall eat you utterly up.'

Hector with his dying breath then said, 'I know you what you are, and was sure that I should not move you, for your heart is hard as iron; look to it that I bring not heaven's anger upon you on the day when Paris and Phœbus Apollo, valiant though you be, shall slay you at the Scæan gates.'

When he had thus said the shrouds of death enfolded him, whereon his soul went out of him and flew down to the house of Hades, lamenting its sad fate that it should enjoy youth and strength no longer. But Achilles said, speaking to the dead body, 'Die; for my part I will accept my fate whensoever Jove and the other gods see fit to send it.'

As he spoke he drew his spear from the body and set it on one side; then he stripped the blood-stained armour from Hector's shoulders while the other Achæans came running up to view his wondrous strength and beauty; and no one came near him without giving him a fresh wound. Then would one turn to his neighbour and say, 'It is easier to handle Hector now than when he was flinging fire on to our ships' – and as he spoke he would thrust his spear into him anew.

When Achilles had done spoiling Hector of his armour, he stood among the Argives and said, 'My friends, princes and counsellors of the Argives, now that heaven has vouchsafed us to overcome this man, who has done us more hurt than all the others together, consider whether we should not attack the city in force, and discover in what mind the Trojans may be. We should thus learn whether they will desert their city now that Hector has fallen, or will still hold out even though he is no longer living. But why argue with myself in this way, while Patroclus is still lying at the ships unburied, and unmourned – he whom I can never forget so long as I am alive and my strength fails not? Though men forget their dead when once they are within the house of Hades, yet not even there will I forget the comrade whom I have lost. Now, therefore, Achæan youths, let us raise the song of victory and go back to the ships taking this man along with us; for we have achieved a mighty triumph and have slain noble Hector to whom the Trojans prayed throughout their city as though he were a god.'

On this he treated the body of Hector with contumely: he pierced the sinews at the back of both his feet from heel to ancle and passed thongs of ox-hide through the slits he had made: thus he made the body fast to his chariot, letting the head trail upon the ground. Then when he had put the goodly armour on the chariot and had himself mounted, he lashed his horses on and they flew forward nothing loth. The dust rose from Hector as he was being dragged along, his dark hair flew all abroad, and his head once so comely was laid low on earth, for Jove had now delivered him into the hands of his foes to do him outrage in his own land.

Thus was the head of Hector being dishonoured in the dust. His mother tore her hair, and flung her veil from her with a loud cry as she looked upon her son. His father made piteous moan, and throughout the city the people fell to weeping and wailing. It was as though the whole of frowning Ilius was being smirched with fire. Hardly could the people hold Priam back in his hot haste to rush without the gates of the city. He grovelled in the mire and besought them, calling each one of them by his name. 'Let be, my friends,' he cried, 'and for all your sorrow, suffer me to go single-handed to the ships of the Achæans. Let me beseech this cruel and terrible man, if maybe he will respect the feeling of his fellow-men, and have compassion on my old age. His own father is even such another as myself – Peleus, who bred him and reared him to be the bane of us Trojans, and of myself more than of all others. Many a son of mine has he slain in the flower of his youth, and yet, grieve for these as I may, I do so for one – Hector – more than for them all, and the bitterness of my sorrow will bring me down to the house of Hades. Would that he had died in my arms, for so both his ill-starred mother who bore him, and myself, should have had the comfort of weeping and mourning over him.'

Thus did he speak with many tears, and all the people of the city joined in his lament. Hecuba then raised the cry of wailing among the Trojans. 'Alas, my son,' she cried, 'what have I left to live for now that you are no more? Night and day did I glory in you throughout the city, for you were a tower of strength to all in Troy, and both men and women alike hailed you as a god. So long as you lived you were their pride, but now death and destruction have fallen upon you.'

Hector's wife had as yet heard nothing, for no one had come to tell her that her husband had remained without the gates. She was at her loom in an inner part of the house, weaving a double purple web, and embroidering it with many flowers. She told her maids to set a large tripod on the fire, so as to have a warm bath ready for Hector when he came out of battle; poor woman, she knew not that he was now beyond the reach of baths, and that Minerva had laid him low by the hands of Achilles. She heard the cry coming as from the wall, and trembled in every limb; the shuttle fell from her hands, and again she spoke to her waiting-women. 'Two of you,' she said, 'come with me that I may learn what it is that has befallen; I heard the voice of my husband's honoured mother; my own heart beats as though it would come into my mouth and my limbs refuse to carry me; some great misfortune for Priam's children must be at hand. May I never live to hear it, but I greatly fear that Achilles has cut off the retreat of brave Hector and has chased him on to the plain where he was single-handed; I fear he may have put an end to the reckless daring which possessed my husband, who would never remain with the body of his men, but would dash on far in front, foremost of them all in valour.'

Her heart beat fast, and as she spoke she flew from the house like a maniac, with her waiting-women following after. When she reached the battlements and the crowd of people, she stood looking out upon the wall, and saw Hector being borne away in front of the city – the horses dragging him without heed or care over the ground towards the ships of the Achæans. Her eyes were then shrouded as with the darkness of night and she fell fainting backwards. She tore the tiring from her head and flung it from her, the frontlet and net with its plaited band, and the veil which golden Venus had given her on the day when Hector took her with him from the house of Eëtion, after having given countless gifts of wooing for her sake. Her husband's sisters and the wives of his brothers crowded round her and supported her, for she was fain to die in her distraction; when she again presently breathed and came to herself, she sobbed and made lament among the Trojans saying, 'Woe is me, O Hector; woe, indeed, that to share a common lot we were born, you at Troy in the house of Priam, and I at Thebes under the wooded mountain of Placus in the house of Eëtion who brought me up when I was a child – ill-starred sire of an ill-starred daughter – would that he had never begotten me. You are now going into the house of Hades under the secret places of the earth, and you leave me a sorrowing widow in your house. The child, of whom you and I are the unhappy parents, is as yet a mere infant. Now that you are gone, O Hector, you can do nothing for him nor he for you. Even though he escape the horrors of this woful war with the Achæans, yet shall his life henceforth be one of labour and sorrow, for others will seize his lands. The day that robs a child of his parents severs him from his own kind; his head is bowed, his cheeks are wet with tears, and he will go about destitute among the friends of his father, plucking one by the cloak and another by the shirt. Some one or other of these may so far pity him as to hold the cup for a moment towards him and let him moisten his lips, but he must not drink enough to wet the roof of his mouth; then one whose parents are alive will drive him from the table with blows and angry words. "Out with you," he will say, "you have no father here," and the child will go crying back to his widowed mother – he, Astyanax, who erewhile would sit upon his father's knees, and have none but the daintiest and choicest morsels set before him. When he had played till he was tired and went to sleep, he would lie in a bed, in the arms of his nurse, on a soft couch, knowing neither want nor care, whereas now that he has lost his father his lot will be full of hardship – he, whom the Trojans name Astyanax, because you, O Hector, were the only defence of their gates and battlements. The wriggling writhing worms will now eat you at the ships, far from your parents, when the dogs have glutted themselves upon you. You will lie naked, although in your house you have fine and goodly raiment made by the hands of women. This will

I now burn; it is of no use to you, for you can never again wear it, and thus you will have respect shown you by the Trojans both men and women.'

In such wise did she cry aloud amid her tears, and the women joined in her lament.

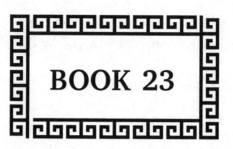

BOOK 23

The funeral of Patroclus, and the funeral games.

Thus did they make their moan throughout the city, while the Achæans when they reached the Hellespont went back every man to his own ship. But Achilles would not let the Myrmidons go, and spoke to his brave comrades saying, 'Myrmidons, famed horsemen and my own trusted friends, not yet, forsooth, let us unyoke, but with horse and chariot draw near to the body and mourn Patroclus, in due honour to the dead. When we have had full comfort of lamentation we will unyoke our horses and take supper all of us here.'

On this they all joined in a cry of wailing and Achilles led them in their lament. Thrice did they drive their chariots all sorrowing round the body, and Thetis stirred within them a still deeper yearning. The sands of the seashore and the men's armour were wet with their weeping, so great a minister of fear was he whom they had lost. Chief in all their mourning was the son of Peleus; he laid his blood-stained hand on the breast of his friend. 'Fare well,' he cried, 'Patroclus, even in the house of Hades. I will now do all that I erewhile promised you; I will drag Hector hither and let dogs devour him raw; twelve noble sons of Trojans will I also slay before your pyre to avenge you.'

As he spoke he treated the body of noble Hector with contumely, laying it at full length in the dust beside the bier of Patroclus. The others then put off every man his armour, took the horses from their chariots, and seated themselves in great multitude by the ship of the fleet descendant of Æacus, who thereon feasted them with an abundant funeral banquet. Many a goodly ox, with many a sheep and bleating goat did they butcher and cut up; many a tusked boar moreover, fat and well-fed, did they singe and set to roast in the flames of Vulcan; and rivulets of blood flowed all round the place where the body was lying.

Then the princes of the Achæans took the son of Peleus to Agamemnon, but hardly could they persuade him to come with them, so wroth was he for the death of his comrade. As soon as they reached Agamemnon's tent they told the serving-men to set a large tripod over the fire, in case they might persuade the son of Peleus to wash the clotted gore from his body, but he denied them sternly, and swore it with a solemn oath, saying, 'Nay, by King Jove, first and mightiest of all gods, it is not meet that water should touch my body, till I have laid Patroclus on the flames, have built him a barrow, and shaved my head – for so long as I live no such second sorrow shall ever draw nigh me. Now, therefore, let us do all that this sad festival demands, but at break of day, King Agamemnon, bid your men bring wood, and provide all else that the dead may duly take into the realm of darkness; the fire shall thus burn him out of our sight the sooner, and the people shall turn again to their own labours.'

Thus did he speak, and they did even as he had said. They made haste to prepare the meal, they ate, and every man had his full share so that all were satisfied. As soon as they had had enough to eat and drink, the others went to their rest each in his own tent, but the son of Peleus lay grieving among his Myrmidons by the shore of the sounding sea, in an open place where the waves came surging in one after another. Here a very deep slumber took hold upon him and eased the burden of his sorrows, for his limbs were weary with chasing Hector round windy Ilius. Presently the sad spirit of Patroclus drew near him, like what he had been in stature, voice, and the light of his beaming eyes, clad, too, as he had been clad in life. The spirit hovered over his head and said:—

'You sleep, Achilles, and have forgotten me; you loved me living, but now that I am dead you think for me no further. Bury me with all speed that I may pass the gates of Hades; the ghosts, vain shadows of men that can labour no more, drive me away from them; they will not yet suffer me to join those that are beyond the river, and I wander all desolate by the wide gates of the house of Hades. Give me now your hand I pray you, for when you have once given me my dues of fire, never shall I again come forth out of the house of Hades. Nevermore shall we sit apart and take sweet counsel among the living; the cruel fate which was my birthright has yawned its wide jaws around me – nay, you too Achilles, peer of gods, are doomed to die beneath the wall of the noble Trojans.

'One prayer more will I make you, if you will grant it; let not my bones be laid apart from yours, Achilles, but with them; even as we were brought up together in your own home, what time Menœtius brought me to you as a child from Opöeis because by a sad spite I had killed the son of Amphidamas – not of set purpose, but in childish quarrel over the dice. The knight Peleus took me into his house, entreated me kindly, and named me to be your squire; therefore let our bones lie in but a single urn, the two-handled golden vase given to you by your mother.'

And Achilles answered, 'Why, true heart, are you come hither to lay these charges upon me? I will of my own self do all as you have bidden me. Draw closer to me, let us once more throw our arms around one another, and find sad comfort in the sharing of our sorrows.'

He opened his arms towards him as he spoke and would have clasped him in them, but there was nothing, and the spirit vanished as a vapour, gibbering and whining into the earth. Achilles sprang to his feet, smote his two hands, and made lamentation saying, 'Of a truth even in the house of Hades there are ghosts and phantoms that have no life in them; all night long the sad spirit of Patroclus has hovered over my head making piteous moan, telling me what I am to do for him, and looking wondrously like himself.'

Thus did he speak and his words set them all weeping and mourning about the poor dumb dead, till rosy-fingered morn appeared. Then

King Agamemnon sent men and mules from all parts of the camp, to bring wood, and Meriones, squire to Idomeneus, was in charge over them. They went out with woodmen's axes and strong ropes in their hands, and before them went the mules. Up hill and down dale did they go, by straight ways and crooked, and when they reached the heights of many-fountained Ida, they laid their axes to the roots of many a tall branching oak that came thundering down as they felled it. They split the trees and bound them behind the mules, which then wended their way as they best could through the thick brushwood on to the plain. All who had been cutting wood bore logs, for so Meriones squire to Idomeneus had bidden them, and they threw them down in a line upon the sea-shore at the place where Achilles would make a mighty monument for Patroclus and for himself.

When they had thrown down their great logs of wood over the whole ground, they stayed all of them where they were, but Achilles ordered his brave Myrmidons to gird on their armour, and to yoke each man his horses; they therefore rose, girded on their armour and mounted each his chariot – they and their charioteers with them. The chariots went before, and they that were on foot followed as a cloud in their tens of thousands after. In the midst of them his comrades bore Patroclus and covered him with the locks of their hair which they cut off and threw upon his body. Last came Achilles with his head bowed for sorrow, so noble a comrade was he taking to the house of Hades.

When they came to the place of which Achilles had told them they laid the body down and built up the wood. Achilles then bethought him of another matter. He went a space away from the pyre, and cut off the yellow lock which he had let grow for the river Spercheius. He looked all sorrowfully out upon the dark sea, and said, 'Spercheius, in vain did my father Peleus vow to you that when I returned home to my loved native land I should cut off this lock and offer you a holy hecatomb; fifty he-goats was I to sacrifice to you there at your springs, where is your grove and your altar fragrant with burnt-offerings. Thus did my father vow, but you have not fulfilled his prayer; now, therefore, that I shall see my home no more, I give this lock as a keepsake to the hero Patroclus.'

As he spoke he placed the lock in the hands of his dear comrade, and all who stood by were filled with yearning and lamentation. The sun would have gone down upon their mourning had not Achilles presently said to Agamemnon, 'Son of Atreus, for it is to you that the people will give ear, there is a time to mourn and a time to cease from mourning; bid the people now leave the pyre and set about getting their dinners: we, to whom the dead is dearest, will see to what is wanted here, and let the other princes also stay by me.'

When King Agamemnon heard this he dismissed the people to their ships, but those who were about the dead heaped up wood and built a pyre a hundred feet this way and that; then they laid the dead all sorrowfully upon the top of it. They flayed and dressed many fat sheep and oxen before the pyre, and Achilles took fat from all of them and wrapped the body therein from head to foot, heaping the flayed carcases all round it. Against the bier he leaned two-handled jars of honey and unguents; four proud horses did he then cast upon the pyre, groaning the while he did so. The dead hero had had nine house-dogs; two of them did Achilles slay and threw upon the pyre; he also put twelve brave sons of noble Trojans to the sword and laid them with the rest, for he was full of bitterness and fury. Then he committed all to the resistless and devouring might of the fire; he groaned aloud and called on his dead comrade by name. 'Fare well,' he cried, 'Patroclus, even in the house of Hades; I am now doing all that I have promised you. Twelve brave sons of noble Trojans shall the flames consume along with yourself, but dogs, not fire, shall devour the flesh of Hector son of Priam.'

Thus did he vaunt, but the dogs came not about the body of Hector, for Jove's daughter Venus kept them off him night and day, and anointed him with ambrosial oil of roses that his flesh might not be torn when Achilles was dragging him about. Phœbus Apollo moreover sent a dark cloud from heaven to earth, which gave shade to the whole place where Hector lay, that the heat of the sun might not parch his body.

Now the pyre about dead Patroclus would not kindle. Achilles therefore bethought him of another matter; he went apart and prayed to the two winds Boreas and Zephyrus, vowing them goodly offerings. He made them many drink-offerings from his golden cup, and besought them to come and help him that the wood might make haste to kindle and the dead bodies be consumed. Fleet Iris heard him praying and started off to fetch the winds. They were holding high feast in the house of boisterous Zephyrus when Iris came running up to the stone threshold of the house and stood there, but as soon as they set eyes on her they all came towards her and each of them called her to him, but Iris would not sit down. 'I cannot stay,' she said, 'I must go back to the streams of Oceanus and the land of the Ethiopians who are offering hecatombs to the immortals, and I would have my share; but Achilles prays that Boreas and shrill Zephyrus will come to him, and he vows them goodly offerings; he would have you blow upon the pyre of Patroclus for whom all the Achæans are lamenting.'

With this she left them, and the two winds rose with a cry that rent the air and swept the clouds before them.

They blew on and on until they came to the sea, and the waves rose high beneath them, but when they reached Troy they fell upon the pyre till the mighty flames roared under the blast that they blew. All night long did they blow hard and beat upon the fire, and all night long did Achilles grasp his double cup, drawing wine from a mixing-bowl of gold, and calling upon the spirit of dead Patroclus as he poured it upon the ground until the earth was drenched. As a father mourns when he is burning the bones of his bridegroom son whose death has wrung the hearts of his parents, even so did Achilles mourn while burning the body of his comrade, pacing round the bier with piteous groaning and lamentation.

At length as the Morning Star was beginning to herald the light which saffron-mantled Dawn was soon to suffuse over the sea, the flames fell and the fire began to die. The winds then went home beyond the Thracian sea, which roared and boiled as they swept over it. The son of Peleus now turned away from the pyre and lay down, overcome with toil, till he fell into a sweet slumber. Presently they who were about the son of Atreus drew near in a body, and roused him with the noise and tramp of their coming. He sate upright and said, 'Son of Atreus, and all other princes of the Achæans, first pour red wine everywhere upon the fire and quench it; let us then gather the bones of Patroclus son of Menœtius, singling them out with care; they are easily found, for they lie in the middle of the pyre, while all else, both men and horses, has been thrown in a heap and burned at the outer edge. We will lay the bones in a golden urn, in two layers of fat, against the time when I shall myself go down into the house of Hades. As for the barrow, labour not to raise a great one now, but such as is reasonable. Afterwards, let those Achæans who may be left at the ships when I am gone, build it both broad and high.'

Thus he spoke and they obeyed the word of the son of Peleus. First they poured red wine upon the thick layer of ashes and quenched the fire. With many tears they singled out the whitened bones of their loved comrade and laid them within a golden urn in two layers of fat: they then covered the urn with a linen cloth and took it inside the tent. They marked off the circle where the barrow should be, made a foundation for it about the pyre, and forthwith heaped up the earth. When they had thus raised a mound they were going away, but Achilles stayed the people and made them sit in assembly. He brought prizes from the ships – cauldrons, tripods, horses and mules, noble oxen, women with fair girdles, and swart iron.

The first prize he offered was for the chariot races – a woman skilled in all useful arts, and a three-legged cauldron that had ears for handles, and would hold twenty-two measures. This was for the man who came in first. For the second there was a six-year old mare, unbroken, and in foal to a he-ass; the third was to have a goodly cauldron that had never yet been on the fire; it was still bright as when it left the maker, and would hold four measures. The fourth prize was two talents of gold, and the fifth a two-handled urn as yet unsoiled by smoke. Then he stood up and spoke among the Argives saying:—

'Son of Atreus, and all other Achæans, these are the prizes that lie waiting the winners of the chariot races. At any other time I should carry off the first prize and take it to my own tent; you know how far my steeds excel all others – for they are immortal; Neptune gave them to my father Peleus, who in his turn gave them to myself; but I shall hold aloof, I and my steeds that have lost their brave and kind driver, who many a time has washed them in clear water and anointed their manes with oil. See how they stand weeping here, with their manes trailing on the ground in the extremity of their sorrow. But do you others set yourselves in order throughout the host, whosoever has confidence in his horses and in the strength of his chariot.'

Thus spoke the son of Peleus and the drivers of chariots bestirred themselves. First among them all uprose Eumelus, king of men, son of Admetus, a man excellent in horsemanship. Next to him rose mighty Diomed son of Tydeus; he yoked the Trojan horses which he had taken from Æneas, when Apollo bore him out of the fight. Next to him, yellow-haired Menelaus son of Atreus rose and yoked his fleet horses, Agamemnon's mare Æthe, and his own horse Podargus. The mare had been given to Agamemnon by Echepolus son of Anchises, that he might not have to follow him to Ilius, but might stay at home and take his ease; for Jove had endowed him with great wealth and he lived in spacious Sicyon. This mare, all eager for the race, did Menelaus put under the yoke.

Fourth in order Antilochus, son to noble Nestor son of Neleus, made ready his horses. These were bred in Pylos, and his father came up to him to give him good advice of which, however, he stood in but little need. 'Antilochus,' said Nestor, 'you are young, but Jove and Neptune have loved you well, and have made you an excellent horseman. I need not therefore say much by way of instruction. You are skilful at wheeling your horses round the post, but the horses themselves are very slow, and it is this that will, I fear, mar your chances. The other drivers know less than you do, but their horses are fleeter; therefore, my dear son, see if you cannot hit upon some artifice whereby you may insure that the prize shall not slip through your fingers. The woodman does more by skill than by brute force; by skill the pilot guides his storm-tossed barque over the sea, and so by skill one driver can beat another. If a man leaves all to his horses, they will go wide in rounding the posts at either end of the course; he has no command over them and cannot keep them from swerving this way and that, whereas a man who knows what he is doing may have worse horses, but he will keep them well in hand when he sees the doubling-post; he knows the precise moment at which to pull the rein, and keeps his eye well on the man in front of him. I will give you this certain token which cannot escape your notice. There is a stump of a dead tree – oak or pine as it may be – some six feet above the ground, and not yet rotted away by rain; it stands at the fork of the road; it has two white stones set one on each side, and there is a clear course all round it. It may have been a monument to some one long since dead, or it may have been used as a doubling-post in days gone by; now, however, it has been fixed on by Achilles as the mark round which the chariots shall turn; hug it as close as you can, but as you stand in your chariot lean over a little to the left; urge on your right-hand horse with voice and lash, and give him a loose rein, but let the left-hand horse keep so close in, that the nave of your wheel shall almost graze the post; but mind the stone, or you will wound your horses and break your chariot in pieces, which would be sport for others but confusion for yourself. Therefore, my dear son, mind well what you are about, for if you can be first to round the post there is no chance of any one giving you the go-by later, not even though you had Adrestus's horse Arion behind you – a horse which is of divine race – or those of Laomedon, which are the noblest in this country.'

When Nestor had made an end of counselling his son he sat down in his place, and fifth in order Meriones got ready his horses. They then all mounted their chariots and cast lots. Achilles shook the helmet, and the lot of Antilochus son of Nestor fell out first; next came that of King Eumelus, and after his, those of Menelaus son of Atreus and of Meriones. The last place fell to the lot of Diomed son of Tydeus, who was the best man of them all. They took their places in line; Achilles showed them the doubling-post round which they were to turn, some way off upon the plain; here he stationed his father's follower Phœnix as umpire, to note the running, and report truly.

At the same instant they all of them lashed their horses, struck them with the reins, and shouted at them with all their might. They flew full speed over the plain away from the ships, the dust rose from under them as it were a cloud or whirlwind, and their manes were all flying in the wind. At one moment the chariots seemed to touch the ground, and then again they bounded into the air; the drivers stood erect, and their hearts beat fast and furious in their lust of victory. Each kept calling on his horses, and the horses scoured the plain amid the clouds of dust that they raised.

It was when they were doing the last part of the course on their way back towards the sea that their pace was strained to the utmost and it was seen what each could do. The horses of the descendant of Pheres now took the lead, and close behind them came the Trojan stallions of Diomed. They seemed as if about to mount Eumelus's chariot, and he could feel their warm breath on his back and on his broad shoulders, for their heads were close to him as they flew over the course. Diomed would have now passed him, or there would have been a dead heat, but Phœbus Apollo to spite him made him drop his whip. Tears of anger fell from his eyes as he saw the mares going on faster than ever, while his own horses lost ground through his having no whip. Minerva saw the trick which Apollo had played the son of Tydeus, so she brought him his whip and put spirit into his horses; moreover she went after the son of Admetus in a rage and broke his yoke for him; the mares went one to one side the course, and the other to the other, and the pole was broken against the ground. Eumelus was thrown from his chariot close to the wheel; his elbows, mouth, and nostrils were all torn, and his forehead was bruised above his eyebrows; his eyes filled with tears and he could find no utterance. But the son of Tydeus turned his horses aside and shot far ahead, for Minerva put fresh strength into them and covered Diomed himself with glory.

Menelaus son of Atreus came next behind him, but Antilochus called to his father's horses. 'On with you both,' he cried, 'and do your very utmost. I do not bid you try to beat the steeds of the son of Tydeus, for Minerva has put running into them, and has covered Diomed with glory; but you must overtake the horses of the son of Atreus and not be left behind, or Æthe who is so fleet will taunt you. Why, my good fellows, are you lagging? I tell you, and it shall surely be – Nestor will keep neither of you, but will put both of you to the sword, if we win any the worse a prize through your carelessness. Hie after them at your utmost speed; I will hit on a plan for passing them in a narrow part of the way, and it shall not fail me.'

They feared the rebuke of their master, and for a short space went quicker. Presently Antilochus saw a narrow place where the road had sunk. The ground was broken, for the winter's rain had gathered and had worn the road so that the whole place was deepened. Menelaus was making towards it so as to get there first, for fear of a foul, but Antilochus turned his horses out of the way, and followed him a little on one side. The son of Atreus was afraid and shouted out, 'Antilochus, you are driving recklessly; rein in your horses; the road is too narrow here, it will be wider soon, and you can pass me then; if you foul my chariot you may bring both of us to a mischief.'

But Antilochus plied his whip, and drove faster, as though he had not heard him. They went side by side for about as far as a young man can hurl a disc from his shoulder when he is trying his strength, and then Menelaus's mares drew behind, for he left off driving for fear the horses should foul one another and upset the chariots; thus, while pressing on in quest of victory, they might both come headlong to the ground. Menelaus then upbraided Antilochus and said, 'There is no greater trickster living than you are; go, and bad luck go with you; the Achæans say not well that you have understanding, and come what may you shall not bear away the prize without sworn protest on my part.'

Then he called on his horses and said to them, 'Keep your pace, and slacken not; the limbs of the other horses will weary sooner than yours, for they are neither of them young.'

The horses feared the rebuke of their master, and went faster, so that they were soon nearly up with the others.

Meanwhile the Achæans from their seats were watching how the horses went, as they scoured the plain amid clouds of their own dust. Idomeneus captain of the Cretans was first to make out the running, for he was not in the thick of the crowd, but stood on the most commanding part of the ground. The driver was a long way off, but Idomeneus could hear him shouting, and could see the foremost horse quite plainly – a chestnut with a round white star, like the moon, on its forehead. He stood up and said among the Argives, 'My friends, princes and counsellors of the Argives, can you see the running as well as I can? There seems to be another pair in front now, and another driver; those that led off at the start must have been disabled out on the plain. I saw them at first making their way round the doubling-post, but now, though I search the plain of Troy, I cannot find them. Perhaps the reins fell from the driver's hand so that he lost command of his horses at the doubling-post, and could not turn it. I suppose he must have been thrown out there, and broken his chariot, while his mares have left the course and gone off wildly in a panic. Come up and see for yourselves, I cannot make out for certain, but the driver seems an Ætolian by descent, ruler over the Argives, brave Diomed the son of Tydeus.'

Ajax the son of Oïleus took him up rudely and said, 'Idomeneus, why should you be in such a hurry to tell us all about it, when the mares are still so far out upon the plain? You are none of the youngest, nor your eyes none of the sharpest, but you are always laying down the law. You have no right to do so, for there are better men here than you are. Eumelus's horses are in front now, as they always have been, and he is on the chariot holding the reins.'

The captain of the Cretans was angry, and answered, 'Ajax, you are an excellent railer, but you have no judgement, and are wanting in much else as well, for you have a vile temper. I will wager you a tripod or cauldron, and Agamemnon son of Atreus shall decide whose horses are first. You will then know to your cost.'

Ajax son of Oïleus was for making him an angry answer, and there would have been yet further brawling between them, had not Achilles risen in his place and said, 'Cease your railing, Ajax and Idomeneus; it is not seemly; you would be scandalised if you saw any one else do the like: sit down and keep your eyes on the horses; they are speeding towards the winning-post and will be here directly. You will then both of you know whose horses are first, and whose come after.'

As he was speaking, the son of Tydeus came driving in, plying his whip lustily from his shoulder, and his horses stepping high as they flew over the course. The sand and grit rained thick on the driver, and the chariot inlaid with gold and tin ran close behind his fleet horses. There was little trace of wheel-marks in the fine dust, and the horses came flying in at their utmost speed. Diomed stayed them in the middle of the crowd, and the sweat from their manes and chests fell in streams on to the ground. Forthwith he sprang from his goodly chariot, and leaned his whip against his horses' yoke; brave Sthenelus now lost no time, but at once brought on the prize, and gave the woman and the ear-handled cauldron to his comrades to take away. Then he unyoked the horses.

Next after him came in Antilochus of the race of Neleus, who had passed Menelaus by a trick and not by the fleetness of his horses; but even so Menelaus came in as close behind him as the wheel is to the horse that draws both the chariot and its master. The end hairs of a horse's tail touch the tyre of the wheel, and there is never much space between wheel and horse when the chariot is going; Menelaus was no further than this behind Antilochus, though at first he had been a full disc's throw behind him. He had soon caught him up again, for Agamemnon's mare Æthe kept pulling stronger and stronger, so that if the course had been longer he would have passed him, and there would not even have been a dead heat. Idomeneus's brave squire Meriones was about a spear's cast behind Menelaus. His horses were slowest of all, and he was the worst driver. Last of them all came the son of Admetus, dragging his chariot and driving his horses on in front. When Achilles saw him he was sorry, and stood up among the Argives saying, 'The best man is coming in last. Let us give him a prize for it is reasonable. He shall have the second, but the first must go to the son of Tydeus.'

Thus did he speak and the others all of them applauded his saying, and were for doing as he had said, but Nestor's son Antilochus stood up and claimed his rights from the son of Peleus. 'Achilles,' said he, 'I shall take it much amiss if you do this thing; you would rob me of my prize, because you think Eumelus's chariot and horses were thrown out, and himself too, good man that he is. He should have prayed duly to the immortals; he would not have come in last if he had done so. If you are sorry for him and so choose, you have much gold in your tents, with bronze, sheep, cattle and horses. Take something from this store if you would have the Achæans speak well of you, and give him a better prize even than that which you have now offered; but I will not give up the mare, and he that will fight me for her, let him come on.'

Achilles smiled as he heard this, and was pleased with Antilochus, who was one of his dearest comrades. So he said:—

'Antilochus, if you would have me find Eumelus another prize, I will give him the bronze breastplate with a rim of tin running all round it which I took from Asteropæus. It will be worth much money to him.'

He bade his comrade Automedon bring the breastplate from his tent, and he did so. Achilles then gave it over to Eumelus, who received it gladly.

But Menelaus got up in a rage, furiously angry with Antilochus. An attendant placed his staff in his hands and bade the Argives keep silence: the hero then addressed them. 'Antilochus,' said he, 'what is this – from you who have been so far blameless? You have made me cut a poor figure and baulked my horses by flinging your own in front of them, though yours are much worse than mine are; therefore, O princes and counsellors of the Argives, judge between us and show no favour, lest one of the Achæans say, "Menelaus has got the mare through lying and corruption; his horses were far inferior to Antilochus's, but he has greater weight and influence." Nay, I will determine the matter myself, and no man will blame me, for I shall do what is just. Come here, Antilochus, and stand, as our custom is, whip in hand before your chariot and horses; lay your hand on your steeds, and swear by earth-encircling Neptune that you did not purposely and guilefully get in the way of my horses.'

And Antilochus answered, 'Forgive me; I am much younger, King Menelaus, than you are; you stand higher than I do and are the better man of the two; you know how easily young men are betrayed into indiscretion; their tempers are more hasty and they have less judgement; make due allowances therefore, and bear with me; I will of my own accord give up the mare that I have won, and if you claim any further chattel from my own possessions, I would rather yield it to you, at once, than fall from your good graces henceforth, and do wrong in the sight of heaven.'

The son of Nestor then took the mare and gave her over to Menelaus, whose anger was thus appeased; as when dew falls upon a field of ripening corn, and the lands are bristling with the harvest – even so, O Menelaus, was your heart made glad within you. He turned to Antilochus and said, 'Now, Antilochus, angry though I have been, I can give way to you of my own free will; you have never been headstrong nor ill-disposed hitherto, but this time your youth has got the better of your judgement; be careful how you outwit your betters in future; no one else could have brought me round so easily, but your good father, your brother, and yourself have all of you had infinite trouble on my behalf; I therefore yield to your entreaty, and will give up the mare to you, mine though it indeed be; the people will thus see that I am neither harsh nor vindictive.'

With this he gave the mare over to Antilochus's comrade Noëmon, and then took the cauldron. Meriones, who had come in fourth, carried off the two talents of gold, and the fifth prize, the two-handled urn, being unawarded, Achilles gave it to Nestor, going up to him among the assembled Argives and saying, 'Take this, my good old friend, as an heirloom and memorial of the funeral of Patroclus – for you shall see him no more among the Argives. I give you this prize though you cannot win one; you can now neither wrestle nor fight, and cannot enter for the javelin-match nor foot-races, for the hand of age has been laid heavily upon you.'

So saying he gave the urn over to Nestor, who received it gladly and answered, 'My son, all that you have said is true; there is no strength now in my legs and feet, nor can I hit out with my hands from either shoulder. Would that I were still young and strong as when the Epeans were burying King Amarynceus in Buprasium, and his sons offered prizes in his honour. There was then none that could vie with me neither of the Epeans nor the Pylians themselves nor the Ætolians. In boxing I overcame Clytomedes son of Enops, and in wrestling, Ancæus of Pleuron who had come forward against me. Iphiclus was a good runner, but I beat him, and threw farther with my spear than either Phyleus or Polydorus. In chariot-racing alone did the two sons of Actor surpass me by crowding their horses in front of me, for they were angry at the way victory had gone, and at the greater part of the prizes remaining in the place in which they had been offered. They were twins, and the one kept on holding the reins, and holding the reins, while the other plied the whip. Such was I then, but now I must leave these matters to younger men; I must bow before the weight of years, but in those days I was eminent among heroes. And now, sir, go on with the funeral contests in honour of your comrade: gladly do I accept this urn, and my heart rejoices that you do not forget me but are ever mindful of my goodwill towards you, and of the respect due to me from the Achæans. For all which may the grace of heaven be vouchsafed you in great abundance.'

Thereon the son of Peleus, when he had listened to all the thanks of Nestor, went about among the concourse of the Achæans, and presently offered prizes for skill in the painful art of boxing. He brought out a strong mule, and made it fast in the middle of the crowd – a she-mule never yet broken, but six years old – when it is hardest of all to break them: this was for the victor, and for the vanquished he offered a double cup. Then he stood up and said among the Argives, 'Son of Atreus, and all other Achæans, I invite our two champion boxers to lay about them lustily and compete for these prizes. He to whom Apollo vouchsafes the greater endurance, and whom the Achæans acknowledge as victor, shall take the mule back with him to his own tent, while he that is vanquished shall have the double cup.'

As he spoke there stood up a champion both brave and of great stature, a skilful boxer, Epeüs, son of Panopeus. He laid his hand on the mule and said, 'Let the man who is to have the cup come hither, for none but myself will take the mule. I am the best boxer of all here present, and none can beat me. Is it not enough that I should fall short of you in actual fighting? Still, no man can be good at everything. I tell you plainly, and it shall come true; if any man will box with me I will bruise his body and break his bones; therefore let his friends stay here in a body and be at hand to take him away when I have done with him.'

They all held their peace, and no man rose save Euryalus son of Mecisteus, who was son of Talaüs. Mecisteus went once to Thebes after the fall of Œdipus, to attend his funeral, and he beat all the people of Cadmus. The son of Tydeus was Euryalus's second, cheering him on and hoping heartily that he would win. First he put a waistband round him and then he gave him some well-cut thongs of ox-hide; the two men being now girt went into the middle of the ring, and immediately fell to; heavily indeed did they punish one another and lay about them with their brawny fists. One could hear the horrid crashing of their jaws, and they sweated from every pore of their skin. Presently Epeüs came on and gave Euryalus a blow on the jaw as he was looking round; Euryalus could not keep his legs; they gave way under him in a moment and he sprang up with a bound, as a fish leaps into the air near some shore that is all bestrewn with sea-wrack, when Boreas furs the top of the waves, and then falls back into deep water. But noble Epeüs caught hold of him and raised him up; his comrades also came round him and led him from the ring, unsteady in his gait, his head hanging on one side, and spitting great clots of gore. They set him down in a swoon and then went to fetch the double cup.

The son of Peleus now brought out the prizes for the third contest and showed them to the Argives. These were for the painful art of wrestling. For the winner there was a great tripod ready for setting upon the fire, and the Achæans valued it among themselves at twelve oxen. For the loser he brought out a woman skilled in all manner of arts, and they valued her at four oxen. He rose and said among the Argives, 'Stand forward, you who will essay this contest.'

Forthwith uprose great Ajax the son of Telamon, and crafty Ulysses, full of wiles rose also. The two girded themselves and went into the middle of the ring. They gripped each other in their strong hands like the rafters which some master-builder frames for the roof of a high house to keep the wind out. Their backbones cracked as they tugged at one another with their mighty arms – and sweat rained from them in torrents. Many a bloody weal sprang up on their sides and shoulders, but they kept on striving with might and main for victory and to win the tripod. Ulysses could not throw Ajax, nor Ajax him; Ulysses was too strong for him; but when the Achæans began to tire of watching them, Ajax said to Ulysses, 'Ulysses, noble son of Laertes, you shall either lift me, or I you, and let Jove settle it between us.'

He lifted him from the ground as he spoke, but Ulysses did not forget his cunning. He hit Ajax in the hollow at the back of his knee, so that he could not keep his feet, but fell on his back with Ulysses lying upon his chest, and all who saw it marvelled. Then Ulysses in turn lifted Ajax and stirred him a little from the ground but could not lift him right off it, his knee sank under him, and the two fell side by side on the ground and were all begrimed with dust. They now sprang towards one another and were for wrestling yet a third time, but Achilles rose and stayed them. 'Put not each other further,' said he, 'to such cruel suffering; the victory is with both alike, take each of you an equal prize, and let the other Achæans now compete.'

Thus did he speak and they did even as he had said, and put on their shirts again after wiping the dust from off their bodies.

The son of Peleus then offered prizes for speed in running – a mixing-bowl beautifully wrought, of pure silver. It would hold six measures, and far exceeded all others in the whole world for beauty; it was the work of cunning artificers in Sidon, and had been brought into port by Phœnicians from beyond the sea, who had made a present of it to Thoas. Euenëus son of Jason had given it to Patroclus in ransom of Priam's son Lycaon, and Achilles now offered it as a prize in honour of his comrade to him who should be the swiftest runner. For the second prize he offered a large ox, well fattened, while for the last there was to be half a talent of gold. He then rose and said among the Argives, 'Stand forward, you who will essay this contest.'

Forthwith uprose fleet Ajax son of Oïleus, with cunning Ulysses, and Nestor's son Antilochus, the fastest runner among all the youth of his time. They stood side by side and Achilles showed them the goal. The course was set out for them from the starting-post, and the son of Oïleus took the lead at once, with Ulysses as close behind him as the shuttle is to a woman's bosom when she throws the woof across the warp and holds it close up to her; even so close behind him was Ulysses – treading in his footprints before the dust could settle there, and Ajax could feel his breath on the back of his head as he ran swiftly on. The Achæans all shouted applause as they saw him straining his utmost, and cheered him as he shot past them; but when they were now nearing the end of the course Ulysses prayed inwardly to Minerva. 'Hear me,' he cried, 'and help my feet, O goddess.' Thus did he pray, and Pallas Minerva heard his prayer; she made his hands and his feet feel light, and when the runners were at the point of pouncing upon the prize, Ajax, through Minerva's spite, slipped upon some offal that was lying there from the cattle which Achilles had slaughtered in honour of Patroclus, and his mouth and nostrils were all filled with cow dung. Ulysses therefore carried off the mixing-bowl, for he got before Ajax and came in first. But Ajax took the ox and stood with his hand on one of its horns, spitting the dung out of his mouth. Then he said to the Argives, 'Alas, the goddess has spoiled my running; she watches over Ulysses and stands by him as though she were his own mother.' Thus did he speak and they all of them laughed heartily.

Antilochus carried off the last prize and smiled as he said to the bystanders, 'You all see, my friends, that now too the gods have shown their respect for seniority. Ajax is somewhat older than I am, and as for Ulysses, he belongs to an earlier generation, but he is hale in spite of his years, and no man of the Achæans can run against him save only Achilles.'

He said this to pay a compliment to the son of Peleus, and Achilles answered, 'Antilochus, you shall not have praised me to no purpose; I shall give you an additional half talent of gold.' He then gave the half talent to Antilochus, who received it gladly.

Then the son of Peleus brought out the spear, helmet and shield that had been borne by Sarpedon, and were taken from him by Patroclus. He stood up and said among the Argives, 'We bid two champions put on their armour, take their keen blades, and make trial of one another in the presence of the multitude; whichever of them can first wound the flesh of the other, cut through his armour, and draw blood, to him will I give this goodly Thracian sword inlaid with silver, which I took from Asteropæus, but the armour let both hold in partnership, and I will give each of them a hearty meal in my own tent.'

Forthwith uprose great Ajax the son of Telamon, as also mighty Diomed son of Tydeus. When they had put on their armour each on his own side of the ring, they both went into the middle eager to engage, and with fire flashing from their eyes. The Achæans marvelled as they beheld them, and when the two were now close up with one another, thrice did they spring forward and thrice try to strike each other in close combat. Ajax pierced Diomed's round shield, but did not draw blood, for the cuirass beneath the shield protected him; thereon the son of Tydeus from over his huge shield kept aiming continually at Ajax's neck with the point of his spear, and the Achæans alarmed for his safety bade them leave off fighting and divide the prize between them. Achilles then gave the great sword to the son of Tydeus, with its scabbard, and the leathern belt with which to hang it.

Achilles next offered the massive iron quoit which mighty Eëtion had erewhile been used to hurl, until Achilles had slain him and carried it off in his ships along with other spoils. He stood up and said among the Argives, 'Stand forward, you who would essay this contest. He who wins it will have a store of iron that will last him five years as they go rolling round, and if his fair fields lie far from a town his shepherd or ploughman will not have to make a journey to buy iron, for he will have a stock of it on his own premises.'

Then uprose the two mighty men Polypoetes and Leonteus, with Ajax son of Telamon and noble Epëus. They stood up one after the other and Epëus took the quoit, whirled it, and flung it from him, which set all the Achæans laughing. After him threw Leonteus of the race of Mars. Ajax son of Telamon threw third, and sent the quoit beyond any mark that had been made yet, but when mighty Polypoetes took the quoit he hurled it as though it had been a stockman's stick which he sends flying about among his cattle when he is driving them, so far did his throw out-distance those of the others. All who saw it roared applause, and his comrades carried the prize for him and set it on board his ship.

Achilles next offered a prize of iron for archery – ten double-edged axes and ten with single edges: he set up a ship's mast, some way off upon the sands, and with a fine string tied a pigeon to it by the foot; this was what they were to aim at. 'Whoever,' he said, 'can hit the pigeon shall have all the axes and take them away with him; he who hits the string without hitting the bird will have taken a worse aim and shall have the single-edged axes.'

Then uprose King Teucer, and Meriones the stalwart squire of Idomeneus rose also. They cast lots in a bronze helmet and the lot of Teucer fell first. He let fly with his arrow forthwith, but he did not promise hecatombs of firstling lambs to King Apollo, and missed his bird, for Apollo foiled his aim; but he hit the string with which the bird was tied, near its foot; the arrow cut the string clean through so that it hung down towards the ground, while the bird flew up into the sky, and the Achæans shouted applause. Meriones, who had his arrow ready while Teucer was aiming, snatched the bow out of his hand, and at once promised that he would sacrifice a hecatomb of firstling lambs to Apollo lord of the bow; then espying the pigeon high up under the clouds, he hit her in the middle of the wing as she was circling upwards; the arrow went clean through the wing and fixed itself in the ground at Meriones' feet, but the bird perched on the ship's mast hanging her head and with all her feathers drooping; the life went out of her, and she fell heavily from the mast. Meriones, therefore, took all ten double-edged axes, while Teucer bore off the single-edged ones to his ships.

Then the son of Peleus brought in a spear and a cauldron that had never been on the fire; it was worth an ox, and was chased with a pattern of flowers; and those that would throw the javelin stood up – to wit the son of Atreus, king of men Agamemnon, and Meriones, stalwart squire of Idomeneus. But Achilles spoke saying, 'Son of Atreus, we know how far you excel all others both in power and in throwing the javelin; take the cauldron back with you to your ships, but if it so please you, let us give the spear to Meriones; this at least is what I should myself wish.'

King Agamemnon assented. So he gave the bronze spear to Meriones, and handed the goodly cauldron to Talthybius his esquire.

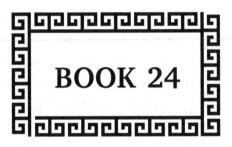

BOOK 24

Priam ransoms the body of Hector – Hector's funeral.

The assembly now broke up and the people went their ways each to his own ship. There they made ready their supper, and then bethought them of the blessed boon of sleep; but Achilles still wept for thinking of his dear comrade, and sleep, before whom all things bow, could take no hold upon him. This way and that did he turn as he yearned after the might and manfulness of Patroclus; he thought of all they had done together, and all they had gone through both on the field of battle and on the waves of the weary sea. As he dwelt on these things he wept bitterly and lay now on his side, now on his back, and now face downwards, till at last he rose and went out as one distraught to wander upon the sea-shore. Then, when he saw dawn breaking over beach and sea, he yoked his horses to his chariot, and bound the body of Hector behind it that he might drag it about. Thrice did he drag it round the tomb of the son of Menœtius, and then went back into his tent, leaving the body on the ground full length and with its face downwards. But Apollo would not suffer it to be disfigured, for he pitied the man, dead though he now was; therefore he shielded him with his golden ægis continually, that he might take no hurt while Achilles was dragging him.

Thus shamefully did Achilles in his fury dishonour Hector; but the blessed gods looked down in pity from heaven, and urged Mercury, slayer of Argus, to steal the body. All were of this mind save only Juno, Neptune, and Jove's grey-eyed daughter, who persisted in the hate which they had ever borne towards Ilius with Priam and his people; for they forgave not the wrong done them by Alexandrus in disdaining the goddesses who came to him when he was in his sheepyards, and preferring her who had offered him a wanton to his ruin.

When, therefore, the morning of the twelfth day had now come, Phœbus Apollo spoke among the immortals saying, 'You gods ought to be ashamed of yourselves; you are cruel and hard-hearted. Did not Hector burn you thighbones of heifers and of unblemished goats? And now dare you not rescue even his dead body, for his wife to look upon, with his mother and child, his father Priam, and his people, who would forthwith commit him to the flames, and give him his due funeral rites? So, then, you would all be on the side of mad Achilles, who knows neither right nor ruth? He is like some savage lion that in the pride of his great strength and daring springs upon men's flocks and gorges on them. Even so has Achilles flung aside all pity, and all that conscience which at once so greatly banes yet greatly boons him that will heed it. A man may lose one far dearer than Achilles has lost – a son, it may be, or a brother born from his own mother's womb; yet when he has mourned him and wept over him he will let him bide, for it takes much sorrow to kill a man; whereas Achilles, now that he has slain noble Hector, drags him behind his chariot round the tomb of his comrade. It were better of him, and for him, that he should not do so, for brave though he be we gods may take it ill that he should vent his fury upon dead clay.'

Juno spoke up in a rage. 'This were well,' she cried, 'O lord of the silver bow, if you would give like honour to Hector and to Achilles; but Hector was mortal and suckled at a woman's breast, whereas Achilles is the offspring of a goddess whom I myself reared and brought up. I married her to Peleus, who is above measure dear to the immortals; you gods came all of you to her wedding; you feasted along with them yourself and brought your lyre – false, and fond of low company, that you have ever been.'

Then said Jove, 'Juno, be not so bitter. Their honour shall not be equal, but of all that dwell in Ilius, Hector was dearest to the gods, as also to myself, for his offerings never failed me. Never was my altar stinted of its dues, nor of the drink-offerings and savour of sacrifice which we claim of right. I shall therefore permit the body of mighty Hector to be stolen; and yet this may hardly be without Achilles coming to know it, for his mother keeps night and day beside him. Let some one of you, therefore, send Thetis to me, and I will impart my counsel to her, namely that Achilles is to accept a ransom from Priam, and give up the body.'

On this Iris fleet as the wind went forth to carry his message. Down she plunged into the dark sea midway between Samos and rocky Imbrus; the waters hissed as they closed over her, and she sank into the bottom as the lead at the end of an ox-horn, that is sped to carry death to fishes. She found Thetis sitting in a great cave with the other sea-goddesses gathered round her; there she sat in the midst of them weeping for her noble son who was to fall far from his own land, on the rich plains of Troy. Iris went up to her and said, 'Rise, Thetis; Jove, whose counsels fail not, bids you come to him.' And Thetis answered, 'Why does the mighty god so bid me? I am in great grief, and shrink from going in and out among the immortals. Still, I will go, and the word that he may speak shall not be spoken in vain.'

The goddess took her dark veil, than which there can be no robe more sombre, and went forth with fleet Iris leading the way before her. The waves of the sea opened them a path, and when they reached the shore they flew up into the heavens, where they found the all-seeing son of Saturn with the blessed gods that live for ever assembled near him. Minerva gave up her seat to her, and she sat down by the side of father Jove. Juno then placed a fair golden cup in her hand, and spoke to her in words of comfort, whereon Thetis drank and gave her back the cup; and the sire of gods and men was the first to speak.

'So, goddess,' said he, 'for all your sorrow, and the grief that I well know reigns ever in your heart, you have come hither to Olympus, and I will tell you why I have sent for you. This nine days past the immortals have been quarrelling about Achilles waster of cities and the body of Hector. The gods would have Mercury slayer of Argus steal the body, but in furtherance of our peace and amity henceforward, I will concede such honour to your son as I will now tell you. Go, then, to the host and lay these commands upon him; say that the gods are angry with him, and that I am myself more angry than them all, in that he keeps Hector at the ships and will not give him up. He may thus fear me and let the body go. At the same time I will send Iris to great Priam to bid him go to the ships of the Achæans, and ransom his son, taking with him such gifts for Achilles as may give him satisfaction.

Silver-footed Thetis did as the god had told her, and forthwith down she darted from the topmost summits of Olympus. She went to her son's tents where she found him grieving bitterly, while his trusty comrades round him were busy preparing their morning meal, for which they had killed a great woolly sheep. His mother sat down beside him and caressed him with her hand saying, 'My son, how long will you keep on thus grieving and making moan? You are gnawing at your own heart, and think neither of food nor of woman's embraces; and yet these too were well, for you have no long time to live, and death with the strong hand of fate are already close beside you. Now, therefore, heed what I say, for I come as a messenger from Jove; he says that the gods are angry with you, and himself more angry than them all, in that you keep Hector at the ships and will not give him up. Therefore let him go, and accept a ransom for his body.'

And Achilles answered, 'So be it. If Olympian Jove of his own motion thus commands me, let him that brings the ransom bear the body away.'

Thus did mother and son talk together at the ships in long discourse with one another. Meanwhile the son of Saturn sent Iris to the strong city of Ilius. 'Go,' said he, 'fleet Iris, from the mansions of Olympus, and tell King Priam in Ilius, that he is to go to the ships of the Achæans and free the body of his dear son. He is to take such gifts with him as shall give satisfaction to Achilles, and he is to go alone, with no other Trojan, save only some honoured servant who may drive his mules and waggon, and bring back the body of him whom noble Achilles has slain. Let him have no thought nor fear of death in his heart, for we will send the slayer of Argus to escort him, and bring him within the tent of Achilles. Achilles will not kill him nor let another do so, for he will take heed to his ways and sin not, and he will entreat a suppliant with all honourable courtesy.'

On this Iris, fleet as the wind, sped forth to deliver her message. She went to Priam's house, and found weeping and lamentation therein. His sons were seated round their father in the outer courtyard, and their raiment was wet with tears: the old man sat in the midst of them with his mantle wrapped close about his body, and his head and neck all covered with the filth which he had clutched as he lay grovelling in the mire. His daughters and his sons' wives went wailing about the house, as they thought of the many and brave men who lay dead, slain by the Argives. The messenger of Jove stood by Priam and spoke softly to him, but fear fell upon him as she did so. 'Take heart,' she said, 'Priam offspring of Dardanus, take heart and fear not. I bring no evil tidings, but am minded well towards you. I come as a messenger from Jove, who though he be not near, takes thought for you and pities you. The lord of Olympus bids you go and ransom noble Hector, and take with you such gifts as shall give satisfaction to Achilles. You are to go alone, with no other Trojan, save only some honoured servant who may drive your mules and waggon, and bring back to the city the body of him whom noble Achilles has slain. You are to have no thought, nor fear of death, for Jove will send the slayer of Argus to escort you. When he has brought you within Achilles' tent, Achilles will not kill you nor let another do so, for he will take heed to his ways and sin not, and he will entreat a suppliant with all honourable courtesy.'

Iris went her way when she had thus spoken, and Priam told his sons to get a mule-waggon ready, and to make the body of the waggon fast upon the top of its bed. Then he went down into his fragrant store-room, high-vaulted, and made of cedar-wood, where his many treasures were kept, and he called Hecuba his wife. 'Wife,' said he, 'a messenger has come to me from Olympus, and has told me to go to the ships of the Achæans to ransom my dear son, taking with me such gifts as shall give satisfaction to Achilles. What think you of this matter? for my own part I am greatly moved to pass through the host of the Achæans and go to their ships.'

His wife cried aloud as she heard him, and said, 'Alas, what has become of that judgement for which you have been ever famous both among strangers and your own people? How can you venture alone to the ships of the Achæans, and look into the face of him who has slain so many of your brave sons? You must have iron courage, for if the cruel savage sees you and lays hold on you, he will know neither respect nor pity. Let us then weep Hector from afar here in our own house, for when I gave him birth the threads of overruling fate were spun for him that dogs should eat his flesh far from his parents, in the house of that terrible man on whose liver I would fain fasten and devour it. Thus would I avenge my son, who showed no cowardice when Achilles slew him, and thought neither of flight nor of avoiding battle as he stood in defence of Trojan men and Trojan women.'

Then Priam said, 'I would go, do not therefore stay me nor be as a bird of ill omen in my house, for you will not move me. Had it been some mortal man who had sent me – some prophet or priest who divines from sacrifice – I should have deemed him false and have given him no heed; but now I have heard the goddess and seen her face to face, therefore I will go and her saying shall not be in vain. If it be my fate to die at the ships of the Achæans even so would I have it; let Achilles slay me, if I may but first have taken my son in my arms and mourned him to my heart's comforting.'

So saying he lifted the lids of his chests, and took out twelve goodly vestments. He took also twelve cloaks of single fold, twelve rugs, twelve fair mantles, and an equal number of shirts. He weighed out ten talents of gold, and brought moreover two burnished tripods, four cauldrons, and a very beautiful cup which the Thracians had given him when he had gone to them on an embassy; it was very precious, but he grudged not even this, so eager was he to ransom the body of his son. Then he chased all the Trojans from the court and rebuked them with words of anger. 'Out,' he cried, 'shame and disgrace to me that you are. Have you no grief in your own homes that you are come to plague me here? Is it a small thing, think you, that the son of Saturn has sent this sorrow upon me, to lose the bravest of my sons? Nay, you shall prove it in person, for now he is gone the Achæans will have easier work in killing you. As for me, let me go down within the house of Hades, ere mine eyes behold the sacking and wasting of the city.'

He drove the men away with his staff, and they went forth as the old man sped them. Then he called to his sons, upbraiding Helenus, Paris, noble Agathon, Pammon, Antiphonus, Polites of the loud battle-cry, Deïphobus, Hippothoüs, and Dius. These nine did the old man call near him. 'Come to me at once,' he cried, 'worthless sons who do me shame; would that you had all been killed at the ships rather than Hector. Miserable man that I am, I have had the bravest sons in all Troy – noble Nestor, Troïlus the dauntless charioteer, and Hector who was a god among men, so that one would have thought he was son to an immortal – yet there is not one of them left. Mars has slain them and those of whom I am ashamed are alone left me. Liars, and light of foot, heroes of the dance, robbers of lambs and kids from your own people, why do you not get a waggon ready for me at once, and put all these things upon it that I may set out on my way?'

Thus did he speak, and they feared the rebuke of their father. They brought out a strong mule-waggon, newly made, and set the body of the waggon fast on its bed. They took the mule-yoke from the peg on which it hung, a yoke of boxwood with a knob on the top of it and rings for the reins to go through. Then they brought a yoke-band eleven cubits long, to bind the yoke to the pole; they bound it on at the far end of the pole, and put the ring over the upright pin making it fast with three turns of the band on either side the knob, and bending the thong of the yoke beneath it. This done, they brought from the store-chamber the rich ransom that was to purchase the body of Hector, and they set it all orderly on the waggon; then they yoked the strong harness-mules which the Mysians had on a time given as a goodly present to Priam; but for Priam himself they yoked horses which the old king had bred, and kept for his own use.

Thus heedfully did Priam and his servant see to the yoking of their cars at the palace. Then Hecuba came to them all sorrowful, with a golden goblet of wine in her right hand, that they might make a drink-offering before they set out. She stood in front of the horses and said, 'Take this, make a drink-offering to father Jove, and since you are minded to go to the ships in spite of me, pray that you may come safely back from the hands of your enemies. Pray to the son of Saturn lord of the whirlwind, who sits on Ida and looks down over all Troy, pray him to send his swift messenger on your right hand, the bird of omen which is strongest and most dear to him of all birds, that you may see it with your own eyes and trust it as you go forth to the ships of the Danaans. If all-seeing Jove will not send you this messenger, however set upon it you may be, I would not have you go to the ships of the Argives.'

And Priam answered, 'Wife, I will do as you desire me; it is well to lift hands in prayer to Jove, if so be he may have mercy upon me.'

With this the old man bade the serving-woman pour pure water over his hands, and the woman came, bearing the water in a bowl. He washed his hands and took the cup from his wife; then he made the drink-offering and prayed, standing in the middle of the courtyard and turning his eyes to heaven. 'Father Jove,' he said, 'that rulest from Ida, most glorious and most great, grant that I may be received kindly and compassionately in the tents of Achilles; and send your swift messenger upon my right hand, the bird of omen which is strongest and most dear to you of all birds, that I may see it with my own eyes and trust it as I go forth to the ships of the Danaans.'

So did he pray, and Jove the lord of counsel heard his prayer. Forthwith he sent an eagle, the most unerring portent of all birds that fly, the dusky hunter that men also call the Black Eagle. His wings were spread abroad on either side as wide as the well-made and well-bolted door of a rich man's chamber. He came to them flying over the city upon their right hands, and when they saw him they were glad and their hearts took comfort within them. The old man made haste to mount his chariot, and drove out through the inner gateway and under the echoing gatehouse of the outer court. Before him went the mules drawing the four-wheeled waggon, and driven by wise Idæus; behind these were the horses, which the old man lashed with his whip and drove swiftly through the city, while his friends followed after, wailing and lamenting for him as though he were on his road to death. As soon as they had come down from the city and had reached the plain, his sons and sons-in-law who had followed him went back to Ilius.

But Priam and Idæus as they showed out upon the plain did not escape the ken of all-seeing Jove, who looked down upon the old man and pitied him; then he spoke to his son Mercury and said, 'Mercury, for it is you who are the most disposed to escort men on their way, and to hear those whom you will hear, go, and so conduct Priam to the ships of the Achæans that no other of the Danaans shall see him nor take note of him until he reach the son of Peleus.'

Thus he spoke and Mercury, guide and guardian, slayer of Argus, did as he was told. Forthwith he bound on his glittering golden sandals with which he could fly like the wind over land and sea; he took the wand with which he seals men's eyes in sleep, or wakes them just as he pleases, and flew holding it in his hand till he came to Troy and to the Hellespont. To look at, he was like a young man of noble birth in the hey-day of his youth and beauty with the down just coming upon his face.

Now when Priam and Idæus had driven past the great tomb of Ilius, they stayed their mules and horses that they might drink in the river, for the shades of night were falling, when, therefore, Idæus saw Mercury standing near them he said to Priam, 'Take heed, descendant of Dardanus; here is matter which demands consideration. I see a man who I think will presently fall upon us; let us fly with our horses, or at least embrace his knees and implore him to take compassion upon us.'

When he heard this the old man's heart failed him, and he was in great fear; he stayed where he was as one dazed, and the hair stood on end over his whole body; but the bringer of good luck came up to him and took him by the hand, saying, 'Whither, father, are you thus driving your mules and horses in the dead of night when other men are asleep? Are you not afraid of the fierce Achæans who are hard by you, so cruel and relentless? Should some one of them see you bearing so much treasure through the darkness of the flying night, what would not your state then be? you are no longer young, and he who is with you is too old to protect you from those who would attack you. For myself, I will do you no harm, and I will defend you from any one else, for you remind me of my own father.'

And Priam answered, 'It is indeed as you say, my dear son; nevertheless some god has held his hand over me, in that he has sent such a wayfarer as yourself to meet me so opportunely; you are so comely in mien and figure, and your judgement is so excellent that you must come of blessed parents.'

Then said the slayer of Argus, guide and guardian, 'Sir, all that you have said is right; but tell me and tell me true, are you taking this rich treasure to send it to a foreign people where it may be safe, or are you all leaving strong Ilius in dismay now that your son has fallen who was the bravest man among you and was never lacking in battle with the Achæans?'

And Priam said, 'Who are you, my friend, and who are your parents, that you speak so truly about the fate of my unhappy son?'

The slayer of Argus, guide and guardian, answered him, 'Sir, you would prove me, that you question me about noble Hector. Many a time have I set eyes upon him in battle when he was driving the Argives to their ships and putting them to the sword. We stood still and marvelled, for Achilles in his anger with the son of Atreus suffered us not to fight. I am his squire, and came with him in the same ship. I am a Myrmidon, and my father's name is Polyctor: he is a rich man and about as old as you are; he has six sons besides myself, and I am the seventh. We cast lots, and it fell upon me to sail hither with Achilles. I am now come from the ships on to the plain, for with daybreak the Achæans will set battle in array about the city. They chafe at doing nothing, and are so eager that their princes cannot hold them back.'

Then answered Priam, 'If you are indeed the squire of Achilles son of Peleus, tell me now the whole truth. Is my son still at the ships, or has Achilles hewn him limb from limb, and given him to his hounds?'

'Sir,' replied the slayer of Argus, guide and guardian, 'neither hounds nor vultures have yet devoured him; he is still just lying at the tents by the ship of Achilles, and though it is now twelve days that he has lain there, his flesh is not wasted nor have the worms eaten him although they feed on warriors. At daybreak Achilles drags him cruelly round the sepulchre of his dear comrade, but it does him no hurt. You should come yourself and see how he lies fresh as dew, with the blood all washed away, and his wounds every one of them closed though many pierced him with their spears. Such care have the blessed gods taken of your brave son, for he was dear to them beyond all measure.'

The old man was comforted as he heard him and said, 'My son, see what a good thing it is to have made due offerings to the immortals; for as sure as that he was born my son never forgot the gods that hold Olympus, and now they requite it to him even in death. Accept therefore at my hands this goodly chalice; guard me and with heaven's help guide me till I come to the tent of the son of Peleus.'

Then answered the slayer of Argus, guide and guardian, 'Sir, you are tempting me and playing upon my youth, but you shall not move me, for you are offering me presents without the knowledge of Achilles whom I fear and hold it great guiltiness to defraud, lest some evil presently befall me; but as your guide I would go with you even to Argos itself, and would guard you so carefully whether by sea or land, that no one should attack you through making light of him who was with you.'

The bringer of good luck then sprang on to the chariot, and seizing the whip and reins he breathed fresh spirit into the mules and horses. When they reached the trench and the wall that was before the ships, those who were on guard had just been getting their suppers, and the slayer of Argus threw them all into a deep sleep. Then he drew back the bolts to open the gates, and took Priam inside with the treasure he had upon his waggon. Ere long they came to the lofty dwelling of the son of Peleus for which the Myrmidons had cut pine and which they had built for their king; when they had built it they thatched it with coarse tussock-grass which they had mown out on the plain, and all round it they made a large court-yard, which was fenced with stakes set close together. The gate was barred with a single bolt of pine which it took three men to force into its place, and three to draw back so as to open the gate, but Achilles could draw it by himself. Mercury opened the gate for the old man, and brought in the treasure that he was taking with him for the son of Peleus. Then he sprang from the chariot on to the ground and said, 'Sir, it is I, immortal Mercury, that am come with you, for my father sent me to escort you. I will now leave you, and will not enter into the presence of Achilles, for it might anger him that a god should befriend mortal men thus openly. Go you within, and embrace the knees of the son of Peleus: beseech him by his father, his lovely mother, and his son; thus you may move him.'

With these words Mercury went back to high Olympus. Priam sprang from his chariot to the ground, leaving Idæus where he was, in charge of the mules and horses. The old man went straight into the house where Achilles, loved of the gods, was sitting. There he found him with his men seated at a distance from him: only two, the hero Automedon, and Alcimus of the race of Mars, were busy in attendance about his person, for he had but just done eating and drinking, and the table was still there. King Priam entered without their seeing him, and going right up to Achilles he clasped his knees and kissed the dread murderous hands that had slain so many of his sons.

As when some cruel spite has befallen a man that he should have killed some one in his own country, and must fly to a great man's protection in a land of strangers, and all marvel who see him, even so did Achilles marvel as he beheld Priam. The others looked one to another and marvelled also, but Priam besought Achilles saying, 'Think of your father, O Achilles like unto the gods, who is such even as I am, on the sad threshold of old age. It may be that those who dwell near him harass him, and there is none to keep war and ruin from him. Yet when he hears of you as being still alive, he is glad, and his days are full of hope that he shall see his dear son come home to him from Troy; but I, wretched man that I am, had the bravest in all Troy for my sons, and there is not one of them left. I had fifty sons when the Achæans came here; nineteen of them were from a single womb, and the others were borne to me by the women of my household. The greater part of them has fierce Mars laid low, and Hector, him who was alone left, him who was the guardian of our city and ourselves, him have you lately slain; therefore I am now come to the ships of the Achæans to ransom his body from you with a great ransom. Fear, O Achilles, the wrath of heaven; think on your own father and have compassion upon me, who am the more pitiable, for I have steeled myself as no man has ever yet steeled himself before me, and have raised to my lips the hand of him who slew my son.'

Thus spoke Priam, and the heart of Achilles yearned as he bethought him of his father. He took the old man's hand and moved him gently away. The two wept bitterly – Priam, as he lay at Achilles' feet, weeping for Hector, and Achilles now for his father and now for Patroclus, till the house was filled with their lamentation. But when Achilles was now sated with grief and had unburthened the bitterness of his sorrow, he left his seat and raised the old man by the hand, in pity for his white hair and beard; then he said, 'Unhappy man, you have indeed been greatly daring; how could you venture to come alone to the ships of the Achæans, and enter the presence of him who has slain so many of your brave sons? You must have iron courage; sit now upon this seat, and for all our grief we will hide our sorrows in our hearts, for weeping will not avail us. The immortals know no care, yet the lot they spin for man is full of sorrow; on the floor of Jove's palace there stand two urns, the one filled with evil gifts, and the other with good ones. He for whom Jove the lord of thunder mixes the gifts he sends, will meet now with good and now with evil fortune; but he to whom Jove sends none but evil gifts will be pointed at by the finger of scorn, the hand of famine will pursue him to the ends of the world, and he will go up and down the face of the earth, respected neither by gods nor men. Even so did it befall Peleus; the gods endowed him with all good things from his birth upwards, for he reigned over the Myrmidons excelling all men in prosperity and wealth, and mortal though he was they gave him a goddess for his bride. But even on him too did heaven send misfortune, for there is no race of royal children born to him in his house, save one son who is doomed to die all untimely; nor may I take care of him now that he is growing old, for I must stay here at Troy to be the bane of you and of your children. And you too, O Priam, I have heard that you were aforetime happy. They say that in wealth and plenitude of offspring you surpassed all that is in Lesbos, the realm of Makar to the northward, Phrygia that is more inland, and those that dwell upon the great Hellespont; but from the day when the dwellers in heaven sent this evil upon you, war and slaughter have been about your city continually. Bear up against it, and let there be some intervals in your sorrow. Mourn as you may for your brave son, you will take nothing by it. You cannot raise him from the dead, ere you do so yet another sorrow shall befall you.'

And Priam answered, 'O king, bid me not be seated, while Hector is still lying uncared for in your tents, but accept the great ransom which I have brought you, and give him to me at once that I may look upon him. May you prosper with the ransom and reach your own land in safety, seeing that you have suffered me to live and to look upon the light of the sun.'

Achilles looked at him sternly and said, 'Vex me, sir, no longer; I am of myself minded to give up the body of Hector. My mother, daughter of the old man of the sea, came to me from Jove to bid me deliver it to you. Moreover I know well, O Priam, and you cannot hide it, that some god has brought you to the ships of the Achæans, for else, no man however strong and in his prime would dare to come to our host; he could neither pass our guard unseen, nor draw the bolt of my gates thus easily; therefore, provoke me no further, lest I sin against the word of Jove, and suffer you not, suppliant though you are, within my tents.'

The old man feared him and obeyed. Then the son of Peleus sprang like a lion through the door of his house, not alone, but with him went his two squires Automedon and Alcimus who were closer to him than any others of his comrades now that Patroclus was no more. These unyoked the horses and mules, and bade Priam's herald and attendant be seated within the house. They lifted the ransom for Hector's body from the waggon, but they left two mantles and a goodly shirt, that Achilles might wrap the body in them when he gave it to be taken home. Then he called to his servants and ordered them to wash the body and anoint it, but he first took it to a place where Priam should not see it, lest if he did so, he should break out in the bitterness of his grief, and enrage Achilles, who might then kill him and sin against the word of Jove. When the servants had washed the body and anointed it, and had wrapped it in a fair shirt and mantle, Achilles himself lifted it on to a bier, and he and his men then laid it on the waggon. He cried aloud as he did so and called on the name of his dear comrade, 'Be not angry with me, Patroclus,' he said, 'if you hear even in the house of Hades that I have given Hector to his father for a ransom. It has been no unworthy one, and I will share it equitably with you.'

Achilles then went back into the tent and took his place on the richly inlaid seat from which he had risen, by the wall that was at right angles to the one against which Priam was sitting. 'Sir,' he said, 'your son is now laid upon his bier and is ransomed according to your desire;

you shall look upon him when you take him away at daybreak; for the present let us prepare our supper. Even lovely Niobe had to think about eating, though her twelve children – six daughters and six lusty sons – had been all slain in her house. Apollo killed the sons with arrows from his silver bow, to punish Niobe, and Diana slew the daughters, because Niobe had vaunted herself against Leto; she said Leto had borne two children only, whereas she had herself borne many – whereon the two killed the many. Nine days did they lie weltering, and there was none to bury them, for the son of Saturn turned the people into stone; but on the tenth day the gods in heaven themselves buried them, and Niobe then took food, being worn out with weeping. They say that somewhere among the rocks on the mountain pastures of Sipylus, where the nymphs live that haunt the river Acheloüs, there, they say, she lives in stone and still nurses the sorrows sent upon her by the hand of heaven. Therefore, noble sir, let us two now take food; you can weep for your dear son hereafter as you are bearing him back to Ilius – and many a tear will he cost you.'

With this Achilles sprang from his seat and killed a sheep of silvery whiteness, which his followers skinned and made ready all in due order. They cut the meat carefully up into smaller pieces, spitted them, and drew them off again when they were well roasted. Automedon brought bread in fair baskets and served it round the table, while Achilles dealt out the meat, and they laid their hands on the good things that were before them. As soon as they had had enough to eat and drink, Priam, descendant of Dardanus, marvelled at the strength and beauty of Achilles for he was as a god to see, and Achilles marvelled at Priam as he listened to him and looked upon his noble presence. When they had gazed their fill Priam spoke first. 'And now, O king,' he said, 'take me to my couch that we may lie down and enjoy the blessed boon of sleep. Never once have my eyes been closed from the day your hands took the life of my son; I have grovelled without ceasing in the mire of my stable-yard, making moan and brooding over my countless sorrows. Now, moreover, I have eaten bread and drunk wine; hitherto I have tasted nothing.'

As he spoke Achilles told his men and the women-servants to set beds in the room that was in the gatehouse, and make them with good red rugs, and spread coverlets on the top of them with woollen cloaks for Priam and Idæus to wear. So the maids went out carrying a torch and got the two beds ready in all haste. Then Achilles said laughingly to Priam, 'Dear sir, you shall lie outside, lest some counsellor of those who in due course keep coming to advise with me should see you here in the darkness of the flying night, and tell it to Agamemnon. This might cause delay in the delivery of the body. And now tell me and tell me true, for how many days would you celebrate the funeral rites of noble Hector? Tell me, that I may hold aloof from war and restrain the host.'

And Priam answered, 'Since, then, you suffer me to bury my noble son with all due rites, do thus, Achilles, and I shall be grateful. You know how we are pent up within our city; it is far for us to fetch wood from the mountain, and the people live in fear. Nine days, therefore, will we mourn Hector in my house; on the tenth day we will bury him and there shall be a public feast in his honour; on the eleventh we will build a mound over his ashes, and on the twelfth, if there be need, we will fight.'

And Achilles answered, 'All, King Priam, shall be as you have said. I will stay our fighting for as long a time as you have named.'

As he spoke he laid his hand on the old man's right wrist, in token that he should have no fear; thus then did Priam and his attendant sleep there in the forecourt, full of thought, while Achilles lay in an inner room of the house, with fair Briseis by his side.

And now both gods and mortals were fast asleep through the livelong night, but upon Mercury alone, the bringer of good luck, sleep could take no hold for he was thinking all the time how to get King Priam away from the ships without his being seen by the strong force of sentinels. He hovered therefore over Priam's head and said, 'Sir, now that Achilles has spared your life, you seem to have no fear about sleeping in the thick of your foes. You have paid a great ransom, and have received the body of your son; were you still alive and a prisoner the sons whom you have left at home would have to give three times as much to free you; and so it would be if Agamemnon and the other Achæans were to know of your being here.'

When he heard this the old man was afraid and roused his servant. Mercury then yoked their horses and mules, and drove them quickly through the host so that no man perceived them. When they came to the ford of eddying Xanthus, begotten of immortal Jove, Mercury went back to high Olympus, and dawn in robe of saffron began to break over all the land. Priam and Idæus then drove on towards the city lamenting and making moan, and the mules drew the body of Hector. No one neither man nor woman saw them, till Cassandra, fair as golden Venus standing on Pergamus, caught sight of her dear father in his chariot, and his servant that was the city's herald with him. Then she saw him that was lying upon the bier, drawn by the mules, and with a loud cry she went about the city saying, 'Come hither Trojans, men and women, and look on Hector; if ever you rejoiced to see him coming from battle when he was alive, look now on him that was the glory of our city and all our people.'

At this there was not man nor woman left in the city, so great a sorrow had possessed them. Hard by the gates they met Priam as he was bringing in the body. Hector's wife and his mother were the first to mourn him: they flew towards the waggon and laid their hands upon his head, while the crowd stood weeping round them. They would have stayed before the gates, weeping and lamenting the livelong day to the going down of the sun, had not Priam spoken to them from the chariot and said, 'Make way for the mules to pass you. Afterwards when I have taken the body home you shall have your fill of weeping.'

On this the people stood asunder, and made a way for the waggon. When they had borne the body within the house they laid it upon a bed and seated minstrels round it to lead the dirge, whereon the women joined in the sad music of their lament. Foremost among them all Andromache led their wailing as she clasped the head of mighty Hector in her embrace. 'Husband,' she cried, 'you have died young, and leave me in your house a widow; he of whom we are the ill-starred parents is still a mere child, and I fear he may not reach manhood. Ere he can do so our city will be razed and overthrown, for you who watched over it are no more – you who were its saviour, the guardian of our wives and children. Our women will be carried away captives to the ships, and I among them; while you, my child, who will be with me will be put to some unseemly tasks, working for a cruel master. Or, may be, some Achæan will hurl you (O miserable death) from our walls, to avenge some brother, son, or father whom Hector slew; many of them have indeed bitten the dust at his hands, for your father's hand in battle was no light one. Therefore do the people mourn him. You have left, O Hector, sorrow unutterable to your parents, and my own grief is greatest of all, for you did not stretch forth your arms and embrace me as you lay dying, nor say to me any words that might have lived with me in my tears night and day for evermore.'

Bitterly did she weep the while, and the women joined in her lament. Hecuba in her turn took up the strains of woe. 'Hector,' she cried, 'dearest to me of all my children. So long as you were alive the gods loved you well, and even in death they have not been utterly unmindful of you; for when Achilles took any other of my sons, he would sell him beyond the seas, to Samos, Imbrus, or rugged Lemnos; and when he had slain you too with his sword, many a time did he drag you round the sepulchre of his comrade – though this could not give him life – yet here you lie all fresh as dew, and comely as one whom Apollo has slain with his painless shafts.'

Thus did she too speak through her tears with bitter moan, and then Helen for a third time took up the strain of lamentation. 'Hector,' said she, 'dearest of all my brothers-in-law – for I am wife to Alexandrus who brought me hither to Troy – would that I had died ere he did so – twenty years are come and gone since I left my home and came from over the sea, but I have never heard one word of insult or unkindness from you. When another would chide with me, as it might be one of your brothers or sisters or of your brothers' wives, or my mother-in-law – for Priam was as kind to me as though he were my own father – you would rebuke and check them with words of gentleness and goodwill. Therefore my tears flow both for you and for my unhappy self, for there is no one else in Troy who is kind to me, but all shrink and shudder as they go by me.'

She wept as she spoke and the vast crowd that was gathered round her joined in her lament. Then King Priam spoke to them saying, 'Bring wood, O Trojans, to the city, and fear no cunning ambush of the Argives, for Achilles when he dismissed me from the ships gave me his word that they should not attack us until the morning of the twelfth day.'

Forthwith they yoked their oxen and mules and gathered together before the city. Nine days long did they bring in great heaps of wood, and on the morning of the tenth day with many tears they took brave Hector forth, laid his dead body upon the summit of the pile, and set the fire thereto. Then when the child of morning rosy-fingered dawn appeared on the eleventh day, the people again assembled, round the pyre of mighty Hector. When they were got together, they first quenched the fire with wine wherever it was burning, and then his brothers and comrades with many a bitter tear gathered his white bones, wrapped them in soft robes of purple, and laid them in a golden urn, which they placed in a grave and covered over with large stones set close together. Then they built a barrow hurriedly over it keeping guard on every side lest the Achæans should attack them before they had finished. When they had heaped up the barrow they went back again into the city, and being well assembled they held high feast in the house of Priam their king.

Thus, then, did they celebrate the funeral of Hector tamer of horses.

THE END

Endnotes

1 The aegis is the shield belonging to Jove or Minerva.
2 Sparta and Lacedæmon appear to be here treated as different places. This seeming error is repeated Od. iv 1 – 10, though the writer of the Odyssey is generally aware that Sparta and Lacedæmon are one place.
3 'Astyanax' means 'king of the city'.
4 'His son' is a reference to Hercules.
5 Cyanus is a type of deep blue glass paste or enamel.
6 A grip is a ditch.
7 A tripod is a cauldron standing on three feet.
8 The Linus-song is a lament sung by people harvesting corn or grapes, mourning the death of the crops being harvested. There are a number of myths relating to Linus, in one of which he is a musician who was killed by Apollo.
9 Orion's Hound is the Dog Star, Sirius.

THE
ODYSSEY

Contents

Translator's Note

The twenty-eighth English rendering of the Odyssey can hardly be a literary event, especially when it aims to be essentially a straightforward translation. Wherever choice offered between a poor and a rich word richness had it, to raise the colour. I have transposed: the order of metrical Greek being unlike plain English. Not that my English is plain enough. Wardour-Street Greek like the Odyssey's defies honest rendering. Also I have been free with moods and tenses; allowed myself to interchange adjective and adverb; and dodged our poverty of preposition, limitations of verb and pronominal vagueness by rearrangement. Still, syntax apart, this is a translation.

It has been made from the Oxford text, uncritically. I have not pored over contested readings, variants, or spurious lines. However scholars may question the text in detail, writers (and even would-be writers) cannot but see in the Odyssey a single, authentic, unedited work of art, integrally preserved. Thrice I noted loose ends, openings the author had forgotten: one sentence I would have shifted in time: five or six lines rang false to me: one speech seems to come before its context. These are motes in a book which is neat, close-knit, artful, and various; as nearly word-perfect as midnight oil and pumice can effect.

Crafty, exquisite, homogeneous – whatever great art may be, these are not its attributes. In this tale every big situation is burked and the writing is soft. The shattered Iliad yet makes a masterpiece; while the Odyssey by its ease and interest remains the oldest book worth reading for its story and the first novel of Europe. Gay, fine and vivid it is: never huge or terrible. Book XI, the Underworld, verges toward 'terribilità' – yet runs instead to the seed of pathos, that feeblest mode of writing. The author misses his every chance of greatness, as must all his faithful translators.

This limitation of the work's scope is apparently conscious. Epic belongs to early man, and this Homer lived too long after the heroic age to feel assured and large. He shows exact knowledge of what he could and could not do. Only through such superb self-criticism can talent rank beside inspiration.

In four years of living with this novel I have tried to deduce the author from his self-betrayal in the work. I found a book-worm, no longer young, living from home, a mainlander, city-bred and domestic. Married but not exclusively, a dog-lover, often hungry and thirsty, dark-haired. Fond of poetry, a great if uncritical reader of the Iliad, with limited sensuous range but an exact eyesight which gave him all his pictures. A lover of old bric-a-brac, though as muddled an antiquary as Walter Scott – in sympathy with which side of him I have conceded 'tenterhooks' but not railway-trains.

It is fun to compare his infuriating male condescension towards inglorious woman with his tender charity of head and heart for serving-men. Though a stickler for the prides of poets and a man who never misses a chance to cocker up their standing, yet he must be (like writers two thousand years after him) the associate of menials, making himself their friend and defender by understanding. Was it a fellow-feeling, or did he forestall time in his view of slavery?

He loved the rural scene as only a citizen can. No farmer, he had learned the points of a good olive tree. He is all adrift when it comes to fighting, and had not seen deaths in battle. He had sailed upon and watched the sea with a palpitant concern, seafaring being not his trade. As a minor sportsman he had seen wild boars at bay and heard tall yarns of lions.

Few men can be sailors, soldiers and naturalists. Yet this Homer was neither land-lubber nor stay-at-home nor ninny. He wrote for audiences to whom adventures were daily life and the sea their universal neighbour. So he dared not err. That famous doubled line where the Cyclops narrowly misses the ship with his stones only shows how much better a seaman he was than his copyist. Scholiasts have tried to riddle his technical knowledge – and of course he does make a hotch-potch of periods. It is the penalty of being pre-archaeological. His pages are steeped in a queer naïvety; and at our remove of thought and language we cannot guess if he is smiling or not. Yet there is a dignity which compels respect and baffles us, he being neither simple in education nor primitive socially. His generation so rudely admired the Iliad that even to misquote it was a virtue. He sprinkles tags of epic across his pages. In this some find humour. Rather I judge that here too the tight lips of archaic art have grown the fixed grin of archaism.

Very bookish, this house-bred man. His work smells of the literary coterie, of a writing tradition. His notebooks were stocked with purple passages and he embedded these in his tale wherever they would more or less fit. He, like William Morris, was driven by his age to legend, where he found men living untrammelled under the God-possessed skies. Only, with more verbal felicity than Morris', he had less poetry. Fashion gave him recurring epithets, like labels: but repetitions tell, in public speaking. For recitation, too, are the swarming speeches. A trained voice can put drama and incident into speeches. Perhaps the tedious delay of the climax through ten books may be a poor bard's means of prolonging his host's hospitality.

Obviously the tale was the thing; and that explains (without excusing it to our ingrown minds) his thin and accidental characterisation. He thumbnailed well; and afterwards lost heart. Nausicaa, for instance, enters dramatically and shapes, for a few lines, like a woman – then she fades, unused. Eumaeus fared better: but only the central family stands out, consistently and pitilessly drawn – the sly cattish wife, that cold-blooded egotist Odysseus, and the priggish son who yet met his master-prig in Menelaus. It is sorrowful to believe that these were really Homer's heroes and exemplars.

T.E. Shaw

O DIVINE POESY
GODDESS-DAUGHTER OF ZEUS
SUSTAIN FOR ME
THIS SONG OF THE VARIOUS-MINDED MAN
WHO AFTER HE HAD PLUNDERED
THE INNERMOST CITADEL OF HALLOWED TROY
WAS MADE TO STRAY GRIEVOUSLY
ABOUT THE COASTS OF MEN
THE SPORT OF THEIR CUSTOMS GOOD OR BAD
WHILE HIS HEART
THROUGH ALL THE SEA-FARING
ACHED IN AN AGONY TO REDEEM HIMSELF
AND BRING HIS COMPANY SAFE HOME

VAIN HOPE – FOR THEM
FOR HIS FELLOWS HE STROVE IN VAIN
THEIR OWN WITLESSNESS CAST THEM AWAY
THE FOOLS
TO DESTROY FOR MEAT
THE OXEN OF THE MOST EXALTED SUN
WHEREFORE THE SUN-GOD BLOTTED OUT
THE DAY OF THEIR RETURN

MAKE THE TALE LIVE FOR US
IN ALL ITS MANY BEARINGS
O MUSE

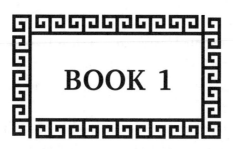

BOOK 1

By now the other warriors, those that had escaped headlong ruin by sea or in battle, were safely home. Only Odysseus tarried, shut up by Lady Calypso, a nymph and very Goddess, in her hewn-out caves. She craved him for her bed-mate: while he was longing for his house and his wife. Of a truth the rolling seasons had at last brought up the year marked by the Gods for his return to Ithaca; but not even there among his loved things would he escape further conflict. Yet had all the Gods with lapse of time grown compassionate towards Odysseus – all but Poseidon, whose enmity flamed ever against him till he had reached his home. Poseidon, however, was for the moment far away among the Aethiopians, that last race of men, whose dispersion across the world's end is so broad that some of them can see the Sun-God rise while others see him set. Thither had Poseidon gone in the hope of burnt offerings, bulls and rams, by hundreds: and there he sat feasting merrily while the other Gods came together in the halls of Olympian Zeus. To them the father of Gods and men began speech, for his breast teemed with thought of great Aegisthus, whom famous Orestes, the son of Agamemnon, had slain.

'It vexes me to see how mean are these creatures of a day towards us Gods, when they charge against us the evils (far beyond our worst dooming) which their own exceeding wantonness has heaped upon themselves. Just so did Aegisthus exceed when he took to his bed the lawful wife of Atrides and killed her returning husband. He knew the sheer ruin this would entail. Did we not warn him by the mouth of our trusty Hermes, the keen-eyed slayer of Argus, neither to murder the man nor lust after the woman's body? "For the death of the son of Atreus will be requited by Orestes, even as he grows up and dreams of his native place." These were Hermes' very words: but not even such friendly interposition could restrain Aegisthus, who now pays the final penalty.'

Swiftly there took him up Athene, goddess of the limpid eyes. 'Our Father, heir of Kronos, Lord of lords! That man Aegisthus has been justly served. May everyone who slaughters a victim after his fashion go down likewise into hell! But my heart is heavy for Odysseus, so shrewd, so ill-fated, pining in long misery of exile on an island which is just a speck in the belly of the sea. This wave-beset, wooded island is the domain of a God-begotten creature, the daughter of baleful Atlas whose are the pillars that prop the lofty sky: whose too are the deepest soundings of the sea. The daughter has trapped the luckless wretch and with subtle insistence cozens him to forget his Ithaca. Forget! Odysseus is so sick with longing to see if it were but the smoke of his home spiring up, that he prays for death. I marvel, my Lord of Olympus, how your heart makes no odds of it. Can you lightly pass over the burnt offerings Odysseus lavished upon you, by the Argive ships in the plain of Troy?'

'My child,' protested Zeus, the cloud-compeller, 'what sharp judgements you let slip through your teeth! As if I could overpass the merit of Odysseus, who stands out above the ruck of men as much for worldly wisdom as for his generous offerings to the Gods that eternally possess the open sky. It is Poseidon the world-girdler who is so headily bitter against him, for the sake of that Cyclops whom Odysseus blinded, even the god-like Polyphemus, their chief figure and Poseidon's very son: – for his mother Thoosa (daughter to Phorkys, an overlord of the ungarnered sea) conceived him after she had lain with the God under the beetling cliffs. Because of this, Poseidon the land-shaker, though he dare not quite kill Odysseus, at least implacably frustrates his every effort to get back to the land of his fathers. But come, let us put all our heads together and contrive the man's return; then will Poseidon have to swallow his bile. Against the concert of the Immortals he cannot stand alone.'

Athene the clear-eyed, the Goddess, answered and said: 'Father and Lord of all, Kronides, if indeed the ineffable Gods now judge it fit that prudent Odysseus should return, then let us call Hermes, our usher, the killer of Argus, and despatch him straight to Ogygia, the island of that nymph with the lovely hair: to warn her how it is become our fixed act that the dauntless one be allowed to set out homeward forthwith. For my part I shall go to Ithaca and rouse his son Telemachus, instilling some tardy purpose into his spirit, so that he may call his Greek exquisites to council and give check to the mob of wooers besetting his mother Penelope, the while they butcher his wealth of juicy sheep and rolling-gaited, screw-horned oxen. I will send the youth to Sparta – yes, and to sandy Pylos – to ask those he meets for news of his dear father's return: not that he will hear anything, but his zeal will earn him repute among men.'

She ceased, and drew upon her feet those golden sandals (whose fairness no use could dim) that carried their mistress as surely and wind-swiftly over the waves as over the boundless earth. She laid hold of her guardian spear, great, heavy, and close-grained, tipped with cutting bronze. When wrath moved the goddess to act, this spear was her weapon: with it, and stayed by her pride of birth, she would daunt serried ranks of the very bravest warriors. Downward she now glided from the summit of Olympus, to alight on Ithaca before Odysseus' house, by the sill of the main gate. With that war spear in her fist she seemed some traveller seeking hospitality: she had a look of Mentes, a chief in Taphos.

The gateway was thronged with the self-assertive suitors, whose pleasure for the moment was to sit there playing at chequers on the hides of the oxen they had killed and eaten. Round them bustled their criers and nimble pages, some mixing wine and water in the parent-bowls ready to drink, others wiping down table-tops with soft sponges or re-laying them for the next meal, while yet others were jointing huge sides of meat. If the suitors saw her they did not move or look before handsome Telemachus gave sign. He sat despondent in the hurly, fancying to himself his honest father's sudden arrival from somewhere, somehow: and the scatter there would be, through the palace, of these wasters when they saw him stride in to regain men's respect and king it honourably once more over his household.

As he so dreamed amidst the unheeding suitors he became aware of Athene waiting by the threshold; and went straight to her, vexed to the heart that any guest should be delayed at their door for lack of welcome. He clasped her right hand, relieving her of the metal spear, and spoke to her these winged words: 'Accept, O guest, the friendliest greetings. Enter and taste our food: and thereafter make known to us your every need.'

Whereupon he led the way into the noble house. Pallas followed until he set her spear in the polished spear rack beside a high pillar, amongst weapons once used by the long-suffering Odysseus. Then he spread smooth draperies over a throne of cunning workmanship and seated her upon it. For her feet there was a foot-stool, while for himself he drew up a painted lounge-chair in such a way that they were shut off from the suitors. Telemachus feared lest that roistering mob's impertinences might disgust the stranger and turn his stomach against eating. Then too he wished to put some privy questions about his missing father.

A maid came with a precious golden ewer and poured water for them above its silver basin, rinsing their hands. She drew to their side a gleaming table and on it the matronly house-keeper arranged her store of bread and many prepared dishes, making an eager grace of all the hospitality. A carver filled and passed them trenchers of meat in great variety, and set out on their table two golden beakers which the steward, as often as he walked up and down the hall, refilled for them with wine. The suitors swaggered in. One after the other they seated themselves on the thrones and long chairs. Their retainers poured water for their hands, and the maids of the house heaped loaves of bread in each man's table-basket while the serving lads brimmed the wine-cisterns with drink. Every hand went out to the abundance so laid ready.

But when their lusting for food and drink had been assuaged the suitors began to mind them of other things; of singing and dancing, those twin glories which crown a feast. The steward returned with a very splendid lyre for Phemius, whose hap it was to play the bard for them, under compulsion. He ran his hands over the strings, plucking out an exquisite air, under cover of which Telemachus bent towards clear-eyed Athene and said softly, that the company might not overhear: –

'Honoured stranger, will my words offend? I pray not. They now have their minds easy for music and verse, these suitor-maggots who freely devour another man's livelihood. Freely indeed, without let or fine! Ah, if they did but catch a glimpse of the Master returning to Ithaca, how they would beseech high heaven for the gift of swifter running rather than more wealth in gold or raiment. But alas, his bones whiten to-day in some field under the rain: or the swell rolls them through the salty deep. Yea, he has perished dreadfully: nor would a glow of hope kindle in our hearts if the wisest man on earth told us he was coming home. The sun of his return has utterly gone down.

'Enough of this – instead, tell me, I pray you, and exactly, who you are: of what state and stock? You came, I suspect, by ship; for I am very sure that by dry land you found no road. But what were the sailors who put you ashore in Ithaca, or rather, what did they profess themselves to be? I ask all this in order to satisfy myself that you are really a new-comer, tasting our hospitality for the first time, and not a guest entailed on us by my father: for so great a traveller was he, you know, that our house is honoured by throngs of his acquaintance from every land.'

Then said the clear-eyed Goddess, 'I will meet all these questions of yours frankly. My name is Mentes. My father Anchialus was a noted warrior. I am a leader of the oar-loving islanders of Taphos. I put in here with my ship and crew on our way across the wine-dark sea to

Temesa, where we hope to barter a cargo of sparkling iron ore for the copper of those foreign-speaking people. My ship is berthed well away from the city, in Reithron, that lonely inlet which lies below tree-grown Neion.

'Between our families there is a long tradition of friendship and guesting, which father Laertes will confirm, if you ask him: though they tell me that he now comes no more to town, because of the infirmities of his advanced years. Wherefore he buries himself in his secluded vineyard, among his vine-stocks on their ordered terraces: up and down which the old man drags himself, slow step after step, cherishing the grapes, until the feebleness of age once again takes him sorely by the knees. Then he rests, for the old woman, his sole attendant, to wait on him with restoring meat and drink.

'And the reason for my present visit? Because I heard that he was back. I mean your father: for be assured that the marvellous Odysseus has in no wise perished off the face of the earth: though it seems the Gods yet arrest him in midpath of his return. And therefore (albeit I am by trade no teller of fortunes, nor professed reader of the significance of birds), therefore I am about to prophesy to you what the Deathless Ones have put into my heart and made my faith: – namely, that the day of Odysseus' coming again to his native place is near. He may be penned within some surf-beaten islet ringed by the wide sea: or some rude tribe of savages may hold him in durance. But only for the time. Infallibly he will find means of escape, though they fetter him in fetters of the purest iron. The man is fertility itself in his expedients. – Now tell me something, plainly, as I have told you. Are you real and very son to Odysseus, you who are so well grown of body? His head and fine eyes you have exactly, as I remember him in our old association; for we were much together in the days before he set out for Troy in the hollow ships with all the chivalry of Greece; since when we have not met.'

Careful Telemachus answered thus: 'Indeed you shall have it very plain, my friend. My mother says I am his son: for myself I do not know. Has any son of man yet been sure of his begetting? Would that I had been the child of some ordinary parent whom old age had overtaken in the quiet course of nature on his estate! But as it is, since you press it, they do name me the child of that vaguest-fated of all men born to death.'

Athene put to him one more question. 'I think when Penelope conceived so goodly a son it was meant that the Gods had not appointed a nameless future for your stock. But give me the straight truth again. What feast or rout of a feast is this which rages about us? What part in it have you? Is it a drinking bout or some sort of marriage? No sodality would be thus indecent. A mannered man now, entering by chance, might well forget himself with disgust at seeing how outrageously they make free with your house.'

Soberly Telemachus answered her again, saying, 'Stranger, since you probe into this also and put it to me, I must confess that our house looked to be rich and well-appointed while my father ruled it as master. But the Gods saw fit to order it quite otherwise when they spirited him away with an utterness beyond example. Had he plainly died I should not have taken it so hardly: above all had he died with his likes on the field of Troy in his friends' arms, after winding up the pitch of battle to its height. For then the fellowship of Greece would have united to rear his funerary mound and the fame of his prowess would have been (for his son) a glorious, increasing heritage.

'Instead we have this instant vanishment into blind silence, as though the Harpies, winged Scavengers of the Wind, had whirled him into their void: and I am left weeping with pain. Nor do I weep only his pain. The Gods have gone on to invent other evils for my count. Every man of authority in the islands, from Doulichion, and Same, and Zacynthos of the woods, as well as every figure of this rugged Ithaca – all, all, are come wooing my mother. It seems that she can neither reject the horrible offers, out and out, nor accept any one of them. So here they sit, for ever eating up my substance and making havoc of the house. Surely soon they will devour me too.'

Athene heard him out and then said fiercely, 'A shameful tale! Here's a crying need for Odysseus, to man-handle these graceless suitors. Would that he might appear now in the outer gate, erect, helmeted, with shield and two stabbing spears, the figure of a man I saw enter our house the first time we entertained him on his way up from Ephyra. He had been down in his war-vessel to get from Ilus, son of Mermerus, some deadly poison to smear on the bronze heads of his arrows. Ilus feared to affront the everlasting Gods and refused him any. So it was my father, carried away by the huge love he bore him, who furnished it. If only that Odysseus we knew might to-day thrust in among the suitors! Indeed their mating would be bitter and their shrift suddenly sharp. However such things rest on the knees of the Gods, whose it is to appoint whether he shall re-enter his halls and exact vengeance, or no.

'Wherefore instead I counsel you to take most earnest thought in what way you shall by your single self expel the suitors from the house. Listen to this plan of mine which I would urge upon you. Tomorrow assemble all the Greek chiefs. Address them bluntly, calling the Gods to witness how you order; firstly, that the suitors disperse, every man to his place; and secondly, that your mother (if her nature yet inclines toward marriage) betake herself to the palace of the mighty man her father. It shall be for them, there, to make the new match for her, regulating rich dues and providing such wedding festivities as befit the alliance of a favourite daughter.

'There remains your personal duty, on which also I have a word to say, if you will hear it. Get yourself a ship of twenty rowers, the very best ship you can find. Set forth in this to seek news of your long-overdue father. Even if no mortal tells you anything, yet who knows but there may steal into your mind that divine prompting by which Zeus very often gives mankind an inkling of the truth. Go to Pylos first and consult its revered Nestor; thence to Sparta where you will find brown-haired Menelaus, latest of all the mail-clad Achaeans to get back from Troy. If you learn that your father is living and has his face towards home, then steel your temper to one more year of this afflicted house. But if you learn that he is no more – that he is surely dead – then return and throw up a mound to his name, with the plenishing and ceremonial befitting a great fallen warrior: after which do you yourself give his widow, your mother, to some man for wife.

'These things first. Yet also it must be your study and passion to slay these suitors in your house, either by fair fight or by stratagem. Childishness no longer beseems your years: you must put it away. My friend (I wish to call you that, for you are man in frame and very man in form), my friend, be brave, that generations not yet born may glorify your name. Consider young Orestes and the honour he has won in all men's mouths by putting to death his father's murderer, the crafty blood-boltered Aegisthus who trapped noble Agamemnon. No more – I must back to my swift ship: its waiting crew will be grumbling because I have delayed them all this weary while. Only a parting word – make it your instant and main effort to do as I have said.'

Heedful Telemachus replied, 'Sir, the kindness of your advice to me has been like a father's to his son: and I will ever gratefully remember it. But I beg you, however urgent your business, to delay your setting out till you have bathed and refreshed yourself. Then go to your ship, spirit-gladdened, with a gift from me in your hand: for it shall be a worthy gift to remind you of me always: some very beautiful treasure such as only great friend gives to friend.'

The Goddess Athene, the clear-eyed, refused him. 'Do not try to hold me. I long to be on the way. As for this token which your friendly interest prompts, let it be mine on the return journey when I can carry it straight home. Choose your richest gift. It shall be matched by what I give you in exchange' – and having so said she went, suddenly and elusively as a sea bird goes; leaving the young man quick with ardour and decision and more mindful of his father than ever of late. Telemachus, as he felt this change come to his spirit, was amazed. The persuasion took him that his visitant had been in some way divine. Accordingly his carriage as he went once more among the suitors reflected God-head.

To that audience the great singer still sang: and they sat round, hanging on the song which told of the woeful return entailed by Pallas Athene upon such Greeks as had gone to Troy. In her upper storey, Penelope, that most circumspect daughter of Icarius, caught rising snatches of the minstrelsy. Her wit pieced these together into their sense. Down she came by the high stairs from her quarters and entered the great hall: not indeed alone, for always two waiting women closely followed her. So, like a stately goddess among mortals, she descended upon the suitors: to halt there where the first great pillar propped the massy roof. As veil for her face she held up a fold of her soft wimple: and the ever watchful maidens covered her, one on either side. Thus stood she and wept, till she found words to address the inspired bard.

'Phemius,' she cried, 'do you not know many other charmed songs for people's ears? Songs in which poets have extolled the great deeds of Gods or men? Sing one of those, here from your place in the company which will, none the less, sit silently drinking and listening. But this lamentable tale give over: the sorrow of it slowly melts my heart within my bosom; for you tell of the event which has brought down upon me – me above all women – this unappeasable pain. So continually does my memory yearn after that dear head. O my lost hero! whose glory had spread throughout Hellas and Argos, the very heart of the land!'

Telemachus decently cut her short. 'My Mother, why take it amiss that our trusty singer should entertain us as the spirit moves him? I think it is not poets who bring things to pass, but rather Zeus who pays out to men, the Makers, their fates at his whim: we have no cause against Phemius for drawing music out of the hard fate of the Danaans. A crowd ever extols the song which sounds freshest in its ears. Harden your heart and mind to hear this tale. Remember that Odysseus was not singular in utterly losing at Troy the day of his return. There were others, many others, who in the Troad lost their very selves. Wherefore I bid you get back to your part of the house, and be busied in your proper sphere, with the loom and the spindle, and in overseeing your maids at these, their tasks. Speech shall be the men's care: and principally my care: for mine is the mastery in this house.' She, astonished, went back up the stairs, laying away in her breast this potent saying of her son's. But when she had regained the upper storey with her serving women she began to weep for Odysseus her lost husband, and wept until the grey-eyed Goddess Athene cast a pitying sleep upon her eyelids.

Behind her back the wooers broke into riot across the twilit hall, everyone swearing aloud that his should be the luck of lying in her bed: but to them the dispassionate Telemachus began, 'Suitors of my mother and lewd ruffians: – tonight let us forgather and feast: but no shouting, please, to spoil our privilege of hearing this singer with the divine voice. Tomorrow I vote we go early to the assembly and all take seat there. I have to unburden my soul to you formally and without stint on the subject of your quitting this house: and to suggest that you remember your own banqueting halls in which you may eat your own food-stuffs and feast each other in rotation from house to house. But if you deem it meeter and more delightful to waste the entire substance of a solitary man, scot-free and for nothing – why then, waste away! Only I shall pray to the Gods – the ever-lasting Gods – on the chance that Zeus may decree acts of requital. In which case you will all be destroyed in this house, scot-free and for nothing.'

So he spoke: and they curbed their lips between their teeth to contain their astonishment at Telemachus' daring to taunt them with such spirit. At last Antinous, son of Eupeithes, undertook to reply. 'Why, Telemachus, those very Gods must have been giving you lessons in freedom of speech and heady taunting! All the same I doubt Zeus ever making you king of sea-girt Ithaca, even if that dignity does happen to be your birth-right.'

Said Telemachus with restraint, 'Antinous, take not my words against the grain. If Zeus willed it I would assume even that charge ungrudgingly. You imply it is the worst thing that could happen amongst us men? Let me tell you it is not so bad a fate to be King: quickly does a royal house grow rich, and himself amass honour. However, since the mighty Odysseus is dead, surely this headship will fall to some one of the swarm of kings young and old now infesting this land of Ithaca. My determination and aims are bounded by this house – to be lord in it and over its bond-servants whom the triumphant might of Odysseus led in from his forays as thralls.'

Eurymachus son of Polybus then put in his word. 'Telemachus, the question of which Greek shall reign over this island lies on the lap of the Gods. Yet assuredly you shall possess your belongings and have the lordship in your own houses: nor against your will shall any man come and strip you of them forcibly while Ithaca holds an inhabitant. But my good lad, let me question you about that visitor of yours who slipped away so suddenly that none of us had time to make him out. Yet his face was not the face of a negligible man. Whence came he and what country gave he as his own? Where do his kindred live and where are the corn-lands of his family? Did he come with news of your father, or on some business of his own?'

Discreetly Telemachus reassured him: 'Eurymachus, the time of my father's return is long over. I do not now credit any messages regarding him, whatever their source. Nor does any soothsaying take me in: though my mother may at whiles call some noted diviner to the palace and seek sooth of him. As for the stranger, he is a former friend of our family from Taphos called Mentes, whose father was old wise-minded Anchialus. Mentes is a man of authority among the seafaring Taphians.' So he said: but secretly Telemachus was sure of the immortal Goddess. Howbeit the suitors turned to dance and to the enthralling song, making merry while the evening drew down; and they celebrated until evening had darkened into night. Then the longing for sleep took them and they scattered, each man to the house where he lodged.

The mind of Telemachus was perplexedly brooding over many things as he also sought his bed within his own room, which was contrived in the highest part of the main building, that stately landmark of the country-side. Eurycleia the daughter of Ops son of Peisenor, attended him, lighting his way with flaring slips of pine-wood – Eurycleia the trusted, the adept, who, in the flush of her youth, had been bought by Laertes, out of his great wealth, for the price of twenty oxen. In the house Laertes had esteemed her even as his beloved wife, but never dared have intercourse with her, fearing the temper of his wife. Of all the servants it was Eurycleia who most loved Telemachus, for she had nursed him when he was a tiny child. Accordingly it was she who lighted him to his well-built room.

He flung open its doors and sat himself on the couch. There he pulled off his long clinging tunic, which the old woman received into her skillful hands and folded and patted into smoothness before she hung it on the clothes-peg beside his fretted, inlaid bedstead. Then she quitted the chamber, pulling-to the door after her by the silver beak which served as handle and sliding the bolt across by its leathern thong. And there Telemachus lay all night, wrapped in a choice fleece, pondering in his heart how he should compass the journey enjoined upon him by Athene.

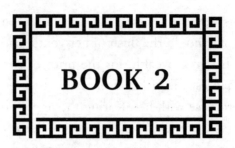

BOOK 2

So soon as rosy-fingered morning came forth from the first grey dawn, the beloved son of Odysseus sprang from bed, dressed, threw the sling of his cutting sword over one shoulder, and tied the rich sandals round his nimble feet: stately as a God he stepped out and down from his bed-chamber. On the moment he had called his heralds and told them to sound, with their ringing voices, the assembly amongst the long-haired Achaeans. As he bade, the heralds sounded: and as they bade, the Achaeans assembled speedily. Telemachus waited till all had come together into place and then, tightly gripping his copper-bladed spear, he strode through their throng. For company he had just his two flashing-footed dogs at heel: but Athene poured about his form so significant a glory that upon his approach the eyes of the crowd were held at gaze. The elders yielded him way and in his father's great chair he sat him down.

Debate was opened by honoured Aegyptius, an aged councillor of ten thousand wiles, whose years bowed him double. He was quick to speak because his favourite son, Antiphos, expert with the spear, had gone away with Odysseus in the capacious ships to Ilios, that land of good horses. To tell truth, Antiphos was even now dead, barbarously slain in the vaulted cave by the Cyclops, who had cooked him, too, and eaten him for his latest, and his last, feast. Aegyptius had yet three other sons. One of them, Eurynomus, had thrown in his lot with the suitors; and two kept the house, helping with the husbandry: but the consolation of these did not still the old man's inward aching and outward lamentation for the one who had not returned. Therefore it was that he now rose up and spoke through his tears: –

'Hear now, O men of Ithaca, and attend my words. Never once since the day that mighty Odysseus sailed from us in his ribbed ships, has our assembly met in session. Who is now our convenor? Is some one of the new generation in extreme urgency? Or one of us elders? Perhaps an army approaches, of which a man has had warning and would make us share his certain knowledge? Or is it some matter touching the common weal, which he would disclose and expound? Anyway I judge his zeal timely: may the event turn to his advantage, and Zeus ensure him the good thing for which his soul yearns.' – Thus far: and the dear son of Odysseus rejoiced at the auspicious phrase. The longing to deliver his mind pricked him to his feet in the midst of the gathering. Peisenor the herald, past master by experience of public conduct, thrust into his hands the gavel which gave right to speak: and Telemachus began, addressing himself first to the old councillor.

'Venerable Sir, the man who convened the people is not far to seek. Here he stands, in your eye. I am compelled to action by the burden of my pains. I have no word of any army coming, no advance or exclusive news affecting that or the common estate. The need, the motive, is personal. A two-headed evil has stricken me and struck my house. I have lost my noble father who was once your king, the king of all present: but also my very gentle father. And upon this harm comes far heavier harm, one which bodes the early wasting of my home and an utter ruin of my livelihood.

'My reluctant mother is plagued by suitors, sons of the leading men in this and other islands. Their honest course would be to interview her father, Icarius, and ask him to fix his daughter's marriage terms and give her to the man he liked or found fittest from among them. But they shrink in a twitter from such plain dealing. Instead they have fallen to haunting our place day after day, at the expense of my sleek cattle. Oxen and sheep and goats must be sacrificed to feast their greed. They gulp our wine – stuff with the glint of sunlight in it – like ordinary drink. Everything is being spent.

'Odysseus, now, was a man who could defend his house against the spoiler: but there is nothing of his build about us. So long as we live we shall remain feebly untrained bodies, incapable of such defence. Not for want of willing: it is strength I lack, to meet this intolerable provocation; the grim, slow sack of my innocent house. Will not a fellow-feeling for people who are living beside you, neighbours, make you share their vexation and ashamedly pity their plight? Pray you, Sirs, begin to fear the anger of the Gods a little, lest they be aghast at the evil already wrought and turn to requite it. I beseech you by Olympian Zeus, and by Themis, in whose justice courts like this are gathered together and, after session, released. No. Rather, my friends, let me be. Leave me to wear myself out with the misery of my own grief. Perhaps Odysseus, the father who was so good to me, in reality hated his panoplied Greeks and did them deliberate injuries; which you now in turn deliberately repay by cheering on my afflictors. Better hap for me, by far, if yours were the appetites emptying my storehouses and byres. For then how soon there would be a counter-stroke! We should go through the city with our tale, clinging as suppliants to all we met, demanding our monies, till everything had been given back. But as it is, you heap up in my heart these irremediable pains.'

So he spoke through his gathering rage: and here, in a gust of tears, he flung the gavel to the ground. The audience were seized with pity and sat still and silent, all of them, lacking face to return angry words to these words of Telemachus. Finally Antinous gave tongue as follows: –

'Your lost temper and haughty lips, Telemachus, conspire to smirch our conduct and link us with disgrace. Yet I tell you it is not the suitors who are guilty, among the Achaeans, but your respected mother, that far-fetched artful mistress. For these three years – nay, longer: in the fourth year now – she has rapt away the wits of the Achaean men. She has led every one of us to hope, given each his privy assurance, let fall little messages: while her heart all this while has been harbouring quite other designs. One trick her subtlety devised was to instal in her apartments a huge loom, and set up on this a fine wide weave; and ever she would say to us, "Sweet hearts, go slow. Allay your burning intent to have me married. The death of royal Odysseus lays on me the duty of completing this linen shroud, to save its gossamer threads from being scattered to the winds. It is for the burial of Laertes, the aged hero: and it must be ready against the inevitable day when fate will pull him to the ground and death measure out his length. If I leave it undone, and in consequence the corpse of this old, once-wealthy man lie bare of cerement, I shall be the pointing-block of every Achaean woman within our neighbourhood."

'So she protested, and our manly hearts credited her tale. Daily she laboured at the vast loom, weaving: but each night she had torches brought in and unravelled the day's woof. Thus for the space of three years she deceived us and cheated the Achaeans: but when the fourth year was wearing through its sequence of seasons one of her maids, who knew the whole truth, told on her. Then we caught her in the act of unpicking the glorious web: and forced her against her inclination to finish it right off. Hear, therefore, Telemachus, the suitors' reply to you: hear and understand it to the bottom of your heart, and all the people of this country with you. Send away your mother. Order her to be wedded straightway, as her father will command, to the man who best pleases her.

'But if, instead, she insists on continuing to wreak havoc among the bachelors of Achaea, then let her do so – at the price. Athene has bestowed on her an armoury of graces (skill in all the housewifely crafts, and such arts and airs as her guileful wit adeptly turns to personal advantage) beyond parallel among the famous beauties of old time: not Alcmene, nor Tyro, nor diademed Mycene could match this Penelope in intriguing charm. Yet, for the time, you shall see that her intrigues are not opportune. The suitors will swallow up your goods and sustenance for just so long as she persists in this frowardness which heaven has let possess her mind. She gains her notoriety: you regret your substance, vainly lost. We shall not go about our business nor go home till she has made her choice and been married to some one of us Achaeans.'

With measured words Telemachus answered him. 'Antinous, in no way can I forcibly expel from our house the mother who bore me and gave me nourishment. Besides, there is my father somewhere in the earth – if he lives – or perhaps he is dead. At any rate, consider the terrible expense if mine were the hand which put her away: I should have to pay back her dowry to Icarius. And to what end? I should be evilly entreated by her father. More evil would fall on me from above, for as she was driven from our door my mother would imprecate against me the dread furies. Also my fellow-men would condemn me out of their mouths. So I shall never stoop to give her such order.

'But listen – you and the other suitors. Do our family affairs jar your sense of niceness? Then get out of my guest-quarters. Arrange to entertain each other from your own resources, turn and turn about among your houses. Yet, if you find it pleasanter and better to go on scathelessly destroying the entire livelihood of a lone man – then go on. Meanwhile I shall be praying to the everlasting Gods, if perchance Zeus may grant that due penalties be paid. For then will our house, unscathed, see all of you destroyed within its walls.'

So did Telemachus invoke Zeus: and the All-seeing, in answer to his prayer, sent forth two eagles from his mountain top. Swift as the storm-blast they flew, wing-tip to wing in lordly sweep of pinions, until they were over the midmost of the many-tongued assembly. There they wheeled in full flight, with quivering, outstretched, strong wings, and glazed down with fatal eyes upon the upturned faces. Next they ripped with tearing claws, each at the other's head and neck, swooping quickly to the right over the houses of the citizens. So long as eye could follow them everyone stood wondering at the birds and musing what future history this sign from heaven could mean.

While they mused came the voice of Halitherses, son of Mastor, an elder of great standing who surpassed all his generation in science of bird-reading and the foretelling of dooms. Out of this deep of knowledge he now held forth: 'Hear me, islanders of Ithaca: hear me out. Especially the suitors, for what I portend concerns them most. Great evils are rolling down upon them. Odysseus will not longer remain sundered from his people. Even now, it may be, he approaches, carrying within him the seeds of bloody doom for every suitor. He will be deadly, too, for many others of us substantial men in this island of the pellucid skies. Wherefore before the event let us devise a plan by which the offence of the suitors shall be removed – unless they forthwith remove their own offence, which, did they study their interests, would be their wiser choice.

'I speak of what I know surely. This is not my first essay in divination. Everything has come to pass of what I prophesied to Odysseus, when that resourceful leader was sailing for Ilios with the Argive host. I foretold that after enduring many disasters and the loss by death of his whole fellowship, he would at the last find himself again made free of a home, where no one knew his face, in the twentieth year from his setting out: and today all this mounts to its fulfilment.'

Him, in turn, Eurymachus son of Polybus denied. 'Come, come, dotard. You will do better to stay at home and prophesy to your children, saving them from this wrath to come. In practical affairs I am the master-prophet. Multitudes of birds flit hither and thither in our bright sunshine: but not all bear messages from heaven. Odysseus, of whom you prate, died long ago and far enough away. If only you had gone and died with him! Then we should have escaped these oracles of yours, and you would not have had this chance of perhaps making future capital for your family by egging on the vexed Telemachus to publish his griefs.

'Yet, I fear, your family will never receive from him the reward you envisage. I am about to speak hardly: but what I say shall surely be. When an elder of long and wide worldly experience prostitutes his stored wisdom to abet a young man's anger; then, in first instance, the consequences are very grievous for the young man, who finds himself impotent to bend his hearers to his will. And secondly, for you too, Ancient, the regrets will be bitter. Upon you we shall lay such fine as will make your heart ache to pay it.

'Now, before you all, I have advice for Telemachus. He must order this mother of his back to her parents, for them to decide her re-marriage and assess the sumptuous interchange of gifts which go with a dear daughter. I assure you that till then the cadets of the Achaeans will not desist from their irksome and exigent wooing. Why should they? We fear no one on earth: certainly not Telemachus with his bluster. Nor are we to be moved by the soothsayings which you, old man, mouth over at us, without end – save to make yourself ever more generally detested. Telemachus' goods shall be ruthlessly devoured, and no fair deal come his way while Penelope thwarts the people in this matter of her re-marriage and keeps us dancing attendance on her, day in, day out; our passions too excited by the chance of winning so admirable a bride to cultivate any of the ordinary women who would make us fitting mates.'

'Eurymachus,' said Telemachus in deliberate reply, 'I will not re-open entreaties or discussion upon this subject, with you or any other arrogant suitor. We have deferred our case, in fullest detail, to the Gods: and made it known to all the Achaeans. Instead, I now ask you for a clean-built ship and twenty rowers to man her. In this I purpose to go round Sparta and sandy Pylos, enquiring after my long-lost father. Perhaps news of his return is to be gleaned from men: or a whisper may come to me from Zeus, whose breath oftenest conveys forewarnings of truth to us mortals.

'If I learn that my father is alive and on his homeward way I can endure this wilful spoiling of my house for yet a space: but if it be confirmed that he is dead and gone, then I will turn back to this loved land of mine and heap up for him a barrow to hold the rich tomb-furniture which is seemly for so grand a name. Afterward I will give my mother to a man.'

He ended and sat down: and there rose from the throng Mentor, the comrade to whom stout Odysseus, on sailing for Ilios, had committed his house; enjoining all in it to be obedient to the old man and in his steadfast guard. Wherefore out of his good heart Mentor protested as follows: 'Give heed, now, men of Ithaca to what I say to you. Here is a warning to all sceptred kings, that they wholly abjure clemency and gentleness, and take no thought for just dealing. Instead let them be harsh always, and unseemly in conduct: for glorious Odysseus, your king and the king of all this people, was like our father in his mildness – and lo! not one of you remembers him. Yet I advance no plaint against these haughty suitors, whose ill-nature has led them into deeds of such violence. Indeed this violence I find not excessive, weighed against their risk. They have staked their heads upon a persuasion that he comes home no more. My complaint is rather against the rest of the people, because you have sat by mutely, without word of denunciation or restraint: though you are very many, and the suitors are but few.'

Leocritus, the son of Euenor, opposed him. 'Mentor, you crazy mischief-maker, why waste breath in pleading that the people stop our nuisance? To make war over a matter of feasting would be outrageous, superior numbers or no superior numbers. Even suppose that your Odysseus of Ithaca did arrive in person, all hot to drive from his palace the noble suitors who have made it their banqueting hall. His wife may yearn for his coming: but in that way she would have small joy of it. In his very palace he would encounter horrid fate if he alone attacked so many of us. You babble vainly. Enough of this. Let all the people return to their employments, leaving only Mentor and Halitherses (because they have long been hangers-on of his family) to deal with this youth's journeying. Yet I fancy he will stay long enough in Ithaca, news-gathering still from his chair: and the project of a voyage come to nought.'

He finished, and the assembly was speedily dissolved, the crowd streaming homeward: while the suitors repaired to the palace of magnificent Odysseus. But Telemachus walked by himself far along the margin of the sea, and there laved his hands in the transparent sea-water before praying to Athene. 'Divine One, hear me! Yesterday you came to my house and told me to venture by ship across the shadow-haunted main, seeking news of my absent father. Now see how the Achaeans, and especially these lustful, bullying suitors, thwart my every turn.'

While he prayed Athene drew nigh. She had put on the appearance of Mentor's body, to the life: and it was with Mentor's voice that she exhorted him stirringly, thus: – 'Telemachus, let not your courage and resource fail you now. In your father deed and word notably marched together to their deliberate end. If your body holds a trace of his temper it will suffice to make this effort of yours neither bootless nor aimless. But if, on the contrary, you are not true issue of Odysseus and Penelope then I may abandon hope of your achieving any purpose. Few are the sons who attain their fathers' stature: and very few surpass them. Most fall short in merit. But surely this time you will not, you cannot, prove fainthearted or base: nor can you have failed to inherit some of Odysseus' cunning. Therefore I have good hope that you will attain your goal. Pay no heed to the advice or intentions of these infatuate suitors. With them instinct and decency are alike at fault; nor do they apprehend the death and black fate hovering over them, to overwhelm them all in a day.

'As for this journey of your heart, it shall not be too long denied you. Because I was a friend of your father's, therefore I am myself obtaining you the fast ship: and I shall be of your company aboard her. For the moment do you go back to your house, and mingle cheerfully with the suitors: while you get ready the victuals. Pack everything securely. Let the wine be in wine-jars and the barley meal (the marrow of men's strength) in tough skins. I will very quickly gather from the town our crew of willing fellows. Sea-girdled Ithaca is rich in ships, new and old. I go to survey them and choose the fittest; which we will presently equip and launch into the open sea.'

So said Athene, the daughter of Zeus. Telemachus, hearing the divine accent, made no delay but returned straight home with his heart-ache, to find the suitor-lords in guest-hall or fore court, where they were stripping the skins off his slaughtered goats and singeing his fat pigs for the cooking fire.

Antinous, with a laugh and loudly calling his name, swaggered up to him and took his hand. 'Telemachus,' said he, 'you have just now given your enmity too free tongue against us. Instead, will you not henceforward banish from your mind these thoughts of doing us hurt and forget your injurious words and eat and drink with us as of yore? Meanwhile the Achaeans will be making quite ready for you all you want in the way of ship and crew, to take you most quickly to hallowed Pylos for news of your august father.'

Well-advised was the reply of Telemachus, as he gently drew his hand from the grasp of Antinous. 'It is not possible for me to dine softly in your too-proud company: to be at ease and merry-make. O suitors, was it not grief enough that in my callow childhood you shore from me so much of my precious goods? Today I am a grown man and hear from others all this tale; and verily my swelling heart prompts me to visit upon you every evil I can contrive, whether from Pylos or in this place. Therefore will I most surely go on my journey: nor shall it be a barren quest, though by your crafty precaution I travel but as a passenger, without ship or rowers of my own.'

The suitors went on feasting their hardest, where they were, till he had spoken. Then they hooted and jeered at him. One graceless cockerell held forth after this strain: 'Really, Telemachus does mean to kill us all. He now hates us so terribly that he may bring back avengers with him from the sands of Pylos or from far-away Sparta. Or perhaps he plans to visit the luxuriant fields of Ephyra, and procure some life-destroying drug to mix into our wine-bowl and cut us all off together!'

And another youth of the same sort cried out, 'I tell you what, if he goes off in the inside of a ship, perhaps he will wander away from his friends, like Odysseus, and get lost. Then what extra work we poor creatures will have, dividing up all his belongings among ourselves. I vote we give the house-property to his mother, for the man who makes her his wife.'

Thus they japed: but Telemachus went from them to his father's store-chamber. Under its high, wide dome lay heaped up the gold and the copper: also great chests of clothing, and an abundance of pleasant-smelling olive oil. Secured against the wall in ranks, stood jar upon jar of old delicious wine, every jar filled with pure liquor, fit for the Gods but awaiting the day of Odysseus' home-coming – if he was ever to come home, through his toils and pains. This treasure-room had swinging double doors, strong and tight, always shut: and between them, day and night alike, there lodged the woman-guardian, old Eurycleia, the daughter of Ops, Peisenor's son. She in her sagacity stood watch over all its wealth.

Telemachus called her into the chamber and said to her, 'Good mother, pray draw off for me in jars some sweet wine: your second best, that which comes next after the very special vintage you are reserving for him, the unfortunate one, godlike Odysseus, in case he somehow tricks death and fate and wins his way back. Fill me twelve jars, sealing each with its stopper. Then run barley meal into stout-sewn leather sacks. Twenty measures let there be, of your well-kerned barley groats. See that no one spies what you do: but heap up all the things together in one place, whence I can fetch them this evening after my mother has gone up to her room in preparation for bed. I am going to Sparta and sandy Pylos, hoping to learn something of my father's return.'

Eurycleia, the foster-mother who loved him, wailed aloud at the tidings and implored him tearfully: 'Alas, my dearest child, why has such a notion come into your head? How should you hope to make your way over the vast earth, you a shielded only son, when your father Odysseus, the descendant of gods, himself perished there very far away, wandering in some place unknown? Further, so soon as your back is turned these men in your guest-hall will think out some evil to overtake you: and thus you will die in a trap, leaving them to share out your goods between them. Instead, do you sit here in your proper place. It is no duty of yours to stray over the desolate sea in search of misfortune.'

Wise Telemachus answered her: 'Be brave, good nurse. This plan did not come to me without the prompting of Heaven. But swear not to breathe a word of it to my dear mother till eleven or twelve days are passed, or till she misses me and learns that I have gone away. I want to spare her beautiful face from being furrowed with tears.' Thus he spoke, and the old woman swore a great oath by the Gods. He heard her swear and seal the oath: and after it at once she turned to drawing off his wine in jars and filling the stout leathern wallets with barley meal, while Telemachus returned to the living rooms and entertained the suitors.

All this time the clear-eyed Goddess was taking thought for the next stages of her plan. In the guise of Telemachus she traversed the entire city and standing by each of her men said her say, exhorting them to muster at nightfall by the swift ship: the ship itself she asked of Noemon, famed son of Phronius, who granted it heartily.

The sun went down into the sea, and the streets grew obscured. Then Athene had the fast ship run down into the water and stowed aboard her all the gear proper to a well-found galley. She had her brought round to the very mouth of the harbour where the picked crew had rallied, every man of them inspired by the grey-eyed Goddess with her own zest.

Athene, steadily pursuing her course, next visited the great house of Odysseus and there poured out upon the suitors a fond sleep and dazed them as they drank, till the cups slipped from their drowsy hands. Incontinently the banquet broke up, as each man struggled homewards to his bed in the city, with a weight of slumber bearing down his eyelids. Then the Goddess called Telemachus to speak with her outside the comfortable halls. She was again Mentor in speech and body. 'Telemachus,' she said, 'your companions, all armed and ready, sit now on the thwarts abiding only your advent. Let us go, and not hold them longer from the journey.'

With the word Pallas Athene went swiftly in the lead. He followed in her track. When they came out on the beach to the ship, there they found the long-haired company waiting at the water's edge. To them Telemachus, their appointed leader, made his first speech: 'Friends, come with me and lend a hand with the rations. I have everything put together, ready, in the house: and my mother knows nothing of our business, nor do any of the house-maids. I have told just one woman out of them all.'

He spoke and led back: and they went with him. They laded everything on their shoulders to the ship and put it away below, as the beloved son of Odysseus directed. Afterwards Telemachus went on board (Athene having preceded him) and sat down in the stern-sheets, quite near where she had seated herself. The crew loosed the after-warps, clambered aboard, and took their seats on the oar-benches.

Then did Athene, the clear-eyed, summon up for them a favouring breeze, a brisk following West Wind which thrummed across the wine-dark sea. Telemachus roused his followers and bade them get sail on the vessel. They obeyed him: the fir mast was raised aloft and heeled through its pierced cross-beams: the stays were rigged and the white sails hauled up by their halyards of pliant cowhide. The wind caught the sail, bellying it out, and the blue-shadowed waves resounded under the fore-foot of the running ship as she lay over on her course and raced out to sea.

They made fast all the running tackle of the swift dark hull and got out the drinking bowls. These they filled with wine, brim-full, and poured out as offerings to the Immortal Gods that are for ever and ever: honouring especially the clear-eyed Daughter of Zeus: while the ship cleft through the long night towards the dawn.

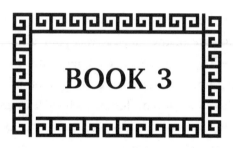

BOOK 3

Forth from the lovely waters sprang the sun into its firmament of brass, thence to shine upon the Immortals, as also upon mortal men walking amid the corn-fields of earth; while the ship drew into Pylos, the stately citadel of Neleus. There upon the fore-shore were gathered the inhabitants, doing sacrifice to the Earth-shaker, Poseidon, the dark-tressed God. Nine congregations they made, each five hundred strong: and every congregation had offered nine victims, jet-black bulls free from any fleck of colour, to the God: in whose honour the leg-bones were now burning with fire while the assembly ate of the entrails and organs.

Straight towards this beach the tight ship was steered. The crew brailed up and furled: then moored her. Afterwards they all issued forth (including Telemachus) in the train of grey-eyed Athene. She turned to him and said, 'Telemachus, here is no room for false modesty: no room at all. Have you not come oversea in quest of your father, expressly to learn where the earth is hiding him or what doom he has drawn upon himself? So you must go up straight, now, to this horse-proud Nestor, and make him yield to you the inmost secrets of his heart. Implore him, yourself, to speak perfect truth: and then he will not deceive us: for his mind is compact with wisdom.'

The cautious Telemachus protested thus: 'Mentor, how dare I approach him, how cling to him in supplication, when I am all unversed in speeches of subtle appeal? It is only right for a young man to be diffident when he importunes an elder.' The Goddess rejoined, 'Your heart will prompt you in part: and other things the spirit will teach you to say. I think if ever anyone was conceived and grew to manhood with the fostering care of the gods, it was yourself.'

Pallas led on swiftly while she spoke. Telemachus followed her divine steps, till they encountered the throng of the men of Pylos. There sat Nestor amongst his sons, with his followers busied about him, arranging the feast or roasting joints of beef or skewering choice morsels on the spits. Yet no sooner did they spy strangers than one and all crowded forward with welcoming hands, to have them take place in the gathering. Peisistratus, Nestor's son, reached them first. He took a hand of Athene and a hand of Telemachus and led them to fleecy sheepskins spread over the sand of the beach beside the platters, where sat Thrasymedes, his own brother, and Nestor their father. He gave them portions of the beasts' inwards: and pouring wine into a gold tankard he raised it to Pallas Athene, daughter of aegis-bearing Zeus, with these words:

'Offer a prayer, O guest, to our lord Poseidon, upon whose feast you have chanced in visiting us now. And after you have made your drink-offering and prayed the due prayer, then pass the honeyed wine to this your friend, that he may offer: for I deem that he, like you, will wish to supplicate the eternal Gods, for lack of whom the hearts of all the world would go desolate. If I give the embossed cup to you, before him, it is only because he is younger, a man of my own generation.'

Thereupon he put the sweet wine into her hand: Athene was gladdened by the right instinct of the man, who had preferred her in serving the storied golden cup; and presently she uttered to kingly Poseidon all her desire in prayer.

'Hear us, World-girdler, nor refuse, as greedy, our prayers for the gaining of our end. Entail upon Nestor, greatest of his line, as for the sons which follow after him, glory. Give to all in Pylos a bountiful return for these hundred victims they have so largely sacrificed. Grant further that when Telemachus and I go back, it may be with a happy issue to the purposes for which we have sailed here in our swift, black ship.' So she prayed, and all the while was bringing her own prayer to pass. Then she gave the rich loving-cup to the dear son of Odysseus and he repeated her prayer.

By now the others had roasted the flesh-meat of the victims and drawn the gobbets off their spits. Portions were shared out to all: and they ate their fill of the noble spread. But when at last the appetites for food and drink had been relieved, to them Nestor, Gerenia's knight, began to speak: –

'When strangers are fully satisfied with food, as now, it is fair to make enquiry of them and find out who they are. Tell us therefore of yourselves, O guests! Where did your journey over the sea-ways begin? Is yours a business venture, or do you cruise at random like those pirates who quarter the salt waves and risk their souls to profit by what others lose?'

Telemachus was inspired to answer him bravely, being heartened thereto by Athene herself, who wished that he might acquire men's respect through diligence in seeking news of his absent father. 'O Nestor, Neleus' son, chief glory of the Achaeans! You ask whence we come. I will make all plain. We are from Ithaca, that lies below Neion: and our motive, which I now set forth, is personal, not public. I cast about for trace of my father, a man of universal fame, the patient and mighty Odysseus. Rumour has it that in the sack of the Trojan capital he fought by your side. We can tally all the others who served at Troy; or mark just where each one died his grievous death: but Zeus has left the fate of this last man a mystery. No one can say for sure where he was lost – on the mainland, borne down by men who hated him, or in the deep, beneath the waves of Amphitrite.

'Because of this I am suppliant at your knees, O Nestor: begging that you relate his pitiful death, as you saw it with your own eyes, or learned it from the lips of such another waif. His death, I say, for even from his mother's womb calamity had marked him for her own. Do not in pity convey to me smooth things, things gentler than the truth: blurt out, rather, all that met your sight. I beseech you if (when you Achaeans were sore pressed by the men of Troy) my father, noble

Odysseus, ever pledged himself to you and fulfilled his bond – that so you now have regard for me and give me the naked fact.'

Then answered him Nestor, knight of Gerenia. 'Dear lad, since you recall to my mind those dreary memories, hear the tale of what we endured in that fatal land – we fierce, ill-disciplined Achaeans; and of what we endured while we strayed after booty over the misty face of the ocean wheresoever Achilles led: as also of our struggles about the great walled city of King Priam. There our bravest died. Aias, the lord of battles, lies there: Achilles himself: and Patroclus, whose wisdom at the council board was godlike. And there too died my lovely son, the strong, clean Antilochus, who was surpassingly swift-footed and a fighter. Ever so many evils we suffered beyond this count. Mortal frailty could not support the whole story, not though you tarried here for five years or six enquiring into all that the Achaean chivalry there lost. Before the end you would have faded back to your native land.

'Nine years we pegged away industriously, entangling the enemy in every kind of evil trick: and, in the event, hardly did Zeus see it through. With one particular man of us, all that time, no one dared compare himself, aloud, as a master of craftiness: for manifestly in stratagems of any sort the palm was borne off by Odysseus, your regal father – if really you are his son. A strange wonder takes me as I gaze on you: though you have his tricks of speech. One would have sworn that never any lad could speak so like him. See now, all the while great Odysseus and I were together, we never, in council-chamber or in open assembly, spoke to two briefs. It was as if we had a single heart from which we expounded to the Argives, with forethought and ripe council, how they should arrange it for the best.

'Even so we destroyed the tall city of Priam. It was afterwards, when the god had dispersed the Achaeans and we had all gone down to our ships, that Zeus contrived in his heart a sorry return for the Argives, because they had not, all of them, been either upright or circumspect. As for the grisly doom which swallowed so many of them up, it arose from the fatal anger of the grey-eyed Daughter of the Great One, who set dissension between the two sons of Atreus. Wherefore these two chiefs summoned all the host together, indecorously and not by rule, near sundown: and they came staggering with wine, did the strong sons of the Achaeans, to hear why the brothers so intemperately sounded the assembly.

'Then Menelaus urged that the Achaeans should be mindful only of an immediate return over the swelling horizon of the sea: but in this advice he did not at all please his brother Agamemnon, whose plan was to hold back the host while he offered hundreds of victims in sacrifice to allay that deadly wrath of Athene. The fool: who did not see that she was not thus to be persuaded. The face of the ever-lasting Gods is not suddenly changed. So did the brothers confront each other in full view, bitterly wrangling: till the Achaeans impatiently sprang up with thrilling tumultuous cry and clang of armour. The opposed councils each found advocates amongst them. Sleep, when it came to us that night, came tossed and broken by hard thoughts of one another; while Zeus aloft brooded over us, quickening the seeds of our iniquity.

'In the morning the faction whereof I was one drew down our ships to the good salt sea. We loaded them with our treasures and our captives, the outlandish, loin-girt Trojan women: while the other faction held back, keeping with Agamemnon, shepherd of the host. We, the journeying half, then set sail and went. Very swiftly did we sail, for the sea in all its hugeness was divinely spread smooth for our keels till we came to Tenedos, where we made sacrifice to the gods as beseemed men homeward bound.

'Yet did Zeus still deny us an unchequered return: indeed he was cruel and for the second time let loose evil dissensions among us. From Tenedos, therefore, some of us turned prow to poop, and rocked off again, back whence they had come. Of these were the party of Odysseus, the myriad-minded, the resourceful, whose judgement veered to favour once more Atrides-Agamemnon.

'For my part I fled away, with a fleet of vessels following me: in my heart I felt that the God was brewing mischief. Diomedes, the fighting son of Tydeus, fled too, and his example carried all his fellowship with him. After we two had gone there pursued after us the high-coloured Menelaus, who found us in Lesbos taking further counsel upon our long voyage: – whether it were best to go wide of cliff-bound Chios, by way of the island of Psyria which we should keep upon our left: or to pass this side of Chios, by stormy Mimas. We asked the god to give us a lead. He answered that to cut across the central sea to Euboea would be our quickest escape from disaster. Then there sprang up and blew a loud following wind, before which the ships scudded fast across the fish-filled ways till they made their landfall on Geraestus in the dead of night. We went ashore and slew many bulls there and burnt their marrow-bones in sacrifice to Poseidon, by token that so great a stretch of open sea was favourably passed. It was no more than four days later that the following of Diomedes, daunter of horses, beached their trim ships in Argos.

'I held on for Pylos, helped thereto by the friendly wind which never once let up on us from the first day when the god caused it to blow. Thus easily, dear lad, did I return home by myself, without learning the fate of the other Achaeans or knowing who was saved and who was lost. What news I have gathered since, sitting quietly in my great hall, that shall you now learn from me without exception, as is your due.

'The Myrmidons, they say, those spearmen, got back in good order under the renowned son of great-hearted Achilles. It was well, also, with Philoctetes, gallant son of Poias: and Idomeneus brought back all his company to Crete: – all, that is, who escaped the war. The sea wrested none from him. Of the fate of Agamemnon, son of Atreus, word must have come, even to those remote fastnesses which are your home, relating the calamity of his return to the woeful fate Aegisthus had schemed for him. Yet Aegisthus paid a reckoning even more terrible. How good it was that a son of the victim survived, and that he should avenge his great father's cruel death upon Aegisthus, the sly murderer! Fortify yourself, my tall and comely friend, upon his example: that your praises may be sung by posterity.'

Telemachus answered him gravely, 'Nestor, son of Neleus, chief glory of the Achaeans: I grant you that young Orestes took the last drop of his revenge; and therefore shall the Achaeans indeed trumpet his fame, for ever and ever. Would that the Gods had endowed me with strength like his, to visit upon the lawless suitors these iniquitous presumptions with which they artfully insult my feebleness. But when the Gods spun the web of fate for me and for my father they made no such blissful provision of power for us. Our part is only to endure.'

Then said Nestor of Gerenia, master of the horse: 'Friend, now you open this matter and make mention of it to me, let me admit that I have heard how your palace is beset by a mob of those who would marry your mother: and that they plot to your disadvantage, in your despite. Tell me, do you willingly yield to them? Or is it that some divine will has made the people of your part to turn against you? Who knows, perhaps one day he will arrive and reward their violence with violence upon themselves: as he can do equally, whether he come alone or with the might of Achaea at his back. Furthermore, should the grey-eyed Athene single you out to cherish, with the loving care she bore famous Odysseus in the Troad where we Achaeans suffered – never saw I such open affection on the part of the Gods as was there displayed by Pallas, who would stand openly by his side – if Pallas will so love you and vex her heart for you, then may one or two of them be distracted clean out of the idea of marriage!' Telemachus replied sadly, 'Reverend Sir, I do not think this word of yours can live. Your saying is too great. So much too great that I grow afraid. Not all my hoping, not the good-will of the Gods, could bring it about.'

Here Goddess Athene broke in. 'Telemachus, it is unseemly to let such words escape past the barriers of your lips. When a God wishes, it is idly easy for him to preserve a man, even in the ends of the earth. For my part I should choose to be vexed with every sort of pain on my way home, so that I reached there at last and enjoyed my return: rather than get back just to meet death at my fireside, as Agamemnon died through the treachery of his wife and Aegisthus. Yet I grant you that not the immortal gods themselves can for ever shield the man they love from the common meed of death, or continually avert that fatal decree which lays every man prone in the grave at the end.'

Telemachus answered after his wont, 'Mentor, we will speak no more of it. Why harrow ourselves imagining returns for him, when already the Deathless Ones have given him death and the dark which follows it? But see, I wish to change the topic; and ask another word of Nestor, as from one whose rulings and conclusions have final authority. They tell me he has been King for thrice the span of ordinary generations. By this virtue he seems to my gaze almost an immortal himself. So Nestor, son of Neleus, give me more true history – how died that great king, Agamemnon, son of Atreus? By what subtleties of device did Aegisthus snare into death a man so much better than himself? Where was Menelaus in the business, that Aegisthus dared to kill? Absent perhaps, wandering abroad in the world far from Achaean Argos?'

Nestor of Gerenia, the exceeding rich in horses, answered, 'My child, I can tell you the whole truth of it. You have rightly guessed how it would have been had tawny Menelaus, Agamemnon's brother, come back from Troy to find Aegisthus alive in his brother's place. There would have been no corpse to need the kindly rites of burial. Dogs and carrion crows would have torn the carcase to tatters in the open fields beyond the city walls: nor would any of our women have keened over him, so abhorrent was the man's crime.

'We were away, you see, fighting our great fights at this siege, while he, comfortable in the heart of Argos and its green horse-pastures, was ever speaking in the ear of Agamemnon's wife, trying to steal her love. For long she would not abide the foul thing, Clytemnestra the divinely fair, the noble-minded. Besides there was ever at her side the family minstrel, whom Atrides, before he left for Troy, had told off to protect his wife.

'Yet the doom of the Gods linked her with disaster after all. Aegisthus lured the singing man to a desert island and there abandoned him to be a spoil and booty for the birds of prey. Whereupon her lust matched her lover's, and he took her into his house. Many thigh-bones of oxen he burned to the gods on their holy altars: and many dedications of tapestries or gold he made, in thankfulness for the momentous success he had achieved beyond his heart's hope.

'Then we came sailing back together, Atrides-Menelaus and I, fast friends. But at Sunium, the sacred headland of Athens, Phoebus Apollo shed down his gentle darts upon Menelaus' navigator and ended his life. He dropped dead, with the steering oar of the moving ship yet within his hands. This Phrontis, son of Onetor, excelled all the men of his trade in skilfully holding a ship to her course when squalls bore down thick and heavy. So Menelaus was delayed there, in spite of his anxiety to be moving, till he had given due and rich burial to his henchman. Then at last he got away across the wine-dark ocean, at the best pace of his hollow ships, as far as the steep slope of Maleia. There however, Zeus the far-seeing swept him grievously astray by loosing upon the fleet a blast of piercing winds and monster waves which grew mountainous.

'The squadron was torn asunder. Some ships the God thrust almost to that part of Crete where the Kydonians live beside the streams of Iardanus. When the wind sets from the south-west, a long swell drives in there against the smooth wall of cliff which sheerly fronts the mist-veiled sea, from the furthest end of Gortyn westward to the promontory by Phaestos: where a low reef stems the whole sweep of the tide. Upon this came the half of the fleet. The ships were shattered by force of the waves against the crags: and the men in them narrowly avoided death.

'As for the rest of the dark-prowed fleet, the other five vessels, – they were borne by wind and water to the coasts of Egypt; in which strange region, with its foreign people, Menelaus lingered, amassing great store of gold and goods, all the while that Aegisthus at home was carrying out his dastard scheme. Therefore it chanced that he had seven years of rule in golden Mycenae after killing Atrides: and all the people served him. But in the eighth year there returned from Athens the goodly Orestes to be his undoing. For Orestes killed the traitor Aegisthus, his father's murderer: a son slaying the sire's slayer. After perfecting his vengeance Orestes gave a funeral feast to the Argives over the bodies of the mother he hated and despicable Aegisthus: and that self-same day there sailed in Menelaus of the loud battle cry, laden down with all the wealth that his ships could carry.

'Learn from this, my friend, not to wander from your home for too long, abandoning your property, when there are men rampaging in the house likely to share out and consume all you have: for so you would find your journey to have defeated itself. Yet I exhort, nay I order, you to visit Menelaus who has so newly come home from abroad, from parts so foreign that the stoutest-hearted would despair of ever returning thence when once driven distractedly by storms across that fearful, boundless sea: a sea so vast and dread that not even in a twelve-month could a bird hope to wing its way out of it.

'Wherefore I would have you visit him, sailing in your own ship with your crew: but if you prefer the road, a chariot and team are at your disposal, with my own sons to guide you to tawny Menelaus, in Lacedaemon the fair. Make your appeal to him with your own lips, for then he will heed and answer truthfully out of his stored wisdom, not thinking to play you false.'

There Nestor ceased: but now the sun was going down and the shadows deepening. So to the company spoke the goddess, grey-eyed Athene. 'Ancient, right well have you told us your tale: but it is time to cut the tongues and mix the wine, that we may complete our offerings to Poseidon and the other immortals: and then must we think of our couches: for it is bedtime. The sun has sunken into the shadow of the world and we should be going, lest we sit unmannerly long at the table of the Gods.'

Her audience approved her. The henchmen poured water on their hands and the serving-boys filled the drinking bowls to the brims with compounded drinks. Then they served round to each a fresh cup. The ox-tongues were cast into the fire, and rising to his feet each man poured his libation in turn. After they had so offered and had drunk of what was left all their hearts' desire, then Athene and godlike Telemachus would have been going back together to their hollow ship: but Nestor stayed them with words of protest: –

'May Zeus and the whole company of the immortals deliver me from your passing by my house, to slight it and sleep in your ship, as if I were a naked, needy man who had at home neither cloaks nor coverlets for the soft sleeping of himself and his guests! Praise be, I have great store of bedding. Never, I swear, while I live shall the beloved son of my comrade Odysseus lie out on the bare boards of his vessel – nor while there are children of mine left in the palace to entertain whatever guests may come under its roof.'

Athene replied, 'Well said, old friend: and Telemachus will do your bidding, as is most fit. Let him even now go with you to sleep in your palace. But my duty is to order and hearten the crew of our black ship by returning to them with our news. You see I am the one man of years in the party. All the rest are young men, fellows in age of stout Telemachus, and they have come with us on this trip for love's sake. Therefore with them I sleep this night through, beside the black shell of the ship: and in the morning I shall push on to the estimable Cauconians, who for no small while have owed me no small sum. Meanwhile let it be your care to send Telemachus, your guest, forward with one of your sons in one of your fast chariots: choosing for him from out your stud two of the lightest footed and deepest chested horses.'

The goddess ended her say, and took flight from them, in the way of a sea-eagle. Astonishment fell on all present and the venerable man was awed at what his eyes saw. He seized Telemachus by the hand, crying his name and saying: 'Friend Telemachus, what fear could one have of your growing up weak or base, when from your youth gods walk with you as guides? Of the great dwellers on Olympus this can be no other than the Daughter of Zeus himself: the Tritonian, the All-glorious: who also was wont to single out your great father for honour, from among the Argives.

'O QUEEN, I pray you, be gracious unto us, and bestow upon me a goodly repute amongst men; for me, and my sons, and for the wife I love and honour. And I vow to you a yearling heifer, broad-browed, uncovered, and never yet subjected to the yoke of man. This beast will I sacrifice to you, after I have caused her horns to be covered with pure gold.'

Such was the prayer that he uttered, and Pallas Athene heard him.

Then did Nestor, Gerenia's knight, lead into the fair hall his sons and his sons-in-law; who there in the palace of that most famous sire sat them down, orderly, each on his seat or throne: while the old lord mixed for his visitors a cup of wine which had mellowed eleven years in its jar before the good-wife broke the sealed wrappings and poured it forth. With such drink did the old man have his cup blended: and he poured the first of it to Athene, praying fervently the while to her, the daughter of aegis-bearing Zeus.

The others again made their drink-offering, and drank till their hearts were satisfied. Then the company dispersed, each to his own quarters in search of sleep: but for Telemachus, godlike Odysseus' son, Nestor the Gerenian horselover had coverlets spread on an inlaid bedstead in the coved entry of the house, under its reverberant roof. For company there was Peisistratus with his good ashen spear: Peisistratus, though a tall man who led his rank in the battle, was yet unmarried, and so, alone of the sons, kept his father's house. The old lord slept apart in the depths of the great building, where his lady wife had made ready their couch and its coverings.

Day-break: and the rosy-tinted fingers of dawn crept up the sky. Nestor, knight of Gerenia, left his bed and came forth to sit before the lofty gateway of his house on the smooth platform there built. Its white stones, all smoothly polished, had been the old-time seat of Neleus, that divinely-unerring counsellor, long since subdued by Death, who had gone down to Hades leaving Nestor as warden of the Achaeans to sit in his place and wield his sceptre of power. About him gathered the cluster of his sons, coming from their private houses: Echephron and Stratius and Perseus and Aretus and magnificent Thrasymedes. Also the sixth son, brave Peisistratus came: and they brought goodly Telemachus too, and set him there amongst themselves as Nestor began to address them:

'Quickly, quickly, dear sons, do my bidding, that I may single out from all the gods for reverence, divine Athene, who visited me in the flesh yesterday at the God's solemn feast. Let one of you, therefore, run to the pastures for a heifer to be brought as quickly as the neat-herd can drive her here. Let another hasten to the black ship of large-hearted Telemachus and bring up all his company save two. Let some one else bid Laerkes the gilder come, to lap in gold the horns of the victim. The rest of you stay in the house to see that its women busy themselves, laying the tables in our famous hall and arranging seats and a proper provision of fire-wood and sparkling water.' So Nestor ordered and they ran to obey. The heifer appeared from the fields and the crew of high-hearted Telemachus arrived from their swift and goodly ship: also the smith came, carrying in his hands the tools of his smithying by which his art was manifested – the anvil, the hammer and the shapely tongs to work his gold.

Athene, too, came to accept her sacrifice.

Then did Nestor, the ancient knight, bring out his gold: and the craftsman cunningly overlaid the heifer's horns in order that the goddess might be glad when she saw the loveliness dedicated to her. Statius and noble Echephron led the beast forward by the horns. Aretos came out from the living rooms, with a lotus-bowl of water for lustration in one hand and the basket of barleymeal in the other. Thrasymedes, strong in battle, stood ready, poising his sharp axe to cut down the heifer. Perseus held the blood-basin.

Venerable Nestor opened the rite of sacrifice by dipping his hands into the water to purify them: then he began to sprinkle the meal, praying earnestly the while to Athene and casting hairs from the forelocks of the heifer into the flame. Then, after they had joined in prayer and in scattering the heave-offering of grain, suddenly the son of Nestor, ardent Thrasymedes, stepped in and struck. His blade cut through the sinews of the neck, and the might of the heifer was undone. The women raised their wavering cry, the prince's daughters and his daughters-in-law and his honoured wife, Eurydice the eldest daughter of Clymenus: while the men strained up the beast's head from the trodden earth, that proud Peisistratus might sever her throat.

The dark blood gushed forth, and life left its bones. Very quickly they disjointed the carcase, stripped the flesh from the thigh bones, doubled them in the customary manner with a wrapping of the fatty parts, above and below, and banked the raw meat over them. Then the elder set fire to his cleft billets of wood and burned the offering while sprinkling ruddy wine upon the flames. So the thigh bones were utterly consumed even as the young men tasted the entrail-meat, crowding about their father with the five-pronged roasting forks in their hands. Afterwards they chopped up the rest of the flesh into morsels which they impaled on their points and broiled, holding the sharp spits firmly out to the fire.

During this sacrifice beautiful Polycaste, the youngest grown daughter of Nestor, son of Neleus, had given Telemachus his bath, washing him and anointing him with rich olive oil before she draped him in a seemly tunic and cloak: so that he came forth from the bath-cabinet with the body of an immortal. He rejoined Nestor, the shepherd of his people, and took place by his side. The flesh-meat was now ready. They drew it off the fork-points and sat down to dine. Men of standing waited on them, filling up with wine their golden beakers: and when they had eaten and drunken till they would no more, Nestor, Gerenia's knight, again opened his mouth and said:

'Now, my sons, it is time to harness to Telemachus' chariot the long-maned, proud-tailed horses, that he may be upon his way.' So he spoke, and heedfully they hastened to do his bidding. Very soon the swift horses were ready beneath the chariot's yoke. The house-keeper packed in bread and wine which she brought from her stores, together with such dainties as kings, the spoiled darlings of the gods, are wont to eat.

Telemachus stepped up into the stately chariot. Peisistratus, Nestor's noble son, stepped up beside him and gathered the reins into his hands. Then he struck the horses with the whip: and these, glad to be loosed, flew down from the steep crag of the citadel of Pylos out on to the plain: which all day long they steadily traversed, with the yoke nodding to and fro over their necks.

Down sank the sun. The road became blind. They were in Therae, by the house of Diocles, son to Ortilochus, who was own son of Alpheus. With him they rested the night, duly entertained: and at the first red pointers of dawn in the sky they were yoking their horses to the gay chariot for their next stage.

Forth they drove through the court-yard gate past the echoing porch. Again the driver swung his whip: again the willing horses flew forward. Presently they entered the wheat-lands, sign that their journey drew towards its close; with such speed had the horses pressed on. Again the sun grew low and the roads were darkened.

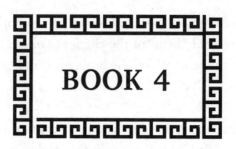

BOOK 4

They came to the country of Lacedaemon, where it nestled among the hollowed hills: and they drove up to the home of famous Menelaus. He was in act of feasting his many kinsmen to celebrate the marriages of his son and of the flawless daughter of his house. The girl he was giving to the son of that breaker of the line of battle, Achilles. It was in Troy that Menelaus first accepted the proposal and bowed his head in agreement that his daughter should go; and now by horses and car he was about to send her to the storied city of the Myrmidons over which her bridegroom was king: for the Gods were causing the fulfilment of the match proposed. As for the son – Menelaus was bringing from the town of Sparta the daughter of Alector to wed his Megapenthes, his strong but only son whom he had got by a slave-woman: for to Helen the Gods vouchsafed no more fertility after she had borne her first adorable child Hermione, who was as fair as golden Aphrodite herself. So they were dining delightedly, these neighbours and kinsmen of the famous Menelaus, under his tall roof-tree. Of the party one was a minstrel who sang divinely to his lyre. As soon as his preluding chords were heard two clowns danced in among the guests and threw cart-wheels upon the hall floor.

Just then in the clear space before the house there reined up the chariot and pair of heroic Telemachus and Nestor's distinguished son. Master Etoneus the lively squire of famed Menelaus happened to see them come. He ran through the palace to bear news of them to the Shepherd of the People. Going up close to him he said pointedly, 'Two men are arriving, my lord Menelaus, nursling of Zeus: strangers, but godlike in look as though they were of Zeus' own kin. Tell me quickly, shall we now unharness their swift horses? Or send them on to some proper man for entertainment?'

Ruddy Menelaus flushed in wrath and cried to him, 'You were not anciently such a fool, O Etoneus, son of Boethus! But herein you babble like a fond child, forgetting how many times we two have eaten hospitably in other men's houses on our way back to this palace, where may Zeus for ever grant us surcease from pain! Hasten to take the horses from the chariot of our guests and bring the two riders in to feast with us.' At his order the squire darted back through the hall bidding the other brisk footboys help him. They loosed the sweating horses from the yoke and haltered them in the horse-stalls, throwing down for them a mixed feed of corn and white barley. They propped the chariot against the polished return of the gateway and led the men into the marvellous house.

Upon first sight of this palace of the heaven-nurtured king the visitors paused in amazement. The lustre that played through it was as though the sun or the moon had risen within the lofty dwelling of far-famed Menelaus. They stared round, feasting their eyes: then went to the polished bath-tubs and bathed: or rather, the house-maidens bathed them and rubbed them down with oil, and after swathed them in warm mantles over tunics; fitting them to take place on their thrones beside Menelaus the son of Atreus.

The washing ewer, a goodly golden ewer, was brought to them by its maid-servant who poured water over their fingers into the silver cistern. She arranged a shining table by their side upon which the aged housekeeper put bread and rich victuals in joyful profusion. The butler came with platters of various flesh-meats and placed golden goblets to their hands. Menelaus waved them to his bounty saying, 'Taste of our food and be glad: so that after you have eaten we may enquire of you who you are. In scions like you the fathers' stock has not gone to waste: patently you are of the breed of kings, sceptred god-children of Zeus. The mean people do not sire sons like you.' With this introduction he picked up and passed to them the luscious loin of beef which had come to him as his privileged portion: then their hands duly made free with the refreshments provided.

Later, when their longings for food or drink had been put away Telemachus leaned his head across near the son of Nestor and whispered in his ear, that the others might not catch his words, 'Son of Nestor and joy of my heart, see what a blaze of polished copper and gold and electrum and silver and ivory goes through this echoing hall. Surely the mansions of Olympian Zeus must be like this, one great glory within of things wonderful beyond all telling. I am awed by the very sight of it.'

Fair-haired Menelaus had overheard his whisper. He opened his mouth to them with momentous words. 'Dear children, with Zeus no mortal man can vie. His houses and his treasures are from everlasting to everlasting. On earth – well, there may be a man as rich as myself, or there may not: but it was only after terrible suffering and eight years of adventure in foreign parts that I won home from overseas with this my wealth. I wandered through Cyprus and Phoenicia and Egypt: I have seen Ethiopians and Sidonians and the Erembi in their native haunts: even Libya, where the ewes bring forth their lambs with horns on and bear them three several times in the cycle of each year. No Libyan, be he king or shepherd, goes short of cheese or mutton or sweet ewe-milk, for the udders are full there all the year round.

'Yet, while I was roaming in such places gathering the wealth you note, another man crept privily upon my unsuspecting brother and murdered him; by connivance of his vile wife. Wherefore my rule over all these great possessions gives me no joy. Probably the story will have been told you by your fathers, whosesoever sons you are: for I have notoriously suffered much and brought to ruin a family which had been flourishing and rich in blessings. Gladly would I cut this wealth to a third if so I might repeople our homes with the men who died years ago in the rolling Troad, exiles from Argos the mother-land of horses. For these my men I am always moaning aloud and making lamentation – or perhaps not quite always, for now and then my heart grows suddenly sated with grief: and thereupon my eyes run dry, even as I sit here in our lordly hall. So abruptly does the comfort of tears turn cold and become a surfeit.

'Yet above and beyond all my company do I especially vex my weeping heart for one, whose memory makes me utterly loathe sleep and food. No man of the Achaeans deserved so greatly or laboured so greatly as great Odysseus laboured and endured. For him it was written that the outcome should be but sorrow upon sorrow: and for me a distress for his sake not ever to be forgotten while he continues missing and we in ignorance of whether he be alive or dead. Without doubt they mourn him too, old Laertes and self-possessed Penelope and Telemachus, who was no more than a child newly-born, left behind by his father in the house.'

Thus he spoke, and his words moved in the son a longing to bewail his father when he heard mention of his name. A tear splashed from his eyelids to the ground and he lifted up the purple cloak with both hands before his eyes: while Menelaus who noted it guessed the significance and pondered in his heart and head whether he should wait and allow him to name his father: or press him and try his every word by cross-questioning.

While thus his heart and mind debated, Helen, like a vision of Artemis of the golden distaff, came out from her high-coffered, incense-laden room with her women; of whom Adraste carried the graceful reclining-chair for her mistress while Alcippe had her soft woollen carpet and Phylo a silver basket given the queen by Alcandre, wife of Polybus, a dweller in Egyptian Thebes, that richest in palaces of all the cities of the earth. Polybus himself had given to Menelaus two bathing-tubs of silver and a pair of three-legged cauldrons and ten talents in gold: while his wife added for Helen other wonderful gifts, such as a spindle all of gold, beside this silver basket which the maid Phylo now brought in and set beside her. The basket was mounted on a wheeled carriage also of silver and the rims of it were carried out in gold. It was heaped full of the smoothest yarn and across it, at the moment, lay the distaff wound with wool of a wood-violet blue.

The queen sat down in her long chair which had a stool to support her feet: then she began to speak with her lord, asking him all that was forward: 'Do we know yet, heaven-nurtured Menelaus, from their own lips the truth about these two men our visitors? Shall I play the ignorant or disclose what my sure instinct tells me? My heart is so full of it that I must speak and discharge my utter astonishment: for never in all my experience saw I man or woman with so extraordinary a likeness as this lad bears to magnanimous Odysseus. Surely he must be Telemachus, that son he left behind him a mere infant in the house, when for the sake of this worthless self of mine all you Achaeans came up breathing savage war against the town of Troy.'

Auburn Menelaus answered her and said, 'Indeed, now I can see the likeness which you limn. Those are the feet of Odysseus and his hands and the flash of his eye and his head with the crested hair atop. And just now when I was casting my mind back upon Odysseus and recounting the bitter toil and woe he suffered for my sake, the young man suddenly let a salt tear drop from his bent brows and raised up the purple cloak to veil his eyes.'

Peisistratus the son of Nestor took up the reply and said 'Menelaus, Zeus-fostered son of Atreus, leader of the common people, my friend here is indeed the son of that man, the one and only, as you say. But he is very slow-spoken and would be ashamed in his heart on first coming here to pour out a flood of words before you, in whose utterance we two are taking such pleasure as if it were the voice of a god! Therefore did Nestor of Gerenia, master of chariots and horses, send me with Telemachus as guide. For Telemachus greatly wished to see you and be prompted by you to some word or work. Heavy griefs fall to the lot of a home-keeping son whose father is absent, if so it be that he can find no guardian to champion him. The father of Telemachus is still absent, and he lacks men at home to ward him from calamity.'

To which the reply of yellow-maned Menelaus was: 'Wonderful,

wonderful! that there should come to this house the son of my most especial friend who endured unnumbered ordeals for my sake. I had promised myself that when Odysseus came he should be embraced above all my Argives: if only all-knowing Olympian Zeus had granted us to return across the salt sea in our running ships. I would have removed him from Ithaca with his goods and his child and all his dependents, and contrived for him in Argos a dwelling place, a house, a city, by emptying completely of inhabitants one of the towns of my lordship which lies round about us. Then continually would we have foregathered here; nor should any force have sundered us, the lover and the enjoyed, before death's black cloud rolled down on us and covered one from other. I think the God himself perhaps envied us that happiness which would have been: at least he decreed that Odysseus, unhappy soul, should not return.'

So spoke he, and his words quickened in them all a longing to weep. Argive Helen, seed of Zeus, burst into tears: Telemachus too and Atrides-Menelaus: nor could the son of Nestor keep dry eyes, for there came to his memory stainless Antilochus whom the glorious son of shining Dawn had slain. Remembering him he said memorably: 'Atrides, that you were fuller of the knowledge of God than any other of mortal men was always the saying of venerable Nestor, whenever in his great house we brought up your name and questioned of you. Yet in this moment, if it be lawful, I would have you take counsel of me. Know that I take no delight in weeping after my supper: and now it is much after supper: the night advances towards the birth of a new dawn.

'Not that I would disclaim the fitness of weeping for any one of the sons of men who has run upon his fate and died. The last homage we can pay to woe-begone humanity is to shear close our hair and let the tears run down our cheeks. See now, I too have suffered loss: my brother who was far from meanest of the Achaeans. It may well be that you knew him. I was too young to meet or set eyes on him: but they tell me Antilochus was remarkable for that he outran other men in his swiftness of foot and fought surpassingly.'

Said fair Menelaus, 'My dear, when you have said so much you have spoken and acted with the discretion of an enlightened man, even were he a generation older than yourself. As the son of such a father naturally you speak with wisdom. It takes no art to pick out the offspring of a man into the texture of whose days the son of Kronos has woven bliss in the marriage bed and in the procreation of fair children. Nestor, to return to him, has had supremely granted him for all his days that he should glide peacefully into old age in his comfortable halls, surrounded by sons well-advised and very adept with their spears. So now we will let be the weeping aloud which before came upon us and remember again our supper. Ho there, pour water once more upon our hands that we may eat! In the morning Telemachus and I will bandy our fill of tales.'

So he spoke: and Asphalion the great man's handiest retainer poured water over their fingers, which they then employed on the rich food set ready. But Helen, of the line of Zeus, called to mind another resource. Into the wine they were drinking she cast a drug which melted sorrow and sweetened gall, which made men forgetful of their pains. Whoso swallowed it mixed within his cup would not on that day let roll one tear down his cheeks, not though his mother and his father died, not though men hacked to death his brother or loved son with the cutting edge before him and he seeing it with his eyes. These drugs of subtle potency had been furnished the daughter of Zeus by the wife of Thon, even Polydamna the woman of Egypt, where the ploughlands excel other plough-lands of earth in bearing abundance of medicines: of which some when compounded are healing and others baneful. Every man of that country is a physician of knowledge incomparable, for they are of the true strain of Paeon the healer of the Gods.

Helen, after she had mixed the Egyptian drug with their wine and bidden them serve it, returned to the conversation and said, 'Menelaus, son of Atreus and godson of Zeus, and you other sons of the great: it is the way of Zeus to dispense good and evil, now to this man and now to that. He is the all-mighty. Your present lot is to feed, sitting in the halls, and to cheer yourselves with tales, of which I will lead off with one that is seasonable, touching a single one of those innumerable adventures of Odysseus; one only, for beyond all my listing or telling were the exploits of that hardy one.

'Marvellous was this adventure which the iron-nerved man conceived and dared to execute in the Troad of unhappy memory to all Achaeans. He punished himself with humiliating stripes and threw a coarse wrap about his shoulders as if he were a bondman: and so went down into the broad streets of the hostile city amongst his enemies, hiding himself in his foreign shape and making believe he was a mendicant, a figure very unlike that he cut in the Achaean fleet. Yet in this disguise he went through the city of the Trojans – and not a soul of them accosted him. But I knew who this man was and challenged him again and again while he cunningly eluded my questions. After the washing and anointing with oil when I was clothing him in new garments I swore to him a mighty oath that I would not declare to the Trojans that it was Odysseus, before he had got back to the swift ships and the bivouacs. Then he told me all the intention of the Achaeans: and get back to them he did, replete with great fund of news, after killing many Trojans on the way with his long pointed sword: whereupon the Trojan women wailed shrilly: but my heart laughed, for now my desire had shifted to get back home, and deplored too late the infatuation engendered by Aphrodite to lead me away from my own dear country, abandoning child and marriage-ties and a lord not poor in wit or looks.'

Fair Menelaus took up the tale: 'Of all these things, my lady wife, you have said what is needful. In my time I learnt the counsel and thought of many brave men, and traversed many countries, but never set eyes on another man as high-hearted as my beloved Odysseus. The sort of deed his bold heart would imagine and dare to do was such an adventure as that carved horse within which all we flower of the Argives lay hidden, with death and destruction our guerdon for Troy. You came to us then, my lady: surely some god prompted you in desire to glorify the Trojans. Godlike Deiphobus had escorted you thither. Three times you circled our packed lair, stroking it with your hands and calling by name upon the leaders of the Greeks. Your voice was the voice of all our absent wives. Myself and the son of Tydeus and stout Odysseus were inside and heard you calling: and of a sooth two of us, Diomedes and I, raged furiously to leap up and call you or quickly to answer you from within. But with main strength Odysseus held us back against our passions. Wherefore all the other sons of the Achaeans were still: save only Anticlus who was about to address you, when Odysseus with his great hands gripped his jaws and held on, thus saving all the Achaeans: until Pallas Athene at last called you away.'

To him staid Telemachus replied: 'Son of Atreus, Menelaus, foster son of Zeus, bulwark of the rank of battle: all the worse is our pain. For this courage did not deliver him from grievous ruin nor would it have availed if his heart had been of unflawed iron. But come now, dismiss us to our beds that we may stretch out and take our fill of the sweetness of sleep.'

At his word Helen of Argos ordered her house-maidens to range beds under the sun-porch, piling them with lovely purple blankets covered smoothly with rugs and thick woollen cloaks on top of all. The maids left the hall, torch in hand, and made ready the beds. Then the usher showed the guests out. So they slept there, in the entry, heroic Telemachus and Nestor's brilliant son: while the son of Atreus lay remote in the great house, and beside him Helen of the flowing robes, fairest of women.

At dawn's first redness in the sky Menelaus of the resounding war-cry arose from bed, clothed himself, belted on a sharp sword and bound gay sandals beneath his lively feet. Like a god he went forth from the married quarters and calling Telemachus to sit by him, greeted him and said, 'What promptings drove you to me, princely Telemachus, here to Lacedaemon the fair, over the broad swelling sea? Public or private need? Confide in me freely.'

Telemachus answered him with advisement. 'Atrides-Menelaus the god-nurtured, pre-eminent when battle is ranged, I come to know if perchance you can give me any rumour of my father. My household is being eaten up and my fat properties ruined. Our home is full of evil-minded men, these inordinately proud suitors of my mother, who ever butcher my numerous sheep and slow swaying oxen with the crumpled horns. Therefore am I come pleading to your knee that you may consent to tell me the story of his pitiful destruction as you saw it with your eyes or as you learnt it from the lips of another wanderer. Indeed his mother conceived him to great misery. Condone nothing and spare me nothing out of misplaced pity: but relate just as much as you saw of him. If the excellent Odysseus my father ever fulfilled word or pledge of his to you in that Troy of unhappy suffering for the Achaeans, then I pray you recompense me now by remembering it and dealing with me as faithfully.'

Menelaus flushed with anger and cried to him: 'The dastards, who would lay their puny selves in the bed of that whole-hearted warrior! It is as if a deer had laid her newborn suckling fawns in a lion's den and gone out searching across the mountain-spurs and green valleys for her pasture. When the strong beast returns to the thicket which is his lair he will fearfully kill those poor intruders: and even such a mean death shall Odysseus deal out to these pests. By Zeus our Father, and Athene, and Apollo! I can remember how once in luxurious Lesbos Odysseus rose up in a rage and wrestled with Philomeleides and threw him strongly: and all the Greeks rejoiced. If only he might confront the suitors with that old strength. How swiftly would fate close on them and turn their nuptials into bitterness! As for these questions you entreat of me I promise you to distort nothing nor let myself speak beside the truth, nor shall I trick you. Yea, not one word will I hide from you or cover up of all that the Ancient of the Sea, the Infallible, told me.

'It was in Egypt. I was eager to return but the Gods delayed me there because I had not perfected their full ritual sacrifice. Ever jealous the Gods are, that we men mind their dues. In the surge that breaks across the mouth of the river of Egypt there lies a certain island which men called Pharos, no further from the land than a laden ship will make in the daylight hours, granted that she has a favouring wind to bluster her squarely forward. In it is a harbour with good landing beaches and clean, deep wells of fresh water, from which, after drawing their fill, men run down the trim hulls into the sea. In this island the gods kept me for twenty days, nor ever did there blow a breath of those sea-breezes which inspire ships to move over the wide ridges of the sea.

'And now would our last rations have been devoured and with them the courage of my men, had not a divinity taken pity on me and been merciful. Eidothea she was, that daughter of stalwart Proteus, the sea's venerable lord. The sad sight of me touched her heart on a time she met me wandering furtively apart from my followers, who daily quartered the island, angling with hooks that they had bent up, for fish to allay the hunger which griped their bellies. Eidothea, however, drawing near called me and put a question: "Stranger, are you foolish or to such a point easy-going that freely you abandon yourself to enjoy the sense of pain? All this long time you are prisoned in the island and put no term to the delay, though the spirit of your company diminishes." Thus she addressed me: and I in my turn replied, "Whatever one of the goddesses you are, let me protest that I am not willingly held here. It would seem that I have transgressed against the immortal gods which are in high heaven. Tell me therefore of your knowledge (for the Gods know all) which deathless one it is who fetters me here and prevents my leaving? Also of my return; how is that to be managed across the swarming deep?"

'So I said: and forthwith the fair goddess answered, "Freely will I inform you, Stranger. This is the haunt of the authentic Ancient of the Sea, Proteus of Egypt, the Immortal One, who knows the unplumbed ocean-pits and is first minister to Poseidon. Rumour makes him my father by course of nature. If you can but summon strength to lie in wait for him and take him, then he will impart to you how and where and when your course should be and what return you will have, riding over the fishes' element. He will even tell you, heaven-nurtured, if you press him, what good or evil has befallen your homes while you have been wearing this weary road."

'Taking her up I said, "This ambush, Goddess, must be of your designing if it is to succeed; otherwise be sure the old divinity will see or hear something suspicious and avoid my snare. It is pain for mortal man to compel a god."

'The glorious goddess acceded instantly. "Hear then this detailed plan. When the climbing sun has reached the zenith of its sky, even then daily does the unerring Ancient of the Sea come forth from his deep with the breath of the west wind to attend him and drape him in its darkling ripple. He comes out, into the wave-worn caves, and lies him down to rest: while drove upon drove of his seals, bred from salt-water by an ocean-nymph, forsake the grey brine and sleep too around him, bitter-scenting the place because their breathing holds the bitterness of the salt abysses of the sea. Thither I will bring you at the break of day and set you properly in ambush; you and three of your companions, carefully chosen as the trustiest men of your staunch ship. And now I will warn you of all the formidable tricks of this old god. First he will muster his seals, to count them: and when he has fingered them all off and recognized each one, then he will lie down in their midst like a shepherd in the midst of a flock. When you see him settle down, at that moment call up your mighty strength and hold him there, though he will struggle vehemently, desperately, to escape you. In his urgency he will assume all shapes, of whatever things there be that creep upon the earth: and he will turn to water and to flaming heavenly fire: but do you hold to him, unflinchingly, gripping ever the tighter: and at the last he will speak in his own nature and as you saw him when he lay down to sleep. Then indeed, hero, cease your effort and let the old man be: while you ask him which of the gods is angry with you and how you shall return home across the fish-quick sea."

'Having spoken she dived beneath the billows: while I plodded away to the ships drawn up on the beach. My mind as I went was all clouded with perplexities. However I did regain the ships and the sea: and by them we made our supper while immortal night came down. Then we stretched out to sleep with the breaking of the surf beside us.

'At the first red finger of daybreak in the east I was again afoot, pacing the verge of the outstretched sea in most earnest supplication to the gods: then I chose three of the company, the three I could most trust in any undertaking. As for the goddess she had been down into the broad bosom of the sea and brought back from the depths the pelts of four seals all newly flayed. She had thought out a way of deceiving her father, and had dug lying-places in the sand of the sea-shore: by them she sat awaiting us. We came to her side and she made us to lie down in these lairs, where she threw a seal-skin over each form. Then indeed our vigil was like to have been most terrible, so hard to bear was the deathly stench of the sea-born seals. Indeed what man would choose to couch beside a monster of the deep?

'The goddess it was who saved us and refreshed us greatly by bringing to each one of us and setting under our noses scented ambrosia, so marvellously sweet that it abolished the animal stink. Thus the whole morning we endured hardily while the seals came out all together from the main and basked in ranks along the water's edge. At noon the Ancient of the Sea himself came forth and found his fat seals and went down the line of them to add up their number; counting us as the first four beasts, his heart not warning him of the fraud afoot. Then he laid himself down. We shouted our cry and leaped upon him grappling him with our hands: to find that the old one had in no wise forgotten the resources of his magic. His first change was into a hairy lion: then a dragon: then a leopard: then a mighty boar. He became a film of water, and afterwards a high-branched tree. We hardened our hearts and held firmly to him throughout.

'At long last the old wizard grew distressed and broke into words, questioning me: "Son of Atreus, which God conspired with you in this plan to ambush me and take me against my will? What is it that you must have?" So he said, and in reply I spoke as follows: "Ancient: you know. Why confuse our issue by questions? I am detained too long in this island and can find no token why: so that my heart grows faint. Therefore do you now, as one of the all-knowing Gods, tell me which of the Immortal Ones hobbles me here and delays my journey. How is my return to be contrived, over the sea and its thronging fish?"

'At once he answered me, "Why, of course your fault was in not paying to Zeus and to the other gods liberal sacrifice before your setting off. This would have ensured the quickest passage to your native land, by ship across the wine-dark sea. Now it is ordained that you shall not see your friends nor reach your well-appointed house in the country of your fathers until once again you have entered the river of Egypt (the divine river fed by heavenly rain) and offered their sacramental hecatombs to the eternal masters of the open skies. Thereafter the gods will give you the road of your desire."

'So he said, and my modest spirit quailed within me when I heard that I must once more cross the shadowy main that long and woeful way to Egypt. Nevertheless I found words to answer him. "I will carry out your bidding, Venerable One: yet I pray you give me also a clear word on this other matter. All those Achaeans whom Nestor and I left when we sailed from Troy – did they get home undamaged with their ships, or were some lost, either by harsh fate in shipwreck or in their comrades' arms, after their war had been well ended?"

'This was my question. And he replied, "Son of Atreus, why enquire too closely of me on this? To know or to learn what I know about it is not your need: I warn you that when you hear all the truth your tears will not be far behind. Of those others many went under; many came through. How many fell in battle your eyes saw: but two only of the chiefs of the bronze-corseletted Achaeans died on the way back. One other is still somehow alive, pent and languishing in the boundless sea. Aias was wrecked amongst his long-oared ships by act of Poseidon, who carried him to the huge cliffs of Gyrae, yet delivered him from the waves. Thus he would have escaped destruction despite the hatred which Athene nursed for him if he, infatuate in his frantic

pride, had not cried out an overweening word – how in the teeth of
the Gods he had escaped the sea's mighty void. Poseidon heard this
high proclaiming and snatched at his trident: with labouring hands
he let drive at the rock of Gyrae and hacked it through. The stump
remained, but the jagged pinnacle on which Aias had first pitched,
boasting and blaspheming, broke off and fell into the sea, carrying
him down into the vasty seething depths: where he died, choked in
its briny water.

"'As for Agamemnon, your brother, he somehow escaped his fates
and got away in his shapely vessels. Our Lady Hera was his saviour,
till he had almost attained to Maleia, that steep mountain. There a
tempest fell upon him and snatched him from his course. It carried
him, deeply groaning, across the fish-infested waves to that butt of
land where Thyestes dwelt of old in his settlements: but now Aegisthus
the son had succeeded him. Yet from here also prospect of a sure return
appeared. The gods once again changed the wind to fair: homeward
they came; and as the joyful leader touched upon his own land he bent
down and kissed its soil with his lips, crying hot tears of gladness, for
that at last he saw his native place.

"'Yet from above, from the look-out, the watchman had seen him
– a sentry posted by guileful Aegisthus with promise of two gold
talents for reward of vigilance. A whole year had he been on guard
lest King Agamemnon get past without being spied and first signal
his return by headlong attack upon the usurpers in his house. The
watchman ran with his news to the house of Aegisthus, the shepherd
of the people, who straightway put his cunning plot in train. A
chosen twenty of the ablest-bodied local men he hid in ambush,
while on the other side of the great hall he had a high feast spread.
Then with welcoming horses and cars, but with iniquity in his hollow
mind, he went forth to meet Agamemnon the king. Into his house
Aegisthus ushered him (all unsuspicious of the death hidden there)
and feasted him, and after cut him down – as a man might cut down
an ox at its stall. Nor was there anyone left of the company of

Atrides: nor even of Aegisthus' company. All of them fell there in the palace."

'Here Proteus ceased his tale: and again my kindly heart failed within me. Down I sank weeping on the sands nor did my spirit any more desire to live on and see the light of the sun. Yet later, when I had indulged to the full in tears, wallowing on the ground, the Venerable One of the Sea, the Infallible, further addressed me: "Persist no more, son of Atreus, in thus stubbornly weeping: we shall not thereby attain an end. Instead try your quickest to devise a return to your country: there you may happen on the criminal yet living: or Orestes may have just forestalled you and killed him: in which case you will be in time for the death ceremonies." So he said: and thereat my heart and stately spirit glowed once more in the breast of my sorrows: and I found winged words to answer him: "These men I have now heard of: but name me that third man who yet lives but lingers somewhere in the broad sea: or dead? I wish to know it, even though my grief be deepened."

'So I said, and he replied again: "The son of Laertes, the lord of Ithaca. I saw him in an island, letting fall great tears throughout the domain of the nymph Calypso who there holds him in constraint: and he may not get thence to his own land, for he has by him no oared ships or company to bear him across the sea's great swell. Hear lastly the fate decreed you, O Menelaus, cherished of Zeus. You are not to die in Argos of the fair horse-pastures, not there to encounter death: rather will the Deathless Ones carry you to the Elysian plain, the place beyond the world, where is fair-haired Rhadamanthus and where the lines of life run smoothest for mortal men. In that land there is no snowfall, nor much winter, nor any storm of rain: but from the river of earth the west wind ever sings soft and thrillingly to re-animate the souls of men. There you will have Helen for yourself and will be deemed of the household of Zeus."

'He spoke and plunged beneath the billows: but I went to the ships with my gallant following: and my heart as I went was shadowed by its cares. Yet we attained the ships and the sea-beaches and furnished ourselves a supper, while ambrosial night drew down, persuading us to stretch out in repose by the fringes of the tide. And with the early rosy-fingered Dawn we first of all ran down our ships into the divine salt sea and placed masts and sails ready in their tight hulls. Then the men swarmed aboard, and sat down on their rowing-thwarts: and having duly arranged themselves they flailed the sea white with their oars. Back once again to the river of Egypt, the water of the gods, where I made fast the ships to make the ordered sacrifice of burnt offerings. When I had so slaked the resentment of the never-dying gods I heaped up a great mound in Agamemnon's name, that the glory of him might never be put out. All things were then accomplished. I turned back. They gave me a wind, did the Immortal Ones, which carried me swiftly to my beloved land.

'But see now, Telemachus. Remain with me in my palace until there dawns the eleventh or twelfth day from now: and then I shall dismiss you nobly, with conspicuous gifts – three horses shall you have and a two-seater chariot of the finest workmanship – yea, and a beautiful embossed cup, that each time you pour an offering from it to the deathless gods you may think of me, for all your days.'

To him said Telemachus, 'Atrides, I beg you, delay me not for all that time. It would be possible for me to sit still here in your presence and forget home or parents throughout a whole year, so wonderfully am I entranced to hear your words and tales. But my companions are already chafing in happy Pylos, and would you hold me yet many days in this place? As for the gift which it pleases you to give me, let it be an heirloom: for to Ithaca I cannot take horses. Better I leave them here to dignify your place. The plain of your lordship is wide, rich in clover and water-grass and wheat and grain and also strong-strawed white barley. In Ithaca we have no broad riding-grounds, no meadow land at all: of these our islands which rise rock-like from the sea, not one is fit for mounted work, or grass-rich: least of all my Ithaca. Yet are its goat-pastures more lovely in my sight than fields for grazing horses.'

So he replied: and Menelaus of the ringing battle-shout smiled and petted him with his hand, and naming him dearly said, 'My child, your gentle words disclose your breeding. Of course I will exchange my gifts. I have such choice. See, out of the store of treasures ranged in my house I give you the fairest and costliest: – Item, a wrought mixing-bowl of solid silver doubled with gold about the rim. Work of Hephaestus. Hero Phaedimus, King of Sidon, endowed me with it when I found shelter in his house on my way back here. I am happy to transfer it now to you.' As they so exchanged their phrases those whose turn it was to provide (and share) the entertainment that night in the palace of the godlike king came near, driving before them the needful sheep and carrying their generous wine. For them too their high-coiffed wives sent a store of wheaten bread.

Here were these men, toiling orderly in the palace to make ready the feast for their night: while over in Ithaca the suitors before the great house of Odysseus were junketing with their established insolence, the whim now being to put the weight or hurl throwing-spears on the level fore-court. Antinous and imposing Eurymachus sat and looked on. These two were the lordliest suitors, pre-eminent in reputation. To them drew nigh Noemon, son of Phronius, who greeted Antinous and asked, 'Antinous, have we any idea in our heads (or none) of when Telemachus is due back from sandy Pylos? He went off with my ship, and now I am wanting her to take me across to Elis, in whose wide lands are twelve mares of mine at milk with stout mule-foals, yet unbroken. I have a design to drive off some one of these and break it in.'

His news amazed their minds. They had never imagined to themselves that the lad might have gone to Neleus' city, Pylos: rather that he was somewhere in the estate, with the flocks or perhaps keeping company with the swineherd. So Antinous son of Eupeithes turned to him and demanded: 'Let me have the whole truth of this. When did he go, and who were the young men who abetted him? Were they chosen Ithacans, or his serfs and house-thralls, of whom he might properly dispose at will? Also answer me this too, categorically, that I may be sure: – did he lift your black ship off you by force, against your will; or did you voluntarily lend her to him because he begged the favour formally?'

Phronius' son Noemon replied: 'I gave her to him freely. What could one do when such a man, having a heart-full of worry, asked a kindness? It would be churlish to refuse compliance. The youths who after us are the best men of the country-side formed his crew. The captain, when they went aboard, I recognized for Mentor, or some god his very image: the point has puzzled me, for I saw goodly Mentor here in the city at the dawning of yesterday, when already he had left in the ship for Pylos.'

He finished, and turned away towards his father's house. The lordly wrath of his two hearers had been kindled. They made the suitors stop their playing and sit in conclave. Then Antinous son of Eupeithes rose to address them. He was deeply moved. His black-bound heart heaved with wild rage and his eyes were flashing fires.

'Heaven and hell!' he cried, 'here's a fine thing Telemachus has carried through in style to its very end – this journey of his. We used to swear it would come to nought: yet the young fellow has slipped clean away against all our wills like this – just launching out a ship and helping himself to the best company in the place. He threatens ever worse and worse for us: may Zeus cut the strength off from him before he reaches the height of manhood! I ask you to supply me a fast ship and a crew of twenty men, with which to watch and waylay him as he comes through the narrow gut between Ithaca and steep Samos: that this gadding about after his father may cost him dear at last.' He spoke: they cried applause and urged him to execution. Then they rose up and returned to Odysseus' house.

Not for very long did Penelope remain unaware of these plots which the suitors were hatching in the evil depths of their minds: for the poursuivant Medon told her what he had overheard of their council, he being just beyond the court-wall while they were thrashing out their schemes within. Medon hasted through the building to bring his news to Penelope who, as he crossed the threshold of her quarters, shrilled at him, 'Herald, why have the famous suitors sent you in here? Perhaps they now give orders even to the house-maidens of godlike Odysseus, and bid them lay aside their duties and prepare them a feast? May they be dining here to-day for their last and latest time, never again to meet, never to go on wooing! You! who ever swarm to spoil the great wealth, the livelihood of shrewd Telemachus. You! who never heard in days when you were children any word from your fathers of how Odysseus bore himself towards your parents, with never an arbitrary deed nor even an arbitrary word, in the city! Yet such are prerogatives of consecrated kings, who will hate this one and love that – all save Odysseus: for he wrought no iniquity upon any man whatsoever. Indeed your temper and ugly works come out plain in this: nor does any grace survive for past favours.'

Medon's enlightened mind advised him. He quietly replied, 'If only that, O Queen, were the worst of our troubles! The suitors discuss an evil deplorably greater; which may Zeus, son of Kronos, forfend: they are fully determined that their sharp swords shall slay Telemachus on his way home: he went to learn news of his father, you see, away to most holy Pylos and sacred Lacedaemon.'

At his speech her knees gave way, and her loving heart: and for a long time stupor cut off her power of speech. Her eyes brimmed with tears and the copious fountain of her voice was stopped. After very long, words came to her for a reply: 'Herald, why has my son gone? He had no call, none whatever, to embark in any one of the swift-going ships which serve men as horses to ride the salt waves: nor to cross the great water. Was he determined that not even his name should survive among men?'

Well-advised again was the saying of Medon: 'I do not know if a god roused him out: or whether it was that his own great heart rushed him to Pylos upon enquiry as to his father's return or fate.' He spoke and turned back through the house of Odysseus: while upon her came down a heart-corroding agony: so that she could not even guide herself to one of the many stools which stood about the house. Instead she sank to the door-sill of her richly-appointed room and wailed aloud in piteous fashion: while round her came crooning all the women-servants of the house, the young ones with the old ones: and across the torrent of her grief Penelope sobbed to them: –

'Hear me, my people. Now the lord of Olympus has given to me greater pain than has been the lot of all the women born and brought up my mates. Of old had I lost my mighty husband, the lion-hearted, most virtuously endowed of all the Greeks; indeed a noble man whose fame was bruited across Hellas and to the heart of Argos. But now the whirlwinds have snatched my beloved son ignobly from our halls without my hearing he had gone. O cruel women whose hearts knew all, but did not think to call me from my bed when the lad went down to his black hollow ship. If I had known that he was intending the journey, very surely he should have stayed, however eager: or gone only by leaving my dead body behind him in the halls. Hasten, some one of you, and call old Dolius, the bondman my father gave me, even before I entered this house, my gardener who keeps the orchard with its many trees. He shall run to Laertes and sitting by his side shall retail to him all these things. Perhaps Laertes may weave some device in his heart for a public appeal to this people who are coveting the final destruction of his seed and the seed of godlike Odysseus.'

Privileged Eurycleia the nurse answered and said, 'My lady, I must declare myself, whether you kill me therefor with your pitiless blade or spare me to live on in your service. I knew all his intent, and what-ever he bade me I gave him of food and sweet wine. He exacted of me a great oath that I should not tell you before twelve days had passed, unless you yourself missed him and heard that he had left: for he would not that you should mar your lovely flesh with tears. Do you therefore bathe yourself and choose clean clothing for your body: and afterward go to your upper room with your attendant maidens and supplicate Athene, daughter of aegis-bearing Zeus: if haply she may then save Telemachus from death. Increase not the affliction of old afflicted Laertes without cause: for I think the seed of Arceisius his ancestor is not so wholly hateful to the blessed gods that there will not be left some one of the house to enjoy its high-ceiled rooms and the fat lands which stretch hence ever so widely.'

Eurycleia's words lulled my lady's weeping, and freed her eyes of tears. She bathed, changed garments, and with her maidens gained the upper floor: and then she put the bruised barley of the heave-offering into its basket and prayed to Athene: –

'Hear me, unwearied Goddess, child of aegis-bearing Zeus: if ever experienced Odysseus burnt to you in these halls fat thighs of oxen or sheep, then be mindful of them now unto me and save my beloved son: deliver him from the suitors and the excesses of their evil will.' Her yearning broke in vibrant cry upon the goddess, who heard the supplication: while below stairs in the dusky halls the suitors were rioting, some rude youth now and again making boast, 'This much-courted queen goes on preparing her marriage with us, never guessing that death is decreed for her son.' The others took up and repeated the saying – they being the infatuates who did not guess how death had been decreed – till Antinous spoke out and said, 'Look here, my masters. Now will we cease uttering these words so pleased and proud, lest someone repeat them in the house. Instead let us rise up silently to carry out the scheme arranged which even now met all our fancies.' Thereupon he chose his twenty leading spirits, who rose up and went to the foreshore and the swift ships, where their first move was to drag down a ship into deep water. They stowed masts and sails into her blackness and refixed round the oars their raw-hide thole-loops, as was due and meet. They strained flat the white sails. The disdainful attendants carried war-harness to them. Then they took her well out to moorings in the road, and came ashore for supper and to wait for the fall of darkness.

All this while circumspect Penelope was lying in her upper room, without eating or even tasting any food or drink, agitated to know if her innocent son would escape death or be overcome by the hands of the intolerant suitors. Her distress was the distress of a lion beset and at bay in a throng of men, seeing with anxious eye how they spread round him in a crafty circle. With just such fears was she wrestling when the swoon of sleep came down on her. She lay back and slept: and all her frame relaxed.

Then the grey-eyed goddess, Athene, provided a fresh resource. She created a phantom, the bodily likeness of another daughter of stout Icarius, Iphthime, who had wedded Eumelus and lived at Pherae. This wraith she sent to the house of godlike Odysseus, to weeping, moaning Penelope, that she might lay aside her lamentation and loud tears. In it came to the wife's chamber, through the thong-hole of the latch, and took stand there behind her head and said its say to her as follows: 'Do you sleep, Penelope, with your loving heart so bruised? Not even the Gods resting at ease above our affairs can bear to let you so weep and suffer, forasmuch as there is a homecoming appointed for your son. He is no transgressor against the gods.'

Cautious Penelope murmured back as she slumbered very sweetly in the gate of dreams: 'Why come now, sister, seeing how rarely you get here from your so-distant home? You tell me to lay aside these many distressful griefs which torture my heart and mind. Why, a time ago I lost my lion-hearted hero husband, whose nobility was noised through Hellas and Argos: and now my beloved boy, a child untempered in affairs or words, has gone in a hollow ship. I sorrow more for him than for my man and tremble in fear of what he may suffer among the strangers he visits or in the wide sea. His many enemies invent snares for him, intending to kill him before he can reach home again.'

The dim wraith replied, 'Be brave: give not fear too large rule over your heart. There goes with him a guide of power such as all men would pray to have stand by them, even Pallas Athene. She takes mercy upon your grief and directly sends me that I may speak to you these comforts.'

Wise Penelope again said, 'If you are divine and have heard the voice of a god, enlighten me now upon my unfortunate husband, whether he yet lives and sees the light of day, or is now a dead man in the house of Hades.'

Said the dim shadow: 'Of that I will not tell you all, not even if he be alive or dead. It were ill to speak airily of that.' With which words the spectre vanished by the latch, and dissolved into the moving air: but Penelope the daughter of Icarius rose up from her sleep, her loving heart warmed by the vividness of the dream which had fallen on her in the gloaming.

The suitors set forth, harbouring sadden death for Telemachus in their hearts, and sailed the water-ways as far as a stony island in mid-sea, equidistant from Ithaca and craggy Samos, even the islet Asteris, no large place: which has a harbour with two approaches and in it a berth for ships. There they drew up to lie in wait for him.

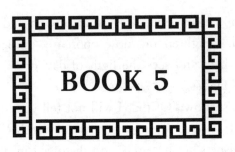

BOOK 5

Dawn rose from her marriage-bed beside high-born Tithonus to bring her daylight to both gods and men. The immortals, with Zeus the high-thundering, their mightiest one, sat down in council: and to them Athene spoke thus, designing to remind them of the many misfortunes of Odysseus, whose long sojourn in the nymph's house lay heavy on her heart: –

'Father Zeus, and you happy ever-living Gods: henceforth let no sceptred king study to be kindly or gentle, or to ensue justice and equity. It profits more to be harsh and unseemly in act. Divine Odysseus was a clement and fatherly king; but no one of the men, his subjects, remembers it of him for good: while fate has abandoned him to languish sorely in Lady Calypso's island, kept there by her high hand, a prisoner in her house. Nor has he power to regain the land of his fathers, seeing that he lacks galleys and followers to speed him over the broad back of ocean. Moreover, there is now a plot afoot to murder his darling son as he returns from sacred Pylos or noble Lacedaemon, whither he went in hope to hear somewhat of his father.'

Zeus the cloud-marshal answered her and said, 'My child, too fierce are the judgements of your mouth. Besides, I think this last move was of your scheming, for Odysseus to avenge himself on those men when he comes. You have the knowledge, the power and the skill to convey Telemachus again to his own place wholly unscathed. See that it is so: and that the suitors come back too in their ship, as they went.'

He turned to Hermes, the son he loved, and said, 'Hermes, hear your commission as our particular messenger. Inform this nymph of the love-locks of my fixed decision that long-suffering Odysseus shall return home as best he can, without furtherance from gods or mortal men. Therefore he is to lash together a raft as firm as may be, on which after twenty days of hazard and disaster he will make rich-glebed Scheria, the Phaeacian land. The Phaeacians, godlike in race and habit, will take him to their heart with all honour as divine: and send him forward to his native place in a ship laden with gifts of copper and gold and clothing of an abundance such as Odysseus would never have amassed for himself in the sack of Troy, even though he had come away intact, and with the full share of booty assigned him by lot. The decree is, that so furnished he shall once again behold his friends and enter his stately house in the country of his fathers.'

Such was the order: and the messenger, the Argus-slayer, made no delay in his obedience. Instantly he laced to his feet the fair sandals of imperishable gold by which he made equal way, swift as a breath of wind, over the ocean and over the waste places of the earth. He took the wand with which at will he could lure the eyes of men to slumber or wake them into activity, and with it in hand the Argus-slayer leaped out upon the air and flew strongly. Over mount Pierus he dived down from the firmament to sea level: and then along the waves he sped like a cormorant which down the dread troughs of the wild sea chases its fish and drenches its close plumage in the salt spume. Just so did Hermes skim the recurring wave-crests.

But when at last he attained that remote island, he quitted the purple sea and went inland as far as the great cave in which lived the nymph of the well-braided hair. He chanced to find her within where a great fire burned on its appointed hearth, perfuming the island far across with the fragrance of flaming cedar-wood logs and straight-grained incense trees. Inside the cavern the nymph's sweet voice could be heard singing as she went to and fro before her loom, weaving with a golden shuttle. All round the cave-mouth there flourished a luxuriant copse of alder trees and black poplars and rich-scented cypresses: therein roosted birds of long wing, owls and hawks and chattering hook-billed crows – birds of the sea whose livelihood was from the waters. A young strong vine loaded with bunches of grapes wreathed the opening of the cave. Four springs quite near together jetted out translucent water in separate rills ingeniously contrived, each to water its own garden-plot. The soft lawns were starred with parsley and violets. Even an immortal coming upon the nook would pause before its beauty and feel his heart made glad: the messenger, Argus' bane, halted in amazement.

When his heart had taken its fill of wondering, he entered the great cave: nor was his figure strange to Calypso, the very goddess, when she saw him come into her presence. (It is a gift to the gods, to know one another when they meet, however distant the home of one of them may chance to lie.) In the cavern he did not find great-hearted Odysseus, who sat weeping on the shore as was his wont, crying out his soul with groaning and griefs and letting flow his tears while he eyed the fruitless sea.

Calypso, the fair goddess, made Hermes seat himself on a splendid polished throne, and asked him, 'Hermes of the gold rod, ever honoured and welcome, from of old you have had no habit of visiting me: why do you come here to-day? Tell me your mind. My spirit is eager to second your desire if its fulfilment be in my gift and such a thing as may lawfully be fulfilled. Yet first enter further into the cave that I may put before you the meed of guests.' With such words did the goddess bring forward a table bounteously set with ambrosia. She blended him ruddy nectar. Then did the messenger, Argus' bane, drink and eat: but when he had dined and made happy his spirit with the food, he opened his mouth and said: –

'As goddess to god you ask me, you order me, to tell why I have come. Hear the truth of it! Zeus commanded my journey: by no choice of my own did I fare to you across so unspeakable a waste of salt water. Who would willingly come where there is no near city of men to offer sacrifice to the gods and burn us tasty hundreds of oxen? Listen: – in no way can another god add or subtract any tittle from the will of

Zeus, the aegis-bearer. He declares that you have with you the unhappiest man of men – less happy than all those who fought for nine years round the citadel of Priam and in the tenth year sacked the city and went homeward. Yet during their return they sinned against Athene, and she worked up against them an evil wind and tall waves by which this man's entire splendid company were cast away. As for himself, the wind blew him and the sea washed him to this spot. Wherefore now the Father commands that you send him hence with speed: for it is decreed that he is not to die far from his friends. On the contrary he is to behold these friends again and is to sit under his lofty roof in his own land.' So he said: and as he spoke Calypso the lovely goddess grew cold and shuddered. Then with barbed words did she reply: 'Cruel are you gods and immoderately jealous of all others; especially do you hate it when goddesses elect to lie openly with men, or fall in love and make a match of it with some mortal. Remember how it was when pink-fingered Dawn chose Orion. You gods at ease in your heaven grudged the union bitterly, even until chaste Artemis of the golden throne killed him in Ortygia by an infliction of her gentle darts. So again it befell when long-tressed Demeter unleashed her passion and coupled herself for love and venery with Iasion in the thrice-broken fallows. Not for long was Zeus unaware: and then He slew him with a cast of his blinding thunderbolt.

'Just in that same way you gods are now envying me this man I live with. Yet it was I who saved him as he clung astride his vessel's keel, alone and adrift in the wine-dark ocean. Zeus had launched a white thunderbolt at his ship and shattered her: and in her wreck were all the worthy henchmen lost. Only it chanced that he himself drifted to my shore before the wind and waves: and I have loved him and cared for him and promised myself he should not die nor grow old all his days. Yet very justly do you say that no lesser god can overpass or make vain the purpose of aegis-bearing Zeus: accordingly, if the impulse and order are from Him, I must let my man go hence across the sterile sea. Yet shall the sending be in no wise mine. Here are neither oared ships nor crews to convoy him over ocean's broad back. Unreservedly however will I furnish him my very best advice as to how he may come safe to his native land.'

The messenger, the Slayer of Argus, answered: 'Of a surety send him away now, in utter obedience and regard for the wrath of Zeus: lest He, being angered against you, later bear malice.' And after this parting word the mighty Argus Slayer went away: while the nymph set out to find great-hearted Odysseus, in accordance with the command which Zeus had sent. She found him sitting by the water's edge: his eyes as ever dewed with tears at this ebbing of his precious life in vain lamentations after deliverance – seeing that the nymph no longer pleased his fancy. True, that every night would he sleep with her: he had no choice while he lived in her vaulted cave. Yet was he not willing, and she willed too much: consequently day-long he haunted the rocks and pebble-beaches of the island's shore, retching up his heart with crying and sighs and misery, his gaze fixed upon the desolate main through a blur of tears.

The goddess approached him and said: 'Ill-fated man, grieve no longer in this place. Your life shall not so fade away: for see, my mind is most ready to send you hence. Up now and fell yourself tall tree-trunks and carpenter them with metal tools into a great raft, substantial enough to carry an upper deck clear of the water, on which you may journey over the misted sea. I will supply food to guard you against hunger, and water and red wine such as you enjoy: and I will put rich robes on you and ensure a mild wind in your wake that you may come without misadventure to your native place – if so the Gods will: for that company of the wide heavens are more potent than myself, alike in purpose and fulfilment.'

Her speech made steadfast Odysseus shiver. He loudly shot back at her, 'Surely, Goddess, something not at all to my advantage, something quite contrary, lies behind this your command – that on a raft I launch out over the great soundings of a sea which is so perilous and difficult that not invariably do the tall swift-running ships pass it in safety: not even when Zeus blesses them and makes them happy with his assisting winds. Understand therefore that I shall not embark upon this raft-venture without your will: not unless you as a goddess consent to swear me a great oath that in this you do not plan further misfortunes for my account.'

His words made Calypso, the beautiful nymph, smile. As she soothed him with her hand, repeating his name, she spoke to him as follows: 'Sharp-witted rogue you are, to imagine and dare say such a thing to me. Bear witness now, Earth, and spacious Heaven overhead, and the river of Styx that slideth downward (which oath is the greatest and most terrible in the use of the blessed gods) how in this counsel I intend no sort of evil against you. Rather am I planning and advising you with the scrupulous care I should have for myself, if ever I stood in such case. Believe me that my understanding is ripe: and the heart in my breast is not made of iron, but very pitiful.'

Having ended, the goddess turned back abruptly. Odysseus followed the divine leader so that they re-entered the cave, immortal and mortal keeping company. There the man sat him down on the throne from which Hermes had lately risen, and the nymph served him a various refreshment of such meat and drink as men usually take. Afterward she took place opposite her great hero, while the maids plied her with nectar and ambrosia. Freely they partook of the cheer at hand till they had had their fill of eating and drinking. Then Calypso the lovely goddess opened her mouth and said: –

'Kinsman of Zeus and son of Laertes, many-counselled Odysseus: is it your true wish, even yet, to go back to your own country? God forgive you: may you be happy there! Ah, did but the mirror of your mind show you what misfortune must yet fill your cup before you attain the home you seek, verily you would dwell here with me always, keeping my house and your immortality; to the utter rejection of this day-long and every-day yearning which moves you to behold your wife. Think not however that I avow myself her less than rival, either in figure or in parts. It were out and out impious for a mere woman to vie in frame and face with immortals.'

𝕽𝕽𝕽𝕽𝕽𝕽𝕽𝕽𝕽𝕽𝕽𝕽𝕽𝕽𝕽𝕽𝕽𝕽𝕽𝕽𝕽𝕽𝕽𝕽𝕽𝕽𝕽𝕽𝕽𝕽𝕽𝕽𝕽

In his worldly wisdom great Odysseus answered, 'O Queen and Divinity, hold this not against me. In my true self I do most surely know how far short of you discreet Penelope falls in stature and in comeliness. For she is human: and you are changeless, immortal, ever-young. Yet even so I choose – yea all my days are consumed in longing – to travel home and see the day of my arrival dawn. If a god must shatter me upon the wine-dark sea, so be it. I shall suffer with a high heart; for my courage has been tempered to endure all misery. Already have I known every mood of pain and travail, in storms and in the war. Let the coming woe be added to the count of those which have been.' The sun fell and twilight deepened as he spoke. They rose and went far into the smooth-walled cave – to its very end: and there by themselves they took their joy of one another in the way of love, all night.

When the child of the first light, rosy-fingered Dawn, appeared then Odysseus clothed himself in tunic and cloak, while Calypso flung about her a loose silver gown, filmy and flowing. She clipped a girdle of fine gold about her loins and covered the hair of her head with a snood. Then she turned to speed the going of high-hearted Odysseus.

First she gave him a great axe of cutting copper, well-suited to his reach. It was ground on both edges and into the socketed head was firmly wedged the well-rounded handle of olive-wood. Then she gave him a finished smoothing-adze and led the way to the end of the island where the trees grew tall, the alders and the poplars with heaven-scaling pines, withered long since and sapless and very dry, which would float high for him. She showed him where the loftiest trees had grown, did Calypso that fair goddess: then she returned to her cavern while he busily cut out his beams, working with despatch. Twenty trees in all he threw and axed into shape with the sharp copper, trimming them adeptly and trueing them against his straight-edge.

Then his lovely goddess brought to him augers with which he bored the logs for lashing together: firmly he fastened them with pegs and ties. As broad as a skilled shipwright would design and lay down the floor of a roomy merchantship, just so full in beam did Odysseus make his raft. To carry his upper deck he set up many ribs, closely kneed and fitted, and he united the heads of these with long rubbing-strakes, for gunwales. He put a mast into his craft, with a yard in proportion: also a stern sweep with which to steer her. To defend himself from breaching seas he fenced in the sides of the raft with wicker work, wattling it cunningly all of osiers like a basket and adding a lavish reinforcement of stanchions. Calypso came again with a bolt of cloth for sails, which he stitched strongly. Then he set up stays and sheets and halyards, and at last with levers he worked the raft down into the sacred sea.

By the fourth evening the work ended: and on the next, on the fifth day, beautiful Calypso sent him away from her island, having washed him and adorned him with sweet-smelling clothes. On his raft the goddess put provisions; one skin of dark wine, another (a very large one) of water; like-wise a leather sack of foodstuffs which included many dainties dear to his heart. She called forth a kindly warm wind in his favour. The delighted Odysseus spread wide his sail to this fair breeze and sat down by the stern oar, most skilfully steering. Nor did sleep once take possession of his eyelids, so continually he kept gazing on the Pleiades, or on Arcturus that goes down so late, or on the Great Bear (they call it also Wain) which revolves in constant narrow watch upon Orion and alone of stars will never enter the bath of ocean. Goddess Calypso had exhorted him to keep this star always on his left while he voyaged, as he did for seventeen days; and on the eighteenth day the loom of the nearest mountain top of the Phaeacian land rose up into his sight. Over the clouded face of the sea it appeared as it were a lifted shield.

Yet then the God, the Earth-shaker, spied him from far off by the mountains of the Solymi, by which way he was returning from Aethiopia. The mind of Poseidon was mightily enraged when he saw who was sailing his sea. With a wagging of the head he began to mutter to himself, 'There now, while I have been away amongst the Aethiopians these gods have changed their mind about Odysseus. Alas, he nears the land of the Phaeacians where the decree runs that he shall escape the balance of the miseries he has encountered. However I think I can give him yet a long excursion into sorrow.'

With this he drove the clouds into a heap and, trident in hand, tossed together the desolate waters. He summoned all the violent gusts that were in all the winds and let them loose, blind-folding sea and land with storm-clouds. Night leaped into heaven. Mightily the surge rolled up, for east wind clashed upon south wind, the ill-blowing west with the north wind from the upper sky. Therefore the knees and warm heart of Odysseus shook and heavily did he commune with his own high courage.

'Ill-fated one, what is this latest misery in the path? I fear the goddess spoke no more than truth when she said I should fill the cup of my disasters in the deep before I reached home. Surely this is the end at last. See with what storms Zeus has wreathed all his heaven and how the deep sea is moved. Squalls rush down from the four corners of the world: utter and inevitable is my doom. Thrice blessed, four times blessed were the Greeks who perished in the plain of Troy to oblige the sons of Atreus. Indeed I should have met my end and died there on that day when the throng of Trojans made me the anvil of their copper-bladed spears round the dead body of the fallen son of Peleus. So dying I should have won my funeral rites and the Achaeans would have bruited my glory: but now fate traps me in this ignoble death.'

Just as he ceased a huge rushing wave towered, toppled, and fell upon the raft, whirling it round. The winds came down confusedly in fierce turmoil and snapped the mast across in the middle. Yard and sail flew wide into the deep. Odysseus let the steering oar jerk from his hand and was himself thrown far from the raft into the body of the wave, whose weight of water long time buried him: nor did his struggles easily avail to get him out from under its wash, because of the hampering heavy clothes of honour in which divine Calypso had dressed him.

Yet at the last he did emerge, spewing bitter brine from his lips while other wet streams ran gurgling down his face. Yet not even in such dire distress did he forget his raft, but swam hard after it and caught it amongst the breaking waves and crouched down in its centre to escape, for the moment, the imminence of death.

His refuge was tossing hither and thither in the eddies of the waves, as when in autumn's stormy days the North wind pitches dried thistles along the fields, so that they lock spines into each other as they roll. Just in this way did the winds bowl the raft hither and thither across the face of the water. Sometimes the South wind flung it across to the North wind to carry, or the East wind would let the West wind chase it back.

But Ino of the slim ankles had seen him, – Ino the bright, a daughter of Cadmus. She had been born mortal in the beginning: just a simple-speaking girl: but she had attained honour amongst the gods and now was made free of wide ocean's salty depths. She pitied Odysseus so carried to and fro in anguish. Easily, like a sea gull, she rose from the level of the sea to light on the raft and say, 'Unhappy man, why is Poseidon so cruelly provoked against you as to plant these many harms in your path? Yet shall you not wholly perish, for all his eager hate. See: – if, as I think, you are understanding, this is what you must do. Strip off these clothes that are upon you and abandon the raft to go with the winds, while instead you try by swimming to gain the Phaeacian shore, your destined safety. Further, take this divine veil of mine and strain it round your chest. While you wear it you need not be harmed, or die: and afterwards, when you have solid land in your possession, unbind the veil from you and fling it far out from shore into the wine-dark sea, yourself turning away the while.'

The goddess spoke, gave him the scarf, and with bird-swiftness sprang back again into the breakers: and the blackness of the water closed over her. Then was staunch Odysseus sore perplexed, and he thus held debate in his brave heavy-laden heart: 'Travail upon travail for me. This may be some new snare set for me by a grudging goddess who would have me abandon my raft. I dare not obey her at the moment: for with my own eyes I saw how far off was the coast to which she would have me escape. Perhaps it will be my best course if, so long as the logs cling together in their setting, I remain here and put a bold face on my plight: but when the waves have battered the frame of the raft to pieces, then will I swim for it; for by that time the wit of man could not devise a better scheme.'

While his judgement and instinct pondered thus Poseidon the Earth-shaker heaped up against him a wave of waves, a terror and tribulation, so high and combing it was. With this he smote him. It flung the long baulks of the raft apart as a powerful wind lays hold on a heap of dried chaff and whirls its straws everyway in confusion. Odysseus leaped astride a single beam, riding it as a man rides a plunging horse: while he tore off the clothes which had been fair Calypso's gift. Then he wrapped the veil about his breast and headlong leaped into the waves, striking out with his hands and urgently swimming. The proud Earth-shaker saw him, wagged his head and gloated to himself thus: 'Everywhere in trouble, all over the seas, wherever you go! In the end doubtless you are to slip in amongst those Zeus-favoured people and be happy: yet I trust you will never complain that your punishment has been inadequate.' He whipped up his glossy-coated horses and departed to Aegae, to his splendid place.

And now did Athene the daughter of Zeus take counter-measures. She bound fast the other winds in full career, ordering every one to be hushed and fall to sleeping: all but the impetuous North wind. Him she encouraged and by his power she laid the waves flat, that Odysseus, kinsman of Zeus, might indeed attain the sea-faring Phaeacians and escape death and the fates.

Nevertheless for two nights and two days he strayed across the waves and the currents, and many, many times did his heart presage to him of his death: but when at last well-tressed Dawn fairly brought in the third daylight then the gale died away and an ineffable quietness held air and sea. Still the mighty rollers rolled: but when he was upon the crest of one of these he happened to glance quickly up, and behold! land was only just ahead. To Odysseus the sight of those fields and those trees was welcome as is to a man's children the dawning of life once again in the father who has been outstretched on a sick bed, pining all too long in severe agony beneath the onslaughts of some angry power. As the children rejoice when the gods relax their father's pain, so also did Odysseus gladly swim hard forward to set his feet on the dry land. But when it was no further distant than the carry of a good shout, he could hear the heavy boom of surf against a broken shore and see how the great billows thundered down upon the naked coast in terrible clouds of spray which spattered all the sea with salty foam: for here were no inlets to welcome ships, nor roadsteads: but tall headlands, crags and cliffs. Then did the knee-joints and courage of Odysseus fail him, and sadly he questioned his own brave spirit: –

'Woe is me! Has Zeus let me behold this land only to make me despair? See, I have won my way from the depths of the tide, to find that here is no escape out of the foaming waters. There face me walls of sheer cliff, about which tumultuous seas clash loudly; and smooth the rocks run up, steep-to, so that nowhere is there lodging for my feet to bear me free from disaster. Should I try to climb, the next wave would take me and fling me against the broken rocks; and my effort have been in vain. As for swimming further, on the chance of gaining some sheltered beach or quiet inlet of the sea, then there is fear that a fresh storm-blast may drive my groaning body again far into the fish-haunted deep: or some god may rear up against me leviathan from the sea: for illustrious Amphitrite breeds many such, and I have proof how the Earth-shaker, her lord, is wrought up against me.'

He was still weighing such things when a huge wave flung him upon the rugged shore. There would his flesh have been torn off him and his bones shattered had not the goddess Athene prompted him to seize the rock hastily in both hands. To it he held, sobbing, until the force of the wave had passed him by. So he evaded that danger; but afterwards the backwash enveloped him and cast him once more into deep water. Exactly as when a squid is dragged out from its bed the many pebbles come away in the suckers of its arms, so did the skin peel off Odysseus' strong hands against the stones. Then the billows closed over his head.

And there of a surety had woe-begone Odysseus died, contrary to fate's decree, had not grey-eyed Athene now given him a deeper wisdom, by light of which when he once more came to the surface he swam out beyond the breaking surf and along, closely eyeing the shore to see if he might achieve a sheltered landing by help of some spit or creek: and so swimming he encountered the mouth of a fair-running river which seemed to him the best spot, forasmuch as it was clear of reefs and sheltered from the wind. He felt then the outward-setting current of the river's flow and prayed to its god in his heart: –

'Hear me, whatever lord you be! I come to your worshipful presence, a fugitive from the threats of Poseidon – from the sea. Immune and respected even by the deathless gods, are wanderers like me, who now very weary come to your stream and knees. Have mercy upon me, Lord. I pray that my supplication be acceptable in your sight.'

Thus his petition: and the god forthwith allayed the current, smoothed out the eddies and made his way calm, safe-guiding him within the river's mouths. Odysseus' knees gave way together, and his sinewy arms: for his reserve of manhood had been used up in the long fight with the salt sea. The flesh had puffed out over all his body and the sea water gushed in streams from his nostrils and mouth. Wherefore he fell helpless, not able to breathe or speak, and terrible was the weariness which possessed him.

But when at last he breathed again and some warmth rallied in his heart, then he loosed from his body the veil of the goddess and let it down into the river as it was running towards the sea. The fast current bore it back, down-stream, where lightly and gladly did Ino catch it in her hands. Then Odysseus struggled up from the river, to collapse in a bed of reeds: there he embraced the fruitful earth, the while he strove to rouse his great heart to action, saying, 'Alas, what next am I to do? What will become of me, after all? If I watch through the anxious night, here by the river, it may be that the joint severities of hoar-frost and heavy dew will be too much for my feebly-panting heart: surely the reek off the river valley will blow chill towards the dawn. Yet if I climb the slope to the dark wood and take cover there in some dense thicket, perhaps cold and its exhaustion may be spared me and a sweet sleep come on: but then I have to fear lest the wild beasts make me their prey and prize.' Yet, as he turned the choices over in his mind, this seemed the more profitable. He forced himself up into the wood which he found standing high and not far from the water. He got under a double bush, two trees with a single root: one wild olive, the other a graft of true olive. So closely did they grow together and supplement each other that through them no force of moist winds could pierce: nor could the shining of the sun cast in any ray: nor would any downpour of rain soak through.

Beneath them did Odysseus creep, and set to scraping together with his own hands a broad bed for himself: for inside there had drifted such a pile of dry leaves as would have covered two or three men well enough for a winter-time, however hard the weather. When bold Odysseus saw the leaves he rejoiced and laid himself down in the midst of them and fell to pouring the litter by handfuls over his body, till he was covered: – even as a neighbourless man in a lonely steading, before he goes forth covers his charring log under black wood-cinders: and thus hoards all day against his return, a seed of flame, which otherwise he would have had to seek for himself from some other place. Just so did Odysseus lie while Athene shed down sleep upon his eyes, to shroud the dear eyelids and the sooner deliver him from the pains of his weakness.

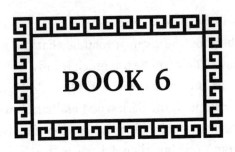

BOOK 6

So at last long-suffering Odysseus yielded to his weariness and slept there; while Athene proceeded to the district and chief town of the Phaeacian people. These had formerly occupied broad lands in Hypereia near the Cyclopes, that race of rude bullies who, being brawnier than the Phaeacians, were wont to plunder them. Wherefore godlike Nausithous rose up and removed his people to Scheria beyond reach of the world's covetousness. There he threw a wall around the new town-site and built houses and erected temples to the gods and apportioned the plough-lands.

Nausithous in due time yielded to fate, and went down to Hades: so now Alcinous reigned; wisely, for the gods prompted him. Therefore it was to his house that the goddess, grey-eyed Athene, descended to plan the reception of great-hearted Odysseus: and of his house she chose to enter the precious room where slept Nausicaa, daughter of royal Alcinous, a girl beautiful as an immortal in nature and form. Beside her, on each side of the entry, slept two hand-maidens whom the Graces had blessed with the gift of loveliness: and the gleaming doors were shut. Yet through them Athene swept like a sharp wind to the girl's head. For the sake of her message the goddess had assumed the likeness of a playmate of Nausicaa's own age and dear to her, the daughter of Dymas a famous sea captain. In this character then the grey-eyed Athene said: –

'O Nausicaa, how careless has your mother's daughter grown! These rich clothes all lie neglected, while your marriage season draws near: and that is the very time when you must clothe yourself rarely and have other things to give those who will take you in the bridal procession. By trifles like these is a good name won in the world, and fathers and mothers made proudly happy.

'Therefore let us go washing to-morrow at the break of day: for I will lend you my aid, as fellow-worker, that you may be the sooner decked ready for that near time when you shall cease to be a maid. Do not the best lads of the Phaeacians, your kith and kin throughout the countryside, already ask your hand? So remember now to beg your father, first thing in the morning, to give you the mules and a waggon big enough to hold the men's body-wrappers and your dresses and the glossy bed-covers. It will be better if you ride in it, too: for the washing pools are a very long foot-journey from the town.'

Having thus fulfilled her purpose Athene went away to Olympus where evermore they say the seat of the gods stays sure: for the winds shake it not, nor is it wetted by rain, nor approached by any snow. All around stretches the cloudless firmament, and a white glory of sunlight is diffused about its walls. There the blessed gods are happy all their days: and thither, accordingly, repaired the grey-eyed One after clearly imparting her message to the maiden.

High-throned Dawn came to rouse Nausicaa of the goodly robe. She, waking, wondered at her dream and went straight through the house to tell her dear father and mother. She found them within. Her mother sat by the hearth with her serving women, twirling on the distaff yarn which had been dipped in sea-purple dye: while her father she crossed in the doorway as he went out to consult with the illustrious princes of the people – a council to which the noblest of the Phaeacians had summoned them. She went near to this father she loved, that she might softly say: –

'Dear Father, will you not let me have the deep easy-wheeled waggon, that I may take all the good soiled clothes that lie by me to the river for washing? It is only right that you, whenever you go to sit in council with the leaders, should have clean linen to wear next your skin: while of your five sons begotten in the house only two have taken wives: and the three merry bachelors are always wanting clothes newly washed when they go out to dances. Thinking about all these things is one of my mind's cares.'

So much she said, too shy to name to her dear father the near prospect of her marriage: but he saw everything and answered in a word: 'My child, I do not grudge you mules, or anything. Go: the bondsmen will get you the tall, light waggon with the high tilt.'

As he spoke he called his men, who obeyed. They brought the easy-running mule cart to the outside of the palace and led forth the mules and yoked them to it, while the girl was carrying down the gay clothes from her bed-chamber and heaping them into the smooth-sided cart. The mother packed tasty meats in a travelling-box; all sorts of good things to eat, including relishes: and filled a goat-skin with wine. Then as her daughter climbed into the cart she gave to her a golden phial of limpid olive oil, that she and the hand-maidens might anoint themselves after bathing. Nausicaa took up the whip and the polished reins. She struck the beasts to start them: there came a clitter-clatter from the mules who laid vigorously into the collar and bore off the linen and the girl – not alone, of course: her maids went too.

At journey's end they came to the flowing stream of the lovely river and found the washing-places, within which from beneath there bubbled up such abundance of clear water that its force was sufficient to clean the very dirtiest things. There they loosed the mules from the cart and drove them down to the rippling water, where was honey-sweet herbage for their cropping. Then they took the garments from the waggon in armfuls and laid them in the shadowed water of the washing pools: where they danced on them in emulation, each striving to out-knead the rest. Afterward, when all the dirt was worked right out, they stretched the linen wide and smooth upon the foreshore, even on the pure shingle where the sea had washed it clean.

The work being done they fell to bathing, and then anointed themselves to sleekness with their olive oil before carrying their provisions to a nook which overlooked the sea; where they ate and waited as the clothes lay out in the sunlight drying. The food having satisfied their appetites the hand-maids and their young mistress next threw off their scarves and turned to playing with a ball. The white forearms of Nausicaa, leading the chorus, beat time for this ball-dance. She moved with them, as arrow-loving Artemis goes down the mountain-steeps of supreme Taygetus or Erymanthus when she is pleased to chase wild boars or flying stags with all her rout of nymphs (those shy ones, daughters of our lord of the aegis, Zeus): and then the heart of her mother Leto delights in Artemis for that she bears her head so high, and her brows, and moves carelessly notable among them all where all are beautiful – even so did this chaste maiden outshine her maids.

When at last it was time for her to fare homeward they set to yoking-in the mules and folding the fair garments: then the grey-eyed goddess Athene took thought how to arouse Odysseus from sleep that he might see the fair maiden who should lead him to the city where the Phaeacians lived: – which was why, when the girl next flung the ball to one of her retinue, she threw wide of her and put the ball into a deep eddy. Whereat their shrieks echoed far: and awoke great Odysseus who sat up and brooded dully in his heart and head. 'Alack now, and in what land of men do I find myself? Will they be inhospitable and savagely unjust; or kind to strangers, of god-fearing nature? How it plays round me, this shrilling of girls or of nymphs who hold the inaccessible heads of the mountains and the springs of rivers and water-meadows of rich grass. By the voices I do think them human. Let me go forward, and if I can see . . .'

Thus muttering Odysseus crept out from his bushes, snapping off in his powerful hands from the thick tree one very leafy shoot with which to shield from sight the maleness of his body. So he sallied forth, like the mountain-bred lion exulting in his strength, who goes through rain and wind with burning eyes. After great or small cattle he prowls, or the wild deer. If his belly constrain him he will even attempt the sheep penned in solid manors.

So boldly did Odysseus, stark naked as he was, make to join the band of maidens: for necessity compelled him. None the less he seemed loathsome in their sight because of his defilement with the sea-wrack; and in panic they ran abroad over all the spits of the salt beaches. Only the daughter of Alcinous remained; for Athene had put courage into her heart and taken terror from her limbs so that she stood still, facing him, while Odysseus wondered whether he had better clasp her knees and entreat this handsome girl or stand away by himself and cajole her with such honeyed words as should bring her to clothe his necessity and introduce him within her city. Even as he weighed these courses, it seemed to him most likely to benefit him if he stood off and coaxed her: for by taking the girl's knees he might outrage her modesty. Wherefore he began in soft wheedling phrase: –

'I would be suppliant at your knees, O Queen: yet am I in doubt whether you are divine or mortal. If a goddess from high heaven, then Artemis you must be, the daughter of great Zeus and your nearest peer in form, stature and parts. But if you are human, child of some dweller on this earth of ours, then thrice blessed your father and lady mother, thrice blessed your family! What happy joy in your regard must warm their hearts each time they see this slip of perfection joining in the dance: and blessed above all men in his own sight will be that most fortunate one who shall prevail in bridal gifts and lead you to his home! Never, anywhere, have I set eyes on such a one, not man nor woman. Your presence awes me. Yet perhaps once, in Delos, I did see the like – by the altar of Apollo where had sprung up just a slip of a palm-tree. For I have been at Delos, in my time, with many men to follow me on this quest which has ended for me so sorrily. However as I said, there by the altar of Apollo, when I saw this palm-sapling my heart stood still in amaze. It was the straightest spear of a tree that ever shot up from the ground. Likewise at you, Lady, do I wonder. With amazement and exceeding fear would I fain take your knees. I am in such misery. Only yesterday, after twenty days, did I escape from the wine-dark sea. That long the surges have been throwing me about, and the tearing storms, all the way from the island of Ogygia. And now some power has flung me on this shore where also it is likely I shall suffer hurt. I dare not yet look for relief. Before that comes the gods will have inflicted on me many another pain.

'Yet, O Queen, have pity. The sport of many evils I come to you, to you first of all, for of the many others who hold this town and land I know not a soul. Show me the city: give me a rag to fling about my body – the wrapper of your washing bundle would do, if you brought one here – and to you may the Gods requite all your heart's desire; husband, house, and especially ingenious accord within that house: for there is nothing so good and lovely as when man and wife in their home dwell together in unity of mind and disposition. A great vexation it is to their enemies and a feast of gladness to their friends: surest of all do they, within themselves, feel all the good it means.'

To him replied Nausicaa of the white arms: 'Stranger – for to me you seem no bad or thoughtless man – it is Zeus himself who assigns bliss to men, to the good and to the evil as he wills, to each his lot. Wherefore surely he gave you this unhappiness and you must bear it: but inasmuch as you have attained our place you shall not lack clothing nor the other things which are the due of a battered suppliant, when he has been received. I will show you the city and name those you see there. The town and the district belong to the Phaeacians whose strength and might are vested in Alcinous, their king: and I am his daughter.'

She spoke, and cried orders after her maidens with the braided hair. 'Rally to me, women. Why run because you see a man? You cannot think him an enemy. There lives not, nor shall there live, a man to come upon this Phaeacian land to ravage it. The gods love the Phaeacians too well. Also we are very remote in the dashing seas, the ultimate race of men: wherefore no other peoples have affairs with us. This man appeals as a luckless wanderer whom we must now kindly entertain. Homeless and broken men are all of them in the sight of Zeus, and it is a good deed to make them some small alms: wherefore, my maids, give our bedesman food and drink and cleanse him in the river at some spot shielded from the wind.' So she said. Slowly they stood firm, and each to the other repeated her order. Soon they had set Odysseus in the sheltered place according to the word of Nausicaa, daughter of large-minded Alcinous. They laid out clothes, a loose mantle with a tunic, and gave to him their pure oil in its golden phial and urged him to be washed in the waters of the river: but noble Odysseus up and spoke to the serving maids, saying, 'Handmaidens, stand you thus far off, in order that I may myself cleanse my body of the sea-stains and anoint it with oil. Too long has my skin been a stranger to ointment. Yet in your sight I will not bathe. I am shy of my nakedness among maidens so carefully tressed.' Thus he said: and they went to tell it to their young mistress.

Meanwhile great Odysseus in the river scrubbed the salt crust from the flesh of his back and broad shoulders and cleaned his hair of the frothy scum dried in it from the infertile sea. When he had so thoroughly washed and anointed himself smoothly and put on the clothes given him by the girl, then did Athene daughter of Zeus contrive to make him seem taller and stronger, and from his head she led down the curls of his hair in hyacinthine tendrils. As when some master craftsman (trained by Hephaestus and made wise by Pallas Athene in all the resources of his art) washes his silver work with molten gold and betters it into an achievement that is a joy for ever – just so did the goddess gild his head and shoulders with nobility. Then he went far apart and sat down by the margin of the sea, radiant with graciousness and glory, so that the girl in wonder said to her well-coiffed maidens:

'Hush now and listen, my white-armed attendants, while I speak. Not all the gods inhabiting Olympus have opposed the entering in of this man among the sanctified Phaeacians. At first he appeared to me not a seemly man: but now he is like the gods of spacious heaven. O that such a man might settle contentedly in our city, and agree to be called my husband! But come now, women, give the stranger food and drink.'

They most willingly obeyed. They placed refreshment before daring divine Odysseus who had been so long without tasting food that he fell upon it and ate and drank greedily: while Nausicaa of the white arms passed to her next concern. The folded clothes were duly restored to the splendid waggon and the strong-hoofed mules harnessed up. Then the maiden mounted and calling Odysseus spoke to this intent.

'Rouse yourself now, Stranger, to go as far as the city, where I shall show you the house of my wise-thinking father: in whose halls, as I assure you, acquaintance with all the best of the Phaeacians will be yours. Yet have a special care to do as follows if, as I think, you are a man of judgement. While we are passing people's fields and country-places do you march briskly forward with my maids after the mules and their cart. I will lead the way, so far: but at the entering in of the city – easy to know for its high towers – a good haven lies on either hand and the fairway between them is narrow, for it is lined by the swelling hulls of ships berthed or drawn up high and dry in the spaces allotted each ship-owner for his vessels. There is the assembly-ground round the temple of Poseidon, and it is fitted with stone slabs very solidly pitched into the earth. Hereabout they manufacture tackle for the black ships, cables and canvas: also they shave down the blades of oars. For know that amongst us Phaeacians the bow and the quiver get no honour. All delight is in masts and ships' oars and trim vessels in which to cross the foaming sea.

'I shrink, stranger, from the rude scoffing of these seafarers: lest someone later chide me – there are too many ill-natured tongues amongst the crowd – lest some rascal accuse me, sneering, "Who is this grand tall stranger following Nausicaa? Where did she pick him up? He will be the husband, doubtless, to her taste. Some wandering castaway of a foreigner rescued off a ship, perhaps: for we have no neighbours of that sort. Or he may be some god who after long entreaty has come down from heaven to answer her, and keep her for ever and ever. Good riddance, if she has dug out some mate for her own from somewhere: for she has never seen good in Phaeacians of her own sort, the many young excellencies who have courted her.' Thus will they speak, and these things become a reproach to me: indeed I too would blame another girl who did such things as consort with men before she had come to public marriage, against the will of her friends while her father and mother were still alive.

'Therefore, stranger, consider well these directions from me that you may secure from my father your earliest safe-conduct and carriage homeward. You will find a stately grove of Athene near the road: a grove of black poplars. Within it is an eye of water: and about it meadows. That is an estate of my father's and his abundant garden, no further from the town than a man's voice can carry. Sit in it and wait, while we pass into the city and attain my father's house. Then, when you judge me home, do you enter the city of the Phaeacians and ask for the palace of my father, Alcinous the Generous. It is easily to be distinguished, or the veriest child will guide you to it. In no way worthy to be compared therewith is the style of the citizens' houses: not like the palace of King Alcinous.

'But when the buildings and court have swallowed you up, then hurry your fastest through the great hall, till you find my mother. She will be sitting at the hearth in a glare of firelight spinning yarn tinctured with sea-purple, a marvel to the eye. Her chair will be backed against a pillar and her maidens all orderly behind her. My father's throne is propped beside hers, and on it he sits, drinking his wine and sitting like an immortal. Pass him by and throw your hands about my mother's knees, if you wish to ensure the dawning, fair and soon, of the day of your return. For no matter how distant your land, if only my mother favours your impression in her heart you may hope to see your friends and come to your stately home and fatherland.' She ceased and struck the mules with her shining whip. Quickly they left the valley of the river and neatly their feet plaited in and out as they paced onward, with Nausicaa reining them in and laying on the whip discreetly, so that her attendants and Odysseus could keep up with them on foot. The sun sank and they were at the famous grove dedicated to

Athene, where Odysseus tarried and at once prayed a prayer to the daughter of great Zeus.

'Hear me, Unwearied One, child of Zeus who holds the Aegis. Especially I pray you now to hear me, forasmuch as you did not lately when I was broken – when there broke me the famous Earth-shaker. Give me to find love and pity among the Phaeacians.'

So he prayed. Pallas Athene heard him but would not yet show herself to him, face to face, out of respect for her father's brother, whose furious rage against Odysseus lasted till he regained his own shore.

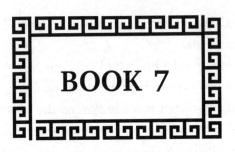

BOOK 7

Wherefore proud Odysseus waited in his place and prayed, all the time that her two strong mules were drawing the girl into the city as far as the palace of her illustrious father. Before its door she halted: her brothers, men like gods, came out and clustered round her. They freed the mules from the wagon and carried the washed clothes into the house: but she went up to her room, where a fire had been lit for her by the old woman of Aperaea, her chambermaid, whose name was Eurymedusa and who had been captured from Aperaea during a raid over-sea. Afterwards she had been set aside as prize of honour for Alcinous, because he was supreme ruler among the Phaeacians, obeyed by the common people as if he were a god. She had tended the infancy of white-armed Nausicaa in the palace; and now was wont to kindle the fire and lay her supper in her bower.

At length Odysseus bestirred himself and moved towards the city: whereupon Athene for the love she bore him muffled his shape in a wreath of mist to prevent any swaggering Phaeacian from standing in his road and trying by jeers and questions to find out who he was. For further care there met him in the entrance of the gracious town Athene herself, grey-eyed and goddess but now subdued to the likeness of a quite young girl bearing a water-jar. She hesitated, when she was very near him, and of her Odysseus begged, 'Child, will you not guide me to the dwelling of Alcinous, King over the people here? I am a stranger and have met and endured sore tribulation on my way from a distant land. Nor do I know this people, not one citizen or house-holder from among them all.' To him the Goddess answered: 'Very readily, father and stranger, will I show you the house you want, the more so because it stands next to my revered father's home. Yet I pray you to follow me in dead silence along the way I show, not staring at any men we meet, nor accosting them. The people here are short with strangers and do not use any love towards foreigners. Their trust is in the swiftness of their ships (a grace granted them by the Earth-shaker) in which they overpass the deepest seas with the speed of wings or of a thought.' Upon this exhortation Athene tripped forward hastily, Odysseus treading so closely in the divine footsteps that the Phaeacians, those famous seamen, were not aware of his passage through their midst. The goddess, remote and awful beneath her coronal of hair, forbade their knowing it; out of her heart's friendliness towards him she closed about him that supernatural mist.

Odysseus was astonished at the havens and ships he saw; as at the assembly-grounds of the heroes. Astonishment took him also at the long, lofty walls with palisades atop: a marvellous sight: but when they reached the famous palace of the king, Athene again broke into speech: –

'This is the house, venerable stranger, which you asked me to point out. Within it you shall find kings, god-children of Zeus, feasting in the hall. Thrust in fearlessly: however foreign a man may be, in every crisis it is the high face which will carry him through. Haply you may light first upon the Queen (Arete her name) whose lineage is the same as the King's, a line which began in Nausithous, son of Poseidon the Earth-shaker by Periboea, the fairest woman of her time. She was the youngest daughter of magnificent Eurymedon, anciently king of the too-proud giants, whom he served to destroy in their impiety; yet with their destruction was himself destroyed. Poseidon however lay with the daughter, who conceived this son, large-hearted Nausithous, afterwards king of the Phaeacians. Nausithous begat two sons, Rhexenor and Alcinous, of whom Rhexenor died soon after marriage, smitten by the silver archer, Apollo; and left no son, but one daughter Arete, an infant. Her, later, Alcinous made his consort, treating her as no woman on earth has been entreated, with consideration above the lot of all wives who keep house for their men. So she has been and is honoured amazingly in her dear children's eyes; as by Alcinous her lord and by all his people, who revere her as divine and acclaim her devoutly whenever she makes progress through the city. Nor is she less gifted in qualities of mind. She will resolve the disputes of those for whom she has countenance, even when the affair is an affair of men. If she can be brought to look kindly upon you, then may you entertain real hope of again seeing your friends, your lofty house and native land.'

With this saying Athene left him. She left lovely Scheria, and went over the sterile sea to Marathon and the broad ways of Athens, where she entered the massive house of Erectheus. Odysseus the while lingered before the gate of Alcinous' renowned dwelling. He stood there, not crossing its copper threshold, because of the host of thoughts thronging his heart. Indeed the brilliance within the high-ceiled rooms of noble Alcinous was like the sheen of sun or moon: for the inner walls were copper-plated in sections, from the entering in to the furthest recesses of the house; and the cornice which ran around them was glazed in blue. Gates of gold closed the great house: the door posts which stood up from the brazen threshold were of silver, and silver, too, was the lintel overhead: while the handle of the door was gold. Each side the porch stood figures of dogs ingeniously contrived by Hephaestus the craftsman out of gold and silver, to be ageless, undying watch-dogs for this house of great-hearted Alcinous. Here and there along the walls were thrones, spaced from the inmost part to the outer door. Light, well-woven draperies made by the women of the house were flung over these thrones, and on them the chiefs of the Phaeacians would sit to drink and eat: for the hospitality of the palace was unstinting. The feasters in the great hall after dark were lighted by the flaring torches which golden figures of youths, standing on well-made pedestals, held in their hands. Of the fifty women servants who maintain this house, some are ever sitting to grind the golden grain in querns, some weave at the looms, while others sit carding wool upon distaffs which flutter like the leaves of a tall poplar: and so close is the texture of their linen that even fine oil will not pass through it. For just as the seamen of Phaeacia are the skilfullest of human kind in driving a swift ship through the water, so are their women marvellous artists in weaving. Athene gave them this genius to make beautiful things.

From outside the court, by its entry, extends a great garden of four acres, fenced each way. In it flourish tall trees: pears or pomegranates, stone fruits gaudy with their ripening load, also sweet figs and heavy-bearing olives. The fruit of these trees never blights or fails to set, winter and summer, through all the years. A west wind blows there perpetually, maturing one crop and making another. Pear grows old upon pear and apple upon apple, with bunch after bunch of grapes and fig after fig. Here, too, a fertile vineyard has been planted for the King. A part of this lies open to the sun, whose rays bake its grapes to raisins, while men gather ripe grapes from the next part and in a third part tread out the perfected vintage in wine-presses. On one side are baby grapes whose petals yet fall; on another the clusters empurple towards full growth. Beyond the last row of trees, well-laid garden plots have been arranged, blooming all the year with flowers. And there are two springs, one led throughout the orchard-ground, whilst the other dives beneath the sill of the great court to gush out beside the stately house: from it the citizens draw their water. Such were the noble gifts the gods had lavished upon the palace of Alcinous.

Great Odysseus stood there and gazed: but when he had studied all and seen it with his understanding, swiftly he passed the threshold and was swallowed up within the house. He found the chiefs and leaders of the Phaeacians emptying their beakers to the keen-eyed slayer of Argus: for it is their custom, when their minds turn towards bed, to pour a last cup of the night to Hermes. He strode across the hall, and the thick vapour which Athene had condensed about his form wrapped him round till he came to Arete and King Alcinous. Then Odysseus threw his arms about the knees of Arete. The god-given mist rolled back from him: throughout the house men's voices failed them when they saw the hero there. They gaped, dumb-founded; and Odysseus prayed: –

'O Arete, daughter of godlike Rhexenor, to your husband and to your knees I come, in my extremity. And to these guests too. May the gods give them happiness, while they live; and permit each to hand down his goods and houses to his children, together with such consideration as the world has rendered him. But for me, I pray you, hasten my despatch by the quickest way to my native place. Now for so long have I been sundered from my friends and in torment.' After speaking he crouched down on the hearth among the ashes of the fire: and for a time the hall was very still.

At last there sounded the voice of manful old Echeneus, an elder Phaeacian who excelled in speaking and knew the ancient wisdom. Heartily he addressed them, protesting as follows: 'Alcinous, it does not conduce to your credit, nor is it right that this stranger should sit upon the ground among the ashes of our hearth. Yet must every other voice hold back, awaiting your lead. Up then, and set the stranger on a silver-studded throne. Command the servers to mix wine ready for us, that we may pour offerings to Zeus the thunder-lover, patron of all self-respecting suppliants; and let your housekeeper give the stranger a supper of whatever she has at hand within.'

When Alcinous the consecrated king had heard this counsel, he took deep, devious Odysseus and raised him from the hearth to the seat nearest himself, a silver-studded throne from which he displaced Laodamas, his own well-grown son whom he dearly loved. The serving woman from her rich golden ewer poured the water for rinsing hands over its silver basin, and drew up a polished table on which the sober housekeeper displayed her bread and many dainties, freely offering all the cheer she had. Grave Odysseus drank and ate: and then the king's majesty commanded the herald: 'Pontonous, dilute us wine in the mixing bowl and hand round drink to all in the house, that we may pour general libation to Zeus the thunder-lover, who tends all deserving suppliants.'

He spoke. Pontonous mixed the honeyed wine and served afresh to each man's drinking cup. They poured forth and afterward drank their hearts' fill, when Alcinous again addressed them, beginning: 'Hear me, you leaders of the Phaeacians in peace and war, while I declare the prompting of my heart. We have feasted: and now it is fitting that you go home and woo your beds. In the morning let us summon a larger gathering of elders and fulfil for this stranger in our guest-hall the whole rite of hospitality, together with worthy sacrifice to the gods: and after these ceremonies let us deliberate upon his escort, to see how we may quit him of further travail and accident and ensure his blissful return home, instantly. This home may be very far away: none the less we must guard him from evils or penalties in mid-passage, and until he disembarks on his native land. Once there, our part is done. He must suffer whatever haps the grave Fates spun for him in his thread of life, when his mother bore him. Perhaps, though, he is one of the immortals come down from heaven? Yet, if so, have the gods utterly changed their grace towards us. Always in the past they have been wont to appear plainly, after we had consummated some outstanding sacrifice; and plainly would they feast with us, sitting in our midst in their true forms. Why, even when a simple traveller journeying alone has happened upon a god, it has been a manifest undisguised God: after all, are we not their near of kin, near as the Cyclopes or the lawless tribe of Giants?'

Then subtle Odysseus took up the word and answered him thus: 'Alcinous, think some other thought than this! I am not like the Immortals of spacious heaven, either in my body or in my nature, which are altogether mortal and bound to suffer death. Think, rather, of those men who in your experience have been most vexed with pains and griefs: for it is to them that I would liken myself in my miseries. Indeed I might drool on and on, telling the tale of all that I have suffered, of the manifold trials inflicted on me by the will of the Gods. But instead I will ask leave to obey my instincts and fall upon this supper, as I would do despite my burden of woe. See now, there is not anything so exigent as a man's ravening belly, which will not let him alone to feel even so sore a grief as this grief in my heart; but prefers to overwhelm his misery with its needs for meat and drink, forcibly and shamelessly compelling him to put its replenishment above his soul's agony. None the less will I beseech you to be stirring at the break of day, to scheme how you may put this unlucky, toil-worn self of mine ashore in the land of my fathers. Let life leave me then – so that my dying eyes behold my property, my men and my wide stately house.'

So he said. All men applauded the speech and cried that indeed the stranger must be sent on to his home, as he so justly claimed. By now had they offered and drunk to the fill of their bent, so away went the company homeward to sleep, leaving great Odysseus, with Arete and Alcinous sitting by him, in the hall where the serving women went to and fro clearing away the plenishings of the feast. Forthwith Arete began a questioning, for she had recognised the tunic and cloak upon Odysseus as part of the goodly raiment which she and her maidens were used to fashion. So she flung at him these searching words: 'Stranger, this have I to ask of you, from myself; first, What man are you, and where from? Who gave you those clothes? Your tale to us just now was of your coming here from adventure in the deep.'

Resourceful Odysseus answered: 'It is grievous for me, O Queen, to give you a connected history of my pains: the celestial gods have given me too many. Yet this I will say to meet your questioning. There is an island, Ogygia, lying afar in the ocean, and in it the daughter of Atlas, subtle fair-haired Calypso, dwells. She is divine, and strange: no one, either of gods or men, has traffic with her. However, it was a divine power which carried my hapless self into her house-hold – myself alone: for Zeus had let drive with a dazzling thunder-bolt at our good ship and riven it in the wine-dark unbounded sea. All my good comrades died then: only I clung with both arms about the keel of the curved ship and rode it for nine days. On the tenth, in black night, the gods brought me near to this island, Ogygia, where was Calypso. The awesome goddess took me in and loved me passionately and tended me, vowing that she would make me immortal and ageless for ever and ever. Withal she did not wholly beguile the heart in my breast. Nevertheless for seven years did I endure, years without end. Ever I would water with my tears the clothes (immortal clothes) in which Calypso did me honour. But when the eighth year had duly come, then suddenly she ordered and hastened my going. I know not if some message reached her from Zeus, or if her own inclination at last had changed.

'It was on a raft, most firmly put together, that she despatched me, loaded with gifts; food and sweet liquor and divine clothes to wear: also there was a warm mild wind to favour me, before which I sailed for seventeen days, and for the eighteenth until the hill-crests of your land loomed up through the haze. My heart exulted – too soon: for it was written that I should yet know the further dour griefs allotted me by Poseidon the Earth-shaker, who stirred up the winds to block my passage and raised such seas as not even the gods could tell of. The breakers raged so that they unseated my unhappy self from the raft I rode. Yes, the squalls scattered its beams every way: while for me, I swam with my hands, swam right across the gulf, until between wind and water I approached your coast. There I was climbing out upon the beach when a wave violently took me and flung me against the huge reefs of this dreadful shore. Wherefore I had to give up that plan and swim back, till I found a river mouth which looked to me auspicious for a second attempt, seeing that it was free of rocks and covered from the wind. So it proved. I escaped out and began to collect my courage: then immortal night came down.

'I left behind me the heaven-watered river and struck into the underwood where I slept marvellously well under a pile of leaves. For the God poured down over me, the heart-sick and sorry, so profound a sleep that there I slept all that night among the leaves, and the next morning and half that day. As a fact, the sun was going down the west before that sweet sleep let me go – to discern the attendants of your daughter playing on the beach, with her in their midst, like any goddess. I supplicated her. She proved the mistress of a sounder judgement than is to be expected of the young: the coming generation is so commonly thoughtless. However, she gave me a fill of bread and sparkling wine, and a wash in the river and these clothes you see. Now I have told you the truth, though it put me in disfavour.'

Alcinous replied, 'Stranger, where my daughter's thought fell short of your desert in this was that she did not bring you here to our place directly, in her train. It was her duty, as the one to whom you first appealed.' Odysseus at no loss answered: 'Hero, blame not the blameless maiden therein. She did tell me to follow with her attendants, but I shrank from it lest I be disgraced if your heart took offence at the sight of me there. We sons of men are in our generation so exceeding suspicious.' To which Alcinous cried out: 'Stranger, this heart of mine is not so light in my breast as to be moved for an idle cause. Yet I grant you that it is better to observe a certain seemliness in all things. Ah me! by Zeus the Father, and Athene and Apollo! Would there might be found some man like you, my double in niceness and sentiment, to accept my daughter and the name of my son-in-law, and to live here for good. It would delight me to provide house and property, if you would stay! Yet fear not that any one of us Phaeacians will detain you here by foul means. It would not be pleasing in the sight of Zeus. On the contrary, that you may know for certain, I shall here and now fix the actual day of your going. To-morrow, let it be. To-morrow you shall lie down and slumber soundly, while the oars of your crew smite the smooth sea, bringing you all the way to your land and house, those things you love. It matters not how far they be: let them be further than Euboea, which some of our fellows maintain is the last land of the world. Euboea they saw when they took pale Rhadamanthus to meet Tityus, the son of Earth. They reached it effortlessly, so attaining their goal in the one day: and got right the way home here, too. Let your heart understand from this the surpassing goodness of my ships, and how my lads churn the salt sea with their oar-blades.'

So he said: Odysseus became happy. He opened his mouth and prayed a short prayer, invoking the God: 'All-father Zeus, grant it that

Alcinous fulfils all things even as he says: then may his glory never be dimmed on this bountiful earth, and I come to my own.' In such wise they talked among themselves, till white-armed Arete told her maids to arrange bedsteads under the sun-porch, piling them with fine purple blankets, over which were rugs, and thick mantles on top of all as upper covering. Away went the women from the hall, torch in hand. Diligently they smoothed the soft couch and then summoned Odysseus, standing by his chair and murmuring: 'Rise up now and come to sleep, Stranger. Your bed is prepared.' When he heard their saying he felt that sleep would be right welcome. So he slept there, did tried Odysseus, on his fretted and inlaid bedstead under the echoing porch: but Alcinous retired into the depths of the great house where in his place his lady wife had also laid out bed and bedding.

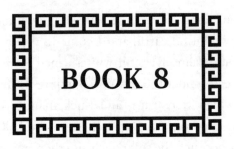

BOOK 8

At the first show of Dawn, great Alcinous left his couch, as did that ravager of cities, Odysseus, kinsman of Zeus. The anointed King led him to the formal meeting place of the Phaeacians, where it had been contrived amongst the shipping. There they sat them down side by side on benches of polished stone: while Pallas Athene in the guise of the King's herald went up and down the city furthering her scheme for getting brave Odysseus home. She accosted for a moment everyone she met, saying urgently: 'Go across now to the council, all you leaders of the Phaeacians, wise men and warriors; there to make up your minds upon this stranger who has just come in from wandering through the deep, and claims the hospitality of our wise Alcinous: he has an air with him, like the Deathless Ones.' By such words she sharpened the zeal and curiosity of everyone, so that in a trice the standing ground and seats were thronged with burgesses. To many of these the look of Laertes' cunning son was wonderful: for Athene had endued his head and shoulders with a benediction of glory, and made his figure tower up and bulk to fill the eye. The goddess would have him win the love of every Phaeacian, and their reverence and awe: and therefore had empowered him to perform miracles of strength when they put him to the test.

After all men were assembled in their places, Alcinous lifted up his voice and said: 'Hear me, leaders of the Phaeacians in war and peace, as I utter the bidding of my heart. This stranger (for I know him not) has wandered into my house with no one to vouch for him: not even to say if he is from the peoples of the dawn or of the sunset. He asks a passage, and presses that it be assured him: and I say that according to precedent we should hasten his going. Never, never shall any visitor to my house linger there in distress for want of setting forward. Wherefore let us pull a black ship down to the sacred sea, a new ship for the maiden voyage, and choose from among the people fifty-two young oarsmen of proven excellence; and these shall be their present orders: "Lash the sweeps firmly into place by the benches: then make haste ashore, every one of you, back to my house where by my care you shall find a banquet ready for your falling-to." Unto the rest, to the sceptred kings, I would say, "Repair now to my goodly house; there will we kindly entertain the stranger in the great hall." Let no one of you fail this tryst. Nay, further, let some one bid to the gathering our divine minstrel Demodocus, to whom the God has given such gift of music that he charms his hearers with every song to which his heart is moved.'

The King ceased and led on. The sceptred ones followed him and a herald sought the godlike musician, whilst the chosen youths, the fifty and two, went down to the brink of the waste of waters. When they were arrived at the sea and the ship they launched the black hull into the briny deep, stepped the mast, carried her sails aboard, and fixed the sweeps into their raw-hide loops, all proper. They bent the white sails and moored her, high-riding on the swell. Afterward they took their way to the palace of profound Alcinous, whose courts and galleries and rooms were now all a press of men, citizens of every age having thronged in. To entertain them Alcinous devoted twelve sheep, eight boars with gleaming tusks, and two heavy-gaited oxen, which they flayed and prepared busily for a heart-warming feast.

The herald came to hand leading the beloved minstrel, whom the Muse did especially love: yet had her gifts to him been mixed, both good and evil. She had taken from him the sight of his eyes, and given him a power of harmony. Pontonous backed a silver-studded throne against a tall pillar in the midst of the feasters and set it for the musician and put him on it; then hung the resonant lyre on a peg above him and guided his hand to the place, so that later he might know to reach it down. Beside him he set a food basket and a goodly table and a wine-cup ready, that he might drink as his spirit prompted. The company plunged hands into the bounty provided, until they had satisfied their lust for drink and meat. Then the Muse pricked the musician on to sing of the great deeds of heroes, as they were recounted in verses whose fame had already filled the skies: telling of the feud between Odysseus and Achilles son of Peleus, and how once at a splendid feast of the gods they had accused each other with terrible words; whereat the king of men, Agamemnon, secretly was glad, gleeful that the best of the Achaeans thus fell out: because Phoebus Apollo had prophesied it to him that day Agamemnon crossed the precinct of naked rock at most holy Pytho to consult his oracle. Those were the beginnings of that tide of sorrow which was to whelm down Trojans and Danaans alike; as Zeus, the all-mighty, willed.

Of this was the song of the very famous minstrel: but Odysseus with two strong hands drew the broad purple cloak over his head to hide his goodly face. He was ashamed to let the tears well from his deep-set eyes publicly before the Phaeacians. Each time the divine singer broke off his song Odysseus dashed away the tears, freed his head from the cloak, and poured from his loving cup a libation to the God. But as soon as the song began again, at the bidding of the Phaeacian chiefs to whom the verses were unalloyed delight, then would Odysseus again hide his head and stifle his sobs. The other company failed to see how his tears ran down: only Alcinous remarked it, for he sat next to him, and could not but notice and overhear his deep-drawn agony. Wherefore at an early chance he broke in upon the oar-loving Phaeacians: 'Pay heed, champions and councillors. We are glutted with feasting together and with the lyre which is the complement of splendid food. Instead let us sally out and divert ourselves with feats of strength, that when the stranger goes home he may tell his friends how we surpass others in boxing and wrestling and jumping and foot-racing.'

He spoke and went out. They followed. The herald hung the sounding lyre upon its peg, took Demodocus by the hand, and led him forth from the hall by the way which the other Phaeacian leaders had taken to witness the exercises. An immense company, a concourse of thousands, followed them to the appointed place: and many gallant youths stood up as contestants. Acroneus rose up and Ocyalus and Elatreus; Nauteus and Prymneus with Anchialus and Eretmeus; Ponteus, Proreus, Thoon and Anabesineus with Amphialus son of Polyneus son of Tekton: also Euryalus son of Naubolus (the match of deadly Ares) who in face and proportions excelled all the Phaeacians except noble Laodamas. Three sons of royal Alcinous stood up also, Laodamas, Halius and godlike Clytoneus.

Their first trial was of running: the course was laid out straight from its start, for speed. The field of them raced across the flat land in a storm of dust. However noble Clytoneus surpassed all in this. When he came back to the crowd his advantage in lead was as that of a yoke of mules in breaking unbroken ground: so distant were the others behind him. Then they wrestled their hardest: and Euryalus proved champion of champions. Amphialus carried off the jumping and Elatreus easily won the weight-throwing: while the boxing fell to Laodamas, Alcinous' doughty son.

When every spirit had been delighted with the sports, then said Laodamas the son of Alcinous, 'Come with me, friends, and let us question the stranger, to learn if he is skilled in games and can show us any feats. He is not in any sense ill-built: those thighs and calves, bull-neck and vigorous hands are tokens of enormous power. Nor has he lost his prime: it is only that he is broken by excess of hardships. I give you my oath that for wreaking havoc upon a strong man, even the very strongest, there is nothing so dire as the sea.' Euryalus answered him and said, 'Laodamas, you have spoken to the point: go up now, declare yourself and call him out.' Upon which the honest son of Alcinous moved through the crowd and addressed Odysseus: 'Will you not, father stranger, now attempt some feat, if you have the skill I credit you? For there is no surer fame, in a man's own life-time, than that which he wins with his feet and hands. Also at this juncture you may well purge your heart of care and prove yourself, for soon you will be on your journey. Is not your ship launched and your crew told off?'

Wily Odysseus replied: 'Laodamas, why do you thus invite me, in mockery? The fashion of my heart is more like grief than games. For long I have been a toiling and a suffering man: my very purpose here in your gathering is only as a suppliant before your king and people, to crave my passage homeward.' Euryalus took him up and sneered in his face: 'Truly, stranger, I do not reckon you a man good at games, like the generality of real men: but rather a master of peddling sailors, one who traffics up and down in a heavy merchantman, mindful always of cargo and husbanding freights, with a sharp eye on gain. You are not built like a champion.'

Deep Odysseus glared at him and thundered: 'You, whoever you are, do not speak well. You behave like a low fellow. So true is it that the Gods do not lavish graciousness entire, their whole endowment of beauty and wit and eloquence, upon all men alike. There will be one rather feebler than average in build, and yet the God will so crown what he says with a bloom of beauty that all who look on him are moved. When he holds forth in public it is with assurance, yet with so honey-sweet a modesty that it makes him shine out above the ruck of men who gaze at him whenever he walks their city as if he were a god. Another will be handsome as the Immortals, yet will lack that strand of charm twined into his words. Take yourself – a masterpiece of body in which perhaps not even a god could see amendment : yet naught in mind. Your reviling made the heart beat faster in my breast. I am no ninny at sports, as you would have it. Indeed I think I was among the best, in my time, while I yet heard the prompting of my youth and hands. In my time – for here I subsist in pain and misery, having risked and endured much in the wars of men and the wearisome seas. Yet despite the ravages of these evil things I will essay your tests of strength: for that sneer galled me and your word has stung me to the quick.'

He spoke and sprang to his feet. All cloaked as he was he seized a throwing weight, a huge heavy stone far bigger than those with which the Phaeacians had been competing. He whirled it up and flung it from his mighty hand, and the stone sang through the air. Down they quailed to the earth, those Phaeacians of the long oars, those master mariners, beneath the hurtling of the stone which soared so freely from the hero's hand that it overpassed the marks of every other. Athene, in her human shape, appeared suddenly and marked the place where it touched earth. Loudly she cried to Odysseus: 'Stranger, even a blind man's dim groping hand would pick out the dint of your stone: because it does not lie confused among the crowd of marks, but is alone, far in front of all. Be confident, for this event at least. No Phaeacian will reach your throw, much less exceed it.' So the goddess cried, and great Odysseus was glad, at the pleasure of finding in the assembly one stout-hearted friend. Wherefore gaily he challenged the Phaeacians: –

'Now, my young athletes, match me this throw; and very soon after you do, I think I will send down another as long or longer. For the rest, let any man whose spirit or temper prompts him come out and take me on in boxing or wrestling or foot-racing, as you will. To such a pitch have you wrought me that I shall not flinch from anything, nor refuse any single Phaeacian, except only Laodamas, my host. For who but a shallow-pated fool would strive with his benefactor? To challenge one's host, while being kindly entreated in a foreign land, would be to spite one's self. But for the others, I refuse none and shirk nothing. I shall look all in the face and prove them. In none of the sports which men use do I disgrace myself. I can well handle the polished bow. In the thick of each fight I would be ever the first to loose arrow and bring down my man, no matter how many followers of mine were there, shooting at the enemy. In the Trojan plain, where the Achaeans made such trial of shooting, only Philoctetes surpassed me with the bow. Wherefore I avouch myself more adept therein than any other man who now eats earthly food. With the men of old time I do not wish to rate myself; not with Herakles, nor with Eurytus of

Oechalia, who would make a shooting match with the Immortal Gods: of which ambition great Eurytus early died, cut off young from his house: for Apollo slew him in rage at being challenged to a bout in archery. I will send my spear further than any man his arrow. I fear only that in swiftness of foot some of the Phaeacians may beat me; for I have been shamefully mauled by incessant waves on a ship destitute of comfort. Therefore are the joints of my knees enfeebled.'

So he protested, and they all waited in a hush: only Alcinous answered and said: 'See now, Stranger, we do not resent these words you have uttered because you, in anger at such a fellow's facing you in the ring and upbraiding you, have been pleased to make so plain to us your inbred prowess that no mortal man who knows what words are worth may question it. Yet listen now to what I say and remember our accomplishment and the skill Zeus has given us – from our fathers' times even until now – that you may tell the tale to some other hero when you sup in your own house with your wife and children: for my part I confess that we are not polished fighters with our fists, nor wrestlers: but we can run swiftly on our feet and are experts on shipboard: we love eating and harp-playing and dancing and changes of clothes: and hot baths and our beds. Wherefore, my people, bestir yourselves and cause the best dancers of the Phaeacians to dance before us, so that when the stranger is got home he may acquaint his friends with our surpassing goodness in seamanship and running and dancing and singing. Let someone go quickly to our house and fetch for Demodocus that sounding lyre which he will find hung up somewhere.'

At the word of Alcinous his herald ran to find the polished lyre in the palace. Other nine men stood up, the elect and appointed stewards of the crowd, whose duty was to set the stage. They levelled the dancing ground, making its ring neat and wide. The herald arrived with the minstrel's singing lyre. Demodocus advanced into the cleared space. About him grouped boys in their first blush of life and skilful at dancing, who footed it rhythmically on the prepared floor. Odysseus watched their flying, flashing feet and wondered.

Then the lyre-player broke into fluent song, telling of the loves of Ares and coiffed Aphrodite in the house of Hephaestus. How they first came together by stealth and of the many gifts that Ares gave her, until he was able to defile the bed and marriage of Hephaestus the King: and of the eventual coming of Helios, the Sun, to the King, with word of their loving intercourse as he had witnessed it. When Hephaestus had heard the dismal tale he hastened to his forge, elaborating evil for them in the depths of his breast. He set the great anvil in its stock and wrought chains which could be neither broken nor loosed, that the guilty pair might be gyved in them for ever and ever. Out of his bitter rage against Ares was born this device. He went then into his marriage chamber, where stood the bed he had cherished, and about its posts he interlaced his toils. Others, many of them, hung down from aloft, from the main roof-tree over the hearth; gossamer chains so fine that no man could see them, not even a blessed God, with such subtlety of craft had they been forged. When Hephaestus had meshed all the bed in his snare he pretended to set forth for Lemnos, that well-built city which in his eyes is much the dearest land of earth. Nor was it a loose watch that Ares of the golden reins was keeping upon Hephaestus. As soon as he saw the great craftsman leave he took his journey to the famous house, chafing for love of well-crowned Cytherea. She was but newly come from Zeus, her mighty father, and had just sat down when Ares was in the house, grasping her hand and saying: 'Come, darling, let us to bed and to our pleasure; for Hephaestus is now abroad, visiting in Lemnos among the barbarous-spoken Sintians.'

His word of their lying together gave her joy. They went to their bed and snuggled deep into it, whereupon the springes of artful Hephaestus closed about them and tightened till they were not able to lift a limb nor move it. At last they understood there was no escape. Then the great God of the mighty arms drew near again and re-entered: he had turned back short of Lemnos when Helios, the spying Sun, had given him word. As he made heavily toward his home grief rooted in his heart: but when he stood there in its entry savage passion gripped him so that he roared hideously and declaimed to all the Gods: –

'Father Zeus and every other Blessed Immortal, hither to me, and see a jest which is unpardonable. Because I am crippled, Aphrodite daughter of Zeus, does me dishonour, preferring Ares the destroyer, Ares being beautiful and straight of limb while I was born crooked. And whose fault is that, if not my parents'? Would they had not brought me into life! Look how these two are clipped together in love's embrace, here, in my very bed. To watch them cuts me to the heart. Yet I think they will not wish to lie thus, not even for a very little while longer, however mad their lust. Soon they will not wish to be together, yet shall my cunning bonds chain them as they are until her father has utterly repaid the marriage fee – every single thing I gave him for this bitch-eyed girl: though indeed his daughter is beautiful, despite her sin.'

His mouthing gathered the gods to the house of the brazen floor. Poseidon the Earth-girdler, beneficent Hermes and royal Apollo the far-darting, came: but the Lady Goddesses remained at home, all of them, quite out of countenance. In Hephaestus' forecourt collected the Givers of Weal: and unquenchable was the laughter that arose from the blessed Gods as they studied the tricky device of Hephaestus. One would catch his neighbour's eye and gibe: 'Bad deeds breed no merit. The slow outrun the speedy. See how poor crawling Hephaestus, despite that limp, has now overtaken Ares (much the most swift of all divine dwellers upon Olympus) and cleverly caught him. Ares will owe him the adulterer's fine.' Words like this one whispered to the other: but of Hermes did Zeus' royal son Apollo loudly ask: 'Hermes, son of Zeus, messenger and giver of good things: would you not choose even the bondage of these tough chains, if so you might sleep in the one bed by golden Aphrodite?' And to him the God's messenger, Argus-bane, replied: 'If only this might be, kingly, far-darting Apollo! If there were chains without end, thrice as many as are here, and all you Gods with all the Goddesses to look on, yet would I be happy beside the Golden One.'

At his saying more laughter rose among the Immortals: only Poseidon laughed not but was still entreating lame Hephaestus the craftsman to let Ares go. Now he spoke out, with winged words: 'Loose him: and for him I promise whatever you require; as that he shall discharge the penalty he has incurred before the undying Gods.' The famous strong-thewed God answered him: 'Do not thus constrain me, Poseidon, Earth-girdler. The bonds of a worthless man are worthless bonds. How could I hold you liable before the Immortals, if Ares gets away free of his debt and this snare?' And to him replied the Earth-shaker: 'Hephaestus, even if Ares absconds, leaving his debt unpaid, I myself will discharge it to you, wholly.' And the lame master said, 'I cannot refuse: nor would it be seemly to refuse such surety.' So saying great Hephaestus loosed the chain and the couple when they were freed of the trap and its restraint swiftly fled away – he to Thrace and smiling Aphrodite to Cyprus, to Paphos, her sanctuary with its incense-burning altar. There the Graces bathed her and anointed her with ambrosial oil, such as is set aside for the ever-living Gods. There they put upon her glorious clothing, till she was an enchantment to the eye.

Such was the song of the famous minstrel. Like the Phaeacians, the long-oared notable mariners, Odysseus had rejoiced in heart as he listened. Then Alcinous ordered Halius and Laodamas to dance, by themselves, for never did any one dare join himself with them. They took in their hands the fine ball, purple-dyed, which knowing Polybus had made them, and played. The first, bending his body right back, would hurl the ball towards the shadowy clouds: while the other in his turn would spring high into the air and catch it gracefully before his feet again touched ground. Then, after they had made full trial of tossing the ball high, they began passing it back and forth between them, all the while they danced upon the fruitful earth. The other young men stood by the dancing ring and beat time. Loudly their din went up: and great Odysseus turned to Alcinous, saying, 'O my lord Alcinous, ruler of rulers, you did assure us that your dancers were the best: and now it is proved true: this sight is marvellous.' Thereat

Alcinous the sacred King rejoiced and quickly said to the Phaeacians: 'Hear me, war-lords and statesmen of the Phaeacians: this stranger seems a man of singular understanding. Let us bestow on him the stranger's meed, in due form. Here are twelve noble kings who rule among the people, with myself the thirteenth. Let each generously contribute a fresh robe and a tunic and a talent of precious gold. If all these gifts are brought promptly the stranger will have them in hand before supper and will go to it gallantly. As for Euryalus, let him atone for his ill manners by words of satisfaction and a gift.'

All accepted his counsel and enjoined it. The pursuivants went forth to collect and bring the gifts, while Euryalus said: 'My lord Alcinous, leader of our rank, right truly will I make amends to the stranger, as you bid. See this short sword of the true metal: that I give to him with its silver hilt and the scabbard of new-sawn ivory which contains it. It shall be worth much to him.' At the word he put the silver-mounted weapon into the hands of Odysseus and spoke wingedly therewith: 'Hail, father stranger: and if some too-harsh word has slipped out, may the storm winds take it and cast it afar. For yourself, the Gods grant that you reach your land and see your wife: all too long have you been afflicted and far from the solace of your friends.' Readily Odysseus answered him, saying, 'To you too, my friend, a warm greeting: may the Gods give you happiness: and may you never feel the lack of this sword which you to-day give me, with the balm of healing words.' He slung the silver-mounted weapon about his shoulder. The sun went down and the presentation of the costly gifts began. In state the heralds bore them to the palace, where the great king's sons received them for Odysseus and bestowed them for safe keeping with their revered mother, while the king himself led in the guests to take places on the lofty thrones.

Then did Alcinous call to Arete his wife: 'Woman, bring hither a very rich chest, your noblest. Put in it a newly-washed robe and tunic. Then warm a copper for the guest by the fire and heat water, that he may bathe himself before he views this show of gifts which the Phaeacian leaders have presented to him: and afterward he will be able to enjoy the feast and our minstrel's music. Stay: to his treasure I will also add this my very beautiful wrought cup of gold, that he may call me to mind always when in his house he pours drink-offerings to Zeus and the other Gods.' So he said, and Arete told her maids to set, as soon as might be, a great three-legged pot by the fire. They placed over the roaring flames the cauldron which served for the bath, and poured water into it and piled kindling wood beneath. The fire licked round the pot's belly and the water warmed, while Arete brought out of the bed-chamber a fair coffer for the visitor and put into it the splendid gifts, the clothing and the gold, which the Phaeacians had given. From her own store she added a fine tunic and outer garment and then addressed him succinctly, as follows: 'See to the lid now, yourself: and quickly contrive a sure fastening about it lest anyone rob you on your way as you are enjoying the sweetness of sleep while your black ship glides on.' Odysseus at once fixed the cover to her asking, and secured it with that intricate knot which Dame Circe had taught him. Then straightway the housewife bade him go to the bath place and wash. It gladdened him to see the steaming water, for it had not been his good fortune to meet such comfort since he left the dwelling of bright-haired Calypso, with whom he had had the entertainment of a god, continually.

When the maids had washed and anointed him they draped him in a rich robe and tunic; and he went out from the bath-house to join the men at their wine-drinking. On the way, by the pillar of the massy roof, stood Nausicaa in her god-given beauty, admiring Odysseus with all her eyes: until words came and she addressed him directly: – 'Farewell, Stranger; and when in your native land think of me, sometimes: for it is chiefly to me that you owe the gage of your life.' Odysseus answered her, saying, 'Nausicaa, daughter of high-souled Alcinous: if Zeus, Hera's Lord, the Thunderer, wills that I reach home and see the day of my return, there and then will I pay vows to you, as to a Divine One; and for ever and ever throughout all my days. For you gave me life, Maiden.'

He ended and passed to his throne beside King Alcinous. The servers were mixing wine and distributing meats. The herald drew near, leading Demodocus the sweet singer whom the people honoured into the midst of the feasters; he set him there with his back to a tall column: and to the herald wily Odysseus called, having cut off from the chine of a white-toothed boar (there was abundance and to spare) a piece rich all round with fat. 'Herald,' said he, 'take and offer this portion of flesh to Demodocus that he may eat it with a greeting from me that not even the depth of my misfortunes can chill; for it is right that bards should receive honour and reverence from every man alive, inasmuch as the Muse cherishes the whole guild of singers and teaches to each one his rules of song.'

When the hero had made an end of speaking, the herald bore his meat in hand to Demodocus who received it and rejoiced. All stretched out and helped themselves to the ready cheer; and when they were filled with drink and food then Odysseus addressed Demodocus. 'Demodocus, I laud you above all mortal men: I know not if it was the Muse, daughter of Zeus, that taught you, or Apollo himself. Anyhow you have sung the real history of the mishaps of the Achaeans, their deeds, their sufferings, their griefs, as if you had been there or had heard it from eye witnesses. But now change your theme and sing of how Epeius with the help of Athene carpentered together that great timber horse, the crafty device, which wise Odysseus got taken into the citadel after packing it with the men who were to lay Troy waste. Tell me all this in order, and then I will maintain everywhere that the God's grace has conferred the bounty of inspiration on your singing.'

So he said; and the minstrel, fired by the God, gave proof of his mastery. He took up his tale where the main body of the Argives embarked on their well-decked ships after setting fire to their hutments, and sailed away; leaving the remnant, the companions of famous Odysseus, enclosed in the heart of Troy-town, in the meeting-place, hidden within the horse which the Trojans themselves had dragged up to their citadel. There the horse stood while the people hung about it arguing this way and that, uncertainly. They were of three minds: – either to prize open its wooden womb with their pitiless blades; or to drag it to the cliff's edge and roll it down among the rocks; or to leave it there dedicated as a mighty peace offering to the Gods. In the end this last counsel had it, for it was fated that they should perish when their city gave lodgement to the monstrous beast in which crouched all the flower of the Argives with their seeds of death and doom for Troy. He sang how the sons of the Argives quitted their hollow den, and poured out from the horse, and made an end of Troy. He sang the share of each warrior in the wasting of the stately town, and how Odysseus, Ares-like, attacked the house of Deiphobus with great Menelaus. There, he said, Odysseus braved terrible odds but conquered in the end, by help of resolute Athene.

Thus ran the famous singer's song: but Odysseus melted and tears from his eyelids bedewed his cheeks. So it is when a loving wife flings herself, wailing, about the body of her man who has fallen before his township and fellow-citizens, defending the town and his children from their cruel day of sack and rapine. The sight of him labouring his last breath and dying makes her wail aloud and wind herself about him. Yet do the enemy from behind beat her with their spear-shafts across her bowed shoulders and lead her into servitude, to her fate of toil and grief. Just as that woman's cheeks are ravaged with despair, just so piteously did the tears fall from Odysseus' brows. Yet this time, too, his falling tears were missed by all the company, save only Alcinous who sat by him and marked his grief, unable not to hear the moaning deep within his breast. Alcinous at once spoke to the oar-loving Phaeacians: –

'Lend me your ears, captains and councillors. It is for Demodocus now to let be his echoing lyre: his song does not delight us all. From supper-time when the divine singer began, the Stranger has not ceased from bitter grieving. Some sore pain besets his heart. Wherefore cease, that we may all, hosts and guest, make merry as we fairly ought: for have we not contrived in our guest's honour just what he required of us – an escort – and further added to him love-tokens in proof of our regard? Any sufficient man who has the wit to pierce a little beneath the surface will entertain a stranger or a suppliant as his brother. Wherefore, Stranger, do not in crafty purpose conceal the news I seek: but make a virtue of frankness. Tell us by what name they call you there at home – your mother and father and the others in your city and district. For all parents fit names to their children as soon as these are born, so that there is no one so poor or so gentle that he is nameless. Tell me your land and district and city, that our sentient ships may get their bearing for your journey. Understand that the Phaeacians do not carry steersmen or steering oars, like ordinary ships. Their vessels know what men think and purpose. They know the cities and rich lands of every people and swiftly cross the ocean-gulfs, through the thickest veils of rain-cloud or mist. Nor are they troubled by panic or disaster, ever. Yet did I hear my father Nausithous once say that Poseidon was vexed with us for giving safe-conduct impartially to all mankind: and would one day shatter a trim Phaeacian ship homeward bound across the misty sea from such a sending, and would shroud our city under a high mountain on every side. So the old man said. The God may do it, or may forbear. It shall be as He wills.

'But open your heart now, and inform me plainly whither you wandered and what coasts of men you have visited. What were the peopled cities like, and what the peoples? Whether harsh, savage and unjust; or humane men, hospitable and god-fearing. Tell us why you wept so bitterly and secretly when you heard of the Argive Danaans and the fall of Ilion. That was wrought by the Gods, who measured their life's thread for those men, that their fate might become a poem sung to generations yet to be. Did some kinsman of your wife's die before Ilion, some one of those worthy relatives by marriage who become nearest to us after our own flesh and blood? Or perhaps it was a friend, some man loving and true? Friends with understanding hearts become no less dear to us than brothers.'

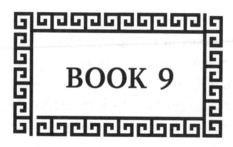

BOOK 9

Many-sided Odysseus then began: 'Lord Alcinous, most eminent, we are in very deed privileged to have within our hearing a singer whose voice is so divinely pure. I tell you, to my mind the acme of intelligent delight is reached when a company sits feasting in some hall, by tables garnished with bread and meat, the while a musician charms their ears and a cup-bearer draws them wine and carries it round served ready for their drinking. Surely this, as I say, is the best thing in the world.

'Yet, lo, at such a moment your heart prompts you to seek the tale of my dismal fortunes: whose telling will wring from me yet deeper tears. How shall I rank my sorrows, to put this first, that afterwards? The Gods of heaven have given me such excess of woe. I will begin with my name to make you sure of me, that when this cruel spell is past I may become your host in my house – my very distant house, alas! I am Odysseus, son of Laertes: a name which among men spells every resource and subtlety of mind: and my fame reaches heaven. I live in pellucid Ithaca, the island of Mount Neriton, whose upstanding slopes are all a-quiver with the wind-blown leaves. About it lie many other islands very near to one another, Dulichium and Same and wooded Zacynthus. My island stands deep in the sea and nearer the west than its neighbours which rather face the dawning and the sun. It is a harsh land, yet it breeds good youths: but perhaps in every man's sight there is nothing better than his native land. Take my case: Calypso the fair goddess sought to keep me in her hollow cave and would have used me as her husband: and likewise Circe, the wily lady of Æaea, tried to detain me in her house, she too wanting me for a husband: but neither the one nor the other could pervert the heart in my manly breast. Wherefore I say that no matter how rich a man's circumstances may be abroad, among foreign parts, there is no sweet in life to compare with home and parents. However, let me hark back to the tale of the calamitous homeward journey with which Zeus had afflicted my return from Troy.

'From Ilion the wind served me to near Ismarus of the Cicones. I sacked the city and slew them. Their wives and wealth we took and divided precisely, so that no one of us, through me, should go short of his just share. I suggested then that we all flee, hot-foot: but my utter fools of men would not obey. There was much wine for the drinking, yet; and mutton or beef from the great droves of sheep and heavy screw-horned kine that they had butchered by the shore. Whilst they so dallied, our Cicones cried for help to the inland Cicones, their neighbours, but more numerous and better men of their hands; men who could fight mounted, but also (when need was) on foot with footmen. They were upon us, thick as the leaves and buds of spring-tide, at the first show of morning; while over us there hung a foreboding of disaster, by doom of Zeus who had further pains in store for our ill-fated heads. The troops set themselves to battle by the swift ships and rained thickly at one another their copper-bladed spears. So long as the dawn lasted and while the blessed day increased, just for so long we stood firm and repulsed their swarms; but when the sun had crossed his stage and brought near the hour for loosing plough-oxen homeward in the evening, then finally the Cicones caused the Achaean lines to waver and give way. Six warriors perished out of each ship's complement. We others who for that time fled our death and doom sailed from the spot with mixed feelings; rejoicing to have avoided fate, yet mourning our comrades for whose sake not one of those full-bellied ships of mine stirred thence till we had thrice invoked the name of each unhappy victim of the Cicones' violent hands, on the flats there by the shore.

'Next Zeus, the cloud-marshal, incited against our fleet a North wind, with screaming squalls. He blinded land and sea alike with clouds. Night plunged down from heaven. The ships were swept aside before the blast and their sails shredded into tatters by the gale. We had to strike them in instant fear of death, and take to the oars. Vehemently we tugged our ships shoreward. For two days and two nights we lay there, making no way and eating our hearts out with despair and the unceasing labour: but on the third morning bright-haired Dawn achieved clear daylight; wherefore up went our masts and white shining sails, enabling us to sit there at our ease watching how the winds and the steersmen held us to our course. Indeed, that time I nearly came unscathed to my father-land; only for the swell and the seacurrents and a north wind which united against me as I beat round Cape Maleia and deflected me wide of Cythera. Thereafter for nine days I was driven by ravening winds across the sea. On the tenth day we made the land of the Lotos-eaters, men who browse on a food of flowers. We landed there to fill our water-butts, while my crews snatched a meal on the shore, beside their likely vessels. As soon as the first hunger for food and drink had passed, I chose out two fellows and added to them a third, as runner, that they might go inland to spy out and enquire what were the human beings there existing. Off they went at once and met a party of these Lotos-eaters, who had no notion of slaying my emissaries: instead they gave them a dish of their Lotos-flower. And so it was that as each tasted of this honey-sweet plant, the wish to bring news or return grew faint in him: rather he preferred to dwell for ever with the Lotos-eating men, feeding upon Lotos and letting fade from his mind all memory of home. I had to seek them and drag them back on board. They wept: yet into the ships we brought them perforce and chained them beneath the thwarts, deep in the well, while I constrained the rest of my adherents to hurry aboard, lest perhaps more of them might eat Lotos and lose their longing for home. They embarked promptly and sat to the rowing benches; then in their proper ranks, all together, they swung their oars and beat the sea hoary-white.

'We left in low spirits and later came to the land of the arrogant iniquitous Cyclopes who so leave all things to the Gods that they neither plant nor till: yet does plenty spring up unsown and unploughed, of corn and barley and even vines with heavy clusters: which the rains of Zeus fatten for them. They have no government nor councils nor courts of justice: but live in caves on mountain tops, each ruling his wives and children and a law unto himself, regardless. Across the bight of the Cyclopes' country extends a fertile island, a wooded island; not very far, yet not close. In it there harbour uncounted wild goats. No trace of man scares these, nor do hunters with dogs track them out, fighting their way through the bush to explore the summits of the hills. The herbage is not grazed down by flocks of sheep nor broken by any plough. Rather the spot continues in solitude, wholly uncultivated, a paradise for the bleating she-goats, by reason that the Cyclopes have no ruddle-cheeked ships, nor ship-wrights to make them such seaworthy vessels for pleasuring among the cities of mankind, like those ordinary men who tempt the seas to know others and to be known. Otherwise they might have made this island theirs, it being not at all bad land. Anything would grow well there in season, in the soft moist meadows behind the dykes of the silvery sea: and its vine-stocks would bear for ever. The crop to be harvested at the due time from such smooth plough-loam would be heavy, seeing that the undersoil is fat. Its haven is a natural port requiring no such gear as anchors or warps. Ships can be beached directly, to lie there in peace while the sailors screw up their hearts to venture farther or until the winds blow kind. And at the head of this inlet is pure running water from a spring rising in a cave. Black poplars shadow it.

'Thither we sailed, some God assuredly guiding us, for the night was utterly dark, without glimmer. The ground-fog shrouded our boats nor could any moon-beam from the sky pierce the low-lying clouds. Wherefore no one of us saw anything of the island, or of the long slow waves rolling unbroken upon its shelving beach. All we knew was that our good ships gently grounded. As they touched we struck sail and climbed out: and there, just beyond the water's edge, sunken in a depth of sleep, we waited the goddess of Dawn. When She came, rosy-fingered, we began in amazement to compass the island, exploring it: and the nymph-daughters of Zeus himself flushed for us the wild goats of the hills, to give my men whereon to dine. We ran to seek our carved bows and long-tanged throwing spears from the ships and began shooting, after forming ourselves into three bands. Very quickly did the God provide us game to our hearts' content: so great was the bag that nine goats could be shared out to each of the twelve ships that made up my command. For my own ship, as a special allowance, ten were allotted. Afterwards throughout the live-long day and until the sun went down we sat about feasting; for the meat was unlimited and the drink good, the red wine being not yet altogether exhausted within our ships, since we had carried off a great store in jars from the hallowed little capital of the Cicones when we sacked it. While we ate we stared across at the land of the Cyclopes, so near that we could see its smoke going up and hear the sounds of its men and the bleating of their sheep and goats; until at last the sun sank and dusk drew down, causing us to stretch out in slumber where we were, on the margin of the sea.

'At dawn I met my men in council and delivered myself as follows: "You, my trusty ones, will remain here while I with my ship and crew run over to try those men and find out if they are brutal savages or kindly to guests, reverent and just." After giving these orders I went up into my ship and told her crew to get aboard when they had let go the hawsers. They obeyed at once and manned the rowing benches smartly. The sea turned pale beneath the flailing of their oars. As we came to the nearest point of land we could see a cave at its seaward extremity – a lofty cave, embowered in laurels. There were signs that large flocks of sheep and goats were wont to be penned within it for the night. Round the cave-mouth a strong-walled yard had been contrived of rocks deeply embedded, with a fence of logs from tall pines and spreading oaks. Actually it was the lair of a giant, a monstrous creature who pastured his flocks widely from that centre and avoided traffic with any man. He was a solitary infidel thing, this ogre, and fearfully made; not in the fashion of a bread-eating man but altogether singular and out-standing like a tree-grown crag of the high mountains.

'I ordered my faithful crew to stand by the ship and guard the ship, while I picked the twelve men I judged best and set off with them. I took, as an afterthought, a goat-skin of potent wine, very mellow, which I had been given by Maron son of Euanthes, the priest of Apollo tutelary God of Ismarus. Maron lived in his dense grove (sacred to Phoebus Apollo) and when we sacked the town we had piously spared him and his wife and child. In reward he paid me valuable gifts – seven talents of refined gold and a mixing bowl of pure silver, over and above this great wine which he drew off neat for us into twelve wine-jars. Liquor for gods, it was. Only himself and his wife and the housekeeper knew of its existence; he had told none of his women slaves or housemaidens: and when he broached it he would draw off just the one cup of deep delight and pour it into twenty measures of water: whereupon there would waft abroad from the bowl a smell so sweet that it was heavenly: and to hold back from drinking, then, would indeed have been no joy. A great skin I filled with this drink and took with me; also corn in a leathern wallet; for at this very moment some masterful instinct warned me that we might have to do with a strange fierce being of vast strength, knowing neither right nor wrong, and ungovernable.

'Soon we were within the cave, to find its owner absent, grazing his goodly flocks in their pastures. So we explored the cave, staring round-eyed at cheese racks loaded with cheeses, and crowded pens of lambs and kids, each sort properly apart, the spring-younglings in this, mid-yearlings there, and the last born to one side. There were pails, buckets and tubs all brimming with whey: well-made vessels too, these milk-vessels of his. My men's first petition was that they might lay hold of the cheeses and make off with them, to return at a run and drive kids and lambs from the pens to the ship, in which we should then put hastily to sea. This advice, in the issue, would have profited us: but now I would not heed it, so set was I on seeing the master and getting (if he would give it) the guest's-present from him. Yet was his coming to prove disastrous to my party.

'We built up a fire, made a burnt offering, helped ourselves to cheese and ate as we sat there inside the cavern waiting for our man to come home from the pastures. He brought with him an immense burden of dried wood, kindling for his supper fire, and flung it upon the cave's floor with a crash that sent us scurrying in terror to its far corners. Then he drove under the arch his splendid flock, or rather those of them that were in milk. The rest, rams and he-goats, he left in the broad yard before the entry. Next he lifted into place and fixed in the cave's mouth a huge tall slab of stone, gigantic like himself. Two and twenty stout four-wheeled waggons would not have shifted it along the ground, so huge was it, this rock he used to block his door. Then he sat down to milk his ewes and bleating goats, all orderly, later putting her young lamb or kid beneath each mother-animal. One half of this white milk he curdled and put to press in the wicker cheese-baskets. The other half he left standing in the buckets as provision against his supper-time when he would drink it and satisfy himself.

'So far he had been wholly engaged in work, but now he rebuilt the fire and looked around and saw us. "Why, strangers," said he, "who are you and where have you come from across the water? Are you traders? or pirates, those venturers who sea-prowl at hazard, robbing all comers for a livelihood?" So he asked, and our confidence cracked at the giant's dread booming voice and his hugeness. Yet I made shift to speak out firmly, saying, "We are waifs of the Achaeans from Troy, intending homeward, but driven off our course haphazard across the boundless ocean gulfs by adverse winds from heaven: it may be by the will and decree of Zeus. We can vaunt ourselves companions of Atrides, Agamemnon's men, whose is now the widest fame under heaven for having sacked earth's greatest city and brought such multitudes to death. Here therefore we find ourselves suppliant at your knees, in hope of the guesting-fee or other rich gift such as is the meed of strangers. Have regard for the Gods, Magnificent! We are your suppliants: and Zeus who fares with deserving strangers along their road is the champion of suppliants, their protector and patron-God."

'Thus far I got: but the reply came from his pitiless heart. "Sir Stranger, you are either simple or very outlandish if you bid me fear the Gods and avoid crossing them. We are the Cyclopes and being so much the bigger we listen not at all to aegis-bearing Zeus or any blessed God: so if I should spare your life and your friends' it would not be to shun the wrath of Zeus, but because my heart counselled me mercy. Now tell me where you moored the stout ship when you came. On the far shore was it, or the near? I want to know." With these words he laid a crafty snare for me, but to my subtlety all his deceits were plain. So I spoke back, meeting fraud with fraud: "My ship was broken by Poseidon the Earth-shaker, who swept her towards the cape at the very end of your land, and cast her against the reefs: the wind drifted us in from the high sea. Only myself with these few escaped." So I said.

'His savagery disdained me one word in reply. He leapt to his feet, lunged with his hands among my fellows, snatched up two of them like whelps and rapped their heads against the ground. The brains burst out from their skulls and were spattered over the cave's floor, while he broke them up, limb from limb, and supped off them to the last shred, eating ravenously like a mountain lion, everything – bowels and flesh and bones, even to the marrow in the bones. We wept and raised our hands to Zeus in horror at this crime committed before our eyes: yet there was nothing we could do. Wherefore the Cyclops, unhindered, filled his great gut with the human flesh, and washed it down with raw milk. Afterwards he stretched himself out across the cavern, among the flocks, and slept.

'I was wondering in my bold heart whether I should now steal in, snatch the keen sword hanging on my hip, and stab him in the body; after making sure with my fingers where was that vital place in the midriff, below the heart and above the liver. Yet my second thoughts put me off this stroke, for by it I should finally seal our own doom: not enough strength lay in our hands to roll back the huge block with which he had closed the cave. So we sighed there night-long with misery, awaiting Dawn: upon whose shining the giant awoke, relit his fire, milked his flock in due order and put each youngling under its dam. After his busy work was done, he seized two more of us, who furnished his day-meal. Then he drove his sleek beasts out of the cave, easily pulling aside the great door-block and putting it back, as one of us might snap its lid upon a quiver. With loud halloos to the flock the Cyclops led them into the hills, leaving me imprisoned there to plot evil against him in the depths of my mind, wherein I sought means to pay him back, would but Athene grant me the opportunity for which I prayed.

'Of what came to me this seemed best. There lay in the sheep-pens a great cudgel belonging to Cyclops, or rather a limb of green olive wood from which he meant to make himself a staff when it had seasoned. In our estimation we likened it to the mast of a twenty-oared black ship, some broad-beamed merchantman of the high seas – it looked so long and thick. I straddled it and cut off about a fathom's length which I took to my fellows, bidding them taper it down. They made it quite even while I lent a hand to sharpen its tip. Then I took it and revolved it in the blazing flame till the point was charred to hardness. Thereafter we hid it under the sheep-droppings which were largely heaped up throughout the cave. Lastly I made the others draw lots, to see who would have the desperate task of helping me lift up our spike and grind it into his eye when heavy sleep had downed him. The luck of the draw gave me just the four men I would have chosen with my eyes open. I appointed myself the fifth of the party.

'Cyclops came back at evening shepherding his fleecy flocks and straightway drove them into the wide-vaulted cave, the whole fat mass of them, leaving no single one in the outer yard. Something on his mind, was it, or did some God move him? Then he lifted up the great door-stone and propped it into place before he sat down to his milking, dealing in turn with every ewe and noisy milch-goat and later setting their young beneath them. Briskly he attacked his household work; only after it to snatch up two more of us and dine off them. Then I went up to the giant with an ivycup of my dark wine in hand and invited him, saying, "Cyclops, come now and on top of your meal of man's flesh try this wine, to see how tasty a drink was hidden in our ship. I brought it for you, hoping you would have compassion on me and help me homeward: but your unwisdom is far beyond all comprehending. O sinful one, how dare you expect any other man from the great world to visit you, after you have behaved towards us so unconscionably?" I spoke: he took and drank. A savage gladness woke in him at the sweetness of the liquor and he demanded a second cup, saying, "Give me another hearty helping and then quickly tell me your name, for me to confer on you a guest-gift that will warm your heart. It is true our rich soil grows good vines for us Cyclopes, and the moisture of heaven multiplies their yield: but this vintage is a drop of the real nectar and ambrosia." Thus he declared and at once I poured him a second cup of the glowing wine: and then one more, for in his folly he tossed off three bowls of it. The fumes were going to his Cyclopean wits as I began to play with him in honeyed phrase: – "Cyclops, you ask me for my public name: I will confess it to you aloud, and do you then give me my guest-gift, as you have promised. My name is No-man: so they have always called me, my mother and father and all my friends."

'I spoke, and he answered from his cruel heart, "I will eat No-man finally, after all his friends. The others first – that shall be your benefit." He sprawled full-length, belly up, on the ground, lolling his fat neck aside; and sleep that conquers all men conquered him. Heavily he vomited out all his load of drink, and gobbets of human flesh swimming in wine spurted gurgling from his throat. Forthwith I thrust our spike into the deep embers of the fire to get it burning hot: and cheered my fellows with brave words lest any of them hang back through fear. Soon the stake of olive wood despite its greenness was almost trembling into flame with a terrible glowing incandescence. I snatched it from the fire, my men helping. Some power from on high breathed into us all a mad courage, by whose strength they charged with the great spear and stabbed its sharp point right into his eye. I flung my weight upon it from above so that it bored home. As a ship-builder's bit drills its timbers, steadily twirling by reason of the drag from the hide thong which his mates underneath pull to and fro alternately, so we held the burning pointed stake in his eye and spun it, till the boiling blood bubbled about its pillar of fire. Eyebrows, with eyelids shrivelled and stank in the blast of his consuming eyeball: yea, the very roots of the eye crackled into flame.

'Just as a smith plunges into cold water some great axe-head or adze and it hisses angrily – for that is the treatment, and the strength of iron lies in its temper – just so his eye sizzled about the olive-spike. He let out a wild howl which rang round the cavern's walls and drove us hither and thither in terror. He wrenched the spike of wood from his eye and it came out clotted and thick with blood. The maddening pain made him fling it from his hands, and then he began to bellow to the other Cyclopes living about him in their dens among the windy hills. They had heard his screaming and now drew towards the closed cave, calling to know his trouble: "What so ails you, Polyphemus, that you roar across the heavenly night and keep us from sleep? Do not pretend that any mortal is driving your flocks from you by force, or is killing you by sheer might or trickery." Big Polyphemus yelled back to them from within his cave, "My friends, No-man is killing me by sleight. There is no force about it." Wherefore they retorted cuttingly, "If you are alone and no one assaults you, but your pain is some unavoidable malady from Zeus, why then, make appeal to your father King Poseidon."

'They turned away and my dear heart laughed because the excellent cunning trick of that false name had completely taken them in. Cyclops was groaning in his extremity of torment. He groped with his hands until he had found and taken the stone from the entrance. Then he sat himself in the cave's mouth with his fingers extended across it, to catch anyone who tried to steal through with the sheep. In his heart he judged me such a fool as that: while I was thinking my very hardest to contrive a way out for myself and my fellows from destruction, we being truly in the jaws of death. Many notions and devices I conceived thus for dear life, and the best of them seemed finally as follows. Some rams there were of big stock, fleecy great splendid beasts with wool almost purple in its depth of colour. I took them by threes silently and bound them abreast with the pliant bark-strips from which the wicked monster's bed was plaited. The middle beast could then take a man and the one on either side protect him from discovery. That meant three rams for each shipmate: while for myself there remained the prize ram of all the flock. I took hold of him, tucked myself under his shaggy belly and hung there so, with steadfast courage: clinging face upwards with my hands twisted into his enormous fleece. Thus we waited in great trepidation for the dawn.

'At its first redness the rams rushed out towards their pasture: but the ewes hung about their pens unmilked, bleating distressfully with bursting udders. The lord, distraught with his terrible pains, felt the back of each sheep as it stood up to march straight past him. The dullard suspected not that there were men bound beneath their fleecy ribs. Last of all the prime ram came to go out, walking stiffly with the weight of his wool and me the deep plotter. Strong Polyphemus stroked him and said, "Beloved ram, why are you the last of all my flock to quit the cave? Never before have you let yourself lag behind the others; but have been always the first to stride freely across the sward nibbling its smooth buds, and first into the hill-streams to drink: while at evening, which was homing time, you would be ever the first that wanted to turn back. And now you come last! Are you feeling the loss of your lord's sight, blinded by that villain with his knavish crew after he had made me helpless with wine? That No-man, who I swear has not yet got away from death. If only you could feel like me and had the gift of speech to tell where he skulks from my wrath. How I would dash his brains out against the ground and spill them over the cave, to lighten my heart of the pains which this worthless No-man has inflicted!"

'He pushed the ram gently from him through the doorway. When we were a little space from the cave and its surrounding yard I loosed myself and then set free my men. Often turning head to look back we drove the leggy flock, the fat ripe beasts, down to the ship where the sight of us gladdened the others at thought of the death we had escaped. They would have stayed to lament the fallen: but I would not have it. Sternly I bent my brows and checked each man's weeping: and set them instead by sharp gestures to tumbling the glossy-fleeced animals into the ship and launching out for the open sea. At once they were aboard and on their benches. Smartly they sat and gave way, so that the sea paled beneath their oar-strokes: but when we were just as far from the land as a man's shout might carry, then I hailed the Cyclops in malignant derision. "So, Cyclops, you were unlucky and did not quite have the strength to eat all the followers of this puny man within your cave? Instead the luck returned your wickedness upon yourself in fit punishment for the impiety that had dared eat the guests in your house. Zeus has repaid you, the other Gods agreeing."

'My cry stung his heart more terribly yet. He tore the crest from a great mountain and flung it at the black-prowed ship, but overcast by a hair's breadth. The rock nearly scraped the end of the tiller. The sea heaped up above its plunging, and the back-thrust, like a tidal wave from the deep, washed us landward again very swiftly, almost to shore. I snatched a long pole and used it as a quant, while I signed with my head to the crew how they must lay to it over the oar-looms if we were to avoid disaster. They put their backs into it and rowed till we were twice our former distance from the coast. Then I would have taunted Cyclops once more, but my followers each in his vein sought with gentle words to restrain me, protesting, "Hothead, why further provoke this savage creature who with his last deadly shot so nearly brought our ship to shore that we did already judge ourselves dead?

Had he caught but a whisper or sound from us just now, he would have crushed our heads and our ship's timbers flat beneath some jagged stone, the marvellous thrower that he is." Thus ran their plea, but my pride was not to be dissuaded. Wherefore once again I spilled my heart's malice over him: "Cyclops, if any human being asks of you how your eye was so hideously put out, say that Odysseus, despoiler of cities, did it; even the son of Laertes whose home is in Ithaca."

'Thus I shouted, and his answer came back in a pitiful voice: "O miserable day, which sees the ancient oracle come true! We had a good and a great prophet living with us, Telemus, the son of Eurymus best of soothsayers, who passed all his life amongst us Cyclopes, practising that art. He told me it should so come to pass after many days, and I lose my sight by the hand of one Odysseus. Wherefore ever I watched for some tall man, bristling with might, to move impressively upon me: and instead there comes this mean poor pigmy and steals my eye after fuddling my wits with his drink. See here, my Odysseus, come back to me and take my guest-bounty together with a god-speed I will win you from the great Earth-shaker: for Poseidon avows himself my father, and so I dare call myself his son. He, if he be kind, will heal my hurt, which no other of the blessed Gods nor any man can do." "Heal your sight," I cried back at him, "never: not even the Earth-shaker will do it. Would God I had power to strip you of life and soul and send you down to Hades, so surely as I know that!"

'So far – but he lifted up his hands to the starry firmament and prayed to his Lord, Poseidon. "Hear me, dark-haired Girdler of the earth, if indeed I am yours and you my sire. Grant that there be no homecoming for this Odysseus, son of Laertes of Ithaca. Yet if it is fated that he must see his friends once more in his stately house and fatherland, let it be late and miserably, in a strange ship, after losing all his crews. And let him find trouble there in the house." So he made his petition and the dark God heard him. Then the giant bent to another stone (much larger than before) whirled it with immeasurable force and let fly. It too fell very near but this time a little short of the ship, just failing to shatter the rudder. The sea swelled over the bulk of the falling stone and a wave boiled up and swept us right across to the far side; to the island where were all my other well-decked ships, with their crews sorrowing near-by for that we had failed them so long. We ran our keel hard up on the sand and came ashore driving the sheep of the Cyclops. These we shared out, I being very exact to see that no one lacked his part in the division. My warrior company decreed the prize ram to me, as gage of honour, and I devoted him to cloud-wrapped Zeus, son of Cronos and Universal King, to whom I consumed the choice parts of the thighs with fire. Yet did Zeus not care for my offering, but was inventing ways to destroy all my trim ships and staunch company.

'However, the sun went down upon us while we sat there, filling ourselves with flesh in incredible abundance and with sweet wine. After the sun had gone and the shadow fallen we lay down by the water's brink till dawn's rosy showing: when I roused the force and bade them embark and cast off. Soon they were aboard and ready on their thwarts, sitting to the oars and frothing the sea with their well-timed strokes: our voyage being sad, insomuch as we had lost a part of our fellowship; and glad, that we had delivered our own souls from death.'

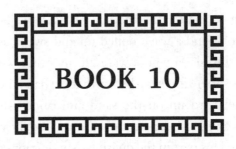

BOOK 10

So we came to the Aeolian island. In that sea-cradled fastness, within a bulwark of invincible bronze from which the cliff falls sheer, lived Aeolus son of Hippotas, a friend of the eternal Gods, with his twelve children, six daughters and six stalwart sons. Aeolus had so ordered it that the daughters served his sons for wives. They all eat at the one board with their father and revered mother and before them a myriad of dainty dishes are heaped up. Day-long the steaming house echoes festively even to its court: but by night they sleep, each man and his bashful wife between soft rugs on ornate bed-steads.

'To this splendid palace and home we came, to find entertainment for a month on end while Aeolus plied me with questions upon Troy and the Argive ships and the varied accidents of their journey home: all which things I recounted as they had happened. Afterwards I broached my own hope of returning and made appeal for his favour thereto. He showed no disposition to refuse me, nor failed to furnish his parting-gift, the hide of a nine-year-old bull, flayed expressly, in which he confined for my sake the complete range of every bursting wind that blew – Zeus having made him keeper of the winds to still them or excite them as he pleased. This leathern sack he fastened with a shiny silver cord into my hull so tightly that not even the very littlest puff of wind might leak out. Besides, he gave a firm and fair West wind to blow my ships and ourselves along, though not to the easy issue he had meant. Our own heedless folly betrayed us to disaster.

'Nine whole days, nine nights and days, we happily sailed. On the tenth we raised our land's green slopes and came so near that we could see the figures tending its fires. Then at last I surrendered myself gladly to overwhelming sleep, for my strength was utterly gone with having myself managed the sheets throughout this voyage: not letting any man of my ship's company spell me, so keen was I to crack on to our native land. Whilst I slept my crew began to mutter of the gold and silver gifts I was bringing home from generous Aeolus. Said each to his mate, regardfully, "Strange how the world loves this man and runs to do him honour as soon as he arrives in any part or place. Think of the stored treasure he carries with him from the sack of Troy, while we, his part- ners in every last tribulation and danger of the way, return with empty hands. To crown it here is Aeolus loading more and more upon him in token of regard. Let us have a quick peep to see what wealth of gold and silver is hidden in this ox-hide" – thus their jealous words. The counsel of envy mastered my crew. They untied the skin and out rushed the winds in a heap, to smite them all at once. Away the storms swept us into the wide sea, away from the fatherland, while the crew burst into loud crying. I awoke to this scene and for a moment pondered in my heart whether to slip overboard and drown were not easier than prolonged life among the living with so great a burden of ill-luck to bear in silence. However I settled to endure and to survive; but for the present lay down in the ship and covered my head. All about me my men made lament continually while the fierce squalls carried the ships right back, even to the island of Aeolus. There we landed and watered; the crews prepared a quick meal where we beached.

'When hunger and thirst were satisfied I took one seaman and one attendant and climbed again to the famous house of Aeolus, reaching it as he sat at meat with his wife and the children. We pushed in as far as the pillars of the hall-entry and there sat down. They wondered to see me again and asked, "How now, Odysseus? Is this return some new freak of ill-fortune? Surely we despatched you heartily enough, equipped to attain your country or anywhere you wished?" I confessed sorrowfully: "My evil companions let me down – they and an untimely sleep which overcame me. Yet repair it, friends, of your ability." I had tried to make this plea persuasive, using my humblest tone. They stared at me in silence: only the father found words, and he hurled out: "Get off the island instantly, you vilest thing alive! Am I to make a habit of maintaining and fitting out one whom the Gods hate? Your being returned proves that you have incurred the abhorrence of those Deathless Ones. Out! out!" His words drove me from the house in grief. Our sailing was gloomy; and now we had no helping wind, wherefore we must labour continually at the oars, by which futile pain my men's fortitude was sapped.

'Six days and six nights was this voyage. On the seventh day we made the fortress of Lamos, which is nicknamed Tall-tower by its people, the Laestrygons. In their region the extremes of day and night so nearly meet that the shepherd coming back with his full ewes exchanges greetings with the shepherd going out to pasture. A sleepless man could there earn double wage, by doing neat-herd one half his time and shepherding small cattle for the remaining hours. Its harbour is good, for an unbroken wall of rock shelters it from side to side; while parallel headlands jut forth to mask the entrance which is rather narrow. Upon our arrival my other shipmasters steered straight into the cove and there moored their ships, each tightly to the next, together: not that it mattered, for inside the haven there was never any swell, small or big, but a white calm constantly prevailed. I however kept my own ship outside, yet near; making fast our lines to a rock at the extreme end of the point. I climbed its craggy slope to look out from the crest, but could see no trace of man's work or beasts': only there was smoke rising from behind a fold of land.

'I told my fellows they must discover what the bread-eaters of this part were like and chose two of them to go, with a third for messenger. They went ashore and along a beaten waggon road, used for lading wood from the uplands to the town. A little short of the settlement proper they chanced upon a girl drawing water. The well-grown daughter of Antiphates the Laestrygonian had come down to this fountain of Artacia because it was the fashion of the town to water from its clear-running stream. They saluted her, asking after the king of the island and his subjects: she quickly pointed the way to the tall roofs of her father's hall: but when they came to that great house they found his wife inside, a mountainous woman whose ill-aspect struck them with horror. She summoned Antiphates, her powerful husband, from the assembly. His notion was to murder my men in cold blood. He seized hold of the first and proceeded to eat him for his dinner out of hand. The other two sprang away in headlong flight and regained the ships, while the master of the house was sounding an alarm through the city. This brought the stout Laestrygons in their thousands pell-mell together – not human-looking creatures, these, but giants. They gathered missile stones each a man's weight and cast them down on us off the cliffs. There went up from the fleet the ghastly sounds of splintering hulls and dying men, while the natives were busy spearing my people like fish and collecting them to make their loathsome meal.

'As they were so engaged in killing all within the close harbour I drew the sharp hanger from my side and cut the hawsers of my dark-prowed ship, shouting orders the while to her honest crew how they must be urgent upon their oars if we were to escape a terrible fate. Like one man they spumed up the water in dread of death, and my ship darted out from the over-shadowing cliffs into the welcome main. All the other vessels which had gone inside went down together: so it was in very disheartened mood that we rowed on, having lost every one of our dear comrades (yet with the consolation that we were still alive), till we came to the island of Æaea, where lived a formidable Goddess – though she spoke our speech – Circe of the luxuriant tresses, own sister of the warlock Æetes. Both were children of Helios, the Sun that lights mankind, and their mother was Perse, daughter of Oceanus.

'We floated into its land-locked harbour silently by divine guidance, right up on the beach: and disembarked to lie where we had landed for two days and two nights, our hearts devoured by fatigue and pain. But when Dawn with shining hair had made the third day bright then

I took my thrusting spear and sharp sword and walked briskly from the ship to the nearest commanding height, hoping to catch sight of human-kind or to hear human voices. My look-out rock showed me smoke rising from the ample landscape, out of an oak-thicket in the forest where lay Circe's house. My heart and mind debated if I should go at once to explore this place where I had seen the flame-shot smoke, or not. It seemed wisest to go first to the shore and ship, issue rations, and after choose some of my men for a search-party. I was going down and already near the ship when surely some God took compassion on my forlorn state by sending a great stag with branching horns across my very path. The sun's heat had driven the beast from the grove where he had been feeding, down to the stream to drink. He was coming up from the water when I hit him in the spine, half-way along the back. My copper weapon went clean through, and with no more than a sob he fell in the dust and died. I put one foot on the carcase and drew my point from the wound. Then I laid the shaft on the ground near-by while I broke off and twined twigs and withies into a rope some six feet long, well-laid throughout. With this I bound together the four feet of my noble kill, passed my head through, and went staggering under the load and staying myself on the shaft of my spear, down to the ship. The burden was far too great for me to heave it to my shoulder and balance it there with the disengaged hand as usual, the beast being hugely grown.

'I dropped it on the shore before my vessel and summoned each individual man with honeyed words. "Friends, by no excess of grief can we get down to the House of Hades one day before our time. Therefore so long as there is meat and drink in the ship let us remember our stomachs and preserve ourselves from wasting away with hunger." They quickly accepted my counsel. All heads came out from the cloaks; upon the edge of the sea they stood to admire the stag, my wonderful great trophy. After they had looked their fill they cleansed their hands and prepared a glorious feast over which we sat till sundown eating the abundant venison and drinking wine. When the sun set and darkness came we slept by the sea: but with the Dawn I called a council of all hands to say: –

'"Hear my words, fellows; we are in desperate case. My friends, now we cannot find out which is East and which is West, or distinguish the dawn lands from the shadowed: nor where the Sun, our light, sinks beneath the earth and rises from it. Wherefore if anyone have counsel let him quickly give tongue. I confess I have no plan and think that none exists. Understand that lately I climbed the hill to look out, and saw that this is an island which the limitless sea encircles like a wreath. The island itself is flat and my eyes perceived how in its heart smoke rose from the midst of a dense wood." By my news their soft natures were distressed, for they recalled the outrage of Laestrygonian Antiphates and the over-weening cannibal cruelty of the Cyclops. They lamented shrilly, pouring out big tears: yet there was no use in this lamentation. So I numbered off my mail-clad followers and divided them into two sections, each with its leader. One would be mine and godlike Eurylochus took the other. The two of us tossed at once in a copper head-piece to see which should go. His counter jumped out, so tall Eurylochus marched off his two and twenty men, all of them weeping aloud. The twenty and two who stayed with me cried in sympathy.

'The party threaded the woodland glades till they found the hewn walls of Circe's house on a site which overlooked the country-side. Wolves from the hills and lions, victims of her witch's potions, roamed about it. These made no onslaught against my men but wagged their long tails and pawed them fondly, as dogs fawn at the feet of masters who bring them from feasts some toothsome pickings in the hand: with such delight did these lions and strong-clawed wolves leap round my men, who were timid amongst the strange formidable pets. From outside the house-gates they heard Circe, the Goddess with the comely braided hair, singing tunefully within by the great loom as she went to and fro, weaving with her shuttle such close imperishable fabric as is the wont of goddesses, some lively lustrous thing. Polites, a file-leader very near and dear to me, then said to the others: "Shipmates, this voice at the loom, singing so heartily that the floor resounds again, is a female voice – either of a woman or a goddess. Let us give her a hail back." They agreed and shouted loudly. She came at once, opening her doors to bid them in. In their simplicity all went in to her: all except Eurylochus who suspected some trick and stayed behind. She showed them to thrones and seats and confected for them a mess of cheese with barley-meal and clear honey, mulched in Pramnian wine. With this she mixed drugs so sadly powerful as to steal from them all memory of their native land. After they had drunk from the cup she struck them with her wand; and straightway hustled them to her sties, for they grew the heads and shapes and bristles of swine, with swine-voices too. Only their reason remained steadfastly as before; so they grieved, squealingly, at finding themselves penned in sties. Presently Circe cast before them such provender of acorns, chestnuts and cornel-fruit, as rooting swine commonly devour.

'Eurylochus slowly turned back to the ship to report his fellows' unsavoury end. Again and again he tried to tell us while we grouped round him, but his heart was too broken with grief: his eyes brimmed with tears: all his spirit went out in great longing to lament. At last he was able to meet our shower of questions and relate the disaster. "We went through the woods as you ordered, Odysseus, Sir: and in the glades we found a noble house of dressed stone, standing high. From a loom inside rose a singing voice, of goddess or woman. We shouted. She opened the door and invited us to enter. All crowded in, unthinking, except myself who imagined guile: and from that moment they vanished completely. Not one came back though I sat there long enough." At his news I belted my long silver-mounted sword with its heavy blade of copper over my shoulder: and then my bow: telling him to lead on, the way he had taken. He caught my hands and knelt to embrace my knees, imploring me with tears and flying words: "Zeus-born, do not force me back again. Let me stay here: or rather let us (such as are yet alive) flee at once and even now escape the evil day.

Surely if you go you will not return – much less bring back the rest."
I replied loudly: "Stay here if it pleases you, Eurylochus, in the ship,
eating and drinking: but I am going. I must."

'I left ship and shore and plunged into the solemn wood, till near
the great house of drug-wise Circe; when there came from it to meet
me Hermes of the gold rod, seeming to be a quite young man, of that
age when youth looks its loveliest with the down just mantling his
cheeks. He called my name and took my hand, saying: "O unhappy
one, do you again hazard the wild-wood alone? Your followers, no
other than hogs to all appearance, are penned in the deep sties of
Circe's house. Do you come to set them free? I tell you, yourself shall
not get away but will join the others and be pent with them. But listen:
I can save you and deliver you from this evil by a potent drug in whose
virtue you can enter Circe's house and yet be immune. Hear the manner
of Circe's deadly arts. She will prepare you refreshment, and hide a
poison in it: but against you her spells will not avail, forbidden by this
saving charm I give you. Let me explain your course of action. When
Circe strikes you with her long thin wand draw the sharp sword that
is on your hip and make for her as if you had a mind to run her
through. She will cower, and implore you to be her bed-mate instead:
and your best suit is not to spurn this divine paramour but to make
the lying with her a lever to free your followers and win kindly treat-
ment for yourself. Be sure though that she swears the Gods' great oath
not to attempt more evil against you, lest she take advantage of your
nakedness to unman you shamefully."

'Upon such explanation the Slayer of Argus plucked from the ground
the herb he promised me. The Gods call it Moly, and he showed me
its nature, to be black at the root with a flower like milk. It would be
difficult for men and mortals to dig up Moly; but the Gods can do
anything. Thereupon Hermes quitted the wooded island for high
Olympus; and I went on, unquiet in mind, to the house of Circe. I
halted at her gate and called. The Goddess heard, opened and bade
me in. Reluctantly I entered. She set for me a silver-embossed throne,

with foot-rest, of fair and cunning workmanship. She prepared me a drink in a golden cup, dropped into it a draught for my destruction and gave it to me. I took and drank it, scatheless; but she rose and struck me with her wand, crying: "Get you to your stye, wallow there with your friends!" Instead I drew sword sharply and leapt up, feigning to make an end of her. She gave a shrill scream, ran in under my stroke and clasped my knees in a flood of tears, while she wailed piercingly, "What kind of a man are you; from what city or family? It is a miracle how you have drunk my potion and not been bewitched. Never before, never, has any man resisted this drug, once it passed his lips and crossed the barrier of his jaws. How firmly seated must be your indomitable mind! Surely you are Odysseus the resourceful, who will come here (as Argusbane of the gold rod often tells me) on his way from Troy in his ship. I pray you sheath that sword and let us two go lie together, that we may mingle our bodies and learn to trust one another by proofs of love and intercourse."

'But to her appeal, I made answer: "How dare you request my favour when you have changed my retainers in your house to hogs, and when you invite me to your bed only in subtile contrivance to have me by you naked, to be mutilated and robbed of my manhood. Wherefore I shall not enter that bed of yours except you deign, Goddess, to swear a great oath that you harbour no further mischief against me." So I declared, and she instantly swore the oath I needed. As soon as she had taken it I went up to the splendid bed of Circe.

'Meanwhile the four maidens who keep her house were at their duties in the hall. They are children of the running springs and the coppices and the sacred rivers that run down to the salty sea. The first was draping the seats in noble purple palls, over a thin under-housing. The second was putting silver tables ready to these seats and laying them with baskets of gold. The third was mixing honey-hearted wine in a silver cistern and setting out golden goblets. The fourth had brought water and kindled fire under a huge copper till the water warmed. At last it seethed with heat in the polished cauldron. Then she put me in a tub and washed me with water from the great tripod, diluted to a pleasant warmth; sluicing my head and shoulders till the life-destroying weariness had melted from my limbs. When she had washed and anointed me with pure olive oil she wrapped me in a tunic and cloak and set me again on the silver-bossed intricate throne, with the footstool under my feet. The damsel of the ewer caught the water from her golden vessel in its silver basin as I rinsed my hands. She drew a shining table to my side: while a matronly woman offered me wheaten bread and a choice of her good things, cheerfully. She pressed me to eat, but eating was no pleasure to my heart whose thoughts were otherwise engaged. So I sat there, brooding unhappily.

'Circe saw me sitting still without helping myself to food because of the distress that lay upon me. She came near and asked, urgently, "Why, O why, Odysseus, do you sit there like a dumb man, gnawing your heart away but not touching my food and drink? Do you still suspect me of guile? Fear not: indeed the oath I have sworn to you is binding." I answered, "Circe, how could any decent man bear to eat or drink till he had freed his company and restored them to his sight? If truly you wish me to feast then deliver them and let these men I love come before my eyes." At the word Circe went out from the house wand in hand, opened the doors of the piggery and let out what seemed a drove of nine-year-old fat hogs. When they were all before her she went down amongst them and smeared each with a particular unguent. Then from their parts dropped away the coarse hairs which had sprouted in the might of the poison given them by the Goddess. They turned to men again as they had been before, but younger now, fresher, and much taller to the eye. They knew me, too: each and every one came up to put himself between my hands. A sorrow that was love's yearning so thrilled through them all, that the great house echoed with their sobbing. Even the Goddess was touched.

'Later she came to me and said, "Son of Laertes, go now to your ship by the beach and drag her out on dry land, first: then store her fittings and cargo in my caves. Do it quickly and return with all your comrades." My high judgment marched with hers: so I went to the sea-side where my men were in sore grief and shedding great tears. Upon my arrival they ran to me, as the stalled calves of the country to the cows when the herd, glutted with hay, comes back to the muck-yard from grazing. At the sight of their mothers the calves skip so wildly that their pens can no longer hold them: they break loose, lowing all the while and gambolling. Just so my fellows cried and crowded round me when they saw me plain. To their hearts my coming was for one moment almost as though they had reached homely Ithaca, the city and place of their birth and upbringing. Their sorrow burst out in touching phrase: "Over your return, Heaven-born, we rejoice as if we saw again Ithaca our fatherland. Yet now tell us of those others, our friends, how they died."

'I sought to give them comfort in replying: "Nay: instead we will first draw our ship up the beach and store her gear and tackle in the caves. Then shall you follow me, one and all, to see those others feasting and pledging each other in the sacred house of Circe. They are in luxury." This was my word and presently all gave me credence but Eurylochus, who stood out and would have stayed the rest. He chided them sharply: "Poor fools, what next? Do you so love suffering that you would go again to Circe and all be turned into pigs or wolves or lions, forced to keep watch over her great house? It was so that Cyclops got his chance when some of us went into his private cave with insensate Odysseus: by that man's rashness they were cast away." His words so angered me that I had it in mind to whip the long sword from my huge thigh and smite him, to send his head rolling in the dust, though he was my near kinsman, the husband of my sister: but the others parted us and soothed me, promising, "Zeus-born, we await your guidance to Circe's sacred dwelling. As for this man, if you think fit, we can leave him here as ship-keeper by the ship." They spoke and set off from the sea. Yet was Eurylochus not left behind by the hulk. He came along too, trembling from my savage abuse of him.

'Meanwhile Circe had commanded baths for the others of my company in her house, with olive oil and fleecy tunics and outer garments for each one. So we found them attired at all points and feasting in the hall. When each saw the others and recognized them face by face, the tears ran afresh and they cried so shrilly that the rooms re-echoed through and through. The Goddess approached me with: "Son of Laertes, do not permit longer indulgence in such grief. Of course I know how sorely you were afflicted in the fish-haunted seas, and the outrages wreaked upon you by violent men along the coasts. But let that be. Eat my cheer and drink my wine till your courage returns to your breasts, as in rugged Ithaca long ago when you first quitted your ancestral homes. See how haggard and heart-sick you are with ever brooding on the evil of your wanderings! So long and terrible have been your pains that your hearts have become strangers to feasting and gladness." Our pride accepted her advice and we tarried day by day till an entire year had lapsed, sitting to table and delighting in her untold wealth of flesh and mellow wine. Slowly the year fulfilled itself, as the seasons turned about and the months died, bringing down the long days once more. Then my men took me aside, saying: –

'"Master, it is time you called to memory your native land, if fate will ever let you come alive to your well-built house and ancient estate." So they said, and my nobility assented to them. For that last day we sat and feasted on the abundant meat and wine till the sun went down. But when night had fallen and the men had stretched out in the darkling halls, I climbed to the lovely bed of Circe and prayed her by her knees, in supplication. The Goddess heeded me and the winged words I used: "O Circe, now grant me fulfilment of the promise you so largely made, to aid me towards my home. My heart pants with the thought, and my men's hearts too. When you are absent they come round me and shatter my contentment with their longing to be gone." Thus I made prayer. The beautiful Goddess of Goddesses answered me: "Zeus-kin, son of Laertes, ingenious Odysseus: against your will you must not be kept in my house. Yet learn that your next journey will be to a strange destination, even so far as the House of Hades and dread Persephone, to seek counsel of the spirit of Teiresias of Thebes, that sightless prophet whose integrity of judgement has survived death. For him Persephone has ruled that he alone, though dead, should know: all others of the dead are shadows that drift ineffectually."

'She ceased: and again my loving heart gave way. I wept as I sat there on her bed, nor did my soul any longer desire to feel or see the shining of the sun: till I had wept and wallowed myself impotent. Then I ventured again, asking: "But who, O Circe, can guide us by this way? No human being ever reached Hades in one of our black ships." Whereupon the Goddess of Goddesses replied, "Let not the need of a pilot for the ship concern you at all. Set mast, hoist sail, and then sit quietly. The northern airs will bring you thither. When you have cut across the river of Ocean you will find Persephone's shore and her grove of tall poplars and seed-blighted willows. Beach your ship there by the deep eddying Ocean stream and make your own way down to the dank house of Hades. There Pyriphlegethon (with Cocytus a tributary of the water of Styx) runs into Acheron; by a rock the two roaring rivers meet. When there, hero, step very near the face of the stream and dig a pit – like this – about a cubit each way, and pour a drink-offering around it to all the dead, of milk-in-honey first and then sweet wine and lastly water. Over it all sprinkle white pearl-barley. Then cry earnestly upon the wan muster of the piteous dead, promising that when in Ithaca again you will devote to them in your house a clean heifer, your best, on a pyre made rich with votive offerings: while for Teiresias particularly you will further sacrifice an all-black ram, the worthiest among your flocks. When thus with prayers you have entreated the grave's worshipful populations, slay for them a ram and a black sheep, pointing them towards Erebus while you yourself turn to face the stream of the river. Then many wraiths will repair to you of the dead who have died. At once straitly enjoin your fellows to flay the two sheep which lie there, butchered by your pitiless sword, and burn them: while they pray all the time to the Gods and to great Hades and to dreadful Persephone. Draw the sharp sword from your hip and sit with it ready, sternly preventing any one of the shambling dead from coming near the blood till you have had your word with Teiresias. Nor will the prophet be long in coming to you, O leader of the people; and he will explain to you your road and its stages and how, in returning, you may get across the teeming deep."

'She ceased, and then came gold-throned Dawn. The nymph put on a flowing silvery gown of light and lissom stuff, clasped her middle with a splendid golden girdle and hid her hair in a veil. She clad me in my under-garment and cloak and I went through the house, finding each of my men and rousing them with soft-spoken words: "No longer lie and dream in quiet sleep. Let us go. See, Lady Circe has told me the way." Their courage rose to my summons. Yet was I not to get every last one of them safely off. There was Elpenor the youngest (no great fighter, and loose-minded) in whom over-much drink had put a longing for cool air. So he had left his fellows and lain down on the roof of Circe's house. Hearing the bustle when the others rose and the trampling of their feet he leaped up all of a sudden with his wits too astray to think of coming down again by the long ladder. Instead he tumbled from the roof and broke his neck-bone, just where it joins the spine. His soul flew to Hades.

'As we went out together I said to my men, "You think that we are now heading for our loved country. But Circe has detailed us a quite different course, which will take us down to the House of Hades and to dread Persephone in search of the spirit of Teiresias the Theban." The news broke their hearts. They sat down where they were and tore the ringlets of hair by the roots from their heads, lamenting. Not that it was any good, the moan they made.

'So sorrowfully we proceeded towards the sea, shedding floods of tears. Yet meanwhile had Circe lightly outstripped us, gone down to the ship and tethered by it a ram and a black ewe. What mortal eye can see a God going up and down if He wills not to be seen?'

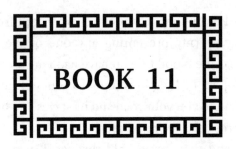

BOOK 11

At length we were at the shore where lay the ship. Promptly we launched her into the divine sea, stepped the mast, made sail and went: not forgetting the sheep, though our hearts were very low and big tears rained down from our eyes. Behind the dark-prowed vessel came a favourable wind, our welcomed way-fellow, whom we owed to Circe, the kind-spoken yet awesome Goddess: so when each man had done his duty by the ship we could sit and watch the wind and the helmsman lead us forward, day-long going steadily across the deep, our sails cracking full, till sundown and its darkness covered the sea's illimitable ways. We had attained Earth's verge and its girdling river of Ocean, where are the cloud-wrapped and misty confines of the Cimmerian men. For them no flashing Sun-God shines down a living light, not in the morning when he climbs through the starry sky, nor yet at day's end when he rolls down from heaven behind the land. Instead an endless deathful night is spread over its melancholy people.

'We beached the ship on that shore and put off our sheep. With them we made our way up the strand of Ocean till we came to the spot which Circe had described. There Perimedes and Eurylochus held the victims while I drew the keen blade from my hip, to hollow that trench of a cubit square and a cubit deep. About it I poured the drink-offerings to the congregation of the dead, a honey-and-milk draught first, sweet wine next, with water last of all: and I made a heave-offering of our glistening barley; invoking the tenuous dead, in general, for my intention of a heifer-not-in-calf, the best to be found in my manors when I got back to Ithaca; which should be slain to them and burnt there on a pyre fed high with treasure: while for Teiresias apart I vowed an all-black ram, the choicest male out of our flocks.

'After I had been thus instant in prayer to the populations of the grave I took the two sheep and beheaded them across my pit in such manner that the livid blood drained into it. Then from out of Erebus they flocked to me, the dead spirits of those who had died. Brides came and lads; old men and men of sad experience; tender girls aching from their first agony; and many fighting men showing the stabbed wounds of brazen spears – war-victims, still in their blooded arms. All thronged to the trench and ranged restlessly this side of it and that with an eerie wailing. Pale fear gripped me. Hastily I called the others and bade them flay and burn with fire the sheep's bodies which lay there, slaughtered by my pitiless sword. They obeyed, conjuring without cease the Gods, great Hades and terrible Persephone, while I sat over the pit holding out my sharp weapon to forbid and prevent this shambling legion of the dead from approaching the blood till I had had my answer from Teiresias.

'The first I knew was the spirit of my fellow, Elpenor, whose body was not yet interred under the ample ground. We had left him unwept and unburied in the halls of Circe, for that these other labours came upon us urgently. When I saw him I had compassion and sharply cried across to him: 'Elpenor, how come you here into the gloomy shades? Your feet have been quicker than my ship.' He in a thin wail answered me: 'Son of Laertes, ready Odysseus, the harsh verdict of some God sealed my doom, together with my own unspeakable excess in wine. I had lain down on Circe's house-top to sleep off this drunkenness, but awoke still too confused to descend from the roof by the long ladder. Instead I plunged headlong over the parapet and broke my neck-bone in its socket: hence my spirit has come down here to Hades. Yet I implore you, my Lord, to remember me as you go past homeward; for of my sure knowledge your returning must be by Æaea. My Lord, I adjure you by those left behind, those not among us – by your wife and by the father who cared for you when you were a little child, as by Telemachus, the babe you had to leave in your house alone – do not abandon me unwept and unburied, lest I be the pawn to bring upon you God's wrath: but consume my body in fire, with those arms and armour which remain mine, and heap over the ashes a mound at the edge of the sea where the surf breaks white, for a token telling of an unhappy man to aftertime; and when the rites are completed fix above my mound the oar that in life I pulled among my fellows.'

'Thus he said and I promised him: "Luckless one, all these things will I see done, exactly." So we two sat there, exchanging regrets, I with my sword held out stiffly across the blood-pool and the wraith of my follower beyond it, telling his tale. Then advanced the spirit of my mother who had died, even Anticleia, daughter of kindly Autolycus. I had left her alive when I started for the sacred city of Ilios, so now the sight of her melted my heart and made me weep with quick pain. Nevertheless I would not let her near to touch the blood, for I awaited Teiresias to speak with me. And at last he came, the spirit of Theban Teiresias, gold sceptre in hand. He knew me and said, "Heaven-born Odysseus, what now? O son of misfortune, why leave the lambent sunshine for this joyless place where only the dead are to be seen? Stand off from the pit and put up your threatening sword that I may drink blood and declare to you words of truth." So he said and I stepped back, thrusting my silver-hilted sword home into its scabbard: while he drank of the blackening blood. Then did the blameless seer begin to say: –

'"You come here, renowned Odysseus, in quest of a comfortable way home. I tell you the God will make your way hard. I tell you that your movements will not remain secret from the Earth-shaker, whose heart is bitter against you for the hurt you did him in blinding the Cyclops, his loved son. Yet have you a chance of surviving to reach Ithaca, despite all obstacles, if you and your followers can master your greed in the island of Thrinacia, when your ship first puts in there for refuge from the lowering sea. For in that island you will find at pasture the oxen and wonderful sheep of Helios our Sun, who oversees and overhears all things. If you are so preoccupied about returning as to leave these beasts unhurt, then you may get back to Ithaca, very toil-worn, after all: but if you meddle with them, then I certify the doom of your men and your ship; and though yourself may escape alive, it will not be till after many days, in a ship of strangers, alone and in sorry plight, that you win back, having suffered the loss of all your company: while in your house you shall find trouble awaiting you, even overbearing men who devour your substance on pretext of courting your worshipful wife and chaffering about her marriage dues. Yet at your coming shall you visit their violence upon them, fatally. After you have killed these suitors, either by cunning within the house or publicly with the stark sword, then go forth under your shapely oar till you come to a people who know not the sea and eat their victuals unsavoured with its salt: a people ignorant of purple-prowed ships and of the smoothed and shaven oars which are the wings of a ship's flying. I give you this token of them, a sign so plain that you cannot miss it: you have arrived when another wayfarer shall cross you and say that on your doughty shoulder you bear the scatterer of haulms, a winnowing-fan. Then pitch in the earth your polished oar and sacrifice goodly beasts to King Poseidon, a ram and a bull and a ramping boar. Afterward turn back; and at home offer hecatombs to the Immortal Gods who possess the broad planes of heaven: to all of them in order, as is most seemly. At the last, amidst a happy folk, shall your own death come to you, softly, far from the salt sea, and make an end of one utterly weary of slipping downward into old age. All these things that I relate are true."

'So he prophesied and I, answering, said: "O Teiresias, surely these things are threads of destiny woven in the Gods' design. Yet tell to me one other thing. Before me is the ghost of my mother, dead. Lo there, how she crouches by the blood and will not look upon me nor address me one word. Tell me, King, how shall she know that I am her son?" So I said and he replied, "A simple thing for my saying and your learning. Any of these ghosts of the dead, if you permit them to come near the blood, will tell you truth: and to whomsoever you begrudge it, he shall go back, away." The spirit of King Teiresias ended his soothsaying and departed to the House of Hades, but I remained firmly there, while my mother came up and drank of the storm-dark blood. Then at once she knew me and wailed aloud, crying to me winged words: "My child, what brings you to visit here, a quick man in this darkness of the shadow? It is sore travail for the living to see such things, because of the wide rivers and fearful waters that run between: especially Ocean's flood, that mortals cannot cross on foot but only by ship, in a well-found ship. Are you still errant, you and your men, from Troy? The time has been long if you have not yet reached Ithaca nor seen your wife in the house."

'So she said and I returned: "My mother, I had no choice but to come down to Hades. I must needs consult the spirit of Theban Teiresias, inasmuch as I have not yet drawn nigh Achaea, not yet set foot upon my own land, but have strayed ever painfully from that day I followed great Agamemnon to fight the Trojans at Ilios of the fine horses. But tell me now plainly – by what fateful agency did Death strike you down? Was it a slow disease, or did arrow-loving Artemis slay you with a stroke of her gentle darts? Inform me of the father and son I left. Is my position still safe in their keeping, or has a stranger assumed it on the rumour that I shall not return? Also of my wife – what is her mood and conduct? Does she abide by the child and guard all things as they were, or has she married some noble Achaean?" My lady mother exclaimed: "Why, she is ever in your house, most patiently. The nights drag through for her heavily and her days are wet with tears. Your fair position has not fallen to another. Telemachus holds the estate unchallenged, feasting amongst his peers at all such entertainments as magistrates may properly attend. He is invited everywhere. For your father – he now-a-days dwells wholly in the country and does not come to town. Old age grows crankily upon him. He will not suffer for his own use any bed or couch, quilts or glossy blankets: nor aught but rags upon his body. In winter-time he sleeps at home as bondmen sleep, by the hearth in the ashes of the fire: but when the summer brings its rush of harvest-tide and all through his rich vine-terraces the dead leaves are strewn for him in ground-carpets, upon them will he lie distressfully, sighing for your return with a sorrow that ever waxes in his heart. Also my death and doom were of that sort. No archer-goddess with piercing sight came upon me in the house and felled me with gentle arrows: nor any set disease, with a sorry wasting to drain the life from my limbs. Rather it was my longing for you – your cunning ways, O my wonderful Odysseus, and your tenderness – which robbed me of the life that had been sweet."

'She ceased her say. While my heart pondered the word a longing rose in me to take in my arms this spirit of my mother, though she were dead. Thrice I stepped toward her for an embrace, and thrice she slipped through my grasp like a shadow or a dream. The pain conceived in my heart grew very bitter and I cried to her in piercing words: "Mother mine, can you not abide the loving arms of one who yearns so sorely after you, that here, even here in Hades, we may tearfully sate ourselves with icy shuddering grief? Or are you only some phantasm which great Persephone has sent to increase the misery of my pain?" So I said; but my mother lamented: "Alas my hapless child! Here is no mockery from Persephone, daughter of Zeus: it is the common judgement upon all mortals when they die. Then the nerves will no more bind flesh and frame into one body, for the terrible intensity of searing fire subdues them till they vanish, as the quickening spirit vanishes from the white bones and the soul flies out, to hover like a dream. Therefore make your best speed back into daylight, noting all things as you go, for rehearsal hereafter to your wife."

'As we two asked and answered, the women arrived in multitude, famous Persephone having sent up all those who had been wives or daughters of great men. They eddied and thronged about the dark blood while I was wondering how to get word with each. The best plan seemed to draw the sharp-edged sword once again from my strong thigh and with it prevent their drinking the blood in one rush: by my so doing they came up singly, each declaring her origin, and I questioned them, one and all.

'The first was nobly-born Tyro who avouched herself daughter of pure Salmoneus and former wife of Cretheus, Aeolus' son. She loved a river, the divine Enipeus, much the fairest of earth's streams. Wherefore she would haunt its reaches continually, till the God who shakes and girdles the earth put on the shape of Enipeus and lay with her in the outpouring of the swift-eddying river. Round them a dark-blue wave arched itself hugely and bowed like a mountain wall to hide the God and his mortal woman. Then he unclasped the girdle of her maidenhead and put her into a sleep. When he had achieved love's labour he took her by the hand, calling her by name and saying, "Rejoice, O woman, in my love: and forasmuch as the couching of the Deathless Ones is never barren you will bear splendid children when the year has turned. Your task must be to care tenderly for these yourself. Till when, go home and set a watch upon your lips, not uttering my name. Yet know that I am Poseidon, Shaker of the Earth." He plunged beneath the frothing sea and in due time she conceived and bore Pelias and Neleus. When they grew up they both served Zeus heart and soul. Pelias, a sheep-master, lived in the plains of Iolcos: the other in sandy Pylos. The queenly woman also bore sons to Cretheus – Aeson and Pheres and Amythaon the chariot-knight.

'After her I saw Antiope daughter of Aesopus. She boasted that she had spent one night clasped in Zeus' own encircling arms: and had two children by him, Amphion and Zethus, first founders of Thebes-with-the-Seven-Gates: its fortifiers, too, for not even men of their might could dwell in that open domain except it were walled and towered. After her came Alcmene, wife of Amphitryon, who from the embraces of great Zeus gave birth to lion-hearted Heracles, the bravely-patient; and Megara came, the daughter of proud Creon, whom that strong and hardy son of Amphitryon took in wedlock.

'I saw Epicaste, the mother of Oedipodes. She in ignorance sinned greatly when she let herself be married to her own son; the son who murdered his father, he it was that wedded her. Presently the Gods made their state notorious to all men. By their dooming he must linger in distress as king of the Cadmaeans in lovely Thebes: whereas she went down to Hades, that strong keeper of the gate of Hell. She tied a running noose to the high beam across her hall and perished, mad with remorse: leaving her son alone to face all the pains and obloquy which the avengers of a mother can impose.

Then came shining Chloris whose amazing beauty made Neleus pay fabulous marriage gifts for her and wed her. She was the last daughter of Amphion son of Iasus, once a great king in Minyan Orchomenus. Chloris became queen of Pylos and amongst her famous issue were Nestor and Chromius and lordly Periclymenus; besides a daughter, Pero the magnificent, a wonder of the world, whom all the neighbours wooed: but Neleus announced he would not part with her except to one who could recover from Phylace the cattle that great Iphiclus had taken. A hard task to win back these lurching broad-fronted beasts; so hard and dangerous that no one was found to try, but the ingenuous Prophet himself; and he got no joy of it, for the Gods visited his attempt upon him by gyving him cruelly under guard of the boorish cowkeepers. Yet after lapse of time, as days and months were accomplished and the year revolved to perfect the destined hour, eventually did strong Iphiclus let him go, when he had uttered all his soothsaying: that the purpose of Zeus might be fulfilled.

'I saw Leda, the consort of Tyndareus: she bore him two strong-willed sons, Castor the breaker of horses, and Polydeuces who was good with his fists. This pair are now under the fertile earth; yet in a sense alive, by the great dispensation of Zeus who has endowed them with alternating life and death, to live one day and to die the next. Honours are paid to them even as to the Gods. After Leda came the wife of Aloeus, Iphimedia, to say that she had slept with Poseidon and got by him two sons; short-lived, alas, but the tallest children that our quickening earth ever nourished on its bread, and the handsomest after peerless Orion. These were godlike Otus and far-famed Ephialtes. At nine years old they were nine fathoms high and nine cubits across. They vowed to carry the din and shock of battle into Olympus, to spite the Immortal Gods. They strained to put Ossa on top of Mount Olympus, and Pelion with its shivering forest trees upon Ossa again, to be their stepping-stones to heaven: and would have done it, too, had they but come to man's estate. As it was, Zeus' son by fair-haired Leto slew them both, their cheeks yet innocent of hair, their chins not shaded with the bloom of down. I saw Phaedra and Procris: also fair Ariadne, daughter of vicious Minos. Theseus was carrying her from Crete towards the fair hill of holy Athens: yet did not reap his enjoyment of her, because Artemis killed her first in sea-cradled Dia on the evidence of Dionysus. I saw Maera and Clymene: horrible Eriphyle too, she that took gold to sell her lawful husband.

'But how can I even name to you, much less describe, all those I saw? There were so many wives of heroes, so many daughters. Before I ended my tale the divine night itself would have worn through. Indeed, already it is time for sleep, though I know not if I should lie in the ship with the crew you have appointed me, or stay in the house. The hour of my starting rests in the hands of the Gods and in your guardian hands.'

Here Odysseus broke off his history: but the Phaeacians none the less stayed silent, spell-bound as it were, amidst the dim-lit hall: till Arete the white-armed suddenly broke out: 'Now, Phaeacians, what think you of this man, the cut and scale of him and his heart's poise? My stranger, look you, and my guest: though in the privilege of entertaining him all of you may share. Be in no haste to forward him hence, nor stint your gifts to so needy a man. Remember how the signal favour of the Gods has filled your homes with treasure.' After her rose the old hero Echeneus, whose age made him august among the Phaeacians. 'My friends, not far off the point nor unbecoming are these words from the mouth of our prudent Queen. Consider them favourably: yet with us must act and authority alike vest in Alcinous.'

The King cried back: 'So long as I am to have lordship and life amongst you, sea-faring Phaeacians, be it understood that the word of the Queen holds good. Wherefore, however he may crave to get home, let the stranger possess himself fairly till the morrow. Tomorrow I will round off the gifts he has received and complete his fortune. For his escort back, doubtless it is everybody's business: but mine especially, I being sovereign in this land.' Odysseus answered him with judgement and said: 'Alcinous, famous Lord, had you directed me to tarry a whole year more while you increased my gifts – with assurance of eventual passage – why I should placidly choose that course as the profitable course. The more nearly full my hands on landing (if I do attain my beloved country) the better held and esteemed I shall be of all who meet me in Ithaca.'

Alcinous loudly replied: 'O my Odysseus, we who have you before our eyes will not be persuaded that you are a pretender or thief, like those many vagrant liars our dark earth breeds to flourish and strut behind so thick a mask of falsehood that none can pierce it to read their worth. In your words is a formal beauty to match the graceful order of your ideas: you frame and bedeck this tale of the Argives' hardship and your toils as knowingly as any bard. Yet tell me one thing more and let us have the truth of it – did you see your comrades in the under-world, any of those godlike ones who served with you before Ilion and there found death awaiting them? The night is still long, immeasurably long. No need yet to clear the hall for sleep: wherefore continue these marvellous histories. I would listen till the full dawn, here in the house, had you voice to set forth to me the tale of all your woes.' Odysseus answered saying, 'Most famous Lord: surely there is a time for long speaking and a time for sleep. But if you still ardently desire to hear me I shall not spare you the recital of sadder things than any I have told, a history of the ultimate agony of ill-starred men who survived the Trojan battle and its death-dealing clamour only to perish at their journey's end by an evil woman's resolve.

'To my tale. From the herd of women-ghosts chaste Persephone at last delivered me, driving them off helterskelter; and in came, despondent, the spirit of Agamemnon son of Atreus. Round him were grouped the wraiths of those others who had fallen upon their fate and died with him in the house of Aegisthus. The chief knew me instantly, after he had drunk of the black blood: and greatly he sobbed, with tears running down his face. He stretched out his hands to me in longing to fold me to his breast: vainly, for no longer had he substance to stand firm or the vigourously free movements, such as once had filled his supple limbs. When I saw this the pity in my heart moved me also to tears and I lamented. "Most famous Atrides, my King of Men, say now by what throw Death the champion flung you at the last? Did Poseidon overwhelm you in your ship by rousing against you terrible gale upon terrible gale: or did foemen beat you down on the shore, while you were cutting out their oxen and their goodly flocks of sheep or disputing with them some walled city and its women?"

'So I asked, but he replied: "Odysseus, Poseidon excited against me no too-great gale to destroy me in my ships nor did savages slay me on any coast. Aegisthus achieved my death and doom with the connivance and aid of my accursed wife, after inviting me to his house and setting me at table. Yes, I was killed feasting – struck down as one butchers an ox at stall. Inglorious, pitiful death! They slaughtered my men around me one by one and laid them out like white-tusked boars brittled for some banquet, or feast of peers, or wedding in a rich lord's house. You have stood by many killings, in single combats or in mellays; but never have you seen one gruesome as ours between the plenished tables, round the mixing bowl of wine, in a hall whose floor swam with blood. My bitterest pass was to hear the death-shriek of Cassandra, Priam's daughter, whom traitorous Clytemnaestra slew just over me. Verily I tried to raise my hands for her, but they fell back to earth again. I was dying then – dying upon the sword. The brutish woman turned her back nor would spend so much pity (though I was fast on my way to Hades) as to draw down my eyelids with her hands, or bind up my jaw. I tell you, there is nought more awful and inhuman than a woman who can fondle in her heart crimes so foul as this conception of my wife's to murder the husband of her youth. I was coming home, promising myself the joyous greeting of my children and my household: and then she, by her depth of villainy, smirches the whole breed of womanhood for ever and ever, even those yet unborn and virtuous."

'He ended and I rejoined: "Alas and woe is me! From the beginning has wide-seeing Zeus dreadfully visited the seed of Atreus through women's arts. What an army of us died for Helen; and now Clytemnaestra spins this web of death for you, while you are far away." So I said and he once again urged me, saying: "Never be very gentle, henceforward, with your wife, Odysseus. Tell her only a part of anything you know, and hide the rest. Yet need you not look for a bloody death from your wife: Penelope is so careful, knowing, and of such excellent discretion; the dear daughter of Icarius. Let me see, a young wife was she not, when we left her for the war? The infant then feeding at her breast may now be sitting with the men, one of them: a happy son to see his father's return and dutifully fold him in his arms. Upon my son Clytemnaestra gave me no time to feed my eyes. Before he came she slew me; slew her lawful husband. Now I will tell you something else to lay up in your heart. You must bring your ship to shore secretly and covertly, in your beloved land. There is no putting faith in women. In return, do you tell me something, bluntly. Have you heard of my son's activity either at Orchomenus or in sandy Pylos or guesting with Menelaus in Sparta? Noble Orestes has not yet died upon earth."

'To his question I returned, "Atrides, why trouble me for news? I know not even if he is alive or dead: and touching life and death I will not vainly invent." As we two stood thus in sorrowful talk, weeping freely, up came the ghost of Achilles, son of Peleus, with Patroclus and gallant Antilochus. Also Aias, the handsomest man and goodliest figure of the Danaans – except for Achilles himself, that swift-footed descendant of Aeacus, whose spirit recognized me and gloomily flung out: "Ingenious son of Laertes, Odysseus of the seed of Zeus, daring unhappy soul! How will you find some madder adventure to cap this coming down alive to Hades among the silly dead, the worn-out

mockeries of men?" So he questioned, bitterly, and I replied, "O
Achilles, son of Peleus, mightiest man of valour among the Achaeans!
Of dire necessity I came, to hear from Teiresias how best to arrive
back in rocky Ithaca. In all this time I have not neared Achaea nor
seen my country. Ill luck dogs me everywhere. How I envy your lot,
Achilles, happiest of men who have been or will be! In your day all
we Argives adored you with a God's honours: and now down here I
find you a Prince among the dead. To you, Achilles, death can be no
grief at all." He took me up and said, "Do not make light of Death
before me, O shining Odysseus. Would that I were on earth a menial,
bound to some insubstantial man who must pinch and scrape to keep
alive! Life so were better than King of Kings among these dead men
who have had their day and died. Enough – give me news of my
admirable son! Did he get to the war and prove himself a leader; or
not yet? Also of noble Peleus, if you have heard – do the Myrmidons
still honour him or is he despitefully seen from Hellas to Phthia,
because old age has crippled his hands and feet? No longer can I stand
up in the eye of day his champion, the prodigy who succoured the
Argives in the plains of Troy and brought death upon the stoutest
Trojans. O if I could be, just for the briefest moment, in my father's
house! How I would make my great strength and invincible hands a
reproach and horror to all those who forcibly let him from his glory!"

'I replied, "Of illustrious Peleus I have not heard; but of your dear
son Neoptolemus I can tell you the whole truth, just as you wish. It
was with me, in my capacious ship, that he came up from Skyros to
join the panoplied Achaeans. So often as we bandied counsel by the
town of Troy he would be quickest to speak, and spoke ever to the
point. Godlike Nestor and myself were the only two to talk him down.
And when we Achaeans joined battle in the plain of Troy he would
never rest in the rank or ruck of men, but dashed ahead allowing no
valour to outstrip his. He slew many men in mortal fight. I cannot
remember even the names of all the chiefs who fell by his hand while
he was aiding the Argive cause: but with what a sword-stroke did he

cut down Eurypylus, heroic son of Telephus, about whom died many of his Ceteian company, victims of a woman's bribe! Royal Memnon apart, I saw no better man among them. Further, when the time came for us Argive leaders to mount into the horse that Epeius built, they charged me with the responsibility of closing or opening the trap-door of our crowded lair. The other chiefs and champions were wiping away tears and trembling in every limb: but though I gazed at him with my whole eyes never once did his comely skin turn white or a tear need dashing from his cheek. Repeatedly he begged me to let him sally forth from the horse: and he kept fondling his sword-hilt and heavy spear-blade, in deadly rage against the men of Troy. After we had sacked the hill-built city of Priam he departed in his ship with his full share of loot, escaping without a wound, for the flying shafts all missed him and the sword-play left him unhurt. The luck of war, that was: Ares often fights too haphazardly to give each one his due." So I said, and the wraith of swift-footed Achilles strode with large strides across the field of asphodel, exultant because I had told him that his son was famous.

'There hung about me others of the departed, each sadly asking news of his loved ones. Only the spirit of Aias the son of Telamon kept aloof, he being yet vexed with me for that I had been preferred before him when by the ships we disputed the harness of Achilles, the arms which his Goddess-mother had set as prize, and which the sons of the Trojans and Pallas Athene adjudged. Would I had not won that victory, since by it earth closed above so excellent a head. Verily, in sheer beauty of form and for prowess, great Aias stood out above every Danaan, the noble son of Peleus excepted. So to him I spoke very gently, thus: "Lord Aias, son of great Telamon, can you not even in death forget your anger against me over those cursed arms? Surely the Gods meant them as a plague upon the Argives. What a tower fell in your fall! For you we Argives mourn as for our lost crown, Achilles; because you died. Prime cause of it was Zeus, who in his terrible hatred of the Danaan chivalry laid upon you their guilty desert. I pray you,

King, draw near to hear the things we say. Vail your fierce pride of heart." So I appealed, but he answered not a word: only went away towards Erebus with other spirits of the departed dead. Yet likely he would have spoken despite his wrath – or I to him again – only my heart was wishful to see other souls of the many dead.

'Thus I saw Minos, Zeus' illustrious son, with his golden sceptre, enthroned in the broad gate of the house of Hades to judge the dead, who sat or stood before his seat enquiring of the King upon their sentences. I picked out, too, gigantic Orion where he chased wild beasts across the meadows of asphodel: ghosts of the same beasts he used to slay among earth's lonely hills. His fist brandished a club of solid copper, unbroken and unbreakable. I saw Tityus, son of Gaia the famous Earth, lying outstretched over a flat ground. He covered nine roods. A vulture sat each side of him and tore at his liver, piercing deeply even to the bowels. With his hands he might not drive them off. This was because he had maltreated Leto, the stately mistress of Zeus, as she went through park-like Panopeus toward Pytho.

'There too was Tantalus in sorry plight, put to stand chin-deep in a pool. He gaped with thirst: but could not reach the water to drink it. As often as the old man bent towards it in his frenzy, so the water disappeared, swallowed into the ground which showed blackly below his feet. A God made it dry. Over the pool high-foliaged trees hung down their fruit, down to his head. Pears there were, and pomegranates, rosy apples, sweet figs and leafy olives. Yet every time the old man eagerly stretched out his hand to grasp, the wind would toss them cloud-high away. Another whom I saw in torment was Sisyphus, wrestling double-handed with a giant stone. He would thrust with hands and feet, working it towards the crest of his ridge: but when he was almost at the top, it would twist back irresistibly and roll itself down again to the level, the shameless stone. Once more he would go push and heave at it, with sweat pouring down his limbs, and a dust cloud mantling higher than his head.

'Also I distinguished great Heracles – I mean his ghost. Himself is happy with the Immortal Gods at their festivals, with his wife Hebe of the slim ankles, the daughter of all-mighty Zeus and golden-shod Hera. About this ghost eddied the dead, clangorously whirling like wild birds this way and that in bewildered fear. He stood, dark as night, naked bow in hand and arrow ready on the string, glaring fiercely like one about to shoot. His breasts were bound with a baldric, a striking work of solid gold, marvellously wrought with images: of bears, wild boars and bright-eyed lions; of fights and wars, slaughter and murderings of men. Its craftsman had surpassed himself by putting into the design all his mastery. Never might he produce its peer. As soon as I came within range Heracles knew me and greeted me compassionately: "So you too, deep-witted Odysseus, are in the toils of ill-luck and lead a life as cruel as mine was while I subsisted in the eye of the Sun. I might be a child of Zeus: yet was my lot a misery beyond belief, for I was subjected to a man meaner than myself who shamefully misused me upon inordinate labours. Why, he sent me down here to fetch their hound away! It was, he thought, the worst task he could devise. Yet I did it and carried the beast up from Hades to him: with Hermes to give me a start and grey-eyed Athene's help." Heracles spoke and went back into the house of Hades; while I lingered yet, to see some of the long-dead antique heroes: for I was very desirous of such dim and distant ones as Theseus or Pirithous, legendary children of the Gods. But before they could come, there beset me ten thousand seely ghosts, crying inhumanly. I went pale with fear, lest awful Persephone send me from Hades the Gorgon's head, that fabulous horror. So I turned to my ship and told the companions to get in and let go the cables. They were quickly embarked and on their thwarts: when the current of the flood bore us down to the river of Ocean, along which at first we rowed, but later found a helpful breeze.'

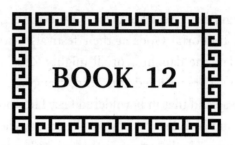

BOOK 12

From Ocean's pouring stream our ship measured the open rolling seas even to Æaea, the isle of sunrise where Dawn the fore-runner has her house and dancing-floor: there we grounded the ship among the sand-banks and went out upon the beach, to sleep and wait for day. When the light came I sent a party up to Circe's house to bring down dead Elpenor's body. We hewed logs and built his pyre upon the tallest headland where it runs out above the sea: duly we made his funeral, bewailing him with bitter tears. After body and armour were quite burned away we piled a mound over them, and to crown it dragged up a monolith, on top of which we fixed his goodly oar. The busy work was scarcely done when Circe came, decked to receive us: our departure from Hades had not been hidden from her. Attending her were maids laden with bread and meat in plenty and red wine with a fiery sparkle to it. She stood in our midst, saying: –

"'A hardy adventure, men, this going down to Hades alive. Now you will twice encounter death, whereas others do die but once. So I pray you rest here in the island all to-day, eating my food and drinking this wine. If you sail to-morrow at the daybreak I shall have time to plot you a course and detail its leading-marks: that you may be saved the hurt and pain of untoward, unforeseen accidents by sea or land." Her counsel convinced our prides. We sat and feasted all day till the sun went down, the flesh being plenteous and the wine excellent. When sunset had darkened into the shadows of night, the others stretched themselves to sleep among the mooring ropes: but the lady Circe took me by the hand apart from my friends, made me sit, and set herself by my side asking me to tell her our story as it had happened. After which she said: –

'"So much has been well done. Now heed what I say and the God himself will quicken it in your memory. Your next land-fall will be upon the Sirens: and these craze the wits of every mortal who gets so far. If a man come on them unwittingly and lend ear to their Siren-voices, he will never again behold wife and little ones rising to greet him with bright faces when he comes home from sea. The thrilling song of the Sirens will steal his life away, as they sit singing in their plashet between high banks of mouldering skeletons which flutter with the rags of skin rotting upon the bones. Wherefore sail right past them: and to achieve this successfully you must work bees-wax till it is plastic and therewith stop the ears of your companions so that they do not hear a sound. For your own part, perhaps you wish to hear their singing? Then have yourself lashed hand and foot into your ship against the housing of the mast, with other bights of rope secured to the mast itself. Ensure also that if you order or implore your men to cast you loose, their sole response shall be to bind you tighter with cord upon cord. That way you may safely enjoy the Sirens' music. And after your crew have rowed you past these sisters, there will come a stretch upon which I do not advise you in so many words how you should steer. The decision must be yours, on the spot. Hear the alternatives: –

'"On this side tower up precipitous cliffs, against which the giant swell of dark-eyed Amphitrite breaks with a shattering roar. The blessed Gods call these rocks the Skurries. Between them not even a bird may slip unhurt; no, not All-Father Zeus' own shy ring-doves carrying his ambrosia. From each flight of them the sheer rocks rob some bird or other and the Father has to add one more to maintain the tale. Suppose a ship of men drives in thither. It is lost. Scattered planks and the corpses of its crew will be descried tossing in the bitter waves amid the lightnings which flash from out the whirlwinds there. Only one ship of all the ships on the sea has threaded this passage: it was Argo the world-famed, on her voyage from Æetes; and she, like the rest, would have been quickly dashed to death against those mighty reefs, had not Hera passed her through because Jason was her love.

'"On the other side stand two huge crags, one of which thrusts into heaven its sharp peak, which yet is covered always by a sombre cloud-cap that never melts away. So there is never any clear light to sparkle round its crest, not even in summer or in autumn's heat. No mortal man could scale that height or ever keep his footing there – not with twenty hands and feet – for its sides are smooth, like well-polished rock. Half way up the cliff on the western side, facing Erebus the land of death, opens a murky cave. By it, noble Odysseus, you can take a bearing to check your course. Yet no archer born is mighty enough to flight an arrow from a ship into that deep cave, within which lurks dread yelping Scylla – yelping, for she squeals like a new-born puppy, being in truth no puppy but a repulsive monster on which not even a God could look without dismay, should his path cross hers. She has twelve splay feet and six lank scrawny necks. Each neck bears an obscene head, toothy with three rows of thick-set crowded fangs blackly charged with death. She keeps herself bedded waist-deep in the bowels of her cave but sways her heads out across the dizzy void, and angles with them, sweeping the reefs ever and again keenly for dolphins or dog-fish or some greater quarry from among the countless droves which breed in loud Amphitrite's thundering waves. Particularly she battens on human-kind, never failing to snatch up a man with each one of her heads from every dark-prowed ship that comes. No sailors yet can boast to have slipped past her in their craft, scot-free.

'"The second, lower crag you will observe, Odysseus, near this one. Quite near, only a bow-shot off. Mark its wild fig tree, florid with leaves, for beneath that is the spot where enormous Charybdis blackly sucks down the sea. Three times a day she sucks it down and three times she spews it out: an awful sight. May you not be there while she sucks in! No power, not the Earth-shaker's own, could then deliver you from ruin. Better bear sharply across towards Scylla's rock, hug it, and coast by at speed. It is less grievous to mourn six men gone from a crowd than for all to be lost together." She paused and I broke in, "Goddess, I must ask you a plain question about all this. Is there no way for me, while avoiding deadly Charybdis, to fight off that other as she tries to harry my men?" So I asked. "Presumptuous wretch!" cried the Goddess, "how your nature leaps at once to thoughts of action and of bloodshed. Will you not give even the Gods best? I tell you, Scylla is not mortal, to be fought off, but an immortal blain: unpitying, fierce, fiendish, invincible. Resign yourself: to flee from her is the better part of valour. Should you linger below her rock to array yourself against her I fear lest she let fly her heads a second time at you and again pick off one man in each. Your best course is to push hard past her, invoking Crataiis, Scylla's dam, who whelped this curse of humanity. Crataiis, if called upon, will keep Scylla from a second plunge.

"'Afterwards you will make the island of Thrinacia, a grazing ground of the many cattle of the Sun and of his noble sheep. The cattle are seven herds and there are as many flocks of sheep, with fifty head in each. Upon these neither birth nor death can pass. Two divine creatures tend them, Phaethusa and Lampetie, fair-tressed nymph-daughters of Neaera and exalted Helios. Their mother, the Goddess, after they had been weaned, sent them to live apart in this Thrinacian island, where they keep their father's flocks and his rolling-gaited kine. Should you be so bound up in the thought of returning home that you leave these beasts unharmed, then through much tribulation you may indeed attain Ithaca at the end of all: but if you hurt them I solemnly predict the certain doom of your ship and men. You may yourself escape, but your return will be at the least tardy and miserable, effected only with the loss of your whole company."

'As Circe spoke Dawn assumed her golden throne. Back into the island went the Goddess, while I rejoined the ship and summoned my men aboard to loosing the hawsers. Soon they embarked, sat to their tholes and dipped the oars in unison, whitening the sea to spray. After the ship Circe sent us a kindly way-fellow, a fair wind which filled our sails. Each man performed his duty in the ship and afterward we sat at ease, while wind and helmsman took us along.

'After a while to my crowd I spoke gravely: "Friends, I do not mean to keep to myself, or among just one or two, the disclosures now made me by Circe, Goddess of Goddesses: but I will publish them freely in order that we may die – if we die – informed: or else trick death and fate to get clean away. Her first warnings concern the marvellous Sirens and their flowery meadow. Our prime duty will be to turn a deaf ear to their singing. Only myself may listen, after you have so fastened me with tight-drawn cords that I stand immovably secured against the tabernacle of the mast, with further short lashings dependent from the mast itself: and if I beg you or bid you let me loose, then must you redoubly firm me into place with yet more bonds." I repeated this till all had heard it well, while our trim ship was borne swiftly towards the island of these Siren-sisters by the breath of our fair breeze. But suddenly this flagged. A breathless calm supervened, some higher power lulling all the waves. My crew rose to take in the canvas, which they stowed in the capacious well: then sat down again to row, frothing the water with their blades of polished pine. I took a great round of wax, chopped it small with my sword-edge and worked it with all the power of my hands. Soon the wax grew warm by this dint of kneading in the glare of the lordly Sun: when it was soft I filled with it the ears of all my party. Then they tied me stiffly upright to the tabernacle, with extra ends of rope made fast to the mast above. Once more they sat and their oar-beats whitened the sea.

'Speeding thus lightly we arrived within earshot of the place. The Sirens became aware of the sea-swift vessel running by them: wherefore they clearly sang to us their song – "Hither, come hither, O much-praised Odysseus: come to us, O Glory of Achaea. Bring your ship to land that you may listen to our twin voices. Never yet has any man in a dark ship passed us by without lending ear to the honey-sweet music of our lips – to go away spirit-gladdened and riper in knowledge. For we know all the toils wherewith the Gods did afflict Argives and Trojans in the broad Troad: and we know all things which shall be hereafter upon the fecund earth." Such words they sang in lovely cadences. My heart ached to hear them out. To make the fellows loose me I frowned upon them with my brows. They bent to it ever the more stoutly while Perimedes and Eurylochus rose to tighten my former bonds and wreathed me about and about with new ones: and so it was till we were wholly past them and could no more hear the Sirens' words nor their tune: then the faithful fellows took out the wax with which I had filled their ears, and delivered me from bondage.

'We had left that island behind when I began to see smoke and broken water: the thundering of breakers came to my ears. My crew took fright: the oars slipped from their grasp to swing with an idle clatter in the ship's wash. We lost way, as the moulded blades ceased their even stroke. I went about the ship, appealing to man after man and bracing them with these hearty words, "Fellows, surely we are not quite novices at danger? This evil which faces us is no blacker than our pass in Cyclops' cave, when he held us there in his mighty toils. We escaped him, thanks to my intrepid resourcefulness and energy of mind. I fancy some day we may look back upon to-day's adventure like that. To which end let each one do exactly as I bid. You others, sit well into your benches and grip the sea's swelling fullness with your oars. We shall see if Zeus will not accord us rescue and deliverance from this extremity. For you, quartermaster, I have a special charge. Impress it on your heart, because you hold the tiller of the ship that holds us all. Keep her away from this smoke and broken water, and skirt the rock lest the ship surprise you by yawing suddenly to that other side. So should you cast us into the danger." These were my orders. All heeded them. Scylla I did not mention: for had I added her hopeless horror to my men's burden, they might have deserted their oars in panic and run below decks to hide themselves away. Also I did not honour Circe's hard saying that I must not arm myself. I dressed all in my famous armour, took two long pikes in hand and mounted to the fore-sheets of the ship, thinking it the best place to watch for cliff-dwelling

Scylla's raid upon my crew. However, I could see nothing, though I stared my eyes bleary with trying to pierce the shadows of the gloomy cliffs.

'We went on up the narrow strait, thus anxiously. On this side lay Scylla, while on that Charybdis in her terrible whirlpool was sucking down the sea: and vomiting it out again like a vat on a hot fire. The briny water did gush from her abysses in such a seethe that the froth of it bespattered the tops of both rocky walls. Whenever she swallowed-in the yeasty ocean one could see right down the whorl of her maw. At its very bottom the sea's floor showed muddy and dark with sand. The cliffs about thundered appallingly. My crew turned sallow with fright, staring into this abyss from which we expected our immediate death. Scylla chose the moment to rape from the midst of the ship six of our party – the six stoutest and best. I happened to cast my eye back along the thwarts, over the crew, and thus marked their dangling hands and feet as they were wrenched aloft, screeching my name for the last time in voices made thin and high by agony. So may a longshoreman be seen, on some cape of rock which he has ground-baited for the lesser fish, darting down into the sea his very long shaft with its rustic cow-horn tip. As he hurls shoreward each wriggling prize to gasp for life, so did they swing writhing upward to the cliffs; where in her cave-mouth she chewed and swallowed them, despite their screaming and stretching of hands in final appeal to me for help in their death agony. This was the most pitiful thing of all the sorrows that ever my eyes did see while I explored the by-ways of the deep.

'Now we were through the danger of the Skurries and of Scylla and Charybdis. We neared the God's good island, where Helios Hyperion kept his broad-browed splendid cattle and many flocks of fat sheep. Even from our decks out at sea I could hear the lowing of cattle driven to stall, and the bleating of sheep. The sound revived in my memory the words of the blind prophet Teiresias of Thebes, and of Æaean Circe. Both had rigidly adjured me to be wary of this island of the

Sun-God who gladdens with light the hearts of men. So I spoke earnestly to my followers: –

'"Hear me, long-tried and suffering ones, while I tell you a thing. In their warnings Teiresias and Circe were very stringent with me to beware this island of Helios, Delighter of Mankind. She foretold that here might be our last and deadliest peril. Wherefore let us drive right past the place and avoid it." So I said, but their hearts were too broken with hardship. Eurylochus mutinously voiced to me their discontent. "You are enduring, Odysseus, and uncommonly strong, nor do your joints grow tired: but if you can prevent us your crew from setting foot on this shore in whose sea-bound security we might sup at ease and heal our weariness in sleep – why then must you indeed be wholly a man of iron. Would you have us plunge into the oncoming night and abandon this island, to wander, all broken as we are, through the dark misty deep? Of Night are born the fierce ship-wrecking winds. How shall any of us be saved from utter destruction, if some sharp gust unlicensed by the Gods our masters come suddenly out of the South or from the windy West, those two quarters most rife in fatal gales? Wherefore let us bow before the power of darkness, sup well, and rest peacefully near the ship till daylight lets us sail across a clear sea."

'Thus Eurylochus, and the others sided with him. I felt that here was some Power intending evil, and cried out to them very greatly with barbed words: "Eurylochus, I am one and you are many, and you will have me yield. But at least let each man swear before me a binding oath that should we find on shore some herd of cattle or great flock of sheep, no one of you will be mad enough or bad enough to slaughter any single beast: but will in all quietude rest contented with the vict-uals that immortal Circe gave." So I urged and presently they took the oath. After all had been duly sworn we brought our staunch ship to rest in the sheltered haven by a spring of fresh water. The company landed and skilfully made our supper. But when they had discharged the needs of drink and food then they minded and bewailed their loved companions whom Scylla had plucked from the ship and eaten alive. Sleep the consoler came on them while they wept.

'We were at the third watch of the night and the stars were going down when cloud-marshalling Zeus brought on a gusty wind so full of the wildest squalls that storm-clouds mantled earth and sea, and night reigned in heaven. Wherefore at the earliest daylight we dragged our ship up the beach and secured it in a hollow cave beneath whose shelter stretched fair dancing-places for the nymphs, with cunning seats about them. Thither I called my men to council and exhorted them saying, "Friends, we have food and drink stored in our hull: accordingly to avoid trouble let us abstain from the cattle of this island. They and its goodly sheep belong to a jealous God, Helios the Overseer and Over-hearer of all." Their high hearts bowed to my word: but for a whole month the wind blew always from the South without abatement and steadily, veering only some points towards East and back again. So long as the corn held out and the red wine, so long my crew, in the wish to survive, kept their hands from the cattle: but there dawned the day when the ship's supplies all failed. Hunger came to rack their bellies. Under the spur of necessity they scattered abroad in search of provender, to try for fish with barbed hooks, or for birds – avid of anything that might fall within their dear hands. As for me, I went up into the island to pray to the Gods on the chance that one of them might disclose a way out. After going far enough to throw off the rest I washed my hands in a calm spot and supplicated the chapter of the Olympian Gods: who sent down a sweet sleep upon my eyelids.

'Meanwhile Eurylochus was preaching treason to his fellows: "Hear me, afflicted and unfortunate ship-mates. No variety of death is pleasing to us poor mortals: but commend me to hunger and its slow perishing as the meanest fate of all. Up therefore; let us take our pick of the Sun's cattle and dedicate them in death to all the Gods of heaven. If ever we do reach Ithaca, our own, there can we quickly erect some splendid fane for Helios Hyperion and fill it with every precious gift. But if he is angered enough by the loss of his high-horned cattle to want the ruin of our ship, and if the other Gods cry yea to him – why then, I choose to quit life with one gulp in the sea rather than waste to death here by inches in this desert island." So said Eurylochus and the rest agreed. The cattle of the Sun were there to hand, gorgeous lurching-gaited broad-horned beasts, browsing quite near the ship. Forthwith the fellows drove aside the choicest and stood round them in a ring praying to the Gods. For heave-offering they plucked and strewed fresh leaves from a branching oak, in place of the white barley no more to be found in the ship. They prayed and cut the beasts' throats: then flayed them, jointed the legs, wrapped the thigh-bones above and below with fat and set bars of flesh on them to grill. They had now no wine left to pour over the flaming sacrifice; instead they kept on sprinkling water for libation. The entrails they roasted whole. When the thighs had burned right down and they had touched the offal with their lips, they sliced the other flesh small and spitted it for cooking. It was then that the burden of sleep was lifted from my eyelids and I rose to regain the ship and the beach. While I went, when I was near the curved ship, there came all about me the savoury smell of roasted fat. Wherefore I groaned and protested to the deathless Gods: "Father Zeus and all Blessed Ones that are from everlasting to everlasting! By this cruel sleep you have cozened me to doom. My crew, left to themselves, have imagined and done the awful thing."

'Swiftly to Helios with the news ran Lampetie of the trailing robes. She told him how we had slain his cattle: wherefore in a fury he declaimed to the Immortals: "Father Zeus and you other blessed Gods: I cry for your vengeance upon the followers of Odysseus, son of Laertes, because they have insolently dared to kill my cattle, the sight of which was my chief joy whenever I mounted the starry sky or swung back from the height of heaven, earthward. If they do not pay me a full retribution, I shall quit you for Hades and shine my light there upon the dead." Zeus answered him and said: "Nay, Helios: do you go on shining amongst the Gods and for the mortals who go their ways about the fertile earth. Upon me be it to smite their ship with one cast of

591

my white thunderbolt and shiver it amid the wine-dark sea." [These sayings were reported to me later by Calypso, who heard them from Hermes the Guide.]

'When I reached the ship in its bay, I upbraided each man for the guilty deed, but there was no amending it. The cattle were dead, and for another six days my comrades fed off the finest of these beasts of Helios which they had driven off. Yet the Gods were not slow to manifest portents. The hides of the slain beasts crawled slowly along, and the meat (alike the raw and the cooking) bellowed with a lowing like the lowing of a herd. When Zeus had brought the seventh day, then the wind ceased its unreasonable blowing. We leaped aboard and made for the open sea, stepping our mast and hoisting sail. We lost the isle and after it saw no more land, only sky and seas: but then the son of Cronos caused a lowering cloud to gather and stand over our hollow ship. Beneath it the deep turned thunder-dark. Nor did we scud much longer on our course: for suddenly a hurricane shrieked upon us from the West, ravening with mad gusts of wind, whose tearing violence carried away both our forestays. The mast toppled aft and all its gear ruined down into the waist; while the mast itself stretched backward across the poop and struck the helmsman over the head, smashing his skull to pulp. He dropped from his high platform in one headlong dive, and the brave spirit left his bones. Then Zeus thundered and at the same moment hurled a bolt of lightning upon the ship. Her timbers all shivered at the shock of the levin of Zeus. She filled with choking sulphur and brimstone smoke: her crew pitched out of her. For one instant they rode black upon the water, upborne like seafowl on the heaving waves past the black ship. Then the God ended their journey home.

'I reeled up and down the hulk for yet a little, while the smashing seas stripped the plankings from the keel till it floated off bare by itself. The heel of the mast had torn out from the keelson – to which, however, the backstay (a thong of raw bull's-hide) had been made fast. It still held; so that I could draw mast and keel together and lash them into one. Athwart them I drifted through the raging storm.

'At last the West wind ceased its frantic blowing: only to be succeeded by a South wind whose strengthening brought more pain to my heart; for it meant my measuring back each wave towards fatal Charybdis. All night I was sea-borne, and sunrise found me opposite Scylla's cliff facing dire Charybdis as she gulped down the ocean. Her eddy whirled me upward to the tall fig-tree. I caught and clung there like any bat: not able, though, to find a foothold or any standing-place thereon: so far beneath were the roots and far above me the boughs. Long and vast these boughs were, shading all Charybdis. I held on grimly waiting for her to disgorge my mast and keel. Very late it was before my hopes were answered and they came: as late as the supper-rising of a justice from the courts, who has stayed to settle the many suits of his hot-blooded litigants: so late it was before the spars reappeared. I let go and dropped with sprawling hands and feet, to splash heavily into the water on the lee side of these great beams. Across them I sat and paddled hard with my hands. The Father of Gods and men spared me further sight of Scylla, else should I inevitably have died.

'So I drifted for nine days. In the tenth darkness the Gods cast me ashore on Ogygia, where lives Calypso, the high but humane-spoken Goddess who greeted me kindly and tended me. Yet why rehearse all that? Only yesterday I told it within to you, O King, and to your famous wife. It goes against my grain to repeat a tale already plainly told.'

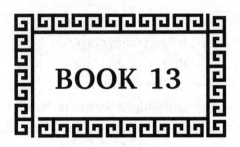

BOOK 13

He ceased, but his audience were so entranced by the tale that no one moved in the hushed twilit hall. At last the voice of Alcinous replied to him across the silence: 'Lord Odysseus, however great your misfortunes hitherto, now that you have eventually attained my bronze-floored house, my stately house, I think you will not suffer further deflection from your way home: touching which I have a charge for all you frequenters of my palace, who come to hear our minstrel and drink our ruddy aldermanic wine. Already a polished coffer has been packed with the clothes and gold ornaments and other gifts brought in for the stranger by the Phaeacian councillors. Let all of us here, as from ourselves, now present him with a great tripod complete with cauldron. Later we can strike a levy from the common herd and recoup our costs, for it would be a sore business if such liberality fell unrelieved on any single party.' So said Alcinous and he was warmly approved. The gathering dispersed sleepily homeward; but in the dawn light they were hastening toward the ship with their copper treasures. To ensure everything being shipshapely stowed His Majesty himself came down to the ship and saw them packed beneath the thwarts, where they would not foul the crew tugging at their oars. Thence the crowd rallied to Alcinous' house and prepared a banquet. Publicly for them the King sacrificed an ox to the cloud-mantled son of Cronos, Zeus the lord of all. After the thighs had been duly burnt they fell to feasting joyously, while in their admiring midst Demodocus plied his rich minstrelsy.

Yet was Odysseus ever turning his head toward the all-glorious sun, as though to urge it earthward by the fervency of his longing for home.

A husbandman yearns in this fashion toward supper, if he has been all day attendant upon his two dun oxen breaking a fallow land with the curved plough they drag. Because it dismisses him in quest of supper the sunset gladdens such a man, for all that his knees are sagging beneath him as he goes. So Odysseus felt relief as the light of the sun faded and died. Abruptly he broke out among the sailor Phaeacians, addressing himself primarily to Alcinous: 'Admirable King, perfect your offering! Then send me duly forth and God give you joy of it. Now is fulfilled my heart's desire – escort with endowment. May the heavenly Gods turn it to my good, and grant me to find my noble wife safe at home amid the unbroken circle of my friends: while you dwell here to fill the pleasant cup of your faithful wives and your children. The Gods shower down their grace upon this people, so that no evil harbour among them for ever and ever.' All clamoured applause and judged that the stranger must be given the god-speed he rightly claimed. Royal Alcinous commanded his herald: 'Pontonous, stir the mixing bowl and carry drink to the entire hall, that our despatching the stranger to his land may be with prayer to Zeus the Father.' At his bidding Pontonous mixed the honey-natured wine and served the company. From their seats, as they were, all offered libation to the blessed host of heaven. Only Odysseus the Great rose to his feet and reached his loving cup into Arete's hand while his voice rang out: 'May your happiness endure, O Queen, until the coming of Age and Death, those twin presences which wait for all mankind. Now will I be going. Gladness attend you in this house, with your children and people and Alcinous the King.'

Odysseus ended. His stride cleared the threshold of the door; but as far as the beach, where his vessel waited, Alcinous had a herald conduct him; while Arete sent one of her serving women to carry his laundered vest and robe, another in charge of the stout casket, and yet a third with victuals and ruddy wine. So he came to the sea; where the proper men, his escort, quickly took the baggage, the food and the drink, and stowed all within their ship. They spread for Odysseus a tappet and smooth sheet on the poop deck right aft where he might sleep undisturbed. Then did he also embark and lie down, saying never a word. The crew took station along their thwarts. They cast off the cable from its ring-stone and bent to their work, spuming the sea high with their oar blades: while a sleep that was flawless closed down upon the eyes of Odysseus – a most sweet sleep, profound, and in semblance very near to death. As he slept the stern of the ship towered, shuddered, and sank again towards the huge dark waves of the clamorous sea ever rushing in behind. So a team of four stallions yoked abreast will rear and plunge mightily beneath the lashing of the whip, as they strain forward to run their level course in the twinkling of an eye. Like them the ship heaved, and unfalteringly sped forward in her race, lighter than the circling hawk, though that is swiftest of the things that fly. So she went, cleaving the ocean surges and bearing within her a man deep-witted as the Gods, one who had in the past suffered heart-break as the common sport of men's wars and the troublous waves, but who now slept in tranquil forgetfulness of all he had endured.

Upon the rising of that most brilliant star which is the especial harbinger of early dawn, the ship in her rapid seafaring drew toward the island, toward Ithaca. On its coast is an inlet sacred to Phorkys, the ancient of the sea, where two detached headlands of sheer cliff stand forth and screen a harbour between their steeps against the great breakers which rage without whenever the harsh winds blow. Once they are berthed inside this port even decked ships can lie unmoored. By the creek's head is a long-leaved olive tree and very near it a cave set apart for those nymphs they call Naiads; a charming shadowy place containing store-bowls and jars of stone in which the honey-bees hive and lay up their sweetness. There on great long looms of rock the nymphs weave sea-purple robes, marvellously beautiful; and its springs of water never fail. The cave's entries are two: one with doors opening northward, by which men come in; while the other entry faces the south and is holy indeed. No human foot trespasses there; it is the pathway of the Deathless Ones.

The mariners knew this bay of old: they drove in with such way on their ship that she took the ground for full half her length: judge by this the stroke they pulled. They filed down off her benches, raised Odysseus from the hollow hull and bore him to land just as he was, on his sheet and gay carpet. He was yet lost in sleep as they bedded him gently on the sand. Then they passed ashore his belongings, the treasures with which by Athene's contriving the Phaeacian nobles had speeded his parting. These they piled in a little heap against the olive-trunk, aside from the road for fear some wayfarer might pass while Odysseus still slept; and plunder him. Then they pushed off for home.

The Earth-shaker had not yet forgotten his fateful word against great Odysseus long ago. Wherefore he began to sound the mind of Zeus, saying, 'Father Zeus, now the Eternal Gods will regard me no more, seeing that I can be slighted by mortals, even by the Phaeacians, that race of men so lately issued from my loins. I did announce that Odysseus should not get home before he had exhausted the sum of miseries. That I allowed him a return at all was for your sake, because when it was first broached you had acceded to it and signified assent. But now while he sleeps at ease these fellows ferry him swiftly across the ocean and set him down in Ithaca, after enriching him beyond my telling with gifts of bronze and gold and woven garments in great store, more wealth than ever he could have amassed for himself had he got away from Troy in good order with all his loot.'

The Cloud-compeller rejoined: 'This complaint of yours is too great and grievous, potent Earth-shaker. In no sense dare the Gods cease from honouring you. How could they? It would go sorely against them to diminish the prestige of their gravest senior. As for men, if any so purblindly follow the dictates of their passion and self-will as to scamp your due reverence – the remedy is yours and ultimate revenge awaits your bidding. Unleash yourself: do what your heart inclines.' To him Poseidon: 'That, Cloud-shadowed One, is exactly what I should have done of my own accord, only I ever weigh and respect your feelings. My present impulse is to destroy this splendid Phaeacian ship as she sails back from her mission across the hazy sea. So shall I teach them modesty, and to leave off escorting every sort of man. Also I would mew their city up behind a wall of mountain.'

To him Zeus answered: 'Why, friend, if you hear my counsel you will smite this good ship into a rock of her own size and shape quite near the shore, while the whole populace gaze from the quays upon her arrival. So will every man be wonder-struck. Then close your hill about the city.' Poseidon embraced the advice and betook himself to Scheria, the Phaeacian home-town, where he waited till the trim vessel in its light coursing had almost made the land. Then he leant over to her and with a single sweep of the flat hand turned her into a rock firmly rooted upon the bottom of the sea. After that he went away. The Phaeacians, famous masters of great-oared galleys, gazed into one another's faces. Knots of them stammered such quick words as these: 'Tell me, who arrested our swift ship like that amidst the waves at the very entrance of the home port? Only now we saw every detail of her plain.' They might well ask. It remained a mystery till Alcinous proclaimed aloud: 'Alas, my people, now are fulfilled the antique prophecies my father used to tell me, how Poseidon was so contraried by our granting free passage to all and sundry that upon a time he would destroy one of our best ships as she came in through the ocean-haze to land: and then would obscure our city within a wall of hills. So the old man would say, and here it comes true. Yet pay heed, everyone; let all of us obey the word. From now, give up this passing onward any stranger who happens to enter our city. Also we will sacrifice twelve picked bulls to Poseidon on the chance that he may repent from hiding our place under the shadow of some huge peak.'

They heard him and feared greatly: forthwith they prepared the bulls. So it was that all the chief men and warriors of the Phaeacians were standing in supplication about royal Poseidon's altar as Odysseus stirred and woke from sleep in the land of his fathers. Not that he knew his whereabouts. Partly he had been absent for so long; but in part it was because Pallas Athene had thickened the air about him to keep him unknown while she made him wise to things. She would not have his wife know him, nor his townsmen, nor his friends, till the suitors had discharged their frowardness.

So to its King Ithaca showed an unaccustomed face, the pathways stretching far into the distance, the quiet bays, the crags and precipices, the leafy trees. He rose to his feet and stood staring at what was his own land, then sighed and clapped his two palms downward upon his thighs, crying mournfully, 'Alas! and now where on earth am I? Shall I be spurned and savaged by the people of this place, or find them pious, hospitable creatures? Why do I lade all this wealth about? Come to that, what do I here myself? Would the stuff had stayed with its Phaeacians, if only I might have reached some lord strong enough to befriend me and pass me to my home. Now I have no place to store it, yet cannot leave it a prey for others. I fear that both right instinct and honesty of judgement must have been to seek among the Phaeacian chiefs and councillors, for them to abandon me in this strange country. They swore to land me on prominent Ithaca, and are forsworn. May Zeus the surveyor of mankind and scourge of sinners visit it upon them in his quality as champion of suppliants: and now, to make a start, let me check my belongings and see if the crew took off anything in their boat when they vanished.'

Whereupon he totted up his tripods and their splendid cauldrons, the gold and the goodly woven robes. Not a thing was gone. So his lament must be entirely for his native land as he paced back and forth in bitter grieving beside the tumultuous deep-voiced waves, till Athene in male disguise manifested herself and drew nigh, seeming a young man, some shepherd lad, but dainty and gentle like the sons of kings when they tend sheep. She had gathered her fine mantle scarf-like round her shoulders and carried a throwing spear; on her lovely feet were sandals. Odysseus, glad to see anyone, went forward with a swift greeting: 'My friend – for in you I hail the first soul to meet me in this place – all hail! and may your coming be with good will: for I would have you save these things of mine and save myself, entreating you as a God and making my petition at your beneficent knees. I pray you teach me for sure what land, what government, what people we have here. Is it some distinct island, or a thrusting spur from the mainland which leans out its fertile acres into the deep?'

Said the Goddess in answer: 'Stranger, you must be untutored or very strange if you ask me of this spot, which is not obscurely nameless but a familiar word across the populous lands of the dawning east, and towards the twilight and its peoples of the declining sun. Rugged it may be and unfit for wheels, but no sorry place, for all that it is straitened. The corn-yield here has no limit and wine is made. The rains never fall short nor the refreshment of dews. Goats find plenteous grazing and cattle pasture. The isle has every sort of timber-tree and perennial springs. Because of all these things, stranger, the name of Ithaca is rumoured abroad, even to Troy which is said to be so far from our Achaean coasts.'

Her word made great Odysseus' heart leap for happiness in this his native land, now divine Athene made him aware of it. To her he again uttered winged words; yet not true words, for he swallowed back what had been on his lips to make play with the very cunning nature instinctive in him. 'Of Ithaca I had heard, indeed, even from far Crete's wide land behind the seas: and have I now reached it myself? I, and this portion of my wealth, though as much again rests with the children in my house, whence I have fled for killing Idomeneus' dear son, Orsilochus the runner, who was fleeter-footed than any of the gainful men in ample Crete. I killed him because he wished to rob me of all the loot I brought from Troy at great pains to myself, loot which I had won by fraying me a path through the wars of men and the difficult seas. My offence lay in having failed to oblige his father, who would have had me serve in his retinue for the Trojan war. Instead I went at the head of my own men-at-arms. Wherefore with just one follower I lay in wait by the roadside and caught him with my bronze spear-head while he came down from the country. At the very dead of night it was, a black night which held all heaven in fee. Wherefore no human eye saw us as I privily took away his life. Immediately after the deed I made for a Phoenician ship and laid suit to its grave masters, paying them liberally from my warspoil to receive me aboard and set me down either at Pylos or in Elis the Epean headquarters. However the force of the wind forbade them this goal, though they tried for it their hardest without a thought of cheating me. Instead we beat up and down, till after dark last night we made this place, getting into the harbour by dint of rowing. After having beached we came straight ashore and lay down as we were, regardless of supper despite our great need of food. I was so tired that sleep came heavily upon me where I lay out on the sand; and I slept while the seamen were discharging my stuff from the ship's hold and heaping it by my side. Then they pushed off for Sidon, that nobly-sited port. But I am left in some distress of mind.'

As he was running on the Goddess broke into a smile and petted him with her hand. She waxed tall: she turned womanly: she was beauty's mistress, dowered with every accomplishment of taste. Then she spoke to him in words which thrilled: 'Any man, or even any God, who would keep pace with your all-round craftiness must needs be a canny dealer and sharp-practised. O plausible, various, cozening wretch, can you not even in your native place let be these crooked and shifty words which so delight the recesses of your mind? Enough of such speaking in character between us two past-masters of these tricks of trade – you, the cunningest mortal to wheedle or blandish, and me, famed above other Gods for knavish wiles. And yet you failed to recognize in me the daughter of Zeus, Pallas Athene, your stand-by and protection throughout your toils! It was thanks to me that you were welcomed by the entire society of the Phaeacians, and now I join you to invent further stratagems and help hide these treasures where-with by my motion and desire the great men of Phaeacia enriched your homeward voyage. Further, I have to warn you plainly of the grave vexations you are fated to shoulder here in your well-appointed house. So temper yourself to bear the inevitable and avoid blurting out to anyone, male or female, that it is you, returned from wandering. Subdue your pride to plentiful ill-treatment and study to suffer in silence the violences of men.'

Fluently Odysseus answered: 'Your powers let you assume all forms, Goddess, and so hardly may the knowingest man identify you. Yet well I know of your partiality towards me, from the day that we sons of the Achaeans went to war against Troy until we plundered Priam's towering city. But after we had embarked thence and the might of the God scattered the Achaeans – since that day I have not set eyes on you, O daughter of Zeus, nor been aware of you within my ship to deliver me from evil. So it became my lot to wander broken-heartedly waiting for the Gods to end my pain: until at long last you did appear in the Phaeacians' rich capital and heartened me by your bold words to venture in. Accordingly I now conjure you for your father's sake . . . surely I am not in clear-shining Ithaca? I think I have lighted on some foreign land, and you are telling me it is Ithaca only in mockery, to cheat my soul. If in very deed this is my native land, assure me of it.'

Said Athene: 'Your mind harps on that, and I cannot leave on tenterhooks one so civil, witty and shrewd. Any other returned wanderer would have dashed home to see his children and his wife. Only you choose to be sceptical and to reject the evidence till you have further proved the wife who as from the beginning sits awaiting you in the house, miserable through the long nights and tearful all her days. I was never one of those who despaired for you, because I knew for certain you would return, though not till after losing all your party. Wherefore I refrained from open warfare with Poseidon, my uncle, who always wished you ill because of his rage at your blinding his dear son. But now let me show you the substantial Ithaca, to convince you. This is Phorkys' bay, haunted by that ancient of the sea: there at its head stands the spreading olive tree, near which is the mouth of that cool and dusky cave consecrate to the nymphs that are called Naiads. How often under its broad vault have you sacrificed full hecatombs of choice victims to the Nymphs! And lo, where Mount Neriton rears its tree-clad flanks.' As she spoke the Goddess thinned away her mist and the landscape plainly appeared. The joy of seeing his own place so wrought upon Odysseus that he fell to kissing its bounteous soil, before invoking the Nymphs with up-stretched hands. 'O Naiad-nymphs, daughters of Zeus, I had told my heart that I had set eyes on you for the last time: wherefore I now greet you most dearly in this prayer. Verily will we lavish gifts upon you even as of old, if the providence of Zeus' daughter, the Reiver, allows me life and adds to me my beloved son grown to manhood.'

The grey-eyed Goddess exhorted him: 'Be bold and dismiss these concerns from your mind, while we turn to laying up your goods in the hinder end of this cave of marvels, where they will be safe for you. Then must we ponder and advise ourselves the best course of action.' Athene spoke and plunged into the gloom of the cavern to search it for hiding-holes, while Odysseus carried in the Phaeacian gold, the tempered bronze, the goodly raiment. After everything had been carefully laid by, Pallas sealed the passage with a rock. Then they sat together by the bole of the sacred olive to plot the doom of the extravagant wooers, Athene opening thus: 'Son of Laertes, next you must settle how to get these shameless suitors into your hands, for it is now three years that they have been lording it in your palace, plaguing your glorious wife with their suits and proffering marriage settlements; while she, despite heart-racking anxieties over your return, still keeps them all in play by giving each one hope and separate promises and privy messages, with her mind set constantly elsewhere.'

Wily Odysseus replied: 'My hard fate on reaching home, Goddess, would have been such another pitiful death as Agamemnon's, but for your timely acquainting me with the true situation. Wherefore extend your bounty and disclose how I may avenge myself upon these suitors. Stand by me, Mistress, fanning my valorous rage as on the day we despoiled shining Troy of its pride of towers. With your countenance, august One, I would fight three hundred men together: only buoy me up with your judicious aid, O wise-eyed Goddess.' Athene answered him: 'Surely I shall be by your side always taking thought for you, so soon as we undertake this deed. As for these wooers of your wife and wasters of your substance, I feel that some are about to be-spatter the great earth with their blood and brains. But now I must so work on you that no human being will know you; by parching the fair flesh of your agile limbs and laying waste the yellow locks on your head. I shall even make dim your eyes which are so lovely, and afterward clothe you in tatters to affront every eye. Then your guise will repel the united suitors, as also the wife and son you left in the house. You will begin by joining company with the swineherd who keeps your swine: a man of single heart toward yourself and devoted to your son and judicious Penelope. You will find him watching his beasts grubbing round the Raven's Crag and Arethusa's fountain. Thereby they grow into fat and healthy pigs, by virtue of the acorns they love and the still waters of the spring they drink. Sit with him and wait, learning all his news till I have been to Sparta, the land of fair women, and recalled your dear son Telemachus who went to the house of Menelaus, there in wide Lacedaemon, trying to find out if you are still alive.'

He said to the Goddess: 'Why did you not tell him so much, out of your all-knowing heart? Must he, too, painfully roam the barren seas while others devour his living?' The grey-eyed one replied: 'Take it not so much to heart. I was his guide, even I who stirred him up to win favour by this activity. He suffers no hardship, but rests tranquilly in Atrides' palace, lapped in abundance. Admitted, the cadets of the suitors lie in ambush with their black ship, hot to kill him before he can regain his fatherland. Yet I think this will not be: instead, the earth will cover certain suitors who devour your estate.'

Athene touched him with her rod, withering the firm flesh of his active limbs, robbing his head of its fair hair and making the skin over all his body old, like an aged man's. She quenched the sparkle of his handsome eye and flung round him for covering foul and sorry rags, all crusted with a sooty reek. Over these she draped a great deerskin from which the hair was quite worn off. She gave him a stick and a shameful leather pouch, of stiff, cracked leather, slung from a common cord. Then, having reached agreement upon their plans, they separated; her intention being for Lacedaemon, to summon home the son of Odysseus.

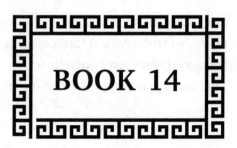

BOOK 14

Meanwhile Odysseus strode up the hill-path that climbed straight from the timbered plains into the highlands, the way Athene had pointed him to that devoted swineherd who cared more for his lord's substance than any other of the serfs Odysseus owned.

He found him sitting in the lodge of his high-walled steading which was a landmark because it stood by itself and was well built and large. Without telling his lady or grandfather Laertes, the swineherd had made it himself for his absent master's pigs by lining up boulders from round about and topping them with a dense hedge of prickly pear. For outer fence he had run round it a stiff, very close-set paling of heart-of-oak, the tree's dark core. All in a row inside the pound he had contrived twelve sties to lodge his beasts. Fifty each sty held, of the brood sows be it understood, supine on beds of litter in their pens: as for the boars, they were kept in the yard outside and were far fewer because of the drain of the suitors' appetites which forced the swine-herd to keep them daily supplied with a prime fatted hog. So these now came to just three hundred and sixty. They were always watched by four wild-looking dogs of the accomplished swineherd's own breeding.

The man himself was shaping to his feet a pair of sandals, cutting them from the hide of what had been a stout ox. Of his men, three happened to be out somewhere or other with their herds of swine, while the fourth the swineherd had sent perforce to the city with a boar whose sacrifice might appease the proud suitors' lust for flesh.

When the noisy dogs saw Odysseus they plunged suddenly towards him, baying: but he cunningly let fall his staff and sank to the ground. Yet even so he risked a savage onslaught there in his own estate, but was saved by the ready swineherd who flung aside the slab of leather and rushed towards him through the gate on flying feet, shouting and raining stones at the dogs to drive them off. Then said he to the prince: 'One moment more, father, and the dogs would have killed you. Quickly too: and thereby you would have added disgrace to me whom the Gods have already afflicted with a variety of griefs and pains. Here I languish, mourning a god-like master and tending his fat pigs for others to eat, while he maybe starves for food, adrift in some land or place of strangers – if, that is, he yet lives under the sun. However follow me inside to our quarters, old man, where our food and wine will nerve you to tell us of yourself and the hardships you have survived.' With no more ado the honest swineherd led him to the inner room and there shook down for him a couch of springy twigs, which he covered with the great thick hairy goat-skin that was his own sleeping-mat. Odysseus rejoiced at being thus received and thanked him saying: 'Host, may Zeus and the other immortal Gods concede your dearest wish in return for this ready welcome you proffer.'

And what was it, O Eumaeus the swineherd, that you answered? 'My guest, I should sin if I failed in attention to any stranger, even one poorer than yourself. The needy and the strangers are all from Zeus; and with the likes of us a quite slender gift can convey good-will, for alas the state of bondmen is never wholly free from fear when their lords and masters are young. My proper lord has, I think, been denied his return home by the Gods. Surely he would have favoured me with the endowment a good master gives his house-men (things like a cottage with its scrap of garden, and a prudent woman) in reward for faithful labour whose fruits God has multiplied and blessed, as He has blessed and multiplied my unremitting toil. Indeed my lord would have largely benefited me as years came upon him in the house; but he has perished – and I would that every one of Helen's kind might be beaten to the knee and broken, in revenge for all the manhood she has undone. See you, my master was one of those who went to Ilium of the goodly horses to fight the Trojans for Agamemnon's fair name.'

As he was speaking he hitched the slack of his smock quickly into his loin-cord and betook himself to the sties that held the piglet clans. From their mass he chose two young ones for butchery, singeing and chopping them up before spitting them to roast. When they were done he carried them to Odysseus and set them in front of him, still on the spits and piping hot. He dusted them over with barley meal and in an ivy-bowl diluted wine till it was sweet for drinking. Then he sat down face to face with Odysseus and invited him, saying: "Eat now, my guest, of our bondman's ration, this young pork. All fatted hogs go to feed those suitors devoid of ruth or any sense of shame. Yet lawlessness does not commend itself to the blessed Gods, who lean towards justice and human integrity. Why even foemen-freebooters feel a foreboding of vengeance and retribution stealing into their hearts' core when ever Zeus has let them raid a strange coast and collect plunder enough to bring their ships heavy-laden home. Therefore surely some whisper from a God must have given these men a certainty of my lord's sad fate, for them to have no care either of wooing with decency, or of ceasing to woo and going home. Instead they devour and devour all that we produce, with a calm insolence that has no bounds. During each Zeus-given night or day they will have their victims, not limiting themselves to just one or two, either. As for our wine, they spill it and lavish it wantonly. The master's wealth was beyond computation. No hero from Ithaca proper or from the dark mainland possessed so much – why, not twenty of them conjoined could match his fortune! Let me recite it you. On the mainland twelve droves of cattle, twelve flocks of sheep, twelve herds of swine, twelve large troops of goats: hired men and his herding-thralls keep all these at pasture. In the extremity of our island are other great troops of goats, eleven in all, each in hand of trusty watchmen: and daily a herdsman will drive the ripest beast of all these to the roisterers in the house. But my plan with the swine is to pen them here out of the way under guard, only sending in, out of the herd, what beast I judge suitable." So he explained to Odysseus who ate his meat and drank his wine in a burning silence, while his longing to injure the suitors grew mightily within him.

But after he had dined and was heartened with the food, then did the swineherd fill to the brim and pass the cup, his own cup he always used. Odysseus took it with an inward thankfulness, while aloud he questioned him shrewdly, saying: 'Now, friend, who was this wealthy man who bought you, this master whose power and riches you so laud? You say he died vindicating Agamemnon's honour. As one of those, maybe I met him. Pray you, his name: for so widely have I roamed that only Zeus and his fellow immortals can say for sure if I have news of seeing him, or no.' Said the swine-herd, that prince of servants, 'Old man, no vagrant body's tale of seeing him will get past me to win credence of his widow and son. It is too much the yarn any conscience-less waif might spin to earn him board and lodging. Wanderers land in Ithaca and go to my mistress with their moonshine. She welcomes them ever so kindly and enquires of this and that, while the tears a woman should shed for her husband fallen in a far country rain griev-ously downward from her eyes. You too, my ancient, would soon pitch some story, if it was to be paid in kind with a cloak and tunic. Whereas in very deed his spirit fled long since, abandoning his bones either to the dogs and birds of prey to pick clean or to lie shrouded in deep sand upon some shore after the fishes of the sea have fed upon him. And this death of his has brought down upon me directly, as upon all who loved him, a load of care: for go where I may, never shall I light upon so gentle a lord, not though I was to regain the home of my birth and the father and mother who reared me. Yea, deeply as I yearn to set eyes on them and on my own place, to-day my deeper grief is for my lost Odysseus. See, stranger, how I blush only to pronounce his name, though he is far away. Truly he cared for me beyond measure and cherished me in his heart, wherefore despite his extreme absence I title him with all respect.'

Odysseus replied: 'My friend, with your unbelieving heart so certain sure that he will never come again I shall not merely assert the returning of Odysseus but seal it with an oath: and I shall claim my guerdon (make it robes of honour, within and without, glorious) the day his feet bring him home. Till then despite my need I shall accept nothing, for hateful to me as the mouth of Hell is one who tells lies out of poverty. So I call upon Zeus, God of Gods, and upon this table of my host and upon the hearth of famous Odysseus to which I have attained! Bear me witness that all things shall happen according to my word; during this very year Odysseus will arrive, between the waning of this moon and the rise of the next, to take his revenge upon those who dishonour his wife and brilliant son.'

And your reply to this, O Eumaeus? You said: 'Ancient, I shall never have to pay this guerdon of yours. Nor will Odysseus regain his house. Be at peace and drink, while we mind ourselves of other things; for I would have you spare these memories, to save me the heartache which comes whenever anyone brings back the thought of my dear lord. So we will let pass your oath. Yet how grateful would be the coming of Odysseus to me and to Penelope, as to old Laertes and Telemachus! See, that godlike young Telemachus is now grown into one of my quick griefs. When the Gods made him flourish like a young tree I said to myself "He will be his loved father's peer, of a form and features to make men marvel," and then some earthly or heavenly thing touched his wits and off he went to Pylos, seeking news of his father. Whereupon the suitor-lords set themselves in ambush against his return, that even the name of the royal race of Arcesius might be rooted out of Ithaca. However we will let pass his affair too, whether he is to be caught or to gain some refuge. Perhaps, indeed, the son of Cronos will shield him with his arm. Instead give me the history, aged one, of your ill-fortunes, first clearly explaining who you are and your city and parents, and what ship you came in and how the sailors brought you to Ithaca, or what sailors they called themselves: for I think you found no dry way hither."

Odysseus answered advisedly: 'I will be plain with you. Yet I wish we had food and good wine enough to let us sit here at our quiet entertainment all through the others' working hours. Easily could I fill a year and still not end the recital of my heart's griefs and the pains the Gods have given me. Let me admit to being a Cretan, the son of a rich man in whose house were born and brought up many other sons of his marriage – whereas my mother was a bought woman, his concubine. Still, Castor the son of Hylax, whose seed I declare myself, made no distinction in honour between me and his lawful issue. Amongst the other Cretans he was held almost divine, having such estate and fortune and splendid family. In time his fate of death came and bore him away to the House of Hades: then the sons made bold to divide his property and draw for their shares. They gave me a very meagre portion but assigned me a house; and to it I brought the wife (daughter of a leading land-owner) whom my prowess had won me: for I was no sluggard and never shirked a fight. To-day my strength has been cropped away by my too-plentiful tribulations: but perhaps from the look of the stubble you can guess what my ripeness was. Ares and Athene granted me a courage which carried me through the press of battle. When once I had determined my tactics against an enemy, no inkling of death would visit my high heart. I would post a chosen party in ambush and then thrust far beyond its leaders to bring down with my spear any opponent less nimble than myself upon his feet. That was the fighting me: but labour I never could abide, nor the husbandry which breeds healthy children. My fancies were set upon galleys and wars, pikes and burnished javelins, the deadly toys that bring shivers to men of ordinary mould. I think such tastes came to me from heaven. Each man sports the activity he enjoys.

'Before the prime of Achaea went up to battle against Troy I had nine times commanded men and warships on foreign expeditions, at great profit to myself, with the leader's first choice of the booty to increase my individual share. So my house rapidly filled with wealth and I became formidable and respected among the Cretans. Consequently, when far-seeing Zeus finally imagined this dread course which has enfeebled the knees of so many men, people clamoured for me and for famous Idomeneus to lead their fleet to Ilium: and so firmly was the popular mind made up that we had no option. Wherefore we sons of the Achaeans stayed fighting for nine years. In the tenth we sacked Priam's city and afterwards embarked for home, a God dispersing the host.

'My unhappy lot, though, was to be vexed anew by an invention of Zeus the Disposer, after only one month's enjoyment of my children and faithful wife and goods: for then my heart prompted me to take my faithful companies and sail against Egypt, after properly refitting the ships. So I commissioned nine vessels. Crews for them rallied quickly to me and to my feast which was sustained for six whole days by the many divine sacrifices I provided to furnish the tables. On the seventh day we launched out from the coast of Crete and sailed with so fair and filling a north wind that it made the sea run like a stream in our favour. We just sat there in careless ease; nor did any ship meet harm with that wind and the helmsmen to steady us. On the fifth day we made the smoothly-flowing river which is Egypt and into its stream I brought our imposing fleet, anchoring it there and ordering my trusty fellows to stand by on ship-guard while I put out watchers into picket posts about. But the men gave themselves up to their baser instincts and the prompting of their own ungovernable passions. In a trice they were ravaging the rich Egyptian countryside, killing the men and carrying off women and children. An instant alarm was given in the town: and the war-cry roused the townspeople to pour out against us at the first show of dawn. The entire valley filled with footmen and horsemen and the glint of bronze. Thunder-loving Zeus crumbled my men into shameful flight, leaving no single one of them the courage to stand firm and face it out. Disaster seemed to beset us on every side. Many of our company perished there by the Egyptians' keen weapons: many others were led living into captivity, there to labour under duress. As for me, I had an inspiration from Zeus himself – yet would rather I had then died and met my final end in Egypt there; for since that day my continued abiding has been in the house of sorrow. My well-wrought helm I hurriedly did off, and let fall the shield from my shoulders. Away went the spear from my hand, while I ran over to the King's car to embrace his knees and kiss them. He drew me to him and had mercy upon me, seating me all tearful as I was on the floor of his own war-chariot. Then he took me to his palace, through the hate-maddened throng whose blood-lust set every spear in rest against my life. But he drove them all back in his reverence for our Lord Zeus whose wrath soonest rises when strangers in his protection are outraged.

'So there for seven years I remained amassing great wealth, for all Egypt gave me gifts. But the eighth year brought in its train a very subtile Phoenician, one of those subverters who have wrought such havoc in the world. His plausibility won me to keep him company even so far as Phoenicia, where lay his house and interests. I stayed with him the round of a year: but when with the march of months and days the season returned he decoyed me into a ship bound overseas for Libya, on the pretence of my running a cargo with him: whereas really he was exporting me for sale as a slave at some incredible profit. My mind misgave me, yet my hands were tied. I had no choice but to embark with him. Our ship ran before a fair freshening wind as far as the open passage south of Crete; where Zeus had taken counsel to destroy her complement. So soon as we sank the Cretan hills and had only sea and sky in view he massed over our ship a deep purple cloud which shadowed the sea in gloom. Then Zeus thundered and at the same instant struck the ship with his lightning. She reeled from stem to stern at the divine stroke and was filled with brimstone-fumes. All fell from her and were tossed like gulls past the black hull on the huge waves. That was the end to their journey which the God gave them: but between my hands Zeus thrust the ship's mast, that despite my heart-load of misery I might yet avoid final bane. I twined myself about this mast and drifted at mercy of the savage winds for nine days: for it was not till the tenth black night that the great rolling swell approached me to the land of the Thesprotians, where the king, Pheidon, received me generously. It was his son who happened to find me lying helpless from exposure and exhaustion; and he lifted me with his own hands and bore me home to his father's palace, where they clothed me anew.

'At their place I got my news of Odysseus. The lord of the house told me he had been their honoured guest on his way home, and showed me treasures of bronze and gold and well-purified iron, laid up by Odysseus within the royal palace, in bulk to satisfy ten generations of heirs. Their owner, the King said, had gone to Dodona to hear what Zeus would counsel him out of the God's tall leafy oak, whether it were better, after so long an absence, to re-enter fertile Ithaca publicly or privily. Besides this the King swore to me, while he made libation in his house, "that the ship to take Odysseus home to his loved country was launched and her crew equipped and ready." Only a chance made him despatch me first, because there was a Thesprotian ship clearing for granaried Dulichium. He charged her masters to convey me most surely to its King, Acastus; but they preferred to follow their own evil imaginings, which plunged me to the very depths of despair. For when the ship had put far out and was in the mid-sea they schemed to enslave me then and there, stripping me naked to exchange my good clothes against these rags of a tunic and cloak you see. In the evening they made the tilled coasts of vivid Ithaca and hurried out upon its foreshore to prepare their supper, after securing me in the well of the hull with coils of stranded rope.

'I think it was the Gods themselves who let the knots slip off me easily. I piled my clothing on top of my head, lowered myself down the slippery after-part and launched out into the sea on my breast with an arm-over-arm stroke that quickly carried me to land beyond their party. I pushed up country as far as a particularly dense thicket and there huddled into its full-leaved bushes. They were wildly distressed over my escape and beat here and there for me: but at last understood that a wider search was unprofitable and went back into their ship. Only the Gods made my hiding so easy; and by their mercy, again, I have found myself the guest of an enlightened man. It seems I am granted a new lease of life.'

And your answer, Eumaeus the pig-keeper? 'My unhappy guest, these sufferings you narrate touch me to the heart, save and except your tattle about Odysseus which is all awry and unconvincing. Why feel constrained by your plight to invent so wild a lie? My mind is definitely made up on this point of my lord's return, knowing for sure that the Gods all hated him, in that they did not grant him death at the climax of the war, in his friends' arms and amid the Trojans: for then every Achaean would have helped set up his tomb and he would have devolved great after-glory upon his son: whereas now the random winds have borne him meanly away. So it is that I hold myself withdrawn here amongst my pigs, never visiting the city except when bidden by circumspect Penelope to hear some news which has casually blown in. Then how they sit round and ply the tale-bearer with questions, not merely those who sorrow for their absent lord but also those others who are enjoying a free run of their teeth in his substance! Only I have lacked heart to query or chop questions, since that day an Aetolian cheated me with his tale. He had killed his man and wandered over the face of the earth till he reached my place. I tended him with all kindness and he told me he had seen Odysseus in Crete with Idomeneus, patching his storm-battered ships. By the summer or at harvest-time he would be back, he said, enriched and with his noble following. But you, old misery whom Fortune has brought to my door, have no need of lies to ingratiate yourself or to warm my heart: that is no road to my regard and charity, which derive from fear of Zeus, the strangers' patron, and from pity for yourself.'

Odysseus the subtle replied: 'Your heart must indeed be froward if this my sworn testimony fails with you and is discredited. See, we will make a bargain and have the Gods of Olympus as witnesses between us. If your lord regains this house you shall clothe me freshly in mantle and tunic before sending me forward to Dulichium, my goal. And if he does not return as I say, then bid your bondmen hurl me from that great crag to teach the next beggar not to invent.'

'Why,' cried the honest swineherd, 'what public name and fame should I have for ever and ever after that, if I brought you into my quarters and entertained you only to set on you and rob you of dear life? With how clean a heart, then, would I supplicate Zeus son of Cronos! See, it is the supper hour. I hope my fellows come back to time, that we may cook something choice for supper here in our place.' As they spoke of it the drovers and their swine appeared. Very shrilly the clamour went up from every sty while the beasts were being herded into their yards for the night; but kindly Eumaeus called to his men, saying, 'Pick out the best of the porkers for devoting to this my foreign guest. And we will have our share too. Over long have we put ourselves to great labour and vexation in keeping these white-tusked boars, only to see others eat for nothing the product of our pains.' While he called to them he was cleaving firewood with his trenchant axe. The others dragged in a fat boar of five years old. They set it by the flaming fire, while the swineherd's ripe understanding prompted him to fulfil his exact duty towards the Deathless Ones. He began by pulling hairs from the head of the tusker and throwing them into the fire, while he implored of all the Gods a home-coming for wise Odysseus. Then he drew himself up and with a billet of wood spared from his chopping he clubbed the beast. It died. They slit its throat, singed it and quickly quartered it for the swineherd to cut a first slice from every limb, of lean doubled in fat. These offerings he dusted with barley groats and flung into the fire, while they were cutting up the rest for threading on the spits to roast with care. Afterwards they drew away the spits and heaped the flesh upon platters. The swineherd stood up to apportion it, for his eye was just. Most precisely he divided the whole into seven helpings. With an invocation he set the first aside for the nymphs and for Hermes, son of Maia: the rest he handed round. For Odysseus he picked out the most noble part, the long back of the white-tusked beast.

The spirit of the king was so gratified thereby that he cried: 'I am praying, Eumaeus, that Father Zeus may love you even as I do, for your conferring this signal portion upon a lone man.' To which you, O Eumaeus, replied, 'Eat, my fine Sir, and be happy with what there is: the God gives and withholds at pleasure, being almighty.' So he pronounced, dedicating his first sacrings to the Eternal Gods. Then he made libation and passed the dark wine to Odysseus the waster of cities, before sitting to eat his own portion. Their bread was brought to them by Mesaulius, the swineherd's private slave, whom he had bought out of his own means from some Taphians during his master's absence, without telling his lady or old Laertes. They reached out and made play amongst the prepared dishes until their appetites for meat and drink had been assuaged: then their replete instincts veered towards bed, even as Mesaulius was clearing the remains of food away. However the night proved dirty. The moon was wrapped in clouds and Zeus rained through all the dark hours; while a powerful west wind, that wet wind, never ceased to blow.

Odysseus had in mind to prove his swineherd by seeing if he would doff his cloak to lend it him, or require a cloak of one of his fellows for the guest he had so entertained. Wherefore he said: 'Hear me now, O Eumaeus and you others, while I let myself go as your wine's intoxication tempts me. Drink will set the most solid man singing or giggling with laughter; if indeed it does not push him forward to dance or make him blurt out something better left unsaid. However now I have loosened my tongue I had best go through with it.

'I wish I were young, with the enduring vigour that was mine in the days when we imagined and took on a surprise raid against Troy. Odysseus was one of our leaders: with him was Menelaus, son of Atreus, and for third in command (by their arranging) went myself. We worked our way round the city till we reached its massive wall and there we lay by the swamp beneath the citadel, our panoply weighing us down into the reeds and dense brake. As we waited the night turned very foul. The north wind came down and it froze hard. Then snow began to fall, chill and dry like rime, while ice plated our shields. The others all wore cloaks over their tunics and so slept well enough, hunched up with their shields over their shoulders; but I had left my cloak with my fellows before setting out, having been fool enough to think I should never feel cold. So there I was with just a gay jerkin and my shield. When the third part of the night had come and the stars were going down I nudged with my elbow against Odysseus who lay next to me, and whispered to his attentive ear: "Son of Laertes, surely I will not be counted long among the living, for this cold is more than I can bear without my cloak. Something possessed me to come out only in my vest and now there is no helping it."

'Even as I spoke a notion flashed into his mind, for he was in a class by himself when either scheming or fighting were in question. He hissed at me sharply: "Be quiet, lest some other Achaean hear you." With that he propped his head on his bent arm and said in a low carrying voice: "Listen, friends. I fell asleep and God has sent me an important dream to show how much too far from the ships we have come. I would have someone bear warning to Agamemnon son of Atreus, the shepherd of the people, that he may move us reinforcements from the leaguer." At his word Thoas son of Andraemon leaped up nimbly, flung aside his purple cloak and broke into a run for the ships, while I snuggled into his garment till Dawn shone from her golden throne. Now, as I remarked, if only I could be young and strong again like that. For then some swineherd of the manor would lend me his cloak, from the double motives of charity to a guest and pity for a stout comrade: but as it is I look for no regard, because of these rags disfiguring my body.'

To which you replied, Eumaeus: 'Old man, that was a really good story you told of him; not one word amiss or wasted. So to-night you shall not be stinted of a coverlet, nor of anything a luckless client may reasonably expect from those with power to help him. Only for to-night, of course; in the morning you must flap away in your own rags again. We have here no store of cloaks nor changes of tunics, but just the suits in which we stand. Yet when Odysseus' darling son comes back he will present you with outer garment and under garment and speed you whither your heart's longing claims.'

He rose as he spoke and pitched a bed by the fireside, covering it with sheepskins and goatskins; and after Odysseus had lain down he drew over him a thick and ample cloak that he kept by him for change in the worst weather. So there Odysseus slept with the lads beside him. Only the swineherd had no heart to lie there apart from his swine, in comfort. Wherefore, to the joy of Odysseus who marked this diligence for the welfare of his absent lord's estate, he girded himself for going out to them, looping a sharp sword about the breadth of his shoulders and wrapping himself in a wind-defying cloak of solid weave, about which went a broad tough goat-skin. Also he took a sharp javelin as defence against dogs or men and so sallied forth to lay himself under the overhang of the crag where the white-tusked boars slept in shelter from the north wind.

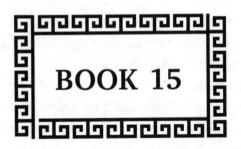

BOOK 15

Meanwhile Pallas Athene had gone to Lacedaemon of the broad acres to prompt the son of Odysseus to a quick return. She found him and Nestor's noble son asleep in the porch of great Menelaus' house – or rather Nestor's son lay in gentle slumber while Telemachus stirred with anxious thoughts about his father all through the divine night.

Pallas stood by him and said: 'My Telemachus, with those bold men behind you in your house you dare not prolong your wandering abroad, to the neglect of your affairs. This journey will have been useless if during it they share out your wealth and devour it. Make stentorian Menelaus speed you homeward at once, while your mother is yet to be found there: for her father and his sons are urging her to accept Eurymachus, who has proved more lavish than any other of the suitors and has largely increased his wedding-bids. If you return she cannot carry off from the house things you would regret to lose: for you know what a woman's nature is and how an eagerness to enrich her actual husband makes her cease speaking or thinking of her once-dear lord and the children she bore him. So back with you and put your gains for safety in hand of the house-maiden you most trust, till the Gods designate some stately woman to be your consort.

'Other news I have for you, and heed it carefully. An ambush of picked men from the suitors is hiding in the gut between the reefs of Samos and Ithaca, with intent to kill you before you regain home. I do not fear it: they are likelier to die themselves, some of these suitors who batten on your livelihood. Yet give those islands a wide berth and sail day and night in your staunch ship – for that Immortal who watches over you for good will vouchsafe you a fair wind. Get ashore on the hither end of Ithaca and send your ship and company round to the city, while you make straight for where your loyal and devoted swineherd lives with his beasts. Lodge with him that night and send him to tell Penelope how you are spared to her and safely come out of Pylos.'

She departed for the peak of Olympus, while Telemachus let drive with his heel against the son of Nestor and woke him, to say: 'Up, Peisistratus, and harness your sure-stepping horses to the chariot, that we may be on our way,' but the son of Nestor replied: 'Telemachus, no matter what the urgency, there is no driving in the dead of night. See, dawn is near. I vote we stay to take the warm farewells and god-speed of the son of Atreus, that master spearsman, as also for the gifts with which this hero Menelaus will load our car. A guest should be ever considerate of the host who has lovingly entreated him.'

Thus he advised: and Dawn assumed her golden throne. Clarion-voiced Menelaus quitted fair Helen's side and came towards them. When the son of Odysseus perceived this he flung the bright tunic about his glossy body and draped his great shoulders in a cloak to go through the gates to meet him: and then he said, 'O royal Menelaus! Here and now send me home; my heart is yearning to be in my own dear country,' and to him Menelaus replied, 'Telemachus, if you so want to go I shall not hold you back. Hosts, to my mind, should be neither importunate nor abrupt. There is always the happy mean. It is as wrong to despatch a reluctant guest as to detain the impatient. Cherish the stranger in the house and speed him so soon as he has the mind. Yet wait while I display the beauty of my gifts to you, while I pack them in the chariot; and let me tell the women to set out in the hall a refection of what meats they have ready. It is a point of credit and honour with us, and of benefit for you to set out with full bellies across these boundless plains. Or would you make the tour of Hellas and mid-Argos in my company, me furnishing the horses and directing you among the towns? Verily not one man would send us away as we came, but every time there would be a gift, some tripod or tub of real bronze, some yoke of mules or golden cup.'

Tactful was the reply of Telemachus: 'Menelaus, I want to go to my own land so quickly because when I left it I did appoint no warden over my goods; and to lose some prized ancestral treasure would suit my taste no better than dying myself in quest of my glorious father.' So soon as stentorian Menelaus understood him he commanded his wife and her maids to contrive a luncheon from the victuals that lay plenteously to their hands. Then came in Etoneus the son of Boethus, all new from bed, for he lived near-by. Menelaus had him light the fire and cook meat: which he obediently did. Next the king went down into his sweet-smelling treasure house; not unattended, for Helen and Megapenthes kept him company. At the treasure heap Atrides picked out a double cup and made Megapenthes his son take a mixing bowl of silver. Helen hesitated by the clothes-chests with their bright store of variegated garments of her own needle-working. Finally from them this fairest of women chose the amplest and richest vestment of all. It had been buried deeply beneath the others and glittered like a star. Then they marched back through the palace till they found Telemachus. Menelaus addressed him saying: 'O Telemachus, may Zeus the Thunderer, who is Hera's lord, allow you this return home you covet. Meanwhile I am giving you the choicest and rarest treasure in my house. Here it is: the storied mixing bowl, of pure silver but for its lip of gold, which Hephaestus made and His Majesty the King of Sidon, Phaedimus, gave me as I was sheltering under his roof on my homeward journey: it pleases me to confer it upon you.'

With such words the warrior son of Atreus presented him the double-cup. Then sturdy Megapenthes brought forward his polished silver bowl, while Helen in her beauty advanced with the robe and naming him said, 'This, dear child, is to be my gift, a keepsake from Helen's hand for your bride to wear on the day of expectation, your wedding-day; till then lay it up with your mother in the house. May gladness go with you homeward to your own place and land.' She gave it him and he was glad. Staunch Peisistratus marvelled at the sight of all the gifts, even while he was stowing them away in the chariot's locker.

Again the tawny-crested king led them within his palace, where they sat enthroned while the maid poured the cleansing water for their hands from her golden ewer over its basin and set out their polished table, which the matron bountifully spread with wheaten loaves and cooked meats. The son of Boethus carved and helped the flesh while Menelaus' son poured out their wine. So they fed till they were satisfied. Then Nestor's son and Telemachus harnessed their horses and in their brilliant chariot swept through the echoing portal and its porch. But there, full in the track of the horses, stood the son of Atreus with a golden beaker, the stirrup-cup of honeyed wine, in his right hand; calling out, 'Your healths, young men! Pledge me to Nestor the people's shepherd who was such a father to me when we young Achaeans were fighting in the Troad.' To which Telemachus properly replied: 'We will repeat him all your message as you have given it, bantling of Zeus, when we arrive; and as my setting out from you has been upon such loving usage and weighted with this wealth of gifts, even so may my return to Ithaca discover Odysseus surely in the house, to hear my tale.'

Upon the word there flew out from the right an eagle whose talons held an enormous white goose, one of their fowls from the yard. After it rushed the farm-hands and maids, yelling; but the eagle sheered again to the right, just by their horses. The sight gave them joy and excited every heart, till Peisistratus said: 'Interpret it, O royal Menelaus, if the God means this portent for us two or for you.' Fighting Menelaus fell on thought, how he should properly read it and reply; but Helen took the word from him and said, 'Hear me, while I declare the meaning (surely the true meaning) which the Gods have flashed into my mind. As that eagle from the mountain eyrie which the eagles haunt has borne off in one swoop our farm-fattened goose, so shall Odysseus come back from his sore wandering and avenge himself: unless perhaps he is already home and brooding ruin for the suitors.'

Telemachus thanked her saying, 'Zeus grant it so, Lady; and I shall reverence you as a divinity.' He whipped up the horses and they raced through the town to the open country where day-long the yoke nodded over their steady pacing till night-fall darkened the roads. They had attained Pherae, by the house of Diocles, son of that Orsilochus whom Alpheus begot; and there they stayed the night, fitly entertained. Rosy dawn saw them harnessing the horses. They climbed into their decorated chariot and drove through the loud gateway. Telemachus laid on with the whip and the willing pair flew onward, so that soon they reached frowning Pylos. There he said to Nestor's son: 'How shall I persuade you now to promise me what I want? Friends we are by reason of our fathers' old acquaintance: also we are of an age and have had this trip together to confirm our love. So do not drive me past my ship, O favoured of Zeus, but set me down beside her, that the old man's sense of hospitality may not have power to keep me chafing in his house. I would speed homeward.'

The son of Nestor pondered if this was a thing he could properly accept and perform. Reflection showed it to be best. So he turned his team out of the way to the water's edge and transferred to the after-part of the ship all the noble gifts of Menelaus, the clothing and the gold. Then he said to Telemachus urgently: 'Now get aboard and have your crew mustered before my reaching home warns the old man. My heart and head assure me that his wilfulness will take no excuse. He will himself come here and hail you; refusing, as I say, to go back alone. This will fling him in a rage.'

With that he turned his long-maned horses back to the town of the Pylians and quickly was at home: while Telemachus was busied greeting his men and bidding them make all ready in the black ship for an instant start. They heeded him and hurriedly obeyed, climbing aboard and taking their places to row. Telemachus was ordering them and praying and sacrificing to Athene in the stern-sheets when there appeared an utter stranger, fugitive from Argos for having killed a man. He was a prophet, being indeed kin to Melampus who had had a splendid house and been rich among the people of sheep-breeding Pylos, where he lived until forced to quit his land and settle abroad for having offended Neleus over his daughter. That haughtiest of nobles laid violent hands on all Melampus' property and kept it, during the long year its owner lay painfully gyved in the house of Phylacus – a spirit-breaking penalty he suffered by decree of the grim fury and Goddess, Erinys. At length Melampus avoided his doom and avenged his wrongs upon the mighty Neleus by driving off to Pylos the loud-ly-lowing cattle from Phylace: with which deed he won the daughter and brought her home to be his brother's wife. Afterwards he banished himself to Argos, that land of thoroughbreds, where fortune made him, a chance-comer, acquire lordship over very many of the Argives. He built a palace there, married and had two stout sons, Antiphates and Mantius.

Antiphates' son, Oicles, was the father of Amphiaraus inspirer of peoples, who though beloved of Zeus and Apollo yet attained not the quiet of old age but died in Thebes for a woman's gifts, leaving Alcmaeon and Amphilochus as issue. Mantius, the other son of Melampus, had a child Cleitus who was so very lovely that gold-en-throned Dawn snatched him up to be with the Immortals: also another son, Polypheides, who by grace of Apollo succeeded Amphiaraus as the greatest prophet alive. But he fell out with his father and so transferred himself to Hyperesia where he lived and prophesied publicly. It was his son, by name Theoclymenus, who now approached Telemachus as he made prayer and libation beside the black hull of his ship, to say earnestly, 'My friend, whom I find in act of sacrifice, tell me truthfully I pray you, by that sacrifice and God, upon your head and your followers' heads – who are you? where from? what city and family?'

Telemachus replied: 'Actually I am from Ithaca and my father is Odysseus, or was Odysseus if he existed, ever. Anyway he died in misery long ago. I took these companions and sallied out to solve the mystery of his disappearance.' Then said Theoclymenus, 'And I too have left my country, for manslaughter of a kinsman whose powerful family bears sway over the Achaeans of the Argive plain. I fled their dark sentence of death, thereby dooming myself to wander across the habitable world. Hear a fugitive's prayer. Admit me to your ship and save my life. I think the pursuers are not far behind.'

Said Telemachus, 'If you really wish to sail with us I shall not refuse you. Come to our home and welcome to your share of what we have.' He took the bronze spear from him and laid it on the deck, then stepped aboard himself and had Theoclymenus sit by him in the stern-sheets. As they cast off the warps he gave order to rig the boat. Zealously they raised their pine-tree mast, stepped it, trapped it in the thwart and tautened its stays. Then they hoisted the white sails by their halyards of plaited hide. Athene gave them a fair wind which sang shrilly through the cloudless firmament so that the ship scudded most quickly towards her goal across the salt sea-water. By Crouni and by Chalcis of the running brooks they went, till sunset and the darkness fell. The ship coasted Pheae in the might of Zeus' wind and raised Elis, the Epeans' strong sanctuary. As he drove thence past each jagged islet Telemachus asked himself if he would escape death or be trapped.

Meanwhile Odysseus was supping in their homestead with the honest shepherd and his men. When appetite had been appeased he spoke again, in wish to find out the swineherd's real mind towards him and if he would extend him longer hospitality there in the farm, or compel him city-wards. 'Now Eumaeus and you others, listen. So as not to exhaust your kindness I would go at crack of dawn to the town, where I can beg my way. Only give me hints and skilful guidance thither: for once arrived I must work by myself if I am to win bread and sup from someone. My special idea is to pass a word with wise Penelope at Odysseus' house and meet the graceless suitors. Perhaps they will fill my mouth out of their superfluity; and it is likely I may prove useful to them for I tell you – heed me and believe it well – that by help of Hermes (whose is the dignity that graces human labour) no man equals me in service, at building fires and chopping wood for them, at carving or roasting meats, at serving drink, at anything you like to mention that menials can do for their betters.'

Ah then, Eumaeus, how your heart sank while you answered him. 'Alas, my guest, that this notion should have come to your mind. You must thirst for your own destruction if you would push among that mob of suitors whose rank cruelty affronts the steely sky. Their lackeys are not men like you, but young rufflers in gay cloaks and robes, sleek-headed and blooming-cheeked. Already their tables groan with bread and meat and wine. So stay with us. No man here, not myself nor any of these my fellows, grudges your tarrying: and when Odysseus' good son returns he will clothe you newly and forward you whither your spirit bids.' To this Odysseus said: 'May Father Zeus love you, Eumaeus, as I do for your sparing me further distressful vagabondage, that saddest of human fates. For their loathly bellies' sake do men incur these pains and griefs of vagrancy. But now, if I am to settle here till the son returns, tell me about the mother of Odysseus and of the father whom his going left behind stricken in years. Are they yet living in the eye of day, or dead and in Hades' mansions?'

Said the excellent swineherd: 'I will tell it you in detail. Laertes lives: but prays ever and ever that Zeus will let the life flicker from his limbs in the hall. So bitterly does he lament his missing son and the long-proven wife whose death has been a main grief to age him before his time. Know too that she herself fell on death for grieving after her famous son. A tragic end hers was, such as I would wish to no kindly neighbour who had entreated me well. Despite her sorrow I was careful and glad to ask after her while she lived: for I was brought up by her with tall long-gowned Climene, her youngest daughter. Together we grew up, the mother honouring me almost like her own child, until both of us came to blissful adolescence. Then they parted with her (for a high wedding-price) to a man of Same, while me my lady clothed and shod fairly and put to work on the farm. Her love toward me ever grew, and it is that which I now miss, despite the Gods having prospered me in the work which is my livelihood, so that I have my food and drink and can give alms to the deserving. But since the shadow fell on the great house and ruffians beset it there is no more cheerfulness in the mistress, neither kind word nor kindly deed – whereas it is the way of servants to take great satisfaction in meeting their mistress, to pass the time of day and gossip, perchance to eat or drink somewhat and carry off to their fields a trifle which warms their loyal hearts.'

Odysseus rejoined: 'Was it as an infant, Eumaeus, that you went astray from your home and kin? Take this chance to tell me all your story. Did they sack and ruin that spacious city where your parents lived, or were you alone, herding sheep or cattle for instance, when raiders caught you and shipped you overseas for sale at a stiff price into a master's household?' The swineherd replied, 'Stranger, if you will open up that topic, settle yourself comfortably into your seat, refill your cup and listen to me closely. These nights are inordinately long and afford us time for diverting tales and for sleep too. Nor is there point in sleeping over soon: that way lies boredom. Of the others let anyone who feels like it go off to bed. At daybreak there will be a snatch-meal and then away out with our lord's swine. But we two snugly indoors here may drink and eat and revel in an interchange of sorrows – sorrows that are memories, I mean; for when a man has endured deeply and strayed far from home he can cull solace from the rehearsal of old griefs. And so I will meet your questioning.

'There is an island called Syria, if you have heard of it, beyond Ortygia where the sun has its turning. No populous place, but good, with its bounties of cattle and sheep, corn and wine; so that its people are never straitened nor made miserable by disease. When a generation has grown old Apollo of the silver bow and Artemis come with kindly darts to end their term. Politically the whole island is comprised in two cities, and my god-like father, Ctesius son of Ormenus, was king of both.

'Ours was a place where profit-seeking Phoenician master mariners would come to chaffer the ten thousand gew-gaws in their ships: also my father had a Phoenician woman among his bond-maids. Beautiful and tall she was and an accomplished seamstress: but passion will lead astray the very best of women, and she fell, seduced by a wily fellow-countryman, actually while she did our laundry. The Phoenician who lusted and lay with her was from a near-by ship; and afterward he asked her about herself. She pointed to my father's towering roof with "Yet I swear I am from the mart of bronze, from Sidon itself, own daughter to Arybas, that source of wealth. Taphian pirates captured me as I was strolling down the country road. They brought me here and sold me into this king's establishment. No small sum he paid."

'Then the sailor who had secretly enjoyed her said, "And would you like to come back with us, to see again the tall house of your father and mother, and be with them once more? They live still and are reputed rich." The woman replied, "Let it be so, indeed, if you sailors will pledge your word to bring me honourably home." They all swore it as she wished and after the oath was taken she began again: "Be mum now and see that never a one of you speaks to me on the highway or even at the fountain, should we meet. Someone might go and tell the old man in the palace, and on the suspicion he would fetter me savagely and compass your destruction. So keep it to yourselves while you drive your cargo-bargain. Afterwards, when the ship is fully freighted, make sure that a swift word finds me in the palace: for I would bring with me every scrap of gold within reach, together with another sort of goods that I will most gladly give you for my fare. I play nurse to my master's child, a priceless boy, who toddles by my side in and out the house. If I bring him aboard he should fetch you a huge sum from some foreign buyer."

'Thus she said and returned within the mansion. The seafarers delayed amongst us for a whole year till their trading had brought together great wealth in the ship. When all the holds were filled ready for departure they sent up a messenger to warn the woman. The crafty fellow came to my father's house hawking a golden collar beaded here and there with amber. As the serving women in the hall and my lady mother were offering him bids for this, fingering it and devouring it with their eyes, he nodded silently to the woman. Then he went back towards his ship, while she took me by the hand and led me out through the hall door. In its porch she found cups and tables where the men in attendance upon my father had refreshed themselves before going out to Assembly for their debate. Swiftly she snatched up three goblets and hid them in her bosom, me tripping along meantime in all innocence. As we hurried towards our familiar harbour the sun set and the roads grew obscured. The Phoenician vessel lay ready. The crew embarked us and sailed across the waters, Zeus affording a fair wind. We sailed for six days and nights on end: but as the son of Cronos created the seventh day Artemis the archer smote the woman, who dropped with a sea-gull's headlong dive into the bilges. They flung her overboard to feed the seals and fishes, leaving me disconsolate. Wind and currents at length brought them up in Ithaca where Laertes purchased me with his wealth. So I came to see this land.'

Odysseus in his answer said: 'Eumaeus, your tale of all these haps and sorrows sadly borne touches my heart. Yet surely Zeus has given you good to set off against the evil, in bringing you at the end of your distress to this house of a gentle man who has so well provided you with meat and drink as to let you live wholesomely. While I have arrived only as a waif, errant among the haunts of men.' So they chatted, till at last they slept away the little remnant of the night. Little it was, for Dawn was soon enthroned.

In this same dawn the crew of Telemachus, off shore, lowered first their sails and then their mast, smartly, and rowed their ship to land. They let go the anchors and bitted their hawsers, before going out upon the margin of the sea to prepare the day-meal and mix their sparkling wine. After they had well eaten and drunken Telemachus exhorted them prudently: 'Now you must take our black ship round to the city, while I go up-country to my herdsmen. By evening I shall have checked my affairs and got back to the city: where early to-morrow I will discharge your journey-fee in a worthy feast of meat and good wine.'

Here reverend Theoclymenus broke in to say, 'And where am I to go, dear lad? Whose house should I make for, in this rugged Ithaca with all its chiefs? Or shall I go straight to your mother's house, which is yours?' Telemachus pensively replied: 'Normally I would have you come to ours, where guests are welcomed; but now it might be unsuitable, with me away and my mother invisible – for she likes not to be seen much among the suitors in the hall, but keeps her upper room, weaving. However there is one man I can commend to you as host, and that is Eurymachus, wise Polybus' distinguished son. In the eyes of the Ithacans he is rather more than mortal, being beyond cavil their greatest figure. It is his ambition to espouse my mother and succeed to the honours of Odysseus: but that only Zeus, in his Olympian firmament, can judge. The God might cause their day of wrath to come before their wedding day' and as he finished speaking a bird (one of the hawks that are Apollo's speedy messengers) swooped past upon the right hand with a dove in its claws and tearing at it so that the feathers came fluttering to earth midway between Telemachus and the ship.

Theoclymenus called him apart from the crowd, gripped his arm and said: 'Telemachus, as soon as I saw it I knew that bird was significant. Only by the God's warrant did it fly past on the right. There is no family more royal than yours in all Ithaca. To you will ever be its sovereignty.' Upon which sober Telemachus rejoined: 'Ah, stranger, if only this word come true. My love and generosity would then so light upon you in swift measure that every one who met you would pronounce you blessed.' Then he summoned Peiraeus, one of his trusted ones, and said, 'Son of Clytius, during this voyage to Pylos you have proved most heedful of my wishes. Now I would have you take this stranger home and tend him with kindly honour till I come,' and Peiraeus the doughty spearman answered, 'Telemachus, I will receive him and not pinch his entertainment, however long you tarry.' He turned to the ship and had the others embark and cast off. They hurried to their rowing stations while Telemachus was doing on his neat sandals. Then he lifted from the deck his great spear with its keen bronze tip. The crew cast off their cables, pulled out to sea and sailed for the port, as the son of Odysseus had enjoined: while his feet sped him inland to the penfold where slept his swarms of swine about their herdsman, that loyal servant of his master's weal.

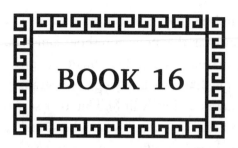

BOOK 16

At dawn, after they had sent out the drovers with their pigs, Odysseus was helping the honest swineherd light the fire within their hut and prepare breakfast, when suddenly the restless noisy dogs hushed their baying to fawn about the approaching Telemachus. Odysseus, hearing foot-falls, noted this quiet welcome that the dogs were giving, and exclaimed to Eumaeus, 'Friend, here comes a mate of yours, or someone so familiar that the dogs instead of barking play round him in friendship. Now I hear his footsteps.' With the words yet in his mouth his dear son appeared at the door. The astonished swineherd let drop the jars in which he had been mixing wine and sprang to his feet. With tears of joy he met his lord, to kiss his head, his eyes, his hands, as a good father greets the darling of his heart, his only and beloved son, home after ten long anxious years. Just so the good swineherd clung to the prince and embraced him like one snatched from death, while he cried out: 'Your coming, O Telemachus, is sweetness and light. After you had sailed for Pylos I whispered to myself that I had seen you for the last time. Come in, my child, come in to the house, that my heart may be gladdened by the wanderer's return. You keep yourself so closely in the town, to the neglect of your estate and husbandmen, as if you liked to watch that swarm of suitors devouring everything in view.'

'Have it your way, father,' protested Telemachus. 'Yet here I come to see you with my own eyes and hear from your lips if my mother is still at home. Or has she yielded to another, and abandoned the bed of Odysseus for spiders to defoul with their webs?' The swineherd replied, 'She abides constantly in the house, though the nights wane for her wearily and her days are wet with tears,' and as he spoke he was ushering him over the stone threshold and relieving him of his brazen spear. Odysseus, the father, made to give him place, but Telemachus motioned him back, saying, 'No, stranger, rest where you are. This farm is ours and we will find another seat. Here is the man to arrange it.' So Odysseus sat still while the swineherd strewed green twigs and covered them with a fleece on which the dear son of Odysseus set himself. Then the swineherd brought out on platters what was left of yesterday's baked meats, busily arranging with them baskets of bread and sweet wine mixed in an ivy-bowl. He sat to face Odysseus and they made play with the cheer till appetite was stayed. Then said Telemachus to Eumaeus, 'Father, how did this stranger reach you, in what ship's company and whence their declaration? Surely he has not just tramped in?'

Then you, O swineherd Eumaeus, said, 'I will inform you, son. He calls himself a native of the Cretan coast and a wanderer through earth's cities, that being his destiny. Actually he reached the farmstead as runaway from a Thesprotian ship. To you I convey him for disposal: yet he would be your suppliant.' Telemachus replied soberly, 'This word of yours cuts deep, Eumaeus; for how can I entertain a stranger in my house? I am still young and unversed in defending myself against aggressors. My mother is in two minds, at one time wanting to stay carefully at home keeping true to her husband's bed and public opinion, and another time ready to accept whichever of her Achaean parties shows himself the most generous wooer. Yet now you have received this guest, I will clothe him fairly with robe and tunic, give him a stabbing-sword and shoes, and send him whither he wishes: or if you prefer to look after him here, I will supply you his clothes and full rations, to prevent his being a drain upon you and your fellows. Only amongst the suitors I will not have him come, lest their vile rudeness undo me by offering him insult. It is hard for one man, however eminent, to assert himself against the odds of a crowd.'

Odysseus took up the word. 'Friend, it is my place to answer that, I think. I am desolated to hear you tell how unconscionably these suitors spite you at home. Explain – do you suffer it, or have the local people heard a God bidding them turn against you? Or perhaps you have been let down by the blood-relations upon whose armed help a man naturally counts in his greatest need? Ah, if only I were your age or as young as I feel, and could be the son of Odysseus or the great man himself back from wandering, as yet might happen! Anybody might cut my head off if I failed to go to the palace of Laertes' son and visit my fury upon every soul within it. And if their numbers prevailed over my solitary self, why I would be happy to die there in my house rather than passively witness such outrages as guests insulted and serving women violated in the stately halls, my wine spilt wantonly and my food wasted, day after day.'

Telemachus gravely replied: 'Stranger, I can explain it all. The people do not hate me, nor have I been deserted in extremity by kinsmen on whom I did rely. The son of Cronos made our house single-fruited. Arcesius had the one son, Laertes. Odysseus was the only son of his father, and his sailing to the war left me as sole heir at home – to his loss, for now his house is beset with these innumerable enemies. The pick of all the island gentry from Dulichium and Same and leafy Zacynthus (not to mention rugged Ithaca itself) are courting my mother and eating the estate bare. She cannot either reject the horrid match or get it over. So to the ruin of the house they eat and eat, till soon they will eat me too. However such things lie in the lap of the Gods. Father swineherd, I pray you hurry to Penelope and tell her I am safely arrived out of Pylos for her sake. Till you get back I shall stay here. Be sure you see her apart and let no Achaean overhear you: I have only too many ill-wishers.'

And you said, Eumaeus, 'I know. I understand. You speak to a man who thinks: but continue and direct me plainly. Shall I push my journey a little further and inform poor Laertes, who till lately through all his griefs for Odysseus kept the supervision of the property, eating and drinking whenever he thought it advisable with the household staff? They tell me now that since you sailed for Pylos he has never once feasted thus nor cared for the farm-work; but sits in grief and lamentation, letting the flesh waste off his bones.'

Telemachus replied: 'Our misfortunes grow; but very sadly we must let him be: though had mankind the faculty of choice we would plump for my father's return. So just do your errand and come back, without seeking over the country-side for the aged man – yet warn my mother to send her old hand-maiden quickly and secretly across to him with the news.' So he despatched the swineherd, who picked up his sandals, put them on and struck out for the city. His departure was watched by Athene who then repaired to the farm herself, in the guise of a tall, splendidly accomplished woman. She stood before the living quarters and revealed herself to Odysseus; but Telemachus saw nothing there, the Gods having the power not to be manifested except at will. However Odysseus perceived her, and the dogs, who instead of barking slunk in whining terror to the back of the yard. She frowned biddingly towards Odysseus. He rose and went past the outer wall to stand before her.

She said, 'God-begotten, cease hiding from your son. Open yourself to him and concert a way to slaughter the suitors. Then start together for the famous town. Nor will I lag behind. I am longing for the fray.' She touched him with her golden rod and clothed his body anew in laundered robes. She restored his stature and presence. His flesh took on colour, his cheeks filled out. The dark beard bushed once more about his chin. When her work was perfected she went away, leaving Odysseus to re-enter the hut. His son, who took him for a God, was astounded and withdrew his face, saying urgently, 'Stranger, you are not what you seemed to me just now. Your clothes are different, even your flesh is changed. Surely you are a God, a denizen of heaven. Be propitious; while we set before you gold offerings beautifully wrought, and sacrifices. Spare us, Lord.'

But Odysseus said, 'I am no God: liken me not with the Immortals. In very deed I am your father, the Odysseus for whose sake you have grieved and endured adversity and suffered indignities from men.' He spoke and kissed the lad, yielding to the tears he had hitherto held back; but Telemachus could not credit that it was his father, so he said, 'You are not Odysseus, not my father, but some subtile devil plaguing me worse till I cry with pain. No mortal man can so alter his fashion by taking thought; nor may it be, unless some very God come down and arbitrarily change him between youth and eld. You were aged and degraded: and now you are like the Gods in their wide heaven.' Odysseus replied, 'My Telemachus, do not let yourself be amazed or shaken beyond measure by your father's return. No other Odysseus than I will ever come to you now. As for my state, that is how I reach my own land after twenty years of woes and wanderings. This changing me to old or young is the whim of Athene the Reiver, who can make me at one time a sorry beggar and at another a youth of fashion. It costs the Gods of high heaven no pains to exalt or to abase plain men.'

Upon this he sat down: but Telemachus with a cry folded his father in his arms and burst out weeping. The longing for tears welled up in them both at once so that their cries rose conjoined, longer drawn and more piercing than the din of vultures or hook-taloned sea hawks whose nests have been plundered of their fledgelings by country-folk. So sorrowfully did the tears rain down from their eyelids and so unstaunched that the sun might have set upon their lamentations, only for Telemachus suddenly saying to his father, 'But in what manner of ship, father, did your crew bring you to Ithaca, and whence did they avouch themselves? You cannot have come afoot.' And Odysseus answered, 'My child, in truth they were the famous Phaeacians, those stout seamen who convey all comers. I slept the quick voyage through and was yet sleeping when they landed me in Ithaca with their wonderful rich gifts of bronze and gold and clothing. By the Gods' care all these things are bestowed in caves: and Athene's behest brings me here for us to plan the destruction of our enemies. So recite to me the sum of these suitors and let me know their quality and quantity, that my noble heart may ponder and determine if we two can take them on, alone and unsupported; or must seek allies.'

Telemachus soberly replied, 'Father, I know your reputation as a man of your hands, but shrewd. Surely you have said too much. It appals me. Two men cannot fight a company of champions. These suitors are not just ten men or twenty even, but a crowd. Listen while I count them off. From Dulichium fifty-two men of standing with six varlets. From Same twenty-four. From Zacynthus twenty noble Achaeans; while from our Ithaca there are twelve of the best men, besides Medon the usher, the inspired bard and two skilled waiters and carvers. If we come upon all these in the house, beware lest your vengeance recoil altogether too bitterly. Rack your wits for the name of some doughty one who would stand by us manfully.'

Dauntless Odysseus replied, 'Indeed I can give you a name. Heed me and mark it carefully. Will Athene, supported by Father Zeus, do for us two, or must I think of another helper?'

Telemachus said gently, 'This pair rule all mankind, with the Immortals to boot, and are indeed mighty helpers; but their seat is very far away amongst the clouds.' 'It may be,' said Odysseus, 'yet when the ordeal by Ares is staged between us and the suitors in the hall, those two will not hold back from the din and press. Our first move is for you to go home at daybreak and rejoin the haughty suitors, whither the swineherd a little later will conduct me in my beggarly guise, seeming old and broken. Should they insult me in the house, harden your heart's love for me against my pains, even if they hurl at me or drag me feet-first across the floor to cast me out. Endure all such scenes, only reasoning sweetly with them to moderate their wildness – which they will not do. Their fateful day looms near. Now remember my next words carefully. When the wisdom of Athene prompts me I will nod to you. Watch me closely for this and when you see it, carry off all the deadly weapons within reach to that recess in the solar upstairs; and when they miss them put the suitors off with some such likely excuse as "I took them away out of the smoke, for they have become so tarnished by fire-reek as hardly to look like the same things Odysseus left here when he went to Troy. Also the son of Cronos prompted me with this deeper reason, that iron of itself tempts man's frailty. In wine you might quarrel and a scandal of wounds follow to mar this junketing and courtship." Just leave for the pair of us where we can snatch them suddenly, two swords, two spears and two hide shields. Pallas and deep-planning Zeus will do the rest, to confound them. Only I tell you – and again pay attention – if you are my own true-blood son let no one know Odysseus is back, not Laertes nor the swineherd nor any servant; not Penelope herself. We will study the women, you and I alone: and test the serfs also, to divide those with some respect for discipline from the froward who disparage even your dignity.'

His famous son spoke up and said, 'My father, you will prove my courage by and by, I know, and find me steadfastness itself. But I would have you reconsider this plan, in which I see nothing to our joint advantage. If you run round the properties to test each serf, you will spend ever so much time during which those others sitting in our house will go on using up our wealth with the coolness of effrontery. The women I would indeed have you prove, to see which have disgraced you and which are innocent; but the men in the farms I would postpone till later; if you can truly pin your reliance on aegis-bearing Zeus.'

While they discussed their plans the staunch ship and company of Telemachus were putting in to Ithaca. Deep within the harbour they beached her and drew up the dark hull. Pages carried their arms proudly homeward, and took the splendid gifts to Clytius' house. They sent a herald to the palace of Odysseus to tell careful Penelope (lest the pround queen's fears set her weeping) how Telemachus had sent the ship round to the port, while he struck overland. This herald and the honest swineherd ran into one another on the same errand to their lady: but the herald, from amongst the serving-women in the room, proclaimed aloud, 'Your dear son, O Queen, has just come back to you,' while the swineherd went near to Penelope herself and privily imparted her son's message. As soon as he had said his say he quitted the house and its precincts, to regain his swine.

The news vexed and depressed the suitors who flocked out from the hall through the high-walled court to its gate where they sat in conclave; Eurymachus opening thus: 'My friends, Telemachus has made an insolent success of his difficult task, this voyage, which we decided he must not complete. Now our job is to launch as good a vessel as there is, with deep-sea oarsmen for crew, to bid our others homeward at their best speed.' Even while he spoke Amphinoumus looked aside and saw their ship in the deep harbour, with its crew striking sail and gathering up their oars. So he laughed shortly and proclaimed, 'We will send no such message. Here they are. Either some God warned them or they saw the other ship go by and could not catch her.' All rose and trooped to the sea-front where the crew were drawing the black hull quickly up the foreshore while haughty lackeys took their weapons home. Then the united body of suitors moved to the assembly-place, strictly excluding old and young from their number, for Antinous, son of Eupeithes, to make this speech: –

'It is a sad blow, the Gods' letting this man escape his predicament. Our scouts in quick reliefs crowned the windy headlands, on the look-out all day; nor did we pass one night ashore. With sunset we ever put out in the ship and lay at sea in wait for Telemachus till dawn, to catch and kill him. Yet some power has brought him home. So here and now let us determine his bloody end, and prevent his slipping through our hands: for I think we shall never achieve our purpose while he lives. The crowd grow less partial to us as he shows himself persuasive and resourceful. We must act before he can gather the Achaeans into council; for I feel sure he will not spare us or mince matters. He will get up and blurt out how we meant to murder him, but underreached: and they will not support us when they hear our treachery. They may even turn on us and banish us to find our living in some land of strangers. Let us anticipate, by catching him somewhere apart from the city or on his way thither. Then shall we possess his livelihood and wealth for even division amongst ourselves, leaving the house itself to his mother for him who marries her. If you will not have this course, but decide to let him live and have all his father had, then must we leave off devouring his riches and disperse to our own houses, thence to woo the woman and tempt her with gifts until she weds the designated best payer.'

After his word came a stillness till Amphinomus rose amongst them and spoke – Amphinomus, the famed son of royal Nisus son of Aretias, chief suitor from grassy and granaried Dulichium. His company was specially agreeable to Penelope because of his poise and judgement, which expressed themselves as he said, 'Friends, I would not kill Telemachus. It is heinous to spill royal blood. Let us first consult the Gods. If the oracles of great Zeus commend it, then will I be the executioner myself, and halloo you on: but if not, I will bid you hold.' His saying pleased them. They rose and returned to the palace and resumed their polished thrones.

The notion came to wise Penelope that she must face the suitors in all their brutal pride, for Medon the usher who knew their plans had told her of the plot to kill her son in the house. So down to the hall-full of suitors went the stately lady with her two tiring-women and stood by a pillar of the mighty roof. She held the thin head-veil before her face and by his name rebuked Antinous, saying, 'Ill-mannered trickster, do they call you prime amongst your peers of Ithaca in eloquence and resource? You show it not. Crazy, I call you, for daring to flout those who have petitioned great Zeus to have Telemachus in his care. And you would kill him? Plotting murder is a deadly sin. Have you forgotten your father's taking refuge in this house from the people who rose against him when he joined the Taphian pirates to harry our Thesprotian friends? They were set upon killing him and plundering his great wealth; but Odysseus beat down their fury. And now you rudely devour his home and court his wife and would murder his son, all to my sore hurt. I bid you hold; and hold back the rest.'

Eurymachus, son of Polybus, intervened: 'Penelope, wise daughter of Icarius, take heart. Be not so distressed. The man who would lift hand against Telemachus is not, shall not be, cannot be, while I exist in the light of day! So I proclaim and ensure it, for quickly would such a fellow's blood drip down my spear. How often has Odysseus, that breaker of cities, dandled me on his knees and put scraps of roast meat into my fingers and made me taste the ruddy wine! Wherefore to me is Telemachus particularly dear, and I bid him have no thought of death at the wooers' hands. From the Gods, of course, there is no avoiding fate.' He spoke to calm her, with death hidden in his heart: and the queen turned back to her glorious upper room where she bewailed Odysseus, her loved husband, till Athene of the grey eyes shed merciful sleep upon her.

At dusk the good swineherd rejoined Odysseus and his son, to find them contriving supper from a yearling pig they had sacrificed. Again had Athene come to the son of Laertes, and with a stroke of her wand aged him anew before wrapping him in his body-rags, for fear of the swineherd's recognizing him and running to Penelope to betray his news. Said Telemachus, 'You have come, dear Eumaeus. What news in town? Are the suitor-lords back from ambush, or still waiting for me?' And to him you replied, O swineherd, 'To wander down town and gossip was no part of my duty. I thought to deliver my message and come straight home, only there met me a herald coming from your crew in haste, and he forestalled me with your mother. Yet this I do know, for I saw it from the head of Hermes' ridge above the city, on my way back – a fast ship entering our harbour, crowded, and bristling with shields and double-edged spears. I think it was them, though I cannot be sure.' His saying made great Telemachus smile and glance aside to catch his father's eye.

Now their preparations were ended and the meal was ready. So they feasted to their common content. When hunger and thirst were put away they remembered their beds and took the boon of sleep.

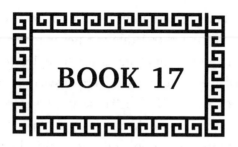

BOOK 17

Dawn saw Telemachus, the son Odysseus loved, binding on his rich sandals. He picked up the heavy spear that so well fitted his grasp and turned his face townwards, saying to the swineherd, 'I am for home, father, to show myself to my mother, for I think she will not stop her tearful lamenting till she has seen me in the flesh. Now for my orders. You are to bring this poor creature to the city where he can beg his bite or sup off the charitable. My heart is too distracted to care for every chance-comer. If the stranger resents my saying so, that is his misfortune. I like blurting out the truth.' But Odysseus replied composedly, 'Why, friend, I have no wish to dally here. There is better begging in a town, where those who feel inclined will give me things. I am no longer of an age to live in quarters, obedient to my superior's every nod. So go; and this man will bring me along as you have ordered, when I have warmed myself through at the fire and the day has heated up. The morning frosts might be too sharp for me, in these poor clothes: also it seems the city is quite a journey off.'

After he had heard him out Telemachus strode vigorously from the farm, maturing schemes against the suitors by the way, till he reached his substantial house and paused to prop his spear against the tall column before stepping across its stone threshold. Eurycleia his nurse was quickest to see him, from her job of spreading sheepskins over the ornate seats. She ran to him in a flurry of tears, and the other maids of the household followed her to flock about him with loving kisses for his head and shoulders. Forth from her chamber issued heedful Penelope, fair as Artemis or golden Aphrodite, to clasp her son and kiss his face and both his beautiful eyes, while she sobbed, 'Are you back, Telemachus, dear light? I thought never to see you more after you sailed secretly and without my leave to Pylos for news of your father. Quick, tell me what you saw.' He answered, 'Mother mine, I have barely missed death. Do not ruffle my heart or set me crying again, but bathe yourself and change your clothing: then go upstairs with your women into your room and vow victims by hundreds to the Gods, on the day Zeus will vouchsafe us perfect vengeance. I am for the assembly to recover a stranger who came back with me, but whom I had to send on with my devoted crew after getting Peiraeus to take him to his place and care for him honourably till I arrived.' His speech stifled the questions on her lips. She performed her libation, put on clean garments and vowed whole hecatombs to the Gods if Zeus would ever let their revenge fructify.

Telemachus left the house spear in hand, with two fleet hounds at heel, and upon him such grace from Athene that all the people adored as he came. The suitor-lords bustled up with welcomes that covered the malice in their hearts; but he avoided them, to sit by Mentor and Antiphus and Halitherses, his old family friends. They questioned him eagerly: but at the instant Peiraeus the spearsman appeared, leading his guest through the town to the assembly, Telemachus went over to be greeted thus: 'Telemachus, send your women promptly to my house and collect the gifts of Menelaus.' But he replied, 'Peiraeus, we cannot yet see how things will go. If the suitors manage to kill me traitorously in the palace and split up my heritage, I would rather you held these gifts. But if I succeed in dooming them to death, then shall I be just as glad to get them as you to let them go.'

He led the way-worn Theoclymenus to the house. Within its massy walls they threw down their cloaks upon some settle or throne and went to wash themselves in the polished baths. The ministering women bathed and anointed them and clothed them warmly. Forth they came once more to their seats, where the maid of the ewer poured for them the hand-water over its basin and drew up their table which the housekeeper hospitably spread with loaves and many dishes. But Penelope placed herself in a reclining chair against the pillar opposite, and spun fine yarn on her distaff all the while they fed themselves full.

At last she broke out, 'Telemachus, I am returning to my room; to that bed of sorrow which I have kept bedewed with tears since the day Odysseus went to Ilium with the sons of Atreus; seeing that you will not move yourself to tell me, now before the suitors come in, what the news is of your father's return – if you did hear anything.' Said Telemachus, 'Nay, mother, listen. We went to Pylos where Nestor the king welcomed me like a child who had been long abroad. He and his sons were so kind: but of Odysseus, alive or dead, he had no news at all. He found me well in chariot and horses and sent me across to Menelaus the son of Atreus, in whose house I met Helen, the cause, under God, of all the Argive-Trojan travail. Menelaus enquired why I had come, and when I explained he said, "For those cowardly suitors to aspire after Odysseus' bed is for a hind to lay her unweaned fawns in a lion's den while she ranges abroad for food. As the lion on his return makes sad work of them, so will Odysseus grimly slay the suitors. If only the Gods would bring him upon them in the might whereby he flung Philomeleides at Lesbos, to the general joy, what a short sharp issue they would have to their wedding! Your query I will best meet by telling you exactly what I learnt from the old man of the sea. He said he had seen Odysseus in an island, Nymph Calypso's prisoner, miserable in her house but unable to escape for lack of shipping and men to ferry him across the swelling sea." That is what Menelaus said. Having achieved my mission I sailed for home and the Gods gave me a fair wind which brought me quickly here.'

His tidings fluttered her heart: but godlike Theoclymenus interposed, 'Hear my word, O august consort of Odysseus. Indeed he had no certain knowledge, but I will prophesy to you most clearly and exactly. I testify by Zeus in first instance, as by this hospitable board and the hearth of Odysseus at which I stand, that already he is in his native place, active it may be or else lying low; but surely hearing of these disorders and meditating vengeance upon all the suitors. The bird I saw by the decked ship pointed the future so plainly that then and there I declared it to Telemachus.' To him Penelope replied, 'May your word be fulfilled, stranger; then I would show you how lavish my gratitude could be, even till every passerby did praise your fortune.' While they thus talked the suitors on the flat land before the palace were heedlessly amusing themselves with the discus or spear-throwing. Supper-time came and homeward after their appointed shepherds came the flocks from the outlying pastures. Then did Medon, the favourite attendant who was always at the feasts, proclaim: 'Lordlings, now that you have played to your hearts' content, turn back to the house; and we shall feast. Nothing is better than a timely meal.' They sprang up and went as he advised into the stately house, where they piled their cloaks on the high seats and slaughtered great sheep, fat goats and pigs, even a bull from the stock, to furnish their table.

Odysseus and the swineherd were ready to leave the country for the town. The exemplary swineherd remarked, 'Stranger, you are keen on moving today to the city, as my prince ordained. Yet I would have left you here in charge, only for regard of my master, and in fear of the rebuke which would follow from him. Very terrible are the rebukes of kings. So let us away. More than half the day has sped and you will feel the chill towards nightfall.' Odysseus answered, 'I understand. I agree. You address an enlightened man. Indeed let us set off under your sole guidance. Yet if you have a trimmed staff give it me, to steady my steps over this road which you describe as difficult.' He slipped on his mean wallet, that tattered thing with its shoulder-cord, and Eumaeus gave him the stick he wanted. Off they went together, leaving dogs and herding-men to keep the farm. In such state, like an aged and sorry pauper hobbling on a staff and deplorably dressed, did the swineherd bring his King home.

They threaded the awkward path till hard by the town, when they found the running spring, steyned round, which Ithacus, Neritus and

Polyctor had built. From this fountain the citizens drew their water. A grove of black poplars completely encircled it and the water, ever so cold, ran down thither from a crag crowned by an altar to the Nymphs. Every wayfarer paid reverence there. Here it was they encountered Melanthius the goat-herd, son of Dolius, who with two herd-boys was bringing in the pick of all his goats for the suitors' supper. When he saw the pair he broke into abuse, calling them every vile and shameful name; which put Odysseus mightily about. 'See one beast escorting another!' he cried. 'How the God joins like with like. Whither, you rogue of a pig-keeper, will you take that hang-dog beggar, that gorbel-lied mar-feast? His sort hang about, scratching their backs against ever so many door-posts, and whine not for swords or cauldrons but for orts of food. If you lent him to me for helping at my place to clean stalls or fodder the kids, why he could drink much butter-milk and plump out his spindle-legs. But having acquired none but bad habits he will not attempt a job so long as he can go begging through the town and pester everyone to feed his gross paunch. Yet listen to my telling you what will surely happen if he ventures to the great palace of Odysseus: showers of foot-stools flung by manly hands will whizz round his head or crack sharply against his ribs while they pelt him through the hall.'

So he reviled; and in passing he back-heeled Odysseus savagely in the rump, but nevertheless failed to jolt him off the path, so solidly he stood. Odysseus was in two minds, if he should not lift his cudgel to bludgeon him out of his senses, or tackle him low and bang his head against the ground. However he mastered himself to take it quietly; but the swineherd with a glare of disgust lifted his hands to pray aloud: 'O fountain-nymphs who are daughters of Zeus, if ever Odysseus burned on your altar the fat-smothered thighs of rams or kids, then grant my petition and let him return; let some God restore him. How he would toss to the winds all this sham splendour with which you deck yourself to parade the city; while faithless shepherds let your flock run to ruin.' Melanthius called back, 'Beshrew me, but the dog talks as if he would bewitch us. Upon a day I shall take him far from Ithaca in a fast dark ship and let his sale bring me a fat profit. O that Apollo of the silver bow would strike Telemachus today in his house, or the suitors settle his account, even so faithfully as Odysseus has died in some far land.' With that parting shot he left them to plod on, while by a short cut he gained the palace, entered it and sat amongst the suitors opposite Eurymachus who was very partial to him. The servers brought him meat and the housekeeper bread, for his eating.

Step by step Odysseus and Eumaeus were drawing near. They halted when the music of the polished harp broke on their ears as Phemius struck up his song to the company. The hero caught the swineherd's hand and said, 'Eumaeus, of a truth this dwelling of Odysseus is noble, easily picked out and recognizable amongst many. See how it rises stage beyond stage with its courts all properly walled and coped, and its double doors so securely hung. No man could reckon it cheap. And I can tell there are many men banqueting within, for the smell of roast hangs round, and loudly rings the lyre which the Gods have made to chime so well with feasts.' To which you, Eumaeus, answered, 'Well may you notice that, if you have any wit at all. But now let us think what to do. Will you go first into the great house and join the suitors, while I stay here? or you remain without and I precede you? Settle it quickly, for if they see you dawdling outside, they may smite or throw something. Weigh my words.'

Odysseus replied, 'I have you: you address a sensible man. Go in front while I wait here. I have no more to learn about beatings or stonings. With all those accidents of sea or battle my heart is grown wholly callous. Let what may be go on the reckoning. Yet it is deplorable there is no hiding humanity's chief curse, this clamorous belly which launches so many proud ships to the affliction of enemies beyond the sterile seas.' As they talked a dog lying there lifted head and pricked his ears. This was Argos whom Odysseus had bred but never worked, because he left for Ilium too soon. On a time the young fellows used to take him out to course the wild goats, the deer, the hares: but now he lay derelict and masterless on the dung-heap before the gates, on the deep bed of mule-droppings and cow-dung which collected there till the serfs of Odysseus had time to carry it off for manuring his broad acres. So lay Argos the hound, all shivering with dog-ticks. Yet the instant Odysseus approached, the beast knew him. He thumped his tail and drooped his ears forward, but lacked power to drag himself ever so little towards his master. However Odysseus saw him out of the corner of his eye and brushed away a tear, which he covered by quickly saying to Eumaeus in an off-hand way:

'Strange, that they let such a hound lie on the dung-hill! What a beauty to look at! though of course I cannot tell if he has speed to match, or is merely one of those show-dogs men prize for their points.' Eumaeus answered, 'That is the hound of a man who died far from home. If only he could recover the fire and life that were his when Odysseus left for Troy, how your eyes would open at seeing such speed and power. Put him on the trail and no quarry ever escaped him, not even in the densest thickets, so keen he was of scent. Now he has fallen low, his master having perished abroad and the heartless women caring for him not at all. Slaves, when their master's control is loosed, do not even wish to work well. Ah, the day a man's enslaved, Zeus robs him of half his virtue!' With this word he plunged into the house, going straight along the hall amidst the suitors; but Argos the dog went down into the blackness of death, that moment he saw Odysseus again after twenty years.

Telemachus, being the first to notice the swineherd come in, waved and called him forward. He peered about till he saw the trestle on which the carver would sit whenever he had much meat to divide amongst the feasting suitors. This he carried to the other side of Telemachus' table and there straddled it. The usher served him a portion, with bread from the basket. On his heels Odysseus entered, a miserable aged beggar to all seeming, halting on a stick and ragged. He sat down on the door-tread, a beam of ash, and leant against the cypress wainscot which the old-time carpenter had planed so smoothly and plumbed upright. Telemachus called up the swineherd, gave him a whole loaf from the fair basket and a double handful of meat and said, 'For the newcomer, with my instructions to go round and beg of all the suitors. Shyness and destitution are poor bed-fellows.' The swineherd on hearing this went across and said emphatically, 'These, stranger, from Telemachus, who bids you go round and beg of all the suitors. Modesty, he says, sits ill on beggars.' Odysseus for response prayed aloud: 'O royal Zeus, make Telemachus happy on earth and ensure his heart's desire.' He took the present in both hands, laid it on the sorry wallet between his feet and made his meal there, while the musician sang. When he was satisfied, the song had ended and the clamour of the suitors was loud across the hall: but then Athene's spirit visited Odysseus and prompted him to solicit hunks of bread off them, as a test to distinguish the just from the lawless – though not even so would she save one man of them all from fate.

Accordingly he set off by the right, to beg from each man in turn with outstretched palm like a trained mendicant. They had compassion and began to give, in surprise asking one another who and whence this man was. Melanthius the goat-man then gave tongue, crying, 'Hear me, suitors of our great Queen, and I will tell you about this stranger whom I have seen before. The swineherd introduced him here. As to who or what he is, that I cannot say.' The news made Antinous short with Eumaeus. 'Infamous swineherd,' he called out, 'why bring this thing to town? Have we not vagabonds enough, paupers whose pestering turns our stomachs while we feast? Do you reck so little that they swarm here and eat up your lord's substance as to add another to the list of them?' Eumaeus replied, 'An ungenerous speech, Lord Antinous, be you ever so noble. Who invites or constrains a stranger to his board, unless he happens to be some creative man, a prophet or healer or worker in wood, or perhaps some surpassing musician with power to give joy by song? Such men are asked the world over. But beggars – who invites them to prey on him? You are always harshest of the suitors against the servants of Odysseus, and especially against me. Yet I complain not while staid Penelope and godlike Telemachus remain in the palace.'

Telemachus hushed him. 'Hold your peace, Eumaeus. Never enter into discussion with Antinous, whose custom it is to rail upon us angrily and inflame the company.' Then to Antinous: 'Is it out of love, Antinous, with a father's feeling for his son that you would have me arbitrarily expel this stranger from our house? God forbid. Instead I pray you take somewhat and give it him yourself. Far from grudging this, I urge, I enjoin you so. Disregard Penelope and my great father's servants. No? Your heart prompts you this way not at all? Truly you would rather feed yourself than give a crumb away.' Antinous retorted, 'Telemachus, pride and temper run away with your tongue. If all the wooers gave him what I am going to give, this house would be quit of him for three months or so' – and as he spoke he hooked out into view from under the table and poised in his hand the footstool on which his lithe feet had rested during the feast.

But all the others were giving Odysseus presents and stuffing his wallet with bread and meat. Really it seemed he might regain his door-sill unscathed after feeling the temper of the Achaeans: only he paused facing Antinous to adjure him direct. 'Alms, my kind sir: for you seem to me not the meanest of the Achaeans but their kingliest. As such you owe me a greater hunk of bread than any, and so should I hymn your praise the length and breadth of the earth. Once I had my house and was rich, with crowds of servants and what else composes a decent life. Charity to waifs of all kinds and degrees was then my habit. But Zeus stripped me – surely it was Zeus – when he sent me roving with pirates to distant Egypt and disaster. In Egypt's mighty river I stationed my fleet and commanded my stout companions to bide by their ships, on guard while the scouts went ashore to spy. But the scouts began wantonly plundering the land, killing its people and carrying off its women and children. An alarm was raised and there came against us great hordes that filled the country-side. Panic took hold of my followers. They broke, and were slain or taken: but my lot was to be sent away by the Egyptians to Cyprus, as a gift to Dmetor, son of Iasus its valiant king, who happened to be with them. From Cyprus am I come to you so miserably.'

Antinous roared back: 'What murrain brought this kill-joy here to curdle our feast? Leave my table. Stand away there, clear, or again you will find yourself in a bad Egypt and bitter Cyprus. The impudence of the beggar! to visit unabashed every man here and solicit alms, which they heap upon you so freely and carelessly because it happens to be another man's property, and plenty still remains!' Odysseus drew off a little and said, 'It grieves me that your breeding should not compare with your looks. If you, thus sitting in another's house, refuse me one crumb from his plenty, it follows that at your own place, with you there, no suppliant would get even a grain of salt.' At this saying fury possessed the heart of Antinous. With sinister leer he ground out, 'For your saucy speaking I shall make sure you do not get away from the hall in good order'; and upon the word he swung his footstool and hurled it to hit him on the right side, just where the arm roots into the back.

Odysseus stood up against the blow like a rock; only he wagged his head in silence, while a black rage swelled within him. He reached his doorstep, laid the bursting wallet on the floor and sat down to say, 'Listen, O suitors of the great Queen, while I unburden my mind. There is no soreness or rancour over wounds received in battle, where a man defends his neat or his grey wethers. But here Antinous assaults me in an affair of the belly, that pestilent member which everlastingly afflicts us. If there are Gods and Avengers for the poor, may the crisis of death overtake Antinous before his wedding day.' Antinous rejoined, 'Keep your place, stranger, and eat, and hold your tongue: or else quit, lest the lads punish your words by dragging you hand and foot through the house till you are torn in ribbons' – but actually he had greatly vexed the company so that in succession these reckless young lords were protesting to him and saying, 'Your striking this unhappy waif was a sin, Antinous, which will seal your fate so surely as there is a

God in heaven. Not to mention that these very Gods are always disguising themselves as travellers from abroad and roaming our settlements to note human good or ill.' However he would not abide the others' remonstrances. As for Telemachus, though the anger grew within him, yet he too only shook his head dumbly at witnessing his father assaulted.

When Penelope heard of a man's having been beaten in the guest-hall she cried before her maidens, 'Oh that the great archer, Apollo, may smite you, Antinous, as you have smitten!' and matronly Eurynome observed, 'If our prayers were answered, never a one of these would see another Dawn fairly enthroned.' Penelope said to her, 'Ah, mother, every one of them is hateful and all their desires are evil: but Antinous is black doom itself. A wretched stranger under spur of necessity wanders round the house to beg, and all give him something and fill his wallet, until he comes to that one, who smites him with his stool behind the right shoulder.'

So she held forth to her handmaidens from her chair in her room, while Odysseus was eating. Then she summoned the swineherd and said, 'Good Eumaeus, bid the stranger come up to receive my hearty greeting and be asked if he has heard anything of Odysseus, or seen him, perchance; for he looks a much-travelled man.'

And your reply to that, O Eumaeus, swineherd? 'Ah, Queen, if only the Achaeans would grant you a moment's peace! How his tales would enchant your very wits. I had him for three nights and kept him three days in my homestead: for he came straight to me when he escaped his ship. Yet he could not exhaust this history of his mishaps. Spellbound he held me at my own fireside while I yearned for him to go on for ever, as the sight of a bard with the god-given art of entrancing song makes men yearn to hear him so long as he will sing. He claims a family acquaintance with the house of Odysseus, and to be a Cretan of Minos' race, made by misfortune to roll round the world till he reached here. He says he has heard of Odysseus near-by, in the rich Thesprotian land, alive and bringing all kinds of treasure home with him.'

Then Penelope cried, 'Bring him quickly to tell me this to my face, while those others sit in our gates or house, rejoicing to the top of their bent. Intact in their homes lies all their wealth, bread and sweet wine, with none but their house-thralls to consume it: while they haunt us day by day, sacrificing our oxen and sheep and fat goats, and bibbing our precious wine in their revels. Our entire wealth goes to wrack for need of one like Odysseus to defend it from ruin. Ah, if only he might regain his country! How very soon he and his son would repay these men their outrages!'

While the words were yet on her lips Telemachus sneezed so vehemently that the house resounded. Penelope laughed. Then she hastily repeated to Eumaeus, 'Now call the stranger instantly. Did you not hear how my son sealed all I said with that sneeze? It spells no half-measures for the suitors, but utter death and doom for every individual man. Note this too: if I find that what he says is truth I shall clothe him in tunic and cloak most handsomely.'

Off went the swineherd on his urgent errand, to say, 'Venerable stranger, Penelope the wise, the mother of Telemachus, calls you; having a mind to enquire about the lord for whose sake she has suffered so much: and if she approves your good-faith she will give you the clothing you sorely need and let you go on begging in the town, to profit your belly amongst all the well-disposed.' Odysseus replied, 'I would readily tell Penelope what I know and I have good information upon Odysseus, having endured ill-luck in his company: but I fear this horde of irritable suitors with their rude arrogance towering into the iron skies. Just now that man yonder struck me very sorely as I went inoffensively through the house; and neither Telemachus nor any other saved me. So let Penelope bridle her eagerness and wait upstairs till the sun goes down. Then let her find me a seat nearer the fire – my clothing, as you well know from my first coming to you, being threadbare – and question me upon her lord's returning home.'

Back went the swineherd with this message: but hardly had he crossed her threshold than Penelope cried, 'Not bringing him, Eumaeus? What ails the tramp? Is he too afraid of someone or does our palace scare him? A timid man makes a sorry beggar.' Eumaeus answered, 'What he says is only what everyone feels about keeping clear of these bullies' violence. He wants you to delay till sunset; and that would benefit yourself, O Queen, by letting you be alone when you question him and get his news.' Wise Penelope said, 'Perhaps the stranger's caution is right. Surely of all living men these suitors are the most outrageous and extravagant.' So the queen: but the swineherd had said all he wished.

Back he went to the suitors' gathering, to put his head close to Telemachus' ear and whisper so that none overheard: 'Beloved, I am going. I must see to the swine and all – my livelihood and yours. I leave you to manage here: but make it your first concern to guard yourself and ensure no harm befalls you. They wish you all the evil there is, this mob of Achaeans. Zeus confound them before their mischief reaches us!' Said Telemachus, 'Amen, father: go after the time of supper, but return early tomorrow with sound beasts for sacrifice. The Immortals and myself will regulate this business.'

The swineherd sat once more on his smooth trestle till contented with meat and drink. Then he forsook the courts and hall-full of banqueters. The day was ending, and their merriment broke out into dancing and singing: while he went back to the pigs.

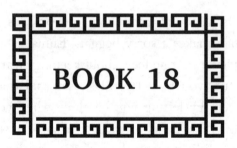

BOOK 18

Then arrived on the scene a vulgar tout who used to cadge his living everywhere round Ithaca and had the champion gluttonous belly of the world, that put no bounds to his eating or drinking: yet he got no muscle and no vigour by it, for all his bulky look. Arnaeus, his respectable mother had called him at birth; but all the lads nicknamed him Irus, because there was never an errand he would not run. His coming now was to pick a quarrel with Odysseus and expel him from his own house. So he floutingly began, 'Outside the porch, old one, or you may be haled forth by the leg. Cannot you see how all these give me the wink to throw you out? But I should be sorry to do that. So off with you instantly, before our difference turns to blows.'

Deep, devious Odysseus eyed him hard and replied, 'Sir, I am doing you no hurt and saying nothing; nor do I resent the bounty these reserve for you, however liberal it be. The door-sill is amply wide for both of us and you have no call to be close with strangers' goods. You seem, like me, a wanderer: just as dependent on the Gods for happiness. Wherefore do not rouse me with show of fists, lest I forget my years, lose temper and sully your breast and mouth with blood. Yet thereby should I gain a calm tomorrow: for afterward, I think, you would never frequent the house of Odysseus again.' This angered Irus the tramp. He cried, 'Tut, tut! the pot-belly nags away like an old cinder-quean. I shall play on him my wicked trick, that two-handed chop; to spatter the teeth of his jaw about the ground as a boar in the crops rattles down grains of corn. Gird yourself, then, to let all these see our fight – yet how dare you stand up to a much younger man?'

Thus vigorously did each abuse the other on the polished threshold under the high entry, till the dignified Antinous became aware of them. He laughed out right musically and called to the rest, saying, 'My dears, here is such luck as we never had before; real sport from God. Irus and our stranger are challenging each other to fisticuffs. Let us make a match of it, instantly.' Then they sprang up, laughing, and pressed round the two scare-crow tramps; but Antinous called, 'Just a moment, Sir suitors. Roasting there by the fire lie those goat-paunches we stuffed with fat and blood and reserved for supper. Suppose we let the better man, after he has won this fight, go over to take his pick of them, and make him ever after free of our feasts; to be the only beggar allowed inside, begging?'

His proposal gained favour, till Odysseus, with crafty intent, said, 'But, friends, an old man worn with toil cannot fairly fight a young one. It is my mischief-making belly that eggs me on to earn this thrashing. So promise me on oath, everyone, not to foul me for Irus' sake with some heavy hand-stroke that will lay me at his mercy.' All solemnly swore as he wished; and after the oath Telemachus said, 'Stranger, if your pride and pluck move you to mate this man, have no concern for any Achaean. He who strikes you will have the crowd upon him. Witness myself, your host; and thereto agree Prince Antinous and Prince Eurymachus, men of judgement.'

All approved. Odysseus kilted up his rags like a loin-cloth, baring his massive, shapely thighs, his arching shoulders, chest and brawny arms. Attendant Athene magnified the limbs of the shepherd of the people. The suitors were startled out of their wits and stared at each other, saying, 'Such hams has the old fellow brought out from his rags that soon our tout will be outed by an evil of his own procuring.' Their boding shook Irus to the core. The workmen had to truss him forcibly: they brought him on with the flesh of his limbs quaking in panic. Antinous spoke to him sharply: 'Now, bully, you were better dead or not born, maybe, if you will start so in terror of an old man crippled with suffering. Let me tell you this, for certain. Should he best you and win, I shall thrust you into a black ship for export to the continent; to King Echetus, bane of the earth, who will hack off your nose and ears with his cruel knives and tear away your privy parts for throwing all raw to his dogs as food.' These words gave the trembling a deeper hold upon his limbs.

However they haled him into the open, and there the two squared off. Royal Odysseus was puzzling himself if it were better to smite the other so starkly that life would leave him where he fell, or to tap him gently and just stretch him out. On the whole the gentle way seemed right, to save himself from too close notice by the Achaeans. So when they put up their hands and Irus hit at his right shoulder Odysseus only hooked him to the neck under the ear and crushed the bones inward, so that blood gushed purple from his lips and with a shriek he fell in the dust, biting the ground and drumming with his feet. The suitor lords flung up their hands and died of laughing; but Odysseus took him by the leg and dragged him through the entrance, across the yard and to the outer-gate, where he propped him with his back against the precinct-fence and his beggar's crutch between his hands, remarking bitterly, 'Sit there and play bogy to the dogs and pigs: but unless you want a worse beating never again set up your silly self as beggar-king.' Then he reassumed his sorry wallet, the poor burst thing with a mere string for strap, and walked back to the door-step where he sat once more. The suitors, still laughing merrily as they trooped past into the hall, hailed him with, 'Zeus and his Immortals grant you your ambition, stranger, and fulfil your heart's wish, for your having ended that insatiable tramp's begging up and down. Now will we trade him to the mainland, to King Echetus, mankind's worst enemy.' Odysseus rejoiced at this fair omen; and Antinous set beside him the great tripe-pudding all bubbling with its blood and fat, while Amphinomus picked him two loaves from the basket and pledged him thus in a golden loving-cup: 'Your health, venerable stranger. May there be happiness for you hereafter, in place of the many woes you now endure.'

Odysseus replied, 'Amphinomus, apparently you take after your enlightened father: for I have heard how Nisus of Dulichium was decent and rich. You whom they call his son seem approachable. So now attend closely and mark what I say. Of all that creep and breathe upon her, Earth breeds no feebler thing than man. While the Gods grant him vigour and limber joints he says that evil can never overtake him: and when the blessed Gods doom him to sorrow he must harden his heart and bear that too. Man's free-will on earth is no more his than the daylight Zeus ordains. Once I might have held a place in society, only that I (with infatuate reliance upon my father and kinsmen) let my pride and strength run wild. Might everyone take example thereby to abjure lawlessness and accept God's providence evenly and without cavil! Yet here are the suitors just as lawlessly employed in spending the substance and pestering the wife of a man who, I tell you, will soon regain his friends and country. Indeed he is near. May some power waft you away home, to miss meeting him when he stands at last beneath his roof-tree – for I think he and the suitors will not be separated, then, till blood has flowed.' He ended and spilled the ritual drop before setting his lips to the honeyed wine. Then he restored his cup to that marshal of the people who went back down the hall with bowed head in distress of mind. A foreboding of evil chilled his spirit; yet it did not save him from fate, for Athene had appointed him to meet death at the hands and spear of Telemachus. For the while he sank once more upon the throne from which he had risen.

Goddess Athene now put it into the mind of Penelope, the royal daughter of Icarius, to appear before the suitors and inflame their hearts – while gaining distinction with her husband and son. So the Queen laughed mirthlessly and said, 'Eurynome, my heart urges me to visit these suitors in all their hatefulness: and I would also speak a timely word to my son, adjuring him (for his good) not to haunt the company of intolerant men whose kindly speaking is only a mask for infamy.' The old dame replied, 'Your proposal, my child, is fitting. Exhort your son and spare not: only first wash yourself and make up your cheeks, so as not to show him this tear-stained face. Unrelieved grief is not wholesome, and your son is now a man. Have you not much prayed the deathless ones to let you see him bearded?' Said Penelope, 'Your partiality, Eurynome, must not flatter me to cleanse and anoint myself with unguent. The Gods of high Olympus took away what appeal I had the day my man embarked. Summon Antonöe and Hippodameia to support me in the hall. Unattended I go not amongst the men: modesty forbids.' The old crone went off down the house to call these women and speed them.

Another notion came to Athene, who breathed down sweet sleep upon the daughter of Icarius, so that she leaned back in slumber on the long couch, with all her joints relaxed. As she thus lay the Goddess was giving her immortal gifts to bewilder the Achaeans. First of all she refined the beauty of her face with the imperishable salve used by well-crowned Cytherea whenever she goes featly dancing with the Graces. She made her taller and fuller to the eye and whiter than ivory freshly sawn: so having worked her pleasure the Goddess departed as the white-armed maids chattered in from their room. Drowsiness left Penelope, who said, rubbing her cheeks, 'That was a pretty trance which overlaid my sorrow. Would but chaste Artemis grant me, here and now, a death as calm; and save me an eternity of heartgrief and sickness for my peerless lord, who surpassed the Achaeans in all nobility.' With this on her lips the fairest of women went down from her shining upper room (not by herself, for the two maids attended her) till she reached the suitors. She took her stand by the great column which upheld the roof; she spread her bright head-veil before her face. One to either side stood the trusted maids. The vision of such loveliness enfeebled her courtiers' knees and filched away their hearts with desire. Each man prayed that his might be the luck to lie abed with her.

She addressed her dear son: 'My Telemachus, your feelings and your reason are not so stable as they were. Your childish nature was particularly knowing: but now that you are grown of age, your instincts and judgements fail. Yet any stranger setting eyes on your tall beauty would know you for some great man's heir! Consider what has just now passed, in your letting this stranger be mishandled. What would be the outcome of a guest's suffering brutal injury in our halls? You would incur public obloquy and contempt for ever and ever.' Telemachus answered reasonably: 'My mother, I do not resent your being vexed at this. Agreed that lately I was a child; but now I can distinguish good and evil and comprehend them. Yet I cannot order all things according to reason, for these men's wicked imaginings pull me hither and thither and I get help from none. Still, this broil between Irus and our guest did not end in the least as the suitors wished, for the stranger proved the doughtier. By Zeus and Athene and Apollo! would that these suitors in our palace might every one lie vanquished in house or court with hanging head asprawl, as Irus now squats by the precinct-gates lolling his drunk-like head, not able to stand upright or make off home (wherever home may be) because his limbs are all abroad.'

So the one answered the other: but Eurymachus rose to compliment Penelope. 'O daughter of Icarius, if only the remaining Achaeans of Iasian Argos might see you, this press of suitors feasting in your halls would be augmented by tomorrow's sunrise. You outshine your sex in features, stature and intellect.' But Penelope sadly rejoined, 'My charms of face and form, Eurymachus, the Immortals reft from me, what time the Argives, with lord Odysseus, sailed for Ilium. If he were back to shelter my existence I should have a fairer and a wider fame: but now I am made sad by all these ill-fortunes God has imposed. Listen: when he left his native strand he took me by the wrist, by this right wrist, and said, "Dear wife, I fear not quite all of us mail-clad Achaeans can live through this campaign: for the Trojans are described as fighters, good with javelin or bow, and expert managers of the swift-pacing horses that oftenest decide the issue of a well-matched fight. So I cannot tell if heaven will grant me a home-coming or retain me in the Troad. Hence you must take charge here. Study my father and mother in the house as you do now; or even more, perhaps, to replace my absence. But when you see our son a bearded man, then feel free to marry again as you will and leave your home." Thus he enjoined; and his period is accomplished. The night comes which will see me a victim of the wedlock I loathe, one more misfortune for this ill-starred soul bereft of happiness by Zeus and further harried by this new-fangled courtship. Such conscienceless devouring of another's livelihood is clean contrary to rule. Properly, when rivals compete for the hand of a lady of family and fortune they should bring their own fat flocks and beeves to feast her friends, and give her costly gifts.'

As he listened Odysseus laughed to hear her cozening gifts from them and speciously keeping their hearts' lust in play, while preserving her very different purpose: for Antinous replied, 'O discreet Penelope, take what gifts the Achaeans will willingly bring in. No decent man shirks giving. Yet understand that we are not going to our own places, or elsewhere, till you have married the worthiest Achaean.' All cried assent; and charged their attendants to collect her gifts. The page of Antinous brought a lovely ample robe, embroidered throughout. It was fitted with twelve toggles of pure gold, each pin complete with looped fasteners. From Eurymachus there arrived an elaborate chain, strung with beads of amber like golden sunshine. The attendants of Eurydamas fetched a pair of triple-drop pendants, so clear that they sparkled brilliantly: while the squire of Peisander, King Polyctor's son, brought from his place a necklace that was a choice jewel. Every Achaean contributed something. Her maids took up the precious tribute and away she went to her room upstairs.

The company whiled away the evening hours with dancing and joyous singing, very well amused; and the darkness of night came down upon their gaiety. Then three fire-stands were set out along the hall to light it, and about them piles of kindling wood, good dry stuff, long seasoned but freshly split. Into each heap were sorted firebrands and the house-maidens took turns to feed their blaze until bold Odysseus said to them: 'Maids of the long-absent King, away with you to your honoured mistress' quarters. Sit there to divert her while you twirl yarn on the distaffs or comb wool for her with your fingers. I will maintain these men's light, nor yield to weariness though they should fancy to outwear the enthroned Dawn. I have stout endurance.'

His words made them exchange glances and giggle. Only fresh-faced Melantho mocked him vilely. She was Dolius' child, reared and tended by Penelope like a daughter and indulged with every bauble she set her heart on. Yet did she have no feeling for her lady's woes, but was Eurymachus' light of love. 'O shabby guest!' she now rudely cried, 'are your wits unhinged that instead of seeking fit lodging in some smith's booth or public house, you thrust in here and impudently enlarge your mouth amongst our lords? Or perhaps drink has gone to your head; or maybe you are a natural and so talk gustily always. Or did your over-coming beggarman Irus unbalance you? If so beware lest one stronger than Irus arise and hurl you forth all bloody from great buffets on your pate.' Odysseus glared back and said, 'Bitch, I shall instantly find Telemachus to tell him your words; and he will hew you in pieces where you stand.' His fierceness appalled the women, who believed what he said and scattered through the house with terror in every shivering limb: while he took his stand beside the flaring braziers, tending them and staring round, yet with his thoughts far away, fixed on what would be.

Athene was determined to provoke the suitor lords to sharper scorning, whose sting should pierce the heart of Laertes' son; so Eurymachus began to sneer at his expense in the others' hearing, to excite their ridicule. 'Listen, O suitors of the famous queen, while I speak my mind. Surely this fellow's coming to the hall of Odysseus is a godsend. I fancy the main blaze of torchlight shines from him, from that polished head unruffled by the littlest hair!' Then he turned to the stormer of cities and asked, 'Stranger, would you enter my service if I hired you for my outlying farm, to build dykes of dry stone or plant timber trees? You should be sufficiently paid and get rations all the time, good clothes and shoe-leather. But alas! I fear you are a mere waster, through and through, who will refuse employment while you can tout round the country-side and cadge to gratify your bottomless appetite.'

Odysseus replied, 'Ah, Eurymachus, if only there might be a working match just between us two during the late springtide when the days are long: in a hay meadow, perhaps; me with a well-curved scythe and you with one like mine; our match to last all day, foodless, and far into the gloaming, with grass yet to spare! Or draught oxen of the finest, great flaming beasts lusty with feed, well matched in age and pulling-power, and fresh: also a four-team field of loam that turns cleanly from the coulter. Then should you see what a long straight furrow I would drive. Or Zeus might, this very day, stir us up one of his wars; and I get a target, two spears and a skull-cap of good bronze fitting tight to my temples. Then, when you saw me abreast the forefront of the battle, you would rant no more nor ridicule my belly. Enough of this! You are an ill-natured cad, puffed up to think yourself someone by association with these few weaklings. Ah, if Odysseus came back to his land, how quickly would those wide doors become too narrow for your rush to safety through the porch.'

The retort swelled the anger of Eurymachus, who glared at Odysseus and cried sharply, 'Wretch! I shall see that your big talk before this crowd gets you into instant trouble. Your impudence! – has that wine touched your wits? Maybe you always play the public fool; or are you above yourself through beating poor scapegrace Irus?' While shouting he snatched up his footstool; but Odysseus for fear of him ducked downward by the knees of Amphinomus of Dulichium. So the stool struck the cup-bearer's right hand. He uttered a groan and measured his length in the dust; while his spouted flagon clanged loudly as it rolled. A gasp from the suitors ran the length and breadth of the hall: they exclaimed among themselves: 'O that our foreign visitor had died before he got here, and spared us this disorder and falling out over two beggars! Now the contagion of malice will spread, to spoil our delight in the luscious feast.'

Telemachus rose in reproof. 'My lords, you are mad. Some God excites you, or do you fail to carry your food and liquor? You have feasted too well. Go home now and sleep just as soon as you like –

though of course I force no man away.' As they bit their lips in astonishment at such plain speaking Amphinomus intervened: 'Friends, that is proper comment and we have no ground for offence or tart reply. Hands off the stranger and the servants of the house. Cup-bearer, fill all round that we may offer libation before going away to sleep. We can leave the stranger to Telemachus, his host.' All were pleased with this. Brave Mulius, the squire who attended Amphinomus from Dulichium, mixed them a bowl and served it. They poured to the blessed Gods and themselves drank of its sweetness: then, heart-full, they went to their rest.

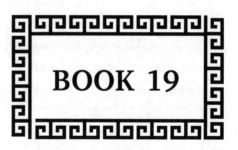

BOOK 19

Odysseus lingered where he was in the hall, nursing his schemes to kill the suitors with Athene's help. Suddenly he spoke out to his son: 'My Telemachus, let us now stow away all the serviceable weapons; and for reasoned excuse, when the suitors ask you why, say, "To save them from the fire-reek: for they have become so tarnished by smoke as not to look like the same weapons Odysseus left here when he sailed for Troy. Also the graver thought came to me from above that some day in wine you might yield to anger and disgrace the hospitality of this courtship by wounds given and taken. Iron has that attraction for men."'

In furtherance of his father's words Telemachus called to Eurycleia the nurse: 'Mother, pray keep me the women in their quarters while I transfer my father's costly war-gear to the store. The things are getting so sooted, with no one to care for them since he went. I was a baby then; but now I would put them where the fumes of the fire will not reach.' Eurycleia answered, 'It would be as well, my child, if you made a habit of caring for the house and the preservation of its goods: but who is going to light you at work, if you will not have the maids whose office that is?' He replied, 'The stranger here. Though a man come to me from the ends of the earth I will not have him idle while he eats at my expense.' This saying cut off her speech: the well-fitting doors clashed behind her. Up sprang Odysseus and his noble son, to start carrying off helmets, bossed shields and sharp spears; while Pallas Athene with a golden lamp made their way beautifully bright.

Telemachus gasped out, 'Father, my eyes behold a miracle. The sides of the hall, its roof-beams and pinewood framing and the tall columns glow with lambent flame. Some God must be here in the midst; one of the heavenly host.' 'Hush,' said Odysseus, 'repress your thoughts and ask no question. This is the mode of the divinities of Olympus. To bed with you, and leave me here to probe the feelings of the serving-women and your mother. Grief will make her question me by and large.' Telemachus duly crossed the hall, under its flaring torch-light, to seek the room where he always lay when sleep's bounty visited him. Through this night, too, he rested on his couch for Dawn to come: while Odysseus waited alone in the hall, still meditating the suitors' destruction by aid of Athene.

Like Artemis or golden Aphrodite Penelope appeared from her room. In its wonted place before the fire they had set her chair, an early piece turned in ivory and silver by Ikmalius the artist, who had added an extension forward from the seat to serve as foot-rest: and this was upholstered with a great fleece. In such state Penelope sat, while from their part of the house her bare-armed maids pressed in to clear the tables of the plentiful broken bread and the cups which those haughty ones had used. They raked out the embers from the braziers and piled them high again with fresh logs, to afford light and heat.

But Melantho began again upon Odysseus: 'Hanging about still, plaguy stranger, to prowl through the darkened house peeping at the maids? Put paid to your supper, wretch, and get outside the gate. Quickly too, or you will be chased out at the point of a fire-brand.' Odysseus, looking at her hardly, said, 'Damsel, why persecute me with such malignity? I know I am dirty. I know I am ragged. I do beg round the country-side, as I needs must. It is the way of paupers and home-less men. Once, like my fellows, I had a house and was prosperous, with crowds of freedmen and the other trappings of an easy life. In those days I often helped such-like waifs, no matter what their need or nature. Only Zeus brought me down: God's will be done. One day, woman, you too may lose this pride of place wherefrom you now dominate the maids, for your lady might fall out with you, or Odysseus return. There is still hope of that: while supposing he is really dead and gone, his son, Telemachus (like him, by grace of Apollo), is old enough now to notice it whenever a servant of the house misconducts herself.'

Penelope overheard his speech and called up the maid for reproof. 'Bold brazen piece!' she rated her, 'the great secret in your life is not hidden from me. Your head shall pay for it. Also you know perfectly (having heard me say it) that the stranger waits in the hall because I mean to question him upon my husband, so grievously lost.' She turned to Eurynome: 'Bring a bench and spread it with a sheep-skin for the stranger to sit and hear me and reply. I want all his tale.' Quickly the place was set and then Penelope opened, with, 'Stranger, my first enquiry must be – whence are you and who? What town and parents?' and Odysseus said, 'Lady, no mortal man could resent your least saying. High and wide as heaven your fame extends, pure as the glory of some god-fearing king of a populous powerful race, by virtue of whose equity and good governance the masses prosper and the dark earth abounds with wheat or barley and the trees bow down with fruit and the ewes lamb infallibly and the sea yields fish. Enquire of me, here in your house, upon every imaginable thing save only those of my race and country. Their memories would fill my heart too full of woe. I am a very melancholy man; but it is unbecoming to sit in another's house sobbing and sighing, for such promiscuous grief makes things worse. Further, one of the maids or even yourself, Lady, losing patience with me, might cry out that the tears in which I wallow derive from an overload of wine.'

Penelope replied, 'Stranger, my beauty went forfeit to the Gods the day my husband sailed with the Argives for Troy. Should he return to cherish me my fortune and favour would improve. As it is Heaven afflicts me too sorely. All the island chiefs court me uninvited and ravage the estate: while I neglect my guests, the suppliants that come and even heralds on mission, to eat my heart out for Odysseus. Men urge my re-marriage: but over that I lead them a fair dance. I was inspired to build me a monster loom upstairs, on which I set up a great, fine-threaded linen weave, telling them by and by, "My lords and suitors, be patient with me (however much you wish me wedded now great Odysseus is lost) till I complete this shroud against the inevitable day that death shall smite Laertes, the aged hero, low. I would not have my threads idly wind-scattered, lest some Achaean woman find me blameworthy – with good reason should this once-wealthy man lie unhoused." They honoured my request. All day I would weave and after dark unravel my work by torch-light. So for three undetected years I fooled them, but by connivance of my traitorous and despicable maids they caught me in the act as the fourth year drew toward its close. Their wrath forced me to finish the winding-sheet incontinently, and now I can find no other excuse or means of shirking this marriage. My parents insist on it; my son resents the inroads upon his income caused by the suitors' forced entertainment and is very conscious of their expensiveness, he being now a grown man, house-proud and honourably endowed by Zeus with wits. Yet do tell me of your family, for you cannot be the fabulous child of some crag or oak-tree.'

Odysseus said to her in answer, 'O honoured wife of Odysseus, must you indeed press me about my family? Very well: you shall have it, though the telling entails great pain, as is ever the way with men who have spent years in sorry vagabondage from city to city. Hear your answer. Amidst the wine-dark sea lies Crete, a fair rich island populous beyond compute, with ninety cities of mixed speech, where several languages co-exist. Besides the Cretans proper there are Achaeans, Cydonians, Dorians of tossing crests and noble Pelasgians. The capital is Knosos, ruled by Minos, who from his ninth year talked familiarly with great Zeus. He was my grandfather, King Idomeneus and myself being the children of Deucalion, his son. I had the honour of being called Aethon but was the cadet, Idomeneus being elder and preferred.

He accompanied the sons of Atreus to Ilion in the war-fleet, so giving me the chance of seeing Odysseus and playing host to him when an adverse wind forced him to leeward of Maleia and ashore in Crete, while Troy-bound. He only just escaped the storm but made the difficult port of Amnisus by the cave of Eileithyia; and there stopped. Presently he visited our city to ask after Idomeneus, claiming close and esteemed friendship. Only Idomeneus had sailed for Ilium ten or eleven dawns before; so I had the bringing of him to our palace where I could entertain him with all courtesy and nobility, because of our abundant wealth. I found him, and the troop that followed him, in barley-meal and dark wine from the public magazines; and collected all the cattle they needed for sacrifice. Twelve days these noble Achaeans passed with us while a northerly gale (excited by some wrathful God) raged so madly that they could not even stand upon the shore. On the thirteenth the wind fell and they put out.'

As he spun them, his lies took on the hue of truth; and as she listened, her tears rained down till her being utterly dissolved, as the snow laid upon the lofty peaks by the west wind melts before the breath of the south-easter and streams down to fill the water-brooks. So did her fair cheeks stream with grief for the husband who was sitting beside her in the flesh. Even Odysseus pitied his unhappy wife, but crafty purpose kept his eyes hard, with never a tremor to break their steady stare from eyelids that might have been of horn or iron. She wept her fill and ceased; to say, 'Now before everything, Stranger, I must test you to make sure it was really my husband and his glorious company you entertained, as you allege. So tell me of his dress. Describe him and the fellows in his train.'

Odysseus answered, 'Lady it is hard after so long; twenty years have passed since he came and went: but I will recite the impression he left on my mind. Odysseus himself wore a heavy purple cloak; lined self, it was. His brooch of wrought gold was double-bowed. Its flat bore the design of a hound holding down a dappled fawn with his fore-paws and watching it struggle. All admired how the dog was made (in the metal) to be eyeing his prey while gripping it by the throat; and how the fawn's feet writhed in convulsive effort to escape. Also I noted the sheen of the tunic that fitted his trunk as closely as clings the sheath to a dried onion, smooth like that and shining like the sun. The many women could not take their eyes from it. Let me recount another thing for you, as there can be no certainty that Odysseus wore these clothes at home and did not have them given him for the voyage by some friend or host, he being greatly beloved, a man almost beyond compare amongst Achaeans. Myself when re-conducting him respectfully to his ship presented to him a bronze sword, another good doubled purple cloak, and a fringed tunic. But he had a herald with him, a man rather older than himself; whom I can describe as well, for he was stooping and dark-faced, with clustering curls. His name? Eurybates. Odysseus, finding him sympathetic, prized him beyond his other men-at-arms.'

His words renewed her longing to weep, for she recognized the authentic proofs he showed. She cried herself out and said, 'Till now, stranger, you have been an object of compassion. Henceforward you shall be privileged and loved here in my house. The garments you describe I furnished from my store and packed for him; adding the burnished pin to be his ornament. Alas that I shall never have him back with me, home in his own dear land! An ill-season took Odysseus in his hollow ship to desTroy, that cursed place whose name shall not pass my lips.'

Odysseus urged her, 'Lady of Odysseus, melt not your heart nor mar your face with further grief for your lord. Though I cannot blame you, seeing how many women lament the dear dead fathers of their children, husbands not to be mentioned in the same breath with Odysseus, who all agree was godlike. Yet dry your tears, to mark what I now say frankly, and with assurance. Very recently I had news of Odysseus returning. He is alive and near-by, no further than the rich Thesprotian land; and well, for he has collected and brings with him great store of choice treasure. Only he lost all his retinue and ship in the sea this side of Thrinacia, when Zeus and Helios were wroth with him for his men's killing the cattle of the Sun. The crew perished to a man in the waves: but the currents brought him ashore riding the ship's keel, to the Phaeacians who are near-Gods by race. These almost worshipped him and gave him great gifts, offering to bring him safely here – in which case he would have been back already: but he preferred to fetch a long compass round and further enrich himself. Odysseus is wiser at profit-turning than any of us. No one matches him there. Pheidon king of the Thesprotians (my informant) swore to me in the act of libation at his house that both ship and crew to bring Odysseus home stood ready. He sent me first only because a merchantman was clearing for Dulichium. He showed me Odysseus' stored wealth; and what was there of his in the royal treasury would suffice his heirs for ten generations. The king said he had gone to Dodona to hear Zeus counsel him, out of the tall leafy oak, upon the manner of his return to Ithaca, whether it should be open or secret, after so long. I assure you, and swear to it, that he is safe, well, near and about to regain his friends and land. Bear me witness Zeus, the supreme and noblest God, as also the hearth of great Odysseus to which I have attained. As I have said, all things shall come to pass. During this cycle of the sun, between the waning of the present moon and the next, will Odysseus arrive.'

Penelope replied, 'Ah, stranger, should that come true my bounty will rain on you till all comers praise your state. But my heart warns me that the contrary will be the way of it. Odysseus will never return, nor you secure your passage hence: for today we have not in our house masterful ones like Odysseus – was there ever an Odysseus? – to greet guests of merit and speed them onward. Let be now. Women, prepare the bath and make down the stranger's bed, with quilt and rugs and glossy blankets, that he may arrive snugly before Dawn's golden throne. And be prompt in the morning to wash and anoint him, that he may sit at table within the hall beside Telemachus. Any one of these bullies who offends him shall learn to his vexation that he has done himself no good in his suit here. But tell me, stranger, how you adjudge me to transcend all women in character and resource, while I leave you sitting here weather-beaten and in tatters at your meal? Man's day is very short before the end, and the cruel man whose ways are cruel lives accursed and is a by-word after death: while the righteous man who works righteousness has his renown bruited across the wide earth by guests, until many acclaim such nobility.'

Odysseus protested, 'O great and grave spouse of Odysseus, I foreswore rugs and smooth blankets that day the snow-clad hills of Crete faded in my long-oared galley's wake. Let me lie as I have lain through many wakeful nights. How many dark hours have I not endured on rough couches till the well-throned Dawn! Baths for my feet appeal to me no more, nor shall any waiting-maid of yours lay hand on me – save you have some aged and trusty woman upon whose head have passed sorrows like mine. Of her tending I should not be jealous.' Penelope said, 'Dear stranger, among all the great travellers received in this house, never has one in speech given proof of such grateful discretion or juster insight than yourself. I have a shrewdly-conducted old dame, the nurse whose arms received my unhappy lord from his mother the day of his birth, and who tended and nourished him devotedly. She is frail now, but can wash your feet. Rise, prudent Eurycleia, to serve this man of your master's generation. Who dare say that the feet and hands of Odysseus are not, today, old like his? Hardship does so soon age its men.'

At the Queen's words the old servant covered her face with her hands and burst into scalding tears, while she bewailed Odysseus: 'My child, my child! And I cannot help. Despite that piety of yours Zeus has hated you worse than all mankind. Never were such fat thighs, such choice hecatombs consumed to the Thunder-lover as when you prayed him for calm declining years in which to educate your splendid son. Yet you alone are denied a home-coming. Is Odysseus, when seeking hospitality in some foreign palace, mocked by its women as all these curs, O stranger, mock at you? For shame of their ribald vileness you will not let them tend your feet; but in me the wisdom of Penelope has found you a glad ministrant. For her sake do I wash your feet; but for your own too, my heart being touched and thrilled. Why thrilled? Because we have had many way-worn strangers here: but never have seen such likeness as yours, I say, to Odysseus, in shape and feet and voice.'

With presence of mind Odysseus exclaimed, 'Old woman, all who have set eye on both of us remark it. They saw what you say, that we are exceedingly like.' While he spoke the hoary woman had taken the burnished foot-bath and poured in much cold water before stirring in the hot. Odysseus had been sitting towards the hearth, but now sharply turned himself to face the shadow, as his heart suddenly chilled with fear that in handling him she might notice his scar, and the truth come to light. Yet so it was, when she bent near in her washing. She knew it for the old wound of the boar's white tusk that he took years ago in Parnassus, while visiting his mother's brother and noble Autolycus, their father, who swore falser and stole better than all the world beside. These arts were conferred upon him by Hermes the God, who lent him cheerful countenance for the gratification of his kids' and goats' thighs burned in sacrifice.

Autolycus once visited Ithaca, to find his daughter just delivered of a son. Eurycleia brought in the baby and set it in his lap at the end of supper, saying, 'Autolycus, invent a name for this your dear daughter's son – a child much prayed for,' and Autolycus had answered, 'Son-in-law and daughter, name him as I shall say. Forasmuch as I come here full of plaints against many dwellers upon earth, women as well as men, so call him Odysseus, for the odiousness: and when he is a man make him visit the palace of his mother's family at Parnassus, which is mine, and I will give him enough to send him joyfully home.' And so it came about. Young Odysseus went for his gifts and Autolycus with his sons welcomed him in open-handed courtesy, while his grandmother Amphithea embraced him to kiss his face and two lovely eyes. Autolycus told his famous sons to order food. Hastily they produced a five-year-old bull which they flayed and flensed, before jointing its limbs to piece them cunningly small for the spits. After roasting them they served the portions round; and day-long till sunset all feasted, equally content. After sunset when the darkness came they stretched out and took the boon of sleep. At dawn they were for hunting, the sons of Autolycus with their hounds. Odysseus went too. Their way climbed steep Parnassus through the zone of trees till they attained its wind-swept upper folds just as the sun, newly risen from the calm and brimming river of Ocean, touched the plough-lands. Their beaters were entering a little glen when the hounds broke away forward, hot on a scent. After them ran the sons of Autolycus, with Odysseus pressing hard upon the pack, his poised spear trembling in his eager hand. A great boar was couching there in a thicket so dense and over-grown as to be proof against all dank-breathing winds; and proof, too, against the flashing sun-heat and the soaking rain; while its ground was deep in fallen leaves. About this rolled the thunder of their chase. When the tramp of men and dogs came close the boar sprang from his lair to meet them. With bristling spine and fire-red eyes he faced their charge. Odysseus in the van eagerly rushed in to stick him, brandishing the spear in his stout hand: but the boar struck first with a sideways lift of the head that drove in his tusk above the man's knee and gashed the flesh deeply, though not to the bone. Odysseus' return thrust took the beast on the right shoulder, the spear-point flashing right through and out. Down in the dust with a grunt dropped the boar, and its life fled. Then the sons of Autolycus turned to and skilfully bound up the wound of gallant godlike Odysseus. They staunched the dark blood with a chanted rune and made back at once to their dear father's house, and then Autolycus and the sons completed his cure, made him great gifts (delighting a delightful guest) and punctually returned him to his own land of Ithaca. Laertes and his lady mother, in welcoming him home, enquired of everything and especially of how he suffered that wound: and he recounted the whole story of the boar's gleaming tusk that ripped his leg while he hunted Parnassus with the sons of Autolycus.

Now as the old woman took up his leg and stroked her hands gently along it she knew the scar by its feel. She let go the foot, which with his shin splashed down into the tub and upset it instantly with a noisy clatter. The water poured over the ground. In Eurycleia's heart such joy and sorrow fought for mastery that her eyes filled with tears and her voice was stifled in her throat. So she caught Odysseus by the beard to whisper, 'You are my own child, Odysseus himself, and I never knew – not till I had fondled the body of my King.' Her eyes travelled across to Penelope, meaning to signal that her beloved husband was at home: but Penelope failed to meet this glance or read its meaning, because Athene momently drew her thought away. Odysseus' right hand shot out, feeling for Eurycleia's throat, and tightened about it, while with his left he crushed her to him and muttered, 'Would you kill me, nurse, you who have so often suckled me at your breasts, when I at last return after twenty years of manifold misfortune? Now you have guessed this and the God has flashed its truth into your mind, keep it close, not to let another soul in the house suspect. Otherwise, believe me – and I mean it – if Heaven lets me beat the suitor lords I shall not spare you, my old nurse though you be, when I slaughter the other serving-women in my hall.'

Wise Eurycleia protested, 'My child, what a dreadful thing to say! You should know my close and stubborn spirit and how I carry myself with the starkness of iron or rock. Allow me, in turn, to suggest a point for your considering. If the God delivers you the bold suitors, then let me rehearse to you which women of the house disgrace you and which are innocent.' He replied, 'Nurse, why trouble? There is no need: on my own I can note them, and class each one. Keep your news to yourself and commend the issue to the Gods.' Thereupon the beldam hobbled off through the house for water to replace what had been spilled; and Odysseus after being washed and anointed with smooth olive oil dragged his bench nearer the fire to warm himself, carefully hiding the scarred leg beneath his rags.

Then said Penelope, 'Stranger, only a trifle have I to put to you now: for soon it will be the hour of happy sleep which comes so graciously to man, however sad. But not to me; Heaven has overburdened me with griefs beyond measure. During the daytime I glut myself with sorrow and lament, having my own duties to see to, and my house-maidens' work: but night falls and the world sleeps. Then I lie in my bed and the swarming cares so assail my inmost heart that I go distraught with misery. You know how the daughter of Pandareus, the sylvan nightingale, lights when the spring is young amidst the closest sprays and sings marvellously; the trills pouring from her colourful throat in saddest memory of the son she bore King Zethus, darling Itylus, whom she unknowingly put to the sword and slew. My troubled mind quavers like her song. Must I stay by my son and firmly guard all my chattels, my maids, the towering great palace itself, out of reverence for my lord's bed and what people say? Or shall I go off with the best of these Achaeans who court me here and proffer priceless gifts? While my son was an unthinking child his tender years forbade my leaving home to take a new husband: but he, tall now and come to man's estate, prays me to leave for my father's house, so greatly does he grudge the sight of the Achaeans swallowing up his substance. Wherefore listen, and read me this dream of mine. I have twenty geese on the place, wild geese from the river, who have learned to eat my corn: and I love watching them. But a great hook-billed eagle swooped from the mountain, seized them neck by neck and killed them all. Their bodies littered the house in tumbled heaps, while he swung aloft again into God's air. All this I tell you was a dream, of course, but in it I wept and sobbed bitterly, and the goodly-haired Achaean women thronged about me while I bewailed my geese which the eagle had killed. But suddenly he swooped back to perch on a projecting black beam of the house and bring forth a human voice that dried my tears: "Daughter of Icarius, be comforted," it said. "This is no dream but a picture of stark reality, wholly to be fulfilled. The geese are your suitors; and I, lately the eagle, am your husband come again, to launch foul death upon them all." With this in my ears I awoke from my sleep, to be aware of the geese waddling through the place or guzzling their food from the trough, just as ever."

Odysseus replied to her, 'Lady, this dream cannot be twisted to read otherwise than as Odysseus himself promised its fulfilment. Destruction is foredoomed for each and every suitor. None will escape the fatal issue.' But wise Penelope responded, 'Stranger, dreams are tricksy things and hard to unravel. By no means all in them comes true for us. Twin are the gates to the impalpable land of dreams, these made from horn and those of ivory. Dreams that pass by the pale carven ivory are irony, cheats with a burden of vain hope: but every dream which comes to man through the gate of horn forecasts the future truth. I fear my odd dream was not such a one, welcome though the event would be to me and my son. Let me tell you something to bear in mind. Presently will dawn the illfamed day which severs me from the house of Odysseus. To introduce it I am staging a contest with those axes my lord (when at home) used to set up, all twelve together, like an alley of oaken bilge-blocks, before standing well back to send an arrow through the lot. Now will I put this same feat to my suitors: and the one who easiest strings the bow with his bare hands and shoots through the twelve axes, after him will I go, forsaking this house of my marriage, this very noble, well-appointed house that surely I shall remember, after, in my dreams.'

Odysseus uttered his opinion again: 'August wife of Odysseus, do not hesitate to arrange this trial in the hall; for Odysseus of the many sleights will be here before these men, for all their pawing of the shapely bow, shall have strung it and shot the arrow through the gallery of iron.' Said Penelope, 'If only you would consent, stranger, to sit by me all night, entertaining me, sleep would not again drown my eyes. Yet mortals cannot for ever dispense with sleep, the deathless ones having appointed its due time to each thing for man upon this fertile earth. So I will away to my room and lie on its couch, the place of my groaning, which has been wet with my tears all the while since Odysseus went to destroy that place I never name. There shall I be lying while you rest here in the hall. Either spread something on the floor, or have them arrange you a bed.'

She ceased and went off to her shining upper room; not alone, for the maids trooped after her. So she lamented Odysseus, her dear husband, till Athene's kindly sleep closed her eyelids.

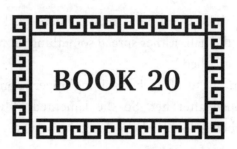

BOOK 20

Eventually noble Odysseus made his bed in the entrance hall, by stretching an untanned ox-hide on the floor and piling upon it many fleeces of the sheep sacrificed to Achaean appetite. Eurynome drew a mantle over him after he had lain down. Yet sleep would not come, because his heart was too active in planning evil against the suitors: for whom, besides, after a while those women that nightly played the strumpet poured out with laughter and loud jest from the servants' quarter. His gorge rose then: impulse and reason warred within him, now wanting to charge forth and give each whore her death, now to yield them a latest and last chambering. Over this his secret self snarled like a bitch standing guard over her helpless litter, when she stiffens with a growl to fly at any approaching stranger. So the anger rumbled within Odysseus at their lechery: but he smote his breast in self-rebuke, saying, 'Be patient, heart. You stood a grimmer trial, that day the bestial Cyclops devoured my splendid fellows. Steadfastly you bore it, till your cunning had frayed you a path from that cave you thought your death-trap.'

He so conjured himself and rated his passions that his soul's patience survived to the end: but the strain tossed his body about, like the basting paunch stuffed with blood and fat that a man who wants it immediately cooked will turn over and over before a blazing fire. In such fashion did Odysseus roll to this side and to that in the throes of wondering how his single self could get the many shameless suitors into his grasp. Upon his perplexity Athene in her woman's shape came down from Heaven, to stand above his head and say, 'Why still awake and watchful, O sorriest man of men, now you lie at last in your own house where are your wife and also your son – such a lad as everyone would wish his son to be?' And to her Odysseus replied, 'Alas, Goddess, your rebuke is justified: but my heart's debate was how one man might lay hands upon these wasters who keep the house in droves. And out of that rises the second and stiffer problem. Supposing the grace of Zeus, with yours, lets me slay them, where afterwards may I find sanctuary? Inspire me, pray.'

'Exigent wretch,' said the Goddess, 'others trust friends so much feebler than me, creatures all too human and not various: whereas I am very God and your buckler to the end of toil. Let me state you a naked truth. Though fifty troops of humans hemmed us round, all mad to kill outright, yet should you win through to lift their flocks and herds. So let yourself sleep. Watching all night is very wearying and presently you will be quitted of evil.' She spoke, shed a slumbering upon his eyelids and left for Olympus. Odysseus sank into the arms of sleep, a nerve-allaying sleep which ravelled out the tangles of his mind. But his loyal wife awoke and sat up in her soft couch to weep, before praying directly to Artemis: –

'Artemis, Goddess, daughter of Zeus! Only strike me through now with your dart and take my life utterly away – or let a whirlwind hurtle me down the darkling ways and fling me where the under-tow of Ocean joins the main! The whirlwinds thus paid the daughters of Pandareus, who had been orphaned in their home by the Gods' killing their parents. Aphrodite nourished them with goat-milk cheese and sweet honey and wholesome wine, Hera gave them beauty and insight above all women, and Artemis made them buxom; while Athene dowered them with every grace and art. Yet as Aphrodite was journeying to high Olympus to beg their crowning glory of fortunate marriages – and beg it of Zeus the Thunder-lover, who knows what is or is not destined for mankind – even then the Harpies of the storm snatched the girls away and cast them to serve the terrible Furies. O that the dwellers on Olympus would so blot me from human sight, or well-tressed

Artemis thrust me through, that as I went to my grave under the hateful earth I might yet carry with me the image of Odysseus unsmirched by dalliance with some baser man! I call that pain endurable if it makes one mourn day-long from the heart's great ache but permits sleep of nights, the sleep which assoils all good and ill concern, once it has lidded the eyes. But for me even the dreams vouchsafed by the powers are an affliction. Tonight, for example, there lay by me the image of my man as when he left for the war; and my heart leapt up, thinking it no dream, but truth at last.'

So ran her complaint till Dawn came, golden-throned: but then her sobbing pierced to the ears of Odysseus and mingled with his waking thoughts, to make him fancy she had discovered him and was there by his side. He rose to fold the cloak, and the sheepskins on which he had slept; then laid them on a hall-throne: but the ox-hide he took out of doors and spread for his praying to Zeus with uplifted hands: 'O father Zeus, if heaven's good will has led me safely home across the waters and the wilderness, despite terrible danger, then let the welkin yield some sign thereof from you, and waking humanity confirm it with an important word.'

This prayer Zeus the contriver heard. He pealed from out the mists veiling the radiant peak of Olympus, and made Odysseus glad; while the momentous word was uttered by a woman slaving at her quern near-by, in the mill-room attached to the palace of the people's shepherd. There all day twelve women strove their hardest, grinding barley-meal and flour, the marrow of man's strength. They were sleeping now with their stint of grain well ground – all save the feeblest one, who yet laboured: but at the thunder she too let her mill run down, to sigh out the word for which her King was waiting: 'O father Zeus, ruler of gods and men, this loud peal from a star-spangled sky without one wisp of cloud – do you thereby show some sign for man? Grant it import, I pray, even for wretched me. Let today's be the final and ultimate easy feast of the suitors in Odysseus' halls. To mill groats for them must my limbs be wrung with this excruciating toil. Make it their last supper, Lord!'

She breathed this out, and great Odysseus rejoiced for its aptness and for the thunder of Zeus. He told himself he had won his revenge upon the wrong-doers. Meantime the other maids of the great palace were stirring. They rebuilt the undying fire upon the hearth. Telemachus rose from his couch, a godlike figure of a man as he put on his clothes, before slinging his sharp sword about his shoulders and binding the handsome sandals to his lissom feet. He picked up his massive bronze-tipped spear and stood by the outer door to ask Eurycleia, 'Dear nurse, about our guest – was he honourably entreated as regards bed and food or left anyhow to fend for himself, as is so much my mother's way, woman of the world though she be? She falls over herself to please some worthless fellow and leaves a worthy man in utter neglect.' Faithful Eurycleia answered back, 'Child, you find fault where no fault is found. The man sat and drank all the wine he wished: but refused food on the plea of no appetite, though she pressed him. She would have had the maids make down a bed against his wanting to sleep: but he seemed so beaten and hopeless that he would not lie between blankets on a couch. Instead he had an undressed ox-hide and fleeces in the entrance hall. We put a cloak over him, too.'

After hearing her Telemachus, carrying his spear, left the house with two swift dogs at heel, making for the assembly-ground to meet the warrior Achaeans: while the dame began to hustle her maids, calling out, 'Rally round now and fall to work, some of you, on the floor, sweeping till your breath is spent – but first put water down – and then smooth the thrones' purple housings; while you others take sponges and clean down all the tables, swilling out the mixing-bowls and the handsome double-handled cups. All the rest fetch water from the spring, briskly there and briskly back. Very soon this morning will the house see its suitors again, today being the public festival.' She rained orders upon them and freely they obeyed. Full twenty set off for the fountain where the dark water flowed, while the others skilfully did out the hall. Then the freedmen began to appear. Some of these adeptly split kindling-wood till the women should return from the spring: but when they did come Eumaeus the swineherd was of the party, with his three fattest hogs. He left these rooting in the precincts, to address Odysseus in all courtesy: 'Stranger, have the Achaeans come to look upon you with more favour, or are they yet despiteful as they were?' and Odysseus rejoined, 'Ah, Eumaeus, may the Gods punish their outrages and the way these nefarious ruffians misuse another's house.'

So far they had got when Melanthius the goat-man appeared with two herders and the finest of their goats for the suitors' table. He tied his beasts under the echoing porchway and remarked to Odysseus with a sneer, 'You still pester the household, stranger, by your begging and refusal to leave? I think our affair will not be closed without you get a taste of fist. Importunity like yours is not decent. This is not the solitary Achaean banquet.' Roundly he abused him, but crafty Odysseus made no reply, only hanging his head in silence: yet within him his enmity increased. A third party arrived, Philoetius, a man of mark, who had with him a heifer for the suitors and more prime goats. He had been brought across by the boatmen of the public ferry. After tethering his charges securely in the porch he came over to Eumaeus, asking, 'Swineherd, who is this fresh stranger in our house? What race does he claim? Where are his people and their lands? Shabby he may be but his build is royal. A man meshed in the web of the Gods' wrath and made homeless soon shows the strain, even if he have been a King.'

He turned to Odysseus and held out a right hand, saying cordially, 'Greeting, sir stranger: may the future bring you happiness; for patently you are now in the toils of misfortune. Father Zeus, you are the deadliest of all Gods, in that you make no allowance for the men you have created, but tangle them in such sad and sorry pains. I sweat only to think of it and my eyes grow moist, remembering Odysseus, who if yet alive and in the sunshine may be ragged and adrift like this. But if he is dead, and gone down to Hades' mansions, then hear me bemoan the excellent Odysseus, who while I was yet a boy promoted me over his herds in Cephallenia. Yes, and these have so increased as to be beyond number, like ears of standing corn for multitude. Never did any man's broad-fronted cattle breed better. But these outsiders, disregarding the son of the house and slighting the Gods, make me bring in my beasts ever and again for their banqueting. Their latest freak is to share out the whole fortune of our missing King. I keep on turning the affair over in my mind, well aware how wrong it would be to go off, beeves and all, to a stranger's service while the heir lives; but certain that it is worse still to sit down here under such iniquities and herd my cattle for the benefit of men who have no claim to them. My position is unbearable. Long since I should have run off and engaged myself with some other mighty King, only that I keep thinking of this unhappy man and of how he might suddenly turn up from nowhere and chase the suitors helter-skelter through his house.'

Said Odysseus in crafty reply, 'Cow-herd, you display a goodly discretion. My judgement assures me upon the rightness of your instincts: so I shall tell you a thing on my solemn and lawful oath. O Zeus, greatest of the Gods, be my witness, and the hospitable table and hearth of great Odysseus by which I stand! You shall be yet in this place when Odysseus comes home. Your eyes shall see the fate you invoke meted these officious suitors.' The cow-man replied, 'May the son of Cronos fulfil your word, Stranger, to let you see how my hands should gratify my strength.' Eumaeus echoed his prayer to all the Gods that Odysseus might return: while the suitors in their place were again conspiring a death by violence for Telemachus.

But an eagle stooped from the heights of the sky and flew past on their left, bearing off a pitiful dove: whereupon Amphinomus rose and said, 'Friends, our plot to assassinate Telemachus is misjudged. Let us feast instead.' They accepted his verdict and marched to the palace of Odysseus, where they laid their cloaks aside upon seats before turning to slaughter the sheep, the goats, the swine and the heifer from the stock. They roasted the inwards and passed them round, then mixed wine in the bowls. The swineherd gave out the cups, stately Philoetius helped them to bread from the fair baskets and Melanthius poured wine. All set to and feasted.

௵௵௵௵௵௵௵௵௵௵௵௵௵௵௵௵௵௵௵௵௵௵௵௵௵௵௵

With subtile intent Telemachus had brought Odysseus within the hall, arranging him a small table and plain settle by the stone entry. He helped him to the inward meats and poured him wine in a golden cup, pronouncing, 'Rest you there and drink your wine among the men. Should abuse or assault follow from the suitors I shall be your defence. This place is not a public house but the palace of Odysseus which he won for me: so you, suitors, must govern your hearts and hands, to prevent breach of the peace.' Such bold speech from Telemachus made them bite their lips in amazement; but Antinous rallied them: 'What Telemachus says is severe and he threatens us starkly, Achaeans. Yet take it quietly. Zeus was not willing – or already we should have cut off his peevish railing in the hall.' However, Telemachus paid no heed to this, for already the heralds were going in procession through the town with the long array of beasts to be slain in the Gods' honour: and the long-haired Achaeans were gathering within the shady grove of Apollo, lord of the bow. There they roasted the flesh and drew it off the spits for division. Nobly they feasted, the servers helping Odysseus to his portion just like their own or another's: for that was the ruling of Telemachus, his dear son.

However Athene did not mean to let the suitors rest from provoking Odysseus, for she wanted their contempt to make his heart ache. Among the suitors was one especial ruffian, Ctesippus of Same, whose enormous wealth had emboldened him to woo the wife of absent Odysseus, and he now bayed forth in their midst: 'Hear me, suitor-lords, hear what I suggest! The stranger has had his share like the others, as is fitting. To stint a guest of Telemachus, whatever his sort, would be unjust and indecorous. But it is quite a while since he had it: so now I am adding my guesting-gift which will let him spare his old foot-washing hag a trifle, or tip some other palace servant.' Therewith he snatched a cow's foot from the dish before him and hurled it with a strong hand: but Odysseus inclined his head lightly to one side and avoided it, with a wry smile. It crashed harmlessly against the solid wall.

Telemachus was up to rate Ctesippus soundly. He cried, 'Very profitable for your peace of mind, Ctesippus, that you missed the stranger! Had he not dodged your shot I should have thrust you through the midriff with my war-spear and given your father the pains of your funeral, not your marriage, here. Let me finally warn you all against displaying violence in my house. I used to be a child; but have now come to the knowledge of good and evil. Necessity may lead us to stand impotently by while our sheep are butchered and our wine and food wasted, for one man can scarcely make head against many. Only make sure your enmity stops short of actual crime – otherwise, if you must persist in your murderous intent against me, hear my deliberate conviction; that death is better than longer looking upon your villainies – this outraging my guests and man-handling my servant-women all through the stately palace, to their shame.'

His outburst stilled them for a while. At last Agelaus, son of Damastor, said, 'My friends, when there has been plain speaking it is not a man's part to lose temper or complain. Let be the stranger and the servants of Odysseus' household. I would offer Telemachus a soft answer – meant for his mother too – hoping it may move them. So long as your hearts kept a vestige of hope for the return of Odysseus, your delaying and excusing the suitors vexed nobody. Clearly it was expedient, while a chance remained of his survival and return. But now it is plain that he is gone. So sit down beside your mother and put it to her that she must wed the best man and highest bidder. Then she will take over that other's house and let you comfortably assume your whole inheritance in free enjoyment of your food and drink.'

Telemachus protested, 'Indeed, Agelaus, I swear to you by Zeus and by all the pains my father suffered in dying or straying far from Ithaca, that the obstacle to my mother's marrying lies not in me. I implore her to choose whom she prefers and take him. I go so far as to offer countless presents if but she will. Only I shrink from ordering her unwillingly from the house. God forbid it should come to that.' Upon these words of Telemachus, Pallas Athene fired the suitors to a laughter that ran on and on till it crazed them out of their wits. Now they were laughing with mouths that were not their own, while blood oozed from the flesh they ate. Their eyes filled with tears and their souls were racked in agony. Godlike Theoclymenus wailed aloud, 'O unhappy men, what is this horror come upon you? A night shrouds your heads, your faces: it creeps down to your knees. Weeping and wailing flash back and forth. Cheeks stream with tears and a dew of blood beads over the smooth wall-panels. Ghostly forms throng the entrance and pack the hall itself, shuffling in long file through the murk towards hell. The sun is lost out of heaven and a dire gloom prevails.'

Laughter rang loud from the company as he unburdened himself, and Eurymachus son of Polybus rose to say, 'Our new-come visitor from alien parts has lost his senses. Quick, young men, escort him out and to the market-place. He fancies it is black night here.' Theoclymenus retorted, 'Eurymachus, I want none of your guiding. Eyes I have and ears, my two feet and a spirit not of the meanest. In their power will I pass the threshold, for I feel that evil – evil not to be shunned or avoided – looms over each single one of you suitors whose brutal and perverse imaginings pollute the house of Odysseus.' He quitted the hall, to receive honest welcome from Peiraeus in his house; while the suitors after an interchange of stares began to tease Telemachus by poking fun at his guests, repeating despitefully, 'Indeed, Telemachus, there can be no unluckier host. First you take in this lousy unknown tramp without profession and without prowess but insatiably bellied for eating and drinking, a perfect cumberer of the earth: and then your second guest stands up to play the prophet! Have my advice and make something by them. Let us pack them for sale aboard some many-oared galley bound for Sicily. You would get a good price that way.' Thus the suitors: but he ignored them, in the intensity of his silent gaze upon his father, awaiting the moment to lift hand against his tormentors.

Decorous Penelope had put her state chair just over against them and so heard all that passed. Not that their laughter had hindered the slaughter of many victims to furnish their juicy abundant meal. Though what ghastlier banquet could be dreamed of than this which the Goddess and the valiant man – trapping them after their own villainous example – were now about to provide?

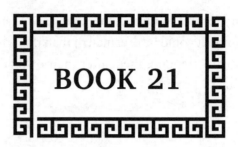

BOOK 21

For Athene chose this moment to introduce the means of bloody death, by prompting wise Penelope to ordain bow and pallid iron as gages of prowess for her suitors in Odysseus' halls. With her throng of escorting women the queen stepped from her room by the tall stairway firmly carrying the curved key (a noble key, bronze forged, with ivory shank) as far as the store chamber in the depths of the house, where the treasures of her king were laid up, his bronze, his gold, his patient-ly-wrought iron. Among them were the recurved bow with its arrow-case that yet held many arrows, each a groan-maker.

These had been given Odysseus years ago by a fellow-guest in Lacedaemon, at the hospitable house of Ortilochus in Messene where a whim of fate threw him into the company of godlike Iphitus, son of Eurytus. Odysseus had come thither on a suit affecting the whole community, for the men of Messene had lifted in their ships three hundred Ithacan sheep with the thralls minding them: and his father and the other elders had commissioned Odysseus (still a lad in years) to make this long journey on their behalf. As for Iphitus, he was in search of strayed horses – a dozen mares with sturdy mule-foals at milk. Later, these same beasts were to be the death of him, by bringing upon him that supreme man of action, Herakles, Zeus' bold son, who flouted the Gods and stained his hospitable board by the dastardly killing of Iphitus while a guest under his roof; and after the crime Herakles kept the strong-hooved horses in his palace for himself.

While thus searching, Iphitus met Odysseus and presented him with the bow which great Eurytus had carried before his time and, dying, left to the son of his lofty house. The return gifts of Odysseus were a keen sword and formidable spear – earnests of a cherished acquaintanceship that however failed to ripen into mutual entertainment because the son of Zeus too soon murdered godlike Iphitus, the giver of the bow; which great Odysseus preserved in his house as an abiding memorial of this beloved fellow guest, and never took with him on foray in his dun vessels. He would carry it only when he went about his own lands.

The fairest of women held on her way to the treasury till she stood on its oak threshold which had been dressed so skilfully smooth by the old-time workman – squared it, he had, by rule and trued the jambs upon it and set up his gleaming doors – and there she swiftly unbound the thong from the hook of the latch and thrust the key home with such decision that the door-fastenings snapped open. The roar with which the splendid doors sprang wide at the stroke of her key resounded like the bellow of a bull afield at grass; so abruptly they opened for her. She climbed to the high stand supporting the chests in which the clothing was laid away in spices. She reached up to its peg and unhooked the bow, all proper in its shining case, and sat herself there with it across her knees; and taking out her lord's bow cried bitterly a while. Then after her tearful sorrow had exhausted itself she proceeded again to the hall of the proud suitors, holding the recurved bow in one hand and also bearing its quiver-load of woeful arrows. Her women brought along in its chest the iron and bronze gear used by the king when he would play.

Once more in the suitors' presence the queen stood by the roof-pillar with her gauzy veil before her face and two trusty women flanking her. She called to her suitors and said, 'Hear me, my lords and courtiers that have haunted and beset this house and eaten and drunk here all the long time the master has been away, with only excuse and burden of talk your lustful desire to wed me and possess me for wife. Now, my suitors, see your test plain. Here I set the huge bow of godlike Odysseus. Whoso easiest strings the bow with bare hands and shoots an arrow through the twelve axes – after him will I follow, forsaking this house, my husband's home, a house so goodly and stocked with all life's comforts that remembrance thereof will come back to me, I think, hereafter in my dreams.'

Upon that she bade Eumaeus, the master swineherd, arrange the bow and the grey iron axes for the suitors: but Eumaeus burst into tears as he received them for handing over, and the cowherd in his place wept too at sight of the royal bow. They brought upon themselves the rebuke of Antinous who called out, 'You silly yokels with day-cribbed imaginations, twin fools, how dare you by floods of tears further distress that womanly heart which already lies prostrate in agony at losing a beloved husband? Sit you down and eat in silence or take your lamenting out of doors, being careful, however, to leave us that bow, the suitors' dire and infallible test. Not easily, I think, will that smooth bow be strung. In all this crowd there is never a match for the Odysseus I remember. How that peep at him sticks with me, child though I was.' This was what he said aloud: but in his heart of hearts he fancied his own chance of notching the string and shooting through the irons. Yet his actual destiny was to get the first taste of arrow from great Odysseus whom now he was himself contemning and egging on his fellows to contemn, there where he sat in his own hall.

Princely Telemachus cut across them with the cry, 'Alas and woe is me! Zeus drives me crazy. My beloved mother in her wisdom proclaims that she will forsake this house and cleave to a stranger – and I laugh out and go gay in my heart's folly. Step up, you suitors, with this prize in view. The lady has no peer in the Achaean country: not in Pylos the holy nor in Argos nor Mycenae: nowhere in our Ithaca or on the dark mainland. You know it all. What have I to do, praising my mother? Up with you; let us see what we shall see. Away with excuses for hanging back or putting off the bow-bending. Stay, why should I not try it myself? If I can string it and shoot through the iron I shall not so regret my mother's leaving home in some stranger's train, for I shall at least be living here and man enough to bear my father's arms.'

With this he slipped the keen sword and blood-red cloak from his shoulders, to heave himself upright. He began to set up the axes, hollowing one long trench for them all, getting them exactly in line and firming the earth about them with his foot. Every onlooker was amazed at how regularly he set them, despite his never having seen it done before. Then he took his stand by the main threshold and essayed the bow. Three times it quivered under his frantic efforts to string it, and three times he had to rest his muscles, though still the hope buoyed him of notching the cord and sending a shaft between the irons. Perhaps he might have summoned all his forces and succeeded at the fourth try, only Odysseus frowned him off it and checked his zeal. Whereupon Telemachus sighed that all could hear, 'Alas, must I go on being a feeble failure, or am I still too young to trust to my own hands for safety against attack? However, to it you with the stouter thews. Attempt the bow and let us get this contest over.' With this he laid aside the bow, propping it between the floor and the close-joined door frame: while the keen shaft he leaned against the showy crook of the latch.

As he resumed his throne Antinous the son of Eupeithes called out, 'Up with you in turn from left to right, fellows, the way our wine goes round.' His notion pleased them and so Leodes the son of Oenopus was the first to rise. As their augurer he had the end seat beside the splendid mixing bowl: but their violence so repelled him that he kept by himself in solitary loathing of the suitors. Yet now he led off by picking up the bow and its sharp arrow, over there by the threshold, where he felt the bow's stiffness but could not string it. Before ever it bent his hands gave way; his soft, untried hands. So he cried to the suitors, 'I cannot bend it, friends: let some other try. Indeed this bow will break many princes, body and soul: yet how much better is it that we die, than live in the failure of that ideal which holds us yearning here, day after day! Doubtless some one aspires with his whole heart's strength to marry Penelope, the bedmate of Odysseus. Let such a one try this bow and learn its lesson; and then divert his gifts to winning another of the well-robed Achaean women, while this one weds her fated best-bidder.' He, also, put down the bow to lean against the smooth doors, with the arrow against the door-handle, before going straight back to sit on the seat he had left; but Antinous named him in sharpest rebuke and said:

'Leodes, it shocks me to hear this dismal judgement escape your lips. Merely because you fail to bend it must this bow cost our bravest ones their lives or souls? In very truth your lady mother, when she conceived you, was not making a master-bowman: yet there are some amongst the distinguished suitors who will soon manage the stringing.' He turned to Melanthius the herder of goats, saying, 'Bestir yourself, Melanthius, and quicken the hall-fire. Put before it a broad trestle with sheepskin a-top, and fetch that great ball of tallow from within. Then after it has been warmed through and well greased we young men can prove this bow to conclude our test.' At his bidding Melanthius quickened the never-dying fire and brought near it the trestle with its sheepskin and the big ball of tallow from inside the house. The young men warmed the bow and did their best to string it, but failed. They showed themselves not nearly strong enough; but Antinous and Eurymachus kept themselves out of it – and they were the leading suitors, their best in general merit.

While this was happening the neatherd and swineherd of royal Odysseus had quitted the palace together. Odysseus himself followed them out through the courtyard and its gates, where he cleared his throat and said to them ever so smoothly, 'O herder of cattle and you, swineherd, am I to tell you something or keep it to myself? My impulse is to say it out. If Odysseus were to appear, somehow, suddenly – shall we say a God bringing him – how far would you help? Would you be for the suitors or for Odysseus? Show me the working of your hearts and minds.'

The keeper of his cattle then burst out: 'Ah, Father Zeus, only let that hope come true and him return, led by the spirit. So shall you witness how my hands would serve my might,' and Eumaeus echoed him in praying to all the Gods for the home-coming of resourceful

Odysseus. Thus assured of their hearts he quickly replied. 'But I am back again, my own true self, here at home after twenty years of hardship: to realise that of all my servants only you two long for my coming. From the rest I have not heard one prayer breathed for my return. So let me lay down to you what will follow upon God's giving me the victory over the haughty suitors. I shall find you a wife each and an endowment of chattels and houses built next to mine: and you shall rank with me hereafter as the fellows and blood-brothers of Telemachus. Now I will show you a sure and certain sign, to make you credit me from the bottom of your hearts. See my scar, given me by the boar's white tusk so long ago, as I went upon Parnassus with the sons of Autolycus.'

As he spoke he opened his rags to betray the great scar: and when the pair of them had studied it and knew it for sure, they wept and flung their arms about Odysseus, with most loving kisses for his head and shoulders. Odysseus had answering kisses for their heads and hands, so that truly the sun might have gone down upon their emotion, only for Odysseus pulling himself together to say: 'Now stop this sorrow and weeping, lest some one coming from the house espy us and report it within. Instead, go you back, not together but one by one, me first and you afterward, with a procedure fixed up between us. Understand that those suitor lords will one and all refuse me a loan of the bow and quiver: so you, Eumaeus, as you carry it up and down the hall must put it into my hands and then go tell the women to close the stout doors of their quarters, and should they hear men's voices from our side groaning or in dispute, let there be no running out of doors but a steady holding to their work within. While you, noble Philoetius, I tell off to shut and bar the gates of the court, lashing them together as quickly as you can.' Upon which he turned back into the stately house, to resume the seat he had left. Then the two serfs came in.

Eurymachus' hands still held the bow and turned it every way before the blazing fire to warm it; but nevertheless he utterly failed at the stringing. Deeply he groaned in his pride of heart and woefully he exclaimed, 'Alas, I sorrow for my own sake and for the general! It is bitter to forfeit this marriage, yet that is not the worst. There are plenty more Achaean women here in sea-girt Ithaca, and others in other cities. What I chiefly regret is our appearing to fall so short of godlike Odysseus in strength as not to be able even to bend his bow. The tale will disgrace us generations hence.'

Antinous the son of Eupeithes protested: 'Not so, Eurymachus, and you know why. To-day is sacred to the Archergod and his public feast. On it who will be bending bows? Put it down and leave it, and the axes too. We can let them stand. I fancy no one will venture into the great hall of Odysseus, son of Laertes, to lift them. Come on, have the server fill once more our cups that we may offer libation before the bow as it lies there in a hoop. To-morrow morning we will have Melanthius the goat-keeper fetch in the best goats of his whole flock, for us to offer thigh-pieces to the mighty archer Apollo before our trial of the bow and the ending of this contest.' Thus Antinous, and his advice pleased. The heralds poured water on their hands and their squires brimmed the bowls with wine all round; everyone offered and afterwards drank his fill.

But then craftily and subtly Odysseus spoke out, saying,

'Hear me, suitors of the famous queen, while I retail the promptings of my heart, making my main appeal to Eurymachus, and to godlike Antinous for his fitting counsel just now to leave the bow to the Gods' reference. In the morning the God will give mastery to whom he wills. Yet for the moment pass me this polished bow that I may test my hands and strength while you watch, to see whether there yet lies in me the virtue that once inhabited my supple limbs, or if the privations of a wandering life have wasted it right away.'

His words enraged them all and instantly, for fear lest he string the polished bow. Loudly Antinous rebuked him, 'Foreign wretch, are you utterly devoid of sense? Is this dining in our high company not enough for you? We let you eat your full share unmolested and hear our debate and conversation, which no other beggared stranger overhears. It is wine that plays the mischief with you, the sweet wine which ruins all who drink with deep and greedy gullet. It was the downfall of Eurytion the famous Centaur, in the house of brave Peirithous, during his visit to the Lapithae. The wine took away his senses and maddened him so that he did terrible things in Peirithous' house. The heroes went wild with rage and flung him out of doors after slicing his ears and nose with their cruel weapons; and away with shattered wits he went, hag-ridden by the burden of his folly. So began the feud between the Centaurs and mankind, the original injury being self-inflicted by immoderacy in wine. Wherefore let me warn you against the painful consequences of your stringing that bow. You will find no grace from anyone in this country, but we shall ship you promptly in a dark hull to King Echetus, that mutilator of the human race; and once with him you are doomed beyond hope. So drink up in all quietness and avoid challenging the younger generation.'

Decorous Penelope complained to him, 'Antinous, it is neither fair nor seemly to browbeat in this house any visiting guest of Telemachus, whatever his quality. Do you really envisage the stranger's taking me home and lying with me, if by prowess and sleight of hand he strings the great bow of Odysseus? Why he, in his own heart of hearts, has no hope of that. Let not a thought so ugly vex the soul of any one of you feasters. It would never, never do!' Eurymachus the son of Polybus replied to her, 'Wise Penelope, we do not contemplate his carrying you off. That is unthinkable: only we shrink from what some low-down Achaean – man or woman – might later say; such as "Poor creatures, these courtiers of the hero's widow, with their efforts and failures to string his polished bow until a beggarman came wandering by and strung it easily and shot through the iron." They will gossip so, to our shame.'

Penelope retorted, 'Eurymachus, the men who devour and dishonour a nobleman's house will not anyhow be accorded public respect: so why thus nice upon a detail? Our guest, this tall personable figure, claims that his father was a man of breeding. Up with you, therefore, and hand him the polished bow, to let us see. I tell you, I will make a firm offer. If he (by the ordering of Apollo) bends it I shall clothe him fairly in tunic and cloak, and give him a sharp spear and double-edged sword for defence against dogs and men; and also shoes for his feet and passage withersoever his spirit bids.'

Telemachus thus answered her: 'My mother, in the disposal of the bow there lives not an Achaean with more rights than I; to grant it or refuse, at my pleasure. If it so pleases me no chief from this craggy Ithaca, or from any other island right down to Elis of the stud-farms, shall prevent my giving these arms outright to the stranger, for his taking away. Off with you, then, to your quarters and your duties, the weaving and the spinning and the ordering of your maids' work. The bow is man's business and especially my business, as I am master here.' She turned, bewildered, into the house with this pregnant phrase of her son's laid up in her heart, and when upstairs again with her serving women she bewailed Odysseus, her sweet husband, till Athene shed a balm of sleep upon her eyes.

The worthy swineherd took up the bow; but then the whole crowd of suitors in the hall roared against him, stuttering in their young pride: 'Miserable half-wit of a pig-keeper, where would you carry that recurved bow? Let but Apollo and the other Immortal Gods hear our petition and soon shall those swift hounds you breed eat you alive amongst your swine, far from man's help.' Their threats so frightened him that he dropped his burden where he stood, all mazed with their many-voiced clamouring in the hall: but now Telemachus menaced him loudly from the opposite part, shouting, 'Carry on with the bow, ancient; if you obey all these you will be instantly sorry, when I take advantage of my youth and greater strength to chase you into the open country with volleys of flung stones. There is someone else I would as soon send sorrily packing from the house for their evil designs, had I only a like margin of power over the suitors.'

His outburst made them laugh so merrily together that their anger against Telemachus passed: and the swineherd went along through the hall with the bow till he reached Odysseus and put it into his hands. Then he called Eurycleia the nurse aside and charged her: 'Telemachus orders you, wise Eurycleia, to shut tight the stout doors of your quarter; and if any one of the women inside should hear the sound of groaning men from our part of the house, see that she comes not out but keeps quietly at work.' These words made her speech flutter and fall. She fastened the doors of the stately place, while Philoetius slipped stealthily out-doors to secure the gates of the courtyard. In its loggia there chanced to be lying the grass hawser of a merchantman. This he used to make all fast before he went in again to sit as he had sat, on his settle; watching Odysseus who still felt the bow, turning it round and round and testing it throughout, to make sure that worms had not riddled the tips during its lord's absence. Men turned to their neighbours and muttered, 'The fellow is a bow-fancier or expert, what? Perhaps he has something of the kind laid by at home; or is the ill-conditioned beggar planning to make one, by the way he twists it over and over in his hands?' – to which the next young scoffer might reply, 'May his luck, in that, end like his bow-stringing effort.'

Thus the suitors: but Odysseus the master of craft had by now handled and surveyed the great bow up and down. Calmly he stretched it out with the effortless ease of a skilled musician who makes fast both ends of a piece of twined cat-gut and strains it to a new peg in his lyre. Changing the bow to his right hand he proved the string, which sang to his pluck, sharp like a swallow's cry. Distress over-whelmed the suitors and they changed colour. Zeus declared himself in a loud thunder-peal; and long-suffering royal Odysseus rejoiced that the son of devious-counselled Cronos should make him a sign. He snatched up the keen arrow which lay naked there upon his table – all the others which the Achaeans were so soon to feel being yet stored in their quiver – and set it firmly upon the grip of the bow. He notched it to the string and drew; and from his place upon his settle, just as he sat, sent the arrow with so straight an aim that he did not foul one single axe. The bronze-headed shaft threaded them clean, from the leading helve onward till it issued through the portal of the last ones.

Then he cried to Telemachus, 'Telemachus, the guest sitting in your hall does you no disgrace. My aim went true and my drawing the bow was no long struggle. See, my strength stands unimpaired to disprove the suitors' slandering. In this very hour, while daylight lasts, is the Achaeans' supper to be contrived: and after it we must make them a different play, with the dancing and music that garnish any feast.' He frowned to him in warning: and Telemachus his loved son belted the sharp sword to him and tightened grip upon his spear before he rose, gleaming-crested, to stand by Odysseus, beside the throne.

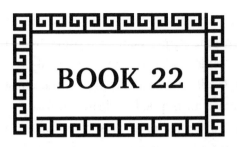

BOOK 22

Therewith the wily Odysseus shed his rags, grasped the bow with its filled quiver and made one leap to the door-sill, where he tumbled out the swift shafts at his feet before calling in a great voice to the suitors, 'At last, at last the ending of this fearful strain! Before me, by favour of Apollo if my luck holds, stands a virgin target never yet hit.' He levelled the bitter arrow at Antinous whose two hands were raising the splendid golden wine-cup to his lips, without suspicion of death in his heart – for who, at a thronged banquet, could conceive of any single man being bold enough to dare compass his violent death and bloody destruction? However Odysseus shot, and took him with the shaft full in the throat. Right through his graceful neck and out again went the point. He rolled over sideways, letting the cup fall from his stricken grasp and thrusting back the table with a jerk of the foot that threw his food, the bread and the cooked meats, to pollution on the floor. The life-blood spurted thickly from his nostrils.

One outcry broke through the house from the suitors when they saw the man fall. They sprang in terror from their thrones, and gaped all about the smooth walls, to find never a shield or great spear they could snatch up. They rained abuse upon Odysseus – 'Stranger, your wicked shooting at people makes this the last trial of strength in which you compete. It seals your doom. You go as carrion to the vultures, for having slain the crown of all Ithaca's young manhood.' They clamoured so, because they were persuaded his killing was not deliberate, their infatuation hiding from them the toils of death that enlaced each and every one: but Odysseus glaring at them cried, 'Dogs that you are, you kept harping on your conviction that I would never return from the Troad, and in that strong belief let yourselves ravage my house, ravish my house-maidens and woo my wife, while I was yet alive. You have flouted the Gods of high heaven and the consequent wrath of men: so now you are all trapped in death's toils.'

His words chased the pallor of fear from man to man, and wildly each one stared round for escape from this brink of disaster. Only Eurymachus found tongue, and he said, 'If you are indeed Odysseus of Ithaca come back to us, then you have substance for protest against the many offences committed by the Achaeans in your palace and estates. But the begetter of all your hurt lies there – Antinous, whose true spring of action was no great need or necessity for marriage, but a very different motive, ambition, which entailed the waylaying and killing of your son to make himself king over the whole of prosperous Ithaca. Cronos prevented him, and now he has met the death he deserved: wherefore your part should be one of forbearance towards this people who are your people, and a chance for us to make good publicly all that has been eaten and drunk in your guest-rooms, each of us subscribing as much as twenty oxen to recoup you with bronze and gold till your heart warms toward us. Meanwhile no man can make a stricture upon your rage.'

There was no softening of that glare as Odysseus rejoined, 'Eurymachus, not if you gave away to me your whole inheritance, all that you now own and yet may earn, would I relax my hands from slaughtering until the suitors have paid the last jot for their presumptions. Only flight or fight confront you now as escapes from ultimate death: and some of you, I think, will find no way of avoiding doom's abyss.'

The menace of him shook their hearts and knees; but Eurymachus had yet a word for them. 'O my friends,' he said, 'this man will not curb his ruthless hands. He would shoot us down from the polished threshold with that goodly bow and quiver that he has until we all be slain. Wherefore let us whip up the thrill of battle. Out swords, and hold the tables up as bulwark against his deadly arrows. Let us have at him in one rush to drive him off his doorstep, maybe: that way we can attain the city and raise an instant alarm, to ensure this man's never bending bow again.' Upon the word he bared his keen, two-edged bronze sword and sprang forward with an awful cry: but instantly Odysseus launched at him a flying arrow which struck him by the nipple of his chest and lodged deep in his liver. The sword fell from his hand and he went down doubled and writhing over his table, to spill the food and loving-cup upon the floor. His heart's agony made him hammer his brow against the ground and flail his two legs about till the throne rocked: then dimness veiled his eyes.

Amphinomus, naked sharp sword in hand, followed him in the rush to edge glorious Odysseus off the doors; but for him Telemachus was too quick, catching him behind the shoulders so fair and square that the bronze spear-point transfixed his breast. He crashed earthward full on his face, while Telemachus abandoning his weapon sprang away in fear that some Achaean might stab him whilst he was tugging at the long shaft, or cut him down while he stooped for it. So he ran off quickly to his father and paused by him to say excitedly, 'Father, now let me fetch you a shield and pair of spears and a bronze skull-cap with cheek-pieces. At the same time I can equip myself and provide for the swineherd and cowman. We had best be properly armed'; and Odysseus the man of judgement replied, 'Run for them, then, while I still have arrows; or they will force my unsupported self off from the doors.'

To obey his dear father's word Telemachus raced to the side chamber where the famous weapons lay. He snatched up four shields and eight spears and four of the bronze helmets with their heavy horse-hair crests, and came running with them back to his father. There he first arrayed his own person in the brazen arms; then the two freedmen put on the like noble panoply; and they all lined up by wary, cunning Odysseus who made great shooting whilst the arrows held out for his defence, each time bringing down an enemy until they lay in swathes;

but when the royal archer had no arrows left he put the bow aside against a polished return of the massive hall-entrance, while he passed a four-ply shield over his shoulders and dressed his great head in a close-fitting helmet, grim under the towering menace of its nodding horse-hair crest. He took up two brave bronze-pointed spears.

It chanced that through the main wall had been contrived a hatch with a shutter of framed boards, opening into a narrow passage beyond the top landing. Odysseus had ordered the trusty swineherd to take post there on guard, it being but a one-man approach: and now Agelaus spoke up, suggesting generally, 'Comrades, might not someone clamber through the hatch and thence warn the world outside, to get the alarm immediately raised? So this fellow will have shot his last.' But Melanthius the goatherd answered, 'That will not do, high-born Agelaus. The main gates to the court are dangerously near and the alley-way too narrow. One man of courage could hold it against all comers. Yet I think I can find you body-armour from the inner chamber: for surely there, and nowhere else, did Odysseus and his high-born son hide away their arms.'

Whereupon up went goatherd Melanthius through the smoke-vents of the hall, into the back chambers, whence he picked twelve shields with spears and crested bronze helms to match, and was soon back amongst the suitors, issuing them out. When Odysseus saw his enemies doing-on hauberks and brandishing spears he shook at the heart and knees, realising how heavy his task grew. He called to Telemachus in a sharp quick tone, 'My Telemachus, evidently one of those women inside is weighting the odds against us – or is it Melanthius?' And Telemachus answered from what he knew, 'O my father, the real blame for this lies on me and wholly on me. My faulty hand left the store-chamber's stout door unfastened, and they have spied after me too well. Now, good Eumaeus, go close it; and note if the meddler in our business is one of the women or that son of Dolius, Melanthius, as I guess.'

While they settled the plan, Melanthius the goatherd made his second journey to the chamber after other useful arms. The stout swineherd recognising him reported at once to Odysseus who stood close by. 'Royal son of Laertes, the villain is the man we suspected, and he is once again on his way to the store. Tell me plainly – shall I kill him if I can better him in fight; or bring him here, to pay for all the wickedness he has committed in your house?' Odysseus weighed his reply and concluded, 'However fiercely they attack, Telemachus and I can hold the raging suitors at bay inside the hall. So away with both of you and fling him down amidst the store-room, pinion his hands and feet behind him and lash him, back down, on a plank. Then make fast a twisted cord about him and hoist him up the pillar high into the roof-beams, where leave him to ebb out his life in lingering torture.'

They heard these orders eagerly and obeyed. They reached the chamber without the man inside it knowing, for he was right at the far end groping after more weapons. The two of them took stand either side the doorway and waited for Melanthius, who at last made to cross the threshold with a noble casque in the one hand and in the other a great old shield, now all warped with mildew, for it had belonged to the hero Laertes in his prime and the stitching of its straps had given from lying by so long. Then they leapt at once upon him, gripping his hair and haling him back into the room; where they cast him in terror upon the floor and bound him tightly, hand and foot, twisting the joints painfully behind him just as great Odysseus ordered, before they passed the stranded rope about his body and hauled him up the pillar to the rafters. And then how you baited him, O Eumaeus the swineherd! You said, 'There you are, Melanthius, fixed in the soft bed you deserve, where you can stretch out on watch all night long, sure to see golden Dawn ascend her throne from out the ocean streams, in warning that you must now drive your goats to the palace for the suitors' feasting.' So they left him, racked in bonds of agony.

They armed themselves again, fastened the shining door and came back to wary Odysseus; and then from the threshold these four men, breathing battle, faced the many champions that held the body of the hall. To them came Athene the daughter of Zeus, but like Mentor in form and voice: and Odysseus in his gladness at the sight of her cried out, 'Mentor, remember we were friends who grew up together, and I helped you often. Rescue me from ruin.' Though he spoke thus, he felt sure it was Athene, the inspirer of peoples; but the suitors booed from down the hall, especially Agelaus the son of Damastor, who threatened, 'Mentor, I warn you against letting Odysseus' smooth tongue lure you into helping him fight the suitors; for I think that will not in the long run defeat our aim to kill them both, father and son. After which we shall put an end to you, taking your head in payment for your foolish dream that you can affect things here. And when our swords have lopped away your strength we shall treat all your possessions, indoor and outdoor, as one with the wealth of Odysseus; forbidding your sons and daughters the use of your mansion, and your devoted wife any longer abiding in the town of Ithaca.'

That they should so threaten her made Athene's heart swell with rage into angry words, wherewith she turned and rent Odysseus, saying, 'How are your strength and manhood fallen, O Odysseus, since those nine years on end you battled with the Trojans for white-armed gentle Helen's sake, and slaughtered them by heaps in the deadly struggle, till Priam's spacious city bowed to your design! Dare you appeal for pity before the suitors' faces and let your courage fail you amidst your home and chattels? Hither, dear heart; stand by me and watch my work, to see how Mentor the son of Alcimus requites, even into the teeth of the enemy, the kindnesses he has received.' She gave him only words like these, and not unchallenged victory, because she had it in her mind yet to prove the force and fervour of Odysseus and his aspiring son. Away she flitted in the guise of a swallow to the smoke-dimmed rafters of the hall, and there perched.

So heavily had the arrows rained down that very many had fallen; but Agelaus the son of Damastor, Eurynomus, Amphimedon, Demoptolemus, Peisander (Polyctor's son) and wise Polybus still survived and stood out as natural leaders to hearten those suitors yet fighting for dear life. Now Agelaus exclaimed so that all his fellows heard, 'Aha, my friends, those peerless hands are ceasing to avail him any. Mentor has mouthed some empty words and gone. They are left by themselves up there on the landing before the doors. So be careful not to volley your long spears at random, but begin hurling, six at a time, and maybe Zeus will grant that Odysseus is hit and glory won. The rest amount to nothing, once he goes down.'

So he said; and they regulated their throwing according to his orders: but Athene made everything miscarry. One hit the massive door-jamb, another the great door itself, while the heavy bronze head of yet another's ashen shaft crashed upon the wall-face; and after his party had lived through this volley all unhurt, stout Odysseus prompted them, 'My friends, I say it is now our turn to fling into the thick of these suitors who deepen their former wickedness by such lust to spoil us.' They took careful aim and let fly their sharp spears. Odysseus killed Demoptolemus, Telemachus Euryades, the swineherd Elatus and the cowman Peisander. As all these tumbled to the immense floor and bit its dust the suitors fell back to the rear of the hall, while the others ran down and recovered their spears from the corpses. Then came the suitors' second critical cast of spears, most of which Athene again made to fall idly against door-post, door or wall: but Amphimedon's shot caught Telemachus on the wrist (only a graze, the blade just breaking the outer skin) while the long spear of Ctesippus ripped Eumaeus across the shoulder above the rim of his shield and glanced upward before falling to the ground.

The party led by wary Odysseus then threw back into the crowd, the waster of cities himself striking Eurydamas, Telemachus killing Amphimedon and the swineherd Polybus: while after them the herdsman flung, to hit Ctesippus in the heart and vaunt himself, saying, 'You loved your jibe, son of Polytherses, but the Gods are greatest: wherefore another time give them the word and let not your folly talk so big. This gift squares the neats-foot hospitality you gave divine Odysseus lately, while he was begging through his house.' As the keeper of the screw-horned herds declaimed, the others were stemming the rush hand to hand, the long shaft of Odysseus stabbing the son of Damastor; and Telemachus thrusting Leocritus, son of Euenor, in the pit of the stomach so shrewdly that the bronze spear-point went right through and he tipped headlong to earth, face down: while at that moment Athene from the high roof brandished her death-dealing Aegis. Their souls were terrified and they stamped down the long hall like a herd of cattle distracted and put to flight by some dancing gad-fly in the rush of the year when the days grow long: but the onslaught the four made upon them was a stooping from the mountains of crook-taloned, hook-billed vultures upon small birds, forcing them out of the skies to cower along a plain which yet affords no cover and no escape; so there they are harried to death, and men love the sport of it. Like that were the suitors buffetted every way up and down the hall, while the dismal crunch of cracking skulls increased and the whole floor seeped with blood.

Leodes in his extremity caught at the knees of Odysseus, loudly imploring, 'By your clasped knees, O Odysseus, pity me and show mercy. Never once, I swear, did I offend any woman in your house by word or deed. Rather would I give pause to the other suitors with such intent, though they would not be persuaded to restrain their hands from evil and therefore has this shameful death caught them amidst their sins. But am I, their wholly guiltless sacrificing priest, to be confounded in their number and perish with them, the good which I have done not being counted to me for charity?' Odysseus scowled down at him and cried, 'If you admit yourself these men's sacrificing priest, then how often have you not prayed in my own house for the happy issue of a homecoming to be removed from me, that my dear wife might follow you and bear you children? For that you shall not escape the grave's strait couch.' As Odysseus cried it, one powerful hand grasped the sword that still lay where Agelaus had dropped it, dying, and swung it free at his throat. So his head, yet praying for mercy, was confounded in the dust.

The bard, Phemius son of Terpes, who had sung for the suitors by constraint, had thus far escaped black fate. He was hesitating – and still fingering his loud lyre – near the hatch, in doubt whether he had best spring in and conjure Odysseus by his knees or flee the house to sit by the altar, so fairly builded outside to great Zeus of the Court, upon which Laertes and Odysseus had burnt many thigh pieces of oxen. As he turned it over, the better way seemed to clasp the knees of Laertes' son: so he set down the fragile lyre between the mixing bowl and his silver-mounted chair and himself darted forward to embrace the knees of Odysseus and beseech him with fluttering words: 'At your knees, Odysseus, I seek consideration and mercy. Remorse will overtake you hereafter should you kill, in me, a bard fit to sing to Gods as well as men: and from innate genius I do it, God having sown in me the seeds of every mode. I am like to hymn you divinely: where-fore curb your rage to cut off my head. Also Telemachus, your loved son, can vouch that in my case neither good-will nor avarice kept me in your house as musician for the suitors' feasts. They were so many and so violent that they could compel my attendance.'

God-fearing Telemachus who had heard his protestation called quickly to the father by his side, 'Let be, indeed, and keep your sword off this one: for he is truly innocent. Let us save our usher Medon, too, the guardian of my boyhood in the house; unless he has already fallen before Philoetius or the swineherd or met you raging through the house.' His word reached the ears of Medon, that discreet man, where he lay beneath a throne with the hide of a freshly-flayed ox wrapped round him to ward off the darkness of death. At once he crawled from under the throne, flung the ox-skin aside and darted forward to embrace the knees of Telemachus with the fervent prayer, 'O my dear, here I am. Master yourself and keep exhorting your father, lest he destroy me with that sharp sword in his excessive strength and rage against these suitors who wasted his worldly goods and ignored you in their recklessness.'

Odysseus smiled then and said to him, 'Take heart; Telemachus has redeemed you and preserved you for this time to learn in your heart of hearts and testify aloud the advantage of virtue over vice: but see that you and the full-throated bard leave the house and sit outside in the court away from the killing, till I have ended all that yet lies for me to do within'; and as he said it they were out of the hall and sitting by the altar of great Zeus, their eyes yet staring wildly with the instant sense of death; while the gaze of Odysseus went ranging the house, on the chance that some living man still hid there, to dodge his fate. However he found them all weltering in dust and blood, many as the fish dragged forth by sailors from the grey sea in seine nets up the beach of some bay, where they lie heaped on the sand and languishing for the briny waves, while the sun's shining saps their life away. Just so were the suitors heaped together.

Then said the guileful Odysseus to Telemachus, 'Go now and call nurse Eurycleia: for I have a word near my heart to speak with her.' Telemachus obeyed his dear father's orders and rattled at the door to summon the nurse, crying, 'Up with you now, aged dame and supervisor of our house-women. Come hither. My father calls you for somewhat he has to say.' Not a word could she launch in reply. She opened the doors of the stately hall and paced in (Telemachus ushering her) to where Odysseus stood in a slaver of blood and muck amidst the corpses of his victims, like some lion that has devoured an ox at grass and prowls forth, terrible to the eye, with gory breast and chaps. So was Odysseus bedabbled from his hands right down to his feet. She, when she saw the corpses and the pools of blood, knew how great was the achievement and opened her mouth to raise the woman's battle-wail: but Odysseus checked her excitement and stilled her with these trenchant words, 'Rejoice within yourself, beldam, and quietly. Keep back that throbbing cry. To make very glad over men's deaths is not proper. These fell by doom of the Gods and through the wickedness themselves had wrought, in disregarding good and bad alike amongst their earthly visitors. To such infatuation they owe their ignominious death. Now, instead, name me the full roll of house-women, those that disgrace me and the innocent ones.'

Then his good nurse Eurycleia said to him, 'Indeed, my child, I will tell you the very truth. In the palace you have fifty serving women whom we have broken to your service and taught such duties as carding wool. Of them just twelve ran to shamelessness, despite me and the orders of the Queen: – not of Telemachus, for his growing to account is a new thing; never did his mother let him touch the women servants. But now let me mount to that bright upper room and bear tidings to your wife where she lies plunged in a god-given sleep.' But cunning Odysseus forbade her. 'By no means call her yet. Bid me in those women who have been disorderly'; and away at his word went the old dame through the house, warning the women and hustling them forward: while Odysseus called to Telemachus, to the stockman and to the swineherd, saying with energy, 'Start to clear away the dead, making the women do the work; and then swill down the rich seats and tables with water and fibrous sponges. Afterwards, when you have restored the whole house to order, take these servants outside the stately hall to that spot between the round vault and the courtyard's strong boundary wall and there slaughter them with your long swords till the last life is spent and their love-passages with the suitors are wholly out of mind.'

So he bade them, and the erring women trailed in, all huddled together and crying great bitter tears of woe. First they bore out the dead and laid them in heaps along the portico of the walled court – Odysseus directing that work himself and driving them, for it took force to make them do it – and then they cleaned down the noble thrones and tables with water and soft sponges, while Telemachus with the swineherd and cattle-man scraped down the floor of the strong house with hoes, the maids carrying for them to a dump out of doors. When the house was tidy they led the women servants beyond the great hall and penned them in that blind place between vault and boundary wall, whence escape was impossible; and then Telemachus began to speak thoughtfully. 'It irks me,' he said, 'to give any sort of clean death to women who have heaped shame on my head and my mother's, and have wantoned with the suitors.' That was what he said. He made fast a dark-prowed ship's hawser to a pillar and strained it round the great spiral of the vault, at too great a height for anyone to touch the floor with her feet. Sometimes in a shrubbery men so stretch out nets, upon which long-winged thrushes or doves alight on their way to roost: and fatal the perch proves. Exactly thus were the women's heads all held a-row with a bight of cord drawn round each throat, to suffer their caitiff's death. A little while they twittered with their feet – only a little. It was not long.

Melanthius they dragged through the entry and the court, sliced his nose and ears with their cruel swords and tore out his privates, which they fed raw to the dogs. Their spite made them also cut off his hands and feet, after which they rinsed their own feet and hands and rejoined Odysseus in the house, all their achievement perfected. Wherefore he called to Eurycleia the beloved nurse, 'Bring me purifying brimstone, dame, and bring fire, for me to smoke the place through: also summon Penelope with her handmaidens. Have all the women of the house in here at once.' Devoted Eurycleia answered him, 'In this, my child, you follow precisely the right course: yet suffer me to bring you tunic and cloak for covering. You lower your dignity by standing in your hall with mere rags about your broad shoulders.' To which Odysseus only said, 'Light me the fire in the hall first . . .' and Eurycleia had no choice but to obey. Whereupon Odysseus carefully purged the hall, the private rooms and the court, with the fire and brimstone of her furnishing.

Afterwards the old woman went through the noble house to notify the women and bid them hastily attend. They came forth from their quarters, torch in hand, poured round Odysseus and embraced him with kisses and loving handclasps for his head, shoulders and hands: and, as his heart recalled each one of them, sorely his temptation grew to burst out weeping and wailing.

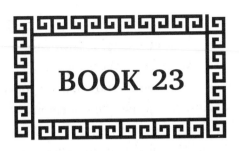

BOOK 23

But it was with a cackle of laughter that the old dame climbed towards the upper room, to warn her mistress of the beloved husband's return. Her knees moved nimbly and her feet tripped along to the lady's bed-head where she stood and spoke her part. 'Awake dear child, Penelope: open your eyes upon the sight you have yearned for all these days. Odysseus has appeared, at this end of time. He has reached his home and in it slaughtered the recalcitrant suitors who for so long vexed the house, ate his stored wealth and outfaced his son.'

Circumspect Penelope replied to this: 'Dear mother, the Gods have driven you frantic. They turn to foolishness the ripest judgements and the flighty into sober ways. From them comes this derangement of your old true understanding: – but why tease with fantasies a heart already brimmed with grief? Why wake me from this sleep whose sweetness held me in thrall and veiled my eyelids; the best sleep I have enjoyed since Odysseus went away to view that ill city never-to-be-named. Off with you below, instantly, to the women's quarters. Had any other of my housemaidens roused me with news of this sort I should have sent her smartingly back into her place. Just for this once your great age shall excuse you.'

Eurycleia persisted. 'Dear child, I am in very earnest with you. Odysseus, I say, is here. He came back to the house as that stranger who met such scurvy treatment at all hands. Telemachus long since learnt his identity but very properly hid the knowledge, to let his father's revenge take shape against those proud rough men.'

This time her word transported Penelope who leaped from the couch and clasped the old woman, crying shrilly through the tears that rained from her eyes: 'Ah, dear mother, but tell me, tell me truly – if as you say he is really come home, how has he coped single-handed with the shameless suitors, who mobbed our house continually?' And the good nurse told her, 'I did not see, I do not know: but I heard the groans of their slaying. We all shrank trembling into a corner of our safe room – its doors wedged fast – until your son Telemachus came and called me forth at his father's bidding. There in the hall I found Odysseus, stalking amidst the bodies of his slain that littered the beaten floor. Your heart would have glowed to see him so lion-like, all battle-stained and steeped in blood. Now the corpses are piled up outside, by the courtyard gates, while he has had a great fire lighted and purges the lovely house. He sent me to summon you; so come, that at the end of all the sorrow you two may enter your hearts' gladness hand in hand. Surely your lingering hope is now fulfilled. He reaches his fireside alive and finds you and your son still there; while upon each and every one of those suitors who served him ill in the house he has wreaked revenge.'

'Hush, mother,' said Penelope the decorous. 'Do not sing too loud or soon. You know how grateful his reappearance in the house would be to everybody, particularly to me and to his son and mine: but what you proclaim does not ring true. This massacre of the overbearing suitors has been the work of some Immortal, inflamed by their heart-breaking wanton insolence which had regard for no soul they met, neither the bad nor the good: so they have been punished according to their sins. But meantime Odysseus in some far land has lost his way to Achaea – yea, lost himself.' Nurse Eurycleia replied: 'My child, why let fall that dull word of your husband's never coming home, when he is here already and by his fireside? Your heart was always stubborn in unbelief. Why I can quote you a sure proof, that scar from the boar's white tusk long years ago, which I noted as I washed him. I wanted to tell you upon the instant; but he, careful for his own interests put his hand over my jaw and silenced me. Come with me now – and I pledge my life on it. If I mislead you, then slay me by the meanest death you know.'

Penelope responded: 'Even your storied wisdom, mother dear, hardly equips you to interpret the designs of the eternal Gods. Howbeit let us away to my son, for I would see the suitors lying in death; and their slayer.' She was going down as she spoke, her heart in a turmoil of debate whether to keep her distance while she examined her dear lord, or go straight up at once to kiss his head and clasp his hand. So when at length she came in across the stone threshold it was to take a seat in the fire-light facing Odysseus, but over against the further wall. He sat at the base of a tall pillar, waiting with drooping eyelids to hear his stately consort cry out when she caught sight of him. But she sat there in a long silence, with bewildered heart. One moment she would look and see him in his face; and the next moment fail to see him there, by reason of the foul rags he wore – till Telemachus named her in disapproval. 'Mother mine,' he cried, 'unmotherly mother and cruel-hearted, how dare you hold aloof from father, instead of running to sit by his side and ply him with questions? No other woman could in cold blood keep herself apart, when her man got home after twenty years of toil and sorrow. Your heart remains harder than a stone.'

But Penelope explained: 'Child, my heart is dazed. I have no force to speak, or ask, or even stare upon his face. If this is Odysseus in truth and at last, then shall we soon know each other better than well by certain private signs between us two, hidden from the rest of the world.' At which the glorious long-suffering Odysseus smiled and said hastily to Telemachus, 'After that, leave your mother alone for the test in her room with me presently. Soon she will come to fuller under-standing. The filth of my body, these shabby clothes – such things make her overlook me and deny it can be myself. Meanwhile you and I must discuss our best policy. In a community the slaying of even a single man with few surviving connections to avenge him entails outlawry from home and family; and we have been killing best part of the young men of Ithaca, its pillars of state. I would have you ponder it' – but Telemachus rejoined, 'Let that be your business, father dear. They call you the clearest-headed man alive, supreme in your generation. We others will support you whole-heartedly: and I fancy whatever our strength may be, courage at least will not fail us.'

Said Odysseus, 'Then hear what I think best. Wash now and dress, and have the house-women deck themselves. Then let the inspired minstrel with his resounding lyre lead off for us in a dance so merry that all hearing it from outside the walls, neighbours or passers-by, will say, "There is a wedding toward." Thus rumour of the suitors' deaths will not spread across the city before we have got away to our tree-clad country place, there to weigh what means of advantage the Olympian may offer to our hands.' They had all listened intently and moved to do his bidding. They washed and put on tunics: the women were arrayed: the revered musician took his hollow lyre and awoke their appetite for rhythm and the gay dance, till the great house around them rang with the measured foot-falls of men and well-gowned women. Outside the house one and another hearing the harmony did say, 'I swear someone has wedded the much-courted queen! Callous she was, and lacked the fortitude and constancy to keep the house of her lawful husband until he came.' Such was the gossip, in ignorance of the real event.

Meanwhile, within, old Eurynome washed and anointed Odysseus, draping upon him a fair tunic and cloak, while Athene crowned him with an especial splendour that filled the eye; she made the hair of his head curl downward floridly, like bloom of hyacinth. As a craftsman lavishly endowed with skill by Hephaestus and Pallas washes his silver-work with fine gold until its mastery shines out, so the grace from Athene glorified his head and shoulders and made his figure, when he left the bath-chamber, seem divine. He retook his former throne opposite his wife and declared, 'Proud lady, the heart that the lords of Olympus gave you is harder than any true woman's. None but you would pitilessly repulse the husband who had won his way home after twenty years of toil. Old dame, favour me now by arranging my bed somewhere apart, that I may lie solitary: for the heart in her breast has turned to iron.'

Said Penelope with reserve, 'Proud lord, I neither set myself too high nor esteem you too low: nor am I confused out of mind. It is that I remember only too well how you were when you sailed from Ithaca in your long-oared ship. So Eurycleia, when you make up his great bed for him, move it outside the bridal chamber that he built so firmly. Have forth the heavy bed-frame and pile it high with fleeces and rugs and glossy blankets.' This she said to draw her husband out; and indeed Odysseus was ruffled into protesting to his wife, 'Woman, this order pains my heart. Who has changed my bed? It would task the cunningest man – forbye no God happened to shift it in whim – for not the stoutest wight alive could heave it up directly. That bed's design held a marvellous feature of my own contriving. Within our court had sprung a stem of olive, bushy, long in the leaf, vigorous; the bole of it column-thick. Round it I plotted my bed-chamber, walled entire with fine-jointed ashlar and soundly roofed. After adding joinery doors, fitting very close, I then polled the olive's spreading top and trimmed its stump from the root up, dressing it so smooth with my tools and so knowingly that I got it plumb, to serve for bed-post just as it stood. With this for main member (boring it with my auger wherever required) I went on to frame up the bed, complete; inlaying it with gold, silver and ivory and lacing it across with ox-hide thongs, dyed blood-purple. That was the style of it, woman, as I explain: but of course I do not know whether the bed stands as it did; or has someone sawn through the olive stem and altered it?'

As Odysseus had run on, furnishing her with proof too solid for rejection, her knees trembled, and her heart. She burst into tears, she ran to him, she flung her arms about his neck and kissed his head and cried, 'My Odysseus, forgive me this time too, you who were of old more comprehending than any man of men. The Gods gave us sorrow for our portion, and in envy denied us the happiness of being together throughout our days, from the heat of youth to the shadow of old age. Be not angry with me, therefore, nor resentful, because at first sight I failed to fondle you thus. The heart within me ever shook for terror of being cheated by some man's lie, so innumerable are those who plot to serve greedy ends. See, it was that way our life's sorrow first began. Argive Helen, the daughter of Zeus, did not in her own imagination invent the ruinous folly that let a strange man lie with her in love and intercourse. A God it was that tempted her astray. Never would she have done it had she known how the warrior sons of the Achaeans would fetch her back once more to her native land. But now with those authentic details of our bed, seen by no human eye but yours, mine and my maid's (Actor's daughter, given me by my father before I came here and ever the sole keeper of our closed bed-chamber-door) you have convinced my heart, slow though you may think it to believe.'

This word increased by so much his inclination to tears that he wept, even with his arms about his faithful, lovely wife. So at sea when Poseidon has swamped a good ship by making her the target of his winds and mighty waves, the sight of land appears wonderfully kind to the few men of her crew who have escaped by swimming. How they swarm ashore from the grey sea, their bodies all crusted with salt spume, but happy, happy, for the evil overpassed! Just so was she happy to have her husband once more in sight and clasped in her white arms which lingered round his neck, unable to let him go. Rosy dawn might have found them thus, still weeping, only that grey-eyed Athene otherwise ordained. She retarded the night a long while in transit and made Dawn, the golden-throned, tarry by the eastern Ocean's edge; not harnessing Lampus and Phaethon, the sharp-hooved young horses that carry her and bring daylight to the world.

At last provident Odysseus said to his wife: 'My dear one, we have not yet reached the issue of our trials. In store for us is immeasurable toil prescribed, and needs must I fulfil it to the end. The day I went down into Hades' realm, the ghost of Teiresias warned me of everything when I asked after my home-coming and my company's. Wherefore let us to bed, dear wife, there at long last to renew ourselves with the sweet meed of sleep.' To which Penelope answered, 'Bed is yours the instant your heart wills, for have not the Gods restored you to your own great house and native land? But now that Heaven has put it in your mind, tell me of this ordeal remaining. Later I must know; and forewarned is forearmed.'

Odysseus in reply assured her, 'Brave spirit, I shall tell you, hiding nothing: but why press me insistently for knowledge that will no more please you than me? He gave me word that I must take my shapely oar and wander through many places of men, until I find a people that know not the sea and have no salt to season their food, a people for whom purple-prowed ships are unknown things, as too the shaped oars which wing their flight. An infallible token of them he told me, and I make you wise to it. When another wayfarer passes me and says I have a winnowing fan on my stout shoulder, even there am I to strike my oar into the ground and offer for rich sacrifice to King Poseidon a ram, a bull and a ramping boar. Thence I may turn homeward, to celebrate the Gods of high heaven with hecatombs of victims, and all things else in order due. While death shall come for me from the sea, very mildly, ending me amidst a contented people after failing years have brought me low. He assured me all this would be fulfilled.' And Penelope's wise comment was, 'If the Gods will make old age your happier time, then there is prospect of your ill-luck passing.'

Thus they chatted while Eurynome and the nurse under the flaring torchlight arranged the soft coverlets upon the bed. When they had busily made it comfortable and deep, the old nurse returned to her sleeping-place, while Eurynome the chambermaid conducted them bedward with her torch. She ushered them to their chamber and withdrew; and gladsomely they performed their bed-rites in the old fashion: Telemachus and the herdsmen staying their feet from the dance and staying the women, so that all slept in the darkling halls.

After the first thrill of love had passed, the pair began to exchange histories for mutual entertainment, the fairest of women telling what she had put up with in the house, watching the suitors' greedy swarming, and the multitudinous sheep and cattle they slew for sake of her, and all the broached jars of wine: while heaven-born Odysseus told of every hurt he had done to others and the woes himself had suffered, detailing thing by thing; and eagerly she heard him, slumber never weighing down her eyelids until all was told. He began with the conquest of the Cicones, thence to Lotos-land, and of what Cyclops did and the price exacted for his cruelly-devoured friends: then how he got welcome and help from Aeolus, but unavailingly, for further storms drove him sadly adrift: also of Telepylus, where the Laestrygonians destroyed all the ships and crews except his own: next of Circe's wiles and of his ship's voyaging to Hades to consult Teiresias, where he saw all his dead company and the mother who had cherished him when young: then of the Sirens' song, the clashers, Scylla and Charybdis those fatal ones: of his crew's killing the cattle of the Sun wherefore Zeus' lightning destroyed the ship and all aboard but himself: of Ogygia and his kindly durance in the cave with Calypso whose promised immortality did not seduce his love: of his pains to reach Phaeacia where he got worshipful hospitality, gifts and transport home: – and as the tale ended sleep fell gently upon him, relaxing his limbs and delivering his mind from care.

Athene was not at the end of her plans: the instant she judged Odysseus satisfied with love and sleeping she let golden Dawn rise from the Ocean to light mankind. With her rose Odysseus and held forth to his wife: 'Lady mine, hitherto we have both travailed exhaustively, you in lamenting the hindrances to my return, I in the sorrows wherewith Zeus and the other Gods afflicted me, homesick, far away: but now that we have both reached the bed of our desire, do you take my indoor interests under your especial care. As for the sheep butchered by the impudent suitors, I shall go raid a-many, and more will the Achaeans give me till the sheep-folds are full. But my first journey must be to the plantations of our farm where I shall see the good father who has been in grief for me. One prior consideration, however, I would put to your most subtle mind, Lady. Upon the sunrise rumour will run abroad of the suitors I slew within. So get above stairs with all your women and sit there, seeing and questioning none.'

He braced the splendid arms about his shoulders, called Telemachus, the neatherd and the swineherd, and had them all take weapons of war in their hands – not that they required urging. They did on their brazen breast-pieces, opened the doors and marched out, Odysseus in the van. Day lay wide upon the face of the earth, but Athene hid them in obscurity and led them swiftly from the town.

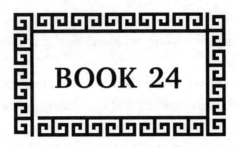

BOOK 24

Hermes the Cyllenian bade forth those ghosts of men that had been suitors. In his hand was the rod of pure gold with which at will he charms men's eyes to rest or stirs them from sleep. By a wave of it he had them afoot and following him with such thin cries as bats use in the fastnesses of their mysterious cave, whenever one falls squeaking from the clustered swarms that hang downward from the rocky roof. So they flocked after, weakly piping, while gentle Hermes led them down the dank, dark passage – by the Ocean Stream and the White Crag, past the portal of the Sun and the land of Dreams – till soon they entered the asphodel meadows where harbour the shadowy ghosts of those that have passed away.

There was to be found the soul of Achilles, son of Peleus, with that of Aias, next after him of all the Greeks for splendid face and figure; also the souls of Patroclus and of brave Antilochus. As these were grouped round Achilles the woe-begone spirit of Agamemnon son of Atreus approached amidst a concourse of those who fell with him in the house of Aegisthus and there miserably died. To him Achilles' ghost began: 'Why, Atrides, we used to fancy you more continually beloved of Zeus the Thunderer than any earthly hero, because you commanded the hosts of brave men in that Trojan land so costly to us Achaeans. Yet was it decreed that the doom of death (which no son of man avoids) must come to you so soon! If only you could have met it in the Troad while your sovranty endured – for then the Concert of Achaea would have raised your tomb and a great glory been earned for your son – instead of this piteous fate which has been your lot.'

The ghost of Atrides answered: 'You happy son of Peleus, god-like Achilles, to have found death near Troy and not near Argos! Some of the noblest youths, both Trojan and Achaean, died about you, furiously contending for your body whose grandeur lay so grandly in the whirling dust, forgetful of its chivalry. Through the long day we battled, and should not even then have ceased but for the storm with which Zeus halted us. Afterward we bore you from the field to our ships, where we set you on a couch and cleansed your beautiful body with warmed water and unguents. Round you the Danaans pressed, shedding hot tears and shearing their love-tresses. Your mother, when she heard, came forth from the waves with her death-less sea-maidens, the cry of them ringing across Ocean so marvellously that a thrill of fear passed over the Achaean host, which would have risen and fled to the ships but for Nestor's stemming them with his rich, rare wisdom, so often tested and approved. Because he knew, he called to them and said, 'Be still, Argives: flee not, you young Achaeans. This is his mother coming from the sea and with her the immortal maidens of the sea, to encounter her dead son.' When they heard him the Achaeans bravely contained their fear, while the daugh-ters of the ancient of the sea circled about you with bitter lamentations and wound your body in imperishable robes. The nine Muses joined to sing your dirge, voice answering sweet voice in harmony; and so movingly rose and fell their clear chant that you would not have found one Argive there dry-eyed. Through seventeen days and seventeen nights we mourned you, deathless Gods and mortal men alike; and on the eighteenth, having sacrificed many good sheep and screw-horned kine, we gave you to the flames and you were consumed, in those divine robes and lapped with a plenty of spices and sweet honey; while panoplied companies of Achaean warriors, mounted or on foot, tramped round your burning pyre with a loud clashing of arms. Then after the fire of Hephaestus had had its way with you, very early in the morning we disposed your white bones, Achilles, in neat wine and unguent. Your mother offered a gold two-handled urn, saying it was Dionysus' gift and a work of famed Hephaestus. In it, brilliant Achilles, rest your white bones with the bones of dead Patroclus the son of Menoetias; while apart but near lie the ashes of Antilochus whom you admired above all your other friends, the fallen Patroclus only excepted. Over you we, the army of devoted Argive spearsmen, piled a great tomb that towers on its jutting headland far over the Hellespont, a mark for seafaring men of our day and days to come. Your mother went to the Gods and begged of them noble trophies which she exhibited in an arena for the Achaean athletes. In your time you have attended the obsequies of many champions, or seen the young men, when some king has died, gird themselves to compete for prizes: but had you seen these treasures your mind would have been astonished, so wonderful were the gages offered in your honour by that fair Goddess, Thetis of the silver foot. The Gods loved you out of measure, Achilles, and even death has not robbed you of your name. Everywhere and for ever you will inherit glory. But for me, what satisfaction did I gain in winding up my war's coil, when Zeus had plotted me so dismal a fate at the hands of Aegisthus and my accursed wife, upon my coming home?'

Thus they communed as the slayer of Argus, the messenger, drew near conducting the ghosts of the suitors Odysseus killed. Amazement at the throng of them led the two forward to watch, and so the spirit of Agamemnon recognised famous Amphimedon, the dear son of Melaneus, by whom he had been entertained in Ithaca. Atrides' spirit called across to him asking, 'Amphimedon, what disaster brings all you picked men in your prime down to this land of shades? Almost might someone have chosen out and gathered the best men of your city. Did Poseidon's harsh winds raise running seas and overwhelm you in your ships? Or did enemies destroy you on some shore while you were busied rounding up their cattle or great flocks of sheep? Or perhaps the fighting was to protect their wives and towns? Tell it me, for I ask as your intimate. Do you not recollect great Menelaus and me coming to your place when we wanted Odysseus to follow with his fleet to

Ilium? A full month we were, before we got across the wide gulf, so hard to persuade was the spoiler of cities, Odysseus.'

'Most renowned son of Atreus, Agamemnon, King of Kings,' answered the spirit of Amphimedon, 'Indeed, Majesty, I do remember it. So here I will give you the full, exact account of our death's deplorable chance. Odysseus was missing: wherefore we fell to courting his wife. She never admitted that our proposals were abhorrent, any more than she would determine upon one of us: nevertheless her heart of hearts kept plotting our black death and doom. For the moment she imagined another device, by setting up a very broad, fine warp on a great loom in her chamber; and pleading to us regarding it, "My lords and courtiers, as great Odysseus is dead, can you not bridle your haste to have me wedded, until I finish this winding-sheet against hero Laertes' burial on the fateful day that all-conquering death lays him low? I would not have my yarns rot unused, lest some Achaean woman of the district censure me for letting a man who had broad possessions lie unshrouded." This was her petition and we lords accepted it. Day-long she wove at her great task but after dark, by torchlight, would unpick it. For three years she maintained this deceit and fooled the Achaeans; but when a fourth year came with its days passing and its months, in seasonal progression, then one of her women (who knew) told on her and we surprised her unravelling the splendid fabric. That forced her, very unwillingly, to finish it. When the immense sheet was washed and displayed, its brilliance was like the sun or moon – but on that very day somehow some unfriendly power led Odysseus back to the isolated homestead where his swineherd lived. Thither also came his son, returned from Pylos after a sea voyage; and the two of them, before ever setting out thence for town, concerted the suitors' murder. Telemachus started first, followed by Odysseus under guidance of the swineherd, like a worn-out wretched beggar, tattered and limping on a crutch. On his sudden appearance in such rags none of us could guess what he was: even our seniors failed to know him. We gave him the rough of our tongues, not to mention blows; and for a time he endured this abuse and pelting in his own halls stolidly enough; but at last inspiration came to him from Zeus, lord of the Aegis. With the help of Telemachus he collected all the house-weapons, hid them in the store-chamber and bolted the doors. Then he ingeniously prompted his wife to set out his bow and irons as test of the suitors' prowess – and also to provide means for our fatal undoing. None of us had strength enough, not by a long way, to notch the string: yet when the bow came round to Odysseus' hands we all vehemently protested against his having it, despite his pleading. However Telemachus stood out and made him try it. When mighty Odysseus got the bow he strung it easily and flashed an arrow through the irons: then he leaped to the threshold, poised himself firmly, tipped the arrows out all ready, glared round him and shot royal Antinous. Afterwards he rained his murderous shafts upon the crowd, shooting so accurately that men fell dead in rows. Evidently some God was aiding his party for they raged at will through the house, slaughtering right and left. Awful was the screaming as the brains were beaten out, while the floor ran with blood. That was the manner of our perishing, Atrides, and our neglected bodies still strew the house of Odysseus, for tidings have not yet reached the friends in our houses who would wash the clotted gore from our wounds, lay out our bodies and raise dirges as the dead deserve.'

The shade of Agamemnon loudly intoned: 'Blessed have you been O son of Laertes, ingenious Odysseus, in winning a wife of such surpassing virtue! So upright in disposition was Penelope the daughter of Icarius that she never forgot Odysseus the husband of her youth: and therefore shall the fame of her goodness be conserved in the splendid poem wherewith the Immortals shall celebrate the constancy of Penelope for all the dwellers upon earth. How unlike the wickedness of that daughter of Tyndareus who slew her husband! In the poem that men sing of her she shall seem abominable, a blot upon even the honest women among her sex.' Things like this the two said to one another where they stood in Hades' mansions, under the hidden places of the world.

Meanwhile Odysseus and his men had passed the town. Soon they reached the flourishing estate of Laertes, acquired by him years before, after great effort. There stood his place, ringed with the hovels in which the slaves who served his purposes ate and sat and slept: while in the house proper he kept an old Sicilian woman who diligently tended her aged master in this farm so far from the town. Now Odysseus had a word for his son and the serfs. 'In with you smartly to the well-built house,' he said, 'and there devote the finest of their hogs to making our dinner; meanwhile, in view of my long absence abroad I shall go to test if my father knows me again by sight, or not.' He handed his arms to the two thralls who went straight in, as Odysseus proceeded through the rich fruit-farm, on his quest.

He went down the great garden, but did not meet Dolius, nor any other of the serfs or serfs' sons. Everybody had gone under that old man's guidance to collect stones for walling up the vines. So what he found was his father alone in the neat vineyard, hoeing round a vine-stock. The greasy tunic upon him was patched and mean. His shins were cross-gartered in botched leggings of cowhide, to save their being scratched, and he wore hedging gloves against the brambles, with a goat-skin cap for his head: all of which made plain his despondency. When Odysseus knew for his father this out-worn old man, lined with heart-sickness, he paused beneath a tall pear-tree to drop a tear, while his heart asked his head if he might not kiss and clasp this father and blurt out how he had returned and regained his native land – instead of catechising him first and trying him every way – but upon reflection he deemed it still expedient to rake him with searching enquiries.

In this mood Odysseus marched up to him: only he had his head down and so went on working carefully about his vine till his famous son was beside him and said: 'Old man, you prove yourself no fool at looking after trees. What a return they make! In all the garden there is not one plant – no fig, vine, olive, pear or vegetable plot – without its contribution to the whole. Yet one remark I would offer, and take it not amiss. Your own state seems less considered. Old age presses ruinously upon you, yet you go wasted and pitifully clad. No idleness gives the master grounds for this neglect: nor do your carriage and demeanour betray the slave. You have a royal air like one who can take his ease abed, after bath and refreshment, as befits great age. So tell me now plainly and well whose serf you are and whose fruit garden is this you tend? I require the truth particularly to satisfy myself that this is really Ithaca, as a fellow just now told me when I met him in my way. A boorish fellow, lacking the manners to answer me fully or hear out my enquiries after a friend of whom I wished to know if he were yet here, alive, or dead and in Hades' domain. Wherefore let me enlarge upon this to your attentive ear. Once in my own dear land I played host to a man that happened along: and never among all the wayfaring creatures that visited me was one more welcome. He acknowledged himself an Ithacan by race: his father Laertes son of Arcesius. I brought him to my home and entertained him lavishly, as I well could from the plenty I possessed. Also I gave him gifts of hospitality agreeable to the event. Seven talents of refined gold I gave, and a petal-bowl of solid silver; twelve cloaks of a piece, so many carpets, over-mantles, tunics: and beside all these four women superbly trained in handicraft and very buxom, those which his own taste chose.'

The father wept as he answered him, 'Stranger, you are in the land you seek, but alas it has fallen into the hands of coarse and ungodly ruffians. Vain have been the gifts you generously gave, your many splendid gifts. Had you found that man living here in his land of Ithaca he would have received you with noble hospitality, as is the due of the prime benefactor, and sent you on with a goodly return of gifts. But tell me this, precisely: – how many years is it since you entertained your guest, your unhappy guest, my son – had I a son? – that ill-starred one whom the fishes of the deep sea may have swallowed, or birds and beasts of the field devoured, far from his friends and country? His mother and his father, we his parents, have not shrouded his body or raised his dirge. His well-dowered wife, faithful Penelope, never wailed as a wife should over her husband's bier, or closed his eyes in pious duty to the dead. Tell me all the truth of what you are: your city and people? Where lies the swift ship with capable crew that brought you? Or did you ferry here in another's ship which landed you and sailed away?'

Devious Odysseus answered and said: 'Yea, hear the truth. I am from Alybas, where my house is famous. My father is Apheidas, son of Polypemon, and royal. My own name is Eperitus. Some involuntary urge drove me hither from Sicania. My ship stands off the open shore beyond the town. As for Odysseus, this is the fifth year since he took leave and left my country. Unhappy man – and yet the bird-omens were favourable, wholly on his right, as he went away. That made me glad to speed him, and him glad to go. Both of us in our hearts were hoping for another meeting to seal our friendship with rich gifts.'

The news shrouded the old man in a black misery. He groaned deep and long and gathered cupped palmfuls of dust which he poured over his grey head. This touched Odysseus to the heart; there stabbed through his nostrils a spasm of pain, to see his dear father thus. He leaped forward and caught him in his arms and kissed him, crying, 'I, my father, I myself am the one you ask after, arrived in this twentieth year at home. Cease your sighs and sobs – for let me tell you, quickly as the need is, that I have killed all those suitors in my house, to punish their burning insolence and iniquity.'

Laertes wailed, 'If you are my son Odysseus returned, then show me some clear sign that I may believe,' and the ready Odysseus answered, 'Set your eyes first on this scar, given me by the boar's white tusk that time I was on Parnassus, when you and my mother had sent me to her father, Autolycus, after the presents which he proposed and promised for me while he stayed in our house. Next I shall repeat to you the tale of trees all down the formal garden – trees which you gave me once when I was but a child following you about and asking for every thing I saw. We were walking amongst these very trees when you told me each one's name and sort. Thirteen pear-trees you gave me, ten apples, forty fig-trees: also you described the fifty rows of vines you would give, each ripening in its time, so that bunches of grapes there would be continually, as the seasons of Zeus swelled them from on high.'

At these words Laertes' knees and heart gave way, for he recognised the manifest proofs furnished by his son. He caught at the great Odysseus who drew the old man, fainting, to his breast and held him thus till the breath came back and the spirit quickened in him once more. Then Laertes called, 'Father Zeus, still there are Gods on tall Olympus, if truly the suitors have paid the penalty of their shocking pride. Yet terribly the fear takes my soul that now all the men of Ithaca will mass against us here, while they send hue and cry through the cities of the Cephallenians.'

'Never fear it,' replied Odysseus, 'nor let it concern your mind. Off with us to the near-by garden house whither I despatched Telemachus with the cowman and swineherd, to prepare a hasty meal:' and away the two strolled, chatting, to the pleasant house, within whose stout walls laboured Telemachus and the herdsmen carving the abundant flesh and mixing rich wine. There his Sicilian dame washed honest Laertes and anointed him, before putting upon him a handsome cloak: while Athene came down, to enhance the stature and build of this shepherd of the people, so dignifying his limbs that the figure which issued from the bath was like an immortal. His amazed son put his wonder into words. 'Father,' he said, 'surely one of the Eternal Gods has made you taller and more impressive to the eye,' to which the wise old man replied, 'Ah, if but Zeus and Athene and Apollo would make me the man I was when as King of my Cephallenians I led them to the capture of Nericus, that great fortress of the mainland! Had that old fighting self of mine been with you yesterday in our house to help you repulse the suitors, I should have made many a one give at the knees, and delighted your heart of hearts.'

They talked till the others, having ended their work of getting the meal, sat down in order upon their thrones or chairs. They were helping themselves to the food when old man Dolius arrived and with him his sons, panting from their toil. Their mother, the old Sicilian, whose zealous cherishing of her age-crippled master yet let her care for them, had run outdoors and hailed them in. When they saw Odysseus and minded him again they stood dumbstruck in the hall: but Odysseus fastened upon them with honeyed words, saying: 'Forget your surprise, aged man, and sit down to eat. For quite a while we have been in the house eager to begin; but we hung about, momently expecting you.' Dolius heard him and ran forward open-armed to take Odysseus' hand and kiss his wrist while he cried excitedly, 'My dear, now you have come back to those who loved and longed and despaired for you – now the Gods bring you home – all hail and very welcome! Heaven grant you happiness. But do assure me that Penelope knows of your return. Else must we send a messenger.' To which Odysseus: 'Ancient man, she knows already; you have no call to meddle there,' and back went venerable Dolius to his polished bench, while the sons pressed round famous Odysseus, greeting him and clasping his hands. Then they sat properly beside their father and were busied on their dinner in the house.

Meanwhile in the city rumour had coursed far and fast, proclaiming the destruction of the suitors by death. When the people heard of it they gathered from all sides to Odysseus' house with wailing and lamentation. Thence party after party bore out the corpses of their dead to burial: while those that came from outlying cities were loaded into swift ships and sent by boatmen home. Afterward the entire populace trooped in deepest mourning to their debating-ground; and when all were in place Eupeithes rose, heart-burdened with inconsolate misery for sake of his son Antinous, the first victim of kingly Odysseus. Tears rained from his eyes as he harangued them, saying, 'O my friends, the vast mischief this man has worked against the Achaeans! Think of the many stout warriors he took aboard with him, only to cast away his ships and all their crews; while he returns only to butcher the very best leaders of the Cephallenians that remained. You must act before he takes swift flight to Pylos or to sacred Elis, the Epeian sanctuary.

Let us forward, or our faces will be for ever bowed with shame. The disgrace of it will echo down the generations, should we fail to punish the murderers of our sons and kinsmen. For me, there would remain no sweetness in life. Rather would I choose death and the company of these dead. Up and strike, before they steal from us oversea.'

This and his tears awoke pity in every Achaean; but now Medon appeared, coming with the inspired bard from the palace of Odysseus where they had just awaked. They strode to the heart of the gaping crowd, and there Medon halted to say temperately, 'O men of Ithaca, hear me. What Odysseus has done was not of his own design, unsupported by the Immortal Gods. With my own eyes I saw a deathless form, in exact guise of Mentor, stand next Odysseus and manifest divinity by thrusting forward to embolden him; and again by an onslaught which drove the suitors in terror about the hall, till they fell side by side.' His words turned them pale with fear, and then old Halitherses, Mastor's stately son, struck in to exhort them, out of his unequalled knowledge of things past and things to be. Very candidly he spoke, saying, 'And now listen to me, men of Ithaca, and to what I say. These disasters have followed upon your negligence, my friends. You would not be persuaded by me, or by Mentor the people's shepherd, to make your sons cease their insensate ways. Wilfully and wantonly they were led to waste the property and insult the wife of a man of virtue, through believing him gone beyond return. But take my advice now and let things be. If we make another move, maybe some will find that evil recoils.' Thus he counselled and a few stayed in their place; but the rest, the majority, preferred Eupeithes' advice and leaped to their feet crying the war-cry. They ran to arms and arrayed their bodies in shining bronze, before assembling in their multitudes outside the broad town. Eupeithes led them, frantic at the slaying of his son and thinking to avenge him: whereas in the event he was to find his own death and never return.

In heaven Athene appealed to Zeus, son of Cronos. 'O Father of us all and King of Kings, answer what I ask and make plain the secret working of your mind. Will you provoke a new cruel war, more din of battle? Or turn them again to loving one another?' Then the Cloud-compellor replied, 'Daughter, why put to Me this question? The affair is of your creating. Did you not plan for the coming of Odysseus to be with vengeance upon the suitors? Now work it as you please, though I will tell you the fitting way. Great Odysseus has revenged himself. Let the parties compose a binding treaty, by virtue of which he shall remain their king: while we will expunge from memory this slaughter of the people's kith and kin. So shall they love one another as of yore and peace abound, with wealth.' His words exalted Athene, already eager. Down she went hurtling from the crest of Olympus.

At the farm the men had glutted their desire for the honey-sweet food. Odysseus began directing them. 'One of you had better look if any enemy approaches,' he said, and accordingly out went a son of Dolius to the threshold: whence he saw the mob quite near at hand. So he cried in haste to Odysseus, 'They are on top of us. Our arms! Quick!' They leaped to their feet and armed. Besides the four with Odysseus, Dolius had six of his sons; while even the hoary-headed Laertes and Dolius harnessed themselves once again to become men of war at the need. They flung wide the gate and marched out, all corseleted in shining bronze, Odysseus leading. Athene, talking and looking like Mentor, joined them, to the delight of Odysseus who admonished his son: 'My Telemachus, you are taking part with men in battle where the best will win. Learn instantly not to disgrace your lineage: ours has had a world-reputation for courage and skill' – and to this Telemachus appositely replied, 'Dear Father, if it pleases you to watch, you will see me in such form as will indeed not disgrace my forbears, the way you put it.' Laertes, who had overheard them, glee-fully cried out, 'Dear Gods, what a day for me! O joy, to have my son and my son's son vying on the point of valour!'

Athene came to Laertes' elbow and whispered, 'Son of Arcesius, whom I love best of all my friends, offer a prayer to the grey-eyed Goddess and to Father Zeus, then poise your long-shafted spear and let fly.' With her words she breathed vigour into him. He invoked the daughter of great Zeus, balanced the weapon a moment and hurled it to strike Eupeithes on his helmet's bronze cheek-piece, which did not resist the spear. The point went through and with a clang of armour the man crashed down.

Odysseus and his brave son fell upon the leading rank, hacking with their swords and thrusting with their spears. They would have cut them off and destroyed every one had not Athene, the daughter of aegis-bearing Zeus, shouted with such force as to halt the array. 'Let be your deadly battle, men of Ithaca,' she cried. 'Without bloodshed is the affair best arranged.' The voice of the Goddess blenched them with fear. In their panic the weapons slipped from their grasp and fell together to the ground, as the Goddess called. They turned their faces toward the town for dear life, while with a roar the great long-suffering Odysseus gathered himself for the spring and launched after them, like an eagle in free air.

But instantly the son of Cronos flung his lurid levin which fell before the grey-eyed Goddess, the dread Father's own child; then did Athene cry to Odysseus, 'Back with you, heaven-nourished son of Laertes, Odysseus of the many wiles. Hold back. Cease this arbitrament of civil war. Move not far-sighted Zeus to wrath.'

So Athene said, she the daughter of aegis-bearing Zeus. Odysseus obeyed, inwardly glad: and Pallas, still with Mentor's form and voice, set a pact between them for ever and ever.